ABOUT THE AUTHORS

Elizabeth Frost-Knappman, left, is the founder and president of New England Publishing Associates, Inc., located in Chester, Connecticut. She is the author of *The World Almanac of Presidential Quotations* (1993) and the *Clio Companion to Women's Progress in America* (1994), selected as an Outstanding Academic Book of the Year (reference) by the American Library Association's

Choice. Under the pen-name Elizabeth Frost, she co-authored, with Kathryn Cullen-DuPont, *Women's Suffrage in America: An Eyewitness History* (1992), described by *The Washington Spectator* as "one of the best recent books on the subject of women and the vote." With David Shrager, she compiled and edited *The Quotable Lawyer* (1986). Frost-Knappman also was the general editor of the Primary Source Media CD-ROM *American Journey: Women in America* (1994).

Until 1982, Frost-Knappman was a book editor for Doubleday, the Natural History Press, William Morrow, and William Collins & Sons. She is a member of the American Society of Journalists and Authors, the Authors Guild, the Association of Authors Representatives, and Network of Entrepreneurial Women. A frequent speaker on publishing topics for libraries, colleges, and universities in New York and New England, she is profiled in *Who's Who of American Women* (20th edition).

Kathryn Cullen-DuPont, right, is the author of *Encyclopedia of Women's History in America* (1996), featured as a selection of the History Book Club, and *Elizabeth Cady Stanton and Women's Liberty* (1992), named a New York Public Library Best Book for the Teen Age. With Elizabeth Frost, she co-authored *Women's Suffrage in America: An Eyewitness History* (1992). She was also a contributor to Gale's *Great American Trials* (1994).

Cullen-DuPont served upon the advisory board for the Primary Source Media CD-ROM *American Journey: Women in America* (1994), and she is the permanent consultant on women's issues for *New Book of Knowledge Encyclopedia*.

This book is dedicated to our parents,

Martin and Arlene Cullen
and
Lorena Launer Frost

WOMEN'S RIGHTS on TRIAL

WOMEN'S RIGHTS on TRIAL

101 Historic Trials from Anne Hutchinson

to the Virginia Military

Institute Cadets

**Elizabeth Frost-Knappman
and Kathryn Cullen-DuPont**

A NEW ENGLAND PUBLISHING ASSOCIATES BOOK

GALE

Detroit New York Toronto London

Edited and prepared for publication by New England Publishing Associates, Inc.
Principals: Elizabeth Frost-Knappman and Edward W. Knappman; **Staff:** Rebecca Berardy, Karen Corriveau, Ron Formica, and Victoria Harlow

Gale Research staff
Managing Editor: Lawrence W. Baker; **Developmental Editors:** Kenneth Estell and Jane Hoehner; **Associate Editor:** Camille Killens; **Acquisition Editors:** Meggin Condino and Christine Nasso; **Production Director:** Mary Beth Trimper; **Assistant Production Manager:** Evi Seoud; **Production Associate:** Shanna Heilveil; **Cover and Page Designer:** Mary Krzewinski; **Production Design Manager:** Cynthia Baldwin; **Image Database Supervisor:** Randy Bassett; **Imaging Specialists:** Mikal Ansari and Robert Duncan; **Photography Coordinator:** Pamela A. Hayes; **Graphic Services Manager:** Barbara J. Yarrow

Library of Congress Cataloging-in-Publication Data
Frost-Knappman, Elizabeth.
    Women's rights on trial : 101 historic American trials from Anne Hutchinson to the Virginia Military Institute cadets / Elizabeth Frost-Knappman and Kathryn Cullen-DuPont.
        p. cm.
    Includes bibliographical references and index.
    ISBN 0-7876-0384-8 (alk. paper)
    1. Trials—United States. 2. Women—Legal status, laws, etc.—United States. I. Cullen-
    DuPont, Kathryn. II. Title.
    KF220.F76 1996
    346.7301'34—dc20
    [347.306134]   96-43656
             CIP

Printed in the United States of America
10 9 8 7 6 5 4 3 2

CONTENTS

Contents (In Chronological Order)   **xi**
Contents (In Alphabetical Order)   **xv**
Preface   **xix**
Introduction   **xxi**

Overview   **1**
Anne Hutchinson's Trials [1637 and 1638]   **3**
Mary Dyer Trials [1659 and 1660]   **7**
Salem Witchcraft Trials [1692]   **11**
Crandall v. Connecticut [1834]   **15**
United States v. Susan B. Anthony [1873]   **21**
The Trials of Alice Paul and Other National
    Woman's Party Members [1917]   **25**
New York v. Sanger [1918]   **29**
Cammermeyer v. Aspin [1994]   **34**

**Section 1:
Crimes of
Conscience and
Nonconformity**

Overview   **39**
The Case of Mary Mendame [1639]   **43**
The Trial of Charles Sheepey [1687]   **45**
Missouri v. Celia, a Slave [1855]   **48**
Massachusetts v. Fogerty [1857]   **53**
The Triangle Shirtwaist Fire [1911]   **56**
Los Angeles v. Stately [1949]   **61**
Pennsylvania v. Daniel and Douglas [1967]   **63**
Coker v. Georgia [1977]   **69**
Oregon v. Rideout [1978]   **73**
Michael M. v. Superior Court of Sonoma
    County [1981]   **77**
New Bedford Rape Trials [1984]   **81**

**Section 2:
Crime and
Punishment**

American Booksellers Association v.
    Hudnut [1986] **86**

Section 3:   Overview **91**
Rights and   Martin v. Massachusetts [1805] **93**
Responsibilities Hester Vaughan's Trial [1868] **96**
of Citizenship Bradwell v. Illinois [1873] **100**
    Minor v. Happersett [1875] **104**
    Breedlove v. Suttles, Tax Collector [1937] **109**
    Reed v. Reed [1971] **112**
    Taylor v. Louisiana [1975] **115**
    Stanton v. Stanton [1975] **119**
    Craig v. Boren [1976] **123**
    Rostker v. Goldberg [1981] **127**
    Mississippi University for Women v.
      Hogan [1982] **131**
    Grove City College v. Bell [1984] **135**
    Roberts v. United States Jaycees [1984] **139**
    United States v. Virginia [1996] **143**

Section 4:   Overview **149**
Reproductive Massachusetts v. Bangs [1812] **151**
Rights   Buck v. Bell [1927] **153**
    United States v. One Package [1936] **158**
    Griswold v. Connecticut [1965] **162**
    United States v. Vuitch [1971] **167**
    Eisenstadt v. Baird [1972] **172**
    Roe v. Wade [1973] **177**
    Harris v. McRae [1980] **185**
    In the Matter of Baby M [1988] **190**
    Webster v. Reproductive Health
      Services [1989] **197**
    Planned Parenthood of Southeastern Pennsylvania
      v. Casey [1992] **202**
    Madsen v. Women's Health Center [1994] **207**

Section 5:   Overview **213**
Marriage,   Carroll v. Warren [1736] **217**
Parenting and Pattison v. Pattison [1737] **220**
Divorce   Burk v. Phips [1793] **223**
    Barnes v. Hart [1793] **226**

Scott v. Scott [1795] **230**

Megrath v. Robertson [1795] **233**

Beall and King v. Woolford [1797] **237**

Fry v. Derstler [1798] **241**

Griffith v. Griffith's Executors [1798] **244**

Dibble v. Hutton [1804] **247**

Fitch v. Brainerd [1805] **252**

Watson v. Bailey [1808] **256**

Kempe v. Kennedy [1809] **260**

Coutts v. Greenhow [1811] **264**

Webster v. McGinnis [1812] **268**

Pennsylvania v. Addicks [1813] **271**

Kenny v. Udall and Kenny [1821] **274**

Peckford v. Peckford [1828] **277**

Prince v. Prince [1845] **280**

Shaw v. Shaw [1845] **283**

Hair v. Hair [1858] **287**

Packard v. Packard [1864] **292**

Birkbeck v. Ackroyd [1878] **296**

McKim v. McKim [1879] **300**

McGuire v. McGuire [1953] **304**

Frontiero v. Richardson [1973] **308**

Weinberger v. Wiesenfeld [1975] **312**

Orr v. Orr [1979] **316**

Marvin v. Marvin [1979] **320**

Califano v. Westcott [1979] **324**

Kirchberg v. Feenstra [1981] **328**

Ireland v. Smith [1995] **333**

Overview **337**

Lochner v. New York [1905] **341**

Muller v. Oregon [1908] **346**

Adkins v. Children's Hospital [1923] **352**

West Coast Hotel v. Parrish [1937] **357**

Goesaert v. Cleary [1948] **361**

Weeks v. Southern Bell [1969] **365**

Bowe v. Colgate-Palmolive [1969] **369**

Phillips v. Martin Marietta [1971] **373**

United States v. Libbey-Owens-
 Ford [1971] **376**

Pittsburgh Press v. Pittsburgh Commission on
 Human Relations [1973] **379**

**Section 6:
Women at Work**

Cleveland Board of Education v.
  LaFleur [1974] **385**
Corning Glass Works v. Brennan [1974] **390**
Geduldig v. Aiello [1974] **394**
Dothard v. Rawlinson [1977] **398**
Los Angeles Department of Water and Power v.
  Marie Manhart [1978] **402**
Personnel Administrator of Massachusetts v.
  Feeney [1979] **406**
Hishon v. King & Spaulding [1984] **410**
Meritor Savings Bank v. Vinson [1986] **414**
California Federal Savings and Loan Association
  v. Guerra [1987] **419**
Johnson v. Transportation Agency [1987] **423**
Automobile Workers v. Johnson
  Controls [1991] **428**
Harris v. Forklift [1993] **433**
The Tailhook Scandal [1994] **436**

Glossary **441**
Appendix of Legal Citations and Sources **447**
Index **453**

CONTENTS

In Chronological Order
(by date of trial)

Anne Hutchinson's Trials [1637 and 1638] **3**

The Case of Mary Mendame [1639] **43**

Mary Dyer Trials [1659 and 1660] **7**

The Trial of Charles Sheepey [1687] **45**

Salem Witchcraft Trials [1692] **11**

1600s

Carroll v. Warren [1736] **217**

Pattison v. Pattison [1737] **220**

Burk v. Phips [1793] **223**

Barnes v. Hart [1793] **226**

Scott v. Scott [1795] **230**

Megrath v. Robertson [1795] **233**

Beall and King v. Woolford [1797] **237**

Fry v. Derstler [1798] **241**

Griffith v. Griffith's Executors [1798] **244**

1700s

Dibble v. Hutton [1804] **247**

Martin v. Massachusetts [1805] **93**

Fitch v. Brainerd [1805] **252**

Watson v. Bailey [1808] **256**

Kempe v. Kennedy [1809] **260**

Coutts v. Greenhow [1811] **264**

Massachusetts v. Bangs [1812] **151**

Webster v. McGinnis [1812] **268**

Pennsylvania v. Addicks [1813] **271**

Kenny v. Udall and Kenny [1821] **274**

Peckford v. Peckford [1828] **277**

Crandall v. Connecticut [1834] **15**

Prince v. Prince [1845] **280**

1800s

Shaw v. Shaw [1845] **283**

Missouri v. Celia, a Slave [1855] **48**

Massachusetts v. Fogerty [1857] **53**

Hair v. Hair [1858] **287**

Packard v. Packard [1864] **292**

Hester Vaughan's Trial [1868] **96**

United States v. Susan B. Anthony [1873] **21**

Bradwell v. Illinois [1873] **100**

Minor v. Happersett [1875] **104**

Birkbeck v. Ackroyd [1878] **296**

McKim v. McKim [1879] **300**

1900s

Lochner v. New York [1905] **341**

Muller v. Oregon [1908] **346**

The Triangle Shirtwaist Fire [1911] **56**

The Trials of Alice Paul and Other National
Woman's Party Members [1917] **25**

New York v. Sanger [1918] **29**

Adkins v. Children's Hospital [1923] **352**

Buck v. Bell [1927] **153**

United States v. One Package [1936] **158**

West Coast Hotel v. Parrish [1937] **357**

Breedlove v. Suttles, Tax Collector [1937] **109**

Goesaert v. Cleary [1948] **361**

Los Angeles v. Stately [1949] **61**

McGuire v. McGuire [1953] **304**

Griswold v. Connecticut [1965] **162**

Pennsylvania v. Daniel and Douglas [1967] **63**

Weeks v. Southern Bell [1969] **365**

Bowe v. Colgate-Palmolive [1969] **369**

Phillips v. Martin Marietta [1971] **373**

United States v. Libbey-Owens-
Ford [1971] **376**

Reed v. Reed [1971] **112**

United States v. Vuitch [1971] **167**

Eisenstadt v. Baird [1972] **172**

Roe v. Wade [1973] **177**

Frontiero v. Richardson [1973] **308**

Pittsburgh Press v. Pittsburgh Commission on
Human Relations [1973] **379**

Cleveland Board of Education v.
LaFleur [1974] **385**

Corning Glass Works v. Brennan [1974] **390**
Geduldig v. Aiello [1974] **394**
Taylor v. Louisiana [1975] **115**
Weinberger v. Wiesenfeld [1975] **312**
Stanton v. Stanton [1975] **119**
Craig v. Boren [1976] **123**
Dothard v. Rawlinson [1977] **398**
Coker v. Georgia [1977] **69**
Los Angeles Department of Water and Power v.
  Marie Manhart [1978] **402**
Oregon v. Rideout [1978] **73**
Orr v. Orr [1979] **316**
Marvin v. Marvin [1979] **320**
Personnel Administrator of Massachusetts v.
  Feeney [1979] **406**
Califano v. Westcott [1979] **324**
Harris v. McRae [1980] **185**
Kirchberg v. Feenstra [1981] **328**
Michael M. v. Superior Court of Sonoma
  County [1981] **77**
Rostker v. Goldberg [1981] **127**
Mississippi University for Women v.
  Hogan [1982] **131**
Grove City College v. Bell [1984] **135**
New Bedford Rape Trials [1984] **81**
Hishon v. King & Spaulding [1984] **410**
Roberts v. United States Jaycees [1984] **139**
American Booksellers Association v.
  Hudnut [1986] **86**
Meritor Savings Bank v. Vinson [1986] **414**
California Federal Savings and Loan Association
  v. Guerra [1987] **419**
Johnson v. Transportation Agency [1987] **423**
In the Matter of Baby M [1988] **190**
Webster v. Reproductive Health
  Services [1989] **197**
Automobile Workers v. Johnson
  Controls [1991] **428**
Planned Parenthood of Southeastern Pennsylvania
  v. Casey [1992] **202**
Harris v. Forklift [1993] **433**
Cammermeyer v. Aspin [1994] **34**
Madsen v. Women's Health Center [1994] **207**

WOMEN'S

RIGHTS

ON TRIAL

The Tailhook Scandal [1994] **436**
Ireland v. Smith [1995] **333**
United States v. Virginia [1996] **143**

CONTENTS

In Alphabetical Order

Adkins v. Children's Hospital [1923]   **352**
American Booksellers Association v.
   Hudnut [1986]   **86**
Anne Hutchinson's Trials [1637 and 1638]   **3**
Automobile Workers v. Johnson
   Controls [1991]   **428**

A

Barnes v. Hart [1793]   **226**
Beall and King v. Woolford [1797]   **237**
Birkbeck v. Ackroyd [1878]   **296**
Bowe v. Colgate-Palmolive [1969]   **369**
Bradwell v. Illinois [1873]   **100**
Breedlove v. Suttles, Tax Collector [1937]   **109**
Buck v. Bell [1927]   **153**
Burk v. Phips [1793]   **223**

B

Califano v. Westcott [1979]   **324**
California Federal Savings and Loan Association
   v. Guerra [1987]   **419**
Cammermeyer v. Aspin [1994]   **34**
Carroll v. Warren [1736]   **217**
The Case of Mary Mendame [1639]   **43**
Cleveland Board of Education v.
   LaFleur [1974]   **385**
Coker v. Georgia [1977]   **69**
Corning Glass Works v. Brennan [1974]   **390**
Coutts v. Greenhow [1811]   **264**
Craig v. Boren [1976]   **123**
Crandall v. Connecticut [1834]   **15**

C

D

Dibble v. Hutton [1804] **247**

Dothard v. Rawlinson [1977] **398**

E

Eisenstadt v. Baird [1972] **172**

F

Fitch v. Brainerd [1805] **252**

Frontiero v. Richardson [1973] **308**

Fry v. Derstler [1798] **241**

G

Geduldig v. Aiello [1974] **394**

Goesaert v. Cleary [1948] **361**

Griffith v. Griffith's Executors [1798] **244**

Griswold v. Connecticut [1965] **162**

Grove City College v. Bell [1984] **135**

H

Hair v. Hair [1858] **287**

Harris v. Forklift [1993] **433**

Harris v. McRae [1980] **185**

Hester Vaughan's Trial [1868] **96**

Hishon v. King & Spaulding [1984] **410**

I

In the Matter of Baby M [1988] **190**

Ireland v. Smith [1995] **333**

J

Johnson v. Transportation Agency [1987] **423**

K

Kempe v. Kennedy [1809] **260**

Kenny v. Udall and Kenny [1821] **274**

Kirchberg v. Feenstra [1981] **328**

L

Lochner v. New York [1905] **341**

Los Angeles Department of Water and Power v.
Marie Manhart [1978] **402**

Los Angeles v. Stately [1949] **61**

M

McGuire v. McGuire [1953] **304**

McKim v. McKim [1879] **300**

Madsen v. Women's Health Center [1994] **207**
Martin v. Massachusetts [1805] **93**
Marvin v. Marvin [1979] **320**
Mary Dyer Trials [1659 and 1660] **7**
Massachusetts v. Bangs [1812] **151**
Massachusetts v. Fogerty [1857] **53**
Megrath v. Robertson [1795] **233**
Meritor Savings Bank v. Vinson [1986] **414**
Michael M. v. Superior Court of Sonoma
    County [1981] **77**
Minor v. Happersett [1875] **104**
Mississippi University for Women v.
    Hogan [1982] **131**
Missouri v. Celia, a Slave [1855] **48**
Muller v. Oregon [1908] **346**

New Bedford Rape Trials [1984] **81**
New York v. Sanger [1918] **29**

Oregon v. Rideout [1978] **73**
Orr v. Orr [1979] **316**

Packard v. Packard [1864] **292**
Pattison v. Pattison [1737] **220**
Peckford v. Peckford [1828] **277**
Pennsylvania v. Addicks [1813] **271**
Pennsylvania v. Daniel and Douglas [1967] **63**
Personnel Administrator of Massachusetts v.
    Feeney [1979] **406**
Phillips v. Martin Marietta [1971] **373**
Pittsburgh Press v. Pittsburgh Commission on
    Human Relations [1973] **379**
Planned Parenthood of Southeastern Pennsylvania
    v. Casey [1992] **202**
Prince v. Prince [1845] **280**

Reed v. Reed [1971] **112**
Roberts v. United States Jaycees [1984] **139**
Roe v. Wade [1973] **177**
Rostker v. Goldberg [1981] **127**

N

O

P

R

S

Salem Witchcraft Trials [1692] **11**
Scott v. Scott [1795] **230**
Shaw v. Shaw [1845] **283**
Stanton v. Stanton [1975] **119**

T

Taylor v. Louisiana [1975] **115**
The Tailhook Scandal [1994] **436**
The Trial of Charles Sheepey [1687] **45**
The Trials of Alice Paul and Other National
    Woman's Party Members [1917] **25**
The Triangle Shirtwaist Fire [1911] **56**

U

United States v. Libbey-Owens-
    Ford [1971] **376**
United States v. One Package [1936] **158**
United States v. Susan B. Anthony [1873] **21**
United States v. Virginia [1996] **143**
United States v. Vuitch [1971] **167**

W

Watson v. Bailey [1808] **256**
Webster v. McGinnis [1812] **268**
Webster v. Reproductive Health
    Services [1989] **197**
Weeks v. Southern Bell [1969] **365**
Weinberger v. Wiesenfeld [1975] **312**
West Coast Hotel v. Parrish [1937] **357**

PREFACE

Women's Rights on Trial provides a fully-rounded portrait of four centuries of women's legal history in America—from colonial times to the present. The book is divided into six topical sections:

Crimes of Conscience and Nonconformity
Crime and Punishment
Rights and Responsibilities of Citizenship
Reproductive Rights
Marriage, Parenting, and Divorce
Women at Work

Each section opens with an overview of the trials covered therein.

We used five criteria in selecting the 101 trials that appear in the book: Does the case set a precedent? Is it representative of an historical period? Is it a judicial landmark? Does it offer an historical contrast to an earlier trial in the book? Finally, is it interesting?

Each chapter opens with a "fact box," which presents the major points at a glance—plaintiff, defendant, crime charged, lawyers, judges, location and dates of trial, verdict, and sentence, and significance of the trial. In these headings, the terms "Plaintiff" (the person who brings the case before the court) and "Defendant" may change to "Appellant" or "Appellee," depending on whether the verdict was appealed by the plaintiff or defendant. "Justice" means a judge sat on the Supreme Court; "Judge" means he or she served on a lower court. "Chancellor" is the title for judges of the early courts of equity, or chancery. The names of all judges appear in alphabetical order, with the name of the person delivering the opinion in italics. Where an attorney's first name is not in the trial or historical record, we give only the last. The date for the decision refers to the last trial to take place.

We have shortened the trial titles in the contents and essays and substituted state names for the term "Commonwealth." However, the reader will find the legal citations in the Appendix of Legal Citations and

Sources. Should an early citation follow a different style from the ones used in the twentieth century, we have left the original wording.

Other helpful features include three contents sections: the first is in chronological order within each of the six topical sections; the second is in overall chronological order; and the third is in alphabetical order, by trial name. In addition, a glossary provides definitions to legal terms, and a comprehensiv index lists key figures, subjects, and areas of law.

There are many people who helped **Women's Rights on Trial** happen. Our gratitude goes to the hardworking staff of New England Publishing Associates. We deeply appreciate the invaluable work of Victoria Harlow, for obtaining nearly all illustrations and trial information that appear in this book; Rebecca Berardy, for helpful proofreading and computer advice; Karen Corriveau, for keeping us financially responsible; and Ron Formica, for reliable trouble-shooting.

Thanks, too, for the hard work of Larry Baker, our editor at Gale Research, Winifred Bonney, our copyeditor, and Roberta Buland, our indexer.

The contributions of the following writers and researchers have greatly enriched this book: Winifred Bonney, Sandy Senior Dauer, Professor Maurice Isserman, Sarah Kurian, and Marco Raffala.

For information and fact-checking, we thank Laura Allan, Esq. (Feminist Majority), Lawrence Cheeseman (Connecticut State Law Library), Mike Hveem (University of Connecticut Law Library), Penelope Petzold, Esq., Dr. Carl Schneider, Fred Shapiro (Yale Law Library), and the staffs of the Connecticut State Library, Russell Library (Middletown, Connecticut), New York Public Library, and the Supreme Court Library.

Professor Francis M. Nevins, Saint Louis University Law School, was thoughtful in bringing Melville Davisson Post to our attention.

Finally, we would like to thank our husbands, Edward W. Knappman and Joseph DuPont, for their stimulating conversation and continued interest and encouragement, and our children, Amanda Frost Knappman, Jesse Cullen-DuPont, and Melissa Cullen-DuPont, for being there.

—Elizabeth Frost-Knappman
Kathryn Cullen-DuPont

INTRODUCTION

Women's Rights on Trial contains 101 key trials of historical importance to American women since the settlement of the colonies. These lawsuits illustrate six themes important to women: crimes of conscience and nonconformity; crime and punishment; rights and responsibilities of citizenship; reproductive rights; marriage, parenting, and divorce; and women at work. The trials highlight disputes over property, custody, wills, deeds, voting, jury membership, education, sexual harassment, residence, salary, work conditions, birth control, and other issues central to women's experiences in America.

Our earliest case is that of Mary Mendame, the first female on record prosecuted for a sexual offense in colonial America, tried in 1639 in Plymouth Colony. The most recent is *U.S. v. Virginia*, which in 1996 decided whether a military academy receiving taxpayer money could exclude women.

We have selected our trials for historical, as well as legal, reasons. For example, the Salem witch trials—not real trials at all, since no attorney was present for the accused—are essential to our understanding of colonial New England. We have chosen trials that set precedents in the law, illustrate important regional practices, and demonstrate common roadblocks women faced on their long march to legal equality.

The trials speak volumes about why women's history is still controversial: Were women any better off after the Revolution? Did the Founding Fathers intend to include women when they met in 1787 to draft the Constitution? Was the era of protective legislation beneficial to women? Is there a right of privacy implicit in the Constitution that protects women's reproductive decisions? Do women still need an Equal Rights Amendment? These are complicated and politically divisive questions, which we hope to illuminate, although not answer.

The trials in **Women's Rights on Trial** also exemplify key changes for women under the law. Throughout the colonial and nationalist eras, the legal position of American women was, in the words of historian Marylynn Salmon, one of "enforced dependence." Although single women were equal to men in property rights, they did not have the same political rights. As historian Eleanor Flexner writes in *Century of Struggle*, "Women had many duties, but few rights." Furthermore, "Married women in particular suffered 'civil death,' having no right to property and no legal entity or existence apart from their husbands." One reason was the legal fiction of "coverture," which considered a married couple "one person" under the law. That "one person" was the husband.

Under English common law, which prevailed in the American colonies, after marriage a woman became a *feme covert* (from the French expression *femme coverte*). In 1632, *The Laws Resolutions of Women's Rights; or The Lawes Provision for Women* explained this term as follows:

> When a small brook or little river incorporateth with Rhodanus, Humber or the Thames, the poor rivulet looseth its name, it is carried and recarried with the new associate, it beareth no sway, it possesseth nothing during coverture. A woman as soon as she is married, is called covert . . . that is, *veiled*, . . . clouded and overshadowed. . . . To a married woman, her new self is her superior, her companion, her master.

Thus the married couple became a *fictive* single person, that person being the husband.

Under coverture, a married women lost her right to her own property, wages, and inheritance. She could not sue or be sued, sign contracts, enact wills, or hold custody to her own children. She could engage in business only with the express permission of her husband. *Megrath v. Robertson* (1795) shows how women—even in a state such as South Carolina, which was tolerant of female participation in commerce—needed the consent of their husbands to engage in business.

In *Burk v. Phips* (1793) the courts specifically refused to grant legal standing to a married woman, separated from her husband, to petition for the return of her kidnapped son. The judges ruled that only a father, not a mother, was entitled to the child's labor. One early rape trial, *Massachusetts v. Fogerty* (1855), demonstrates that the rape of a wife was a legal impossibility. Not until *McKim v. McKim* (1879) did it become accepted judicial policy for a mother to retain custody of a young child because it might be in the child's "best interests."

The Colonial Period

In colonial America, there was only one remedy for these legal disabilities: equity law. In early America two legal systems existed side-by-side, common law and equity jurisprudence. Under the rules of equity, sometimes wives could own and control property separately from their husbands.

Equity law was decided by a judge, not a jury. It was based on the judge's sense of fairness—of what was equitable—rather than precedents, upon which common law is based. Under common law, any personal property a wife brought into marriage or inherited or earned afterward automatically became that of her husband. Her real estate became his to manage as he saw fit. Equity law allowed married women some control over their own property under certain situations.

The colonists imported equity law from England and dispensed it through courts of equity, also called courts of chancery. New York, South Carolina, Maryland, and Virginia had chancery courts, and some legislative bodies, such as Connecticut's, sat as a court of equity as well.

However, in New England, the Puritans believed that a wife's central duty was to submit to her husband and that allowing her any say over the disposal of property could only lead to friction in her marriage. That wives might be concerned about property matters also implied that the marriage was based on economics, not love and respect. Therefore, colonies influenced by the Puritans rejected equity courts.

The 1736 trial of *Carroll v. Warren* is one of the earliest on record to illustrate how the courts of equity tempered the harshness of the common law. The Pennsylvania decision *Barnes v. Hart* (1793) represented an advance in the protection of women's real estate from greedy husbands. Until 1830, equity courts were the only bright spot on the legal landscape for women—for a wealthy few.

Despite the promise of republicanism after the Revolutionary War, women's contributions to the new nation were recognized in neither legislation nor practice. In *Women and the Law of Property in Early America*, historian Marylynn Salmon found only three changes benefiting women that came as the *direct* result of independence: a relaxation of the divorce laws, which gave abused or deserted wives new legal protection; the eradication of the old rules of primogeniture, permitting females to inherit; and the end of the practice of double shares for eldest sons whose fathers died without a will, which entitled women to a fairer share of their father's wealth.

Unlike slaves or Indians, women were not even mentioned in the Constitution. The document's gender-neutral words "person," "people," "elector," and "representative" did not mean to imply that women were included.

After the Revolution, in 1805, *Martin v. Massachusetts* provided a revealing discussion of the relationship between women and the state, showing how the law put wives on the same level as children and the mentally deficient. Federalist lawyer Theophilis Parsons claimed that as a married woman, Anna Martin was not a member of the state, only an inhabitant. He argued, "The real question is, whether the [Massachusetts] statute was intended to include persons who have, by law, no wills of their own. . . . Infants, insane, [married women], all of whom the law considers having no will, cannot act *freely*." The Supreme Court agreed with Parsons, remarking that Martin had "no *political* relation to the *state* any more than an *alien*."

The Victorian Era

The status of early nineteenth-century women was aptly described by Melville Davisson Post in his story "The Heir at Law," published by *American Magazine* in 1927. In this story, the main character is Colonel Braxton, who is practicing law in Virginia before the Civil War. Braxton's adversary is Caleb Lurty, who is about to take over the estate of his dead brother, Marshall, who died without a will, to the exclusion of Marshall's out-of-wedlock daughter. The two men argue over the injustice of the inheritance law. Braxton asks, "Upon what theory of justice, Mr. Lurty, could such a law be founded? In what manner is our paternal ancestor of greater value to us, that a child's estate should go to the father, while the mother who brought him into the world takes nothing?" Lurty responds, "Upon the theory itself, sir, that the man made the fortune." Braxton retorts, "Upon the theory, sir, that the man made the laws!"

Fortunately, improvements in women's legal status evolved during the nineteenth century, usually through the modification of existing laws within each state. Then between 1839 and 1895, a series of property acts radically improved the lot of wives. These property acts guaranteed married women the right to control the property they brought with them into marriage as well as any money or goods they subsequently earned. The state of New York's version became a model for the nation. It read:

> The real and personal property of any female who may hereafter marry, and which she shall own at the time of her marriage, and the rents, issues and profits thereof, shall not be subject to the disposal of her husband nor be liable for his debts and shall continue her sole and separate property as if she were a single female.

This was a huge victory for women, but one of even greater consequence came in 1868 with the passage of the Fourteenth Amendment to the Constitution.

Women's First Attempts to Claim Fourteenth Amendment Protection

After the Civil War, women were organizing and winning the vote in the Wyoming, Washington, and Utah territories. Victoria Woodhull ran for president. Smith and Bryn Mawr colleges opened. Vermont, New York, Michigan, and Minnesota granted suffrage on school issues to mothers. Connecticut admitted the first woman to the bar, and the U.S. Senate debated the Susan B. Anthony amendment.

However, as women made demands upon their legislatures and the courts, judges and lawmakers fought back, actively discriminating against them. In particular, they refused to apply Fourteenth Amendment protection to women's rights. Two examples—*United States v. Susan B. Anthony* and *Bradwell v. Illinois*—involving the right to vote and the right to practice a profession, illustrate the judiciary's prejudice on this point.

When the Fourteenth Amendment was adopted in 1868, women's rights leaders were angered by the wording of Section 2. That section, written to encourage states to give the vote to black males, seemed to place in doubt the citizenship of females by inserting the word "male" into the Constitution for the first time. In the section on the right to vote, the word "male" was used in place of the former words "the people" or "citizens":

> But when the right to vote at any election for the choice of electors for President and Vice President of the United States, Representatives in Congress, the Executive and Judicial officers of a State, is denied to any of the *male* inhabitants of such State, . . . the basis of representation therein shall be reduced in the proportion which the number of such *male* citizens shall bear to the whole number of such citizens twenty-one years of age in such State.

The implication was that women were not citizens. However, Francis Minor, a Missouri lawyer, thought Section 1 of the Fourteenth Amendment was more relevant. It read:

> All persons born or naturalized in the United States, and subject to the jurisdiction thereof, are citizens of the United States and of the state wherein they reside. No state shall make or enforce any law which shall abridge the privileges or immunities of citizens of the United States.

This clause, Minor wrote, *confirmed* the citizenship of women—and, indeed, their claim to all the "privileges" of citizenship, including suffrage.

Elizabeth Cady Stanton and Susan B. Anthony published Minor's opinion in their newspaper, the *Revolution*, and urged women to vote in defiance of any state law to the contrary. Women in at least ten states heeded this advice in 1871 and 1872. A few women—including Anthony—managed to cast their ballots.

Anthony and fourteen women registered to vote in Rochester, New York, and they voted in the presidential election of November 5, 1872. They—and the inspectors who had registered them—were arrested on November 28. Bail was set at $500, and all but Anthony elected to pay it rather than face jail.

Anthony's criminal trial for casting her ballot in 1872, almost fifty years before the ratification of the Nineteenth Amendment, was an act of political defiance. She intended to test whether the recently adopted Fourteenth Amendment would be interpreted as expanding or protecting women's rights. On June 17, 1873, her trial came before Judge Ward Hunt, who instructed the jury to find Anthony guilty:

> I have decided as a question of law . . . that under the Fourteenth Amendment, which Miss Anthony claims protects her, she was not protected in a right to vote. . . . I therefore direct you to find a verdict of guilty.

The Supreme Court considered women's claims under the Fourteenth Amendment for the first time in 1873, in *Bradwell v. Illinois*. Myra Bradwell, editor of the *Chicago Legal News*, passed Illinois' law exam in August 1869. When she applied for admission to the Illinois bar later that year, the state court refused to admit her because she was a woman.

Bradwell countered that her Constitutional rights, especially as protected by the Fourteenth Amendment's guarantee that "no State shall make or enforce any law which shall abridge the privileges and immunities of citizenship," were being abridged by the state of Illinois.

The court did not agree. Bradwell appealed to the U.S. Supreme Court. It ruled that Illinois was entitled to restrict the practice of law—and indeed any other profession—to men. Justice Joseph Bradley offered a particularly biting observation on a woman's place in American society, insisting that the very idea of a woman having a distinct career from her husband would interfere with "family harmony," not to mention that "the paramount destiny and mission of women are to fulfill the noble and benign offices of wife and mother. This is the law of the Creator."

The Fourteenth Amendment was not successfully used to overturn a sex-biased law until *Reed v. Reed*, ninety-eight years later.

The Twentieth Century

In 1908, *Muller v. Oregon* upheld Oregon's right to pass a maximum hour law for women because, like children, they constituted a "special class" in need of protection. When *Muller* was appealed to the U.S. Supreme Court, Florence Kelley, of the National Consumers' League, Barnard tutor Josephine Goldmark, and some male union leaders thought that working long hours was harmful to women, especially as it affected their ability to produce and parent children. Their ideas conflicted with traditional court decisions upholding a person's "liberty of contract."

They turned to Louis Brandeis, a young attorney. Working around the clock, the three wrote a 113-page document marshaling facts and figures that detailed economic, social, and medical statistics to support the argument that the health and morality of *women* workers were *uniquely* affected by their hours of labor. For the first time, a case based on human welfare was made in place of legal reasoning. This new form of legal argument came to be called the "Brandeis brief."

Brandeis argued that it was "common knowledge" that to permit women to work more than ten hours a day was "dangerous to public health, safety, morals or welfare."

Justice David J. Brewer, speaking for the majority, thought:

> That women's physical structure . . . place her at a disadvantage in the struggle for subsistence is obvious. This is especially true when the burdens of motherhood are upon her. Even when they are not, by abundant testimony of the medical fraternity continuance for a long time on her feet at work . . . tends to injurious effects upon the body, and, as healthy mothers are essential to vigorous offspring, the physical well-being of woman becomes an object of public interest and care in order to preserve the strength and vigor of the race.

For these reasons the Court unanimously ruled against Muller. The Brandeis brief had been a huge success. However, its assumptions about women proved to restrict rather than promote their opportunity. This legal fiction—that woman is the weaker sex—was a classic example of winning the battle but losing the war, for it kept women out of decent jobs for years.

After 1908, the Supreme Court and state houses began a period of protectionism for wage-earning women. After the *Muller* decision, other states passed statutes that kept women from working overtime or working certain jobs. *Goesaert v. Cleary* (1948) upheld a Michigan law that barred women from being licensed as bartenders while at the same time making an exemption for wives and daughters of bartenders. Michigan argued—and the Court agreed—that the presence of a male relative was necessary to protect a female bartender from the "hazards that confront a barmaid" and that, in any event, public morals were best served by restricting the bartending trade to men. Other states prohibited women from working in foundries or mines, delivering the mail, operating elevators, lifting certain weights, or working at night.

The Equal Pay Act and Title VII

With the passage of the Equal Pay Act in 1964, and the addition of the word "sex" to Title VII of the Civil Rights Act the same year, America's wage-earning women began to come into their own under American law. The Equal Pay Act states that women must receive the same pay as men for equal work. Title VII of the 1964 Civil Rights Act, known as the Equal Employment Opportunity section, forbids discrimination by private employers, employment agencies, and unions on the basis of race, color, religion, national origin, or sex.

The 1971 case of *United States v. Libbey-Owens-Ford* was the Justice Department's first sex-discrimination suit under Title VII. The federal government accused Libbey-Owens-Ford and United Glass and Ceramic Workers of North America, AFL-CIO Local #9 with hiring women for only one of five glass plants in Toledo, Ohio, and assigning them to the least attractive jobs. The Justice Department also demanded back pay for women as well as a change in that policy.

Libbey-Owens-Ford attributed its inability to comply with Title VII to the fact that Ohio state laws mandated different treatment of women, especially the maximum-hour law and limitation on weight lifting. The settlement came with a consent agreement, and did not resolve the conflict between Title VII and state protective legislation; however, Libbey-Owens-Ford did agree to promote some women immediately, to consider women for more types of jobs, and to educate women about job opportunities.

Three years later, in *Corning Glass Works v. Brennan* (1974), the Supreme Court rendered its first decision in a pay discrimination suit under the Equal Pay Act. Corning paid female day inspectors less than night inspectors, a position from which women were excluded—due to laws prohibiting their nighttime employment—until 1966. The evidence showed that the night staff's higher wages were not an acceptable "night shift differential" but a continuation of the higher wages originally paid to an all-male staff as compensation for performing what they viewed as "demeaning"—"women's work." The Court ruled that this was a violation of the Equal Pay Act which could be remedied only by raising the female day staff's wages.

In other workplace decisions, the Supreme Court abolished the business practice of refusing to hire the mothers of pre-school age children (*Phillips v. Martin Marietta*, 1971); ended sex segregated want ads (*Pittsburgh Press v. Pittsburgh Commission on Human Relations*, 1973); ended the practice of forcing pregnant school teachers to go on unpaid maternity leave (*Cleveland Board of Education v. LaFleur*, 1974); abolished minimum height and weight standards for female workers (*Dothard v. Rawlinson*, 1977); prohibited pension benefit discrimination (*Los Angeles Department of Water and Power v. Marie Manhart*, 1978); and defined sexual harassment as illegal discrimination (*Meritor Savings Bank v. Vinson*, 1986).

From Margaret Sanger's Jail Cell to *Roe v. Wade*

Margaret Sanger opened the first birth control clinic in the nation in 1917, earning herself a jail sentence and a place in the "Crimes of Conscience and Nonconformity" section of this book. A half-century later, in *Griswold v. Connecticut* (1965), the Supreme Court overturned one of the last state laws prohibiting the prescription or use of contraceptives in the case of married couples.

The decision was grounded in the Ninth Amendment to the Constitution, which states that "the enumeration in the Constitution, of certain rights, shall not be construed to deny or disparage others retained by the people." The Court declared that the right to privacy was one of the un-enumerated rights "retained by the people" and ruled that a married couple's contraceptive decisions fell within that right of privacy. The Supreme Court subsequently ruled that the right of privacy encompassed an unmarried person's right to use contraceptives (*Eisenstadt v. Baird*, 1972), and a woman's right to an abortion (*Roe v. Wade*, 1973 and *Planned Parenthood of Southeastern Pennsylvania v. Casey*, 1992).

The Fourteenth Amendment Revisited

Finally, in 1971, the Supreme Court ruled that the Fourteenth Amendment—passed 103 years earlier—did, in fact, protect the rights of women. This pivotal decision was reached in *Reed v. Reed*, a case that challenged a state law giving males automatic preference over females in the selection of executors. Sally Reed, upon rejection of her application to act as executor for the estate of her deceased son, claimed that her right to equal protection under the Fourteenth Amendment had been violated.

Although the Court had rejected similar arguments a number of times during the past century (beginning in 1873 with its decision in *Bradwell v. Illinois)*, it now agreed with Sally Reed. The Fourteenth Amendment's guarantee that "no state shall make or enforce any law which shall abridge the privileges or immunities of citizens of the United States," protected the rights of women as well as the rights of men.

Based on this precedent, the Supreme Court has since ended the practice of requiring female army officers to prove a husband's financial dependency before receiving spousal benefits (*Frontiero v. Richardson,* 1973); overturned laws setting different ages of majority for males and females (*Stanton v. Stanton,* 1975); denied states the right to exclude women from juries (*Taylor v. Louisiana,* 1975); required the payment of Social Security benefits to the surviving male parents of dependent children upon the death of female parents who had paid into the Social Security system (*Weinberger v. Wiesenfeld,* 1975); made wives as well as husbands liable to pay alimony (*Orr v. Orr,* 1979); overturned a state law that designated a husband "head and master" of property owned jointly with his wife and permitted him to dispose of such property without his wife's knowledge or consent (*Kirchberg v. Feenstra,* 1981); ordered a state-funded women's nursing college to admit men (*Mississippi University for Women v. Hogan,* 1982); upheld a state law forbidding sex discrimination in the admission policies of organizations such as the Jaycees (*Roberts v. United States Jaycees,* 1984); and ruled on the exclusion of women from taxpayer-funded military academies (*United States v. Virginia,* 1996).

Our Daughters' America

These legal victories would have delighted the first Fourteenth Amendment plaintiffs, Myra Bradwell and Virginia Minor, and that first brave Fourteenth Amendment defendant, Susan B. Anthony. The decisions since *Reed v. Reed* have, one step at a time, brought women ever closer to true legal equality with men. And yet, it is disconcerting that many of women's rights are "guaranteed" by an amendment that was part of the Constitution for 103 years before it was so construed, while the Equal Rights Amendment's forthright declaration that "equality of rights under the law shall not be denied or abridged by the United States or by any State on account of sex" failed to win ratification.

Is an Equal Rights Amendment necessary? Ruth Bader Ginsburg, during her career as a civil rights attorney, was the central figure in women's successful battles to win Fourteenth Amendment protection of their rights. She addressed this question during her 1993 Supreme Court confirmation hearings.

In answer to preliminary questions, she discussed discrimination faced during her law-student days, including being barred from a section of Harvard's library to which only men were admitted. Newspaper articles also made much of the fact that she had once been denied an interview for a clerkship with Supreme Court justice Felix Frankfurter, who was reportedly unwilling to consider hiring a woman. That she now sits upon that very Court as an associate justice was certainly one measure of just how far American women had come in their struggle for equality. Yet she found it necessary to take a much longer view when asked about the Fourteenth Amendment and the Equal Rights Amendment.

Reviewing the Fourteenth Amendment's history, she said it was a "sad part of our history" that the "great amendment that changed so much in this nation . . . didn't change the status of women" at that time. She acknowledged that it was nothing less than "a bold change from the middle of the nineteenth century until the 1970s when women's equal citizenship was recognized before the law." Then she stated unequivocally:

> I remain an advocate of the equal rights amendment, I will tell you, for this reason: because I have a daughter and a granddaughter, and I would like the legislature of this country and of all the states to stand up and say, "We know what that history was in the *nineteenth* century, and we want to make a clarion call that women and men are equal before the law, just as every modern human rights document in the world does since 1970." I'd like to see that statement made just that way in the United States Constitution.

So would we.

Section 1
CRIMES OF CONSCIENCE AND NONCONFORMITY

American history is replete with tales of women who lived bravely and in defiance of the "rules" of conduct for their sex. Many had to answer for their actions in court.

In 1637, Anne Hutchinson was clearly and willingly at odds with the male Puritan establishment of the Massachusetts Bay Colony. In a society that demanded religious conformity, she dared to hold her own views of Puritan theology. Her society also demanded subordination of its women, but Hutchinson nonetheless dared to preach and publicize her dissenting views—and to believe in her right to do so. She was exiled from the colony following a civil trial and excommunicated from the church following a religious trial. Mary Dyer, likewise, ran spiritually afoul of the Massachusetts Bay Colony's leadership. Convicted and once nearly hanged for her Quaker beliefs, she too was banished from the Colony. Dyer did not enjoy her remaining years away from the Colony. Instead, she returned to "look the bloody (anti-Quaker) laws in the face," an act she knew would result in her certain execution.

Both Hutchinson and Dyer had the benefit of religious conviction, and each evidently went to her punishment believing she suffered for a just cause. Such was not the case for the Salem "witches." While some of the accused may have engaged in healing aids or fortune-telling practices handed down from pagan times—and while they, like many at the time, may have believed in supernatural forces not endorsed by their church—there is no evidence they actually practiced witchcraft. Rebecca Nurse, convicted and sentenced to hang, protested her innocence to Reverend Nicholas Noyes. When he refused to believe her, she wished vengeance upon him: "If you take my life away, God will give you blood to drink."

Lone women can still find their individual consciences in sharp and public conflict with the dictates of a deeply held faith. In 1979, for example, Sonia Johnson was expelled from the Church of the Latter Day Saints for her support of the Equal Rights Amendment (ERA) and two Roman Catholic nuns resigned from their religious order for refusing to retract pro-choice statements published during Walter Mondale's and Geraldine Ferraro's unsuccessful 1984 bid for the White House.

Our earliest non-religious case of female conscience in conflict with the law is Prudence Crandall's, who went to jail in 1834 for teaching young African American girls in her boarding school. Connecticut's "Black Law"—passed specifically to prevent Crandall's operation of her school—was ultimately found unconstitutional by a higher court, but Crandall was forced to give up her school nonetheless.

Margaret Sanger was also moved by the plight of others: among them were her many nursing patients, including a young woman who died following a self-induced abortion, and her own mother, who died too young after eighteen pregnancies. Sanger went to jail at least nine times in her quest to make contraceptives available to American women. A trial in 1873 followed Sanger's opening of the country's first birth control clinic. Although she was convicted and her conviction was upheld by a higher court, the case provided a loophole that later enabled Sanger legally to establish physician-staffed birth control clinics.

Two cases, forty-four years apart, concern women taking desperate measures to secure suffrage. In 1873, Susan B. Anthony was convicted of illegally casting a ballot in a presidential election. Denied the vote because she was a woman, Anthony did not have the right to testify in her own defense because of her sex. In 1917, Alice Paul and 167 other members of the National Women's Party went to jail for obstructing a sidewalk. The sidewalk in question was in front of the White House, and the "obstructing" was actually caused by their picketing to demand suffrage. Although picketing was perfectly legal in the United States—and a sidewalk obstruction would seem a minor infraction of the traffic rules—the women remained in jail up to seven months. They also became the first American citizens to claim that the United States held them as political prisoners.

The final case in this section involves Colonel Margarethe Cammermeyer. The recipient of a Bronze Star for distinguished service in Vietnam, Cammermeyer became the most highly-decorated and highest ranking officer to be discharged from any branch of the military for her sexual orientation. She sued the U.S. Army in the U.S. District Court in Seattle, Washington. District Judge Thomas Zilly ordered Cammermeyer reinstated. He cited, among other things, Cammermeyer's own record, both before and after her acknowledgment of her lesbian orientation. Cammermeyer's illustrious service to the Army, he wrote, was sufficiently compelling proof that "acknowledged homosexuality is not incompatible with military service." As of 1997, the government is appealing the decision.

Anne Hutchinson's Trials: 1637 and 1638

Defendant: Anne Hutchinson   **Crimes Charged:** "Traducing the ministers and their ministry" and heresy   **Chief Defense Lawyer:** None
Chief Prosecutors: Civil trial: John Winthrop; religious trial: the Reverend John Davenport   **Judges:** Civil trial: John Winthrop and the Magistrates of Massachusetts; religious trial: John Wilson and the ministers of the Church of Boston   **Places:** Civil trial: Newtown (Cambridge); religious trial: Boston, Massachusetts   **Dates of trials:** Civil trial: November 7–8, 1637; religious trial: March 22, 1638   **Verdicts:** Guilty   **Sentences:** Banished from the colony and excommunicated from the Church of Boston

SIGNIFICANCE
Anne Hutchinson became the most famous of the women who rebelled against the religious authority of the Massachusetts Bay Colony's male leadership.

When the Puritans established the Massachusetts Bay Colony, they wanted to be free of the prejudice and interference they had experienced in England. As founding governor John Winthrop described it, they wanted a close-to-perfect "citty [sic] upon a hill." But their model of Christian deportment and solidarity did not include religious liberty for others or intellectual freedom for women. Most Puritan ministers preached that a person's "good works" could be construed as an indication, or justification, that God had elected that person for salvation.

Anne Hutchinson—a midwife and herbal healer—arrived in the Bay Colony in 1634 and wasted no time upsetting this "citty" with her strong views on religious doctrine. She shared her ideas in weekly religious meetings with sixty to eighty women and men—and church elders were quickly and seriously alarmed. They objected to "one woman . . . [who] took upon her the whole exercise . . . [as] disorderly, and without rule."

Hutchinson paid no attention. She continued to preach her interpretation of Puritan doctrine—that is, she believed that those so elected experienced not only a spiritual consciousness, but a replacement of their own self-will with the inner guidance of an in-dwelling Holy Ghost. John Cotton, and her brother-in-law, John Wheelwright, also spoke of a "covenant of grace"—the theory that justification could also be determined by an individual's own spiritually experienced consciousness of God's election. She also began to denounce ministers who preached only the Puritans' traditional "Covenant of Works."

An Uppity Woman

In November 1637, Hutchinson was brought to civil trial by Governor Winthrop, who charged her as follows: "Mrs. Hutchinson, you are called here as one of those that have troubled the peace . . . you have spoken of divers[e] things . . . very prejudicial to the honour of the churches and ministers thereof, and you have maintained a meeting . . . that hath been condemned . . . as a thing not tolerable nor comely in the sight of God nor fitting for your sex."

Hutchinson bluntly demanded to know where she had erred. Winthrop finally accused her of supporting Wheelwright: "Why for your doings, this you did harbour and countenance those that are parties in this faction that you have heard of." Wheelwright had been banished following his conviction of sedition and contempt, and she had both signed and encouraged others to sign a petition on his behalf.

Winthrop persisted in his exploration of Hutchinson's support for Wheelwright and his followers, until she asked, "What breach of law is that, Sir?"

"Why, dishonoring of parents," Winthrop quickly replied, implying that the commonwealth's magistrates and governor were "parents" to those they led, including Hutchinson.

She did not dispute Winthrop's view, but inquired: "But put the case Sir that I do fear the Lord and my parents, may I not entertain them that fear the Lord because my parents will not give me leave?"

Winthrop shifted the questioning to her conduct in holding religious meetings. She interrogated Winthrop in turn: "Can you find a warrant [permission] for yourself and condemn me for the same thing?" Claiming that no men had been present, she reminded Winthrop of the apostle Paul's letter to Titus saying, "the elder women should instruct the younger." Winthrop insisted that older women should only instruct the younger "about their business and to love their husbands." When she rebutted his point, saying "it is meant for some publick times," Winthrop took her to task for distracting women from their homemaking duties and therefore wasting their time.

Cotton testified on Hutchinson's behalf the following morning—both on her theological interpretations and the issue of whether she had "traduced the ministers." Just as she seemed close to acquittal, she announced that she had had an immediate revelation from God and that she knew her inquisitors would be destroyed. No further proof of heresy was required, and she was "banished . . . as a woman not fit for our society." She was allowed, however, to stay in the colony until the end of winter.

Banned From the Church

Despite her conviction, Hutchinson continued to preach. Finally, "the Elders of Boston . . . declared their readinesse to deale with Mistris Hutchinson in a Church way." In this religious trial, held March 22, 1683, Cotton testified *against* Anne. He warned her, "Though I have not herd, nayther do I thinke, you have bine unfaythful to your Husband in his Marriage Covenant, yet that will follow upon it." He directed the female members of the church to disregard her teachings. He cautioned, "You see she is but a Woman and many unsound and dayngerous principles are held by her."

At the trial's conclusion, excommunication was added to banishment. Hutchinson was not without support, however. Mary Dyer—who would herself be hanged for religious crimes in the Colony in 1660 (see page 7)—boldly walked to Hutchinson's side and took her hand. Before the two women exited the church, Hutchinson delivered the last word: "The Lord judgeth not as a man judgeth, better to be cast out of the Church than to deny Christ."

After her sentence, Hutchinson "gloried in her sufferings, saying that it [her excommunication] was the greatest happiness, next to Christ, that ever befel her." Her husband, William, who later described himself as "more nearly tied to his wife than to the church," shared her banishment. Their son, Francis, called the church "a strumpet"; he was excommunicated, fined forty pounds, and imprisoned when he refused to pay the fine.

During the eighteen-month period directly following the trials, other women felt similar punishment. Judith Smith was excommunicated in April 1638 for "obstinate[ly] persisting" in "sundry Errors." Katherine Finch was ordered whipped on October 10, 1638, as punishment for having "spoke[n] against the magistrates, against the churches, and against the Elders." She thereafter failed to behave "dutifully to her husband" and was forced to make a public promise of obedience to him. In 1639, Phillip[a] Hammond was excommunicated for "sins" which included her public declaration that "Mrs. Hutchinson neyther deserved the Censure which was putt upon her in the Church, or in the Common Weale."

In this nineteenth-century painting, Anne Hutchinson preaches at her home in Boston. (Prints & Photographs Division, Library of Congress)

Although the Boston clergy failed to end female dissension with Hutchinson's excommunication and exile, they were sure they had acted properly. Indeed, they interpreted later events in her life as divine signs of her guilt: Both Mary Dyer and Anne Hutchinson gave birth to what the clergy described as stillborn "monster[s]." When Hutchinson was killed in 1643 by Native Americans in what would become New York state, the clergy's final verdict was: "Let her damned heresies shee fell into . . . and the just vengeance of God, by which shee perished, terifie all her seduced followers from having any more to doe with her leaven."

For Further Reading

Evans, Sara M. *Born for Liberty: A History of Women in America.* New York: Macmillan, Co., The Free Press, 1989.

Flexner, Eleanor. *Century of Struggle.* Cambridge, Mass.: Harvard University Press, Belknap Press, 1959.

Foner, Eric, and John A. Garraty, eds. *A Reader's Companion to American History.* Boston: Houghton Mifflin, 1991.

Hutchinson, Thomas. *The History of the Colony and Province of Massachusetts Bay.* Edited from Hutchinson's copy of Vols. I and II and his manuscript of Vol. III by Lawrence Shaw Mayo, 1936. Volume II, Appendix II, 366–391, reprinted in *Roots of Bitterness: Documents of the Social History of American Women.* Edited by Nancy Cott. New York: E. P. Dutton, 1972.

James, Edward T., Janet Wilson James, and Paul S. Boyer, eds. *Notable American Women, 1607–1950.* Cambridge, Mass.: Harvard University Press, Belknap Press, 1971.

Koehler, Lyle. "The Case of the American Jezebels: Anne Hutchinson and Female Agitation during the Years of the Antinomian Turmoil, 1636–1640." *William and Mary Quarterly,* 3d ser., 31 (1974): 55–78. Reprinted in *Women's America: Refocusing the Past.* Edited by Linda K. Kerber and Jane DeHart Mathews. New York: Oxford University Press, 1991.

Morgan, Edmund S. *The Puritan Dilemma: The Story of John Winthrop.* Boston: Little, Brown and Company, 1958.

Stanton, Elizabeth Cady, Susan B. Anthony, and Matilda Joslyn Gage, eds. *History of Woman Suffrage,* 1881, reprint. Salem, N.H.: Ayer Co., 1985.

Winthrop, John. *Winthrop's Journal, "History of New England," 1630–1649* (2 vols.). New York: Charles Scribner's Sons, 1908.

Mary Dyer Trials: 1659 and 1660

Defendant: Mary Dyer **Crime Charged:** Quakerism
Chief Defense Lawyer: None **Chief Prosecutor:** No Record
Judge: Governor John Endecott **Place:** Boston, Massachusetts Bay Colony
Dates: October 19, 1659 and May 31, 1660 **Verdicts:** Guilty
Sentences: First trial: death by hanging, commuted to banishment from the colony and hanging should she return. Second trial: death by hanging

SIGNIFICANCE
Mary Dyer, convicted and executed in 1660 for practicing her Quaker faith, was an important "witness for religious freedom" in American history.

In 1638, when the Church of Boston excommunicated Anne Hutchinson (see page 3), Mary Dyer had been the one person to walk to Hutchinson's side and extend her hand in sympathetic solidarity. Twenty-two years later, she once again acted without hesitation and in accord with her own principles.

The Massachusetts Bay Colony had been established to secure religious freedom for its Puritan founders. This religious freedom was not extended to dissenters and they were frequently and energetically ejected from the colony. In 1658, Quakers, or members of the Society of Friends, were identified as a particularly dangerous sect of dissenters. According to the *Records of the Governor,* "The doctrine of this sect of people . . . tends to overthrow the whole gospell & the very vitalls of Christianitie . . . ." The colony responded by passing a law on October 19, 1658, which banished Quakers "on payne [sic] of death."

In 1659, Dyer learned that two of her Quaker friends, Marmaduke Stephenson and William Robinson, were being detained in a Boston jail. She visited the two and was promptly imprisoned herself. The three were then banished from the colony and warned that they faced execution should they ever return. They left the colony when they were released, but within a few weeks they decided to return to "looke [the] bloody laws in the face."

As the governor's records describe it, the three Quakers were imprisoned for "theire rebellion, sedition, & presumptuous obtruding themselves upon us," and for acting "as underminers of this government." They were tried by the General Court on October 19, 1659. When they were "brought to the barre," each of the three "acknowledged themselves to be the persons banished" and

MARY DYER

QUAKER

WITNESS FOR RELIGIOUS FREEDOM

HANGED ON BOSTON COMMON 1660

"MY LIFE NOT AVAILETH ME
IN COMPARISON TO THE
LIBERTY OF THE TRUTH"

ART COMMISSION OF
LTH OF MASSACHUSETTS
Y OF ZENAS ELLIS
ERMONT

ILY 1959

To honor Mary Dyer's missionary efforts for the Quakers, the citizens of Boston erected a statue of her on the grounds of the State House in 1959.
(Massachusetts Art Commission, Boston, Mass.)

previously "convicted for Quakers." Governor John Endecott delivered identical sentences to all of the defendants: "You shall go from hence to the place from whence you came [prison], & from thence to the place of execution, & there hang till you be dead."

Dyer remained calm and said simply, "The will of the Lord be done." William Dyer, her husband, sought earthly intervention. On August 30, 1659, he wrote to the "Court . . . assembled at Boston" to protest the infringement of his wife's religious liberty. He compared the General Court's members to the "Popish inquisitors" of the thirteenth century, pointing out that they, too, had acted as "judge and accuser both." Finally and most saliently, he expressed outrage that the Puritans, who had fled persecution in England, should in their turn persecute Quakers: "Surely you or some of you, if ever you had the courage to looke a bishop in the face [back in England], cannot but remember that the [first, second] or third word from them was, You are a Puritane are you not, & is it not so [here] in N[ew] England, the magistracy having . . . assumed a coercive power of conscience, the first or next word. After [my wife's] appearance [before you] is [the accusation] You are a Quaker." Among the others who protested Dyer's sentence were Dyer's son, William, Governor John Winthrop, Jr., of Connecticut, and Governor Thomas Temple of Nova Scotia.

When the day of her expected hanging arrived, Dyer, Stephenson, and Robinson were paraded in the company of drum-beating soldiers to "the place of execution." Then Dyer, like her fellow convicts, was "made to stand upon the gallowes, with a rope around her necke." Stephenson and Robinson were hanged, but Dyer, to her surprise, was left alive in her untightened noose. She was then granted "liberty for forty eight howers . . . to depart out of this jurisdiction, after which time, being found therein, she is forthwith to be executed."

Dyer enjoyed her liberty for seven months, and then she returned to the Massachusetts Bay Colony. On May 31, 1660, before the General Court and Governor Endecott, "she acknowledged herself to be Mary Dyer, . . . denied our lawe, [and said she] came to bear witness against it." Later that day, "The whole court mett together and voted, that the said Mary Dyer, for her rebelliously returning to this jurisdiction . . . shall . . . according to the sentence of the General Court in October last, be put to death."

Dyer was hanged on June 1, 1660. In 1959, the Massachusetts General Court commemorated and reinterpreted Mary Dyer's actions: It ordered that a seven-foot statue of Dyer be placed on the Boston State House lawn, bearing the inscription "Witness for Religious Freedom."

For Further Reading

Chu, Jonathan M. *Neighbors, Friends, or Madmen: The Puritan Adjustment to Quakerism in Seventeenth-Century Massachusetts Bay.* Westport, Conn.: Greenwood Press, 1985.

Cullen-DuPont, Kathryn. *Encyclopedia of Women's History in America.* New York: Facts on File, 1996.

Dyer, William. *Mary Dyer, Quaker: Two Letters of William Dyer of Rhode Island, 1659–1660*. Printed for Worthington C. Ford by the University Press, Cambridge, U.S.A., n.d.

Frost-Knappman, Elizabeth. *The ABC-CLIO Companion to Women's Progress in America*. Santa Barbara, Calif.: ABC-CLIO, 1994.

James, Edward T., Janet Wilson James, and Paul S. Boyer, eds. *Notable American Women, 1607–1950*. Cambridge, Mass.: Harvard University, Belknap Press, 1971.

Knappman, Edward, ed. *Great American Trials*. Detroit: Gale Research, 1994.

McHenry, Robert, ed. *Famous American Women: A Biographical Dictionary from Colonial Times to the Present*. New York: Dover Publications, 1983.

Shurtleff, Nathaniel B., ed. *Records of the Governor and Company of the Massachusetts Bay in New England*. Boston: From the Press of William White, Printer to the Commonwealth, 1854.

Salem Witchcraft Trials: 1692

Defendants: Two hundred were accused, including Sarah Bishop, Sarah Good, Rebecca Nurse, Sarah Osborn, and Tituba, a slave
Crimes Charged: Witchcraft   **Chief Examiners:** John Hawthorne and Jonathan Corwin   **Place:** Salem Village (now Danvers, Massachusetts)
Dates of Hearings: March 1, 1692 and throughout the Spring
Chief Defense Lawyers: None   **Chief Prosecutors:** None
Judges for the Court of Oyer and Terminer: Jonathan Corwin et al.
Place: Salem Town (now Salem, Massachusetts)   **Dates of Trials:** June 2, 1692–September 1692; a superior court in January 1693 held trials in several cities   **Verdicts:** Twenty-nine guilty of witchcraft
Sentences: Nineteen were hanged and ten imprisoned

SIGNIFICANCE

What prompted these accusations of witchcraft—which were levied primarily against women—has been a matter of intense historical debate for over three hundred years.

Witch-hunts were not uncommon before or during the seventeenth century in Europe or in colonial Massachusetts. Approximately one hundred inhabitants of the Massachusetts Bay colony were formally charged with witch-craft—and fifteen were executed—before 1692. In that year, however, a frenzy of accusation resulted in more than two hundred charges of witchcraft.

Several teenage and adolescent girls fell into a series of fits in February 1692. When questioned by adults who seemed to assume the Devil was in-volved, the girls implicated Sarah Good, Sarah Osburn, and, in particular, Tituba, an enslaved woman from Barbados. Warrants were issued, and the three women were arrested on February 29, 1692.

At a public hearing beginning on March 1 in Salem Village, magistrates Jonathan Corwin and John Hawthorne interrogated the accused women. The impoverished and pregnant Good maintained that she was innocent but cast suspicion upon Osburn. Osburn, who would die in jail before trial, said she was not a witch but suggested that she, like the young girls, might have been bewitched. Tituba—who had been amusing her charges with magical tales and fortune-telling games—at first declared her innocence, but then described "four women and one man [who] . . . tell me, if I will not hurt the children, they will hurt me." She identified Good and Osburn as two of the women but refused to identify the others.

The Trials

Sarah Bishop was the first woman to stand trial. A neighbor testified that Bishop's "spector" (the Devil in Bishop's image and form) had hovered near the cradle of his child who later became ill and died. Found guilty of witchcraft, Bishop was hanged on June 10, 1692. During an eighteen-day recess, ministers warned that "spectral evidence" was suspect, since the "demon may assume the shape of the innocent."

A nineteenth-century rendering of the Salem witchcraft trials of the 1690s. (Prints & Photographs Division, Library of Congress)

The court found the next five women guilty as well, sentencing them to hang. Rebecca Nurse, a well-regarded and deeply religious woman, issued her own verdict to the Reverend Nicholas Noyes, who pressed her to confess: "I am no more a witch than you are a wizard," she said. "If you take my life away, God will give you blood to drink." (Anecdotally, Noyes died hemorrhaging from the mouth.)

Before the trials ended, the court found twenty-nine people guilty and executed nineteen of them. Other fatalities included eighteen-year-old Giles Corey, who was pressed to death for not pleading to the charges, and two people who died in jail awaiting trial. The new royal governor, William Phips, finally suspended the witchcraft court, forbade the carrying out of further executions, and released any "witches" remaining in jail. Five years later, the general court ordered a day of penitent prayer and fasting in memory of the trials' victims. In 1703 and 1710, the legislature—in response to petitions of the "witches" descendants—reversed most of the convictions.

An older woman on trial for witchcraft during the 1630s. (Prints & Photographs Division, Library of Congress)

Why Did They Do It?

Some historians suggest that ergot fungus, a hallucinogenic, may have been present in the colonists' rye flour. Others believe that the young girls permitted their original small fiction to escalate. Others blame the stress caused by shifts in Massachusetts' political status between 1684 and 1688. During this time, the colony became part of the Dominion of New England; had its land titles questioned; and, following the deposing of James II, had been existing "on hold" while William and Mary's policies toward their American colonies slowly evolved.

Feminist scholars have other views. Elizabeth Cady Stanton, Susan B. Anthony, and Matilda Joslyn Gage published volume 1 of the *History of Woman Suffrage* in 1881. Gage outlined in her chapter, entitled "Woman, Church and State," three striking points for consideration in her analysis of witchcraft trials in Europe and in colonial America:

First. That women were chiefly accused, a wizard being seldom mentioned.

Second. That men, believing in woman's inherent wickedness, and understanding neither the mental nor the physical peculiarities of her being, ascribed all her idiosyncrasies to witchcraft.

Third. That the clergy inculcated the idea that woman was in league with the devil, and that strong intellect, remarkable beauty, or unusual sickness, were in themselves a proof of that league.

Many modern historians also view the witchcraft trials in terms of gender issues. Carol Karlsen and Anne Llewellyn Barrow, for example, point out that those most frequently accused have been female inheritors, successful businesswomen, unmarried women, and those who had not produced a son during their child-bearing years. Barrow places particular emphasis upon the fact that Salem widows, unlike most other widows at the time, had the right to hold title to their own property. David Hall notes that women were accused of witchcraft more than men by a ratio of four to one. Men were also less likely to be tried and convicted than women. Women over forty and healers were especially vulnerable. He and Karlsen both note that witch-hunting may have affirmed male authority at a time when women were testing male leadership and experiencing more independence, such as when women without husbands or brothers inherited property.

For Further Reading

Barrow, Anne Llewellyn. *Witchcraze: A New History of the European Witch Hunts.* San Francisco: HarperCollins, Pandora, 1994.

Hall, David D. *Witch-Hunting in Seventeenth Century New England: A Documentary History, 1638–1692.* Boston: Northeastern University Press, 1991.

Hansen, Chadwick. *Witchcraft at Salem.* New York: George Brazillier, 1969.

Karlsen, Carol. *The Devil in the Shape of a Woman: Witchcraft in Colonial New England.* New York: W. W. Norton, 1987.

Stanton, Elizabeth Cady, Susan B. Anthony, and Matilda Joslyn Gage. *History of Woman Suffrage,* vol. 1, 1881, reprint, Salem, N.H.: Ayer Company, 1985.

Starkey, Marion L. *The Devil In Massachusetts: A Modern Enquiry into the Salem Witch Trials.* New York: Alfred A. Knopf, 1949.

Upham, Charles W. *Salem Witchcraft.* Williamstown, Mass.: Corner House Publishers, 1971.

Crandall v. Connecticut: 1834

Appellant: Prudence Crandall **Appellee:** The State of Connecticut
Appellant's Claim: The "Black Law" forbidding the education of blacks in
Connecticut was unconstitutional **Chief Lawyer for Appellee:** Andrew T.
Judson **Chief Lawyer for Appellant:** William Wescott Ellsworth
Justices: Thomas Scott Williams, Clark Bissell, and Samuel Church
(majority); Chief Justice David Daggett (dissent) **Place:** Hartford, Connecticut
Date of Decision: July 18, 1834 **Decision:** The "Black Law" was
unconstitutional

SIGNIFICANCE

In a time when custom kept women from legally defending themselves, Prudence
Crandall's courage tested whether black freedmen, and by implication women,
were citizens under the U.S. Constitution.

In 1831, twenty-seven-year-old Prudence Crandall was a teacher in Plainfield, Connecticut, when seventeen citizens urged her to start a school for their daughters in nearby Canterbury. She agreed, and the town helped her to buy Paine House—a building on the town green—as her residence and school. The Canterbury Female Boarding School opened in early November 1831.

At first, the town praised her work, but within a year, the school was in peril. In September of 1832, Sarah Harris, whom Crandall described as a "colored girl of respectability—a professor of religion—and daughter of respectable [farming] parents," applied to the school. She wanted to learn "enough to teach colored children." Crandall welcomed the young woman, but when word of her action spread, some of the white mothers visited her, threatening that if the "nigger" were not sent away, they would withdraw their daughters, leaving the school to "sink."

Throwing Down the Gauntlet

Needing fifteen girls, at the minimum, to stay open, Crandall sought the advice of William Lloyd Garrison, the publisher of the abolitionist paper *The Liberator*. She had decided to devote the rest of her life to benefiting "people of color," and planned to replace the departing "white scholars for colored ones."

Knowing full well that she dared not make her intentions public—lest her present school fail financially—she begged Garrison to privately help her find "twenty or twenty-five young ladies of color" to attend her school "for the term of one year at the rate of $25 per quarter, including board, washing, and tuition." Garrison referred Crandall to friends in Providence and New York. In Providence, Crandall found six students; abolitionist Arthur Tappen led her to twenty-five more.

On February 20, 1833, Crandall sent her white students home with a message to their parents: If the Canterbury school could not accept black girls, it would deny admittance to whites. Six days later, four of the town's most powerful men told her that they would "destroy [her] undertaking and that they could do it and should do it. . . ." Nonetheless, in the March 2, 1833, issue of the *Liberator*, Crandall announced the opening of her school for "young ladies and little misses of color" on the first Monday in April.

The Town Erupts

The citizens of Canterbury were outraged. It was one thing to interfere with their daughters' education, but quite another to bring in out-of-town black girls—and worse yet, by out-of-town abolitionists. When Crandall could not find a local attorney to represent her, she asked a founder of the New England Anti-Slavery Society, Arnold Buffum, to come to a town meeting with her on March 9. He had some doubts about their safety, but nonetheless, he and her friend, Reverend Samuel May, accompanied Crandall to the Meeting House.

They faced a room packed with nearly one thousand enraged men. Leaders read resolutions condemning the proposed school, fearing "large numbers of persons from other States whose characters and habits might be various and unknown to us." A committee formed to explain to Crandall "the injurious effects and incalculable evils resulting from such an establishment. . . ."

Crandall's next door neighbor, Andrew T. Judson, a candidate for governor and later judge of the U.S. District Court, warned about a drop in property values, lowered morals, intermarriage—all would be caused by "this nigger school." Some men shook their fists in Buffum and May's faces and threatened them with violence if they so much as opened their mouths to speak for her.

Nevertheless, Crandall opened her school on time. The first scholar to arrive was Ann Eliza Hammond from Rhode Island. At the end of April, there were seventeen girls enrolled, aged nine to eighteen years from Providence, Boston, New York, Philadelphia, New Haven, and other Connecticut towns.

Outrageous Acts

During the late spring and summer of 1833, Crandall and her students endured behavior from their neighbors that foreshadowed the hate-inspired acts of whites following the Civil War and during the civil rights movement of the 1960s. With the exception of one store, no one would sell food or other necessities to the school. The Congregational Church barred its doors and stage-coaches would not transport Crandall or her students. Eggs splattered her house; rocks crashed through her windows; her well was poisoned and her father had to haul water from his farm to the school.

Claiming blacks were "an appalling source of crime and pauperism" and the school's existence would invite an influx of blacks from other states who would impose burdens on whites, Judson was determined to drive the school out of the state. He asked the state legislature to create a "Black Law" that would make it illegal for any person in Connecticut to establish a school for "colored persons who are not inhabitants of this State" or teach or board any such person without permission from the majority of "civil authority" and the selectmen of the town in question.

Signed into law on May 24, 1833, "any colored person not an inhabitant of this state" who came for schooling would be treated as a vagrant. In addition to a fine and a public whipping, any student in such a school as Crandall's "shall be an admissible witness in all prosecutions [under the act] . . . and may be compelled to give testimony."

Saturday, June 27, 1833, deputy sheriff George Cady arrested Crandall at Paine House. Judges Rufus, Adams, and Bacon read the complaint, charging Crandall and her sister with willfully and knowingly harboring and boarding out-of-state black girls. Admitting to the charges, Crandall was bound over to the County Court in Brooklyn. She posted not a penny of the bail, preferring to stand on principle.

On a June evening, sometime after eight, the Canterbury sheriff jailed Crandall. May left her with the following words: "The deed is done; completely done. It cannot be recalled. It has passed into the history of our nation and our age." As he predicted, historians remembered her act of passive resistance as one of the most courageous of the nineteenth century.

Her Courage, Men's Battle

Since nineteenth-century customs prevented women from defending themselves, men took over Crandall's battle. William Wescott Ellsworth, Calvin Goddard, and Henry Strong acted as her attorneys. Abolitionists William Lloyd Garrison, Samuel J. May, George Benson and Arthur Tappen, rejected by all the newspapers in surrounding towns—even the Letters page—printed a four-page newspaper, *The Unionist,* to publicize Crandall's case.

There were two charges against Crandall: "that said Prudence Crandall, on the 24th day of June last, with force and arms" taught colored girls and "willfully and knowingly did harbor and board certain colored persons not inhabitants of the town without consent in writing of the Civil Authority or Selectmen." Although her attorneys conceded that their client had broken the "Black Law," they argued that the statute itself was unconstitutional because it affected a particular class of people. Therefore, Crandall plead "not guilty."

When the prosecution began calling Crandall's students to testify, as permitted under the "Black Law," the defense challenged the constitutionality of that law. Were not freemen citizens? If so, did they not deserve the same rights as others?

Judson testified that the "Black Law" was not in conflict with the U.S. Constitution, because "the term 'citizen' does not include colored persons. If 'citizen' does not mean a white person only, then our state constitution is a nullity [nullified] for it allows 'free white males' alone to be electors."

Prudence Crandall, in an 1834 painting.

The jury deadlocked, allowing Crandall to go home and resume classes. But, on September 26, Crandall was arrested again. Her second trial took place at the State Supreme Court in Brooklyn, Connecticut. Chief Justice David Daggett, an advocate of the "Black Law" who had blocked the opening of a college for blacks in New Haven in 1831, instructed the jury that freemen were not citizens: "The *African* race [is] essentially a degraded caste, of inferior rank and condition in society. Marriages are forbidden between them and whites, . . . they are revolting. . . ." This time, the jury found Crandall guilty.

A Higher Court

The defense immediately appealed to the Supreme Court of Errors in Hartford on two grounds: that the superior court did not have jurisdiction and that the particulars of the charges were insufficient. Crandall's lawyers argued that freemen *were* citizens, for: "What shall be the ascertainment of citizenship? Shall one half, one quarter, one twentieth, or the least possible taint of negro blood, be sufficient to take from its possessor the citizen character?"

They pointed out that freemen ran businesses and served in the armed forces. Unlike women—black or white—freemen voted in North Carolina and Tennessee and in *all* of New England, except in Connecticut. As citizens in their respective states, the U.S. Constitution secured them the right of both living in Connecticut and receiving an education there. Ellsworth and Goddard made the case for equality of opportunity regardless of race, a point later raised by Thurgood Marshall when representing the NAACP in *Brown v. Board of Education of Topeka* (1954).

The opposition claimed Crandall willfully broke the law, insisting that the school would "destroy the government itself and this *American* nation." Arguing that the law *was* constitutional, the lawyers declared that white and colored men "composed the grand divisions of the human family." Therefore, *white* men were entitled to civil and political rights to which colored men were not heir. After all, the framers of the Constitution were slave-holders and certainly never meant for descendants of slaves to be *citizens*. Finally, since the 1790 federal naturalization law restricted citizenship to any free *white* alien, states had the right to deny education to aliens from other states.

In a three to one vote, the Court threw out the state's case against Crandall. Knowing the "Black Law" was unconstitutional, Justice Thomas Scott Williams went along with Clark Bissell and Samuel Church—but because he did not want to overrule Daggett's earlier decision openly, he straddled the fence on a technicality: the "Black Law" was aimed only at unlicensed schools, and the complaint failed to state that Crandall's school was unlicensed. Daggett dissented, but his ruling in the second trial would be used as a precedent cited in the infamous Dred Scott decision—a prelude to the Civil War.

A Triumph of Conscience

For two months Crandall's Canterbury school flourished—its headmistress a heroine in liberal circles in America, Canada, and Europe. However, in September, the town's resentment flared again. Crandall's house was set afire and the school was damaged—doors were broken open and ninety panes of glass were shattered. Fearing harm to herself and her pupils, Crandall gave up her school and moved to Ithaca, New York with her new husband, Reverend Calvin Philleo. Eight years later, she left him, moved to Illinois and then to Elks Falls, Kansas, where she died January 28, 1890.

Samuel May was "ashamed of Canterbury, ashamed of Connecticut, ashamed of my country, ashamed of my color." In time, the public's conscience returned. Philip Pearl, the committee chair who had signed the initial papers requesting the Black Law said, "I could weep tears of blood for the part I took in the matter." He helped to repeal the law in 1838. Connecticut became a leader in abolitionist sentiment and supported the 1868 Fourteenth Amendment.

In the January Session, 1886, House Petition No. 48 was filed in the State archives to provide a $400 pension for Crandall. Signed by 112 people, the petition celebrated Crandall for her benevolent work "that now to its great honor, the General Government itself is engaged in."

For Further Reading

Fuller, Edmund. *Prudence Crandall: An Incident of Racism in Nineteenth-Century Connecticut.* Middletown, Conn.: Wesleyan University Press, 1971.

Garrison, William Lloyd, and Francis Jackson Garrison. *The Anti-Slavery Crusade in America,* reprint. New York: Arno Press and *The New York Times,* 1969. (Originally titled *William Lloyd Garrison: The Story of His Life, Volume I.* New York: The Century Co., 1885.)

Strane, Susan. *A Whole-Souled Woman: Prudence Crandall and the Education of Black Women*. New York: W. W. Norton, 1990.

Welch, Marvis Olive. *Prudence Crandall: A Biography*. Manchester, Conn.: Jason Publishers, 1983.

United States v. Susan B. Anthony: 1873

Defendant: Susan B. Anthony   **Crime Charged:** Unlawful voting
Chief Lawyers for Defendant: Henry R. Selden and John Van Voorhis
Chief Prosecutor: Richard Crowley   **Judge:** Ward Hunt
Place: Canandaigua, New York   **Dates of Trial:** June 17–18, 1873
Verdict: Guilty

SIGNIFICANCE

Susan B. Anthony's casting of her ballot almost fifty years prior to the Nineteenth Amendment's national enfranchisement of American women was both an act of political defiance and an attempt to test whether the recently adopted Fourteenth Amendment would be interpreted as expanding or protecting women's rights.

When the Fourteenth Amendment became part of the U.S. Constitution in July 1868, women's rights leaders—who had been actively campaigning through two decades for women's suffrage—were angered by the wording of Section 2. That section, written to encourage states to give the vote to black males, seemed to place in doubt the citizenship of females by inserting the word "male" into the Constitution for the first time.

But Francis Minor, a lawyer and the husband of Virginia Minor (the president of the Woman Suffrage Association of Missouri and a plaintiff in the 1875 trial *Minor v. Happersett* [see page 104]), thought Section 1 of the Fourteenth Amendment was more to their point. It read:

> All persons born or naturalized in the United States, and subject to the jurisdiction thereof, are citizens of the United States and of the state wherein they reside. No state shall make or enforce any law which shall abridge the privileges or immunities of citizens of the United States.

This clause, Minor wrote, *confirmed* the citizenship of women and made it clear that "provisions of the several state constitutions that exclude women from the franchise on account of sex, are violative alike of the spirit and letter of the federal Constitution."

Elizabeth Cady Stanton and Susan B. Anthony published Minor's analysis of the Fourteenth Amendment in their newspaper, the *Revolution*, and urged women to vote in defiance of any state law to the contrary. Women in at least ten states heeded this advice in 1871 and 1872. Although most of the women were sent home, a few—including Susan B. Anthony in 1872—managed to cast their ballots.

The Vote Is Cast

Anthony had consulted Judge Henry R. Selden before attempting voter registration in Rochester, New York. He concurred with Minor's reading of the Fourteenth Amendment and provided a written opinion saying so. Anthony took the written opinion with her and threatened the registrars with a lawsuit if she were turned away. Anthony and fourteen other women registered, and they voted in the presidential election of November 5, 1872.

Anthony and the other women—and the inspectors who had registered them—were arrested on November 28. Bail was set at five hundred dollars, and all but Anthony elected to pay it rather than face jail. Selden arranged Anthony's release until her trial. On January 21, 1873, a U.S. district judge reset her bail at one thousand dollars. When Anthony again refused to pay her bail, Selden paid it, rather than "see a lady I respected put in jail."

Pre-trial Persuasion

Anthony's trial was scheduled to begin on May 13. Not waiting until then to tell her side of the story, she traveled to all twenty-nine postal districts of her county and delivered the same speech:

> Friends and fellow-citizens, I stand before you under indictment for the alleged crime of having voted illegally. . . . We throw to the wind the old dogma that governments can give rights. The Declaration of Independence, the United States Constitution, the constitutions of the several states . . . propose to *protect* the people in the exercise of their God-given rights. No one of them pretends to bestow rights. . . . One half of the people of this Nation today are utterly powerless to blot from the statute books an unjust law, or to write a new and just one. . . . This form of government, that enforces taxation without representation—that compels [women] to obey laws to which they have never given their consent—that imprisons and hangs them without a trial by a jury of their peers—that robs them, in marriage of the custody of their own persons, wages, and children—[leaves] half of the people wholly at the mercy of the other half.

Following her "prejudic[ing] of any possible jury," in Monroe County, Anthony's trial was rescheduled for June 17 and moved to Canandaigua, a town in Ontario County, New York. By June 16, Anthony had delivered her speech in every village in Ontario county.

A Pre-judged Trial

On June 17, 1873, Anthony's trial opened before Judge Ward Hunt. The essence of the government's case was presented by U.S. District Attorney

Richard Crowley: "Miss Susan B. Anthony . . . upon the 5th day of November, 1873, . . . voted. . . . At that time she was a woman."

Beverly W. Jones, one of the inspectors who had been arrested for registering Anthony, testified that he had both registered her and accepted ballots from her on November 5. The poll list containing Susan B. Anthony's name was introduced as further proof that she had voted, and Crowley rested the government's case.

When Selden called Anthony to the stand, Crowley objected, saying (since she was a woman), "She is not competent as a witness in her own behalf." Selden took the stand instead. He testified that he had agreed with Anthony as to the Fourteenth Amendment's protection of women's rights, and that he had counseled her to exercise her right of suffrage. He continued:

> If the same act had been done by her brother under the same circumstances, the act would have been not only innocent, but honorable and laudable; but having been done by a woman it is said to be a crime. The crime, therefore, consists not in the act done, but in the simple fact that the person doing it was a woman and not a man.

As soon as Selden rested the defense's case, Hunt read a statement to the "Gentlemen of the Jury." Written prior to any argument of the case before him, it set forth that:

Susan B. Anthony, who cast a ballot in the 1872 presidential election to test the Fourteenth Amendment. (Prints & Photographs Division, Library of Congress)

> The right of voting, or the privilege of voting, is a right or privilege arising under the Constitution of the State, and not of the United States. . . . If the State of New York should provide that no person should vote until he had reached the age of thirty-one years, or after he had reached the age of fifty . . . I do not see how it could be held to be a violation of any right derived or held under the Constitution of the United States.

When Hunt also directed the jury to deliver a guilty verdict, Selden objected, stating "it is for the jury [to decide]." Hunt turned again to the jury:

> I have decided as a question of law . . . that under the Fourteenth Amendment, which Miss Anthony claims protects her, she was not protected in a right to vote. . . . I therefore direct you to find a verdict of guilty.

Hunt then instructed the clerk to record the jury's verdict as guilty and refused Selden's request to have the jury polled.

A request for a new trial was denied. Hunt then asked Anthony, "Has the prisoner anything to say why sentence should not be pronounced?" but cut off her responses as "a rehearsal of arguments the prisoner's counsel has already consumed three hours in presenting." He then ordered the convicted Anthony to stand for sentencing. "The sentence of this Court," Hunt declared, "is that you pay a fine of $100 and the costs of prosecution."

Anthony responded, "May it please your honor, I will never pay a dollar of your unjust penalty. . . . 'Resistance to tyranny is obedience to God.'"

Hunt did not order her jailed, but released her, saying "Madam, the Court will not order you to stand committed until the fine is paid."

Susan B. Anthony neither paid her fine nor lived to see the Nineteenth Amendment's national enfranchisement of women in 1920. The Fourteenth Amendment was not successfully used to overturn a sex-biased law until *Reed v. Reed* (see page 112), ninety-eight years later.

For Further Reading

Barry, Kathleen. *Susan B. Anthony: A Biography*. New York: New York University Press, 1988.

Flexner, Eleanor. *Century of Struggle*. Cambridge, Mass.: Harvard University Press, Belknap Press, 1959, revised 1975.

Frost, Elizabeth, and Kathryn Cullen-DuPont. *Women's Suffrage in America: An Eyewitness History*. New York: Facts on File, 1992.

Harper, Ida Husted. *Life and Work of Susan B. Anthony*. 1898. Reprint. Salem, N.H.: Ayer Co., 1983.

Stanton, Elizabeth Cady, Susan B. Anthony, and Matilda Joslyn Gage. *History of Woman Suffrage*, Vol. 2, 1882. Reprint. Salem, N.H.: Ayer Co., 1985.

The Trials of Alice Paul and Other National Woman's Party Members: 1917

Defendants: Various members of the National Woman's Party, including Gertrude Crocker, Gladys Greiner, Alice Paul, and Dr. Caroline Spencer
Crime Charged: Obstructing a sidewalk   **Chief Defense Lawyer:** Dudley Field Malone   **Chief Prosecutor:** Mr. Hart   **Judge:** Alexander Mullowney
Place: Washington, D.C.   **Date of Decision:** October 22, 1917
Verdicts: Guilty   **Sentences:** Alice Paul and Caroline Spencer: seven months imprisonment; Gertrude Crocker and Gladys Greiner: five dollar fine or thirty days imprisonment

SIGNIFICANCE

Police arrested nearly five hundred suffragists during their picketing of the White House in 1917 and 1918; National Woman's Party chair Alice Paul and 167 other women were tried, convicted, and jailed for up to seven months for blocking pedestrian traffic on a sidewalk. The women, protesting that they were incarcerated for their political beliefs, became the first U.S. citizens to claim that their government was holding them as political prisoners.

American women began to organize and campaign for their voting rights in 1848 at the Seneca Falls Convention, in Seneca, New York. In 1917, nearly seven decades later, they still could not vote. Alice Paul and members of her National Woman's Party decided that extreme measures had become necessary: On January 10, they began picketing President Woodrow Wilson and the White House.

The government had paid little attention to the women's picketing before the United States' entrance into World War I. However, as soon as war was declared, the District of Columbia chief of police alerted Paul that any picketers would now face arrest. Paul informed the chief that her legal counsel had "assured us all along that picketing was legal," and added that it was "certainly as legal in June as in January."

On June 22, 1917, police arrested the first two Woman's Party picketers. They were charged, however, with obstructing a sidewalk—not with picketing. Released at the station, they did not go to trial. Within four days, twenty-seven more women went through the same procedure. The picketing continued nevertheless. The next six women arrested on June 27 were convicted for obstructing pedestrian traffic. Refusing to pay a fine of twenty-five dollars, they went to jail for three days.

Undeterred, the picketers continued to maintain a daily presence before the White House gates. Among the sixteen women arrested on July 14 were Allison Turnbull Hopkins, the wife of President Wilson's New Jersey campaign coordinator, and Florence Bayard Hilles, the daughter of a former U.S. ambassador to Great Britain. They all came to trial before district court Judge Alexander Mullowney that same day.

Alice Paul and Lucy Burns conducted the National Woman's Party picket of the White House, which began in January 1917. (Prints and Photographs Division, Library of Congress)

Before the trial, Mullowney had consulted the U.S. Attorney about trying the women under the Espionage Act of 1917, which had been passed in June. The act prohibited, among other things, the making of false statements that might compromise the country's war effort. The banners held by the women, Mullowney claimed, were emblazoned with "words . . . [that] are treasonous and seditious." Upon investigation, however, he discovered that the banners quoted President Wilson.

One banner, for example, carried a line from the president's War Message Speech of April 2: "We shall fight for the things which we have always held nearest our hearts—for democracy, for the right of those who submit to authority to have a voice in their own governments." Since presidential quotations seemed unlikely fodder for the Espionage Act and since—as Paul had steadfastly maintained—the United States had no law against picketing, all sixteen women faced trial for obstructing sidewalk traffic. They were each convicted and sentenced to sixty days imprisonment in the Occoquan Work-house.

Dudley Field Malone, collector of the Port of New York, was both a friend and political appointee of President Wilson. When he witnessed the women's unfair convictions and sentencing, he became outraged. He delivered his resignation personally to Wilson, adding that he intended to provide his legal services to the suffragists. Wilson refused to accept Malone's resignation and pardoned all the imprisoned suffragists on July 20.

Picketing continued and, in August, so did the arrests. Malone's next resignation offer to Wilson was accepted without further hesitation. He sent a letter not only to the White House but to several leading newspapers as well. He wrote, "I think it is high time that men in this generation, at some cost to themselves stood up to battle for the national enfranchisement of American women."

Paul, herself, was among the ten women arrested on October 4. When the women went to trial four days later, they refused to be sworn or to acknowledge the legitimacy of the court proceedings. As Paul explained to the judge, "We do not consider ourselves subject to this court since, as an unenfranchised class, we have nothing to do with the making of the laws which have put us in this position." The women were released without sentence, but also without dismissal of the charge.

Alice Paul and other group members celebrate the 1920 ratification of the 19th Amendment, at the National Suffrage Association headquarters in Washington, D.C. (Prints & Photographs Division, Library of Congress)

On October 20, police again arrested Paul, along with Dr. Caroline Spencer, Gertrude Crocker, and Gladys Greiner. The four women faced trial before Mullowney on October 22.

Police Sergeant Lee testified: "I made my way through the crowd that was surrounding them, and told the ladies they were violating the law by standing at the gates, and would not they please move on." Asked by Assistant District Attorney Hart to describe the women's reaction, Lee said, "They did not [move on], and they did not answer either. . . . [I] placed them under arrest."

Paul and Spencer had been holding banners when they were arrested, and the judge sentenced them to seven months in prison. He ordered Crocker and Greiner each to pay a five-dollar fine or face thirty days in jail. They chose imprisonment.

Lucy Burns had been among the first women arrested on June 22, and in September she had been arrested again and convicted. Prior to Paul's imprisonment at Occoquan Workhouse, Burns had organized the other jailed suffragists, and they requested political prisoner status. When their smuggled petition reached the commissioners of the District of Columbia, each of the petitioners were put into solitary confinement. When Paul and Rose Winslow arrived at Occoquan and discovered what had happened, they announced a hunger strike to "secure for [their] fellow comrades treatment accorded political prisoners in every civilized country but our own."

Paul, Winslow, and the many others who took part in the hunger strike, were force-fed. When this failed to break their resolve, officials transferred Paul to a psychiatric hospital, confining her to a room with boarded windows. Malone intervened and had Paul relocated to another, non-psychiatric, medical institution.

All of the imprisoned suffragists were released without official pardon, condition, or explanation on November 27 and 28, 1917. On March 4, 1918, the District of Columbia Court of Appeals ruled on an appeal Malone had made some time before. The court declared that all of the suffragists had been "illegally arrested, illegally convicted, and illegally imprisoned."

American women nationwide won the vote following ratification of the Nineteenth Amendment on August 26, 1920.

For Further Reading

Frost, Elizabeth, and Kathryn Cullen-DuPont. *Women's Suffrage in America: An Eyewitness History.* New York: Facts on File, 1992.

Irwin, Inez Hayes. *The Story of Alice Paul and the National Woman's Party.* Fairfax, Va.: Denlinger's Publishers, 1964.

Lunardini, Christine A. *From Equal Suffrage to Equal Rights: Alice Paul and the National Woman's Party, 1910–1928.* New York: New York University Press, 1986.

Paul, Alice. *Conversations with Alice Paul: Woman Suffrage and the Equal Rights Amendment.* An interview conducted by Amelia Fry. Berkeley, Calif.: Bancroft Library, Regional Oral History Office, University of California, 1976.

Stevens, Doris. *Jailed for Freedom.* 1920, reprint. Salem, N.H.: Ayer Co., 1990.

New York v. Sanger: 1918

Appellant: Margaret H. Sanger   **Respondent:** State of New York
Appellant's Claim: That the Comstock Act of 1873 violates both the federal and state Constitutions; therefore Sanger is not guilty of a criminal act when she opened the first birth control clinic
Chief Lawyer for Respondent: District Attorney Harry E. Lewis
Chief Lawyer for Appellant: Jonah J. Goldstein   **Justices:** William S. Andrews, Benjamin N. Cardozo, Emory A. Chase, Frederick Collin, *Frederick E. Crane,* William H. Cuddeback, Chief Justice Frank H. Hiscock, John W. Hogan, and Cuthbert W. Pound   **Place:** New York, New York
Date of Decision: January 8, 1918   **Decision:** The lower court's guilty decision was affirmed

SIGNIFICANCE

This decision allowed doctors to advise their married patients about birth control for health purposes. In 1923, Sanger interpreted this ruling as grounds for her to start legal doctor-staffed birth control clinics.

Margaret Sanger was born Margaret Louise Higgins in Corning, New York on September 14, 1883, one of eleven surviving children. Believing her mother's eighteen pregnancies caused her death at about age fifty, Sanger founded the American birth control movement—and went to jail at least nine times for her efforts. She lived to see birth control become a legal practice throughout the United States in 1965.

Up From Poverty

After two years of study at Claverack College and Hudson River Institute, the Higgins' finances were exhausted, so their daughter went to work at the White Plains Hospital in New York. There she completed two years of nurse's training, and in 1902, she married William Sanger in a quick wedding that allowed her to report to her 4:30 A.M. shift the next day.

As a home nurse in New York City, Sanger ministered to maternity patients in the slums of the lower east side. However, when a truck driver's wife died painfully from a self-induced abortion, Sanger left nursing forever, turning to birth control education.

During 1910 and 1911, Sanger gave a series of lectures to Socialist Party women on female sexuality. Their popularity resulted in an invitation to become a columnist for the party paper, *The Call*. In one column she explicitly condemned customs that forced women to rely on men for support. In another, she warned about the dangers of syphilis—prompting the U.S. Postal Service's refusal to mail *The Call* under the forty-year-old federal Comstock Act that banned the topic as obscene.

Comstock's Law

After the Civil War, more rigid American attitudes had led to the passage of the Comstock Act in 1873. The law classified contraceptive literature as obscene—illegal to mail through the U.S. Post Office. It stifled the dissemination of birth control information, even in newspaper ads. It also made it a misdemeanor for a person to sell, give away, advertise, or offer for sale, any instrument, article, drug, or medicine that would prevent contraception. It was even unlawful to give someone verbal information on contraception. Until this time, the nation's birthrates had been declining and the sale of contraception devices increasing.

Sanger wanted to flout the Comstock Act so she launched her own monthly magazine, *The Woman Rebel*, publishing it from her dining room table. Because the words "birth control" appeared, and with it the promise to provide women with contraceptive advice, the U.S. Post Office refused to mail the magazine. Sanger could go to jail if she continued publication.

Still Sanger continued. Predictably, police arrested her in August 1914. Indicted on four criminal counts carrying a maximum sentence of forty-five years, she fled to Europe one day before her trial. The next year, she returned. Soon after, her daughter, Peggy, died of pneumonia. In February 1916, perhaps in response to public sympathy for Sanger, prosecutor Harold Content dropped the charges.

Civilly Disobedient

Grieving, Sanger threw herself into promoting birth control. On October 16, 1916, using a fifty-dollar donation, she and her sister, Ethel Byrne, opened the country's first birth control clinic—an act of civil disobedience.

The clinic occupied two rooms on the ground floor at 46 Amboy Street, near Pitkin Avenue in the Brownsville section of Brooklyn, New York. Its staff consisted of Sanger, Byrne, Fania Mindell—who spoke Yiddish—and a social worker, Elizabeth Stuyvesant. During the ten days before police closed the clinic, nearly five hundred women came through its doors.

On the ninth day after the clinic's opening, a "Mrs." Whitehurst walked in to buy a ten-cent sex education pamphlet. A member of the vice squad, she returned the next day with three other officers, shouting, "I'm a police officer. You're under arrest."

According to the *Brooklyn Eagle*, the police "half-dragged, half-carried" the sisters to a paddy wagon. The local station freed them after they posted a five-hundred-dollar bail. A few weeks later, Sanger reopened the clinic, but again police shut it down, charging Sanger with creating a public nuisance. They arrested Byrne soon after.

Sanger immediately hired attorney Jonah J. Goldstein to represent them. During Byrne's trial, he argued that New York's Comstock Law—which permitted the distribution of birth control information only in case of medical need—denied the poor their right to choose the size of their families. Nonetheless, the court found Byrne guilty of distributing "obscene" birth control information, sentencing her to thirty-two days in the workhouse on Blackwell's Island (now Roosevelt's Island).

Byrne announced she would go on a hunger strike, "to die, if need be, for my sex." Four days after she began her fast, New York City's corrections commissioner announced Byrne would be the first inmate in U.S. history to be forcibly fed through a tube inserted in her throat. The *New York Times* daily covered the painful details of her feedings of brandy, milk, and eggs on its front page.

As a result of all the publicity, the National Birth Control League stepped in to defend the sisters. Called the Committee of 100, it held a rally at Carnegie Hall shortly after Byrne's sentencing. Three thousand people showed up to hear Sanger speak. Several days later, some of the group took Sanger to the office of Governor Charles Whitman to plead for her sister's release. Whitman said he would only pardon Byrne if Sanger promised not to reopen the clinic. At first, Sanger refused, but after visiting her weakened sister, she reluctantly accepted the governor's terms. Against her will, Byrne left the workhouse, carried on a stretcher.

Meanwhile, Sanger and Mindell went to trial on January 29, 1917, at the Court of Special Sessions in Brooklyn. The court fined Mindell fifty dollars for selling copies of Sanger's article *What Every Girl Should Know*. Sanger was tried for trafficking in obscene materials. Policewoman Whitehurst testified she had found a box of suppositories and a rubber pessary (a contraceptive device that works something like a diaphragm) in the back room of the Brownsville clinic. Other witnesses implied Sanger had gone beyond verbal instruction to actually fit clients with the devices.

Of the three-man panel, Judge Freschi was the most empathetic. He permitted the defense to call a long list of Brownsville mothers who recounted their problems with venereal disease, poverty, and unwanted pregnancies. Eventually Freschi agreed to suspend Sanger's sentence if she promised not to reopen her clinic. She refused: "I cannot promise to obey a law I do not respect." The court, having found her guilty, allowed her the choice of a five-thousand-dollar fine or one month in the workhouse. She chose the workhouse.

However, Sanger vowed to repeat her sister's hunger strike, so the workhouse on Blackwell's Island refused to admit her. Instead, she went to the penitentiary for women in Queens, New York.

The Door Is Opened

After her release, Sanger filed an after-the-fact appeal. Goldstein argued it before the Court of Appeals of the State of New York, saying: The Comstock Act "violates both the federal and state Constitutions," and by preventing the

> dissemination of information to all persons . . . it fails to make provision for cases of women who suffer from certain infirmities . . . endangers their lives and brings about a condition injurious to their health.

However, the court thought the Comstock Act was within the police powers of the legislature, because it benefited "the morals and health of the community." On the other hand, if the law prevented a "duly licensed physician" from taking proper care of his married patients, then the law *would* be unconstitutional. However, Sanger was not a doctor, and therefore the law did not apply to her. Besides, physicians were "excepted from the provisions of this act."

Nevertheless, warned Judge Frederick E. Crane, the law does not allow even doctors to advertise such matters or to give "promiscuous advice to patients irrespective of their condition." It *does* protect a doctor who "gives such help or advice to a married person to cure or prevent disease."

With these words, Crane upheld Sanger's conviction under the New York obscenity law—laypeople could not distribute information on birth control without violating the 1873 Comstock Act. However, by claiming that the Comstock Act provided for a medical "exception," Crane established the right of doctors to provide contraceptive advice to married women for "the cure and prevention of disease." (Formerly "disease" meant venereal disease and applied to men only. Crane broadened the interpretation of "disease" to include women's ailments.)

Sanger used Crane's decision to launch a nationwide chain of doctor-staffed birth control clinics, and lobbied for state laws allowing "doctors only" to prescribe contraceptive devices. In 1921, her emboldened American Birth Control League tried to remove all state and federal restrictions on the right of physicians to prescribe birth control devices. Not until 1936 in *United States v. One Package* (see page 158), did Sanger achieve her goal of reversing the Comstock Act's classification of birth control literature as obscene. Thirty-five years later Congress rewrote the statute to remove any mention of birth control. Many states banned the use of contraceptives by married couples until 1965's *Griswold v. Connecticut* (see page 162), but not until 1972 could unmarried couples legally use birth control devices *(Eisenstadt v. Baird;* see page 172).

For Further Reading

Chesler, Ellen. *Woman of Valor: Margaret Sanger and the Birth Control Movement in America.* New York: Anchor Books/Doubleday, 1993.

Garrow, David J. *Liberty and Sexuality: The Right to Privacy and the Making of Roe v. Wade.* New York: Lisa Drew Books/Macmillan, 1994.

James, Edward T., Janet Wilson James, and Paul S. Boyer, eds. *Notable American Women, 1607–1950.* Cambridge, Mass.: Harvard University Press, Belknap Press, 1971.

Planned Parenthood. *A Tradition of Choice: Planned Parenthood at 75.* New York: Planned Parenthood Federation of America, 1991.

Cammermeyer v. Aspin: 1994

Plaintiff: Colonel Margarethe Cammermeyer **Defendants:** Les Aspin,
secretary of defense, et al. **Plaintiff's Claim:** That her discharge from
service in the National Guard—based solely on her statement that she is a
lesbian—was in violation of her constitutional rights
Chief Lawyer for Defendants: David M. Glass
Chief Lawyers for Plaintiff: Jeffrey I. Tilden, Michael H. Himes, and Mary
Newcombe **Judge:** District Judge Thomas Zilly **Place:** Seattle,
Washington **Date of Decision:** June 1, 1994 **Decision:** Cammermeyer's
discharge violated her equal protection and substantive due process rights
but not her right to freedom of speech and association

SIGNIFICANCE
As the highest ranking and most highly decorated officer ever to have been
discharged for homosexual status from any branch of the U.S. Armed forces,
Cammermeyer's case represents a milestone for those lesbians and gays who
"serve in silence" and for those who support their efforts.

Margarethe Cammermeyer's fitness to serve as a nurse in the U.S. military
seemed completely self-evident from her record, which included a Bronze
Star for distinguished service in Vietnam. That the government ordered her
discharge following her statement that she was a lesbian—and ordered it over
the protests of her immediate supervisors and Washington governor Booth
Gardner, commander-in-chief of the Washington State National Guard—
prompted intense media attention and public debate as to the merits of the
military's exclusionary policies.

A Military Discharge

Cammermeyer applied to the Army War College in April 1989 to receive
training to further her career goal of becoming chief nurse of the National Guard
Bureau. During a related top secret security check, Cammermeyer—a divorced
mother of four who had recently fallen in love with a female artist—was asked to
disclose her sexual orientation. She answered that she was a lesbian and afterward initialed a statement explaining, "I am a Lesbian. Lesbianism is an

orientation I have, emotional in nature, towards women. It does not imply sexual activity. . . ."

The Washington State National Guard decided not to replace Cammermeyer as chief nurse and told her that "unless forced to do so" by the Department of the Army in Washington, D.C., it would not pursue her discharge. The National Guard also gave Cammermeyer the opportunity to resign quietly, which she turned down.

In October, the U.S. Army began proceedings to withdraw Cammermeyer's federal recognition of her state National Guard rank—based on Regulation AR 135-175. The regulation, which had been in effect since 1982, required the discharge from the military of any "member [who] has stated that he/she is a homosexual or bisexual, unless there is a further finding that the member is not a homosexual or bisexual."

Cammermeyer continued to serve as chief nurse, earning superb evaluations, while a military board conducted a three-year-long investigation. Although she was given several opportunities to retract her statement, she never did so. Telling the truth, she later explained, "was the very premise of everything I stood for in my entire life and career."

She told the truth again at a two-day hearing before the military board in July 1991. At its conclusion, the board recommended that Cammermeyer's federal recognition to serve be withdrawn. Assuming the recommendation was followed, the State National Guard would soon be forced to discharge Cammermeyer.

Colonel Patsy Thompson, former chief nurse of the National Guard Bureau, was clearly reluctant to make this recommendation. Before reading it, she read another statement on behalf of all its members:

> I truly believe that you are one of the great Americans, Margarethe. And I've admired you for a long time and the work that you've done and all that you've done for the Army National Guard. When I was Chief Nurse, I said many times, I am really glad we have Margarethe Cammermeyer. . . . She's doing such an outstanding job. We're really fortunate that she came to us. And I really mean that. And I still do mean that.

Thompson also read statements from "just a few of the people that you've touched in your thirty years of military career," including statements from one nurse who called it "a rare privilege to work under you during your tenure as Chief Nurse" and another who said Cammermeyer's "ability to lead and inspire others was obvious. . . ." Nevertheless, she said, it was also her "sad duty" to read the board's official recommendation that Colonel Cammermeyer's federal recognition be withdrawn—an action that would result in her discharge.

Cammermeyer was honorably discharged on June 11, 1992, and she promptly filed a suit against the U.S. Army in the U.S. District Court, Seattle, Washington.

The Judgment

Cammermeyer claimed that the U.S. government had violated her Fifth Amendment rights because it had unfairly discharged her.

At this time, the Supreme Court used three tests to determine whether or not discrimination was unconstitutional. Discrimination based on race, origin, or religion was absolutely unconstitutional. Such laws received "strict scrutiny" by the courts. The mid-level test applied to sex discrimination (called "heightened security"). In all other cases, the Court used the "rational relationship" test. In these cases, a discriminatory law must only serve a "legitimate purpose," to be constitutional, as when the states deny licenses to blind people. District Judge Thomas Zilly found that the discrimination claims of homosexuals were only entitled to this last level.

Legitimate But Not Rational

The court found that the government's stated purpose, to "maintain the readiness and combat effectiveness of its armed forces," was indeed a legitimate one. It did not, however, agree that discharging Cammermeyer was rationally related to this goal. Dismissing the government's claim that homosexuality is "incompati[ble] with military service and interfere[s] with military mission," Zilly noted that in "Canada, Australia, France, Israel, Spain, Sweden, the Netherlands, Denmark, Finland, Norway, and Japan," homosexuals serve without incident. He also cited several studies commissioned by the U.S. government that found "the presence of homosexuals in the military is not an issue and has not created problems in the functioning of military units."

The court was likewise persuaded by evidence refuting the government's claims that homosexual service would damage discipline, good order, and morale; unit cohesion; heterosexual privacy; and its ability to recruit and retain military personnel. After dismissing these arguments, Zilly turned to polling results indicating that "40 to 79 percent of the public favors allowing homosexuals to serve in the military." However, Zilly wrote, "to the extent public disapproval of homosexual service in the military is based on prejudice, such disapproval would not be a legitimate basis for the government's policy."

Finally, Zilly cited Cammermeyer herself as the strongest argument against the government's contention that homosexuality was not compatible with military service:

> Certainly, the undisputed evidence in this case relating to Colonel Cammermeyer's service strongly supports the conclusion that acknowledged homosexuality is not incompatible with military service. Cammermeyer served in the Army and the Washington State National Guard with distinction. She was a highly trained, decorated and dedicated officer in the military. . . . After she disclosed her lesbian status in April 1989, she continued to perform her military duties for over three years until her discharge. Her final evaluation, dated July 31, 1992 . . . described her as having continued to serve the Washington Army National Guard "with dedicated professionalism." It is ironic that after over three years as an

acknowledged homosexual servicemember, Cammermeyer was evaluated as having "the potential to assume responsibility at NGB level as Chief Nurse," yet she was discharged because of the alleged incompatibility of her sexual orientation with military service.

The court set aside Cammermeyer's claim that the "Constitution confers a fundamental right of privacy upon a person to be a homosexual," saying that it did not need to decide this question in order to resolve her claim. "The court," Zilly wrote, "has already held that the Army regulation challenged here is based solely on prejudice. As such, it cannot withstand even rational basis review. Regulations based solely on prejudice are irrational as a matter of law and serve no legitimate governmental purpose."

The district court ordered that Cammermeyer be reinstated to her former position with all the rights, honors, and privileges accorded an officer of her rank. That order has been stayed pending the government's appeal, and Cammermeyer currently works in a civilian position at a veterans' hospital.

For Further Reading

Cammermeyer, Margarethe, with Chris Fisher. *Service in Silence.* New York: Viking, 1994.

"Lesbians, Long Overlooked, Are Central to Debate on Military Ban." *New York Times*, May 4, 1993.

Shenon, Philip. "Armed Forces Still Question Homosexuals." *New York Times*, February 27, 1996.

Shilts, Randy. *Conduct Unbecoming.* New York: St. Martin's Press, 1993.

Section 2
CRIME AND PUNISHMENT

L abor was scarce in early America, leading colonial lawmakers to enact more lenient criminal penalties than those of England. For instance, unlike the mother country, many colonies refused to prosecute blasphemy, fornication, "crimes against nature," and "man stealing" as capital crimes.

However, neither judges nor magistrates dispensed justice even-handedly. Prosecutions "had a strong gender bias," according to historian Peter Charles Hoffer. To cite one example, courts charged women more often than men for fornication and having out-of-wedlock babies. If the father held a higher status than the mother, her punishment was even more severe—on occasion this even included execution. In Connecticut, for example, single women went to trial five times more often than men for such sexual offenses. Colonial courts also punished poor women, old widows, and young servants—society's most defenseless class—more harshly than men. For instance, women faced the gallows if they had the "devil's mark" on their bodies; men, however, were never examined for them.

As Hoffer points out, "Convicted by all-male juries and sentenced by male judges for crimes that men defined and prosecuted, women were defamed as symbols of the inherent immortality of a weaker sex." One example was Mary Mendame of Plymouth colony, perhaps the first colonial woman to be forced to wear a mark on her clothing for a sex offense. Found guilty of adultery in 1639, Mendame was tied to a cart and whipped repeatedly as the wagon made its way through town. Afterwards she wore a badge on her left sleeve, proclaiming her crime. If found without it, she would have been "burned in the face [with] a hot iron."

Colonial law could be strict concerning crimes against women. Rape, for instance, could be punishable by death. However, convictions were hard to win. Without eyewitnesses, many defendants went free. Men accused of rape usually claimed that their victims had "consented" to the act, making the woman's behavior central to many rape trials. Courts also demanded that violated women "prove" that they had vigorously resisted their attackers. Indeed, these issues were at the heart of the Charles Sheepey trial in 1687. They were not finally resolved until the twentieth century in trials such as *Coker v. Georgia* (1977),

Michael M. v. Superior Court of Sonoma County (1981), and the New Bedford Rape Trials (1984).

Enslaved women, however, had no legal recourse when raped. As the 1855 trial of *Missouri v. Celia, a Slave*, shows, Celia had been repeatedly raped by her master from the time she was fourteen, yet the judge ruled she did not fall within the meaning of a "woman" as used in a Missouri statute forbidding the crime. Instead she was considered "property."

Under the common law, married women could not defend themselves if raped by their husbands, as sexual consent was in effect part of their marriage vows. In the 1857 trial *Massachusetts v. Fogerty*, in which Patrick Fogerty and others faced charges of raping ten-year-old Agnes O'Connor, the defense implied that the child might have been married to one of her attackers, a ruse that nearly worked. Not until after *Oregon v. Rideout* (1978) would marriage cease to be an excuse for violent rape.

The women's movement that began in 1848 at Seneca Falls, New York, led the fight against the law's unequal practices. One of the most important of the early feminists' grievances was the idea of "presumed coercion." Under this common law rule, a wife could not be charged with any non-felonious criminal offense if she acted in the presence of her husband because he, as the head and master, was ultimately responsible for her behavior. Not until 1949, in *Los Angeles v. Stately*, would this presumption that wives had to obey their husbands be challenged.

In the early 1960s, women across the nation once again began to challenge state and local laws that discriminated against them. Many believed that the U.S. Constitution did not protect the equal rights of women as it did men. Lawyers took unfair laws all the way to the Supreme Court, inspired by the civil rights struggle of the time.

President John F. Kennedy established The President's Commission on The Status of Women on December 14, 1961. After reviewing numerous state and federal laws, the Commission advised the federal government to pass legislation preventing states from enforcing the vestiges of the discriminatory common laws that had been in effect since our nation began.

One form of legal discrimination women fought in this new political climate was the discriminatory sentencing—usually longer—for female offenders. Many states, such as Maine, Ohio, Massachusetts, New Jersey, Iowa, Connecticut, and Kansas, had such laws on their books. *Pennsylvania v. Daniel* (1967) launched the attack against discriminatory sentencing for women offenders throughout the United States.

In the latter part of the twentieth century, new criminal issues of importance to women emerged. *American Booksellers Association v. Hudnut* (1986) examined writer Andrea Dworkin and attorney Catharine MacKinnon's contention that pornography harms women. Although anti-pornography laws inspired by the pair were found unconstitutional, serious public examination of the issue continues.

In trials involving "date rape," the enforcement of orders of protection for battered wives, community notification laws, and the self-defense claims of female spouse murderers, women have expressed their opinions with passion. In doing so they have changed their status from victims to reformers.

The Case of Mary Mendame: 1639

Defendant: Mary Mendame **Crime Charged:** Adultery
Chief Lawyer for Defendant: Unknown
Chief Lawyer for Plaintiff: Unknown **Justices:** Unknown
Place: Plymouth Colony **Date of Decision:** September 3, 1639
Decision: Guilty

SIGNIFICANCE

Mary Mendame was the first female on record convicted of a sex crime, specifically adultery, and required to wear a mark on her clothes for her offense.

Plymouth, settled by the pilgrims in 1620, was the site of the first permanent English colony in New England. During the 1630s, Plymouth was dwarfed by the Massachusetts Bay Colony, which eventually absorbed the smaller settlement in 1691. In the early eighteenth century, the Massachusetts Bay Colony expanded its punishments for various crimes to include the use of jails. However, in the early days, punishment was very public.

Crime and Punishment

Whipping, also called flogging, was the most common form of punishment in the colonies. At first, whips were made of knotted rawhide called "knout." Later, bound leather lashes, called "cat o'nine tails," often left criminals crippled and permanently scarred.

Then, in 1773, authorities built Newgate prison in Simsbury, Connecticut, in an abandoned copper mine. As a consequence, prisoners often endured jail as well as whipping. Americans did not abandon whipping until the nineteenth century, although a few states, such as Maryland and Delaware, had the punishment on the books until the twentieth century.

After an initial punishment such as flogging, the guilty had to wear badges proclaiming their crime—sometimes for many years. For example, "A" was for adultery, and "R" for rape. Eventually Plymouth dropped this treatment, considering it too harsh, but in early America, "scarlet letters" and whippings were common.

The Original Hester

One of Plymouth's early residents was Mary Mendame. She and her husband, Robert Mendame, lived in Duxborrow, now Duxborough. In 1639, word spread that Mary Mendame had engaged in sexual relations with an Indian named Tinsin. The authorities brought Tinsin in for questioning. Interrogated by several interpreters, the man finally "confessed."

On September 3, Mendame was brought before the court. According to *The Plymouth Colony Records*, she faced the charges of having had a "dallyance divers tymes" with Tinsin and of "committing the act of uncleanesse" with him. The court found her guilty. It then ordered Mendame be tied to a cart and whipped repeatedly as the wagon made its way through the streets.

Mendame also had to wear a badge on her left sleeve, proclaiming her guilt. If found without it, she would be "burned in the face [with] a hot iron." Tinsin was whipped, and tied to a post with a halter around his neck, as punishment for "alluring and enticing" Mendame into the romance.

Today, while on the books of most states, laws against adultery are among the most unenforced in the nation. In New York, the offense (having intercourse with another while still married) is a misdemeanor, punishable by a maximum of six months in jail or a fine not exceeding $250. South Dakota, Vermont, and Oklahoma allow for a five-year prison term. Maryland and other states levy fines of small amounts, such as $10.

For Further Reading

Faragher, John Mack. *The Encyclopedia of Colonial and Revolutionary America*. New York: Facts on File, 1990.

Plymouth County Commissioners. *Archives of the Plymouth Colony, 1620–1691*. Boston: Massachusetts Archives at Columbia Point.

Sifakis, Carl. *The Encyclopedia of American Crime*. New York: Facts on File, 1982.

The Trial of Charles Sheepey: 1687

Defendant: Charles Sheepey **Crime Charged:** Rape
Chief Defense Lawyer: Unknown **Chief Prosecutor:** Unknown
Judge: Unknown **Place:** Burlington, New Jersey
Date of Decision: December 21, 1687 **Verdict:** Guilty **Sentence:** Three
months in prison, public whippings, a year and nine months parole, and
payment of court costs

SIGNIFICANCE

Historically a rape victim has had a triple burden to bear in court: to prove a rape occurred; to convince the jury she was chaste; *and* to demonstrate she had vigorously resisted her attacker. The Sheepey trial is one of the earliest on record to show how a rapist defended himself by claiming the victim was impure and went along with his attack.

The laws of colonial America were strict concerning rape. For example, in 1668, New Jersey permitted but did not mandate the sentence of death for this crime. However, convictions were hard to obtain. While people despised rape, believing it deserved severe punishment, judges and juries agreed that the accusation was hard to prove in court without eyewitnesses, and so, many defendants went free.

Men accused of rape frequently claimed that their victims "consented" to the act. Therefore, the issue of consent became central to many rape trials, as did the requirement that violated women "prove" that they had vigorously resisted their attackers. These issues constituted the heart of the following case.

Alone in the House

Charles Sheepey was a servant in home of the Hutchesons. After making earlier "improper advances" toward their daughter Elizabeth, he finally determined to rape her. The night of the crime, the Hutchesons had gone out, leaving Elizabeth and her sister Martha alone with Sheepey.

Apparently afraid to tell her father—or any other adult—of her fears, Elizabeth and Martha walked to neighbors to ask if their daughter could come and stay with them. The parents said no, since Sheepey was already at home to protect them! So, the sisters returned home and went to bed together. Having no bolt on their bedroom door, they "thrust in some apron or clothes between the sneck [door latch] to keep it fast." However, this faint effort was no deterrent to the servant.

The court clerk recorded what happened next: "And then in the night the said Charles Sheepey gott in and came into the bedd to her the said Elizabeth and her sister, and that the said Sheepey when said Elizabeth endeavoured to resist him held her hands, and Shee then struggling and crying out awakened her sister Martha, and notwithstanding they did both with all their strength strive to resist and repulse the said Sheepey, yet hee did then against the will of her the said Elizabeth force the said Elizabeth" to have intercourse.

At his trial, Sheepey denied that he had raped Elizabeth. Instead he tried to smear her reputation, claiming that the girl had willingly slept with him in the past, and did not resist him on the night in question. Fortunately, Martha was an eyewitness, and because of her supporting testimony, the jury convicted Sheepey.

A Quaker Sentence

The Quaker court rejected the death penalty, instead sentencing Sheepey to be:

> whipt this day betwixt the howers of Two and three in the afternoon upon thy naked Body at a Carts tayle, from the house of John Butcher in this Towne, to the house where Abraham Senior inhabitteth and from thence downe on the River side to the High Street, and from thence downe to the Markett house, And that thou Shalt have as many stripes laid on as the Magistrates. . . . Shall be thought meet. And from thence thou shall be taken and kept in Irons for the space of three Moneths from this day next ensueing, dureing which tyme thou shall be Whipt at Three several times more, in manner and forme as before is mentioned, that is to say on every third Seventh day in each and every of the said three moneths, betweene the howers of Tenne and twelve of each said day. And that dureing thy said Three Moneths imprisonment thou shall be made worke for thy bread; And shall pay the Court Charges and Fees; And after thy said three Moneths Imprisonment thou shall for the space of one Yeare and nyne Moneths then next ensueing, be brought (when thou canst be found within this Province) to each and every Quarterly Sessions at Burlington within the said tyme, And then and there be whipted in manner and forme as afore is mentioned.

Blaming the Victim

Sheepey's claim that Elizabeth did not resist him, since they had been intimate in the past, has been a common defense of accused rapists since the Statutes of Westminister made rape a felony in the thirteenth century. Too often, it has been successful. Susan Brownmiller writes: "[Juries] make use of such information to form a moral judgment on [a victim's] character, and here all the old myths of rape are brought into play, for the feeling persists that a virtuous woman either cannot get raped or does not get into situations that leave her open to assault.''

Today police report that fifteen percent of rape charges prove to be unfounded. For those remaining, until the 1980s, women had to demonstrate that they resisted their attackers and also produce a witness. Such standards, writes Brownmiller, were reserved for rape victims. They did not apply to the victims of other violent crimes.

National studies show that juries still closely evaluate a woman's conduct before her rape, often harshly judging her behavior: Was she drinking before the rape? Did she know her attacker? Was she sexually active? The presumptions on which these questions rest—that a woman must be virginal and that she must resist her attacker—have ancient roots reflecting, as Brownmiller notes, ''man's eternal confusion, never quite resolved, as to whether the crime was a crime against a woman's body or a crime against his own estate.''

For Further Reading

Brownmiller, Susan. *Against Our Will: Men, Women and Rape.* New York: Simon & Schuster, 1975.

Clark, Anna. *Women's Silence, Men's Violence: Sexual Assault in England 1770–1845.* New York: Pandora (Routledge & Kegan Paul), 1987.

Hoffer, Peter Charles. *Law and People in Colonial America.* Baltimore: The Johns Hopkins University Press, 1993.

Sifakis, Carl. *The Encyclopedia of American Crime.* New York: Facts on File, 1982.

Weiss, Harry B., and Grace M. Weiss. *An Introduction to Crime and Punishment in Colonial New Jersey.* Trenton, N.J.: Past Times Press, 1960.

Missouri v. Celia, a Slave: 1855

Defendant: Celia, a slave owned by Robert Newsom
Crime Charged: Murder **Chief Defense Lawyers:** Isaac M. Boulware, John Jameson, and Nathan Chapman Kouns **Chief Prosecutor:** Robert Prewitt
Judge: William Hall **Place:** Calloway County, Missouri
Dates of Trial: October 9–10, 1855 **Verdict:** Guilty
Sentence: Death by hanging

SIGNIFICANCE

This case only too clearly demonstrates enslaved women's lack of legal recourse against sexually abusive masters. According to the judge who heard this case, an enslaved woman did not fall within the meaning of "any woman" as used in a Missouri statute forbidding anyone "to take any woman unlawfully against her will and by force, menace or duress, compel her to be defiled." Instead, she was considered *property* without a right to defend herself against a master's act of rape.

Widower Robert Newsom bought Celia—only 14 years old—in Missouri's Audrain County in 1850 to help his daughters (he said) do the housekeeping. On the way to his home in Calloway County, Missouri, Newsom raped Celia. Once at his farm, he put her in a cabin only 150 feet from his house. In the next five years, Celia gave birth to two of Newsom's children, both of whom became Newsom's slaves upon birth. (No record exists to indicate whether they were retained or sold away by Newsom.) During that time, she also entered a relationship with George, another of Newsom's slaves. In 1855, she once again found herself pregnant, but this time she was unsure of the father's identity. At this point, George told her that "he would have nothing more to do with her if she did not quit the old man."

Celia asked Newsom's daughters—nineteen-year-old Mary and thirty-six-year-old Virginia—for help. Although she suggested that they might persuade their father to leave her alone at least for the duration of the pregnancy, neither daughter appears to have intervened on Celia's behalf. On June 23, Celia herself spoke with Newsom. He brushed aside her pleas and said "he was coming to her cabin that night." Looking for something to use in self defense, she found a heavy stick—"about as large as the upper part of a Windsor chair, but not so long"—and then she waited.

That night, when Newsom refused to leave the cabin, Celia hit him in the head twice and killed him. Before morning, she had burned his body in her fireplace. She hid the largest bones "under the hearth, and under the floor between a sleeper and the fireplace." With a rock, she smashed and ground the smaller bones into unrecognizable pieces. When Virginia's son, Coffee Waynescot, walked by the cabin later in the day, Celia offered him "two dozen walnuts [to] carry the ashes out." Waynescot agreed, and he unwittingly dumped his grandfather's ashes on one of the farm's "beat down like" paths.

A cabin similar to the one that Celia lived in during the 1800s. (Prints & Photographs Division, Library of Congress)

Celia's Story

The following day—Sunday, June 24—Newsom's neighbors and family became concerned. George was questioned, and he implicated Celia. (He later ran away.) Robert's sons, David and Harry Newsom, traveled from their homes to their father's farm and interrogated Celia with the assistance of a neighbor, William Powell. Celia denied any knowledge or responsibility at first, but then she asked Powell to send Newsom's two sons outside. Once they were gone, she told her story to Powell.

When Powell and the Newsom family searched the fireplace, they found, as Virginia identified them, "buttons my sister [Mary] sewed on my father's breeches a few days before his death," along with some small splinters of bone. The larger bones were then found under the hearth, in the hiding space Celia had described to Powell.

Justices of the peace Isaac P. Howe and D. M. Whyte were alerted to the events by David Newsom's affidavit, delivered June 25. It stated that he "ha[d] cause to believe that one Negro woman named Celia a Slave of the Said Robert Newsom did at the county aforesaid feloniously, willfully, and with malice aforethought with a club or some other weapon strike and mortally wound the said Robert Newsom, of which wound or wounds the said Robert Newsom instantly died." Celia was promptly arrested and "deliver[ed] . . . forthwith to the keeper of the common jail of said County to await her trial."

White Calloway County residents, learning of Newsom's killing, became alarmed that Celia might have had other slave accomplices who were still at large and planning further violence. To quell these fears, County Sheriff William T. Snell sent two men, Jefferson Jones and Thomas Shoatman, to question Celia at length and until they were satisfied that she had acted alone. All that is known of Celia's account of the story comes from her interviews with William Powell, Thomas Shoatman, and Jefferson Jones. Like many blacks in nineteenth-century America, she was not allowed to testify—even on her own behalf—in a criminal trial.

The Trial

Celia was brought to trial on October 9, 1855. Isaac M. Boulware, John Jameson, and Nathan Chapman Kouns acted as her court-appointed attorneys, and they mounted as strenuous a defense as possible. Entering a plea of not guilty on Celia's behalf, they described her as one who was "ready for trial, and prayed herself upon her God and her Country."

Prosecutor Robert Prewitt called Jefferson Jones to testify on October 10. Jones described the events as Celia had related them several months before. He said that Celia had told him she "had been having sexual intercourse" with Newsom and that George said he would leave her unless she managed to end her master's relations with her. He was then cross-examined by Jameson about Celia's report of the rape on the day of her purchase, the sexual demands placed upon her during the following five years, and the two children she bore. Jones was far from emphatic in his answers, responding to the question of rape that he couldn't "say positively whether Celia said the accused had forced her on the way home" and couldn't "know with certainty whether she told me so."

Virginia Waynescot, the daughter who had found her father's buttons in the fireplace, testified about that discovery for the prosecution. On cross-examination, Jameson tried to elicit information about Newsom's sexual exploitation of Celia without bluntly asking the question. When he inquired of Virginia where her father normally slept, she said: "[I] did not notice the [Newsom's] bed. Sister made the bed up." Virginia did admit, though, that Celia "took sick in February. Had been sick ever since." Virginia's son, Coffee, was next called by the prosecution, and he testified about his unintentional disposal of his grandfather's remains. When he was cross-examined by Jameson as to Newsom's sexual relations with Celia, Coffee—like his mother—offered no information.

William Powell also took the stand. He testified for the prosecution that Celia had confessed to killing Newsom. During the defense's cross-examination, he was asked—as Newsom's daughter and grandson had not been—what he knew of Newsom's sexual abuse of his young slave. Powell testified that Celia had described to him Newsom's abuse and her attempt to seek help from Newsom's daughters. He also testified that Celia had told him that her actions stemmed only from a desperate wish to halt Newsom's sexual demands.

Jameson called Dr. James M. Martin, a Fulton physician, to testify for the defense. Jameson asked Martin how long it would take to dispose of a man's body by burning, but prosecution objections were immediately sustained by Hall. Jameson then called Thomas Shoatman to testify for the defense. Shoatman said that "the reason she gave for striking him the second blow was that he threw up his hands to catch her" and "only to hurt him, to keep him from having sexual intercourse with her." Hall ordered both of these statements stricken from the record.

The Verdict

Throughout the testimony, Jameson had attempted to bring Celia's motives before the jury for consideration. Slaves did have the recognized legal right to preserve their lives, even through the use of deadly force. In addition, the second article of Section 29 of the Missouri statutes of 1845 forbade anyone "to take any woman unlawfully against her will and by force, menace, or duress, compel her to be defiled." It was considered justifiable homicide to kill a person while fending off such a crime. When it was time for the defending and prosecuting attorneys to present the judge with proposed instructions for the jury, Jameson asked Hall to instruct the jury that "if they . . . believe from the testimony, that the said Newsom at the time of said killing, attempted to compel her against her will to sexual intercourse with him, they will not find her guilty of murder in the first degree." He also asked Hall to interpret "the words 'any woman'" in Section 29 as to "embrace slave women, as well as free white women."

Jameson's proposed interpretations were at odds with Missouri slave law, which viewed the enslaved woman as *property* and treated the rape of that woman by someone other than her master as *trespass*. This definition invited the conclusion, as Melton McLaurin put it, that "an owner could hardly be charged with trespassing upon his own property."

Hall did not present the jury with the self-defense arguments outlined by Jameson. Celia was found guilty on October 10, 1855, and ordered "hanged by the neck until dead on the sixteenth day of November, 1855."

The Appeal Denied

Jameson appealed to the Missouri Supreme Court. He also requested a stay of execution for Celia, whose pregnancy had ended in a stillbirth either during or shortly after the conclusion of her trial.

To Jameson's dismay—and to the shock of many in Calloway County—the court agreed to hear the case but refused a stay of execution. To prevent Celia's hanging under these questionable circumstances, some never-identified Calloway County residents "kidnapped" her from jail just prior to the execution date and returned her when it had passed. Jameson wrote a personal entreaty to one of the three Missouri Supreme Court judges. He chose Judge Abiel Leonard for a very specific reason: Leonard was the only one of the sitting justices who had not participated in the infamous, proslavery decision *Dred Scott v. Sandford*, which would be upheld by the Supreme Court in 1857. In his letter to Leonard, Jameson wrote that Hall had "cut out all means of a defense." He pleaded for a stay of execution and implored Leonard to "please give the matter your earliest attention."

On December 15, 1855, the Missouri Supreme Court decided:

Upon an examination of the record and proceedings of the circuit Court of Calloway County in the above case, it is thought proper to refuse the prayer of the petitioner—there being seen upon inspection of the record aforesaid no probable cause for such appeal; nor so much doubt as to render expedient to take the judgment of the supreme court thereon. It is thereby ordered by the court, that an order for the stay of execution in this case be refused.

On December 20, Celia spoke to a reporter for the *Fulton Telegraph*. She said, "As soon as I struck him the Devil got into me, and I struck him with the stick until he was dead, and then rolled him in the fire and burnt him up." On December 21, 1855, she was hanged.

For Further Reading

Brownmiller, Susan. *Against Our Will: Men, Women, and Rape.* New York: Simon & Schuster, 1975.

Fox-Genovese, Elizabeth. *Within the Plantation Household: Black and White Women of the Old South.* Chapel Hill, N.C.: University of North Carolina Press, 1988.

McLaurin, Melon A. *Celia, A Slave: A true story of violence and retribution in antebellum Missouri.* Athens, Ga.: University of Georgia Press, 1991.

Sterling, Dorothy. *We Are Your Sisters: Black Women in the Nineteenth Century.* New York: W. W. Norton & Co., 1984.

Massachusetts v. Fogerty: 1857

Defendants: Patrick Fogerty et al. **Crime Charged:** Rape of ten-year-old
Agnes O'Connor **Chief Defense Lawyer:** G. M. Stearns
Chief Prosecutor: D. W. Alvord **Judge:** Bigelow **Place:** Chicopee,
Massachusetts **Date of Decision:** September term, 1857 **Verdict:** Guilty

SIGNIFICANCE
The court upheld the idea of statutory rape defined as felonious intimacy with a
child whose "consent" is immaterial—despite the defense argument that the girl
might have been Fogerty's (or one of the others') wife. If she had been, rape would
have been, by definition, impossible.

The law took a giant step forward in its view of rape under the Statutes of
Westminster put forward by King Edward I at the end of the thirteenth
century. The modern principle of statutory rape dates from these laws. Under
them, the rape of a married woman by a man not her husband became a crime.
Before, only the rape of virgins was criminal. The state extended its jurisdiction
as well: If a raped woman failed to bring a lawsuit against her attacker within
forty days, the right to prosecute went to the Crown.

Parliament passed The First Statute of Westminster in 1275. It set the
penalty for the rape of either a married woman or a virgin at two years in jail plus
a possible fine. The Second Statute of Westminster, passed in 1285, increased
this penalty to death.

Traditionally, a man could not by definition commit rape by having sex
with his wife, even if he used force *and* the act was against her will. This was
because a wife's consent to her husband was a permanent part of her marriage
vows.

As Pure as Caesar's Wife

Between 1765–69, famed English jurist Sir William Blackstone wrote his
Commentaries on the Laws of England—explaining the common laws of England
on which much of American jurisprudence is based.

Reflecting historical suspicions about rape victims' claims, Blackstone
wrote that if a woman "be of evil fame and stand unsupported by others," if she

"concealed the injury for any considerable time," or if she made no outcry when she might have a requirement straight from the Old Testament, "these and the like circumstances carry a strong but not conclusive presumption that her testimony is false or feigned." To be believed, a victim's reputation must be spotless, and she must demonstrate that she had offered the utmost resistance.

These rules were tested in the 1857 trial of *Massachusetts v. Fogerty*. On April 26, 1857, in Chicopee, Massachusetts, Patrick Fogerty, and other men, faced charges of raping ten-year-old Agnes O'Connor. The complaint read that Fogerty and his friends "with force and arms . . . violently and feloniously did make an assault [on] the said Agnes. . . ." They "then and there violently and against her will feloniously did ravish and carnally know [her], against the peace of said commonwealth, and contrary to the form of the statute in such case made and provided."

In this early nineteenth-century British illustration, a woman tries desperately to escape from a man who is forcing his intentions upon her. (British Library)

Taking Exceptions

The defendants were convicted in the court of common pleas. Next they moved to set aside the verdict on the grounds that "it is not alleged in the indictment, that said Agnes O'Connor was ravished &c. by force, as required by law" and "because it is not alleged but that said Agnes O'Connor was the wife of one of the defendants, or which defendant, if any." The court overruled the motion.

Next, G. M. Stearns, the defendants' lawyer, alleged certain "exceptions" applied to their case. For example, to constitute rape, the act had to have been "by force" as well as "against the will" of O'Connor. He disputed that the defendants had used force, insisting that "force was the concomitant, not that it was the means of accomplishment of the act." In other words, "an act may be done 'violently,' and yet not accomplished 'by force.'"

Another "exception" was that a "man cannot commit a rape on his own wife." Stearns argued that since the indictment (written accusations) did not set out to prove that O'Connor was *not* the wife of Fogerty—or any of the others— the charges must be dropped.

Despite these arguments, Judge Bigelow ruled that the indictment was valid. It sufficiently set forth all the elements necessary to constitute the offense of rape by alleging that carnal knowledge was done "violently" and was against the consent of Agnes.

As to the argument that a man cannot rape his own wife, Bigelow commented that "[o]f course, it would always be competent for a party indicted to show, in defence [sic] of a charge of rape alleged to be actually committed by himself, that the woman on whom it was charged to have been committed was his wife." A man was only guilty of raping his wife "as principal in the second degree of a rape on his wife by assisting another man to commit a rape upon her." Nonetheless, it was not necessary to show that the child was not Fogerty's wife in the indictment so the court overruled Fogerty's "exceptions."

Today most states have eliminated marital exemptions from current rape statutes (see, for example, *Oregon v. Rideout*, page 73) and have abandoned the former requirement of utmost resistance.

For Further Reading

Brownmiller, Susan. *Against Our Will: Men, Women and Rape.* New York, Simon and Schuster, 1975.

Cullen-DuPont, Kathryn. *The Encyclopedia of Women's History in America.* New York: Facts on File, 1996.

Frost-Knappman, Elizabeth. *The ABC-Clio Companion to Women's Progress in America.* Santa Barbara: ABC-CLIO, 1994.

The Triangle Shirtwaist Fire: 1911

Defendants: Max Blanck and Isaac Harris   **Crime Charged:** Manslaughter
Chief Defense Lawyer: Max D. Steuer   **Chief Prosecutors:** Charles S.
Bostwick and J. Robert Rubin   **Judge:** Thomas C. Crain   **Place:** New York,
New York   **Date of Decision:** December 4, 1911   **Verdict:** Not guilty

SIGNIFICANCE
The Triangle Shirtwaist fire spurred the efforts of the International Ladies'
Garment Workers' Union (ILGWU) to organize garment workers, and increased
support for the vote among wage-earning women. Politicians passed legislation to
improve sweatshop conditions in the garment industry.

At the turn of the twentieth century, poor working conditions and long hours were standard for most factory employees—especially for female workers. Male unions and employers kept women out of better-paying jobs, forcing them into industries such as garment-making, where sweatshop conditions prevailed, pay was low, and employees had to pay for their cutting and sewing supplies.

Factories had few fire-prevention regulations—no sprinklers, poor ventilation, and almost no usable emergency exits.

The Uprising of the 20,000

The first major strike by working women took place among the shirtwaist makers of New York and Philadelphia on November 22, 1909, and continued until February 15, 1910. Called the Uprising of the 20,000, the walk-out was an important demonstration of women's beginning labor movement.

New York's Triangle Shirtwaist Factory, a maker of women's clothing, became one of the targets. That winter women and girls in their teens left their cramped and filthy work rooms, and marched to Union Square to protest their poor working conditions at a meeting called by the ILGWU. Although the intent of the meeting was not to call a strike, remarks made by teenager Clara Lemlich stirred up members of the group and motivated them to walk out.

She interrupted the speeches of Samuel Gompers, president of the American Federation of Labor (AFL), and Margaret Dreier Robins of the New York Women's Trade Union League (WTUL)—an organization that joined women factory workers with women from the upper and middle classes—to yell: "I am tired of listening to speakers who talk in general terms. What we are here for is to decide whether or not we shall strike. I offer a resolution that a general strike be declared now!" The following day, the women walked out.

Pauline Newman, remembering the day, recalled:

Thousands upon thousands left the factories from every side, all of them walking down toward Union Square. It was November, the cold winter was just around the corner, we had no fur coats to keep warm, and yet there was the spirit that led us out of the cold at least for the time being.

Esther Lobetkin was arrested during the strike:

The officer wouldn't let us girls sit down on the [police] benches because we were strikers. . . . One of our girls got so tired she went to crouch down to rest herself, when one of the officers came over and poked her with his club and says, "Here, stand up. Where do you think you are? In Russia?"

The WTUL aided the strikers. Well-known society leaders Anne Morgan, Alva Belmont, Mrs. Henry Morgenthau, and Helen Taft (President William Howard Taft's daughter) were active members. They joined the picket lines, faced arrest, raised bail money for the factory workers, monitored the courts, and brought charges against police—despite resentment and harassment from policemen.

One policeman yelled at the WTUL's Helen Marot, "You uptown scum, keep out of this or you'll find yourself in jail." A judge told the arrested women, "You are striking against God and Nature, whose prime law is that man shall earn his bread with the sweat of his brow."

Thirteen weeks after it began, the protest against the Triangle Shirtwaist Company ended, but that year also saw 404,000 women petition Congress for the vote. Of 339 shops involved, over 300 settled with the workers. These women won a fifty-two-hour work week, a promise that employers would provide supplies, no punishment for striking, and an equal division of work in slack seasons. (The latter discouraged bosses from firing workers during slow times.)

The Triangle Fire

Located on the ninth floor of a building that overlooked Washington Place on one side and Greene Street on the other, Triangle's workrooms had inadequate fire escapes and no sprinklers—conditions the workers had been protesting. Worse, supervisors locked the doors to the workplace from the outside to prevent the women and girls, crowded next to each other on benches, from taking breaks during working hours or removing materials. Only one stairway led to the roof.

On March 25, 1911, a fire broke out on the eighth floor, rising to the ninth through the Greene Street stairwell. As smoke and flames filled the air, the women rushed to the Washington Place exit. It was locked. About 500 women were trapped; many clung to the breaking fire escapes. Firefighters tried to reach them, but their ladders stopped at the sixth floor. Women jumped hand-in-hand from the windows, crashing through the nets, and smashing on the sidewalk. Other women, caught inside, died of burns or suffocation. That night, the Twenty-sixth Street pier held 146 corpses. Two thousand people searched for their loved ones' bodies.

Police attend to the bodies from the Triangle Shirtwaist fire, which took the lives of 146 employees on March 25, 1911. (Prints and Photographs Division, Library of Congress)

It took one week to identify the dead; seven were unknown. The enraged members of the ILGWU and New York WTUL planned a funeral for the unnamed women. New York's grieving population turned out in full on the rainy, cold April day. Throughout the steady downpour, they marched. The Washington Square Arch was the agreed point of merger for the marchers coming from all across the city to form one parade. There were so many people at that spot by 3:30 P.M. that the last one waited until 6:00 P.M. to pass below the arch.

On December 4, Max Blanck and Isaac Harris, the owners of the company, went on trial for manslaughter. Max D. Steuer was their attorney. Assistant district attorneys Charles S. Bostwick and J. Robert Rubin prosecuted the defendants in the three-week trial.

There were more than 150 witnesses. Kate Alderman told how both she and Margaret Schwartz tried and failed to open the door. Alderman ultimately escaped by covering herself with dresses and a coat and leapt through the flames to where firemen rescued her. Schwartz died.

Despite the dramatic testimony, Judge Thomas C. T. Crain instructed the jury that the key to the case was whether the defendants knew the door was locked:

> If so, was it locked under circumstances importing knowledge on the part of these defendants that it was locked? If so, and Margaret Schwartz died because she was unable to pass through, would she have lived if the door had not been locked . . .?

On December 27, 1911, the jury acquitted both defendants of manslaughter. One jury member said, "I believed the door was locked at the time of the fire. But we couldn't find them guilty unless we believed they knew the door was locked." Another member of the all-male jury remarked that the women—whom they did not believe were as intelligent as those in other occupations—probably panicked, causing their deaths. The court denied a prosecution demand for a retrial so Blanck and Harris went free.

On April 5, 1911, the International Ladies' Garment Workers' Union and the New York Women's Trade Union League organized a memorial parade for employees who perished in the Triangle Shirtwaist fire. (Prints and Photographs Division, Library of Congress)

Out of the Ashes

The tragedy galvanized working women. Despite arrests and beatings, strikes across the nation increased, and the membership of the ILGWU surged. In 1912, women were among 20,000 textile workers to strike in Lawrence, Massachusetts. One of them explained her continued support: "It is not only bread we give our children. . . . We live by freedom, and I will fight till I die to give it to my children.''

Female labor leaders such as Leonora O'Reilly demanded the vote for women so they could protect themselves by electing politicians who would pass laws to change the sweatshop conditions under which they worked. In 1912, when the next New York City suffrage parade took place, 20,000 people marched and another half million lined the sidewalks.

Out of public outrage, officials imposed new laws—requiring strict building codes and inspections on sweatshops, for example. New York City created a Bureau of Fire Prevention that established and enforced stricter safety regulations. Other cities and states did the same during the following years. Finally, the federal government, under the administration of Franklin D. Roosevelt, developed workplace safety measures—forerunners to the Occupational Safety and Health Administration (OSHA).

For Further Reading

Frost, Elizabeth, and Kathryn Cullen-DuPont. *Women's Suffrage in America: An Eyewitness History.* New York: Facts on File, 1992.

Frost-Knappman, Elizabeth. *The ABC-CLIO Companion to Women's Progress in America.* Santa Barbara, Calif.: ABC-CLIO, 1994.

Knappman, Edward W., ed. *Great American Trials.* Detroit: Gale Research, 1994.

Wertheimer, Barbara Mayer. *We Were There: The Story of Working Women in America.* New York: Pantheon Books, 1977.

Los Angeles v. Stately: 1949

Appellant: Cora Elizabeth Stately   **Appellee:** The City of Los Angeles
Appellant's Claim: That under the doctrine of "presumed coercion," she should not have been convicted of a crime committed in the presence of her husband   **Chief Lawyer for Appellee:** City Attorney Ray L. Chesebro
Chief Lawyer for Appellant: T. Ed Scarborough   **Judges:** *Edward T. Bishop,* Hartley Shaw and Jess E. Stephens   **Place:** Los Angeles, California
Date of Decision: April 1949   **Decision:** Cora Stately's case would be reheard and the jury would be instructed to consider evidence that she had been coerced by her husband, but there should be no presumption of such coercion simply because she was in her husband's presence during the commission of a crime

S I G N I F I C A N C E

This decision broke with the common law to recognize that women had made major political and personal gains and could not be presumed to act under husbands' orders.

In 1848, the Seneca Falls Convention gave birth to the women's movement. One of the early feminists' grievances was the idea of "presumed coercion." This legal doctrine held that a woman could not be charged with any non-felonious criminal offense if she acted in the presence of her husband. The insulting rationale was that a husband, as the head and master, was ultimately responsible for his wife's behavior.

One hundred years later, Cora Stately claimed innocence under California's version of this doctrine (Penal Code Section 26): "All persons are capable of committing crimes except: Married women (except for felonies) acting under the threats, commands or coercion of their husbands," among other categories.

Stately had been driving a car, with her husband as her passenger. When his wife stopped rather than approach a crowded crosswalk, he said, "You have got plenty of clearance, take it." She did. A pedestrian jumped to the sidewalk for safety, and police charged the driver with a failure to yield the right of way.

During a lower court trial, the judge refused to instruct the jury that they should presume Stately drove recklessly because of her husband's orders. The jury found her guilty. She appealed the decision to the superior court.

Judge Edward T. Bishop, writing for that court, conceded that "in a majority of states the common law presumption (of coercion) is still applied." However, he also noted with approval that several states refused to apply the doctrine in the twentieth century. These decisions were based on the view, as a Kentucky court expressed it in 1920: "Having sought and obtained . . . new rights and privileges, which have placed her upon a plane of equality with her husband, [womankind] must accept the corresponding obligations and responsibilities which those rights and privileges entail. . . ." Bishop agreed with this reasoning and ruled that:

> . . . the reign of the thousand year old presumption has come to an end. In our society . . . it is not accepted . . . that a wife does what her husband wishes by way of yielding obedience to a dominant will. . . . A presumption that has lost its reason must be confined to a museum; it has no place in the administration of justice.

However, he ruled only against the presumption of a husband's coercion and not against consideration of whether or not it had actually occurred. For a modern wife to escape the consequences of her disobedience of a statute on the grounds that she was obeying her husband, she would have to prove that she had, as the penal code provided, acted under actual "threats, command, or coercion of her husband."

The court remanded Stately's case for retrial according to these guidelines. She thus "won" the right to argue that her illegal conduct had been forced upon her by her husband, but lost the right to have a jury assume she was incapable of acting on her own. The assumption of presumed coercion since the time of the Stately trial has all but disappeared. However, on rare occasions where husbands have used force on their wives, and both commit a crime, the principle is still resurrected.

For Further Reading:

Flexner, Eleanor. *Century of Struggle: The Women's Rights Movement in the United States.* Cambridge, Mass.: The Belknap Press of Harvard University Press, 1975.

Frost, Elizabeth, and Kathryn Cullen-DuPont. *Women's Suffrage in America: An Eyewitness History.* New York: Facts on File, 1992.

Kanowitz, Leo. *Sex Roles in Law and Society: Cases and Materials.* Albuquerque: University of New Mexico Press, 1973.

Stanton, Elizabeth, Susan B. Anthony, and Matilda Joslyn Gage. *The History of Woman Suffrage.* Vol. I., 1882, reprint. Salem, N.H.: Ayer Company, 1985.

Pennsylvania v. Daniel and Douglas: 1967

Appellants: Jane Daniel and Daisy Douglas **Appellee:** Commonwealth of Pennsylvania **Appellants' Claim:** That Pennsylvania's Muncy Act was unconstitutional as it denied women the equal protection of the laws as required by the Fourteenth Amendment
Chief Lawyer for Appellee: Attorney General Frank P. Lawley, Jr.
Chief Lawyer for Appellants: Herman I. Pollack **Justices:** *Chief Justice John C. Bell, Jr.,* Herbert B. Cohen, Michael J. Eagen, Benjamin R. Jones, Michael Musmanno, Henry X. O'Brien, and Samuel J. Roberts
Place: Philadelphia, Pennsylvania **Date of Decision:** July 1, 1968
Decision: The Supreme Court of Pennsylvania ruled that the State's Muncy Act was a violation of the Equal Protection clause of the Fourteenth Amendment

SIGNIFICANCE
Pennsylvania v. Daniel and Douglas launched the attack against the discriminatory sentencing of women offenders.

I n the early 1960s, women across the nation began challenging as never before the state and local laws that discriminated against them. The question of the decade was: Did the Constitution protect the equal rights of women as well as men? Lawyers took these unfair laws all the way to the Supreme Court, inspired by the civil rights struggle of the time and by the formation of the President's Commission on The Status of Women established on December 14, 1961, by President John F. Kennedy.

After reviewing numerous state and federal laws—such as those regulating marriage, property, child custody, Social Security, and jury service—the commission recommended legislation to prevent states from enforcing these old common laws.

The Commission issued a report in 1963 entitled *American Women*, which called for "judicial clarification" of these laws, so that any "remaining ambiguities with respect to constitutional protection of women's rights be eliminated."

One form of legal discrimination women fought in this new political climate was the discriminatory sentencing—usually longer—for female offenders. Many states, such as Maine, Ohio, Massachusetts, New Jersey, Iowa, Connecticut, and Kansas, had such laws on their books. One of these was Philadelphia's so-called "Muncy Act," which involved a convict named Jane Daniel.

Because She Is a Woman . . .

Jane Daniel already had previously been convicted of a violent crime when she stood trial for burglary (of a bar), aggravated robbery, carrying a concealed deadly weapon, and possession of a firearm. (In 1967 the Superior Court of Pennsylvania recorded her name as Daniels, while in 1968 the Supreme Court of Pennsylvania used Daniel. Official documents from the Pennsylvania Department of Corrections spell it Daniel, which is used here.) On May 3, 1966, Judge James L. Stern found Daniel guilty of robbery and sentenced her to a one- to four-year term in Philadelphia County Prison.

Thirty-one days later, Stern changed the sentence, realizing that he had not followed the State's 1913 Muncy Act, formally titled the State Industrial Home for Women Act. This law regulated the sentencing of women offenders. To comply with the statute, on June 3, 1966, Stern resentenced Daniel to an *indefinite* term at the State Industrial Home for Women at Muncy, Pennsylvania. In practice, because of the parole policies at Muncy, this meant that Daniel would serve at least three years in prison or as many as ten years—the maximum term for robbery.

The Muncy Act specified:

> The duration of such imprisonment [of women], including the time spent on parole, shall not exceed three years, *except where the maximum term specified by law for the crime for which the prisoner was sentenced shall exceed that period*, in which event such maximum term, including the time spent on parole, shall be the limit of detention under the provisions of this act. [Italics added]

Daniel appealed her sentence to the Superior Court of Pennsylvania. Her attorneys, Herman I. Pollack and Carolyn E. Temin, argued that if she were a man she would have received a maximum sentence of four years, and would have been eligible for parole sooner. Only one judge, J. Sydney Hoffman, agreed with them:

> In my view, the Muncy Act constitutes an arbitrary and invidious discrimination against women offenders as a class. . . . In the instant case, the trial judge attempted to sentence the defendant to a term of one to four years. Were it not for the fact that she is a woman, she would have become eligible for parole in one year. Even if never released on parole, she would have been completely discharged after four years. Because of the mandatory language of the Muncy statute, however, she may serve a term whose maximum is 10 years. Because of the scheme of parole referral in force at Muncy, she will probably serve a minimum of three years at that institution. It is therefore apparent that the act imposes heavier sentences on women in general and

has worked to impose a more severe punishment on defendant [Daniel] in particular.

However, a majority of the superior court held that the Muncy Act did not violate the equal protection clause, reasoning that there was a rational basis for the legislature's decision:

> [T]he legislature could have concluded that indeterminate sentences should be imposed on women as a class, allowing the time of incarceration to be matched to the necessary treatment in order to provide more effective rehabilitation. Such a conclusion could be based on the physiological and psychological makeup of women, the type of crime committed by women, their relation to the criminal world, their roles in society, their unique vocational skills and pursuits, and their reaction as a class to imprisonment, as well as the number and type of women who are sentenced to imprisonment rather than given suspended sentences. Such facts could have led the legislature to conclude that a different manner of punishment and rehabilitation was necessary for women sentenced to confinement.

Attorney Carolyn E. Temin (now a judge for the Court of Common Pleas in Pennsylvania) played a key role in helping to overturn Pennsylvania's Muncy Act in 1968, which placed no specific term lengths for women convicted of crimes and sent to prison. (Judge Carolyn Engel Temin)

The court also concluded that Daniel had not proven her claim that if she had been a man she would have received a shorter sentence:

> To support her attack on the legislation appellant argues that because she is a woman she has received a maximum sentence of ten years (the maximum for robbery); that if she were a man she would have received a maximum term of four years (the term imposed before the sentence was corrected to conform with the Muncy Act requirements); and that this difference in maximum terms solely because of her sex demonstrates a violation of the Equal Protection Clause of the Fourteenth Amendment. This argument rests on an invalid assumption, viz., that a man committing this crime would have received a maximum term of four years. Stern's prior sentence of one to four years was a sentence imposed on a female, and we cannot speculate as to what the sentence would have been had the person robbing the bar in question been a male.

With Friends Like These . . .

The court's reasoning had its basis in a long tradition of special sentencing provisions for women that began in the nineteenth century. About 1869, Indiana became the first state to set up reformatories for women, who before this, served out their terms in the same county jails or penitentiaries as men.

By 1917, fourteen states had established separate female reformatories, sometimes called "industrial homes." The reformatories reflected a concept popular at the time: women offenders could and should be rehabilitated, while men needed to be punished. It followed that women should be detained as long as it took to rehabilitate them. Therefore, they needed separate sentencing regulations.

In the early twentieth century, jurists thought that the ideal prison sentence for a woman convict should be an indeterminate or general one with no limits on the minimum or maximum time served. Most states limited the maximum sentence, usually the maximum term for the offense in question. As a result of the effort to "help" women by sentencing them to general sentences, female offenders often served longer jail terms than men for the same crime.

However, in 1966, Philadelphia District Attorney Arlen Specter (among others) filed a brief in the Daniel trial that showed the darker motives behind the statute. He quoted a criminologist (female, at that) some fifty years earlier:

U.S. senator Arlen Specter held the position of Philadelphia's district attorney during the Jane Daniel trial. (Senator Arlen Specter)

There is little doubt in the minds of those who have had much experience in dealing with women delinquents, that the fundamental fact is that they belong to the class of women who lead sexually immoral lives. . . .[Such a statute] would remove permanently from the community the feeble-minded delinquents who are now generally recognized as a social menace, and would relieve the state from the ever increasing burden of their illegitimate children. Furthermore, such a policy, thoroughly carried out, would do more to rid the streets . . . of soliciting, loitering, and public vice than anything that could be devised. There is nothing the common prostitute fears so greatly as to know that if she offends and is caught she will be subject to the possibility of prolonged confinement.

Douglas and Daniel Join Forces

During this time, a second attack on the Muncy Act was gathering steam. Daisy Douglas and her codefendant, Richard Johnson, had been convicted of robbery. Despite six earlier convictions for burglary, Johnson received a conviction of not less than three nor more than ten years. Douglas, with prior arrests for prostitution, was sentenced to the State Correctional Institute at Muncy for twenty years, the maximum allowed by law. Douglas's appeal joined that of Daniel. They came before the Supreme Court on January 5, 1968, and July 1, 1968.

The Douglas case strengthened Daniel's. The Superior Court had ruled Daniel had only "speculated" that had she been a man her sentence would have been shorter. Yet in the case of Daisy Douglas, there was no doubt: Johnson and Douglas were both tried jointly and convicted of the same crime. Johnson was sentenced to ten years, Douglas to twenty, even though her background, unlike that of Johnson, showed no past involvement in robbery. Further, records from the Pennsylvania Board of Probation and Parole showed that men on parole, convicted of a similar offense for a second time, rarely served the maximum sentence.

This time, the court agreed. Chief Justice John C. Bell, writing for the court, declared:

... women are deprived of the right to have a Judge fix (a) maximum sentence less than the maximum prescribed by law for the offense committed, or (b) a minimum-maximum sentence, with its inherent advantages, which right the appellants correctly assert is given to the Judge in the sentencing of men. . . .

He pointed out that whether a sentence is given in terms of an indefinite period or in terms of the minimum-maximum period, "the maximum sentence is the real sentence." The court continued:

... a Judge in sentencing a woman has no discretion in fixing the maximum period during which she must be imprisoned. On the other hand, a Judge in sentencing a man . . . may and does consider extenuating facts and factors. It is clear then that an arbitrary and invidious discrimination exists in the sentencing of men to prison and women to [the State Correctional Institution at] Muncy, with resulting injury to women.

Therefore,

... the act of July 25, 1913, . . . is devoid of reasonable differences, and is arbitrary, discriminatory and invalid under the Fourteenth Amendment of the Constitution of the United States.

The Court remanded both cases to the Court of Quarter Sessions of Philadelphia County for resentencing.

Jane Daniel was convicted of robbery and sentenced to a ten-year prison term beginning on January 26, 1966. After serving only twenty-seven months, she was released on May 6, 1968. She continued her criminal career, however, actually plotting to rob her own husband on August 12, 1969. In the course of the crime, Clarence Daniel stabbed his wife, and she died shortly after.

For Further Reading

Hoff, Joan. *Law, Gender, and Injustice: A Legal History of U.S. Women*. New York: New York University Press, 1991.

Kanowitz, Leo. *Women and the Law: The Unfinished Revolution*. Albuquerque: University of New Mexico Press, 1969.

Temin, Carolyn Engel. "Discriminatory Sentencing of Women Offenders: The Argument for ERA in a Nutshell." *The American Criminal Law Review*. Vol. 11, no. 355 (1973).

Coker v. Georgia: 1977

Appellant: Ehrlich Anthony Coker   **Appellee:** The State of Georgia
Chief Lawyer for Appellant: David E. Kendall
Chief Lawyer for Appellee: Assistant Attorney General B. Dean Grindle, Jr.
Appellant's Claim: That the death penalty for rape violates the Constitution's
Eighth Amendment   **Justices:** Harry E. Blackmun, William J. Brennan,
Thurgood Marshall, John Paul Stevens, Potter Stewart, *Byron R. White*
(majority); Lewis F. Powell, Jr. (concurring in part; dissenting in part); Chief
Justice Warren E. Burger and William H. Rehnquist (dissent)
Place: Washington, D.C.   **Date of Decision:** June 29, 1977   **Decision:** In
a split decision, the Court ruled that Georgia's death penalty for rape violated
the Eighth Amendment of the Constitution

SIGNIFICANCE

Many feminists celebrated this decision, believing the death penalty made juries
less likely to convict rapists. They also thought it would discourage the old idea
that a woman was the property of her husband (or father) and became valueless
to him after a rape.

On September 2, 1974, Ehrlich Anthony Coker escaped from the Ware
Correctional Institution near Waycross, Georgia. He had been serving six
separate sentences, including two terms of life imprisonment for assault, kidnapping, rape, and murder. At about 11:00 P.M., he entered an unlatched kitchen
door and attacked the married couple he found inside. He tied up the man and
took his money and car keys. Then he raped the sixteen-year-old woman at
knife point and forced her to accompany him as he continued his flight in the
couple's car. When police caught Coker, they discovered that his female hostage
had no further injuries.

Coker stood trial, a jury convicting him on all counts. At a separate
sentencing hearing, the jury considered whether Coker should receive the death
penalty for rape. Georgia's statutes permitted the death penalty when a rape "(i)
. . . was committed by a person with a prior record of conviction for a capital
felony; (ii) the offense was committed while the offender was engaged in
another capital felony or in aggravated battery; and (iii) the offense was 'wan-
tonly vile, horrible, or inhuman in that it involved torture, depravity of mind, or

an aggravated battery to the victim.'" The first two aggravating circumstances applied to Coker, and the jury sentenced him to death by electrocution.

On Appeal

Coker appealed to the Georgia Supreme Court, which upheld both his conviction and his sentence of death by electrocution. He then appealed to the U.S. Supreme Court, which agreed to examine just one question raised by the case: whether "the punishment of death for rape violates the Eighth Amendment, which [forbids] 'cruel and unusual punishments' and which must be observed by the states as well as the federal government."

On March 28, 1977, Coker's attorney, David E. Kendall, argued that the death penalty was too severe a punishment for rape and therefore violated the Eighth Amendment. Ruth Bader Ginsburg and others filed an *amici curiae*, or friend of the court, brief on behalf of the American Civil Liberties Union and other organizations.

Assistant Attorney General B. Dean Grindle argued that the death penalty was a punishment appropriate for the crime of rape in certain aggravated circumstances and that the Constitution permitted it.

The Verdict

The Supreme Court ruled on June 29, 1977, that Georgia's death penalty for rape was unconstitutional. Coker would go to jail for life instead of facing execution (and be eligible for parole in 2003). Justice Byron White, in a plurality opinion joined by justices Harry Blackmun, John Paul Stevens, and Potter Stewart, ruled that the death penalty for deliberate murder was neither too severe nor "grossly disproportionate to the crime."

However, noting that the Court had "reserved the question of the constitutionality of the death penalty when imposed for other crimes," White turned to the case at hand and wrote: "We have concluded that a sentence of death is grossly disproportionate and excessive punishment for the crime of rape and is therefore forbidden by the Eighth Amendment as cruel and unusual punishment."

He elaborated that while the crime of rape was serious, reprehensible in a moral sense, and showing "almost total contempt for the personal integrity and autonomy of the female victim," still "it does not compare with murder, which does involve the unjustified taking of human life."

He continued, "Although it may be accompanied by another crime, rape by definition does not include the death of or even the serious injury to another person. . . . Life is over for the victim of the murderer; for the rape victim, life may not be nearly so happy as it was, [but] it is not over and normally is not beyond repair." Therefore, "the death penalty . . . is excessive for the rapist who, as such, does not take human life."

Justices William J. Brennan and Thurgood Marshall, in separate concurring opinions, concluded that the death penalty was cruel and unusual punishment prohibited in *all* cases. Justice Lewis Powell agreed that the death penalty was too severe in Coker's case, since the victim did not suffer a serious nor lasting injury. He dissented, however, from the view that a death penalty would be unconstitutional in "the case of an outrageous rape resulting in serious, lasting harm for the victim," a question he said he "would not prejudge."

Nothing Left to Lose

Chief Justice Warren Burger, joined by Justice William Rehnquist, filed a scathing dissenting opinion. Burger outlined Coker's criminal history, noting that he had raped and stabbed to death one young woman; kidnapped, raped, and beat nearly to death another young woman; and, after his escape from prison, raped, threatened with death, and kidnapped the woman from Waycross, Georgia. The ruling that Coker could not be executed, Burger wrote, "prevents the State from imposing any effective punishment upon Coker for his latest rape . . . [and] bars Georgia from guaranteeing its citizens that they will suffer no further attacks by this habitual rapist." Burger agreed that he "accept[ed] that the Eighth Amendment's concept of disproportionality bars the death penalty for minor crimes. But rape is not a minor crime. . . ." Rather, he wrote later in the opinion:

> A rapist not only violates a victim's privacy and personal integrity, but inevitably causes serious psychological as well as physical harm in the process. The long-range effect upon the victim's life and health is likely to be irreparable . . . it is destructive of the human personality. . . . To speak blandly, as the plurality does, of rape victims who are "unharmed" or to classify the human outrage of rape, as does Mr. Justice Powell, in terms of "excessively brutal," versus "moderately brutal," takes too little account of the profound suffering the crime imposes upon the victims and their loved ones.

Burger concluded that "if murder is properly punishable by death, rape should be also, if that is the considered judgment of the legislators."

Ginsburg Revisits Her Brief

Sixteen years later, during the confirmation hearings upon her appointment to the Supreme Court, Ruth Bader Ginsburg discussed her *amicus curiae* brief in the case and her continued support for the decision reached in *Coker v. Georgia*. The death penalty for rape, she said:

> Where there was no death or serious permanent injury apart from the obvious psychological injury—that . . . was disproportionate for this reason: The death penalty for rape historically was part of a view of woman as belonging to the man, as first her father's possession. If she were raped before marriage, she was damaged goods. . . . And if she were a married woman and she were raped, again, she would be regarded as damaged goods.

We've seen [this] . . . in many places in the world, where women in Bangladesh, for example, were discarded, were treated as worthless because they had been raped. And that was what Coker against Georgia came out of, and that's the whole thrust of [my] brief, that this was made punishable by death because man's property had been taken from him because of the rape of the woman.

Pressed by U.S. senator Charles E. Grassley (R-Iowa), who was questioning her, to concede that her brief reflected a view that the death penalty itself was unconstitutional, Ginsburg shot back:

. . . I urge you to read the entire . . . brief. I think you will find it to be exactly what I represented it to be. One of the reasons why rapes went unpunished, why women who had been raped suffered the indignity of having the police refuse to prosecute, was statutes of that order.

According to Linda Fairstein, director of the Sex Crimes Unit in the Manhattan district attorney's office, the conviction rate in rape cases has greatly increased during the last two decades. In addition to the elimination of the death penalty for rape, other measures passed in the 1970s have helped to make this possible. These include the elimination of requirements that a rape be witnessed and its victim use earnest resistance, as well as the passage of rape shield laws which prohibit testimony about a victim's prior sexual history.

For Further Reading

Brownmiller, Susan. *Against Our Will: Men, Women, and Rape.* New York: Simon & Schuster, 1973.

Fairstein, Linda A. *Sexual Violence: Our War Against Rape.* New York: William Morrow and Company, 1993.

Goldstein, Leslie Friedman. *The Constitutional Rights of Women*, rev. ed. Madison: The University of Wisconsin Press, 1989.

New York Times. "Excerpts From Senate Hearings on Ginsburg's Supreme Court Nomination," July 23, 1993.

Oregon v. Rideout: 1978

Defendant: John J. Rideout   **Crime Charged:** First-degree rape
Chief Defense Lawyer: Charles Burt   **Chief Prosecutor:** Gary D. Gortmaker
Judge: Richard Barber   **Place:** Salem, Oregon
Dates of Decision: December 27, 1978   **Verdict:** Not guilty

SIGNIFICANCE

For the first time in modern American history, a man faced trial for raping his wife. A national public discussion of the issue followed: Does a man have an absolute sexual right to his spouse's—or cohabitant's—body? Two other states besides Oregon had passed laws that did not grant married (or cohabitating) men immunity from the rape of their wives—and New Jersey was about to come on board. The Rideout trial led many other states to abolish marital and cohabitation exemptions to rape.

In 1978, Oregon, Delaware, and Iowa were the only states that did not recognize "marital privilege" as a defense against rape. All other states followed common law, which defined rape as "the forcible penetration of the body of a woman not the wife of the perpetrator."

On October 10, 1978, twenty-three-year-old Greta Rideout telephoned the police for help, saying "My husband just got through beating me." When a police officer arrived at her home, Rideout said her husband had raped her. On October 18th, John Rideout was indicted on a charge of first degree rape.

Does Marriage Mean Consent?

In November, a circuit court judge denied Rideout's request to have the case dismissed on constitutional grounds. When it became clear that the criminal trial would proceed, District Attorney Gary D. Gortmaker asked Judge Barber to prohibit "common law defenses," that is, a defense of John Rideout's actions based upon the common law presumption that a wife cannot refuse to have intercourse with her husband. Gortmaker argued that Oregon's law, passed in 1977, had replaced English common law within the state. The judge denied the motion.

Charles Burt, Rideout's lawyer, explained the common law "marital privilege" for prospective jurors on December 19. He said that the issue was not whether the couple had had sex on October 11, but whether there had been "forcible compulsion" and whether a woman's marriage to a man meant she could not say "no."

Dr. Gilbert Geis, a professor of criminology at the University of California at Irvine and a specialist in the issue of spousal exemption, spoke to Les Ledbetter of the *New York Times* during the trial. He traced husbands' immunity from charges of rape to a seventeenth century English jurist, Judge Matthew Hale. Hale's promulgation, as recorded in the 1736 "Historia Placitorum Coronae, A History of the Pleas to the Crown," explains that "the husband cannot be guilty of a rape committed by himself upon his lawful wife, for by the mutual matrimonial consent and contract the wife hath given up herself in this kind unto the husband which she cannot retract." (Dr. Geis also pointed out Hale's other claim to fame was the number of witches hung by his order during the 1660s.)

John Rideout was charged with rape by his wife, Greta, in 1978. (*Statesman Journal*, Salem, Ore.)

No Help from Friends . . .

The lawyers made their opening arguments before Barber and a jury of eight women and four men on December 20. The prosecution told the jury to prepare themselves for Greta Rideout's testimony that her husband had struck and raped her within sight of the couple's crying two-and-a-half-year-old daughter. The defense countered by saying that Greta Rideout had a "serious sexual problem" and that his twenty-one-year-old client "honestly believed if you are married to a woman, you have a right to sex."

During the following two days, a number of the couple's friends, neighbors, and relatives testified for the prosecution. While witnesses agreed that John did, indeed, beat his wife, a few gave testimony that raised questions about Greta's motives for accusing him of rape.

David Lowe testified that during an argument prior to October 10, he had heard Greta warn her husband that she would have him arrested under Oregon's new rape law. The manager of the Rideout's apartment building, Jackie Godfrey, testified that following John's arrest, Greta had mentioned a $50,000 offer from the Warner Brothers film company. Jackie Godfrey's daughter, Eugenia, and her husband, Wayne, also testified as to the conversation.

Testimony given by two other prosecution witnesses, Jenny Reisch and John Rideout's half-brother Jack Hinkle, swore that the Rideouts had a troubled marriage, but they *also* cast doubt on Greta's truthfulness. At the beginning of the trial, Burt had said that Greta Rideout taunted her husband by saying that she, and her friend Jenny, had once had a lesbian relationship. Jenny testified that there had been no such relationship, and that Greta Rideout's story had been "made up" to "bait" John.

Burt told the court that Greta said she had been raped by Hinkle. However, Hinkle testified that he had never raped his sister-in-law. He also testified that the Rideouts had once lived with him, and that they had been in the habit of "play[ing] games" that involved chasing each other through various rooms before having sex.

Other testimony was less open to interpretation. Dr. Lewis Sayers, the physician who examined Greta after the incident, testified that both her mental and physical condition were "probably from a forced act of intercourse." Officer Deborah Cleveland, who arrested John, said his comment about his wife's battered jaw was, "If I'd done it right she wouldn't be here to complain."

Greta was the prosecution's last witness. She testified that her husband routinely demanded sex two to three times a week and violent sex once a week. She also said that her husband frequently kicked and hit her. On October 10, she woke at 9:00 A.M. and did housework while her husband, a student, slept until the afternoon. Upon waking, he demanded that she have sex with him. Greta refused, saying she had to get ready for work. He began to chase her, she recalled. "I was afraid of him. He was very angry. I'd never seen him that angry."

Greta Rideout, 23, arrives at the Marion County Courthouse in Salem, Oregon, on December 27, 1978, after charging her husband, John, with rape. This was the first trial to occur in the United States in which a wife accused her non-estranged husband with the crime of rape. (AP/Wide World Photos)

She testified that her husband had said, "You are my wife. You should do what I want." There was a physical fight, in front of their two-year-old daughter. When John ordered the child to leave the room, she obeyed, but Greta could hear her daughter crying, "Mommy, Mommy!" Finally, having been beaten and hit especially hard in her jaw, Greta gave in.

Afterward, Greta continued, her husband dragged her to the bathroom and forced her to look at her bruised face in the mirror. He told her, "This is what you'll get for not cooperating from now on." He also threatened to tell lies about her if she went to the police and said that if he were ever arrested, "I'll find you and that will be the end of you."

During the prosecution's presentation of its case, the jury also heard the tape of Greta's call to the police on October 10, and visited the couple's apartment.

John was the only defense witness. His excuse was, "She hit me first." He admitted to hitting her, but testified that he had apologized, saying " 'Greta, I'm sorry. I didn't mean to do that.' She said it was all right," he continued, and then they kissed and had "voluntary" sexual intercourse.

Lose One, Win Some

On December 27, 1978, after three hours of deliberations, the jury found John Rideout not guilty. A member of the jury, Pauline Speerstra, told the press afterward that the validity of Oregon's law had not been an issue in reaching their verdict. Rather, she said, since "we didn't know who to trust," the jury had reached its verdict based upon a finding of reasonable doubt.

Although John was acquitted, the publicity his trial afforded Oregon's law made many feel, as one newspaper editorial put it, that "an end to the common-law notion that rape is permissible in marriage is long overdue. A society that considers it a crime for a man to beat his wife should certainly consider it a crime for him to assault her sexually." By the early 1990s, only four states retained marital exemptions for rape.

Many recall that the couple reconciled two weeks after the trial. What is often forgotten is that the Rideouts separated three months later and finally divorced. Moreover, John Rideout later broke into Greta Rideout's home and received a suspended sentence. Continuing to harass her, he later went to prison.

For Further Reading

Brownmiller, Susan. *Against Our Will: Men, Women and Rape.* New York: Simon & Schuster, 1975.

Davis, Flora. *Moving the Mountain: The Women's Movement in America Since 1960.* New York: Simon & Schuster, 1991.

New York Times. December 20–24, 26–28, and 31, 1978.

Michael M. v. Superior Court of Sonoma County: 1981

Appellant: Michael M.   **Appellees:** Superior Court of Sonoma County; The People, Real Party in Interest   **Appellant's Claim:** That the statutory rape law violates the equal protection clauses of both the United States and California constitutions, because it protects only women and prosecutes only men   **Chief Lawyers for Appellees:** George Deukmejian, Sandy R. Kriegler, S. Clark Moore, William R. Pounders, Jack R. Winkler, and Evelle J. Younger   **Chief Lawyers for Appellant:** Gregory F. Jilka and Teresa de la O, Cotati   **Justices:** Harry A. Blackmun, Chief Justice Warren E. Burger, Lewis F. Powell, Jr., *William H. Rehnquist,* and Potter Stewart (majority); William J. Brennan, Jr., Thurgood Marshall, John P. Stevens III, and Byron R. White (dissent)   **Place:** Washington, D.C.   **Date of Decision:** March 23, 1981   **Decision:** Upheld California's statutory rape law

SIGNIFICANCE
In this case, laws that treat women as more vulnerable than men to the consequences of sexual activity were found to survive the "more rigid scrutiny" test enunciated in 1976 in *Craig v. Boren.*

In June 1978, Michael M., seventeen and one-half years old, was charged with the statutory rape of Sharon, who was sixteen and one-half years old. At the preliminary hearing, Sharon answered questions about the night in question.

Sharon described drinking at the railroad tracks and kissing Michael in the bushes. Before long, she asked him to slow down and stop. He agreed but "just kept doing it." At that point, her sister came up to her and told her to get up and come home. She refused.

Michael then asked her to walk to the park. "We sat down on a bench and then he started kissing me again and we were laying on the bench. And he told me to take my pants off."

Sharon refused and as she was trying to get up, he hit her. "I just said to myself, 'Forget it,' and I let him do what he wanted to do and he took my pants off and he was telling me to put my legs around him and stuff."

The district attorney asked if she had sexual intercourse with the defendant, and she answered yes.

"You said that he hit you?"

Sharon explained that he "slugged" her in the face—on her chin—with his fist "about two or three times," causing bruises.

According to Sharon, Michael asked her age, and she told him she was sixteen. She admitted to having been "a little drunk."

On cross examination, Sharon answered a compromising question: Had she wanted to stay with Michael? She said she had not known until he hit her.

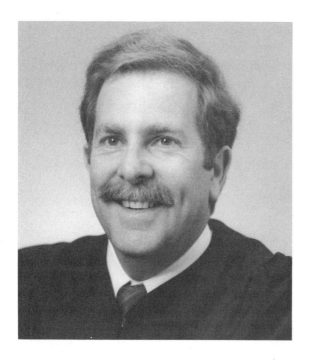

Sandy R. Kriegler, now a superior court judge in California, acted as deputy attorney general for the people during the *Michael M* trial in November 1979. (Superior Court Judge Sandy R. Kriegler)

Statutory Rape Law Justified

When Michael M. was charged with statutory rape, he asked the California Supreme Court to dismiss the charge. He claimed that the statutory rape laws violated the equal protection clauses of both the United States and California constitutions. The statute, Penal Code section 261.5, defined as "unlawful sexual intercourse" any "act of sexual intercourse accomplished with a female not the wife of the perpetrator, where the female is under the age of 18 years."

California's Supreme Court denied the petition. The majority acknowledged that section 261.5 "discriminates on the basis of sex because only females may be victims, and only males may violate the section." The court insisted, however, that:

. . . this obviously discriminatory classification scheme is readily justified by an important state interest. . . . The law . . . challenged is supported not by mere social convention but by the immutable physiological fact that it is the female exclusively that can become pregnant. This changeless physical law, coupled with the tragic human costs of illegitimate teenage pregnancies, generates a compelling and demonstrable state interest in minimizing both the number of such pregnancies and their disastrous consequences. Accordingly, the Legislature is amply justified in retaining its historic statutory rape law because of the potentially devastating social and economic results which may follow its violation.

It further noted that "*all* minors . . . are protected from sexual abuse under sections 272 (contributing to the delinquency of a minor) and 288 (lewd and lascivious conduct upon the body of a child under 14). Women may be prosecuted under these sections if they engage in sexual relations with underage males. Section 261.5 merely provides additional protection for minor females."

Passing Constitutional Muster

Michael M. and his attorneys appealed to the U.S. Supreme Court. On March 23, 1981, the high court held six to three that California's law was constitutional. William H. Rehnquist, in a majority opinion joined by Warren Burger, Potter Stewart, and Lewis Powell, reviewed the level of scrutiny applied to claims of gender discrimination in violation of the Fourteenth Amendment:

> [W]e have not held that gender-based classifications are "inherently suspect" and thus we do not apply so-called "strict scrutiny" to those classifications. See *Stanton v. Stanton* (1975). . . . Our cases have held, however, that the traditional minimum rationality test takes on a somewhat "sharper focus" when gender-based classifications are challenged. . . . [I]n *Craig v. Boren* . . . the Court . . . require[d] the classification to bear a "substantial relationship" to "important governmental objectives."

Rehnquist noted that different members of the California Legislature might have had different motives for passing the statute. Nonetheless, he accepted the prevention of illegitimate teenage pregnancy as "at least one of the 'purposes' of the statute." He wrote:

> We need not be medical doctors to discern that young men and women are not similarly situated with respect to the problems and the risks of sexual intercourse. Only women may become pregnant. . . . The statute at issue here protects women from sexual intercourse at an age when those consequences are particularly severe. . . .

> The question thus boils down to whether a State may attack the problem of sexual intercourse and teenage pregnancy directly by prohibiting a male from having sexual intercourse with a minor female. We hold that such a statute is sufficiently related to the State's objectives to pass constitutional muster.

> Because virtually all of the significant harmful and inescapably identifiable consequences of teenage pregnancy fall on the young female, a legislature acts well within its authority when it elects to punish only the participant who, by nature, suffers few of the consequences of his conduct. . . . A criminal sanction imposed solely on males . . . serves to roughly "equalize" the deterrents on the sexes.

Michael M. had also claimed that statute's protection of prepubescent girls, who would not become pregnant as a result of sexual intercourse, belied the state's supposed purpose of curbing teenage pregnancies. Rehnquist tossed that argument aside in a sentence, stating that the statute "could well be justified on the grounds that very young females are particularly susceptible to physical injury from sexual intercourse. . . ."

Finally, the Court rejected Michael M.'s contention that "the statute is flawed because it presumes that as between two persons under eighteen, the male is the culpable aggressor." On this issue, Rehnquist wrote:

Contrary to his assertions, the statute does not rest on the assumption that males are generally the aggressors. It is instead an attempt by a legislature to prevent illegitimate teenage pregnancy by providing an additional deterrent for men. The age of the man is irrelevant since young men are as capable as older men of inflicting the harm sought to be prevented.

The four dissenting justices found that the law *was* discriminatory. William Brennan—joined by Byron White and Thurgood Marshall—pointed out that "at least 37 States . . . have enacted gender-neutral statutory rape laws . . . and the laws of Arizona, Florida and Illinois permit prosecution of both minor females and males for engaging in mutual sexual conduct. California has introduced no evidence that those states have been handicapped. . . ." John Paul Stevens, in his separate dissent, also indicated that he would have "no doubt about the validity of a state law prohibiting all unmarried teenagers from engaging in sexual intercourse."

For Further Reading

Brownmiller, Susan. *Against Our Will: Men, Women and Rape.* New York: Simon & Schuster, 1973.

Fairstein, Linda A. *Sexual Violence: Our War Against Rape.* New York: William Morrow and Company, 1993.

Goldstein, Leslie Friedman. *The Constitutional Rights of Women*, rev. ed. Madison: The University of Wisconsin Press, 1989.

Roiphe, Katie. *The Morning After: Sex, Fear and Feminism on Campus.* Boston and New York: Little, Brown and Company, 1993.

New Bedford Rape Trials: 1984

Defendants: John Cordeiro, Jose M. Medeiros, Virgilio Medeiros, Victor Raposo, Daniel Silva, and Joseph Vieira **Crime Charged:** Aggravated Rape
Chief Lawyers for Defendants: Edward F. Harrington, Judith Lindahl, Kenneth Sullivan, and David Waxler **Chief Prosecutors:** Ronald A. Pina and Raymond P. Veary **Judge:** William G. Young **Place:** Fall River, Massachusetts **Dates of Trial:** February 23–March 21, 1984
Verdicts: Cordeiro, Raposo, Silva, and Vieira, guilty; Jose Medeiros and Virgilio Medeiros, not guilty **Sentence:** Six to twelve years imprisonment

SIGNIFICANCE

This trial prompted a national debate about whether a rapist should be acquitted if a victim's behavior had been "provocative."

On March 6, 1983, twenty-one-year-old Cheryl A. suffered a gang rape in Big Dan's Tavern in New Bedford, Massachusetts. Eyewitness testimony later substantiated that two men threw the woman on a pool table and raped her. Two other men tried to force her to perform oral sex. One patron physically restrained the bartender when he attempted to telephone for help. Another patron initially ignored the bartender's demand that he call 911—and when he dialed a wrong number, refused to try again. Police eventually arrested six men, who stood trial for rape.

She Asked for It?

Many claimed that the men, all of Portuguese descent, were unfairly accused. The *New York Times* reported:

> By their lights she wasn't raped. Rather, she got herself raped, a very different crime for which they think the victim must take the blame. She did, after all, enter a bar, drink, flirt—behavior which offends a conservative community like theirs. Those demonstrators may not condone her rapists' behavior, but they are more ashamed of hers.

In her 1975 book, *Against Our Will: Men, Women and Rape*, Susan Brownmiller had argued to the contrary, that neither a woman's free behavior nor her independent movement should excuse a rapist. She wrote:

Women have been raped . . . most often by gangs of men, for many of the same reasons that blacks were lynched by gangs of whites: as group punishment for being uppity, . . . or for behavior no more provocative than walking down the wrong road at night in the wrong part of town. . . .

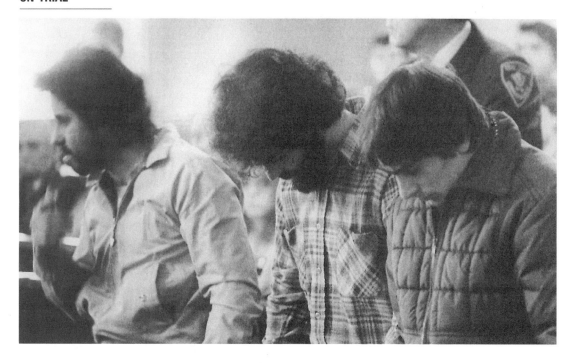

Three rape suspects, from left, Daniel Silva, John Cordeiro, and Victor Raposo, plead innocent to the charge of aggravated assault on March 17, 1983. They were charged in the gang rape at Big Dan's Bar in New Bedford, Massachusetts, on March 6, 1983. (*The Standard Times*)

What Really Happened?

A grand jury charged John Cordeiro and Victor Raposo, both 23, and Daniel Silva and Joseph Vieira, both 26, with aggravated rape. Jose Medeiros, 22, and Virgilio Medeiros, 23 (no relation), were originally charged as accessories, later upgraded to aggravated rape. As alleged participants in a "joint venture" crime, they could be convicted of aggravated rape if it were proved that they encouraged or aided in the crime. The men were tried in two separate groups, since some defendants were expected to incriminate others. The trials of Silva and Vieira were scheduled for afternoon sessions, and the trials of the remaining defendants were scheduled for morning sessions.

On February 23, 1984, Assistant District Attorney Raymond Veary outlined the case against Vieira and Silva. Cheryl A. gave her own testimony the next day. She testified that on March 6, 1983, she had tucked her daughters into bed and then gone out to buy cigarettes. Finding two stores closed, she entered Big Dan's and purchased cigarettes from the vending machine. She then took a seat beside the only other woman in the bar and ordered a drink.

When the other woman left, Cheryl A. also headed for the door. A man yanked her jacket. "What the hell do you think you're doing?" she demanded, but another man grabbed her feet. "They started dragging me across the floor. I started kicking and screaming. . . . I was begging for help. I could hear people laughing and cheering, yelling." She described how the men had thrown her on the pool table and pulled off her pants. One man raped her while another restrained her; then the men traded places, and she was raped a second time.

On cross examination, the victim refuted defense charges that she had made up the story in order to sue the bar's owners or sell book rights. The defense also tried to discredit her testimony by pointing out that her original statement to the police had implicated six men, rather than the four men she now accused. She calmly replied that her original statement was "told when I had not slept and was very upset."

Bartender Carlos Machado testified that he had seen Cheryl A. on the floor and heard her screaming for help when Silva and Vieira took off her pants. He told the court that Jose Medeiros and Virgilio Medeiros were cheering "Do it! Do it! That's it! That's it!" and that one of the two had prevented him from reaching the phone. Cordeiro and Raposo tried to force the victim to engage in oral sex. She was next thrown onto the pool table where, Machado said, Silva "took off his pants and went on top of her."

The prosecution called nineteen witnesses after Machado left the stand. One was the police officer who found Cheryl A. outside of the bar, wearing only her shirt and claiming to have been "repeatedly raped and abused." Another officer, Detective Sandra Grace, met with Cheryl A. shortly after she reported the rape. "She was hysterical and in a state of shock," Grace testified.

When Detective Kenneth Gormley took the stand, he testified that once at the police station, Cordeiro "told us that he wanted to tell us what he did. He said he was sorry. He said he was drunk, but that was no excuse for what he had done." Gormley reported that Cordeiro admitted that "he and Victor held her legs."

Silva's lawyer, Edward Harrington, presented another scenario to the court on March 13, 1984. Harrington then said that "he was talking to her alone," and when he removed her pants they "both fell on the floor." Silva had, Harrington, conceded, placed Cheryl A. atop the pool table, but "his state of mind was that he and she would do something just by themselves. But by then a lot of men came over." Harrington then said that "whatever he was doing with that girl was between he and she. It was consensual, no screaming, crying, or protest."

Four witnesses testified on Silva's behalf. Lizetta Robida, one of the victim's friends, said that she had "told her she should stay home." She also testified that Cheryl A. had two drinks before leaving for Big Dan's. Marie Correia, the other female patron of Big Dan's on the night in question, said that Cheryl A. "was bubbly, she was bouncing around the chair. Her pupils were large and her eyes were very glassy."

Silva testified, "She was, you know, willing." He claimed Cheryl A. had wanted to know if he had any drugs to share. He told her that he did not, but said he'd be willing to "fool around" with her. "She said yes. . . . She looked very happy." According to the remainder of his testimony, the two had kissed and begun to undress when they were interrupted by another of the bar's patrons. He insisted that he had not entered the woman.

The Verdicts

Vieira and Silva were found guilty of aggravated rape on March 17, 1984. As soon as the verdict was read, loud shouts of "Shame!" were heard in the courtroom. In the parking lot, other supporters of the defendants screamed obscenities and punched cars at the first word of the trial's outcome. In contrast, more than two thousand of Cheryl A.'s supporters joined a candlelight march.

Enraged by the March 6, 1983, gang rape at Big Dan's Bar in New Bedford, Massachusetts, a group of women proudly display a banner representing the New Bedford Women's Center. *(The Standard Times)*

The jury for the morning session reconvened on March 19 without having been informed of the first convictions. Cordeiro said that Cheryl A. "was enjoying herself," and the defense attorneys tried to persuade the jury that the woman was nothing more than an intoxicated liar. The jury was not persuaded: On March 22, Cordeiro and Raposo were convicted of aggravated rape. Jose Medeiros and Virgilio Medeiros, who had originally been charged as accessories, were acquitted of aggravated rape. Seven to ten thousand people marched to protest the verdicts. That night, three to four thousand other people joined a second candlelight vigil on behalf of the victim.

Judge William G. Young sentenced the four men to six to twelve years imprisonment. He also gave his answer to the trial's underlying question.

Neither Cheryl A.'s behavior nor her presence in a bar affected the sentences, because that action would "virtually outlaw an entire gender for the style of the dress, the length of their skirts or the choice to enter a place of public refreshment."

For Further Reading

Brownmiller, Susan. *Against Our Will: Men, Women and Rape.* New York: Simon & Schuster, 1975.

Faludi, Susan. *Backlash: The Undeclared War Against American Women.* New York: Crown Publishers, 1991.

New York Times. March 11, 12, 13, 18, 19, 1983; September 1, 3, 4, 1983; February 6, 24, 25, 28, 29, 1984; April 11 and 25, 1984; May 7, 1985; October 7, 1986; and December 18, 1986.

American Booksellers Association v. Hudnut: 1986

Appellants: William H. Hudnut, III, mayor of the City of Indianapolis, et al.

Appellees: American Booksellers Association, Inc. et al.

Appellant's Claim: That the lower courts erred in finding Indianapolis' anti-pornography ordinance unconstitutional

Chief Lawyer for Appellees: Michael A. Bamberger

Chief Lawyers for Appellants: Mark Dall and Kathryn A. Watson

Justices: Harry A. Blackmun, William J. Brennan, Jr., Chief Justice Warren E. Burger, Thurgood Marshall, Sandra Day O'Connor, Lewis F. Powell, Jr., William H. Rehnquist, John Paul Stevens, III **Place:** Washington, D.C.

Date: February 24, 1986 **Decision:** The Supreme Court affirmed the lower court's decision that Indianapolis' anti-pornography law violated the First Amendment of the U.S. Constitution

SIGNIFICANCE

Although the anti-pornography law was found unconstitutional, the Seventh Circuit Court of Appeals and much of the public agreed that pornography harms women.

In 1977, writer Andrea Dworkin and attorney Catharine MacKinnon joined forces to combat violence against women by attempting to outlaw pornography. Minneapolis was the first city to try to adopt their anti-pornography law. In 1983, the Minneapolis City Council held hearings to determine whether, as Dworkin and MacKinnon claimed, pornography prompted violence against women. During two days of hearings, women testified about their first-hand experiences of sexual assaults prompted or influenced by pornography. Rita M. testified about an attack during a Girl Scout camping trip when she was thirteen. Walking through the woods, she said, she had come upon armed hunters reading pornographic magazines. One shouted, "There's a live one," and the group gave chase and gang-raped her at gunpoint. A Native American woman, Carol L., testified that she was gang-raped by men who spoke about the pornographic video game "Custer's Last Stand" during the attack upon her.

Flora Colao, an emergency room nurse, testified that the release of the film *Deep Throat* was followed by an increase in throat-rape victims to her hospital's emergency room and a number of deaths from throat-rape suffocation.

Following these hearings, the city council adopted a law based on Dworkin's and MacKinnon's draft. It defined pornography as sex discrimination in violation of women's civil rights and permitted women to bring lawsuits against its makers and merchants. However, Minneapolis' mayor promptly vetoed it. Immediately, the issue became a matter of intense public debate.

A Blanket Ordinance

In 1984, Indianapolis became the next city to adopt a version of MacKinnon's and Dworkin's proposed law. Kathryn Watson, a lawyer who helped to prepare the ordinance, later reflected that she, the city council, and the city's administration believed from the beginning that their law had "far less than a fifty-fifty chance of surviving a constitutional challenge." However, "the debate the ordinance and any ensuing lawsuit would provoke about the true nature of pornography and its effects on women and their position in society would be worth the fight."

The battle-destined law stated that the city adopted the law in response to its finding that "pornography is a discriminatory practice based on sex which denies women equal opportunities in society. . . . Pornography is central in creating and maintaining sex as a basis for discrimination. . . . The bigotry and contempt it promotes . . . fosters rape, battery, child abuse, kidnapping and prostitution. . . ."

Indianapolis intended, in the words of the law, "to prevent and prohibit all discriminatory practices of sexual subordination or inequality through pornography." And the city left no doubt as to what it considered pornography. "Pornography shall mean the graphic sexually explicit subordination of women, whether in pictures or in words," that show women enjoying "pain or humiliation, . . . being raped, . . . tied up or cut up or mutilated or bruised or physically hurt, . . . being penetrated by objects or animals, . . . [being] shown as filthy or inferior, . . . [being] presented as sexual objects for domination. . . ." Finally, the use of any other human beings—"men, children or transsexuals"—"shall also constitute pornography under this section."

Indianapolis outlawed the "discriminatory practice" of trafficking in pornography, including the "production, sale, exhibition, or distribution" of pornographic works. The city exempted public, college, and university libraries, which were permitted to make pornography "available for study, including on open shelves."

"Coercing, intimidating, or fraudulently inducing any person" into such trafficking likewise became an unlawful discriminatory practice. Indianapolis decided that someone trafficking in pornography could *not* use as a defense a signed contract, a signed statement of a person's "willingness to cooperate," an acceptance of compensation, or an absence of "physical force, threats, or weapons."

At the heart of the law was the view that Indianapolis' citizens should be free from the impact of pornography and any attendant violence, wherever they chose to live, work, study, or walk. The ordinance therefore forbade the "forcing of pornography on any woman, man, child, or transsexual in any place of employment, in education, in a home, or in any public place," as well as any "assault or physical attack" upon such persons "in a way that is directly caused by specific pornography."

The law used broad, sweeping terms to describe those entitled to invoke it: "Any woman," it read, "may file a complaint [against trafficking in pornography] as a woman acting against the subordination of women." (Men, children and transsexuals wishing to file complaints were required to "prove injury in the same way that a woman is injured. . . .")

An Uphill Battle

Almost immediately, the lawsuit Watson had envisioned came before the U.S. District Court. It named William H. Hudnut, the mayor of Indianapolis, and other city and county officials charged with implementing and enforcing the ordinance as defendants.

The district court convened on July 30, 1984. The plaintiffs—the American Booksellers Association and the American Civil Liberties Union (ACLU) among numerous others—asked the court "to preliminarily and permanently enjoin enforcement of [the ordinance], and to declare [it] facially unconstitutional, void and of no effect." They argued that the law, extending as it did beyond the banning of obscenity and other forms of "unprotected speech," required them "to remove . . . materials which are in fact protected by the First Amendment."

The prosecution recalled Supreme Court precedents that denied the right to prohibit speech "simply because its contents may be socially or politically offensive to the majority." They claimed that the ordinance's intrusion into the realm of protected speech would have a self-censoring or "chilling effect" on the general exercise of free speech guaranteed by the First Amendment.

Both Watson and Mark Dall addressed the court for the defendants. On their behalf, they acknowledged that the ordinance extended beyond the regulation of obscene materials. However, they denied that this—or any other aspect or consequence of the ordinance—violated the U.S. Constitution.

A Bedrock Issue

Judge Sarah Evans Barker of the district court ruled on November 19, 1984, that the Indianapolis ordinance violated the Constitution. Indianapolis appealed, and the U.S. Court of Appeals, Seventh Circuit, heard the case on June 4, 1985. It also found the Indianapolis ordinance unconstitutional.

In the court's August 27, 1985 opinion, Circuit Judge Frank Easterbrook quoted a 1943 Supreme Court opinion stressing the bedrock nature of the First Amendment:

> If there is any fixed star in our constitutional constellation, it is that no official, high or petty, can prescribe what shall be orthodox in politics, nationalism, religion, or other matters of opinion or force citizens to confess by word or act their faith within. . . .

> Under the First Amendment, the government must leave to the people the evaluation of ideas. Bald or subtle, an idea is as powerful as the audience allows it to be. A belief may be pernicious—the beliefs of Nazis led to the death of millions, those of the Klan to the repression of millions. A pernicious belief may prevail. Totalitarian governments today rule much of the planet, practicing suppression of billions and spreading dogma that may enslave others. One of the things that separates our society from theirs is our absolute right to propagate opinions that the government finds wrong or even hateful.

Free Speech an Ally

The court acknowledged that pornography harmed women: "We accept," Easterbrook wrote, "the premises of legislation. Depictions of subordination tend to perpetuate subordination. The subordinate status of women in turn leads to affront and lower pay at work, insult and injury at home, battery and rape on the streets."

However, the court ruled the First Amendment could not be violated by those in search of a remedy. The court did not believe that abridgment of freedom of speech would be an effective tool in any fight for change. In other words, Free speech, guaranteed by that amendment, had always been the weapon of choice for those wanting change. In fact, the first thing a government that wishes to *keep* the status quo does is to restrict the speech of those who want change. "Without a strong guarantee of freedom of speech, there is no effective right to challenge what is."

Indianapolis asked for a rehearing, and then a rehearing *en banc* (a rehearing by the entire appellate court), but these requests were denied. The city then appealed to the Supreme Court. That court, by reading the case and not hearing the argument (summary affirmation), upheld the lower court opinion invalidating Indianapolis' anti-pornography ordinance. Pornography continues to be protected as a form of free speech. Nonetheless, the Indianapolis ordinance and the ensuing lawsuit brought serious public consideration to the question of pornography's link to violence against women.

For Further Reading

MacKinnon, Catharine. *Feminism Unmodified: Discourses on Life and Law.* Cambridge, Mass.: Harvard University Press, 1987.

————. *Only Words.* Cambridge, Mass.: Harvard University Press, 1993.

Smith, Dinita. "Love is Strange: The Crusading Feminist and the Repentant Womanizer." *New York Magazine,* March 22, 1993.

Strebeigh, Fred. "Defining Law on the Feminist Frontier." *New York Times Magazine,* October 6, 1991.

Section 3
RIGHTS AND RESPONSIBILITIES
OF CITIZENSHIP

Are American women citizens of the United States? If so, are they entitled to equality of rights under its laws? The courts have given widely divergent answers to these questions. Our review of these controversies begins, rightly enough, with a case concerning citizenship status itself: In *Martin v. Massachusetts* (1805), the state supreme court declared that married women were not citizens—merely inhabitants.

Other nineteenth-century trials show the lack of women's rights. Hester Vaughan's 1868 trial, for example, illustrates that women were denied a place among juries and, therefore, if accused of a crime, denied a trial by their peers.

Bradwell v. Illinois (1873) upheld Illinois' law excluding women from the practice of law. As Justice Joseph P. Bradley stated in his concurring opinion, it was not "one of the privilege immunities of women as citizens to engage in any and every profession, occupation or employment in civil life." He also relied on his belief that "the paramount destiny and mission of women are to fulfill the noble and benign office of wife and mother. This is the law of the creator."

Two years later, in *Minor v. Happersett*, the high court upheld a state's right to deny suffrage to women. In 1920, women finally won the right to vote, with the ratification of the Nineteenth Amendment. Almost two decades later, in *Breedlove v. Suttles* (1937), the Supreme Court upheld Georgia's law exempting unregistered women from the poll tax on the basis that women's payments drained the resources of husbands or fathers. As these cases show, women's new national suffrage rights were not enough to change the justices' traditional view of women.

Both Myra Bradwell and Virginia Minor argued their cases—unsuccessfully—on Fourteenth Amendment grounds. The Fourteenth Amendment was finally found to protect women's rights in 1971. In that year, the Supreme Court ruled in *Reed v. Reed* that a deceased child's mother had equal claim with the father to serve as executor for the estate.

Following *Reed*, the Fourteenth Amendment was found to require women's participation in the jury system in *Taylor v. Louisiana* (1975). The decisions in these two cases also abolished gender distinctions and age requirements. In *Stanton v. Stanton* (1975), the Supreme Court abolished a state law that granted males a larger period of minority and parental support to complete their educations. In *Craig v. Boren* (1976), the trivial issue of disparate drinking age yielded an important judicial precedent—namely, the "heightened security" with which the Supreme Court would now view laws that discriminate on the basis of sex.

Sex discrimination was allowed to stand, however, in *Rostker v. Goldberg* (1981). Here, the Supreme Court relied on the war powers clause of the U.S. Constitution to permit the exclusion of women from a military draft registration. (The armed services have since become an all-volunteer force, and women are well represented in all branches.)

In many other cases during the 1980s and 1990s, the court struck down gender segregation as unconstitutional. In *Roberts v. U.S. Jaycees* (1984), the Supreme Court upheld a Minnesota law that forced a previously all-male business organization to admit women. *Mississippi University for Women v. Hogan* (1982) ordered a previously all-female nursing school to admit men. This ruling set the precedent for the Court's decision more than a decade later in *United States v. Commonwealth of Virginia* (1996). Here the justices ordered the Virginia Military Institute to admit women or forgo public funding. As Justice Ruth Bader Ginsburg summed up in the Supreme Court's opinion, laws discriminating on the basis of sex violate the Fourteenth Amendment in all but a few instances. These include, she wrote, laws passed "to compensate women for particular economic disabilities (they have) suffered, to promote equal employment opportunity, and to advance full development of the talent and capabilities of our nation's people." And, in a fairly clear and welcome warning, she added: "Such clarifications may not be used as they once were, to create or perpetuate legal, social or economic inferiority of women."

Martin v. Massachusetts: 1805

Appellant: James Martin   **Appellee:** Commonwealth of Massachusetts
Appellant's Claim: That lands belonging to Martin's mother and seized by the state under the "absentee act" must be returned because a married woman is not to be held responsible for her husband's treasonous acts
Chief Lawyers for the Appellee: Solicitor General Daniel Davis and Attorney General James Sullivan   **Chief Lawyers for Appellant:** Theophilus Parsons and George Blake   **Justices:** Chief Justice Francis Dana, Thomas Sedgwick, Samuel Sewall, Simon Strong, and George Thacher   **Place:** Boston, Massachusetts   **Date of Decision:** March 14, 1805   **Decision:** A married woman, being obliged to obey her husband, cannot be made to forfeit her real property even if her husband may have committed treason

SIGNIFICANCE

This trial provides a most detailed—and revealing—discussion of the political relationship of women to the state in the nineteenth century. The law put wives on the same level as children and mentally deficient persons, giving them no rights of citizenship—while at the same time, protecting their rights to property they brought to the marriage.

After the American Revolution, were women automatically citizens of their state? During the war, William and Anna Martin had been British loyalists. They had owned land in Braintree and Boston that Anna had brought with her when she married. On March 30, 1776, the Martins fled to Great Britain. Under the "absentee act," passed by Massachusetts on April 30, 1779, the state confiscated their property, selling it in 1781.

Under this act, the state could confiscate the property of those who either had waged or conspired to wage war against the United States, given aid and comfort to the king, or fled to lands under British authority. The state claimed that the Martins had violated this law since April 19, 1775.

In 1801, after the Martins had died, their son James returned to claim the lands, which the commonwealth had sold to William Bosson and others. The young Martin petitioned a lower court to return the property on grounds that his father had only a lifetime interest in it; his mother was the rightful owner. (At this time, under common law, husbands were permitted to manage but not to sell their wives' property.) The first decision went against young Martin, so he appealed.

The case took four years to move from Boston's Inferior Court of Common Pleas to the Supreme Court of Massachusetts. Finally, the five-panel court heard the case under Chief Justice Francis Dana.

Federalist lawyer Theophilus Parsons represented William Martin after he returned to America in 1801 to reclaim land originally owned by his parents. (Social Law Library, Boston, Mass.)

A Brilliant Defense

Theophilis Parsons, representing Martin, owned the largest law library in New England. He had a broader knowledge of English law than any other attorney in the colonies, making him the leading lawyer in the new nation.

Parsons claimed that the "absentee act" applied to every "inhabitant and member" of the state—meaning that it applied only to those who were both inhabitants *and* members of the state. As a "wife," who was legally subservient to her husband, James's mother was not a member of the state, only an inhabitant.

The solicitor general defended the state's right to confiscate the property. He argued, "Cannot a *feme covert* [married woman] levy war and conspire to levy war?" If so, wives might act independently of their husbands.

Parsons countered, "The real question is, whether the statute intended to include persons who have, by law, no wills of their own. . . . Infants, insane, *femes coverts*, all of whom the law considers having no will, cannot act *freely*." The Massachusetts Supreme Court agreed with Parsons.

No Freedom, No Treason

The court decided that Martin had a legitimate claim to his mother's property because she had "no *political* relation to the *state* any more than an *alien*."

Sedgwick pointed out that under the "absentee act" the state had charged both the Martins with treason. However:

> In the relation of husband and wife, the law makes, in her behalf, such an allowance for the authority of the husband, and her duty of obedience, that guilt is not imputed to her for her actions performed jointly by them, unless of the most heinous and aggravated nature. For instance; the law says,

whoever steals shall be punished, and yet if a wife participates in a theft with her husband she is not punishable.

Sedgwich exlained that a wife is exempt from punishment "because she is viewed in such a state of subjection, and so under the control of her husband, that she acts merely as his instrument, and that no guilt is imputable to her."

Dana crystallized the consensus of the court in his closing comments:

On the whole, I am clearly of the opinion that the judgment ought to be reversed, because *femes-coverts*, having no will, could not incur forfeiture; and that the statute never was intended to include them; and oblige them either to lose their property or to be guilty of a breach of the duty, which, by the laws of their country and the law of God, they owed to their husbands.

By a unanimous vote, James Martin won his case.

Four years later a similar case, *Kempe v. Kennedy* (see page 260), came before the U.S. Supreme Court, the only dispute of its kind to do so. Although the Court denied jurisdiction due to a technicality, Chief Justice John Marshall made several comments indicating that he thought Grace Kempe's lawyer, Richard Stockton, was correct when he claimed that New Jersey's confiscation act had been aimed at those who aided the enemy of their own free will, and this Kempe could not have done, because as "a *feme covert*, in the presence of her baron, has no will; and on the subject of residence, she can have no will different from [her husband]."

Women would approach full citizenship with the passage of the Fourteenth (1868) and Nineteenth (1920) Amendments. However, they remained "second-class citizens," until the 1970s, when, in a series of decisions, the Supreme Court abolished many state laws that were inherently discriminatory.

For Further Reading

Flexner, Eleanor. *Century of Struggle: The Woman's Rights Movement in the United States.* Cambridge: The Belknap Press of Harvard University Press: 1975.

Frost, Elizabeth, and Kathryn Cullen-DuPont. *Women's Suffrage in America: An Eyewitness History.* New York: Facts on File, 1992.

Hoff, Joan. *Law, Gender, and Injustice: A Legal History of U.S. Women.* New York: New York University Press, 1991.

Kerber, Linda K. *Women of the Republic: Intellect and Ideology in Revolutionary America.* New York: W. W. Norton, 1986.

Hester Vaughan's Trial: 1868

Defendant: Hester Vaughan **Crime Charged:** First-degree murder
Chief Defense Lawyer: John Guforth **Chief Prosecutor:** No record
Judge: James Riley Ludow **Place:** Philadelphia, Pennsylvania
Dates of Trial: June 10–July 2, 1868 **Verdict:** Guilty **Sentence:** Death

SIGNIFICANCE

One hundred and seven years before the U.S. Supreme Court ruled that women's systematic exclusion from state juries was unconstitutional *(Taylor v. Louisiana,* 1975), women's rights leaders protested a teenage girl's murder conviction without "a trial by a jury of her peers," that is, without a woman's presence on the jury.

Hester Vaughan went to America to begin her married life with the blessings of her family and every expectation of happiness. A year and a half later, her husband, Harris, deserted her. Hester took back her family name and—too ashamed to face her family back in England—stayed in the United States and found work as a housekeeper. Someone in that household raped her. Three months later, finding herself pregnant, she moved to Philadelphia, leased a small room, and supported herself by sewing.

Vaughan gave birth on February 8, 1868, malnourished and alone in a room without heat. Two days later, she asked another roomer for a box for her dead baby—begging her not to say anything to anyone about her circumstances. The woman, however, reported the event to the police and Vaughan was immediately arrested.

Her murder trial began on June 30, 1868. Several witnesses took the stand for the prosecution. As the *Philadelphia Inquirer* summarized their testimony,

> [Vaughan] explained [to the resident from whom she had requested a box] that she had been frightened by a lady going into the room with a cup of coffee, and fallen back upon her child, thus killing it. . . . Dr. Shapleigh [of the Coroner's office], who examined the body, found several fractures of the skull, made apparently with some blunt instrument, and also clots of blood between the brain and skull. The lady who took the coffee to the prisoner heard the child give one or two faint cries.

With that, the Commonwealth of Pennsylvania rested. The judge ordered Hester's lawyer, John Guforth, to present his witnesses the next day. Although

Hester had paid him her last thirty dollars for his fee, he had not so much as interviewed her before the beginning of the trial. All he had to offer in her defense were character witnesses and his own words, saying, "The prisoner should not be convicted of murder in the first degree, because in the agony and pain she must have suffered, she may have been bereft of all reason." He added that the death may even have been by accident. Not surprisingly, Vaughan was convicted of first-degree murder and sentenced to death.

Women to the Rescue

Two of America's first female physicians took an immediate interest in Vaughan's case. Dr. Susan Smith visited the teenaged prisoner several times in Philadelphia's Moyamensing Prison. She interviewed the young woman a number of times and also performed a medical examination. She then wrote to Pennsylvania governor John W. Geary, seeking clemency for Vaughan:

> [Hester Vaughan] rented a third story room . . . from a family who understood very little English. . . . She was taken sick in this room at midnight on the 6th of February and lingered until Saturday morning, the eighth, when her child was born. She told me she was nearly frozen and fainted or went to sleep for a long time. You will please remember, sir, throughout this period of agony she was alone, without nourishment or fire. . . .
>
> My professional opinion in Hester Vaughan's case is that cold and want of attention produced painful and protracted labor—that the mother, in endeavoring to assist herself, injured the head of her child at birth—that she either fainted or had a convulsion, and was insensible for a long time.

Although a witness had testified that cries were heard in the room, both Dr. Smith and another female physician, Dr. Clemence Lozier, raised doubt that the infant had been born alive.

When Governor Geary was not swayed by the physicians' arguments, women's rights leaders Susan B. Anthony and Elizabeth Cady Stanton stepped in. They and members of the Working Women's National Association held a

Elizabeth Cady Stanton, first president of the National Woman Suffrage Association, helped to raise funds for Hester Vaughan when the teen was convicted of murder in 1868. (National Archives)

protest meeting at the Cooper Institute in New York City. Anna Dickinson, a famous orator of the time, described Vaughan's case as emblematic of working women's sexual vulnerability to their employers, especially within the isolated and close confines of domestic service.

Anthony and Stanton just as adamantly objected to Vaughan's "condemn[ation] on insufficient evidence and with inadequate defense." However, it was women's lack of suffrage and their exclusion from jury service—and the impact of these limitations upon women such as Vaughan—that drew their greatest wrath. Those at Cooper Union voted unanimously to petition Pennsylvania's governor for an unconditional pardon or, at the very least, a new trial for Vaughan.

Women's rights advocate
Susan B. Anthony.
(National Archives)

Stanton and Anthony continued to publicize the case in their newspaper, the *Revolution*, and during their travels around the country. Governor Geary finally pardoned Vaughan on the condition that she return to England—with private funds. Passage fare was quickly raised, and Hester Vaughan went home in 1869. Women were not able to serve on juries on an equal basis with men until the 1975 Supreme Court decision in *Taylor v. Louisiana* (see page 115), which declared their treatment unconstitutional.

For Further Reading

Barry, Kathleen. *Susan B. Anthony*. New York: New York University Press, 1988.

Doten, Lizzie. "Hester Vaughan," *Revolution*, March 25, 1969.

DuBois, Ellen Carol. *Feminism and Suffrage: The Emergence of an Independent Women's Movement in America*. Ithaca: Cornell University Press, 1978.

Harper, Ida Husted. *Life and Work of Susan B. Anthony*, Vol. 1, 1898, reprint, Salem, N.H.: Ayer Co., Publishers, 1983.

New York Times, December 4, 1868.

New York World, December 2, 1868; May 21, 1869

Philadelphia Inquirer, July 1–2 and December 2–4, 1868.

Revolution, December 10, 1868–August 19, 1869.

Bradwell v. Illinois: 1873

Plaintiff: Myra Bradwell   **Defendant:** The State of Illinois
Plaintiff's Claim: That Illinois' refusal to admit women to the bar was a violation of Bradwell's constitutional rights
Chief Lawyer for Defendant: None
Chief Lawyer for the Plaintiff: Matthew H. Carpenter   **Justices:** Joseph P. Bradley, Chief Justice Salmon P. Chase, Nathan Clifford, David Davis, Stephen J. Field, *Samuel F. Miller,* William Strong, and Noah H. Swayne
Place: Washington, D.C.   **Date of Decision:** April 15, 1873
Decision: That Bradwell's constitutional rights had not been violated

SIGNIFICANCE
This case was the first to go before the Supreme Court asking that the Fourteenth Amendment protect women's citizenship rights.

Myra Bradwell, editor of the *Chicago Legal News*, passed Illinois' law exam in August 1869. When she applied for admission to the Illinois bar in September 1869, she submitted the required certificate of qualification and also a separate written application addressing the fact that she was a woman. She conceded that the Illinois Revised Statutes described attorneys as males, *"authoriz[ing] him,"* for example, *"to appear in all the courts* [emphasis added]."

She then cited one section of the statutes: "When any party or person is described or referred to by words importing the masculine gender, females as well as males shall be deemed to be included." She pointed out that "Section 3 of our Declaration of Rights says "that all men have a natural and indefeasible right to worship Almighty God,' etc. It will not be contended, that women are not included within this provision."

The Marriage Disability

The Court refused to admit her. The refusal was based ". . . upon the ground that you would not be bound by the obligations necessary to be assumed where the relation of attorney and client shall exist, by reason of the disability imposed by your married condition—it being assumed that you are a married woman . . ."

The disability referred to was a wife's *feme covert* (married woman) status, which was nothing less than her civil and legal death upon marriage. For example, married women—in Illinois up until the year of Bradwell's application—could neither make contracts nor own property. Bradwell took no comfort from the fact that "persons under twenty-one" had also been denied admission "upon the same ground."

Bradwell took another view of her married status. She filed an energetically worded brief with Illinois's Supreme Court the next month. She explained, "Your petitioner admits to your honors that she is a married woman (although she believes the fact does not appear in the record), but insists most firmly that under the laws of Illinois it is neither a crime nor a disqualification." She discussed cases in which married female business owners had operated as *feme sole* traders (single women entitled to conduct business), her own history as the successful editor and an undisputed stockholder of the *Chicago Legal News*, and the Iowa bar's recent decision to admit Arabella Mansfield. She also discussed Illinois' Act of 1869, which had removed some of the *feme covert* "disabilit[ies]" referred to by the Court.

Under that act, married women were no longer to be classed with infants since "a married woman may sue in her own name for her earnings, an infant may not." Bradwell claimed that a woman could now be held "liable as an attorney upon any contract made by her in that capacity." The act also protected a wife's right to any money she earned whether as an attorney or a sewing-women. "Is it for the court to say, in advance, that it will not admit a married woman?" she asked.

Myra Bradwell was the first person to challenge the Fourteenth Amendment; she was denied the right to practice law because she was a married woman. (Illinois State Historical Society)

Bradwell amended her brief a few weeks later to include the claim that her constitutional rights, especially as protected by the Fourteenth Amendment's guarantee that "no State shall make or enforce any law which shall abridge the privileges and immunities of citizenship," were abridged by the State of Illinois.

The Female Disability

The court was not persuaded. It ignored her Fourteenth Amendment argument and claimed only that she had too broadly interpreted the impact of the Act of 1869. Those recent changes in Illinois property law, the Chief Justice wrote, affected only a woman's individual and separate holdings. Their "common law . . . disabilities in regard to making contracts," had not been ameliorated to an extent that would have "invited them to enter, equally with men, upon those fields of trade and speculation by which property is acquired though the agency of contracts."

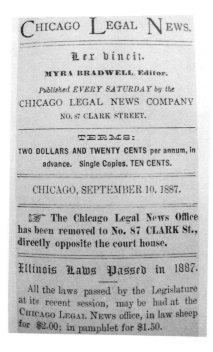

Myra Bradwell founded Chicago's *Legal News* in 1868. It was published every Saturday and was the most widely circulated legal newspaper in the United States at that time.

The court also found that a woman, solely on the grounds of gender and even without her common law legal disabilities, was unfit to practice: "[A]fter further consultation . . . we find ourselves constrained to hold that the sex of the applicant *independent of coverture* [marriage], is, as our law stands, a sufficient reason for not granting this license [emphasis added]." Finally, the court disagreed with Bradwell's interpretation of the Revised Statutes, declaring that females *may* be included in masculine gender words but *not* "where there is anything in the subject or context repugnant to such construction. This is the case in the present instance."

All or Nothing

Bradwell appealed to the U.S. Supreme Court. Matthew H. Carpenter, a U.S. senator from Wisconsin, acted as her attorney. (Illinois did not send an attorney to defend its position.) He argued that Bradwell's Fourteenth Amendment rights had indeed been violated. He asked, "Can this court say that when the XIV amendment declared 'the privileges of no citizen shall be abridged,' it meant that the privileges of no male citizen or unmarried female citizen shall be abridged?"

If Bradwell's choice of profession or employment was not protected by this clause, Carpenter said, then neither was anyone else's. If no female could practice law, then neither could a "colored citizen." "If this provision does not open all the professions, all the avocations, all the methods . . . to the colored as well as the white man, then the Legislatures of the State may exclude colored men from all the honorable pursuits of life, and compel them to support their existence in a condition of servitude." Conversely, if the amendment does protect colored people, then "it protects every citizen, black or white, male or female." On the very same basis, Carpenter declared, the State of Illinois had no right to bar Myra Bradwell from the practice of law.

God's Say So

The Supreme Court ruled that Illinois could restrict the practice of law—and indeed any other profession—to men. Samuel F. Miller, delivering the Court's opinion, said that citizenship was irrelevant to one's admission to the bar and therefore not within the province of Fourteenth Amendment protection.

Joseph P. Bradley, in his concurring opinion, offered particularly biting observations on a woman's place in American society. To agree with Bradwell's claim of Fourteenth Amendment protection, Bradley wrote, would mean ". . . that it is one of the privileges and immunities of women as citizens to engage in any and every profession, occupation or employment in civil life." Explaining his opinion of the impropriety of such a notion, he insisted that the very idea of women having a career distinct from her husband would interfere with "family harmony" not to mention that "the paramount destiny and mission of woman are to fulfill the noble and benign offices of wife and mother. This is the law of the Creator."

He added that "many of the special rules of law flowing from and dependent upon this cardinal principle still exist in full force in most states. One of these is that a married woman is incapable, without her husband's consent, of making contracts which shall be binding on her or him." Therefore, no woman could be an attorney—married or not—because even if there were exceptions to the general rule, society must adapt "to the general constitution of things."

This high court's opinion was maintained until its 1971 decision in *Reed v. Reed* (see page 112). It is less often remarked that the opinion illustrated the force and effect, well into the nineteenth century and even following the passage of various married women's property acts, of a married woman's *feme covert* status—and the fact that even unmarried women felt the legal impact of their wedded sisters' *feme covert* status.

For Further Reading

Cary, Eve, and Kathleen Willert Peratis. *Woman and the Law*. Skokie, Ill.: National Textbook Co. in conjunction with the American Civil Liberties Union, New York, 1977.

Flexner, Eleanor. *Century of Struggle: The Woman's Rights Movement in the United States*. Cambridge, Mass.: The Belknap Press of Harvard University Press, 1959, rev. 1975.

Frost, Elizabeth, and Kathryn Cullen-DuPont. *Women's Suffrage in America: An Eyewitness History*. New York: Facts on File, 1992.

Goldstein, Leslie Friedman. *The Constitutional Rights of Women*, rev. ed. Madison: University of Wisconsin Press, 1989.

Stanton, Elizabeth Cady, Susan B. Anthony, and Matilda Joslyn Gage, eds. *History of Woman Suffrage*, vol. 2, 1882, reprint, Salem, N.H.: Ayer Company, Publishers, 1985.

Minor v. Happersett: 1875

Appellant: Virginia Minor (with Francis Minor, her husband, as required by Missouri law, which did not permit married women to bring suit on their own) **Appellee:** Reese Happersett **Appellant's Claim:** That Virginia Minor's constitutional rights were violated by Happersett's refusal to register her to vote in the election of 1872 **Chief Lawyer for Appellee:** No opposing counsel **Chief Lawyers for the Appellant:** Francis Minor, John M. Rum, and John B. Henderson **Justices:** Joseph P. Bradley, Nathan Clifford, David Davis, Stephen J. Field, Ward Hunt, Samuel F. Miller, William Strong, Noah H. Swayne, and *Chief Justice Morrison R. Waite* **Place:** Washington, D.C. **Date of Decision:** March 29, 1875 **Decision:** The Fourteenth Amendment did not guarantee Virginia Minor's right to vote, although the court ruled she was a citizen of the United States

SIGNIFICANCE

This case marked the second time in two years that the Supreme Court declined to extend Fourteenth Amendment protection to women's rights. Voting rights, the specific "privilege of citizenship" denied in the case, would not go to women nationwide until ratification of the Nineteenth Amendment in 1920.

As Supreme Court justice Sandra Day O'Connor has pointed out, the adoption of the Fourteenth Amendment to the U.S. Constitution in 1868 "introduced sex-specific language into the Constitution: Section 2 of the Amendment, which dealt with the legislative representation and voting, said that if the right to vote were 'denied to any of the *male* inhabitants' of a state aged twenty-one or over [emphasis O'Connor's] then the proportional representation in that state would be reduced accordingly."

Prior to the Fourteenth Amendment, the Constitution referred to the president as "he" but to all other Americans as "citizens" and "persons," without reference to their gender. But the Fourteenth Amendment's "sex-specific language" in Section 2 excluded women and raised questions about women's citizenship. For this reason, Susan B. Anthony, Elizabeth Cady Stanton, and other nineteenth-century women's rights activists fiercely opposed its adoption. (Lucy Stone and other suffragists reluctantly supported the vote for black males, regardless of the perceived cost to women.)

The "New Departure"

After the amendment's ratification and adoption, attorney Francis Minor—husband of Virginia Minor, the president of the Woman Suffrage Association of Missouri—argued that its Section 1 was actually an advance for women. Section 1 of the Fourteenth Amendment states:

> All persons born or naturalized in the United States, and subject to the jurisdiction thereof, are citizens of the United States and of the State wherein they reside. No state shall make or enforce any law which shall abridge the privileges or immunities of citizens of the United States; nor shall any State deprive any person of life, liberty, or property, without due process of law; nor deny to any person within its jurisdiction the equal protection of the laws.

Minor drafted resolutions explaining his view that the Constitution, as amended by the Fourteenth Amendment, now guaranteed the right of suffrage to women:

> Resolved, 1: That the immunities and privileges of American citizenship, however defined, are National in character and paramount to all State authority.

> 2: That while the Constitution of the United States leaves the qualifications of electors to the several States, it nowhere gives them the right to deprive any citizen of the elective franchise which is possessed by any other citizen—to regulate, not including the right to prohibit the franchise.

> 3: That, as the Constitution of the United States expressly declares that no State shall make or enforce any laws that shall abridge the privileges or immunities of citizens of the United States, those provisions of the several State Constitutions that exclude women from the franchise on account of sex, are violative alike of the spirit and letter of the Federal Constitution.

> 4: That, as the subject of naturalization is expressly withheld from the States, and as the States clearly have no right to deprive of the franchise naturalized citizens, among whom women are expressly included, still more clearly they have no right to deprive native-born women of this right.

Missouri's Woman Suffrage Association endorsed Francis Minor's resolutions, and by the end of 1869, so had the National Woman Suffrage Association. Stanton and Anthony published them in their newspaper *Revolution*, and at least 150 women in ten states put them to the test.

They turned out to vote in the 1871 and 1872 elections. Some, including Anthony, were prosecuted for successfully voting; others, like Virginia Minor, sued their states or voting officials for turning them away. The Minor case eventually reached the Supreme Court.

A Constitutional Approach

In their petition filed in December 1872, Virginia Minor's attorneys argued her constitutional rights had been abridged. They drew upon, among other sections from the constitution, Article IV, Section 2, which gave citizens of the states privileges and immunities of citizens in all of the States"; Article IV,

Section 4, guaranteeing to every state a republican form of government and the Fifth Amendment's guarantee that "no person shall be . . . deprived of life, liberty, or property without due process of law."

They also cited the Ninth Amendment, which reserves to the people any rights not expressly granted to the government. The last amendment cited was

A delegation of female suffragists speaks to the Judiciary Committee of the House of Representatives on January 11, 1871. A delegate reads her argument in favor of women's voting, applying the Fourteenth and Fifteenth Amendments. (Prints & Photographs Division, Library of Congress)

the Fourteenth Amendment, Section 1, using the same resolutions Minor had thought out back in 1869.

Reese Happersett's attorney maintained that "the defendant was justified in refusing to register the plaintiff on account of her sex." Both the Circuit Court of St. Louis and the Supreme Court of Missouri agreed. Both courts acquitted Happersett and upheld Missouri's denial of suffrage to women.

All or Nothing

Minor's side presented to the Supreme Court repeated points made before the lower courts and also raised a new claim: "There can be no half-way citizenship. Woman, as a citizen of the United States, is entitled to all the benefits of that position, and liable to all its obligations, or to none." They cited several previous Supreme Court decisions, including *Dred Scott v. Sandford*, the infamous judicial reply to the question of whether "the class of persons who had been imported as slaves [or] their descendants . . . *free or not*," were or ever could be citizens. Chief Justice Roger Taney had written in the majority opinion that they could not (a decision later invalidated by the adoption of the Fourteenth Amendment), but he stressed that a finding of citizenship would have conferred rights no state could abridge:

> If persons of the African race are citizens of a State, and of the United States, they would be entitled to all of these privileges and immunities in every State, and the State could not restrict them; for they would hold these privileges and immunities under the paramount authority of the Federal Government, and its courts would be bound to maintain and enforce them, the Constitution [of an individual state] and the laws of the State to the contrary notwithstanding. . . .

Pointing out that Section 1 of the Fourteenth Amendment granted citizenship to women as well as to black males, Minor's attorneys argued that both groups, by the standards set in *Dred Scott*, were now guaranteed a citizen's "privileges and immunities." They next cited the Supreme Court's 1873 *Slaughter-House* decision as evidence that suffrage was one of the rights of citizenship: "The Negro having by the Fourteenth Amendment been declared a citizen of the United States is thus made a voter in every state of the Union." Therefore, they reasoned, a state's abridgment of its female citizen's right of suffrage was a violation of the United States Constitution.

Unanimously, however, the Supreme Court found otherwise. Chief Justice Morrison R. Waite wrote in the majority opinion that women born or naturalized

Nineteenth-century women struggled for the right to vote and faced a great deal of criticism. This May 16, 1868, *Harper's Weekly* caption reads "How it would be if some ladies had their own way." (Prints and Photographs Division, Library of Congress)

in the United States were in fact—and had been even prior to the adoption of the Fourteenth Amendment—citizens of the United States. He found, however, that the right of suffrage was not one of the privileges and immunities of citizenship, and that the states could exclude women from the polls. It would take nearly a century before the Supreme Court would apply Fourteenth Amendment protection to women's rights.

For Further Reading

Cary, Eve, and Kathleen Willert Peratis. *Woman and the Law*. Skokie, Ill.: National Textbook Co. in conjunction with the American Civil Liberties Union, 1977.

Flexner, Eleanor. *Century of Struggle: The Woman's Rights Movement in the United States*. Cambridge, Mass.: The Belknap Press of Harvard University Press, 1959, rev. 1975.

Frost, Elizabeth, and Kathryn Cullen-DuPont. *Women's Suffrage in America: An Eyewitness History*. New York: Facts on File, 1992.

Goldstein, Leslie Friedman. *The Constitutional Rights of Women*, rev. ed. Madison: University of Wisconsin Press, 1989.

Stanton, Elizabeth Cady, Susan B. Anthony, and Matilda Joslyn Gage, eds. *History of Woman Suffrage*, Vol. 2, 1998, reprint, Salem, N.H.: Ayer Company Publishers, 1985.

Breedlove v. Suttles, Tax Collector: 1937

Appellant: Nolen R. Breedlove   **Appellee:** Tax Collector T. Earl Suttles
Appellant's Claim: That a poll tax exempting women (and three other groups thought to be in need of special protection) violated the Fourteenth and Nineteenth Amendments   **Chief Lawyers for Appellee:** W. S. Northcutt and E. Harold Sheats   **Chief Lawyers for Appellant:** J. Ira Harrelson and Henry G. Van Veen   **Justices:** Hugo L. Black, Louis D. Brandeis, *Pierce Butler,* Benjamin N. Cardozo, Chief Justice Charles Evans Hughes, James Clark McReynolds, Owen J. Roberts, Harlan Fiske Stone, and George Sutherland   **Place:** Washington, D.C.   **Date of Decision:** December 6, 1937
Decision: A Georgia poll tax that exempted any woman who did not register to vote, among others, from the state's poll tax did not violate the Fourteenth or the Nineteenth Amendment

SIGNIFICANCE

The justices' decision exempting women from paying the poll tax rested, in large part, upon men's status as head of the family and upon women's presumed financial dependence upon them. This decision shows that winning the vote did not change the Supreme Court's traditional view of women.

When women won the vote in 1920 as the result of Nineteenth Amendment, they felt they had achieved something close to political or civic equality. Indeed, women's newly found political clout persuaded Congress to pass laws important to them in the years following the "Susan B. Anthony" amendment. For example, the 1921 Sheppard Towner Act authorized money for the improvement of maternal and infant health; the 1921 Packers and Stockyards' bill provided important consumer safeguards; and the 1922 Cable Act permitted women to retain their American citizenship when they married foreigners. In 1923, the Supreme Court also struck down a minimum wage law for women workers in *Adkins v. Children's Hospital* (see page 352), on the basis that the law deprived women of the right to bargain.

Nonetheless, many laws—and much of society—continued to treat women differently from men. For example, a Georgia law made every resident of the state pay a poll tax. However, the statute exempted people under twenty-one or over sixty, the blind, and women who chose not to register. Some felt that this gave women preferential treatment.

On March 16, 1936, a twenty-eight-year-old white man named Nolen R. Breedlove applied to register for the vote in Georgia, saying that he had not paid and would not pay his poll tax. When the clerk refused to let him register, Breedlove sued the tax collector, T. Earl Suttles, claiming that the collector had violated his constitutional rights under the Fourteenth and Nineteenth Amendments. The superior court of Fulton County rejected his claim, and the state supreme court affirmed its decision. Breedlove then appealed to the U.S. Supreme Court, which agreed to hear his case.

Arguments took place on November 16 and 17, 1937. Breedlove did not challenge the law's exemption for the blind, but he did challenge the exception for any woman who did not register to vote. He also objected to the exemption for men younger than twenty-one and older than sixty, and the validity of poll taxes generally.

Poor Folks Denied the Vote

Breedlove's lawyers argued that "if the [poll] tax imposed by Georgia were increased to a high degree, as it can be if valid, it could be used to reduce the percentage of voters. . . . Whatever property and other economic restrictions on the franchise may have been upheld in earlier periods of our history, the admission today that a State has the power to prevent its poorer inhabitants from participating in the choice of federal officials would be totally contrary to the contemporary spirit of American institutions, and inconsistent with the purposes announced in the preamble to the United States Constitution."

The Court rejected this claim; as Pierce Butler explained in his majority opinion, "Levy by the poll has long been a familiar form of taxation . . . laid upon persons without regard to their occupations or property to raise money for the support of government or some more specific end." The Court agreed that payment of the poll tax was a "prerequisite to voting." Nonetheless, it rejected the view that payment or nonpayment of the poll tax conferred or denied a right to vote. In illustration, male aliens between the ages of twenty-one and sixty were both ineligible to vote and yet *still* required to pay the tax.

The Court upheld the exemption of men over the age of sixty as an accommodation similar to the exclusion of older men from road work, jury duty, and military service. The justices also upheld the exception for minor males, because "collection from minors would be to put the burden upon their fathers or others upon whom they depend for support."

Butler then turned to the Nineteenth Amendment, which guaranteed women the right to vote: "The right of citizens of the United States to vote shall not be denied or abridged by the United States or by any State on account of sex." Having already defined the poll tax as one that was unrelated to the taxpayer's right to vote, Butler simply wrote that the Nineteenth Amendment "applies to men and women alike and . . . supersedes inconsistent measures, whether federal or state" but that "its purpose is not to regulate the levy or collection of taxes."

Women as Dependents

The Court then examined the specific issue of exempting women who did not register to vote. Butler, relying on a traditional view of family roles, wrote:

> Women may be exempted on the basis of special considerations to which they are naturally entitled. In view of burdens necessarily borne by them for the preservation of the race, the State reasonably may exempt them from poll taxes. . . . The laws of Georgia declare the husband to be the head of the family and the wife to be subject to him. . . .

> To subject her to the levy would be to add to his burden. Moreover, Georgia poll taxes are laid to raise money for educational purposes, and it is the father's duty to provide for education of the children. . . . Discrimination in favor of all women being permissible, appellant may not complain because the tax is laid only upon some [women] or object to registration of women without payment of taxes for previous years.

The Effect on Women

The stereotyped language of this ruling served to reinforce the role society expected from women. At the same time, the upholding of a poll tax as a condition for voting effectively prohibited many women—and many desperately poor black people—from voting at all. In 1964, the Twenty-fourth Amendment prohibited poll taxes. Stereotyped language and attitudes about women—reflecting the deeply held views of men in America—would remain a fixture of Supreme Court decisions until the 1970s.

For Further Reading

Chafe, William H. *The American Woman: Her Changing Social, Economic, and Political Roles, 1920–1970.* New York: Oxford University Press, 1972.

Goldstein, Leslie Freidman. *The Constitutional Rights of Women: Cases in Law and Social Change,* rev. ed. Madison: The University of Wisconsin Press, 1989.

Reed v. Reed: 1971

Appellant: Sally Reed **Appellee:** Cecil Reed **Appellant's Claim:** That Sally Reed's constitutional rights were abridged by an Idaho law that favored the appointment of a man over a similarly situated woman to act as administrator of an estate **Chief Lawyers for Appellee:** Charles S. Stout and Myron E. Anderson **Chief Lawyers for Appellant:** Allen R. Derr and Ruth Bader Ginsburg **Justices:** Hugo L. Black, Harry Blackmun, William J. Brennan, Jr., *Chief Justice Warren E. Burger,* William O. Douglas, John Marshall Harlan, Thurgood Marshall, Potter Stewart, and Byron R. White **Place:** Washington, D.C. **Date of Decision:** November 22, 1971 **Decision:** That Idaho's law was "based solely on a discrimination prohibited by and therefore violative of the Equal Protection Clause of the Fourteenth Amendment"

SIGNIFICANCE

This was the first time in the Fourteenth Amendment's 103-year history that the Supreme Court ruled that its Equal Protection Clause protected women's rights.

Although Section 1 of the Fourteenth Amendment, adopted in 1868, stated that "No State shall make or enforce any law which shall abridge the privileges or immunities of citizens of the United States . . . nor deny to any person within its jurisdiction the equal protection of the laws," the U.S. Supreme Court refused for a century to apply this guarantee to women.

Reed v. Reed was the first case in which the Supreme Court applied the Fourteenth Amendment to women's rights. This "turning point case," as Ruth Bader Ginsburg termed it, began with the suicide of a teenager, Richard Lynn Reed. Richard's adoptive parents, Sally and Cecil Reed, had earlier separated. The boy spent his "tender years" in the custody of his mother but was transferred into the custody of his father once he reached his teens. At nineteen, using his father's rifle, Richard killed himself. As Ginsburg remembers, Sally Reed had deeply opposed her loss of Richard's custody and had felt that her estranged husband bore some responsibility for their son's death.

Since Richard had died without a will, Sally Reed filed an application to act as administrator of his estate. When Cecil Reed filed a similar petition, the

Probate Court of Ada County ordered that *he* be appointed administrator upon his taking the required oath and filing the required bond.

The court reached this decision without considering the parents' relative merits, but strictly in accordance with Idaho's mandatory probate code. Section 15-312 provided:

> Administration of the estate of a person dying interstate must be granted to some one . . . in the following order:
>
> 1. The surviving husband or wife or some competent person whom he or she may request to have appointed.
>
> 2. The children.
>
> 3. The father or mother. . . .

Section 15-314 stated:

> [O]f several persons claiming and equally entitled to administer, males must be preferred to females, and relatives of whole to those of the half blood.

Win Some, Lose Some

Sally Reed appealed the probate court's order to the District Court of the Fourth Judicial District of Idaho. Her lawyer, Allen R. Derr, maintained that the Idaho law violated her constitutional rights under the Equal Protection Clause of the Fourteenth Amendment. The District Court agreed. It voided the two aforementioned sections of law, and directed the probate court to choose between Richard's parents based upon their relative qualifications, regardless of sex.

Cecil Reed quickly appealed to the Idaho Supreme Court. This court rejected the District Court's ruling. Finding that Idaho's legislature had "evidently concluded that in general men are better qualified to act as an administrator than women," and that this was "neither an illogical nor arbitrary method devised by the legislature to resolve an issue that would otherwise require a hearing as to the relative merits . . . of the two or more petitioning relatives," Idaho's Supreme Court reinstated Cecil Reed as administrator of his son's estate, since he was the male.

Sally Reed, shown soon after the U.S. Supreme Court trial in 1971. (Sally Reed)

Equal Protection

Sally Reed appealed to the U.S. Supreme Court. Ginsburg and others associated with the Women's Rights Project of the American Civil Liberties

Union joined Derr to represent her. The Court also received *amicus curiae*, or "friend of the court," briefs from many other organizations. Derr argued Sally Reed's case on October 19, 1971, continuing to insist—as rights advocates had since the 1870s—that women's rights were protected under the Fourteenth Amendment. In contrast, Cecil Reed's lawyers defended Idaho's law as providing a reasonable means of streamlining the probate court's workload.

This time, the Supreme Court unanimously agreed that women's rights were within the province of the Fourteenth Amendment. Chief Justice Warren E. Burger wrote, "We have concluded that the arbitrary preference established in favor of males . . . cannot stand in the face of the Fourteenth Amendment's command that no State deny the equal protection of the laws to any person within its jurisdiction. . . . This Court has consistently recognized that the Fourteenth Amendment does not deny to States the power to treat different classes of persons in different ways. . . . [It] does, however, deny to States the power to legislate that different treatment be accorded to persons placed by a statute into different classes on the basis of criteria wholly unrelated to the objective of that statute. A classification 'must be reasonable, not arbitrary. . . .' "

Sally Reed and her lawyers thus won for women what Susan B. Anthony, Myra Bradwell, and Virginia Minor had begun to seek in the courts nearly one century before: Fourteenth Amendment protection of women's constitutional rights.

For Further Reading

Carey, Eve, and Kathleen Willert Peratis. *Woman and the Law*. Skokie, Ill.: National Textbook Company in conjunction with the American Civil Liberties Union, 1977.

Davis, Flora. *Moving the Mountain: The Women's Movement in America Since 1960*. New York: Simon & Schuster, 1991.

Goldstein, Leslie Freidman. *The Constitutional Rights of Women*. Madison: The University of Wisconsin Press, rev. ed. 1989.

Lynn, Naomi B., ed. *Women, Politics and the Constitution*. Binghamton, New York: The Harrington Park Press, 1990.

New York Times, November 23 and 28, 1971.

Taylor v. Louisiana: 1975

Appellant: Billy Jean Taylor **Appellee:** The State of Louisiana
Appellant's Claim: That Louisiana's jury selection system violated his right
to trial by an impartial jury under the Sixth and Fourteenth Amendments
Chief Lawyer for Appellee: Kendall L. Vick
Chief Lawyer for Appellant: William M. King **Justices:** Harry A. Blackmun,
William J. Brennan, Jr., William O. Douglas, Thurgood Marshall, Lewis F.
Powell, Jr., Potter Stewart, and *Byron R. White* (majority); Chief Justice
Warren E. Burger concurred in the result without joining the majority opinion
or issuing a separate opinion; William H. Rehnquist (dissent)
Place: Washington, D.C. **Date of Decision:** January 21, 1975
Decision: Louisiana's jury selection process, which excluded women who
failed to register, violated Taylor's Sixth and Fourteenth Amendment rights

SIGNIFICANCE
By overturning gender-based provisions of state laws governing the selection of
jurors, the Supreme Court opened the way for women throughout the nation to
serve on juries equally with men.

On September 28, 1971, police arrested Billy Jean Taylor, a twenty-five-year-old former convict, in the St. Tammany Parish of Louisiana. They charged him with aggravated kidnapping, armed robbery, and rape. Despite having made seven suicide attempts in jail, Taylor was found competent to stand trial.

Jury Concerns

Taylor's trial was to begin at the Twenty-Second Judicial District of Louisiana on April 13, 1972. The day before, he asked the court to throw out the list of available jurors. The law had systematically excluded women from that summoned group, Taylor claimed, by Article 402 of the Louisiana Code of Criminal Procedure, which provided: "A woman shall not be selected for jury service unless she has previously filed with the clerk of court of the parish in which she resides a written declaration of her desire to be subject to jury service."

Because of this requirement, few jurors in St. Tammany Parish were women, even though fifty-three percent of the people who met eligibility requirements were female. More specifically, there were no women among the 175 people drawn for jury service during the criminal term in which Taylor's case would be tried, a situation he claimed violated his right to an impartial jury of his peers—made up of both *women* and men.

The 1975 Supreme Court decision in *Taylor v. Louisiana* denied states the right to prevent women from serving on juries. In the nineteenth century, all-male juries such as this, were the rule.

The court rejected Taylor's motion on the same day he made it and the trial continued. Convicted of aggravated kidnapping by the all-male jury, the court sentenced Taylor to death. Taylor then appealed to the state's supreme court to review whether his motion to quash the list of jurors summoned should have been granted. When Louisiana's Supreme Court ruled that the jury list had been selected by constitutional means, Taylor appealed to the U.S. Supreme Court.

For All Intents and Purposes . . .

Two years later, the case came before the U.S. Supreme Court. Taylor's lawyer, William M. King, argued that his client's constitutional right to "a fair trial by jury of a representative segment of the community . . ." was violated as a result of Louisiana's consideration of only those women who expressly registered their desire to serve as jurors.

He pointed out that from December 8, 1971, to November 3, 1972, there were only twelve women among the 18,000 people drawn for jury service in St. Tammany Parish, and that there had been no women among the 175 people drawn to fill the list for the criminal term during which Taylor's case was tried. In short, whether the intent to eliminate women from the jury was there or not, the fact was that women were excluded.

The state of Louisiana claimed that Louisiana's jury selection system was constitutional and that, in any event, "Taylor, a male, has no standing to object to the exclusion of women from his jury." In other words, since he was not female, he could not object to the lack of women on the jury.

A Fair Cross-Section

Effective January 1, 1975, Louisiana repealed the gender-based provision challenged by Taylor. A decision was nonetheless issued three weeks later, with

Justice Byron R. White pointing out in a footnote to his majority opinion that the repeal "has no effect on the conviction obtained in this case."

White briefly outlined the history of Taylor's case and the Court's jurisdiction "to consider whether the Louisiana jury-selection system deprived appellant of his Sixth and Fourteenth Amendment right to an impartial jury." He then offered the Court's conclusion: "We hold that it did and that these amendments were violated. . . . In consequence, appellant's conviction must be reversed."

Explaining the Court's reasoning, White began by agreeing that Louisiana's "jury-selection system . . . operates to exclude from jury service an identifiable class of citizens constituting 53 percent of eligible jurors in the community. . . ."

White disagreed with the state's claim that Taylor lacked standing to challenge a lack of female jurors, writing that "there is no rule that claims such as Taylor presents may be made only by those defendants who are members of the group excluded from jury service." Recalling earlier court decisions and the Federal Jury Selection and Service Act of 1968, White emphasized that "the requirement of a jury's being chosen from a fair cross section of the community is fundamental to the American system of justice." That requirement, he wrote, "is violated by the systematic exclusion of women. . . ."

White acknowledged that the Court had let stand a similar jury-selection system as recently as 1961, in its decision in *Hoyt v. Florida*. He also acknowl-

An all-male jury from the 1925 John Thomas Scopes Trial (The "Monkey Trial"). Before his kidnapping trial began in October 1974, Billy Jean Taylor claimed discrimination in jury selection, insisting that women had been systematically excluded from jury service. (Prints and Photographs Division, Library of Congress)

edged that "the first Congress did not perceive the Sixth Amendment as requiring women on criminal jury panels. . . ." Nonetheless, he wrote:

> We think it is no longer tenable to hold that women as a class may be excluded or given automatic exemptions based solely on sex if the consequence is that criminal jury venires are almost totally male. To this extent we cannot follow the contrary implications of the prior cases, including *Hoyt v. Florida*. If it was ever the case that women were unqualified to sit on juries or were so situated that none of them should be required to perform jury service, that time has long since passed. If at one time it could be held that Sixth Amendment juries must be drawn from a fair cross-section of the community but that this requirement permitted the almost total exclusion of women, this is not the case today.

Taylor v. Louisiana guaranteed that the states would call women and men to jury service on an equal basis.

For Further Reading

Cary, Eve, and Kathleen Willert Peratis. *Woman and the Law*. Skokie, Ill.: National Textbook Company in conjunction with the American Civil Liberties Union, 1981.

Goldstein, Leslie Freidman. *The Constitutional Rights of Women: Cases in Law and Social Change*, rev. ed. Madison: The University of Wisconsin Press, 1989.

Hoff, Joan. *Law Gender & Injustice: A Legal History of U.S. Women*. New York: New York University Press, 1991.

St. Tammany Farmer, September 30, October 7, November 4, and December 30, 1971; February 17 and April 20, 1972.

Stanton v. Stanton: 1975

Plaintiff: Thelma B. Stanton   **Defendant:** James Lawrence Stanton, Jr.
Plaintiff's Claim: That support for minor children should be the same regardless of sex   **Chief Lawyer for Defendant:** J. Dennis Frederick
Chief Lawyer for the Plaintiff: Bryce E. Roe   **Justices:** *Harry A. Blackmun,*
William J. Brennan, Jr., Chief Justice Warren E. Burger, William O. Douglas, Thurgood Marshall, Lewis F. Powell, Jr., Potter Stewart, Byron R. White (majority); William H. Rehnquist (dissent)   **Place:** Washington, D.C.
Date of Decision: April 15, 1975   **Decision:** Voided Utah's law setting different ages of majority for male and female children

SIGNIFICANCE

The Supreme Court ruled that a law based on the "old notion" that women need less education and preparation for adulthood than men did not pass a rational basis test and was therefore in violation of the equal protection clause of the Fourteenth Amendment.

Thelma and James Stanton married in February 1951. They had two children: Sherri Lynn, born on February 12, 1953, and Rick Arlund, born on January 29, 1955. The couple divorced when Sherri and Rick were seven and five years old. The divorce decree detailed what they had agreed to concerning property, child support, and alimony. James was ordered to pay $100 per month per child and $100 per month in alimony.

Thelma later remarried and, as provided in the decree, James no longer had to pay her alimony. After Sherri turned eighteen, her father stopped paying her child support, but in 1973, when Rick became eighteen, Thelma asked the divorce court for an entry of judgment against her ex-husband for support of both children following their eighteenth birthdays.

The court denied Thelma's request, citing section 15-2-1 of Utah Code Annotated 1953, which set the age of majority at eighteen for females and at twenty-one for males. Thelma then appealed to the Supreme Court of Utah.

"Reasonable" Discrimination

The challenge to Utah's statute was that it was "invidiously discriminatory" and in violation of the due process and equal protection provisions of the Fourteenth Amendment and of similar provisions in Utah's own state constitution. James and his attorney claimed the statute had a rational basis and should be upheld.

The Supreme Court of Utah agreed that "there is no doubt that the questioned statute treats men and women differently." It nonetheless ruled in favor of James, on the basis that disparate treatment is permitted "so long as there is a reasonable basis for the classification, which is related to the purposes of the act, and it applies equally and uniformly to all persons within the class."

The rational basis of Utah's statute was, the court explained, the "old notion" that "generally it is the man's primary responsibility to provide a home and its essentials," and "it is a salutary thing for him to get a good education and/ or training before he undertakes those responsibilities," while "girls tend generally to mature physically, emotionally and mentally before boys" and "generally tend to marry earlier."

In light of this "notion," the court relieved the father of responsibility for Sherri's support after age eighteen, but ordered him to make support payments for Rick until the son turned twenty-one. Thelma appealed to the U.S. Supreme Court.

No Standing to Sue

The case came before the Supreme Court on February 19, 1975. In addition to the argument that Utah's statute was rational in basis, James and his attorney presented several procedural arguments. First, neither mother nor daughter had standing to sue since they both had passed their twenty-first birthdays and couldn't be affected by the outcome of the case. Sherri's support was also a dead issue for the same reason. Finally, Thelma was out of luck because she had signed the divorce decree—which included a reference to her children's majority—and by doing so, she had given up any right to Sherri's support because she had, in effect, been agreeing to Utah's law.

The Court disagreed. The majority opinion noted that "If appellee, under the divorce decree, is obligated for Sherri's support during that period, it is an obligation that has not been fulfilled, and there is an amount past due and owing from the appellee."

Turning to the merits of the case, Justice Harry A. Blackmun wrote, "We find it unnecessary in this case to decide whether a classification based on sex is inherently suspect," in other words, whether claims of sex discrimination were subject to the same "strict scrutiny" as claims of discrimination on the basis of race, religion, or national origin. The "test here . . . is whether the difference in sex between children warrants the distinction in the appellee's obligation to support that is drawn by the Utah statute. We conclude that it does not."

"Old Notions" Aside

Blackmun pointed out that the more frequent early marriages of females "loses whatever weight it might otherwise have, for the statute states that 'all minors obtain their majority by marriage'; thus, minority, and all that goes with it is abruptly lost by marriage of a person of either sex at whatever tender age the marriage occurs." He then set aside the stereotyped "old notions" as a rational basis for the discriminatory statute:

> A child, male or female, is still a child. No longer is the female destined solely for the home and the rearing of the family, and only the male for the marketplace and world of ideas. . . . Women's activities and responsibilities are increasing and expanding. Coeducation is a fact, not a rarity. The presence of women in business, in the professions, in government, and indeed, in all walks of life where education is a desirable, if not always a necessary, antecedent is apparent and a proper subject of judicial notice.

Thelma Stanton in Santa Fe, New Mexico, in 1993. (Thelma Stanton)

If a specified age of minority is required for the boy in order to assure him parental support while he attains his education and training, so, too, it is for the girl. To distinguish between the two on educational grounds is to be self-serving: if the female is not to be supported so long as the male, she hardly can be expected to attend school as long as he does, and bringing her education to an end earlier coincides with the role-typing society has long imposed.

And if any weight remains in this day to the claim of earlier maturity of the female, with a concomitant inference of absence of need for support beyond eighteen, we fail to perceive its unquestioned truth or its significance, particularly when marriage, as the statute provides, terminates minority for a person of either sex.

Finally, Blackmun noted that while the age differential was unconstitutional, it was still within Utah's right to choose what age of majority would apply to both sexes. William H. Rehnquist, the sole dissenter, wrote in his opinion that "if . . . the Utah Supreme Court had concluded that the Stantons intended to bestow more of their limited resources upon a son than a daughter, perhaps for the reasons stated in the opinion of the Supreme Court of Utah, that strikes me as an entirely permissible basis upon which to construe the property settlement agreement." In consideration of this and other factors, he concluded that the appeal should have been dismissed to avoid "unnecessary constitutional adjudication."

The Court decided *Stanton v. Stanton* at a time when long-standing views such as Rehnquist's were being challenged in the political realm as well as the judicial. In 1972, just three years prior to the *Stanton* decision, Congress passed Title IX of the 1972 Higher Education Act to prohibit sex discrimination in federally funded educational institutions—effectively stating that American society would no longer invest more in the education of sons than of daughters. Similarly, the *Stanton* decision, establishing a girl's right to a childhood lasting as long as her brother's, brought home a new precedent: that American families could no longer invest more in the futures of their sons than of their daughters.

For Further Reading

Cary, Eve, and Kathleen Willert Peratis. *Woman and the Law*. Skokie, Ill.: National Textbook Company in conjunction with the American Civil Liberties Union, 1981.

Goldstein, Leslie Friedman. *The Constitutional Rights of Women*, rev. ed. Madison: The University of Wisconsin Press, 1989.

Lynn, Naomi B., ed. *Women, Politics and the Constitution*. Binghamton, N.Y.: Harrington Park Press, 1990.

Weaver, Warren, Jr., "Justices Void Law on Majority Ages." *New York Times*, April 16, 1976.

Craig v. Boren: 1976

Appellants: Curtis Craig, Mark Walker, and Carolyn Whitener
Appellee: David Boren   **Appellants' Claim:** That the law forbidding the sale of 3.2 percent beer to males under the age of twenty-one and females under the age of eighteen infringed upon their Fourteenth Amendment right to equal protection of the laws   **Chief Lawyer for Appellee:** James H. Gray
Chief Lawyer for Appellants: Frederick P. Gilbert   **Justices:** Harry A. Blackmun, *William J. Brennan, Jr.,* Thurgood Marshall, Lewis F. Powell, Jr., John P. Stevens, III, Potter Stewart, and Byron R. White; (majority); Warren E. Burger, and William H. Rehnquist (dissent)   **Place:** Washington, D.C.
Date of Decision: December 20, 1976   **Decision:** The law setting different ages for males and females to buy beer violates the Fourteenth Amendment

SIGNIFICANCE

The Supreme Court announced a new level of heightened or more rigid scrutiny to be applied when determining whether laws differentiating between males and females violate the Fourteenth Amendment or other provisions of the U.S. Constitution.

On December 20, 1972, Curtis Craig and Mark Walker, both between the ages of eighteen and twenty-one, and Carolyn Whitener, a licensed beer vendor, brought suit in the District Court for the Western District of Oklahoma against the governor, David Boren. The three plaintiffs claimed that Oklahoma's law—forbidding the sale of 3.2 percent beer to males under the age of twenty-one and females under the age of eighteen—violated their Fourteenth Amendment right to equal protection of the laws.

Oklahoma argued that young men who drank alcoholic beverages caused more traffic accidents than women who imbibed. Therefore, the law helped society. The federal district court agreed. This "nonweighty interest pressed by thirsty boys," as future Supreme Court justice Ruth Bader Ginsburg would characterize it, then went on appeal to the U.S. Supreme Court.

A New Standard

When the dispute came before the Court on October 5, 1976, James H. Gray—for the state—claimed first that Whitener lacked standing to sue and, second, that the case was now moot (irrelevant), since both young men had turned twenty-one. The Court agreed the case of the men was irrelevant, but ruled that Whitener—as a vendor charged with carrying out the discriminatory law—had a valid third-party right to sue.

As for the law, Gray argued that improving traffic safety was a legitimate government objective, and statistics proved the setting of separate beer-drinking ages for each sex helped reach that goal. He also argued that the Twenty-first Amendment gave states the express right to regulate the liquor trade.

The youths had hired attorney Frederick P. Gilbert, who sought the advice of Ginsburg on how best to tailor his arguments. (Ginsburg also filed an *amicus curiae*, or friend-of-the-court, brief.) The dispute reached the Supreme Court just before the fifth anniversary of the 1971 *Reed v. Reed* (see page 112) decision, which extended Fourteenth Amendment protection to women's rights for the first time.

For more than one hundred years following the amendment's adoption in 1868, the Supreme Court refused to find sex discrimination a reason to extend to women "equal protection of the laws." The 1971 ruling in *Reed* had marked a dramatic transition. As Ginsburg acknowledged during her 1993 Supreme Court confirmation hearings, "It's a sad part of our history, but it is part of our history that . . . the Fourteenth Amendment, that great amendment that changed so much in this nation . . . didn't change the status of women [at the time]. . . . And so it was certainly a bold change from the middle of the nineteenth century until the 1970s when women's equal citizenship was recognized before the law."

Curtis Craig. (Curtis L. Craig)

Nonetheless, the Court applied the Fourteenth Amendment more strictly to some groups than to others. In deciding *Reed v. Reed* and enunciating the first "bold change," the Court did find that sex was "a classification subject to scrutiny under the Equal Protection Clause [of the Fourteenth Amendment]." However, it also mandated that laws classifying people by sex would be subject to a less strict test, than laws classifying people by race, religion, or national origin.

Courts call these latter categories "inherently suspect," and laws classifying people by these criteria are constitutional only if such classifications serve a *necessary* relationship to a *compelling* state interest. (This test is known as "strict scrutiny.") In *Reed*, the Court determined that laws classifying people by sex would be judged by the lower level "rational relationship" test; in other words, such laws would be permitted to stand if they bore a *rational* relationship to a *legitimate* state interest.

Ginsburg, among others, had been working since *Reed* to win a ruling that sex, like race, should be an inherently suspect category. Ginsburg had addressed the issue head-on in her arguments in the 1973 *Frontiero v. Richardson* case (see page 308). To her disappointment, the Court overturned the sex-biased regulation in question, but failed, by one vote, to find that sex classifications were *inherently* suspect. In *Craig,* therefore, Ginsburg advised Gilbert to try to win "heightened scrutiny." Gilbert did so.

When the Court ruled on December 20, 1976, this partial victory was won. The Court established a heightened, intermediate, or mid-level scrutiny test to be applied in cases of laws discriminating because of sex: Such laws could stand only if they bore a *substantial* relationship to an *important* governmental interest. Supreme Court Justice William J. Brennan, Jr., announced the shift in his majority opinion by reinterpreting *Reed* and reviewing subsequent cases in light of the revised standard.

He agreed that "statutory classifications that distinguish between males and females are 'subject to scrutiny under the Equal Protection Clause.'" He added that "classifications by gender must serve important governmental objectives and must be substantially related to achievement of those objectives. . . . Decisions following *Reed* similarly have rejected administrative ease and convenience as sufficiently important objectives to justify gender-based classifications. See, e.g., . . . *Frontiero v. Richardson.*"

Brennan pointed out that *Reed v. Reed* invalidated statutes,

> . . . employing gender as an inaccurate proxy for other, more germane bases of classification. Hence, 'archaic and overbroad' generalizations, . . . could not justify the use of a gender line in determining eligibility for certain governmental entitlements. Similarly, increasingly outdated misconceptions concerning the role of females in the home rather than in the 'marketplace and world of ideas' were rejected as loose-fitting characterizations incapable of supporting state statutory schemes. . . . It was necessary that the legislatures choose either to realign their substantive laws in a gender-neutral fashion, or to adopt procedures for identifying those instances where the sex-centered generalization actually comported to fact. . . .

The Court felt that *Reed* was the deciding factor. "[Does] the difference between males and females with respect to the purchase of 3.2 percent beer warrant the differential in age drawn by the Oklahoma Statute? We conclude that it does not."

Justice William H. Rehnquist and Chief Justice Warren E. Burger dissented, each with a separate opinion. In his opinion, Rehnquist wrote:

> The Court's disposition of this case is objectionable on two grounds. First is its conclusion that *men* challenging a gender-based statute . . . may invoke a more stringent standard . . . than pertains to most other types of classifica-

tions. Second is the Court's enunciation of this standard . . . as being that "classifications by gender must serve *important* governmental objectives and must be *substantially* related to achievement of those objectives. . ." [emphasis added]. The only redeeming feature . . . is that it apparently signals a retreat by those who joined in the plurality opinion in *Frontiero v. Richardson* . . . from their view that sex is a "suspect" classification for purposes of equal protection analysis. I think the Oklahoma statute challenged here need pass only the "rational basis" equal protection analysis . . . and I believe that it is constitutional under that analysis. . . . I would think we have had enough difficulty with the two standards of review which our cases have recognized—the norm of "rational basis" and the "compelling state interest" where a "suspect classification" is involved—so as to counsel weightily against the insertion of still another "standard" between those two.

To date, the standard enunciated in *Craig v. Boren* remains the standard by which the Supreme Court evaluates sex discrimination claims.

For Further Reading

Goldstein, Leslie Friedman. *The Constitutional Rights of Women*, rev. ed. Madison: The University of Wisconsin Press, 1989.

Lynn, Naomi B., ed. *Women, Politics, and the Constitution*. Binghamton, N.Y.: Harrington Park Press, 1990.

New York Times. "Excerpts from Senate Hearing on the Ginsburg Nomination," July 22, 1993.

Von Drehle, David. "The Quiet Revolutionary: Ruth Bader Ginsburg's Odyssey from Convention to Crusade." *The Washington Post National Weekly Edition*, July 26–August 1, 1993.

——. "A Trailblazer's Step-by-Step Assault on the Status Quo." *The Washington Post National Weekly Edition*, July 26–August 1, 1993.

Rostker v. Goldberg: 1981

Appellant: Bernard Rostker, director of the Selective Service System
Appellee: Robert L. Goldberg, acting on behalf of himself and all males
similarly situated   **Appellant's Claim:** That excusing women from registering
for military service did not violate the due process clause of the Fifth
Amendment   **Chief Lawyer for Appellee:** Donald L. Weinberg
Chief Lawyer for Appellant: Wade H. McCree, Jr., the solicitor general
Justices: Harry A. Blackmun, Chief Justice Warren E. Burger, Lewis F.
Powell, Jr., *William H. Rehnquist,* John Paul Stevens, Potter Stewart
(majority); William J. Brennan, Thurgood Marshall, and Byron R. White
(dissent)   **Place:** Washington, D.C.   **Date of Decision:** June 25, 1981
Decision: Under the war powers clause, Congress was well within its
constitutional authority to require only men to register for the draft

SIGNIFICANCE

Congress' refusal to register women for the draft and the Supreme Court's
decision permitting male-only draft registration occurred during the unsuccessful
effort to ratify the Equal Rights Amendment (ERA). Anti-ERA forces used the
decision to bolster its argument that the Constitution should not be amended to
provide equal treatment for men and women.

In 1980, when the Soviet Union invaded Afghanistan, President Jimmy Carter
reactivated the military's draft registration, which had been abolished in 1975.
His request that women register as well as men prompted Congressional hearings and sparked public debate.

Congress always had the undisputed right to draft women if it so chose
and, in fact, had discussed drafting women to fill nursing, industrial, and
agricultural needs during World War II. Moreover, the war powers clause of the
Constitution—which the courts had interpreted as permitting the military to
deprive troops of some of their Bill of Rights protections—also provided the
armed forces with broad discretion to decide whether women would serve in
combat units.

ERA Becomes the Issue

Opponents of the ERA argued that its ratification meant drafting both men and women and deploying women alongside men in combat units. These possibilities—along with the question of whether separate public bathrooms for men and women would be outlawed—became pivotal issues in the ERA debate.

Representative Martha W. Griffiths (D-MI), a sponsor of the ERA, was blunt in her assessment of "all this nonsense about the Army." She said: "The draft is equal. That is the thing that is equal. But once you are in the Army, you are put where the Army tells you are going to go. The thing that will happen with women is that they will be the stenographers and telephone operators."

Unconvinced, leaders of STOP-ERA insisted that the Constitution must not be amended to give Congress power to refuse such presidential requests. However, describing what became the prevailing feminist opinion on the subject, Judy Goldsmith, executive vice president of the National Organization for Women (NOW), said, "War is senseless. Neither the lives of young men nor young women should be wasted. But if we cannot stop the killing, we know we cannot choose between our sons and daughters." Nonetheless, Congress refused Carter's request to register women. The disappointed president ordered male-only registration to begin on July 2, 1980.

From Out of the Past

At this point, the courts were asked to weigh in on the question of drafting women by the sudden resurrection of a decade-old suit. Several young men, unwillingly subject to draft registration during the Vietnam War, had filed suit in 1971 claiming that all-male registration was unconstitutional because it discriminated between men and women.

In 1972, the District Court for the Eastern District of Pennsylvania dismissed the suit. The next stop was the Court of Appeals for the Third Circuit in 1973. It upheld the dismissal of all claims *except* the gender-discrimination claim. A year later, a three-judge panel refused to dismiss the case as moot, since registration was still in progress. However, since the draft had been abolished, the panel did not consider the matter further until June 1979, when there was yet another refusal to dismiss the case.

Then, on July 1, 1980, after Congressional debate had ended and one day before President Carter issued the proclamation reinstating the registration of young men, the court agreed that the 1971 plaintiffs could represent "all male persons who are registered or subject to registration . . . or are liable for training and service in the armed forces. . . ."

The district court, which had dismissed the case originally, reconsidered and found that the male-only registration provisions did violate the due process clause of the Fifth Amendment and "permanently enjoined the Government from requiring registration under the act." The court pointed out that Congress itself did not know what it wanted: Congress claimed it didn't have the funds to register and take care of females, yet it was spending money to recruit female volunteers into the military. Bernard Rostker, director of the Selective Service System, immediately appealed to the Supreme Court. Justice William J. Brennan granted a stay of the District Court's order on Saturday, July 19, 1980, and men-only registration began on Monday, July 21, 1980.

Win Some, Lose Some

On March 24, 1981, Solicitor General Wade H. McCree, Jr., argued before the Supreme Court that the war powers clause of the Constitution permitted broad discretion in matters affecting the military, and that sex discrimination in military staffing served an important governmental interest. That interest, in this case, was registering men to have a readily identifiable group from which to draw in case of possible combat. Therefore, Congress specifically excluded women from combat—since the draft would call up troops for combat, women were not excluded from registering because they were *women* but because women were not allowed in combat.

Attorney Donald L. Weinberg presented the case for Robert L. Goldberg. He argued that the Supreme Court's recent decisions, interpreting the Fourteenth Amendment as prohibiting sex discrimination in other areas, should be applied to military life as well. A number of *amici curiae* (friend of the court) briefs were filed in the case. In one, NOW disputed that women were not able to come to the defense of their country:

> Differences in strength and physical conditioning narrow and disappear when women receive adequate training, and it is a simple fact that some women are stronger than men. Moreover, size and strength are not always synonymous. A person trained in martial arts can defeat a larger opponent. Technological advances also continue to diminish the importance of brute strength. A soldier with a smaller physique can perform certain tasks in today's planes, ships and tanks more providently than a larger person. . . . The evidence is overwhelming—indeed, undisputed—that women are capable of filling current positions that bear "combat" labels.

In the end, in a six-to-three decision, the Supreme Court ruled on June 25, 1981, that the Military Selective Service Act was constitutional and that the war powers clause did grant Congress the authority to decide to register men and not women. The Equal Rights Amendment expired on June 30, 1982, without having won ratification by the states. Nonetheless, in 1993, combat positions began opening up to America's servicewomen.

For Further Reading

Cullen-DuPont, Kathryn. *The Encyclopedia of Women's History in America.* New York: Facts on File, 1996.

Davis, Flora. *Moving the Mountain: The Women's Movement in America Since 1960.* New York: Simon & Schuster, 1991.

Goldstein, Leslie Friedman. *The Constitutional Rights of Women: Cases in Law and Social Change*, rev. ed. Madison: University of Wisconsin Press, 1989.

Mansbridge, Jane J. *Why We Lost the ERA*. Chicago: University of Chicago Press, 1986.

Mississippi University for Women v. Hogan: 1982

Petitioner: Mississippi University for Women   **Respondent:** Joe Hogan
Petitioner's Claim: That the all-female admissions policy of Mississippi University's School of Nursing did not violate the Fourteenth Amendment
Chief Lawyer for Respondent: Wilbur O. Colom
Chief Lawyer for Petitioner: Hunter M. Gholson   **Justices:** William J. Brennan, Jr., Thurgood Marshall, *Sandra Day O'Connor,* John Paul Stevens, and Byron R. White (majority); Harry A. Blackmun, Chief Justice Warren E. Burger, Lewis F. Powell, Jr., and William H. Rehnquist (dissent)
Place: Washington, D.C.   **Date of Decision:** July 1, 1982   **Decision:** The all-female admissions policy of the state-supported Mississippi University for Women's School of Nursing *did* violate the Fourteenth Amendment

SIGNIFICANCE

This was the first Supreme Court decision to find a sex-segregated college admissions policy unconstitutional. It led to *U.S. v. Virginia* (1996), which forced the nation's last two publicly funded male-only colleges to admit women.

The oldest state-supported college for women, Mississippi University for Women (MUW), was founded in 1884 in Columbus, Mississippi, as the Mississippi Industrial Institute and College for the Education of White Girls of the State of Mississippi. In 1971, MUW added the School of Nursing, which ultimately offered both baccalaureate and graduate programs in nursing.

Joe Hogan Wants In

Joe Hogan, a registered nurse without a baccalaureate degree, applied for admission to MUW's School of Nursing in 1979. Although there were two other coed state supported schools at which he could pursue a baccalaureate degree, they were 178 and 147 miles from Columbus, Mississippi, home to both MUW and the medical center at which Hogan worked as a nursing supervisor. The MUW School of Nursing rejected his application on the basis of his sex, although he was otherwise qualified for admission. When he learned that he was welcome to audit classes but not to enroll for credit, Hogan filed a suit claiming that his rights under the Equal Protection Clause of the Fourteenth Amendment had been violated.

The U.S. District Court for the Northern District of Mississippi found that the all-female admissions policy of MUW was reasonably related to the state's legitimate interest "in providing the greatest practical range of educational opportunities for its female student population." The court issued summary judgment in favor of Mississippi.

More Than Rational and Legitimate

The Court of Appeals for the Fifth Circuit reversed the lower court ruling, noting that in cases of sex discrimination, states were required to show more than a *"rational* relationship to a *legitimate* state interest [emphasis added]." The proper test, the court ruled, was whether laws or policies that discriminated on the basis of sex bore a *substantial* relationship to an *important* governmental objective.

The Court of Appeals recognized that the state had an important objective in educating its citizens but found that Mississippi had not proved that providing "a unique educational opportunity for females, but not for males, bears a substantial relationship to that interest." The Court of Appeals held that MUW had disregarded Hogan's Fourteenth Amendment rights, and sent the case back to the district court.

Callaway Hall, the oldest building on the campus of the Mississippi University for Women in Columbus, Mississippi. (Public Affairs Office, Mississippi University for Women)

It's a Historical Policy

On rehearing, Mississippi pointed out that Section 950(a)(5) of Title IX of the Education Amendments of 1972 specifically provided that "in regard to admissions this section [refusing federal funding for any educational program that discriminates on the basis of sex] shall not apply to any public institution of undergraduate higher education which is an institution that traditionally and continually from its establishment has had a policy of admitting students of one sex."

Mississippi argued that when Congress passed this exception to Title IX, it removed such single-sex admission policies from the Fourteenth Amendment's reach. Congress could do this, Mississippi reasoned, because Section 5 of the Fourteenth Amendment gave it the undisputed power to "enforce, by appropriate legislation, the provisions of this [Fourteenth Amendment]." The Court of Appeals flatly rejected this argument, noting that "Section 5 of the Fourteenth Amendment does not grant Congress power to authorize states to maintain practices otherwise violative of the [Fourteenth] Amendment."

Stereotypes Are Out

Arguments took place before the Supreme Court on March 22, 1982. In her opinion for the Court, delivered July 1, 1982, Justice Sandra Day O'Connor pointed out that any statutory policy that discriminates on the basis of sex is subject to scrutiny under the Fourteenth Amendment, whether it discriminated against men or women. She stressed that the proper test of constitutionality in such a case was whether the discrimination was "substantially related to an important governmental interest" and that this test "must be applied free of fixed notions concerning the roles and abilities of males and females."

MUW had claimed that its female-only admissions policy "compensates for discrimination against women and, therefore, constitutes educational affirmative action." O'Connor acknowledged that the Court had in the past upheld certain policies that favored women. She gave as one example *Schlesinger v. Ballard* (1975), which upheld a federal statute giving female naval officers more time than men "to reach a particular rank before subjecting them to mandatory discharge." This, O'Connor stated, directly compensated women for the fact that their exclusion from combat duty gave them fewer promotion opportunities than men.

In contrast, she noted, Mississippi in this case favored women without "showing that women lacked opportunities to obtain training in the field of nursing or to attain positions of leadership in that field. . . ." Women had so dominated the field of nursing, O'Connor wrote, comprising more than 94 percent of its ranks for at least a decade, that

> rather than compensate for discriminatory barriers faced by women, MUW's policy of excluding males from admission to the School of Nursing tends to perpetuate the stereotyped view of nursing as an exclusively women's job. By assuring that Mississippi allots more openings . . . to women than it does to men, MUW's admissions policy . . . makes the assumption that nursing is a field for women a self-fulfilling prophecy.

Mississippi had also argued that the female nursing students were "adversely affected by the presence of men." This argument, O'Connor wrote, was thoroughly refuted by MUW's willingness to have men attend as non-credit earning auditors. Accordingly, the Court held "that MUW's policy of denying males the right to enroll for credit in its School of Nursing violates the Equal Protection Clause of the Fourteenth Amendment."

The only remaining argument to consider was Mississippi's contention that it was not subject to the Fourteenth Amendment, since Congress had passed Title IX with an exemption for historical single-sex admissions policies. O'Connor dismissed this as "requir[ing] little comment. Congress apparently intended, at most, to exempt MUW from the requirements of Title IX," she wrote. Even if Congress had intended to exempt MUW from the Fourteenth Amendment, O'Connor concluded, it had not the power to do so: "Neither Congress nor State can validate a law that denies the rights guaranteed by the Fourteenth Amendment."

The Court concluded that "the state's policy of excluding males from MUW's School of Nursing violates the Equal Protection Clause of the Fourteenth Amendment." It agreed with the Court of Appeals that the nursing college must admit Hogan. This decision heavily influenced the Court in its landmark decision in *United States v. Virginia* (see page 143), which forced the last two publicly funded male-only colleges in America to admit women.

For Further Reading

Goldstein, Leslie Friedman. *The Constitutional Rights of Women: Cases in Law and Social Change*, rev. ed. Madison: University of Wisconsin Press, 1989.

Hoff, Joan. *Law, Gender and Injustice: A Legal History of U.S. Women.* New York: New York University Press, 1991.

Ross, Susan Deller, Isabelle Katz Pinzler, Deborah A. Ellis, and Kary L. Moss. *The Rights of Women: The Basic ACLU Guide to Women's Rights*, 3d ed. Carbondale: Southern Illinois University Press, 1993.

Grove City College v. Bell: 1984

Petitioner: Grove City College   **Respondent:** Terrel H. Bell, Secretary of Education   **Petitioner's Claim:** That although some of their students received Basic Educational Opportunity Grants (BEOG) from the federal government, the college should not be subject to the provisions of Title IX of the Higher Education Act of 1972   **Chief Lawyer for Respondent:** Acting Solicitor General Paul M. Bator   **Chief Lawyer for Petitioner:** David M. Lascell   **Justices:** Harry A. Blackmun, William J. Brennan, Jr., Chief Justice Warren E. Burger, Thurgood Marshall, Sandra Day O'Connor, Lewis F. Powell, Jr., William H. Rehnquist, John Paul Stevens, and *Byron R. White*   **Place:** Washington, D.C.   **Date of Decision:** February 28, 1984   **Decision:** This decision required colleges to follow Title IX provisions of the Higher Education Act of 1972 if their students received federal tuition aid

SIGNIFICANCE

In this 1984 decision, the Supreme Court construed Title IX as prohibiting sex discrimination in only those specific educational programs that were federally funded, rather than throughout an entire educational institution. In the Civil Rights Restoration Act of 1988, Congress responded by specifically requiring the application of Title IX to *entire* institutions if *any part* of an institution or agency received federal-financial assistance.

In 1972, Congress passed Title IX of the Higher Education Act, banning sex discrimination in educational programs that received federal funds. Title IX addresses discrimination in athletics, admission to specific university classes and professional schools, and pregnant students' maternity leaves. Prior to this, for example, schools were legally able to expel pregnant students and to exclude females from athletic participation.

Grove City College v. Bell—and the steps Congress took following the Supreme Court's decision—defined just how broadly Title IX could be applied.

Grove City College Says No

In 1972, Congress directed federal agencies to verify that colleges and other education institutions that received federal aid were not discriminating under Title IX. One provision of Title IX also empowered federal agencies offering assistance to educational institutions to cut off aid "to the particular program, or part thereof, in which . . . noncompliance has been found."

The Department of Education made Basic Educational Opportunities Grants (BEOGs) available to students for use at the colleges of their choice. Since Grove City College enrolled students who used these grants to pay tuition, the Department of Education asked Grove City to sign an assurance of compliance stating that it would:

> . . . comply, to the extent applicable to it, with Title IX . . . to the end that . . . no person in the United States shall, on the basis of sex, be . . . subject to discrimination under any education program or activity for which [it] receives or benefits from Federal financial assistance from the Department.

Grove City refused to sign, saying that it accepted no *direct* federal assistance. However, the Department of Education claimed that federal aid awarded directly to Grove City's students *was* sufficient to subject the college to Title IX's requirements. When Grove City still would not comply, the department began proceedings to strip Grove City College and its students of BEOG eligibility.

Tuition Counts as Aid

An administrative law judge agreed that Grove City did receive federal assistance through the grants made to students and ordered that no further grants be made until the college "corrects its noncompliance with Title IX and satisfies the Department [of Education] that it is in compliance" with its nondiscrimination provisions.

The college and four students who found themselves ineligible for their BEOGs sued Terrel H. Bell, secretary of the Department of Education. In 1980, the District Court for the Western District of Pennsylvania agreed that the students' grants constituted federal financial assistance to their college within the meaning of Title IX. Nonetheless, it ruled "on several grounds," that the students could keep their grants although their college refused to sign an assurance of compliance.

In 1982, the Court of Appeals reversed this decision. Like the District Court, it held that "indirect as well as direct aid triggered coverage" under Title IX, and that a college enrolling students whose tuition was paid by means of BEOGs was a recipient of indirect federal aid. However, the Appeals Court disagreed with the District Court's conclusion that in terminating student grant eligibility, the department had exceeded its authority to compel compliance by ending federal assistance "to the particular program, or part thereof, in which . . . noncompliance had been found." The Court of Appeals' opinion, from which only one judge dissented, held that "where the federal government furnishes indirect or non-earmarked aid to an institution, it is apparent to us that the institution itself must be the 'program.'"

A Rose Is a Rose

The Supreme Court agreed to review the case, hearing arguments on November 29, 1983. Grove City College still claimed that tuition paid by means of student BEOGs—the only type of federal assistance the college had ever accepted—was federal assistance, but not sufficient to subject it to the provisions of Title IX. The Supreme Court, like both lower courts, rejected this argument.

Three months later, Justice Byron R. White delivered the opinion of the Court, affirming the Court of Appeals' decision on slightly different—but very significant—grounds.

As White noted, the BEOG program itself was established by the 1972 Higher Education Act of which Title IX was also a part. "It is not surprising," White reflected, that the language of Title IX "contains no hint that Congress perceived a substantive difference between direct institutional assistance and aid received by a school through its students." In short, whether the college received money from the government directly or indirectly from students using BEOGs, it was still money from the federal government and that was what Congress targeted.

Where the Trouble Arose

While "we have little trouble" concluding that Grove City College was bound to comply with the provisions of Title IX, White wrote, "there remains the question . . . of identifying the 'education program or activity' of the College that can properly be characterized as 'receiving' federal assistance through grants to some of the students attending the College."

Reviewing the legislative history, White conceded that there had been "isolated suggestions that the entire institutions are subject to the nondiscrimination provision whenever one of their programs receives federal assistance." Reading Title IX as it was actually passed, however, the Court said that it could not "accept the court of appeals' conclusion that in the circumstances here Grove City itself is a 'program or activity' that may be regulated in its entirety." The federal assistance, White wrote, was not to the entire college but "to the College's own financial aid program, and it is that program that may be properly regulated under Title IX." On this limited ground, the Court upheld the termination of BEOG eligibility.

As a result, federal funds could thereafter be withheld only from specific discriminating programs and not from an entire institution.

Congress Reacts

Many in Congress became enraged by the *Grove City* decision, which limited what had been intended as an extremely broad measure. With passage of the Civil Rights Restoration Act of 1988, Congress specifically broadened Title IX to prohibit discrimination throughout an *entire* institution or agency if any part of an institution or agency receives federal financial assistance.

For Further Reading

Cullen-DuPont, Kathryn. *The Encyclopedia of Women's History in America.* New York: Facts on File, 1996.

Frost-Knappman, Elizabeth. *The ABC-CLIO Companion of Women's Progress in America.* Santa Barbara, Calif.: ABC-CLIO, 1994.

Goldstein, Leslie Friedman. *The Constitutional Rights of Women,* rev. ed. Madison: University of Wisconsin, 1989.

Hoff, Joan. *Law, Gender and Injustice: A Legal History of U.S. Women.* New York: 1991.

Rix, Sara E. *The American Woman, 1990–91: A Status Report.* New York: W. W. Norton, 1990.

Sadker, Myra, and David Sadker. *Failing at Fairness: How America's Schools Cheat Girls.* New York: Charles Scribner's Sons, 1994.

Roberts v. United States Jaycees: 1984

Appellants: Kathryn R. Roberts, acting commissioner, Minnesota Department of Human Rights, et al. **Appellee:** United States Jaycees
Appellants' Claim: That Minnesota's Human Rights Act was constitutional and required the Jaycees to admit women as regular members
Chief Lawyer for Appellee: Carl D. Hall, Jr.
Chief Lawyer for Appellants: Richard L. Varco, Jr. **Justices:** *William J. Brennan, Jr.,* Thurgood Marshall, Sandra Day O'Connor, Lewis F. Powell, Jr., William H. Rehnquist, John Paul Stevens, and Byron R. White; neither Harry A. Blackmun nor Chief Justice Warren E. Burger participated
Place: Washington, D.C. **Date of Decision:** July 3, 1984
Decision: Minnesota's Human Rights Act was constitutional. Requiring the Jaycees to admit women as regular members in accordance with the act's provisions did not violate that organization's right to freedom of association

SIGNIFICANCE

This was the first in a series of Supreme Court decisions that opened many previously all-male organizations to women.

The United States Jaycees, originally known as the Junior Chamber of Commerce, is a nonprofit membership corporation founded in 1920. Its national headquarters are in Tulsa, Oklahoma. Its purpose is to "promote and foster the growth and development of young men's civic organizations in the United States. . . ." It also meant to encourage "genuine Americanism" and "to develop true friendship and understanding among young men of all nations."

At that time, regular membership was open only to males between the ages of eighteen and thirty-five. Men over the age limit and women could only become associate members. As such, they still paid dues—although somewhat less than regular members—but they could not vote, hold office, or take part in its awards or training programs.

Rebellion in the Ranks

Despite the rule against women, two chapters—one in Minneapolis (1974) and the other in St. Paul (1975)—admitted women to full membership. Women became a significant presence in both local chapters, even serving on their boards of directors. As a consequence, the national organization declared all members of those chapters ineligible to run for the organization's state or national offices, to receive its awards, or to have their votes counted at the Jaycees' national conventions. The chapters then learned that the national board would meet to consider a motion to revoke their charters.

Minneapolis and St. Paul Jaycees immediately filed discrimination complaints with the Minnesota Department of Human Rights, claiming that if they excluded women—as the national board was demanding—they would be infringing upon the state's Human Rights Act. The commissioner agreed and ordered a Human Rights Department hearing examiner to conduct an evidentiary hearing.

The Jaycees' national board fired back with a lawsuit against the commissioner and other state representatives in the U.S. District Court for the District of Minnesota. If the act were enforced, they claimed, male members would be deprived of their constitutional rights of free speech and association. The court dismissed the suit but left the national Jaycees room to sue again if the Human Rights Department examiner ruled against them.

Never Say Die

The department examiner did rule against the national board, classifying the Jaycees organization as a "place of public accommodation" within the meaning of Minnesota's Human Rights Act. Therefore, excluding women *was* an unfair discriminatory practice. The Jaycees renewed its suit before the District Court, which then referred the question to the Minnesota Supreme Court.

Having already ruled in 1981 that the state human rights act applied to any "public business facility," the state supreme court also determined that the Jaycees "(a) is a 'business' in that it sells goods and extends privileges in exchange for annual membership dues; (b) is a 'public' business based on its unselective criteria; and (c) is a public business 'facility' in that it conducts its activities in fixed and mobile sites within the state of Minnesota."

The national Jaycees then amended its district court complaint to add the charge that the act, as interpreted by the Minnesota Supreme Court, was unconstitutional and overly broad. The District Court upheld the act and the Jaycees appealed to the Court of Appeals for the Eighth Circuit.

That court reversed the lower court decision in 1983. The Jaycees' right to determine its membership *was* protected by the First Amendment freedom of association, since "political and public causes, selected by the membership," is a large part of the Jaycees reason for being. The Court of Appeals also held that the Minnesota act was "vague as construed and applied" and therefore in violation of the due process clause of the Fourteenth Amendment.

The Supreme Court Decides

Kathryn R. Roberts, the acting commissioner of the Minnesota Department of Human Rights, appealed to the U.S. Supreme Court. On April 18, 1984,

Richard L. Varco, Jr., argued that the act was not unconstitutionally broad or vague and that Minnesota *could* require the Jaycees to admit women. Carl D. Hall, Jr.—for the Jaycees—argued that the Fourteenth Amendment requires that laws be clearly written and that rights of free speech and association would be violated by a requirement to admit women.

Justice William J. Brennan, Jr., delivered the Court's opinion. He began by pointing out the differences between two aspects of the First Amendment's right of association: "freedom of intimate association" and "freedom of expressive association."

Associations protected by the right of intimate association, Brennan explained, would include family relationships and other associations "distinguished by such attributes as relative smallness, a high degree of selectivity in decisions to begin and maintain the affiliation, and seclusion from others in critical aspects of the relationship." Associations formed in the context of "a

Richard L. Varco, Jr., represented Kathryn R. Roberts in her 1984 trial. Varco presents his case before (l-r) Chief Justice Warren E. Burger and Justices Bryon R. White, Harry A. Blackmun, William H. Rehnquist, and Sandra Day O'Connor. (Richard L. Varco, Jr., assistant attorney general; Manager, Human Rights Division, State of Minnesota)

large business enterprise" did not involve such concerns. The Jaycees—as an organization with no other membership criteria than age and sex, and as an organization with a history of permitting the partial but routine association of women and others deemed ineligible for membership—was "clearly . . . outside of the category of relationships worthy of this kind of constitutional protection."

Turning to constitutional protection of the "freedom of expressive association," Brennan noted that "an individual's freedom to speak, worship, and to petition the government for the redress of grievances" included the "freedom to engage in group effort toward those ends. . . ." So, while the right to engage in such "protected activities" was "plainly implicated" in the case under consideration, Brennan pointed out that the "right to associate for expressive purposes is not . . . absolute. Infringements on that right may be justified by regulations adopted to serve compelling state interests. . . ." Minnesota had a compelling state interest in ending sex discrimination, Brennan concluded, and that interest justified the impact of its Human Rights Amendment on the Jaycees.

To further illustrate the compelling nature of the state's interest, Brennan discussed the nineteenth-century passage of public accommodation laws intended to end racial discrimination, and their expansion over time, "both with respect to the number and type of covered facilities and the groups against whom discrimination is forbidden." He referred to the Court's 1964 decision in *Heart of Atlanta Motel, Inc. v. United States,* which upheld the Civil Rights Act of 1964's prohibitions on racial discrimination in places of public accommodation. In that case, Brennan quoted, the Court recognized that the law's "fundamental object . . . was to vindicate 'the deprivation of personal dignity that surely accompanies denials of equal access to public establishments.' " The Court now recognized that such a "stigmatizing injury, and the denial of equal opportunities that accompanies it, is surely felt as strongly by persons suffering discrimination on the basis of their sex as by those treated differently because of their race." *Roberts v. United States Jaycees* was followed by two other Supreme Court decisions granting women access to previously all-male organizations or establishments: *Rotary International v. Rotary Club of Duarte* (1987) and *New York State Club Association, Inc. v. New York City* (1988).

For Further Reading

Goldstein, Leslie Friedman. *The Constitutional Rights of Women: Cases in Law and Social Change,* rev. ed. Madison: University of Wisconsin Press, 1989.

Hoff, Joan. *Law, Gender & Injustice: A Legal History of U.S. Women.* New York: New York University Press, 1991.

Lynn, Naomi B., ed. *Women, Politics and the Constitution.* New York: Harrington Park Press, 1990.

Mezey, Susan Gluck. *In Pursuit of Equality: Women, Public Policy, and the Federal Courts.* New York: St. Martin's Press, 1992.

Ross, Susan Deller, Isabelle Katz Pinzler, Deborah A. Ellis, and Kary L. Moss. *The Rights of Women: The Basic ACLU Guide to Women's Rights.* Carbondale: Southern Illinois University Press, 1993.

United States v. Virginia: 1996

Appellant: United States of America   **Appellees:** Commonwealth of Virginia, Governor Lawrence Douglas Wilder, and Virginia Military Institute, et al.
Appellant's Claim: That the male-only admissions policy of the state-supported Virginia Military Institute (V.M.I.) violated the Fourteenth Amendment
Chief Lawyer for Appellees: Theodore B. Olsen
Chief Lawyer for Appellant: Deputy Solicitor General Paul Bender
Justices: Stephen G. Breyer, *Ruth Bader Ginsburg,* Anthony M. Kennedy, Sandra Day O'Connor, Chief Justice William H. Rehnquist, David H. Souter, and John Paul Stevens, III (majority); Antonin Scalia (dissent); Clarence Thomas disqualified himself from the case because his son, Jamal, was a V.M.I. student   **Place:** Washington D.C.   **Date:** June 26, 1996
Decision: Excluding women from state-supported schools contravened the Fourteenth Amendment

SIGNIFICANCE

The last two state-supported all-male colleges were forced to admit women or forego state funding.

The U.S. Supreme Court has long grouped race, national origin, and religion as "inherently suspect" classifications for Fourteenth Amendment purposes—meaning that any legislation targeting these groups must pass a "strict scrutiny" test. This test determines if the proposed law serves a *compelling* state interest that cannot be served by any other means. Legislation discriminating on the basis of sex, however, had never been found inherently suspect by the Court.

In 1995, it seemed this might change. President Bill Clinton instructed his administration to file a brief asking the U.S. Supreme Court to use *U.S. v. Commonwealth of Virginia* "as a vehicle for declaring that government actions that discriminate on the basis of sex should be subject to the same strict constitutional scrutiny the Court applies to official distinctions on the basis of race."

Virginia governor L. Douglas Wilder had said that the refusal of the Virginia Military Institute (V.M.I.) to admit women offended his "personal philosophy." He added that "no person should be denied admittance to a state-supported school because of his or her gender." Since he agreed to abide by the court decision, he did not participate in the suit. The state attorney general, also agreeing to abide by the court's ruling, withdrew as well—leaving a *pro bono* counsel (an attorney who works on a case without fee) to seek a "stay of proceedings" on behalf of the college.

Sex Discrimination at V.M.I.

On March 1, 1990, the U.S. Department of Justice under President George Bush sued V.M.I. after a female high school student complained of the school's all-male admissions policy. In the two years prior to this complaint, approximately 300 young women had been rebuffed by the institute.

The United States contended that V.M.I.'s exclusion of women violated the equal protection clause of the Fourteenth Amendment and the precedent established in the 1982 *Mississippi University for Women v. Hogan* decision (see page 131). In that case, the Supreme Court ruled that men could not be excluded from Mississippi's state-supported nursing college.

During a six-day trial, the District Court examined the 150-year history of the institution, which was founded, in 1839, by the Virginia legislature to produce "citizen-soldiers, educated and honorable men who are suited for leadership in civilian life and who can provide military leadership when necessary." The court also looked at the "adversative" method used to produce these "citizen-soldiers." The training "emphasizes physical rigor, mental stress, absolute equality of treatment, absence of privacy, minute regulation of behavior, and indoctrination of values. . . . designed to foster in V.M.I. cadets doubts about previous beliefs and experiences and to instill in cadets new values . . . [in] a hostile, spartan environment. . . ."

In 1991, the District Court ruled that "diversity in education" was a legitimate state interest. Both V.M.I.'s male-only admissions policy and its "distinctive educational methods" were substantially related to this legitimate interest. Therefore, V.M.I.'s exclusion of women was upheld. The United States appealed.

Déjà Vu

Circuit Court judge Paul V. Niemeyer delivered the opinion of the Fourth Circuit Court of Appeals on October 5, 1992. He noted that in May 1864, during the Civil War, V.M.I. cadets bravely fought Union troops at New Market, Virginia. Now, he said, "the combatants have again confronted each other, but this time the venue is in this court." He pointed out that:

> the outcome of each confrontation finds resolution in the Equal Protection Clause. When the Civil War was over, to assure the abolition of slavery and the federal government's supervision over that policy, *all* states, north and south, yielded substantial sovereignty to the federal government in the ratification of the Fourteenth Amendment, and every state for the first time was expressly directed by federal authority not to deny any *person* within the

state's jurisdiction "equal protection of the laws." The [United States] government now relies on this clause to attack V.M.I.'s admissions policy.

A Catch 22

The court ruled that the exclusion of women from the type of education provided men at V.M.I. violated the equal protection clause, but it also found that single-gender enrollment formed the basis of "the unique characteristics of V.M.I.'s program." However, admitting women would so change V.M.I. that their admission would destroy the "unique characteristics" women sought. Therefore, Virginia's violation of the Fourteenth Amendment did not necessarily rest in its failure to admit women to V.M.I. Rather, the violation was its failure to provide women with an equal opportunity to develop the leadership and other skills developed by men at the school.

Niemeyer wrote that the court would "not order that women be admitted to V.M.I. if alternatives are available" but would instead send back the case to the District Court "to give to the commonwealth the responsibility to select a course it chooses, so long as the guarantees of the Fourteenth Amendment are satisfied."

Among the means of forcing V.M.I. to comply with the Fourteenth Amendment, Niemeyer suggested that Virginia "might properly decide to admit women to V.M.I. and adjust the program to implement that choice, or it might establish parallel institutions or parallel programs, or it might abandon state support of V.M.I., leaving V.M.I. the option to pursue its own policies as a private institution."

V.M.I. requested a hearing *en banc*, or by the full circuit court, which was denied. Virginia and V.M.I. subsequently established a state-funded military-style program for women at Mary Baldwin College, a private women's college in Staunton, Virginia. The program was approved by the federal court and began operation in the summer of 1995. The Clinton administration appealed the federal circuit court ruling to the Supreme Court, which agreed to hear the case.

A New Look to the Court

Ruth Bader Ginsburg, a recent appointee to the Supreme Court, shared the president's desire to establish a strict scrutiny standard for sex discrimination. As a civil rights lawyer in the 1970s, Ginsburg had helped to win the first women's rights case by using the Fourteenth Amendment, *Reed v. Reed* in 1971 (see page 112). In the 1973 case *Frontiero v. Richardson* (see page 308), she had come within one vote of persuading the Court to adopt the strict scrutiny standard in sex discrimination cases. She also had helped to win a case in 1976 establishing the alternate "mid-level or *heightened*" scrutiny standard adopted for sex discrimination cases in *Craig v. Boren* (see page 123).

On June 26, 1996, the Court ruled seven to one that V.M.I. must either forgo state funding or admit women. The opinion, written by Ginsburg, stopped short of establishing a strict scrutiny standard for sex discrimination. However, it thoroughly reviewed and perhaps strengthened the just-short-of-strict standard the court demanded. Ginsburg first repeated the Court's ruling in previous cases that sex discrimination must "serve important governmental objectives" and be "substantially related to the achievement of those objectives." Then she added some specifics:

> The justification must be genuine, not hypothesized or invented post hoc in response to litigation. And it must not rely on overboard generalizations about the different talents, capacities, or preferences of males and females. . . . "Inherent differences" between men and women, we have come to appreciate, remain cause for celebration, but not for denigration of the members of either sex or for artificial constraints on an individual's opportunity. Sex classifications may be used to compensate women "for particular economic disabilities (they have) suffered," to "promot(e) equal employment opportunity," and to advance full development of the talent and capacities of our nation's people. But such classifications may not be used, as they once were, to create or perpetuate the legal, social and economic inferiority of women.

Weighing the facts in this case "against the review standard just described," the Court agreed with the lower court that the all-male admission policy of the state-supported school violated the Fourteenth Amendment. The supposed state goal of offering educational diversity, Ginsburg said, was not served by a plan that provided "a unique educational benefit only to males." Such a plan, she continued, while "liberally" providing for "the State's sons . . . makes no provisions whatever for her daughters. That is not equal protection." She also brushed aside Virginia's argument that V.M.I.'s program would be "destroy(ed)" if women were admitted. This was reminiscent of the same "ancient and familiar fear" that had long kept women out of the legal and other professions, she said—and possibly just as misguided. "Women's successful entry into the Federal military academies," she wrote, "and their participation in the nation's military forces, indicate that Virginia's fears for the future of V.M.I. may not be solidly grounded."

Turning to the "parallel program" for females at the Mary Baldwin College, Ginsburg called it a "pale shadow" of V.M.I.'s illustrious and famed schooling. But "generalizations about the way women are, estimates of what is appropriate for most women, no longer justify denying opportunity to women whose talent and capacity place them outside the average description." She said V.M.I. was for the select few of *either* sex by pointing out that Virginia had never tried to claim the program "suited most men."

Ginsburg cited many precedent-setting cases during the reading of her opinion. Many of them, she had argued before the court as a pioneering feminist lawyer. One case in which she was not involved, 1982's *Mississippi University for Women v. Hogan* was the first to prompt a decision that a state could not fund sex-segregated schools. Sandra Day O'Connor, the only other female justice, wrote that decision in 1982. On the morning of June 26, 1996, Ginsburg cited *Hogan*, and than stopped speaking to look toward O'Connor. O'Connor smiled, just a little, and Ginsburg continued reading her opinion: "Women seeking and fit for a V.M.I. quality education cannot be offered anything less under the State's obligation to afford the genuinely equal protection."

Chief Justice William H. Rehnquist issued a concurring opinion. He said he might have been persuaded to let a truly equal parallel program suffice and that he thought the majority decision had needlessly introduced new legal terminology. Justice Antonin Scalia wholeheartedly dissented from the entire decision.

The decision has forced V.M.I. and the Citadel, the last two state-supported, all-male colleges in the country, to admit women or forego public funding. Two days after the ruling, Citadel officials said they would admit women. V.M.I. officials took a few weeks to submit to the inevitable. Four female cadets entered the Citadel in August 1996—under much calmer circumstances than did Shannon Faulkner one year earlier. Faulkner, embroiled in a legal fight and the only woman on campus, was ignored by some male students and taunted by others. She dropped out of the Citadel within a week, as did thirty male cadets.

For Further Reading

Elshtain, Jean Bethke. *Women and War.* New York: Basic Books, 1987.

New York Times, April 4 and 24, 1991; June 18 and 19, 1991; August 13, 1992; October 6 and 14, 1992; November 19, 1992; September 26, 1993; October 13, 1993; June 1, 1995; December 27, 1995; January 18, 1996; and June 27 and 28, 1996.

Sadker, Myra, and David Sadker. *Failing at Fairness: How America's Schools Cheat Girls.* New York: Charles Scribners Sons, 1994.

Smith, Bruce. "No Easy Ride Predicted as Women Enter Citadel." *Detroit News*, August 25, 1996.

Shannon Faulkner, the first female to attend day classes with cadets at the Citadel in Charleston, South Carolina. (AP/Wide World Photos)

Section 4
REPRODUCTIVE RIGHTS

According to common law in England and America, abortion prior to "quickening" (a pregnant woman's detection of fetal movement, usually experienced in the fourth or fifth month) was not illegal. This began to change in the nineteenth century, as anti-abortion laws were passed in the interest of protecting maternal health. In Massachusetts in 1812, before any such restrictive law existed, Isaiah Bangs was prosecuted for attempting to help Lucy Holman abort a fetus. Bangs was acquitted, but his arrest and prosecution indicate that abortion was becoming a crime.

The availability of contraception also diminished in the nineteenth century, after Congress passed the federal Comstock Act in 1873. That law classified contraceptive literature as obscene and made it a crime to mail contraceptive information through the U.S. Post Office. It also became a misdemeanor for any person to provide another with a contraceptive device, and illegal even to offer verbal contraceptive advice. In 1932, Dr. Hannah Stone was the recipient of "one package" of pessaries mailed from Japan. When customs officials confiscated the package, Stone filed suit. The 1936 decision in *U.S. v. One Package* made it legal for physicians to disseminate contraceptive information and devices, provided they were acting to protect the health of their patients. The following year, the American Medical Association urged medical schools to begin teaching contraceptive methods to their students.

Despite the *One Package* ruling, the use of contraceptives remained illegal in some states until well into the twentieth century. The last laws forbidding contraceptive use among married couples vanished in 1965, with the Supreme Court's ruling in *Griswold v. Connecticut*. Laws forbidding such use among single persons ended in 1972, with the Court's ruling in *Eisenstadt v. Baird*. *Griswold* and *Eisenstadt* rested on the Supreme Court's finding of a constitutional right to privacy inherent in the Ninth Amendment's guarantee that the people retained any rights not specifically granted to the government. And, as, Justice William J. Brennan, Jr., wrote in *Eisenstadt,* "If [privacy] means anything, it is the right of the individual, married or single, to be free from unwarranted governmental intrusion into matters so fundamentally affecting a person as the decision whether to bear or beget a child."

Meanwhile, in 1971, the Supreme Court had ruled for the first time on the constitutionality of anti-abortion laws. In language clearly intended to support physicians' discretion in the matter, the court upheld a District of Columbia law making abortion a crime unless it were performed by a licensed physician "for the preservation of the mother's life or health." Interestingly, the District Court had first invalidated the law, leaving Washington, D.C. with no abortion restrictions. Physicians and hospitals—now lacking any guidelines whatsoever regarding a previously criminalized procedure—stopped providing abortions. This brief experience with simple abortion-law repeal convinced activists that only direct legislation or a court decision upholding a woman's right to terminate a pregnancy would make abortions safe and truly legal.

Sarah Weddingtan and Linda Coffee argued what would be the landmark *Roe v. Wade*, with Norma McCorvey as the pseudonymous plaintiff Jane Roe. That 1973 decision abolished state laws restricting women's access to abortions during the first trimester of pregnancy and permitted second trimester restrictions only in the interest of protecting women's health. The Supreme Court has since upheld some fairly harsh restrictions. In *Harris v. McRae* (1980), for example, it upheld the elimination of federal funding for poor women's medically necessary abortions. In *Webster v. Reproductive Health Services* (1989), it upheld Missouri's ban on the use of public facilities, employees, or funds for any abortion-related purposes. However, the essential premise of Roe was upheld in *Planned Parenthood of Southeastern Pennsylvania v. Casey* (1992). In 1994, the Court also upheld an injunction against right-to-life protesters who had impaired the ability of a Florida clinic to provide services.

Supreme Court justice Harry A. Blackmun's decision in *Roe v. Wade* was based, in part, upon the fact that medical advances had made twentieth-century abortions much safer than their nineteenth-century counterparts. Other medical advances in the field of reproduction have raised new questions for ethical debate and legal decision. The 1987–88 "Baby M" case concerns the famous dispute between a "surrogate mother" and a contracting father. Points not emphasized by the media at the time of the trial are highlighted here; for example, the contract gave William Stern the right to determine whether or not Mary Beth Whitehead should undergo an abortion in the event amniocentesis testing revealed congenital or genetic abnormality. (To put this in perspective, the Supreme Court has overturned laws requiring married women simply to consult with their husbands over an abortion decision.)

Finally, it is a 1927 decision that may still define the limits of reproductive freedom. In *Buck v. Bell*, the Supreme Court upheld a state law by which the feebleminded and others "unfit to continue their kind" were forcibly sterilized. Carrie Buck, the young plaintiff, was demonstrably not feebleminded, but she was forcibly sterilized. This decision still stands. In fact, Justice Blackmun cited it in *Roe v. Wade*. There, Blackmun referred to it as he rejected some abortion-rights activists' claims that the privacy right was absolute. As *Buck v. Bell* makes clear, Blackmun wrote, the Court has never held that one is entirely free to do with one's body as one wishes.

Massachusetts v. Bangs: 1812

Defendant: Isaiah Bangs **Crimes Charged:** For the purpose of causing an abortion, committing assault and battery on Lucy Holman and administering a harmful drug to her **Chief Defense Lawyer:** Mr. Fay
Chief Prosecutor: The Solicitor-General **Justices:** Chief Justice Theophilus Parsons, Isaac Parker, and Samuel Sewall **Place:** Cambridge, Massachusetts **Date of Decision:** October term, 1812 **Decision:** That Bangs was not guilty

SIGNIFICANCE

Common law tradition permitted a woman to abort a fetus up until "quickening." This case shows how that began to change in the nineteenth century.

Common law in both England and America held that abortion became a moral issue only after the mother detected fetal movement, or "quickening," which occurs during the fourth or fifth month of pregnancy. In early America, abortions were neither forbidden nor prosecuted under common law. Women used herbal abortifacients and other methods to end their pregnancies, and midwives and doctors performed intrusive procedures.

However, during the nineteenth century, abortion became a crime. *Massachusetts v. Bangs* illustrates how judicial opinion began to change. During the October court term of 1810, Isaiah Bangs stood trial for the assault and battery of a pregnant woman, Lucy Holman, and for forcing her to swallow a drug causing abortion. The jury found Bangs guilty of assault and battery for the abortion, but not for forcing the woman to take the drug. The jury thought she had done this voluntarily.

Therefore, the solicitor-general had to withdraw the assault and battery charge. Bangs now appealed that the prosecutor's indictment (written accusations) did not describe a *criminal* offense.

Bangs' lawyer, Mr. Fay, claimed:

> No abortion was produced; and if there had been, there is no [proof] that the woman was quick with child; both [of] which circumstances are necessary ingredients in the offense intended to be charged in the indictment.

The solicitor-general disagreed, arguing that the woman's consent to take the drug did not make administering it lawful.

The court decided it could not punish Bangs:

> The assault and battery are out of the case, and no abortion is alleged to have followed the taking of the potion; and if an abortion had been alleged and proved to have ensued, the [proof] that the woman was quick with child at the time is a necessary part of the indictment.

In other words, for the indictment to be legal, it had to contain the allegations that Holman was pregnant with a "quickened baby" and that an abortion did take place. Although Bangs got off on a technicality, the severity of the charges showed that public attitudes were becoming more restrictive. During the nineteenth century, a few states began to declare abortion illegal after the fourth month of pregnancy—for example, Connecticut (1821), Missouri (1827), and Illinois (1827). In 1840, ten of the twenty-six states had placed restrictions on abortions. In 1965, the laws in all fifty states prohibited abortion, except in the event of life-threatening situations.

In some states, legislators modified these laws to make exceptions for rape, incest, or fetal deformity. In 1973, the battle to remove all restrictions on abortion resulted in the U.S. Supreme Court's landmark *Roe v. Wade* ruling (see page 177), invalidating all state laws that prohibited abortion during the first twelve weeks after conception.

For Further Reading

Costa, Marie. *Abortion*. Santa Barbara, Calif.: ABC-CLIO, 1991.

Garrow, David J. *Liberty and Sexuality: The Right to Privacy and the Making of Roe v. Wade*. New York: Macmillan/Lisa Drew Books, 1994.

Hoff, Joan. *Law, Gender, and Injustice: A Legal History of U.S. Women*. New York: New York University Press, 1991.

Hymowitz, Carol, and Michaele Weissman. *A History of Women in America*. New York: Bantam, 1978.

Kerber, Linda K. *Women's America: Refocusing the Past*. New York: Oxford University Press, 1991.

Salmon, Marylynn. *Women and the Law of Property in Early America*. Chapel Hill: University of North Carolina Press, 1986.

Wortman, Marlene Stein. *Women in American Law. Vol. I: From Colonial Times to the New Deal*. New York: Holmes & Meier Publishers, 1985.

Buck v. Bell: 1927

Appellant: Carrie Buck   **Appellee:** Dr. J. H. Bell   **Appellant's Claim:** That Carrie Buck's constitutional rights were violated by Virginia's eugenic sterilization law   **Chief Lawyers for Appellee:** Edmund Ackroyd; Aubrey E. Strode   **Chief Lawyer for Appellant:** Irving Whitehead   **Justices:** Louis D. Brandeis, Willis Van Devanter, *Oliver Wendell Holmes,* James C. McReynolds, Edward T. Sanford, Harlan F. Stone, George Sutherland, and Chief Justice William Howard Taft (majority); Pierce Butler (dissent)
Place: Washington, D.C.   **Date of Decision:** May 2, 1927
Decision: Upheld Virginia's compulsory sterilization of young women considered "unfit [to] continue their kind"

SIGNIFICANCE

Some fifty thousand Americans were involuntarily sterilized under Virginia's law and under similar laws in thirty states, still held legal under the Supreme Court's ruling.

Carrie Buck was one of three children born to Emma Buck, a widow who supported her family with the help of charity and prostitution. Following a brief interview with Charles D. Shackleford, a justice of the peace in Charlottesville, Virginia, Emma Buck was committed to the Virginia Colony for Epileptics and Feebleminded in Lynchburg, Virginia. The children were eventually taken from her.

Carrie Buck began living with the family of J. T. and Alice Dobbs when she was three years old. She attended school and progressed through five years without problems. The Dobbses then withdrew Carrie from school to take on additional housekeeping responsibilities.

The Dobbses liked Buck until she became pregnant at the age of 17. She said she had been raped by the Dobbses' son. Their reaction was to bring her before Shackleford with a request that she be found feebleminded and committed to the Virginia Colony along with her mother. The Dobbses, their family physician, and a second physician all testified that Buck was feebleminded. Shackleford signed the commitment order that very day, January 24, 1927. The Dobbses waited until she had given birth; they then institutionalized the teen and raised her daughter Vivian as their own.

In the Name of Humanity

Dr. Albert Priddy was the first superintendent of the Virginia Colony, and he had arrived at his own solution to society's "mental defectives." A proponent of eugenics—the controlled mating of men and women to "improve" humanity—he had sterilized seventy-five to one hundred young women without their consent, ostensibly to cure "pelvic disease." In 1924, the Virginia Assembly made such euphemisms unnecessary by adopting a bill that allowed the forced sterilization of "feebleminded" or "socially inadequate person[s]."

The State Epileptic Colony in Lynchburg, Virginia, circa 1930s, where Carrie Buck was institutionalized. (The Library of Virginia)

Aubrey Strode, who was both the chief administrator of the Virginia Colony and a state legislator, had prepared the bill to conform to a model sterilization act drafted by American eugenicist Harry H. Laughlin. In Laughlin's view, compulsory sterilization was "the practical application of those fundamental biological and social principles which determine the racial endowments and the racial health—physical, mental, and spiritual—of future generations."

Victimized Again and Again

Buck's unhappy fate was to be selected for sterilization under the new law. In a "you-scratch-my-back-I'll scratch-yours" package, Dr. Priddy arranged to have Strode's friend Irving Whitehead, a former board member of the Colony, represent Buck in her legal fight not to be sterilized—his fee to be paid by the Virginia Colony. Strode defended the Colony. *Buck v. Priddy*—which later became *Buck v. Bell* when Priddy died—was argued before Judge Bennett Gordon in the Circuit Court of Amherst County on November 19, 1924.

A district nurse who admitted not knowing "anything very definite about the children, except they don't seem to be able to do any more than their mother," was first on the stand. After disparaging Buck's mother for being unable—or unwilling—to support her children, she felt able to declare that they weren't mentally normal children, despite her admitted lack of direct knowledge about any of them. Upon Whitehead's cross examination, the nurse conceded that "I really know very little about Carrie after she left her mother [at age 3]. Before that time she was most too small."

Three teachers took the stand in turn to discuss the school work of Buck's brother, sister, and cousin, offering such testimony that one was "dull in her books." Others testified about her adult relatives, including one who was described as "right peculiar." Not until Caroline Wilhelm—a Red Cross social worker contacted by the Dobbs family during the young woman's pregnancy—did a witness return to the subject of Buck.

Strode asked Wilhelm if she thought Buck would produce "deficient offspring" if allowed to reproduce. She responded with unintended irony. "I think a girl of her mentality is more or less at the mercy of other people. . . . Her [widowed] mother had three illegitimate children, . . . Carrie would be very likely to have illegitimate children."

Therefore, Strode summarized, the only way to prevent Buck from "increasing her own kind" would be to segregate her or sterilize her. Asked to describe the child Buck had already had, Wilhelm added that Vivian "seems to me not quite a normal baby." (In fact, Vivian made normal progress in school and earned a place on the honor role in 1931. She died at the age of eight from measles.)

Arthur Estabrook of the Carnegie Institute of Washington took the stand and testified about his fourteen years of studies and genetic research involving "groups of mental defectives." He discussed *The Jukes in 1915*, his four-year study of one family (since discredited as fabrication), claiming that "certain definite laws of heredity were being shown by the family, in that the feeblemindedness was being inherited. . . ."

Dr. Priddy testified that sterilizing Buck "would remove one potential source of the incalculable number of descendants who would be feebleminded. [By not reproducing], [s]he would contribute to the raising of the general mental average and standard."

A sworn deposition from Laughlin, author of the model sterilization law, was read into the court record. Without ever having examined the woman, Laughlin apparently formed his opinions from a letter from Dr. Priddy. Buck, the deposition stated, has "a mental age of nine years, . . . a record during her life of immorality, prostitution, and untruthfulness; has never been self-sustaining; has one illegitimate child, now about six months old and supposed to be mentally defective. . . . She is . . . a potential parent of socially inadequate or defective offspring.''

Gordon upheld Virginia's compulsory sterilization law in February 1925 and ordered that Buck be sterilized. When the Virginia Court of Appeals upheld the circuit court decision, Whitehead appealed to the Supreme Court.

Carrie Buck Eagle and her husband, William Eagle. (Mrs. A. T. Newberry, Bland, Va.)

No Justice for Carrie Buck

Whitehead argued that the Fourteenth Amendment to the Constitution guaranteed protection of Buck's "full bodily integrity." He envisioned the "worst kind of tyranny" without "limits of the power of the state (which, in the end, is nothing more than the faction in control of the government) to rid itself of those citizens deemed undesirable." Strode equated compulsory sterilization with compulsory vaccination.

On May 2, 1927, Justice Oliver Wendell Holmes delivered the Supreme Court's nearly unanimous opinion:

> We have seen more than once that the public welfare may call upon the best citizens for their lives. It would be strange if it could not call upon those who already sap the strength of the state for their lesser sacrifices, . . . to prevent our being swamped with incompetence. It is better for all the world, if instead of waiting to execute offspring for crime, or to let them starve for their imbecility, society can prevent those who are manifestly unfit from continuing their kind. The principle that sustains compulsory vaccination is broad enough to cover cutting the Fallopian tubes.

The Evil Lives On

On October 19, 1927, Carrie Buck was sterilized by Dr. J. H. Bell. She was later paroled from the Virginia Colony. She was twice married: to William Davis Eagle in 1932 and, after his death, to Charlie Detamore. Her correspondence with the Virginia Colony in an effort to gain custody of her mother, the recollections of her neighbors, minister, in-laws, and health care providers, as well as the impression she made upon journalists later in her life, all indicate that she was of "obviously normal intelligence."

Thirty other states passed laws similar to the Virginia statute, and more than fifty thousand people—including Buck's sister, Doris—were forced to undergo involuntary sterilization.

When Nazi war criminals were tried after World War II for, among other things, the forcible sterilization of two million people, their attorneys used as an excuse Germany's Hereditary Health Law and the fact that the U.S. Supreme Court had declared such laws constitutional in *Buck v. Bell*. Shockingly, the decision stands to this day.

For Further Reading

Cushman, Robert E. *Cases in Constitutional Law.* 6th ed. Englewood Cliffs, N.J.: Prentice Hall, 1984.

Goldstein, Leslie Friedman. *The Constitutional Rights of Women: Cases in Law and Social Change.* 1979, rev. ed. Madison: University of Wisconsin Press, 1989.

Smith, J. David, and K. Ray Nelson. *The Sterilization of Carrie Buck: Was She Feebleminded or Society's Pawn?* Far Hill, N.J.: New Horizon Press, 1989.

United States v. One Package: 1936

Appellant: United States of America **Appellee:** Dr. Hannah M. Stone, claimant for "one package" (of merchandise) **Appellant's Claim:** That Stone did not have the legal right to import one package of contraceptive devices into the United States, according to the 1930 Tariff Act
Chief Lawyer for Appellee: Lamar Hardy
Chief Lawyer for Appellant: Morris L. Ernst **Justices:** *Augustus N. Hand,* Learned Hand, and Thomas Swan **Place:** New York, New York
Date of Decision: December 7, 1936 **Decision:** Laws prohibiting Americans from importing contraceptive devices or items causing "unlawful abortion" did not apply to physicians who used the items to protect the health of patients

SIGNIFICANCE

This decision allowed contraceptive devices to be imported into the United States, paving the way for the 1937 decision of the American Medical Association that birth control was a medical service that could be taught in schools of medicine.

A nti-obscenity laws became popular in the states after the Civil War. So censorious was public opinion that in 1869 Harriet Beecher Stowe endured widespread criticism for mentioning Lord Byron's incestuous activities with his sister in the *Atlantic Monthly*. In 1873, Congress passed the federal Comstock Act, which made criminal the mailing or advertising of "obscene" materials—including literature on birth control.

No Fun for Anyone

The act was named after Anthony Comstock (1844–1915) of New Canaan, Connecticut. Devotion to his mother—who died when he was ten—compelled him to "protect" women from smut, quack doctors, and other influences he thought harmful to them. In 1872, he joined a YMCA fight against pornographic literature. To persuade Congress to pass the federal obscenity act, Comstock displayed piles of pornography, along with contraceptives, and abortifacients (items that cause abortion), damning them all as *equally* immoral.

Comstock was a busy man. He founded the New York Society for the Suppression of Vice to arrest "criminal offenders," a term that included writers, poets, painters (those who used nude models), abortionists, and advertisers of birth control devices. He prodded government agents to harass druggists and physicians who sold or distributed birth control devices. As special investigator for the post office in New York City, in 1905, he instituted legal proceedings against George Bernard Shaw's play *Mrs. Warren's Profession*. Shaw retaliated by calling his opponent's puritanical endeavors "Comstockery."

Comstock's Nemesis

"Comstockery" resulted in the jailing of Margaret Sanger (1883–1966) at least nine times for campaigning for the right of women to use birth control. Born Margaret Higgins on September 14, 1879, in Corning, New York, the future reformer was one of eleven children. She attributed her mother's early death at about age fifty to her frequent pregnancies.

After the death of her mother, the young teacher turned to medicine, enrolling in White Plains Hospital—a drafty twelve-bed building with no plumbing or central heating—where she completed two years of nurse's training. She became head nurse in the woman's ward, and in 1912, married William Sanger in a quick ceremony—reporting for her 4:30 A.M. shift the next day.

With fifty dollars, Sanger and her sister Ethel Byrne opened the first birth control clinic in America on October 16, 1916—an act of civil disobedience. The clinic occupied two rooms at 46 Amboy Street in the Brownsville section of Brooklyn, New York. In the ten days before police closed the clinic, almost five hundred women arrived to get information about birth control and contraceptive devices. Sanger was arrested and sentenced to thirty days in prison. Her appeal to the New York Court of Appeals resulted in a 1918 ruling that allowed doctors to advise their married patients about birth control for health reasons (see page 30).

Five years after she opened her clinic, Sanger founded the American Birth Control League, which lobbied politicians to make contraception legal. The group urged Congress to exempt doctors from laws that banned the prescription and mailing of contraceptive devices.

To achieve that end, Sanger asked the staff of her American Birth Control League to find proof that the Comstock Act did impede the distribution of birth control materials. They found it in the 1930 amendment to the Tariff Act. This law used original 1873 Comstock Act language prohibiting "the importation into the United States, from any foreign country, any article whatever for preventing conception, or induced abortion."

In 1932, at Sanger's request, a Japanese doctor sent her a package of contraceptive supplies. Customs officers stopped the package. Sanger asked the physician to mail the package again, this time addressing it to her part-time employee, Dr. Hannah M. Stone, a qualified, licensed gynecologist. At the arrival of the package of 120 rubber pessaries (devices placed in the vagina to treat a prolapsed uterus or block conception), agents again confiscated it, ordering Dr. Stone to return it. Sanger, the American Birth Control League, Dr. Stone, the National Committee on Maternal Health, and lawyer Morris Ernst immediately went to court, claiming the supplies were medical exemptions under the law. Using Dr. Stone as the claimant, they filed the case in the U.S. District Court for the Southern District in New York City on November 10, 1933.

Dr. Hannah M. Stone.
(Francis A. Countway
Library of Medicine,
Boston, Mass.)

A Public Sea Change

It took two years before the case came to trial. During this time, contraception was so popular that the government's regulatory agents could not stop birth control items from being bought and sold. Druggists and doctors dispensed them with impunity and even the Sears, Roebuck catalog advertised them as "preventives." In 1935, the *American Medicine* journal noted that mailing contraceptive devices was "as firmly established as the postage stamp."

Polls at this time showed that seventy percent of the American public wanted birth control made legal. One poll, commissioned by *Ladies' Home Journal,* found that seventy-nine percent of readers—fifty-one percent of them Catholic—favored loosening the laws.

Influenced by this change in attitude, the District Court agreed to hear *U.S. v. One Package* in 1935. Dr. Stone testified that she had imported the pessaries for experimental purposes, to test them for reliability in preventing contraception and disease. She said she also prescribed them to women who should not bear children. The United States of America sought a decision directing the forfeiture and destruction of "one package" of pessaries. On January 6, 1936, Judge Grover Moscowitz ruled that the Tariff Act did *not* extend to the prevention of contraceptives intended for medical use.

However, the government appealed, and Ernst, relying on donations to cover his fees, defended his client before a three-judge panel of the Second Circuit Court of Appeals in New York. At the trial, a number of doctors spoke on Dr. Stone's behalf. Even a government witness agreed with them, saying that from a medical standpoint, sometimes it was vital to *prescribe* a contraceptive for some patients to prevent or cure disease.

The judges reached their decision on December 7, 1936. They believed all aspects of the Comstock Act were part of a consistent effort to suppress immoral articles and obscene literature. As for the Tariff Act itself, Section 305(a) had coupled the word "unlawful" with the word "abortion," though *not* with the word "contraception," making the importation of contraceptive items legal. The court also decided contraceptives were necessary for the lawful purposes Dr. Stone had described and allowed them to enter the United States.

Fallout

In 1937, the American Medical Association (AMA) finally reversed its long-held refusal to study contraception and began to support state and federal reforms. As Sanger biographer Ellen Chesler has written, the AMA regarded birth control "as a responsible element of normal sexual hygiene in married life. To this end, it recommended that the subject be taught in medical schools, that scientific investigation of various commercial materials and methods be promoted, and finally that the legal rights of physicians in relation to the use of contraceptives be clarified."

Although the birth control movement claimed victory in *U.S. v. One Package*, not until 1971 would Congress rewrite the Comstock law to remove the specific mention of birth control material. The use of contraceptive devices—even for married couples—remained illegal in many states until 1965, when the Supreme Court overturned the laws with *Griswold v. Connecticut* (see page 162). In 1972, the Court made the use of contraceptive items lawful nationwide for single people as well in *Eisenstadt v. Baird* (see page 172).

For Further Reading

Chesler, Ellen. *Woman of Valor: Margaret Sanger and the Birth Control Movement in America.* New York: Doubleday/Anchor Books, 1992.

Garrow, David J. *Liberty and Sexuality: The Right to Privacy and the Making of Roe v. Wade.* New York: Macmillan Publishing Group, 1994.

Sicherman, Barbara, and Carol Hurd Green. *Notable American Women: The Modern Period.* Cambridge, Mass.: The Belknap Press, 1980.

Griswold v. Connecticut: 1965

Appellants: Estelle T. Griswold and Charles Lee Buxton   **Appellee:** State of
Connecticut   **Appellants' Claim:** That Connecticut's birth control laws
violated its citizens' constitutional rights
Chief Lawyer for Appellee: Joseph B. Clark
Chief Lawyer for Appellants: Thomas I. Emerson   **Justices:** William J.
Brennan, Jr., Tom C. Clark, *William O. Douglas,* Arthur J. Goldberg, John M.
Harlan, Chief Justice Earl Warren, and Byron R. White (majority); Hugo L.
Black and Potter Stewart (dissent)   **Place:** Washington, D.C.
Date of Decision: June 7, 1965   **Decision:** Reversed Griswold's and
Buxton's lower court convictions for providing contraceptive information to
married couples and struck down all state laws prohibiting the use of
contraceptives by married couples

SIGNIFICANCE

This decision set forth a constitutional "right to privacy," which would later be
interpreted as protecting the right of unmarried persons and minors to use
contraceptives, in 1972 with *Eisenstadt v. Baird;* and in 1977 with *Carey v.
Population Services;* the right of women to terminate their pregnancies, in 1973
with *Roe v. Wade;* and the right of families to decide whether or not to terminate
medical treatment, in 1975 with the New Jersey Supreme Court's *In the Matter of
Karen Ann Quinlan.*

In 1879, the Connecticut state legislature passed anticontraceptive legislation
that remained in effect well into the twentieth century:

> Any person who uses any drug, medicinal article or instrument for the
> purpose of preventing conception shall be fined not less than fifty dollars or
> imprisoned not less than sixty days nor more than one year or be both fined
> and imprisoned. . . .

> Any person who assists, abets, counsels, hires or commands another to
> commit any offense may be prosecuted and punished as if he were the
> principal offender.

The U.S. Supreme Court first reviewed the law in 1942, in a lawsuit
brought by the Planned Parenthood League of Connecticut and a physician.
The Court ruled that the physician lacked standing to sue.

Almost twenty years later, when several women brought a suit, the Supreme Court declined to rule, characterizing the law as "dead words" and "harmless empty shadows." Dr. Charles Lee Buxton, chairman of Yale University's obstetrics department, interpreted the Court's action as permitting: "... all doctors in Connecticut ... [to] prescribe child spacing techniques to married women when it is medically indicated." With Estelle T. Griswold, executive director of the Planned Parenthood League of Connecticut, he opened a birth-control clinic in New Haven on November 1, 1961.

Dead Words Come Back to Life

Nine days later, police arrested Buxton and Griswold and closed their clinic. They appeared before Judge J. Robert Lacey of the Sixth Circuit Court on December 9, 1961. Their attorney, Catherine G. Roraback, argued that the 1879 law had breached her clients' constitutional right to freedom of speech.

The six-hour trial began and ended on January 2, 1962. Prosecutor Julius Martez called two police detectives. They testified that when they visited the clinic, they observed a half-dozen women in the waiting room. Griswold acknowledged it was a birth-control clinic and had even offered them contraceptive information and devices. Dr. Buxton testified that he considered "this type of advice" a crucial aspect of women's health.

Martez argued that Buxton and Griswold had broken the law and insisted that the Connecticut legislature—and not the court—should address citizens' objections to the law.

Estelle T. Griswold speaks with Dr. Charles Lee Buxton, Yale professor of Obstetrics and Gynecology. (Planned Parenthood of Connecticut)

Lacey rejected Roraback's free speech argument. He characterized the birth control statute as "absolute," and pointed out that the Connecticut Supreme Court of Errors has upheld it on three prior occasions. The law was, he declared, "constitutional exercise of the police powers of the State of Connecticut." Buxton and Griswold were found guilty and fined one hundred dollars apiece.

Roraback and Harriet Pilpel filed an appeal with the Appellate Division of the Sixth Connecticut Circuit Court on January 12, 1962. The case was heard by a three-judge panel, and a year later, the convictions were upheld. The judges noted, however, that the case raised issues "of great public importance," and they certified it for review by the State Supreme Court of Errors.

Associate Justice John Comley of the Court of Errors issued that court's opinion: ". . . [c]ourts may not interfere with the exercise by a state of the police power to conserve the public safety and welfare, including health and morals." Griswold's and Buxton's convictions were upheld. The next stop: the Supreme Court.

A "Morality" Issue

On March 29, 1964, the Supreme Court heard oral arguments. Griswold and Buxton's attorney, Thomas I. Emerson, argued that Connecticut's anticontraceptive law violated freedom of speech. He also claimed that his clients and their patients had been denied their right to liberty, which, under the Fourteenth Amendment, could not be abridged without "due process of law."

Finally, he argued that the Ninth Amendment protected privacy as one of the rights "retained by the people." He pointed out that Connecticut's declaration that it was "immoral to use contraceptives even within the married relationship" constituted a "moral judgment" not in "conform[ity] to current community standards."

The justices questioned Emerson and Connecticut's attorney, Joseph B. Clark, about sales of contraceptives "under-the-counter" in Connecticut. Clark compared it to illegal bookmaking on horse races, while Emerson explained that contraceptives were sold as "feminine hygiene" merchandise.

Clark was also questioned about whether it would be legal to prescribe contraceptives as a means of preventing disease. This, Clark responded, was a "ludicrous argument," since married persons could be presumed to be free of sexually transmitted diseases. As the *New York Times* reported, "Connecticut requires applicants for marriage licenses to take venereal disease tests, and . . . Connecticut also has laws against fornication and adultery. Thus, [Clark] indicated, there would be no reason to believe that any such disease would spread."

Justices Potter Stewart and Arthur J. Goldberg questioned Clark about the state's motives in passing and retaining the birth control statutes. When Clark explained, "to reduce the chance of immorality [and] [t]o act as a deterrent to sexual intercourse outside marriage," Stewart noted "the trouble with that argument is that on this record it [the clinic] involves only married women."

Questioned further by Goldberg about the state's desire to prohibit sexual intercourse outside of marriage, Clark insisted that anticontraceptive laws made it "easier to control the problem." Besides, Clark claimed, the state had the right to provide for its own "continuity."

A Right to Privacy

On June 7, 1965, the Supreme Court ruled, seven to two, that Connecticut's law violated a constitutional "right to privacy." Justice William O. Douglas, in the majority opinion, wrote that "the specific guarantees in the Bill of Rights have penumbras, formed by emanations from those guarantees that help give them life and substance. . . . Various guarantees create zones of privacy." He cited the Constitution's First, Third, Fourth, Fifth, Ninth, and Fourteenth Amendments.

The Ninth Amendment had previously been interpreted as reserving to the *state* governments any rights not specifically granted by the Constitution to the *federal* government. Interpreting it literally, that such rights were retained by *the people*, Douglas wrote that Connecticut's law could not be enforced without a violation of privacy, which could be assumed to be a right "retained by the people."

Douglas asked, "Would we allow the police to search the sacred precincts of the marital bedrooms for telltale signs of the use of contraceptives?" Such a possibility, he found, was "repulsive to the notions of privacy surrounding the marriage relationship." He concluded, "We deal with a right of privacy older than the Bill of Rights—older than our political parties, older than our school system. Marriage is a coming together for better or for worse, hopefully enduring, and intimate to the degree of being sacred. . . . [I]t is an association for as noble a purpose as any involved in our prior decisions." Only Justices Stewart and Hugo L. Black dissented.

For Further Reading

Carey, Eve, and Kathleen Willert Peratis. *Woman and the Law*. Skokie, Ill.: National Textbook Co. in conjunction with the American Civil Liberties Union, 1977.

Countryman, Vern, ed. *The Douglas Opinions*. New York: Random House, 1977.

Cushman, Robert F. *Cases in Constitutional Law*, 6th ed. Englewood Cliffs, N.J.: Prentice Hall, 1984.

Davis, Flora. *Moving the Mountain: The Women's Movement in America Since 1960*. New York: Simon & Schuster, 1991.

Faux, Marian. *Roe v. Wade*. New York: Macmillan, 1988.

Garrow, David J. *Liberty & Sexuality: The Right to Privacy and the Making of Roe v. Wade*. New York: Macmillan, 1994.

Goldstein, Leslie Friedman. *The Constitutional Rights of Women*, rev. ed. Madison: University of Wisconsin Press, 1989.

Guitton, Stephanie, and Peter Irons, eds. *May It Please the Court: Arguments on Abortion* (live recordings and transcripts). New York: The New Press, 1995.

New York Times. October 27, 1961; November 3, 4, 11, 13, and 25, 1961; December 2 and 9, 1961; January 3 and 13, 1962; October 20, 1962; January 18, 1963; May 17 and 19, 1963; May 12, 1964; December 9, 1964; March 30 and 31, 1965; and June 8, 9, 10, 13, and 15, 1965.

United States v. Vuitch: 1971

Appellant: United States   **Appellee:** Dr. Milan Vuitch
Appellant's Claim: That the governing standard of the District of Columbia's anti-abortion law, which states the mother's ''life'' and ''health'' must be at risk in order for an abortion to be performed, is not unconstitutionally vague
Chief Lawyers for Appellee: Joseph L. Nellis and Norman Dorsen
Chief Lawyer for Appellant: Samuel Huntington   **Justices:** *Hugo L. Black,* Harry A. Blackmun, Chief Justice Warren E. Burger, John Marshall Harlan, and Byron R. White (majority); Potter Stewart and William O. Douglas (dissent); William J. Brennan, Jr. and Thurgood Marshall (abstained)
Place: Washington, D.C.   **Date of Decision:** April 21, 1971   **Decision:** The Supreme Court reversed the judgment of the district court

SIGNIFICANCE

Vuitch was the first decision to rule on the constitutionality of anti-abortion laws. In its aftermath, abortion rights advocates realized that the mere absence of anti-abortion laws was insufficient protection for women. Women would need legislation or court decisions to win their right to end a pregnancy.

In 1971, two years before the historic *Roe v. Wade* (see page 177) legalized a woman's right to end her pregnancy, a U.S. District Court heard the case of Dr. Milan Vuitch. Vuitch was a physician charged with the crime of inducing a medical abortion in violation of the District of Columbia Code. This law, unchanged since 1901, made abortion a crime unless ''done . . . for the preservation of the mother's life or health'' and under the direction of a licensed physician. The statute was typical of anti-abortion laws in many states.

Vuitch had been a Serbian youth who had studied medicine in Hungary before immigrating to the United States in the mid-1950s. In 1962, shortly after receiving his medical license, Vuitch started performing abortions in Washington D.C., Maryland, and Virginia. At a time when abortion was illegal in most states, Vuitch was one of few physicians willing to risk his profession and liberty by taking on referrals from the budding abortion rights movement. By 1964, he was performing abortions on a full-time basis, eventually ten to twenty each week.

Over the next five years, police tried repeatedly to shut down Vuitch's practice, arresting him more than twelve times. However, except for one conviction in Montgomery County, Maryland, on appeal in 1971, courts found Vuitch innocent.

On April 21, 1971, Washington, D.C. charged the fifty-four-year-old physician for violating the District of Columbia Code. In a momentous breakthrough for abortion rights advocates, Federal District Judge Gerhard A. Gesell declared the law unconstitutionally vague, and dismissed the indictments against Vuitch without waiting for a trial. Gesell stated that under this law, "a physician would not know if he was committing a crime when he performed an abortion, because a jury might later disagree with his opinion that the mother's health required it. [Thus] the doctors' problem was particularly acute because the burden was on them to prove that the abortion was justified."

This decision left the district court without any law on abortion. The public hospital on which most of the district's poor residents relied, D.C. General, soon stopped performing abortions. Private hospitals also curtailed them. The National Abortion Rights Action League (NARAL), in conjunction with the American Civil Liberties Union (ACLU), sued D.C. General Hospital twice, obtaining two court orders that forced the hospital to perform more abortions.

In this atmosphere, the Justice Department appealed to the U.S. Supreme Court. Attorneys argued that Vuitch had "performed abortions for any woman who desired one, without considering [if] the woman's health [was in jeopardy]."

Is the Abortion Law Constitutional?

Gesell had found the D.C. abortion law vague for two reasons. First, once an abortion took place, the physician "is presumed guilty and remains so unless a jury can be persuaded that his acts were necessary for the preservation of the woman's life and health." Second, the judge felt disturbed by the "ambivalent and uncertain word 'health.'"

The trial court had examined *Williams v. United States* (1943) to determine that the D.C. law placed the burden of proof on the defendant once prosecutors had proved an abortion had taken place. In that case, the Court of Appeals for the D.C. Circuit Court had held that the prosecution did not have to prove abortion was unnecessary to preserve life or health to win.

However, Justice Hugo L. Black—on behalf of Supreme Court majority—stated that "whether or not this is a correct reading of *Williams* . . . it is an erroneous interpretation of the statute." The D.C. law had "expressly authorized" physicians to perform abortions to preserve a woman's life or health. It did not presume the guilt of a doctor for performing the operation.

The Court also agreed that the word "health" carried an "uncertain" and "ambivalent" meaning, which failed to inform a "defendant of the charge against him and therefore . . . offends the Due Process Clause of the Constitution." Gesell had felt the term vague because it did not account for "varying degrees of mental as well as physical health."

The Supreme Court looked to *Doe v. General Hospital of the District of Columbia* (1970) for guidance. There Judge Joseph Waddy had permitted abortions "for mental health reasons whether or not the patient had a previous history of mental defects." Therefore, the Court found "no reason why this interpretation of the statute should not be followed." Black continued: "Webster's Dictionary . . . defines health as the 'state of being . . . sound in body [or] mind.' Viewed in this light, the term 'health' presents no problem of vagueness."

The majority decided "the District of Columbia abortion law is not unconstitutionally vague," and "the trial court erred in dismissing the indictment on that ground."

Although Black reversed Gesell's decision, he said that the District law should give "physicians considerable latitude [within the law's restrictions] to perform legal abortions." He added that in future abortion trials, the government must prove that the mother's health was *not* endangered.

Opinion of the Minority

While agreeing with the Court's opinion regarding jurisdiction over the appeal, Justice William O. Douglas felt that the D.C. abortion law did not meet the requirements of procedural due process. He insisted that a physician's judgment to determine the necessity of a woman's abortion was "highly subjective [and] dependent on the training and insight of the particular physician." He then raised a question regarding the standard of the D.C. anti-abortion law. "Is the statutory standard so easy to manipulate that although physicians can make good-faith decisions based on the standard, juries can nonetheless make felons out of them?" To further his point, Douglas quoted from *Roe v. Wade*, then making its way through the Texas courts: A court "evaluating the statutory standard" dealing with abortion laws in Texas, was convinced that the law was unconstitutionally vague:

> How *likely* must death be? Must death be certain if the abortion is not performed? Is it enough that the woman could not undergo birth without an ascertainably higher possibility of death than would normally be the case? What if the woman threatened suicide if the abortion was not performed? . . . Is it sufficient if having the child will shorten the life of the woman by a number of years?

Douglas reminded the Court that "abortion statutes [are] heavily weighted with religious teachings and ethical concepts. . . ." This encouraged prejudice in the jury. He felt "the drafting of [new] abortion laws [should] protect good-faith medical practitioners from the treacheries of the present law."

The California Doctor

Douglas also mentioned *People v. Leon P. Belous* (1969). This case involved California physician Belous, who had practiced medicine for thirty-five years and had performed abortions during many of those years. A California court convicted Belous in 1967 for violating the state's anti-abortion law (before the passage of a new reform law). The court found him guilty of having accepted a kickback from another doctor to whom he had referred a pregnant student.

Belous appealed to the three-judge panel of the Second District Court of Appeals, but the panel affirmed the lower court's ruling, believing the physician had indeed accepted kickbacks. Belous then hired civil rights attorneys A. L. Wirin and Fred Okrand to appeal his case to the California Supreme Court. California abortion rights activists quickly rallied around him, believing his case would prove to the state's high court that anti-abortion laws were unconstitutional. The attorneys believed that the principles of 1965's *Griswold v. Connecticut* (see page 162) should protect a woman's privacy and personal autonomy in childbearing. They also felt that states could not interfere with a doctor-patient relationship when it came to the termination of a pregnancy.

Oral arguments took place on March 4, 1969, before the seven-judge California Supreme Court. On September 5, the Court handed down its much anticipated decision. By four to three, Raymond A. Peter's majority overturned the conviction of Belous because California's pre-1967 anti-abortion law was too vague to be unconstitutional.

Dr. Milan Vuitch some years after the 1971 U.S. Supreme Court case that bears his name. (Mrs. Milan Vuitch)

The old law had allowed women to end their pregnancies in only one instance: when necessary to preserve a woman's life. The words "necessary" and "preserve" were unconstitutionally vague. The court explained: "A showing of immediacy or certainty of death is not essential for a lawful abortion."

The California court's majority also ruled that "The fundamental right of women to choose whether to bear children follows from the Supreme Court's and this court's repeated acknowledgment of a 'right to privacy' or 'liberty' in matters related to marriage, family, and sex." The court listed *Griswold v. Connecticut* among other precedents for its decision.

As an ironic footnote, in the District of Columbia, the Supreme Court's overturning of *U.S. v. Vuitch* in 1971 and upholding of the original law restricting abortion yielded greater access to abortion than ever before. As Vuitch emphasized, "This is a big step forward. Now the government lawyer will be in the position of challenging my medical decision. What are the jury members going to decide when a lawyer tries to tell them that the doctor is wrong about a medical matter? What the Supreme Court did," he pointed out, "was throw the whole mess on the shoulders of American physicians; and that is the correct position."

For Further Reading

"Ambivalence on Abortion." *Time*, May 3, 1971.

Davis, Flora. *Moving the Mountain: The Women's Movement in America Since 1960*. New York: Simon and Schuster/Touchstone, 1992.

Garrow, David J. *Liberty and Sexuality: The Right to Privacy and the Making of Roe v. Wade*. New York: Macmillan, 1994.

Graham, Fred, P. "High Court Upholds D.C. Abortion Law." *New York Times*, April 22, 1971.

MacKenzie, John P., and Stuart Auerback. "D.C. Abortion Law Upheld by Supreme Court, 5 to 2." *The Washington Post*, April 22, 1971.

U.S. Supreme Court Reports, 2nd Edition. Rochester, N.Y.: Lawyers Cooperative Publishing, 1971.

Eisenstadt v. Baird: 1972

Appellant: Thomas Eisenstadt, sheriff of Suffolk County, Massachusetts
Appellee: William R. Baird, Jr.   **Appellant's Claim:** That the lower courts
erred in overturning Baird's conviction on charges of distributing
contraceptives without a medical license and to unmarried people
Chief Lawyers for Appellee: Joseph Balliro before the lower courts; Joseph
D. Tydings before the Supreme Court   **Chief Lawyer for Appellant:** Joseph
R. Nolan   **Justices:** Harry A. Blackmun, *William J. Brennan, Jr.,* William O.
Douglas, Thurgood Marshall, Potter Stewart, and Byron R. White (majority);
Chief Justice Warren E. Burger (dissent); (Lewis F. Powell, Jr., and William H.
Rehnquist joined the Court too late in 1972 to participate)
Place: Washington, D.C.   **Date of Decision:** March 22, 1972
Decision: Upheld lower court reversals of Baird's conviction and invalidated
state laws restricting the use of contraceptives to married people

SIGNIFICANCE

In addition to making contraceptives legally available to unmarried people
throughout the United States, the decision described the constitutional right of
privacy in language that foreshadowed the Court's 1973 finding that the right to
privacy protected a woman's right to have an abortion.

Although the Supreme Court struck down state laws prohibiting the use of
contraceptives by married couples in 1965's *Griswold v. Connecticut* (see page
162), furnishing contraceptives to unmarried people in many states continued to
be illegal. Massachusetts prohibited the distribution of contraceptives to anyone
without a medical prescription and to unmarried people under *any* circumstances. Violation was punishable by up to five years imprisonment.

In the spring of 1967, birth control activist William R. Baird, Jr., accepted
an invitation from Boston University students to lecture and "distribute free lists
of abortionists and birth control devices to interested coeds." Prior to Baird's
visit, the *B.U. News* published an article in which Baird, a former medical student
who had once worked for a pharmaceutical company, explained that he had
become a birth control and abortion rights activist after witnessing the death of a
young mother of eight who had been admitted to an emergency room after an
illegal abortion. Saying that more than ten thousand women had died from

illegal abortions in 1966, he condemned laws making contraceptives available only to married women under a doctor's care and declared that he would "test this law in Massachusetts. . . . No group, no law, no individual can dictate to a woman what goes on in her own body."

When Baird took the stage in an auditorium at Boston University on April 6, there were 1,500 to 2,000 people in the audience—and three vice squad officers in the wings. *B.U. News* editor Raymond Mungo introduced Baird, saying, "We are here to test the legal aspects of the birth control and abortion laws in the state of Massachusetts."

When Baird announced his intention to distribute contraceptive foam and a list of places outside the United States where one might secure an abortion, he addressed the vice squad directly, reminding them to "do your duty." Telling the students that "the only way we can change the law is to get the case into a court of law," he urged them to approach and to take the offered information and contraceptive foam. He was arrested as soon as he started handing out the materials.

Among the Lower Courts

Baird stood trial before Massachusetts Superior Court Judge Donald B. Macaulay in October 1967. Represented by attorney Joseph J. Balliro, who took the case without charge, Baird waived his right to a jury trial.

Assistant District Attorney Joseph R. Nolan called police lieutenant Joseph Jordan to the stand. Jordan, who had arrested Baird at Boston University, described Baird's speech and his actions. Balliro argued that the Massachusetts law was unconstitutional. Macaulay found Baird guilty of violating the law, but postponed Baird's sentencing until an appeal was heard.

The Massachusetts Supreme Judicial Court heard the case in November 1968. Nolan characterized Baird's actions at Boston University as "an invitation to promiscuity and sexual license," and he defended the commonwealth's objective of "preventing the distribution of articles designed to prevent conception which may have undesirable, if not dangerous, physical consequences."

In April 1969, the court overturned Baird's conviction for displaying contraceptives, on the basis that this had been part of a speech protected by the First Amendment. However, it affirmed Baird's criminal conviction for distributing the contraceptive foam on the basis that Baird was not a physician, nurse, or pharmacist legally entitled to engage in such conduct in Massachusetts. Returning to the Suffolk County Superior Court, Baird was sentenced to three months. Macaulay agreed to postpone Baird's imprisonment pending an appeal to the Supreme Court, but, to the surprise of many, the Court would not hear Baird's appeal.

Balliro filed a *habeas corpus* petition in federal district court to test the constitutionality of the state's criminal conviction. When U.S. District Judge Anthony J. Julian had not ruled by February 20, Baird went to the Charles Street jail in Boston and surrendered to Suffolk County sheriff Thomas Eisenstadt.

Birth control rights advocate Bill Baird gives a speech at Boston University, September 13, 1967. He challenged the Massachusetts "Crimes against Chastity" law in 1972 by passing out contraceptive foam to several unmarried female students at the school. (Boston University Photo Services)

Julian heard oral arguments at the end of the month and in March 1970, denied the *habeas corpus* petition. The denial entitled Baird to appeal to the First Circuit Court of Appeals. This court ordered that Baird be set free until his appeal could be heard. On July 6, the court ruled that the Massachusetts birth control law was unconstitutional and reversed Baird's remaining conviction.

At the Supreme Court

Eisenstadt appealed to the Supreme Court. This time, the Court announced that it would hear the appeal. Oral arguments were presented on November 19 and 20, 1971, before seven justices. Nolan, arguing for Massachusetts, emphasized Baird's lack of a medical license and claimed that "there are some very dangerous side lights and side effects to the use of many contraceptives."

Nolan dismissed any possible comparison to *Griswold*, which had been decided on the basis of a married couple's "right to privacy," since this case involved a very public display of contraceptives. Joseph Tydings, a former U.S. senator from Maryland, who had replaced Balliro as Baird's attorney, said that the Massachusetts law was "inherently unconstitutional because there is no compelling state reason for it."

On March 22, 1972, the Supreme Court agreed and affirmed the judgment of the First Circuit Court of Appeals. The majority opinion, written by Justice William J. Brennan, Jr., further defined the Ninth Amendment right of privacy first enunciated in *Griswold:*

> If under *Griswold* the distribution of contraceptives to married persons cannot be prohibited, a ban on distribution to unmarried persons would be equally impermissible. It is true that in *Griswold* the right of privacy in question inhered in the marital relationship. Yet the marital couple is not an independent entity with a mind and heart of its own, but an association of two individuals each with a separate intellectual and emotional make-up. If the right of privacy means anything, it is the right of the *individual,* married or single, to be free from unwarranted governmental intrusion into matters so fundamentally affecting a person as the decision whether to bear or beget a child.

In 1973, the right to privacy was found by the Supreme Court to protect a woman's right to terminate her pregnancy, in *Roe v. Wade* (see page 177). Four years later, the Supreme Court, citing *Eisenstadt,* ruled that states could not prohibit the distribution of contraceptives to unmarried minors *(Carey v. Population Services International,* 1977).

For Further Reading

Carey, Eve, and Kathleen Willert Peratis. *Woman and the Law.* Skokie, Ill.: National Textbook Co. in conjunction with the American Civil Liberties Union, 1977.

Faux, Marian. *Roe v. Wade.* New York: Macmillan, 1988.

Garrow, David J. *Liberty & Sexuality: The Right to Privacy and the Making of Roe v. Wade.* New York: Macmillan, 1994.

Goldstein, Leslie Friedman. *The Constitutional Rights of Women,* rev. ed. Madison: University of Wisconsin Press, 1989.

New York Times, December 3, 1968; May 20, 1969; June 2, 1969; July 12, 1970; September 21, 1971; and March 23 and 25, 1972.

Roe v. Wade: 1973

Plaintiff: Norma McCorvey, using "Jane Roe" as an alias, and representing all pregnant women in a class-action suit   **Defendant:** Dallas County, Texas, district attorney Henry B. Wade   **Plaintiff's Claim:** That the Texas abortion law violated the constitutional rights of McCorvey and other women
Chief Lawyers for Defendant: John Tolle, Jay Floyd, and Robert Flowers
Chief Lawyers for Plaintiff: Sarah Weddington and Linda Coffee   **Justices:** *Harry Blackmun,* William J. Brennan, Chief Justice Warren Burger, William O. Douglas, Thurgood Marshall, Lewis Powell, Potter Stewart (majority); William Rehnquist and Byron White (dissent)   **Place:** Washington, D.C.
Date of Decision: January 22, 1973   **Decision:** Invalidated all state laws restricting women's access to abortions during the first trimester (three months) of pregnancy and upheld only those second-trimester (three to six month) restrictions that protected the health of pregnant women

SIGNIFICANCE
This landmark decision made abortion legal in the United States.

Norma McCorvey became pregnant in the summer of 1969. The twenty-one-year-old woman's marriage had failed, and her mother and stepfather were raising her five-year-old daughter. McCorvey did not want to continue her pregnancy. Since Texas law prohibited abortion except to save a woman's life, McCorvey began to look for someone willing to perform one illegally.

Although she was not successful in that search, she did meet Sarah Weddington and Linda Coffee, two attorneys interested in changing the abortion laws. McCorvey agreed to become plaintiff "Jane Roe" in a test case. (Years after the trial, McCorvey came forward under her own name.)

A Constitutional Issue

They faced two difficulties. First, Texas had passed its abortion law in 1859. Like similar laws in other states, it did not target the women who needed abortions, but those who performed them. Therefore, McCorvey might not have "standing to sue." Second, if McCorvey gave birth, or passed the point in her pregnancy where an abortion could be safely performed, the case could become moot (irrelevant). Nonetheless, Coffee wrote a three-page complaint naming Dallas County district attorney Henry B. Wade as the defendant; she filed it at the Dallas federal courthouse on March 3, 1970. Coffee asked the court to declare the law unconstitutional (declaratory relief) and order Texas to stop enforcing it (injunctive relief).

The Right to Privacy

The Ninth Amendment states that "the enumeration in the Constitution, of certain rights, shall not be construed to deny or disparage others retained by the people." Before its decision in the 1965 case *Griswold v. Connecticut* (see page 162), the Supreme Court had interpreted this clause as reserving for the *states* any rights not specifically granted to the federal government by the Constitution. In the majority opinion for *Griswold*, Justice William O. Douglas had articulated another, more literal, view of the Ninth Amendment. He said that rights not explicitly granted to the government by the Constitution were retained by *the people*, and this included a right to privacy. On this basis, the *Griswold* decision invalidated all state laws banning contraceptive use among married couples. Coffee and Weddington would argue that the right to privacy also protected a woman's right to choose whether to bear a child.

The chief judge of the Fifth Circuit federal court, John R. Brown, appointed a panel of three judges to hear *Roe v. Wade:* Irving S. Goldberg, William McLaughlin Taylor, and Sarah Tigham Hughes (formerly Coffee's clerk).

Assistant District Attorney John Tolle, assigned to defend District Attorney Wade's right to enforce the Texas abortion law, submitted his first response to the case on March 23. It was a two-page claim that "Jane Roe" lacked standing to sue, since "the statutes complained of operate only against persons who performed an abortion, not against pregnant women upon whom abortions are performed." A formal hearing before the three-judge panel nonetheless took place on Friday, May 22, 1970, at 2:00 P.M.

Tolle also filed a request to speak with "Jane Roe." McCorvey did not come forward, but on the day before the scheduled hearing, her attorneys filed an anonymous affidavit for her. In it, she stated that she wished to remain anonymous since "the notoriety occasioned by the lawsuit would make it impossible for me to secure any employment in the near future and would severely limit my advancement in any employment which I might secure at some later date." She continued, "I consider the decision of whether to bear a child a highly personal one and feel that the notoriety occasioned by the lawsuit would result in a gross invasion of my personal privacy." McCorvey wrote that she had "wanted to terminate my pregnancy because of the economic hardship which my pregnancy entailed and because of the social stigma attached to the bearing of illegitimate children in our society." Since she could not afford to travel to another state for a legal abortion, she said: "I fear that my very life would be endangered if I submitted to an abortion which I could afford."

Here Come the Judges

By May 22, 1970, Weddington and Coffee had amended the case to a class-action suit so that "Jane Roe" would represent not just McCorvey but all pregnant women. Dr. James Hallford, a Texas attorney who had been charged with performing illegal abortions, had also joined the suit as an "intervenor." Hallford's attorneys, Roy Merrill and Fred Bruner, prepared to defend him on Fourteenth Amendment grounds.

On the defense side, Robert Flowers and Jay Floyd, the respective head and assistant chief of the enforcement division of Texas' attorney general's office, represented the state. Texas had prepared its case based on the argument that the unborn had legal rights and that the state must protect them.

When Goldberg called the hearing to order, Tolle explained for all the attorneys present that there was no testimony to present, since there were no disputes as to the facts in the case. The court gave the plaintiffs one half-hour in which to argue for a "summary judgment" (a ruling on the facts without further discussion). The defense had one half-hour in which to argue for dismissal.

Coffee addressed the procedural points of the plaintiffs' case, including "Roe's" standing to sue. She also had to establish that the case did, indeed, involve a constitutional issue requiring the three-judge court's consideration. The freedoms guaranteed by the First, Ninth, and Fourteenth Amendments led her to conclude: "I think the [abortion] statute is so bad that the court is just really going to have to strike it all down. I don't think it's worth salvaging."

Weddington, addressing the court on the heart of the case (called substantive issues), rebutted the argument presented by state attorneys in their pre-trial briefs. The "justification which the state alleges for the state abortion statute," she said, ". . . is the protection of the life of the child. . . . I would like to draw the court's attention to the fact that life is an ongoing process. It is almost impossible to define a point at which life begins or perhaps even at which life ends."

When Weddington had outlined the right-to-privacy argument, Goldberg asked whether she thought the state had *any* compelling interest that would entitle it to regulate abortions. Weddington responded that the state might require that only qualified physicians perform the procedure. Pressed by Goldberg to evaluate what impact a woman's stage of pregnancy might have on the state's interest, Weddington allowed that "the state of pregnancy gives me some pause. . . . You could recognize life when the fetus is able to live outside the body of the mother."

Goldberg's last question was whether Weddington found "this statute . . . more vulnerable on Ninth Amendment grounds or on [the Fourteenth Amendment grounds of] vagueness."

Weddington responded without hesitation. "I believe it is more vulnerable on the Ninth Amendment basis."

Attorney Bruner, for Dr. Hallford, defended his client on Fourteenth Amendment grounds.

Opening the arguments for the state, Floyd said that since "Roe" must certainly be toward the end of her pregnancy and past the point where the court's decision could affect her, she now lacked standing to sue. Goldberg and Hughes said they found otherwise, and Floyd began to dispute Coffee's First Amendment argument. "I cannot perceive . . . how it would fall under religion, speech or press of the First Amendment," he said. Hughes interrupted, "We agree with you on that," and Goldberg added, "go to the Ninth Amendment and about vagueness." When Floyd began to discuss the Fourteenth Amendment, Goldberg again cut him off, saying, "Skip it."

"Jane Roe" attorney Sarah Weddington, with Texas congressman George Mahon, on December 13, 1971, the day the Supreme Court listened to oral arguments presented in the *Roe v. Wade* trial. (Sarah Weddington)

Turning to the state's goal of protecting fetal life, Floyd then said, "There have been many, many, arguments as to when an embryo becomes a human being. There have been many religious groups that have joined in the controversy, and I'm not setting forth the Catholic faith. . . . But the point is, that the state's interest is [in] whether or not murder occurs, that is, if the embryo is considered a human being."

During an exchange concerning privacy, Goldberg offered his view that "I think its a bad word in this area, but apparently everyone wants to use it. . . . I haven't come up with a phrase myself yet, but I just know 'privacy' won't do."

Tolle followed Floyd, reiterating the claim that "the state has got a right to protect life that is being [i.e., exists] at whatever stage it may be. . . ." He said that any possible change in the relevant law was a matter for state legislatures and not the courts. As to the application of the Ninth Amendment, he claimed that "the right of that child to life is superior to that woman's right to privacy."

The judges found otherwise. In their unanimous opinion issued June 17, 1970, they wrote: "The Texas abortion laws must be declared unconstitutional because they deprive single women and married couples, of their right, secured by the Ninth Amendment, to choose whether to have children."

To the Heights

Because the fifth circuit court issued *declarative relief*, a finding that the law was unconstitutional, without also issuing *injunctive relief*, an order to stop enforcement of the law, the plaintiffs could appeal the case directly to the Supreme Court. The Court scheduled the trial for December 13, 1971.

Forty-two *amici curiae*, or "friend of the court," briefs were filed on behalf of "Roe." They represented organizations as diverse as the American College of Gynecologists and Obstetricians, the New York Academy of Medicine, Planned Parenthood, and the California chapter of the National Organization for Women. A "woman's brief" argued, as author Marian Faux summarizes it, "that even if a fetus were found to be a legal person, a woman still could not be compelled to nurture it in her body against her will." Prominent women such as theologian Mary Daly, Barnard College president Millicent McIntosh, anthropologist Margaret Mead, and former U.S. senator Maurine B. Neuberger (D-Oregon), all signed it.

On December 13, 1971, Weddington argued before the Supreme Court that a woman's right to make childbearing decisions free of government compulsion was fundamental to her right to control her own life. Asking the Court to reject the state's claim that the fetus was entitled to governmental protection, she said, "The Constitution, as I read it . . . attaches protection to the person at the time of birth [not conception]. Those persons *born* [not conceived] are citizens."

Floyd, speaking for the defense, said that "Roe" must certainly have concluded her pregnancy and lost her standing to sue. Asked how the law could ever be challenged by any one of the affected pregnant women, Floyd replied: "There are situations in which . . . no remedy is provided. Now, I think she makes her choice prior to the time she becomes pregnant. That is the time of the choice. . . . Once a child is born, a woman has no choice; and I think pregnancy makes her make that choice as well."

The Court asked Floyd why no states had ever prosecuted the women who obtained abortions if, indeed, abortion was murder. It also asked him to clarify why prosecutors did not charge doctors who performed illegal abortions with premeditated murder, but with the lesser charge of "ordinary felony murder." Finally, the Court asked when life, in the view of the state of Texas, actually began. After several faltering responses, Floyd could only say, "I don't—Mr. Justice—there are unanswerable questions in this field."

Waiting for a Full Court

There were only seven sitting justices when the Supreme Court heard *Roe v. Wade*. Rather than issue an opinion, the justices scheduled the case for re-argument in October 1972, when two justices, Lewis Powell and William Rehnquist, would join the court. Just before the October hearing, the Supreme Court had decided *Eisenstadt v. Baird* (see page 172). As a result, unmarried persons could now use birth control. The Court also further defined the scope of the Ninth Amendment. In the majority opinion, Justice William J. Brennan wrote:

> If the right of privacy means anything, it is the right of the *individual,* married or single, to be free from unwarranted governmental intrusion into matters so fundamentally affecting a person as the decision whether to bear or beget a child.

When lawyers for *Roe v. Wade* went before the nine justices on October 10, 1972, the plaintiffs made all of their earlier points, emphasizing the Ninth Amendment's right to privacy. The state continued to maintain that it had a compelling interest in preserving fetal life.

The Right to Choice

On January 22, 1973, the Supreme Court ruled. Reading from his majority opinion, Justice Harry Blackmun reviewed the history of abortion legislation in the United States, saying "The restrictive criminal abortion laws in effect in a majority of states today . . . are not of ancient or even of common law origin." Rather, he said, it seemed that legislators had designed these laws to protect women from a procedure that was, in the nineteenth century, a risk to their health. That objective was no longer valid, said Blackmun, since abortions were now as safe as or safer than childbirth for women.

Blackmun then turned to a discussion of the "right to personal privacy," before coming to the central point of his decision:

> The right of privacy, whether it be founded in the Fourteenth Amendment's concept of personal liberty and restrictions on state action . . . or . . . in the Ninth Amendment's reservation of rights to the people, is broad enough to encompass a woman's decision to terminate her pregnancy.

Discussing Texas' claim that it had the right to infringe on Roe's rights "to protect prenatal life," Blackmun examined the U.S. Constitution to see if the Founding Fathers had intended to include prenatal life when they used the word "person" in the document. He concluded that nowhere in the document had he found "any possible pre-natal application." He declared, "The word 'person' as used in the Fourteenth Amendment, does not include the unborn."

Addressing "the difficult question of when life begins," Blackmun said, "When those trained in the respective disciplines of medicine, philosophy, and theology are unable to arrive at any consensus, the judiciary . . . is not in a position to speculate as to the answer." He then discussed the wide divergence of thinking on "this most sensitive and difficult question." Blackmun pointed out that "the view that life does not begin until live birth . . . appears to be the predominant, though not the unanimous attitude of the Jewish faith . . . [and] also the position of a large segment of the Protestant community, . . ." while the Roman Catholic Church "would recognize the existence of life from the moment of conception . . . a view strongly held by many non-Catholics as well." Blackmun summarized the impact of these competing views upon the Court's decision by summarizing, "In view of all this, we do not agree that, by adopting one theory of life, Texas may override the rights of the pregnant woman that are at stake."

Continuing, Blackmun cautioned that neither a fetus' ineligibility for state protection nor a woman's right to privacy was absolute:

> The State does have an important and legitimate interest in preserving and protecting the health of the pregnant woman . . . and . . . it has still *another*

important and legitimate interest in protecting the potentiality of human life. These interests are separate and distinct. Each grows in substantiality as the woman approaches term and, at a point during the pregnancy, each becomes "compelling."

Finally, Blackmun outlined a formula to balance these competing interests. During the first trimester of pregnancy, the "abortion decision . . . must be left to the medical judgment of the pregnant woman's attending physician." During the second trimester, a state could "regulate the abortion procedure in ways that are reasonably related to maternal health." During "the stage subsequent to viability, the State . . . may . . . regulate, and even proscribe, abortion except where it is necessary, in appropriate medical judgment, for the preservation of the life or health of the mother."

Doe v. Bolton

The Supreme Court issued another decision in an abortion case, *Doe v. Bolton*, on the same day. It concerned an impoverished Georgia wife and mother of three children. A former mental hospital patient, she had already surrendered one of her children for adoption and had placed the other two in foster care. When she became pregnant again, on doctors' advice, she decided to seek an abortion. When she could not obtain one, she, like Norma McCorvey, became a plaintiff against her state.

Brennan also delivered the majority opinion for *Doe v. Bolton*. Mentioning *Roe v. Wade*, he addressed Georgia's regulations concerning "medically necessary" abortions. In that decision, the Court found the state's "procedural requirements" unconstitutional. These included Georgia's requirement that abortions be performed only in hospitals accredited by the Joint Commission on the Accreditation of Hospitals; the requirement that an abortion be approved by a hospital abortion committee and that two independent physicians confirm the committee's judgment; and that only residents of Georgia might obtain abortions within the state's borders.

Blackmun, at the conclusion of *Doe v. Bolton*, said that the two abortion opinions issued on January 22, 1973, "are to be read together."

While Supreme Court decisions since 1973—including *Harris v. McRae* in 1980 (see page 185) and *Webster v. Reproductive Health Services* in 1989 (see page 197)—have reduced federal spending for abortions, thereby limiting free services for poor women and minors, the basic premise of *Roe v. Wade* was emphatically upheld in 1992, in *Planned Parenthood of Southeastern Pennsylvania v. Casey* (see page 202).

For Further Reading

Cary, Eve, and Kathleen Willert Peratis. *Woman and the Law*. Skokie, Ill.: National Textbook Co. in conjunction with the American Civil Liberties Union, New York, 1977.

Cushman, Robert F. *Cases in Constitutional Law*, 6th ed. Englewood, N.J.: Prentice Hall, 1984.

Davis, Flora. *Moving the Mountain: The Women's Movement in America Since 1960*. New York: Simon & Schuster, 1991.

Ehrenreich, Barbara, and Deidre English. *For Her Own Good: 150 Years of the Experts' Advice to Women*. New York: Doubleday, 1979.

Faux, Marion. *Roe v. Wade*. New York: Macmillan Co., 1988.

Garrow, David J. *Liberty & Sexuality: The Right to Privacy and the Making of Roe v. Wade*. New York: Macmillan, 1994.

Goldstein, Leslie Friedman. *The Constitutional Rights of Women*, rev. ed. Madison: University of Wisconsin Press, 1989.

Guitton, Stephanie, and Peter Irons, eds. *May It Please the Court: Arguments on Abortion* (live recordings and transcripts). New York: The New Press, 1995.

Petchesky, Rosalind Pollack. *Abortion and Woman's Choice*. Boston: Northeastern University Press, 1984, rev. 1990.

Harris v. McRae: 1980

Appellants: Patricia R. Harris, secretary of Health and Human Services, joined by Senators James L. Buckley and Jesse A. Helms, and Representative Henry J. Hyde as ''intervenor-defendants'' **Appellees:** Cora McRae, on behalf of herself and all New York state women similarly situated, and the New York City Health and Hospitals Corp. **Appellants' Claim:** That the Hyde Amendment was constitutional, and that states did not have to pay the costs of indigent women's abortions, even those found medically necessary

Chief Lawyer for Appellees: Rhonda Copelon

Chief Lawyer for Appellants: Solicitor General Wade H. McCree, Jr.

Justices: Chief Justice Warren E. Burger, Lewis F. Powell, Jr., William H. Rehnquist, *Potter Stewart,* and Byron R. White (majority); Harry A. Blackmun, William J. Brennan, Jr., Thurgood Marshall, and John Paul Stevens (dissent)

Place: Washington, D.C. **Date of Decision:** June 30, 1980

Decision: Under the Hyde Amendment, states participating in the Medicaid program could not receive federal reimbursements for even medically necessary abortions and did not have to pay for them

SIGNIFICANCE

This ruling meant that the federal government would not subsidize abortions for poor women—even when a medical necessity.

Following its 1973 decision to make abortion legal in *Roe v. Wade* (see page 177), the Supreme Court ruled on a number of state attempts to limit women's access to (or state support for) abortions. In careful "pick and choose" decisions, the Court found some restrictions—forbidding saline abortions, requiring doctors to try to preserve the life of aborted fetuses, and prior written consent of husbands or minors' parents—unconstitutional.

Others—prohibiting the abortion of a "viable" fetus, certain record-keeping regulations on abortion providers, and requiring pregnant women to furnish written consent prior to an abortion—*were* constitutional. Finally, in 1980, the Court ruled on the constitutionality of an even more severe measure: the federal Hyde Amendment, which withheld Medicaid funding even in cases of medically necessary abortions.

The Hyde Amendment

In 1965, Congress created the Medicaid program for the poor and sick by adding Title XIX to the Social Security Act. Eleven years later, Congress passed the first of yearly Hyde Amendments to Medicaid—imposing varying degrees of financial restrictions on abortions. In 1980, it required that *no* money would be provided for abortions unless the mother's health was endangered by a term pregnancy. Victims of rape or incest—if they reported promptly—could also receive the federally-sponsored medical procedures.

The same day that the first Hyde Amendment was enacted, Cora McRae, a pregnant Medicaid recipient seeking an abortion, filed a legal challenge to the amendment in the District Court for the Eastern District of New York. (Like Norma McCorvey, the plaintiff in *Roe v. Wade,* McRae delivered her child before the suit reached its conclusion.) She claimed that "the Hyde Amendment violated the First, Fourth, Fifth, and Ninth Amendments of the Constitution insofar as it limited the funding of abortions to those necessary to save the life of the mother, while permitting the funding of costs associated with childbirth."

The following day, District Judge John F. Dooling, Jr., issued a preliminary injunction. His decision, issued three weeks later, fully agreed with McRae. The case was also certified as a class action suit on behalf of all Medicaid-eligible New York state women who were pregnant or potentially pregnant and who would seek abortions during the first twenty-four weeks of gestation.

Health and Human Services secretary Patricia R. Harris immediately appealed to the Supreme Court. Having just upheld the withdrawal of funding for "unnecessary" abortions in *Beal v. Doe* (1977) and *Maher v. Roe* (1977), the Court vacated the injunction against Hyde Amendment enforcement and sent McRae's case back to Dooling for reevaluation against these recent decisions.

Back at the District Court

Before reconsidering the merits of the case, Dooling gave permission for a number of additional plaintiffs to intervene. In their amended complaint, the plaintiffs asserted that any state participating in the Medicaid program must provide the means for medically necessary abortions, whether or not they would be reimbursed by the federal government. The plaintiffs also challenged the constitutionality of the Hyde Amendment, claiming that it violated both the religion clause of the First Amendment (because its views reflected those of the Catholic Church) and the Fifth Amendment. (The Courts have interpreted the Fifth Amendment as containing implied due process and equal protection clauses. Thus, the federal government must grant equal protection to its citizens in the same manner as the Fourteenth Amendment requires states to grant equal protection to *their* citizens.)

Dooling—although dissolving his earlier injunction—held a trial on the merits of McRae's claims. He released a 214-page ruling finding that Title XIX *would* have required states to make medically necessary abortions available to poor women—but that the Hyde Amendment, *if constitutional*, would remove that responsibility.

Was the Hyde Amendment constitutional? The judge found that the federal government had not violated the First Amendment's prohibition against a state-sponsored religion. However, the amendment *did* violate the free exercise of speech clause of the First Amendment by prohibiting an affected woman from seeking a medically necessary abortion in accordance with "her religious beliefs under certain Protestant and Jewish tenants."

Finding that the amendment also violated the due process clause of the Fifth Amendment, Dooling ruled that the amendment was invalid in all its versions. He ordered Harris to "authorize the expenditure of federal matching funds" for medically necessary abortions.

Returning to the Supreme Court

Attorney Wade H. McCree, Jr., appealed Dooling's ruling to the Supreme Court. He shifted attention from maternal health to fetal preservation, stating "that the Hyde Amendment is rationally related to the legitimate governmental interests in preserving potential human life and encouraging childbirth."

One of the justices asked him, "Would you make the same rational basis argument . . . if it was her death rather than adverse impact on her health that was involved?"

McCree answered, "I think I would say that you would make the rational relation. . . . It doesn't prevent this woman from obtaining an abortion; it just denies her federal funding. . . ."

The Court pressed, "Don't we have to assume for proposes of analysis at least that some women will be denied abortions if they don't receive federal funding?"

McCree agreed: "Oh, I think we have to. I don't think there is any question about that."

The Court responded: "We therefore must also assume that some of these women will suffer serious medical harm."

That was not Congress's concern, McCree implied: "We must assume that . . . just because *Roe* said that the state could not punish a person . . . for obtaining an abortion . . . that still did not obligate the state or the federal government to reimburse her. . . ."

Did the Hyde Amendment violate the First Amendment? McCree had "difficulty" with the idea that to "refuse funding for them would somehow deny their First Amendment right to freedom of religion and free exercise of religion." To the contrary, he argued "the Free Exercise Clause prevents interference [with religion] . . . but doesn't obligate the state to finance it." He pointed out that the state is not required to give a citizen religious objects—"for example, a Bible or any religious artifacts"—so that the religion may be "freely" practiced.

A Matter of Survival

McRae's attorney, Rhonda Copelon, passionately pled for poor women affected by the amendment:

> This case . . . involves the survival and the health of potentially millions of poor women . . . and it involves reaffirmation of the simple rule of law . . . this Court recognized in *Roe v. Wade.* . . . This case arises in the context of a Medicaid program designed to provide a broad range of medically necessary and essential services for poor people throughout the country . . . but for the Hyde Amendment, it would cover abortions as a mandatory medically necessary service. . . . [The Hyde Amendments] preclude the exercise of sound medical judgment about the health of a pregnant woman or indeed even of fetal life. They prefer fetal life at the expense of maternal health and even maternal life.

Copelon argued that the "strict scrutiny" standard should be applied to the case, rather than the less arduous "rational basis" standard, although she felt even the lesser test could not be met by a law that favored a fetus over a poor woman whose health was endangered by pregnancy. "The . . . Constitution, . . . protects born people, [and] one cannot make that trade-off between people who exist and the potentiality of future life. . . . This is a fundamentally irrational trade-off."

One of the justices asked: "Is this an argument that the fetus is not a person for purposes of the Constitution?"

Copelon answered, "It is not a person for the purposes of the Constitution, and I dare say that in our health-care system, even if some whole person's life is at stake, we don't ask another person to involuntarily sacrifice their health and their life for their well-being."

Turning to the First Amendment aspects of the case, Copelon claimed that "the proponents of the Hyde Amendment sought to take a position . . . on the question of when human life begins. That question, this Court held in *Roe v. Wade,* is impermissible, and I submit that it is impermissible under the Fifth Amendment . . . [and] impermissible under the First Amendment, in both the . . . establishment clause and free exercise clause."

The Decision

However, the Supreme Court ruled in favor of the government. After stating that a state does not *have* to pay for even medically necessary abortions, Justice Potter Stewart turned to the constitutionality of the amendment itself. Referring to *Maher v. Doe,* one of the two 1977 cases in which a state's lack of funding for nontherapeutic abortions had been upheld, he wrote:

> Regardless of whether the freedom of a woman to choose to terminate her pregnancy for health reasons lies at the core or the periphery of the due process liberty recognized in *Wade,* it simply does not follow that a woman's freedom of choice carries with it a constitutional entitlement to the financial resources to avail herself of the full range of protected choices. The reason why was explained in *Maher:* although government may not place obstacles

in the path of a woman's freedom of choice, it need not remove those not of its own creation. Indigency falls in the later category.

Turning to the religious issues, Stewart dealt first with McRae's claim that the Hyde Amendment violated the "Establishment Clause because it incorporates into law the doctrines of the Roman Catholic Church. . . ." Noting that the government was free to pass laws against larceny, even though "the Judaeo-Christian religions oppose stealing," Stewart wrote that "we are convinced that the fact that the funding restrictions in the Hyde Amendment may coincide with the religious tenants of the Roman Catholic Church does not, without more, contravene the Establishment Clause."

The issue of what level of scrutiny ought to be applied was the last addressed. After finding that the "rational relationship" test was sufficient, Stewart concluded:

> The Hyde Amendment, by encouraging childbirth except in the most urgent circumstances, is rationally related to the legitimate governmental objective of protecting potential life. By subsidizing the medical expenses of indigent women who carry their pregnancies to term while not subsidizing abortions (except those whose lives are threatened), Congress has established incentives that make childbirth a more attractive alternative than abortion for persons eligible for Medicaid. . . . Nor is it irrational that Congress has authorized federal reimbursement for medically necessary services generally, but not for certain medically necessary abortions. Abortion is inherently different from other medical procedures, because no other procedure involves the purposeful termination of a potential life.

Congress has passed the Hyde Amendment in one version or another, in every subsequent year. The versions passed in 1993, and since, have reinstated funding for abortions requested by victims of incest or rape.

For Further Reading

Garrow, David J. *Liberty & Sexuality: The Right to Privacy and the Making of Roe v. Wade.* New York: Macmillan Publishing Company, 1994.

Goldstein, Leslie Friedman. *The Constitutional Rights of Women*, rev. ed. Madison: University of Wisconsin Press, 1989.

Guitton, Stephanie, and Peter Irons, eds. *May It Please the Court: Arguments on Abortion* (live recordings and transcripts). New York: The New Press, 1995.

Hoff, Joan. *Law, Gender & Injustice: A Legal History of U.S. Women.* New York: New York University Press, 1991.

In the Matter of Baby M: 1988

Plaintiffs: William and Elizabeth Stern   **Defendant:** Mary Beth Whitehead
Plaintiffs' Claim: That Mary Beth Whitehead should surrender the child she
conceived via artificial insemination with William Stern's sperm, in compliance
with the terms of a "Surrogate Parenting Agreement" made between
Whitehead and Stern prior to the child's conception
Chief Lawyers for Defendant: Harold Cassidy and Randy Wolf
Chief Lawyers for Plaintiffs: Frank Donahue and Gary Skoloff
Justices: Robert Clifford, Marie L. Garibaldi, Alan B. Handler, Daniel O'Horn,
Stewart G. Pollock, Gary S. Stein, and *Chief Justice Robert N. Wilentz*
Place: Trenton, New Jersey   **Date of Decision:** February 3, 1988
Verdict: Mary Beth Whitehead's parental rights were terminated and
Elizabeth Stern was granted the right to immediately adopt William Stern's
and Whitehead's daughter. The New Jersey Supreme Court overturned this
verdict in part on February 2, 1988, when it restored Whitehead's parental
rights and invalidated Elizabeth Stern's adoption, but granted William Stern
custody of the infant

SIGNIFICANCE

This was the first widely followed trial to wrestle with the ethical questions raised
by "reproductive technology."

M elissa Stern's conception took place under an agreement signed at Noel
Keane's Infertility Center of New York on February 5, 1985. There were
three parties to the agreement: Richard Whitehead gave his consent to the
contract's "purposes, intents, and provisions" and to the insemination of Mary
Beth Whitehead, his wife, with the sperm of William Stern. In addition, since
any child born to Mary Beth Whitehead would legally be the child of her
husband, he agreed that he would "surrender immediate custody of the child"
and "terminate his parental rights."

Mary Beth Whitehead agreed to be artificially inseminated and to form no
"parent-child relationship" with the baby. She agreed that she would, upon
delivery of the child, surrender her parental rights to William Stern; and she
acknowledged that she would, during the term of the pregnancy, relinquish her

right to make a decision about an abortion. She was permitted to seek an abortion only if the fetus was "physiologically abnormal" or if the inseminating physician agreed an abortion was required to insure her "physical health." Whitehead then agreed that it was William Stern's right to require amniocentesis testing and that she would "abort the fetus upon demand of WILLIAM STERN should a congenital or genetic abnormality be diagnosed." Despite the limitation of Whitehead's right to seek an abortion, the contract allocated to Stern responsibility for the child in the event that Whitehead refused to fulfill this part of her agreement: "If MARY BETH WHITEHEAD refuses to abort the fetus upon demand of WILLIAM STERN, his obligations as stated in this Agreement shall cease forthwith, except as to obligations of paternity imposed by statute." Finally, the Whiteheads "agree[d] to assume all risks, including the risk of death, which are incidental to conception, pregnancy, [and] childbirth."

Stern agreed to pay ten thousand dollars to Whitehead. Although the ten thousand dollars was described as "compensation for services and expenses" and the contract specifically states that the fee should "in no way be construed as a fee for termination of parental rights or a payment in exchange for a consent to surrender the child for adoption," it was payable only upon surrender of a live infant. If Whitehead suffered a miscarriage prior to the fifth month of pregnancy, she would receive no compensation; if the "child is miscarried, dies or is stillborn subsequent to the fourth month of pregnancy and said child does not survive," Stern agreed to pay Whitehead one thousand dollars. He also paid ten thousand dollars to Noel Keane, for his services in arranging the surrogacy agreement.

Stern's wife, Elizabeth, was not a party to the agreement, nor was she mentioned by name. The contract referred to her only as Stern's wife. The first such reference is the statement that the contract's "sole purpose . . . is to enable WILLIAM STERN and his infertile wife to have a child which is biologically related to WILLIAM STERN." The other reference states, "In the event of the death of WILLIAM STERN, prior or subsequent to the birth of said child, it is hereby understood and agreed by MARY BETH WHITEHEAD, Surrogate, and RICHARD WHITEHEAD, her husband, that the child will be placed in the custody of WILLIAM STERN'S wife."

Events did not go according to the contractual script. On March 27, 1986, Whitehead gave birth to a daughter. She named the infant "Sara Elizabeth Whitehead," took her home, and turned down the ten thousand dollars. On Easter Sunday, March 30, the Sterns took the infant to their home. The baby was back at the Whitehead home on March 31; in the second week of April, Whitehead told the Sterns she would never be able to give up her daughter. The Sterns responded by hiring attorney Gary Skoloff to fight for the contract's enforcement. The police arrived to remove "Melissa Elizabeth Stern" from the Whitehead's custody; shown the birth certificate for "Sara Elizabeth Whitehead," they left. When the police returned, Whitehead passed her daughter through an open window to her husband and pleaded with him to make a run for it.

The Trial Begins

The trial commenced on January 5, 1987, by which time a representative had been appointed for the child, known as "Baby M," which stood for Melissa. The Sterns had received temporary custody. Whitehead, who had been ordered by Judge Harvey Sorkow to discontinue breast-feeding the child, had been temporarily awarded two one-hour visits each week, "strictly supervised under constant surveillance . . . in a sequestered, supervised setting to prevent flight or harm."

Skoloff framed the "issue to be decided" as "whether a promise to make the gift of life should be enforced." He stated that "Mary Beth Whitehead agreed to give Bill Stern a child of his own flesh and blood" and emphasized that Elizabeth Stern's multiple sclerosis "rendered her, as a practical matter, infertile . . . because she could not carry a baby without significant risk to her health."

Harold Cassidy, the attorney for Whitehead, offered an alternative view in his own opening remarks: "The only reason that the Sterns did not attempt to conceive a child was . . . because Mrs. Stern had a career that had to be advanced. . . . What Mrs. Stern has is [multiple sclerosis] diagnosed as the mildest form. She was never even diagnosed until after we deposed her in this case. . . . We're here," Cassidy summed up, "not because Betsy Stern is infertile but because one woman stood up and said there are some things that money can't buy." A neurologist affiliated with the Mount Sinai School of Medicine testified that Elizabeth Stern was afflicted with "a very, very, very slight case of MS, if any."

When the issue of custody was brought up, Skoloff stated that contract law and the infant's best interests dictated that exclusive custody should be awarded to the Sterns: "If there is one case in the United States, where joint custody will not work, where visitation rights will not work, where maintaining parental rights will not work, this is it." He addressed Sorkow directly: "Your Honor, under both the contract theory and the best-interest theory, you must terminate the rights of Mary Beth Whitehead and allow Bill Stern and Betsy Stern to be Melissa's mother and father."

Baby M's representative, Lorraine Abraham, took the stand to make her own recommendation. She told the court that she had relied, in part, upon the opinions of three experts in forming her own conclusion: psychologist Dr. David Brodzinsky; social worker Dr. Judith Brown Greif; and psychiatrist Dr. Marshall Schechter. Abraham stated that the experts "will . . . recommend to this court that custody be awarded to the Sterns and visitation denied at this time." Abraham, required to offer her own opinion as Baby M's representative, added that she was "compelled by the overwhelming weight of [the three experts'] investigation to join in their recommendation."

During Elizabeth Stern's testimony, she was asked by Randy Wolf, one of Whitehead's lawyers, "Were you concerned about what effect taking the baby away from Mary Beth Whitehead would have on the baby?"

Stern responded: "I knew it would be hard on Mary Beth and in Melissa's best interest."

Wolf then said: "Now, I believe you testified that if Mary Beth Whitehead receives custody of the baby, you don't want to visit."

Stern replied, "That is correct. I do not want to visit."

Skoloff next raised questions about Whitehead's fitness as a mother. Whitehead had hidden in Florida with Baby M shortly after the infant's birth, and Skoloff represented this as evidence of instability. He then played for the court a taped telephone conversation between Mary Beth Whitehead and William Stern:

Stern: I want my daughter back.

Whitehead: And I want her, too, so what do we do, cut her in half?

Stern: No, no, we don't cut her in half.

Whitehead: You want me, you want me to kill myself and the baby?

Stern: No, that's why I gave her to you in the first place, because I didn't want you to kill yourself.

Whitehead: I've been breast-feeding her for four months. She's bonded to me, Bill. I sleep in the same bed with her. She won't even sleep by herself. What are you going to do when you get this kid that's screaming and carrying on for her mother?

Stern: I'll be her father. I'll be a father to her. I am her father.

Stern: You made an agreement. You signed an agreement.

Whitehead: Forget it, Bill. I'll tell you right now I'd rather see me and her dead before you get her.

The following day, it was Mary Beth Whitehead's turn to testify. One of her attorneys asked, "If you don't get custody of Sara, do you want to see her?"

Whitehead replied:

"Yes, I'm her mother, and whether this court only lets me see her two minutes a week, two hours a week, or two days, I'm her mother and I want to see her, no matter what."

Expert testimony followed. Dr. Lee Salk, the influential child psychologist, testified for the Sterns. Already termed a "third-party gestator" in court documents, Whitehead would now be called "a surrogate uterus." "The legal term that's been used is 'termination of parental rights,'" Salk began,

"and I don't see that there were any 'parental rights that existed in the first place. . . . The agreement involved the provision of an ovum by Mrs. Whitehead for artificial insemination in exchange for ten thousand dollars . . . and so my feeling is that in both structural and functional terms, Mr. and Mrs. Stern's role as parents was achieved by a surrogate uterus and not a surrogate mother.

Dr. Marshall Schechter testified, as predicted by Abraham, that he believed custody should be awarded to the Sterns. He declared that Whitehead suffered from a "borderline personality disorder" and that "handing the baby out of the window to Mr. Whitehead is an unpredictable, impulsive act that falls under this category." Then, citing (among other things) that Whitehead dyed her hair to conceal its premature whiteness, he added the diagnosis of "narcis-sistic personality disorder."

Boston psychiatric social worker Dr. Phyllis Silverman refuted Schechter's characterization of Whitehead's behavior as "crazy":

> Mrs. Whitehead's reaction is like that of other "birth mothers" who suffer pain, grief, and rage for as long as thirty years after giving up a child. The bond of a nursing mother with her child is very powerful.

"By These Standards, We Are All Unfit Mothers"

Outside the courtroom, 121 prominent women refuted Schechter's con-tentions and the "expert opinions" of Brodzinsky and Greif. On March 12, 1987, they issued a document entitled "By These Standards, We Are All Unfit Mothers." The document quoted from each of the expert's testimony and included the *New York Times'* summary of what commentators called Dr. Schech-ter's "Patty Cake" test:

> Dr. Schechter faulted Mrs. Whitehead for saying "Hooray!" when the baby played Patty Cake by clapping her hands together. The more appropriate response for Mrs. Whitehead, he said, was to imitate the child by clapping her hands together and saying "Patty Cake" to reinforce the child's behav-ior. He also criticized Mrs. Whitehead for having four pandas of various size available for Baby M to play with. Dr. Schechter said pots, pans and spoons would have been more suitable.

Signed by Andrea Dworkin, Nora Ephron, Marilyn French, Betty Friedan, Carly Simon, Susan Sontag, Gloria Steinem, Meryl Streep, Vera B. Williams, and others, the document concluded with the statement that "we strongly urge . . . legislators and jurists . . . to recognize that a mother need not be perfect to 'deserve' her child."

When Cassidy made the closing argument on behalf of Whitehead, he re-emphasized that Elizabeth Stern was not, as Whitehead had been told, infertile. He also stressed that termination of parental rights was permitted by law only in the event "of actual abandonment or abuse of the child." Finally, he warned that a ruling in favor of the contract's enforcement would lead to "one class of Americans . . . exploit[ing] another class. And it will always be the wife of the sanitation worker who must bear the children of the pediatrician."

Sorkow announced his verdict on March 31, 1987: "The parental rights of the defendant, Mary Beth Whitehead, are terminated. Mr. Stern is formally judged the father of Melissa Stern." Elizabeth Stern was then escorted into Sorkow's chambers, where she adopted Baby M.

New Jersey Supreme Court's Opinion

The Supreme Court of New Jersey overturned the lower court's ruling on February 2, 1988. It invalidated the surrogacy contract, annulled Elizabeth

Mary Beth Whitehead, several months after the 1988 New Jersey Supreme Court restored her parental rights. (Faye Ellman Photography)

Stern's adoption of Baby M, and restored the parental rights of Whitehead. Writing for a unanimous court, Chief Justice Robert N. Wilentz said:

> We do not know of, and cannot conceive of, any other case where a perfectly fit mother was expected to surrender her newly born infant, perhaps forever, and was then told she was a bad mother because she did not.

The justices then dealt with the issue as a difference between "the natural father and the natural mother, [both of whose claims] are entitled to equal weight." Custody was awarded to William Stern and the trial court was instructed to set visitation for Mary Beth Whitehead.

The court awarded Whitehead visitation on Tuesdays and Thursdays from 10:30 A.M. to 4:30 P.M.; every other weekend; and two weeks during the summer. (Holidays were also divided: the Sterns are entitled to Melissa's company on her birthday, Christmas Day, and Mother's Day, among other occasions.) Since Melissa is now in school during the week, and the Sterns live in New Jersey and Whitehead on Long Island, Whitehead reports that these circumstances have made it increasingly difficult for her to comply with the court-imposed schedule for visits with her daughter. In a recent interview, she said she would seek either a revision of the agreement's terms or to move the rest of her family closer to Melissa's other home in New Jersey.

The New Jersey Supreme Court decision prohibited additional surrogacy arrangements in that state unless "the surrogate mother volunteers, without any payment, to act as a surrogate and is given the right to change her mind and to assert her parental rights." Seventeen other states have since adopted similar guidelines.

This case elicited a divided response from women. Some asserted the primacy of a mother's claim to her child; others argued that any nullification of the contract would constitute a restriction upon a woman's right to control her own body.

For Further Reading

Brennan, Shawn, ed. *Women's Information Directory*. Detroit: Gale Research, 1993.

Chesler, Phyllis. *Sacred Bond: The Legacy of Baby M*. New York: Times Books, 1988.

Cullen-DuPont, Kathryn. *Encyclopedia of Women's History in America*. New York: Facts on File, 1996.

Davis, Flora. *Moving the Mountain: The Women's Movement in America Since 1960*. New York: Simon & Schuster, 1991.

Evans, Sara M. *Born for Liberty: A History of Women in America*. New York: The Free Press, 1989.

Knappman, Edward, ed. *Great American Trials*. Detroit: Gale Research, 1994.

Sack, Kevin. "New York is Urged to Outlaw Surrogate Parenting for Pay." *New York Times*, May 15, 1992.

Squire, Susan. "Whatever Happened to Baby M?" *Redbook*, January 1994.

Whitehead, Mary Beth, with Loretta Schwartz-Nobel. *A Mother's Story: The Truth About the Baby M Case*. New York: St. Martin's Press, 1989.

Webster v. Reproductive Health Services: 1989

Appellants: William L. Webster, attorney general of Missouri et al.
Appellees: Reproductive Health Services et al.   **Appellants' Claim:** That the
U.S. Court of Appeals for the Eighth Circuit erred in overturning Missouri's
laws restricting access to abortions   **Chief Lawyer for Appellees:** Frank
Susman   **Chief Lawyers for Appellants:** William L. Webster, representing
himself *pro se* (without counsel); Charles Fried for the United States as
amicus curiae (friend of the court)   **Justices:** Harry A. Blackmun, William J.
Brennan, Jr., Anthony M. Kennedy, Thurgood Marshall, Sandra Day O'Connor,
Chief Justice William H. Rehnquist, Antonin Scalia, John Paul Stevens, and
Byron R. White   **Place:** Washington, D.C.   **Date of Decision:** July 3, 1989
Decision: Upheld Missouri's restrictions on access to abortion

SIGNIFICANCE

This decision, while not granting the Bush administration's request to overturn
Roe v. Wade, upheld Missouri's restrictions on abortion and all but invited other
states to pass further restrictive legislation.

In September of 1988, Justice Harry A. Blackmun, author of the 1973 landmark opinion *Roe v. Wade* (see page 177), stunned an audience at the University of Arkansas and made national headlines when he questioned whether abortions would remain legal in America. "Will *Roe v. Wade* go down the drain?" he asked bluntly. He answered his rhetorical question with equal bluntness: "There's a very distinct possibility that it will, this term. You can count votes."

Blackmun's fears dated to the appointment to the Supreme Court of "stealth candidate" Anthony M. Kennedy earlier in the year. Blackmun knew that Kennedy would be the swing vote in a decision that could overturn *Roe v. Wade.* Furthermore, Missouri passed a new tough law in June 1986. The statute began with a preamble setting forth the state legislature's "finding" that "the life of each human being begins at conception," and that "unborn children have protectable interests in life, health, and well-being."

As Chief Justice William H. Rehnquist summarized later, the legislation required "that all Missouri laws be interpreted to provide unborn children with the same rights enjoyed by other persons, subject to the federal Constitution and [the Supreme] Court's precedents." It also included requirements that a physician make "such medical examinations and tests as are necessary to make a finding of the gestational age, weight, and lung maturity of the unborn child" if the physician thought the woman might be twenty or more weeks pregnant. Further, no public facilities or employees were to assist at or perform abortions nor may public funds be used to "encourag[e] or counsel" a woman to obtain an abortion, unless her pregnancy threatened her life.

Before the end of the month, Reproductive Health Services, Planned Parenthood of Kansas City, and five medical providers employed by Missouri challenged the act in the U.S. District Court for the Western District of Missouri. The District Court issued an order restraining enforcement of much of the act, and after a trial in December 1986, declared the act unconstitutional. The Court of Appeals for the Eighth Circuit upheld the lower court decision two years later, and Missouri appealed to the U.S. Supreme Court.

In March 1989, the Supreme Court agreed that the administration of President George Bush could take part in the oral argument on behalf of Missouri. The Bush administration quickly made it clear that it planned to ask for nothing less than the complete overturn of *Roe v. Wade.* In angry response, three hundred thousand demonstrators gathered in Washington, D.C., to demand that abortion remain legal.

Friends of the Court

A record-breaking seventy-eight *amicus curiae* briefs (written arguments by friends of the court) were filed. That was almost double the forty-two such briefs filed in *Roe v. Wade.* This was a clear indication that both sides of the abortion debate viewed the forthcoming decision as a crucial one.

Reproductive Health Services attorney Frank Susman. (Attorney Frank Susman, St. Louis, Mo.)

William L. Webster was first to address the Court. He outlined the three basic areas of Missouri's statute:

The first, the constitutional boundaries on the limitations of public funding; the second, the effect of and the facial constitutionality of legislation declaring that life begins at conception; and, third, the ability of a state to require a physician to perform tests and to make and record findings when determining viability.

He contended that legal decisions at all judicial levels since 1973 had "repeatedly interpreted that *[Roe v. Wade]* mandate, frequently strictly against the states. One result is that states have effectively been forbidden . . . to regulate abortion in any significant way."

Webster defended his state's law forbidding the abortion-related employment of any public facility or person on the public payroll. He argued that "the government is certainly not obligated in and of itself to become an advocate for abortion." He characterized the act's preamble—declaring that Missouri believed human life begins at conception—as "an abstract, philosophical statement of the legislature" which "doesn't affect anyone" and states should be entitled to "have a philosophical statement of when they contend life begins."

Finally, he defended Missouri's requirement that physicians perform specific tests in order to verify fetal viability. Every state has a legitimate and compelling interest, he emphasized, in the fetus, most especially when it becomes viable. Therefore, doctors should perform whatever tests are necessary to protect unborn viable babies.

Dumping *Roe*

Charles Fried, arguing for the Bush administration, asked the Court to overturn *Roe v. Wade.* He insisted that such a ruling would not undermine Americans' other privacy rights and that legislatures and communities were entitled to frame laws based on the assumption that a fetus *was* a person, whether or not the Constitution specifically addressed that question. He insisted that the Court was not being asked to "unravel the fabric of unenumerated and privacy rights which this Court has woven. . . . Rather, we are asking the Court to pull this one thread. . . . Abortion is different."

Abortion means the deliberate ending of a *potential* life, Fried pointed out. To many legislators, it is *actual* life, he added, and "though we do not believe that the Fourteenth Amendment takes any position . . . it is an utter *non sequitur* to say that, therefore, the organized community must also take no position . . . and may not use such a position as a premise for regulation."

Kennedy asked Fried whether he thought the 1965 trial *Griswold v. Connecticut* (see page 162), which legalized the use of contraceptives by married couples and enunciated the right to privacy upon which *Roe* was largely based, should stand. When Fried agreed that *Griswold* should stand, Kennedy asked if there was "a fundamental right involved in that case."

In Fried's opinion, *Griswold* involved a "right which was well established in a whole fabric of quite concrete matters, . . . not an abstraction such as the right to control one's body, an abstraction such as the right to be let alone; it involved quite concrete intrusions into the details of marital intimacy."

Roe Must Not Go

Reproductive Health Services attorney Frank Susman went next into the fray. He immediately attacked the very idea of a reversal of *Roe:* "[Fried] suggests that he does not seek to unravel the whole cloth of procreational rights, but merely to pull a thread. It has always been my personal experience that, when I pull a thread, my sleeve falls off." He argued that the contraceptive rights protected by *Griswold* and the abortion rights protected by *Roe* no longer stood apart:

> It is not a thread he is after. It is the full range of procreational choices that constitute the fundamental right that has been recognized by this Court. For better or worse, there no longer exists any bright line between the fundamental right that was established in *Griswold* and the fundamental right of abortion that was established in *Roe.*

Pressed by Kennedy, Susman conceded that *Roe* granted the state a "compelling interest . . . in potential fetal life after the point of viability," and that this was, as Kennedy phrased it, "a line drawing." But Susman also said that the line between fetal viability and non-viability "was more easily drawn" for "many cogent reasons" than the line between the two landmark decisions.

Susman then discussed the medical safety of legalized abortion, noting that the procedure was "seventeen times safer than childbirth, 100 times safer than appendectomy." He also noted that while thirty percent of all American pregnancies were ended by abortion, the "rate has not changed one whit from the time the Constitution was enacted through the 1800s and through the 1900s." He then discussed the legal history of abortion, pointing out that it had not been a common law crime prior to its criminalization in the mid-nineteenth century.

Justice Antonin Scalia's questions also went back to *Roe*, and its ruling that a fetus was not a "person" within the meaning of the Constitution. Susman responded with an objection to Missouri's preamble declaring that human life began at conception, arguing that it "is not something that is verifiable as fact. It is a question verifiable only by reliance upon faith."

Activists on both side of the abortion debate had gathered to demonstrate outside the courthouse that morning, and Susman referred to them in answering Scalia:

> The very debate that went on outside this morning, outside this building, and has gone on in various towns and communities across our nation, is the same debate that every woman who becomes pregnant and doesn't wish to be pregnant has with herself.

> Women do not make these decisions lightly. They agonize over them. . . . The very fact that it is so contested is one of those things that makes me believe that it must remain as a fundamental right with the individual and that the state legislatures have no business invading this decision.

Both Sides Now

Rehnquist announced the Court's decision. While the nine justices took eight separate positions on some of the questions raised, five agreed that Missouri's prohibition of the use of public facilities and public employees to perform or counsel about abortion, as well as its law requiring doctors to perform tests regarding fetal viability, was constitutional. The Court also permitted Missouri to retain its policy statement that human life begins at conception because the statement had no legal effect.

Roe v. Wade was not overturned, but neither was it wholeheartedly affirmed: Rehnquist, joined by Justices Kennedy and Byron R. White, noted with sorrow that the facts presented in *Webster* "afford us no occasion to revisit the holding of *Roe* . . . [but] [t]o the extent indicated in our opinion, we would modify and narrow *Roe* and succeeding cases." Justice Sandra Day O'Connor said: "When the constitutional invalidity of a State's abortion statute actually turns on the constitutional validity of *Roe v. Wade*, there will be enough time to examine *Roe*. And to do so carefully. . . ." An angry Scalia responded by castigating his colleagues for their failure to use the opportunity to overturn the 1973 decision. In 1992, however, the Court firmly upheld *Roe* in *Planned Parenthood of Southeastern Pennsylvania v. Casey* (see page 202). This time the justices put respect for earlier Court decisions ahead of ideology and political pressure.

For Further Reading

Garrow, David J. *Liberty and Sexuality: The Right to Privacy and the Making of Roe v. Wade.* New York: Macmillan, 1994.

Guitton, Stephanie, and Peter Irons, eds. *May It Please the Court: Arguments on Abortion* (live recordings and transcripts). New York: The New Press, 1995.

Hoff, Joan. *Law, Gender, and Injustice: A Legal History of U.S. Women.* New York: New York University Press, 1991.

Planned Parenthood of Southeastern Pennsylvania v. Casey: 1992

Appellant: Planned Parenthood of Southeastern Pennsylvania
Appellees: Robert P. Casey et al.   **Appellant's Claim:** That under the due
process clause of the Constitution, the 1988 and 1989 amendments to the
Pennsylvania abortion law were illegal   **Chief Lawyer for Appellees:** Ernest
D. Preate, Jr.   **Chief Lawyer for Appellant:** Kathryn Kolbert
Justices: Harry A. Blackmun, *Anthony M. Kennedy, Sandra Day O'Connor,*
Chief Justice William Rehnquist, Antonin Scalia, *David H. Souter,* John Paul
Stevens, Clarence Thomas, and Byron R. White (all concurred and dissented)
Place: Washington, D.C.   **Date of Decision:** June 29, 1992
Decision: Judicial respect for precedent required the Court to reaffirm *Roe v.
Wade,* the Court's 1973 decision making abortion legal in the United States.
The justices declared Pennsylvania's Abortion Control Act law constitutional in
part and unconstitutional in part.

SIGNIFICANCE

In the words of Pulitzer Prize-winning historian David J. Garrow, "*Casey* was a
watershed event in American history." It resolved a national dispute over abortion
by upholding the essentials of *Roe v. Wade* while permitting Pennsylvania to
regulate abortions as long as the state did not place an undue burden on women.

In 1989, the Supreme Court allowed the states more leeway in regulating abortions, in *Webster v. Reproductive Health Services* (see page 197). In its aftermath, anti-abortion groups such as Operation Rescue stepped up their campaign to harass abortion clinics throughout the nation. They threw firebombs, videotaped the children of medical employees, threatened patients, poured glue in keyholes, and distributed posters identifying doctors and nurses as "baby killers."

In 1982, the growing pro-life movement was ready to test the Supreme Court's landmark 1973 decision in *Roe v. Wade* (see page 177), which protects a woman's right to an abortion. That year, Pennsylvania passed the Abortion Control Act, followed by amendments in 1988 and 1989. Governor Robert P.

Casey signed the last one in November 1989, only four months after the *Webster* decision.

1 9 9 2

Planned

Parenthood of

Southeastern

Pennsylvania v.

Casey

The Abortion Control Act required that women seeking abortions give their informed consent—meaning that clinics must provide them with state-scripted information about the abortion at least twenty-four hours before the procedure. The statute also required the informed consent of one parent in order for a minor to obtain an abortion, although it provided "judicial by-pass" steps for the teen to go to court for permission in special cases.

One section of the law required a wife seeking an abortion to sign a statement that she had notified her husband. The statute also imposed reporting requirements on clinics providing abortions. These regulations were lifted only in emergencies.

Before any of the provisions had taken effect, women's groups, clinics, and doctors challenged the law. Five abortion clinics and a doctor representing a class of physicians who provided abortion services went to court to have the law declared unconstitutional. The challenges to the 1988 and 1989 Abortion Control Acts merged into one case—*Planned Parenthood of Southeastern Pennsylvania v. Casey*.

Win Some, Lose Some

The District Court declared the law unconstitutional except for one provision requiring physicians to tell women the age of her embryo. The case then went through two appeals—on October 21, 1991, and October 30, 1992. The Court of Appeals, striking down the husband-notification provision, upheld the others. The stage was set for Supreme Court appeals by both sides.

The oral arguments began on April 22, a month that brought five hundred thousand pro-choice women to the nation's capital. Kathryn Kolbert, an experienced American Civil Liberties Union (ACLU) lawyer, explained the fundamental issue for the plaintiffs:

> [Does] . . . government [have] the power to force a woman to continue or to end a pregnancy against her will? . . . Since . . . *Roe v. Wade*, a generation of American women . . . [have been] secure in the knowledge . . . their child-bearing decisions [are protected]. This landmark decision . . . not only protects rights of bodily integrity and autonomy, but has enabled millions of women to participate fully and equally in society.

Kolbert's opponent, Ernest D. Preate, Jr., followed her to the floor. He had spoken only a few words when Justice Harry A. Blackmun, the eighty-three-year-old author of *Roe v. Wade*, interrupted, "Have you read Roe?" Preate replied, "Yes." Then, before Preate could finish his remarks, Justice Sandra Day O'Connor showered him with critical questions regarding the spousal notification clause. Justices John Paul Stevens and Anthony M. Kennedy continued her skeptical line of questioning, followed by Justice David H. Souter.

Next, U.S. Solicitor General Kenneth W. Starr, representing the administration of President George Bush, came to the lectern to attack *Roe v. Wade*.

According to historian David J. Garrow, Souter "pressed Starr to concede that if his position prevailed, states could outlaw *all* abortions, except perhaps those where a pregnancy directly threatened a woman's life." Souter questioned Starr about whether a complete ban on abortions would meet the *Webster* case's "rational basis" standard. Starr answered that any law would have to include the life of the mother exception or else face "serious questions."

Souter, unsuccessful in getting a clear answer from Starr, remarked in exasperation, "You're asking the Court to adopt a standard and I think we ought to know where the standard would take us." Yet his questions did not really indicate which side he favored.

The Dark Horse

It appeared that the final vote would rest on Souter's actions. From earlier conversations he suspected that O'Connor, Kennedy, and he, himself, could agree that the Pennsylvania law could be upheld *and* still leave *Roe* intact.

However, Chief Justice William Rehnquist had already begun to draft the Court's opinion to overturn Roe, assuming the other judges agreed with him. Then, unexpectedly, Kennedy changed his mind, joining Souter and O'Connor in a compromise. Behind the scenes, Souter began working out the details of the middle ground.

In May, before Rehnquist had finished his opinion, Kennedy, Souter and O'Connor met in Souter's chambers on the far southeastern corner of the main floor. Their private conversations led to a joint decision to uphold *Roe*, derailing Rehnquist's work.

Supreme Court Justice Sandra Day O'Connor, a critical player in the compromise decision that upheld the essence of *Roe v. Wade.* (National Archives)

When they discovered the switch, Rehnquist and Scalia "were stunned," according to the *New York Times.* They had failed to capture the five votes they needed to overthrow *Roe.* Instead, Souter and his allies—along with Blackmun and Stevens—were voting to uphold the landmark decision.

On Monday morning, June 29, 1992, on the final day of the term, observers were unprepared for the results. In a rare action, O'Connor, Kennedy and Souter—on behalf of Blackmun and Stevens—delivered the opinion of the Court, upholding *Roe's* "essential holding."

The three then described "a realm of personal liberty which the government may not enter." Kennedy wrote, "At the heart of liberty is the right to define one's own concept of existence, of meaning, of the universe, and of the mystery of human life." In abortion, "the liberty of the woman is at stake in a sense unique to the human condition and so unique to the law." A woman's "suffering is too intimate and personal for the State to insist . . . upon its own vision of the woman's role, however dominant that vision has been in the course of our history and our culture."

1992

Planned

Parenthood of

Southeastern

Pennsylvania v.

Casey

However, the most original and eloquent opinion came from Souter: "The ability of women to participate equally in the economic and social life of the Nation [for twenty years] has been facilitated by their ability to control their reproductive lives." He noted that the Court's decision on *Roe* had a "dimension" that was present only when a decision "calls the contending sides of a national controversy to end their national division by accepting a common mandate rooted in the Constitution." However, he recognized that there were always going to be efforts—unprincipled or not—to thwart putting such a decision into effect. Therefore, "only the most convincing justification under accepted standards of precedent could suffice to demonstrate that a later decision overruling the first was anything but a surrender to political pressure, and an unjustified repudiation of the principle on which the Court staked its authority in the first instance."

The majority held that the doctrine of *stare decisis*—the rule by which courts are slow to interfere with principles announced in former decisions—required that *Roe v. Wade* be affirmed in its "essential holding," recognizing a woman's right to choose an abortion. The Court also established that an "undue burden test," not Roe's "trimester" framework, be used in evaluating abortion restrictions before viability.

Associate Justice David H. Souter. (Collection, The Supreme Court Historical Society)

The Court accepted the Abortion Control Act except for the spousal notification provision, which did impose an undue burden and was therefore unconstitutional. Therefore, *Planned Parenthood v. Casey* was affirmed in part, reversed in part.

Because of this decision by a Court widely thought to be conservative, a woman's right to an abortion today rests on firmer legal foundations than ever before.

For Further Reading

Garrow, David J. "Justice Souter Emerges." The *New York Times Magazine*, September 25, 1994.

———. *Liberty and Sexuality: The Right to Privacy and the Making of Roe v. Wade.* New York: Macmillan, 1994.

Hoff, Joan. *Law, Gender, and Injustice: A Legal History of U.S. Women.* New York: New York University Press, 1991.

Tribe, Lawrence. *American Constitutional Law*, 2d ed. Mineola, N.Y.: The Foundation Press, 1988.

Madsen v. Women's Health Center: 1994

Appellants: Judy Madsen et al.   **Appellees:** Women's Health Center et al.
Appellants' Claim: That a permanent injunction banning protesters at a woman's health clinic in Florida violated their constitutional rights
Chief Lawyer for Appellees: Talbot D'Alemberte
Chief Lawyer for Appellants: Mathew D. Staver   **Justices:** Harry Blackmun, Ruth Bader Ginsburg, Sandra Day O'Connor, *Chief Justice William Rehnquist,* David Souter, and John Paul Stevens (majority); Anthony M. Kennedy, Antonin Scalia, and Clarence Thomas (dissent)   **Place:** Washington, D.C   **Date of Decision:** June 30, 1994   **Decision:** The U.S. Supreme Court upheld portions of an injunction against right-to-life protesters to protect a Florida abortion clinic

SIGNIFICANCE
The decision balanced a woman's freedom of speech against her freedom to seek an abortion. It put clinics providing abortions and pregnancy counseling on the same footing as hospitals who also need protection from a disruption in services.

Madsen v. Women's Health Center interrupted a continuous and escalating effort by anti-abortion groups to close down the Aware Woman Center for Choice (AWCC), the only women's health clinic in Brevard County, Florida. The clinic, located in Melbourne, is a mid-size medical facility that provides pregnancy counseling to four to five thousand women a year and approximately 1,300 abortions. It operates with a staff of three part-time doctors and fourteen other staff.

Patricia Baird-Windle—a humorous and energetic grandmother—is the clinic's founder and owner. She became alarmed when the demonstrations of Operation Rescue against the clinic became increasingly disruptive and violent.

Operation Rescue stopped cars in the narrow street entrance to the clinic, shoved literature and pictures of fetuses into peoples' faces, and screamed insults and threats—such as "baby-killer." They prayed for the deaths of clinic workers. Operation Rescue garnered license plate numbers from cars, and then obtained names and addresses from the Department of Motor Vehicles. This allowed them to personalize their campaign, climbing on ladders and holding signs with the names of patients over the fence, even sending mailings to their homes. In 1991, AWCC sued the individuals and groups affiliated with Operation Rescue.

In September 1992, Florida's Fifth District Court of Appeals issued an injunction to protect the clinic from the obstruction of its entrances and exits, and staff and patients from physical abuse. This injunction led to increased violence beginning in December—a butyric acid attack, doors sealed with superglue, a doctor threatened with a mock shooting, and lies spread about staff. Right-to-lifers even picketed the homes of clinic workers, tying up their phone lines, videotaping their children, and surrounding their houses with hundreds of threatening picketers.

A Collision Course

In January 1993, the situation worsened when the Institute of Mobilized Prophetic Activated Christian Training (IMPACT) gave classes in Melbourne. Trainees from all over the nation came to learn tactics they would utilize against AWCC in an attempt to close it down. Covenant Presbyterian and other local churches donated space for IMPACT meetings and fund raising activities. For the next three months, IMPACT volunteers waged war on the clinic.

AWCC could not afford to hire security forces and had little reason to expect support from the Melbourne Police. The police, fearful that officers could be injured, said that they would not stop Operation Rescue members who broke ranks and made a dash for the door. If the protesters were chained together with bicycle locks, and they refused to leave, then the police would have to have each lock drilled, and bring in four officers to carry off each protester on a stretcher. If, as had happened before, the police allowed another protester to take the place of the one arrested, the clinic could be shut down all day.

Clinic Seeks a Broader Injunction

Local NOW president Nancy Kohsin-Kintigh shaped strategy with AWCC's Baird-Windle as well as Lisa Sergi and Kathy Spillar from the Feminist Majority Foundation. They collected information from all over the country about the most well-known of the protesters. They discovered a network of hard-core zealots, most between seventeen and thirty-five, two-thirds male, ingenious at recruiting demonstrators and in designing new methods to intimidate women seeking abortions.

One of the founders of the protest, they learned, was Judy Madsen, who later appealed the injunction against the protesters all the way to the Supreme Court. The women categorized hundreds of named tactics, updating them weekly. (This list proved useful as anti-abortion groups duplicated their successful techniques around the country.)

The women also knew that after three years of previous attacks on the clinic by a group known as Operation Goliath, the AWCC was financially drained. The clinic had to turn to volunteers to prevent protesters from blockading doors and keeping out women seeking abortions.

Unitarian Churches helped with that problem by permitting AWCC supporters to hold rallies and training sessions in their facilities, and attendance increased as newspapers and television began to cover Operation Rescue's hostile activities. Soon reporters and documentary filmmakers from many countries began arriving before dawn.

In early spring, IMPACT started arriving before 7:00 A.M. Members began by praying, reading from the Bible, chanting, and swaying, before escalating their protests. On Saturdays, which were surgery days, hundreds more Operation Rescue/IMPACT protesters would appear. They targeted the homes of clinic workers for similar activities on Saturdays.

In April, the AWCC asked the Florida Supreme Court to grant an amended injunction to protect staff and patients by clearly spelling out the bounds of protesters' activities. The clinic listed examples of Operation Rescue/IMPACT's harassment, stressing that health risks increased as patients endured the stress of confronting vocal, threatening protesters who denied them entry to the clinic. Such provocations also harmed patients.

With a video, the AWCC showed how protesters violated the privacy of their clients. The clinic also provided evidence that protesters had stalked staff and their families. A nurse and a doctor resigned under the intense pressures and threats, and possibly because they feared for their lives after the murder of Dr. David Gunn in Pensacola, Florida in March, 1993, by an anti-abortion activist.

Gary Allgeyer, Melbourne police captain of the Detective Division, testified that an amended injunction would help a small town police force maintain public order and safety. He acknowledged that the police had been threatened with lawsuits by protesters. With such compelling evidence, Judge Robert McGregor ruled that a thirty-six-foot buffer zone must surround three sides of the clinic as protection against physical blockades that barred access to the clinic.

The judge also ordered a three-hundred-foot buffer zone around the residences of the clinic staff to give a cordon of safety to workers and their families who had been repeatedly stalked and terrorized, and a three-hundred-foot zone around the clinic to protect patients from unwanted proselytizing and to safeguard their health during surgical procedures.

The final prohibition outlawed the use of bullhorns, sound amplification equipment within earshot, and the exhibiting of images observable to patients inside the clinic during hours of surgical procedure and recovery. Operation Rescue members appealed to the Florida Supreme Court.

Just days before the court issued its unanimous ruling upholding the amended injunction, a confusing decision by the Federal Eleventh Circuit Court struck down the injunction in a separate case brought by an anti-abortion protester who was not a member of Operation Rescue. The Circuit Court stated that existing laws already protected the interests of public safety and order so there was no need to interfere with the first amendment rights of the abortion protesters. The Circuit Court found the injunction to be content-based [prejudicial because the subject was abortion] and too narrowly drawn to achieve an end.

Back to the Drawing Board

The U.S. Supreme Court stepped in to resolve the conflict between the Florida and federal courts. On their last day in session, June 30, 1994, Chief Justice William Rehnquist delivered the majority opinion, arguing forcefully for upholding most of the injunction, yet finding part of it a restriction on the rights of the demonstrators.

The Florida Supreme Court had earlier decided that the injunction protected several important government interests: upholding a pregnant woman's right to medical or counseling services, ensuring safety and order, allowing the free flow of traffic on public streets and sidewalks, and protecting all citizens' property rights. The U.S. Supreme Court reviewed each contested part of the injunction to determine whether it restricted speech more than necessary.

Considering the narrow confines around the clinic, the Court found a thirty-six-foot buffer zone appropriate to allow unfettered entry and exit. The banning of "singing, chanting, whistling, shouting, yelling, bullhorns, auto horns, sound amplification equipment," and other sounds or images observable within earshot from 7:30 A.M. to 12:00 P.M. Monday and Saturday got a split decision.

Rehnquist wrote, "The First Amendment does not demand that patients at a medical facility undertake Herculean efforts to escape the cacophony of political protest." He also stressed that threats to staff and patients violated their rights. However, the Court found the ban on images too broad to prohibit entirely. Signs with threats or veiled threats were unacceptable, but the Court wrote that banning all observable images burdened speech more than necessary in a free society.

The Court also ruled that the three-hundred-foot ban around the clinic was too limiting to freedom of speech unless the protesters used words or threats. In public debate, citizens must tolerate insulting and even outrageous speech in order to provide adequate space to the freedoms protected by the First Amendment.

The final issue was picketing, demonstrating, or using sound equipment within three hundred feet around private residences of clinic staff. Rehnquist, while noting the utmost sanctity of privacy of home in a free society, felt that three hundred feet was too broad a ban. If the injunction had set a smaller zone and set limits on the numbers and duration of protesters, the Court might have upheld it.

Justice Antonin Scalia, in his dissenting opinion, wrote that this was an attempt to silence a particular type of speech. He thought there were no substantiated expressions of violence near the clinic and that a single judge had no right to control free speech by such an injunction. Such injunctions, he wrote, are powerful weapons and should be subjected to greater safeguards. He feared that this decision was a dangerous departure from past rulings of First Amendment speech protection. As a consequence, the AWCC injunction was sent back to the Florida Circuit Court for fine tuning.

The Aftermath

Reactions to this case have been mixed, but among women's groups it is considered a victory for clinic operators and abortion rights advocates. Many women's health clinics have sought similar injunctions to prevent anti-abortion violence, and these have been vital weapons in fighting the pro-life protesters' increasingly aggressive behaviors. Now local courts around the country have some federal guidelines and support for decisions protecting clinics.

According to the Feminist Majority Foundation's 1994 Clinic Violence Survey, over half of the abortion clinics in America were targets of violence during 1994, and almost one-quarter of these clinics reported that a staff member quit as a result of these incidents. One-half of the clinics where staff resigned had difficulty finding a replacement.

The AWCC remained the focus of radical protesters. By May 1993, the AWCC had been embroiled in four separate lawsuits stemming from conflicts with anti-abortion protesters. Beginning August 1, 1994, federal marshals provided assistance to the clinic, but a hard core cadre continued their disruptive activities in Melbourne and around the United States. As of 1996, the injunction was before the Florida Circuit Court in contentious hearings over compliance with the U.S. Supreme Court ruling.

For Further Reading

New York Times, July 30, 1994; July 1, 1994.

Supreme Court in the United States, no. 93-880, October term, 1993.

Washington Post, July 1, 1994.

Section 5
MARRIAGE, PARENTING, AND DIVORCE

Under English common law, marriage and property are intertwined. Brought to America by the colonists in 1607, the law grew from the belief that men could own private property.

Single women could also own property. However, after marriage, wives lost these rights. Wives' status dropped to the level of "children" and the "insane," according to Theophilis Parsons, the most learned lawyer in the colonies. In 1805, Parsons successfully argued before the Supreme Court of Massachusetts that a wife had "no political relation to the state any more than an alien" *(Martin v. Massachusetts).* In 1809, attorney Richard Stockton rested his case in *Kempe v. Kennedy* on the fact that women were not real citizens. Arguing to a sympathetic Chief Justice John Marshall, Stockton said, "A *feme covert* [married woman] cannot properly be called an inhabitant of a state. The husband is the inhabitant."

A bride's wealth went to her new husband, who managed her real property and reaped its profits. Her personal property became his to own and dispense with as he chose. Over the years women tried to contest these losses. Their victories and defeats appear in the trials of *Carroll v. Warren* (1736), *Pattison v. Pattison* (1737), *Barnes v. Hart* (1793), *Megrath v. Robertson* (1795), *Dibble v. Hutton* (1804), *Watson v. Bailey* (1808), *Birkbeck v. Ackroyd* (1878), and *Kirchberg v. Feenstra* (1981). The latter ended the right of the "head of the house" to control marital property.

Another form of property was dower—a widow's right to use one-third of her late husband's real estate and chattel (tangible property). Until the late nineteenth century, the most important laws affecting wives were those regulating their dower rights. Judges and magistrates, having discouraged women from earning wages or running businesses, recognized an obligation to protect them when the family breadwinner died. However, after the American Revolution, this protection eroded as creditors demanded their loans be repaid ahead of widows' shares. These developments are illustrated by *Scott v. Scott* (1795), *Griffith v. Griffith's Executors* (1798), and *Coutts v. Greenhow* (1811).

During the 1830s, women became more publicly active and many complained about the new practice of seizing a widow's property to pay her husband's debts, which left many of them on the dole. However, widows' dependency on public alms also gave men a reason to revise the laws. In response, the states began to pass statutes giving wives control over their earnings and any property they brought with them into marriage. The 1848 New York's Married Woman's Property Act is the most famous of these.

From their loss of property rights flowed the inability of wives to make contracts, especially wills. They could not sue or be sued, buy and sell, or otherwise act as agents for their husbands without his permission. Until the 1820s most married women could not make wills. *Fitch v. Brainerd* (1805), *Beall and King v. Woolford* (1797), and *Webster v. McGinnis* (1812) demonstrate how couples informally drew up premarital agreements to give women these powers. These improvements did include women slaves; sadly, they appear only as bequests in these early property-rights trials.

Common law also treated children and their labor as property. Mothers had no right to claim custody of their offspring or to demand rights to their labor. Fathers were the "natural" custodians of their children; only males could claim the labor of their offspring. *Burk v. Phips* (1793), *Pennsylvania v. Addicks* (1813), and *McKim v. McKim* (1879) demonstrate how custody rights changed over time, culminating in the late nineteenth-century view that during the "tender years" (until about seven), a child's best interest was to live with his or her mother. *Ireland v. Smith* (1995) illustrates new legal challenges faced by working women.

Naturally, husbands assumed their own heavy burdens. They were responsible for feeding, sheltering, clothing, and protecting their families throughout very difficult times. Legally, however, they needed to provide only minimal support to fulfill their obligations, as shown in *Kenny v. Udall and Kenny* (1821) and *McGuire v. McGuire* (1953).

Colonial marriages were hard to dissolve. The colonies granted divorce either rarely or not at all. Permitted by the New England colonies for reasons of adultery, cruelty, and desertion, divorce was illegal throughout the South. Legal separations took their place—without the right to remarry. Only husbands held the right to dissolve a marriage. However, after the American Revolution, divorce increased dramatically—but not necessarily in a way that made the relations between husbands and wives fair. Patriarchal rights were "just," spousal rape was a male entitlement, and jealousy—as a motive for a man's violent behavior—was acceptable.

Throughout American history, women who won separations or divorces risked financial ruin. In colonial courts their alimony hinged on their behavior. If a wife did not seem "submissive" or "obedient," if she refused to follow her husband to another state, or if she traveled without his express permission, her payments could be reduced to one-third of the husband's estate or less. He might be a "ladies' man," but if she did not conform to strict standards of behavior, she would lose her right to spousal support. These practices are demonstrated in *Shaw v. Shaw* (1845), *Peckford v. Peckford* (1828), *Prince v. Prince* (1845), and *Hair v. Hair* (1858).

Today, whichever spouse has the higher income is usually responsible for support payments. In 1979, in *Orr v. Orr,* the Supreme Court ruled that an

Alabama law requiring men, but not women, to pay alimony violated the Equal Protection clause of the Constitution. That year marked the date that unmarried couples could be held responsible for spousal support, as revealed in *Marvin v. Marvin*. By 1993, twenty-nine states had adopted no-fault grounds for divorce, a practice some believe is partly responsible for a growing number of impoverished mothers and children. Their evidence rests mainly on one California study showing that one year after divorce, women experienced a seventy-three percent decline in their standard of living while men improved theirs by forty-two percent.

In 1973, the Supreme Court in *Frontiero v. Richardson* struck down a law that permitted married male members of the armed forces to claim their wives as dependents. Husbands then could receive medical, dental, and housing benefits, even if their wives were earning most of the income. Then-attorney Ruth Bader Ginsburg asked the Court to find sex discrimination as inherently suspect as discrimination based on race, religion, or national origin, and to apply strict judicial scrutiny in this and future instances of sex discrimination. By deciding in her favor, the Court reversed the assumption that "the husband in our society is generally the 'breadwinner' in the family [while] the wife [is] typically the 'dependent' partner." However, it refused—by one vote—to adopt the "strict scrutiny" standard in sex discrimination cases as it used for cases of race, religion, and natural origin.

Weinberger v. Wiesenfeld (1975) repudiated two similar views of married life. The first was "that male workers' earnings are vital to the support of their families, while the earnings of female wage-earners do not significantly contribute to their families' support." The second was that "women as a group would choose to forgo work to care for children while men would not." This decision underscored the finding in *Frontiero* that women's financial contributions to their families merited the same consideration as men's. It also set the new precedent that the Court would not view child-care responsibilities or decisions as being bound by gender.

Today, with about half of all marriages ending in divorce, such issues as custody, property, and alimony, are vital to most couples. Since the 1970s, state and federal discriminatory laws have been overturned by the Supreme Court as the result of lawsuits filed usually by female attorneys. Still many archaic statutes still penalize wives. For instance, in 1991, California, Idaho, Nevada, and New Mexico did not permit wives to will their halves of community property. If a wife died before her husband, he inherited all of their jointly-held property. But if he predeceased her, she was only entitled to one-half. Nonetheless, wives today have an equal playing field more than at any time in the nation's history, with current debates focusing on whether the courts in specific regions of the country are as unbiased as they should be in deciding matters of family law.

Carroll v. Warren: 1736

Plaintiff: Charles Carroll   **Defendant:** John Warren   **Plaintiff's Claim:** That although an officer of the court witnessed the reluctance of Sarah Curtis to sell her lands, the deed was still valid
Chief Lawyer for Defendant: William Cumming
Chief Lawyer for Plaintiff: D. Delany   **Justice:** Samuel Ogle, Esq., chancellor of Maryland   **Place:** Maryland   **Date of Decision:** October 19, 1736   **Decision:** The private examination by a court officer did not mean that Sarah Curtis had freely agreed to let her husband sell her lands

SIGNIFICANCE

This case—one of the earliest on record—shows how the law required court officers to privately examine wives to prevent husbands from forcing or defrauding them into disposing of their property.

In eighteenth-century America, a wife's claim to her property was weak to nonexistent, depending on the colony. For example, the Puritans in New England discarded—in many aspects—English common law. They believed that a wife's central duty was to submit to her husband—and suggested that her control over any property could only lead to friction, even separation.

Maryland, South Carolina, and Virginia were more likely to look to England for legal guidance. To begin with, there were no religious reasons to abandon English law. Most southern male elites came to America for financial reasons, farming large tracts of land to produce crops for export. Many of these "gentlemen" felt inferior to their English relatives in cultural matters. Therefore, they closely followed the laws of Great Britain rather than remake them.

So when it came to protecting the property rights of wives, southerners conformed to the more generous British practices. For instance, the South enforced "private examinations" of married women by court officers to ensure that they had not been forced into selling or mortgaging their lands. Courts also insisted that wives sign the deeds transferring title to their property.

The Misled Wife

In 1711, Sarah Gerard lived in comfort in Saint Mary's County, Maryland—the owner of several thousand acres of real estate, which she had received upon the death of her former husband, Justinian Gerard. Her new spouse, Michael Curtis, tricked her into selling these lands for six hundred pounds sterling to a neighbor, Charles Carroll. Michael told Sarah that he was only leasing her lands. What the neighbor had in mind, however, was buying them outright.

This late nineteenth-century engraving shows a new husband and wife celebrating after their colonial wedding.

Sarah went along with Michael, and the two appeared before the county court on June 26, 1711. The justice of the peace, Samuel Williamson, "a Man of unquestionable Character and Probity," certified that Sarah did sign the deed, although he felt her compliance "was not as Voluntary as it ought to have been."

Later on, John Warren, Sarah's "heir-at-law" (the person who inherits when there is no will), said that when Sarah discovered that Michael had misled her, she "was much troubled in mind" and "the grief thereof broke her Heart." Soon the couple separated.

To protest the sale, Sarah refused to correct several inconsistencies regarding her acknowledgment of the deed, leaving the title open to dispute. She told friends she had "only been askt to join with her Husband in a lease or leases of some Tenements on part of the Lands . . . but never to give away her Right and Title to any part Thereof."

Unfriendly "Perswasions"

A few years later, Sarah died, leaving the title to her lands in turmoil. Charles Carroll's son and heir, Charles, wrote to John Warren, asking for a new "Deed or Conveyance" for the property to clear up the ownership rights. However, since the Carrolls had not yet finished paying for the lands (they owed one hundred pounds sterling), and because of the inconsistencies in Sarah's acknowledgment of the deed, Warren refused. So young Carroll sued him in the court of chancery at the October session, 1737.

The trial hinged on a Maryland law under which a wife who brought property with her into marriage (called separate property) had to agree with or "acknowledge" any sale or mortgage of her lands by signing the deed according to specific steps. Williamson, the justice of the peace who had certified Sarah's acknowledgment of the deed, admitted that "importunate perswasions" had made her sign the papers. This left the court of chancery only the written word of one judge that Sarah Curtis had agreed to the sale.

Therefore, the court—believing that she had improperly signed the deed—ruled in favor of Warren, concluding that the legal steps for selling or mortgaging (conveyancing) married women's estates had not been followed. The court dismissed Carroll's suit and made him pay Warren's court costs.

This early trial shows how southern courts protected the property rights of wives. However, when it came to the misfortunes of divorce and separation, New England showed more compassion.

Suggestions for Further Reading

Hoffer, Peter Charles. *Law and People in Colonial America.* Baltimore: The Johns Hopkins University Press, 1992.

Kerber, Linda K. *Women's America: Refocusing the Past.* New York: Oxford University Press, 1991.

Salmon, Marylynn. *Women and the Law of Property in Early America.* Chapel Hill: University of North Carolina Press, 1986.

Wollstonecraft, Mary. *A Vindication of the Rights of Women.* New York: W. W. Norton, 1975 (original edition, 1792).

Pattison v. Pattison: 1737

Plaintiff: Jane Pattison **Defendant:** Jeremiah Pattison
Plaintiff's Claim: That under the "doctrine of necessities," Jeremiah was
liable for debts Jane contracted even though the two had separated
Chief Lawyer for Defendant: D. Dulany
Chief Lawyer for Plaintiff: Edward Jeninger **Chancellor:** Samuel Ogle,
Esq. **Place:** Annapolis, Maryland **Date of Decision:** February term, 1737
Decision: Although Jeremiah Pattison and his wife were estranged, he was
still responsible for her debts so long as they were the normal "necessaries"
for living

SIGNIFICANCE

Married women in colonial times could not normally make contracts. Only as
agents for their husbands, and under certain circumstances, could they do so.
This case shows how colonial law, under the "doctrine of necessities," held men
responsible for their wives' support even when the couple did not live together.

When colonial husbands left home for long periods, wives charged the "necessaries" of living to their husbands' accounts. These charges however, had to be consistent with the amounts the family normally spent. Wives, people reasoned, were acting as their husband's "agents" when they contracted these debts. However, if a wife "incurred her husband's wrath," he could warn creditors, through newspaper advertisements and public notices, that he would *not* pay the bills. A wife was then left to appeal to the courts.

The "doctrine of necessities" was tested in *Pattison v. Pattison*. In about 1728, widow Jane Abbott married tobacco grower Jeremiah Pattison of Calvert County, Maryland, who was in "very indifferent" circumstances. Jane, however, had received a substantial inheritance from her deceased husband, George Abbott. Under common law, upon marriage, a wife's real estate went to her husband to manage as he saw fit. Her personal property became his entirely. Therefore, Jeremiah profited from his marriage to Jane.

A Marriage Made in Hell

According to Jane, within twelve months of the wedding, Jeremiah began beating her with "tongs and bull whips." He also locked her out of their home, which she had inherited from her first husband.

"Destitute of cloathes and almost naked," Jane met with several of her friends at the home of Dr. James Somerveill. The women begged her to buy new clothes on her husband's account at the shop of Isaac Johns. Jane agreed and visited the store. Johns offered to extend her credit up to fifty pounds in sterling. However, Jane decided she would "contract a debt to the value of about seven pounds sterling."

Learning he was liable for the charges, Jeremiah advertised that he would not be responsible for more of Jane's charges. In a case that would span eight years (1729–37), Jane sued him.

According to Jeremiah

In the Court of Chancery, Jeremiah's attorney argued that his client never married his wife for her money, and had lived free of debt before their union. Jeremiah, he said, was "out of pocket" as a result of his marriage. Jeremiah testified that Jane had treated him with contempt, sworn at him, cut his face with an iron, and even tried to burn down their house. By contrast, Jeremiah felt he "had used the most gentle and persuasive Means he could think of" to convince Jane of the "Dangerous Tendency of her Conduct but without any good Effect."

In this engraving, a woman is "taking the pattern off." *Pattison v. Pattison* permitted a wife to charge merchandise for which her estranged husband was responsible. (Litchfield Historical Society)

Jeremiah said that after the two separated, he had written to Jane asking her to return, but she had refused. When she charged clothes on his account, he feared he could not repay them and announced that he was not responsible.

On the Other Hand

Witnesses supported Jane's story. John Dorrumple, for example, testified that although he had never seen Jeremiah strike Jane, he had "seen several

Bruises upon several Parts of her Body," which he believed Jeremiah had caused.

J. Rigby, an acquaintance of twelve years, swore that he frequently had heard Jeremiah verbally abuse his wife and saw him cut Jane's face with a knife with no provocation. He also testified that far from being "out of pocket" after his marriage, Jeremiah had made a good living from planting large crops of tobacco. Barbara Mackall said she had seen Jane battered and bruised after Jeremiah had locked her out. Eleanor Dorrumple recalled that she had met with Jane and other mutual friends and that they talked Jane into charging a few "necessities," such as clothes, since she had so little.

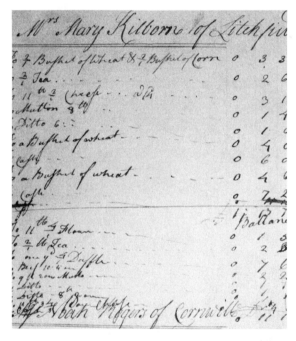

Moses Seymour's 1773 account book shows items charged at his Litchfield, Connecticut, shop by Mrs. Mary Kilborne. (The Litchfield Historical Society)

The Ruling of the Court

The chancellor believed Jane. Accordingly, he ruled that "the Defendant pay to the Complainant the rate of thirty Pounds Current Money per Annum while they live separate, which payment is to commence from April 20, 1736 being the Day of filing her Bill in this Court . . . " He also ordered Jeremiah pay Jane "all her Costs and Charges" for the suit.

This decision upheld the "doctrine of necessities." The law seemed to acknowledge that married women were at a disadvantage in trying to provide for themselves, their primary duties being to bear children and act as helpmates to their husbands. Since Americans held wives neither politically nor legally responsible for themselves—preventing them from making contracts, suing or be sued, managing their property, or winning custody of their children—the courts reasoned that the law was obligated to protect wives when husbands would not.

For Further Reading

Kerber, Linda. *Women of the Republic: Intellect and Ideology in Revolutionary America.* New York: W. W. Norton, 1980.

Salmon, Marylynn. *Women and the Law of Property in Early America.* Chapel Hill: The University of North Carolina Press, 1986.

Spruill, Julia Cherry. *Women's Life and Work in the Southern Colonies.* New York: W. W. Norton, 1938, 1966.

Burk v. Phips: 1793

Plaintiff: Mrs. Burk **Defendant:** Mr. Phips **Plaintiff's Claim:** That Phips indentured the minor Edward Burk to another without his mother's consent, depriving her of Edward's services **Chief Lawyer for Defendant:** Unknown **Chief Lawyer for Plaintiff:** Unknown **Justices:** Andrew Adams, Chief Justice Eliphalet Dyer, Jesse Root, and Erastus Wolcott **Place:** New Haven, Connecticut **Date of Decision:** January term, 1793 **Decision:** Fathers, not mothers, own the services of their sons

SIGNIFICANCE

This case illustrates how few rights eighteenth-century mothers had to their children.

Under English and American common law, fathers automatically gained custody of their children—a source of free labor—after a divorce or separation. Women challenged this inequity in 1848 at the first women's rights convention at Seneca Falls, New York, in their Declaration of Rights and Sentiments. *Burk v. Phips* illustrates how the child custody laws worked.

At the age of sixteen, Edward, a minor, worked on a ship belonging to Mr. Phips, at the port of Charleston, South Carolina. Edward had agreed to work for Phips as a seaman for three months. However, during this period, Phips "sold and executed a bill of sale" to bind [indenture] Edward to work for a Mr. Thomas for several years. Phips forced Edward to go aboard Thomas's ship, which was about to depart for another country.

Edward's mother objected to this, as did her son. Burk said she had lost her son's "person, service, and company." The damage to her, according to a writ dated April 4, 1792, was an inflated fifteen hundred pounds.

A Connecticut jury decided for Burk and awarded her fifteen pounds for damages. However, Phips appealed because of a technicality—the wording of the indictment (a written accusation charging that a crime occurred).

The Connecticut Superior Court agreed. The court noted that Burk was a married woman (with fewer rights than a single woman). Her husband was probably living, as the indictment did not declare him dead. Since her husband must be alive, he—not his wife—owned Edward's labor. Therefore, the court granted Phips' motion to stop the judgment. In the words of the court:

Motion in arrest adjudged sufficient—1st. There is no averment in the declaration that the plaintiff is a *feme sole* [single woman], or but that said Edward's father is living. 2d. It doth not appear that she was guardian or any way entitled to the services of said boy; that as a mother she is not, which differs the case from that of a father's commencing the action, for he is the natural guardian of his minor children, and entitled to their services.

Common law through the 1700s dictated that children under 21 were the property of their fathers, not their mothers. This was significant as children were sources of free labor. In this 1796 lithograph, a girl milks a cow, a daily chore. (Prints and Photographs Division, Library of Congress)

Changes in custody law had already begun before the 1848 Seneca Falls Convention. In 1813, a Pennsylvania decision, *Commonwealth v. Addicks* (see page 271), gave a mother temporary custody during her daughters' "tender years." Then, in 1860, New Jersey codified the "tender years" doctrine. By the late nineteenth century, courts looked at the "best interests of the child" as a guide in most custody battles. By the turn of the century, separated or divorced mothers regularly won custody of their children, as they do today, except when wealthier husbands challenge them.

For Further Reading

Hoff, Joan. *Law, Gender, and Injustice: A Legal History of U.S. Women.* New York: New York University Press, 1991.

Kerber, Linda K. *Women's America: Refocusing the Past.* New York: Oxford University Press, 1991.

Salmon, Marylynn. *Women and the Law of Property in Early America.* Chapel Hill: University of North Carolina Press, 1986.

Wortman, Marlene Stein. *Women in American Law, Vol. I.* New York: Holmes & Meier Publishers, 1985.

Barnes v. Hart: 1793

Plaintiff: William White, lessee of Earles Barnes   **Defendant:** Solomon Hart
Plaintiff's Claim: That common law voids the wills of wives. A simple pre-marital agreement allowing a married woman to own and control her own property is valid *only* if a trust (guardianship) administers it. Wives are incapable of administering it otherwise.
Chief Lawyers for Defendant: Mr. Sergeant and Mr. Wilcocks
Chief Lawyers for Plaintiff: Mr. Rawle and Mr. Bankson   **Justices:** William Bradford, *Chief Justice Thomas McKean,* Edward Shippen Jr., and Jasper Yeates   **Place:** Philadelphia, Pennsylvania   **Date of Decision:** 1793
Decision: The law supports the decision of a husband, before marriage, to make a simple contract with his wife permitting her to will her lands to whomever she chooses. In Pennsylvania it is not necessary for a wife's estate to be administered by trustees to be legal.

SIGNIFICANCE

Barnes v. Hart was one of the earliest decisions in America to strengthen the right of wives to control their own property by making pre-marital contracts with their fiancés. These "separate agreements" represented an important advance in the law.

D erived from broad principles of justice and precedent, rather than written legislation, English common law was the basis of America's legal codes. Under it, the old French word *feme* (the modern version is *femme)* occurs in legal parlance as *feme covert,* meaning a married woman. *Feme sole* means a single woman. The term *covert* comes from the legal doctrine of *coverture* and means that a husband protects or "covers" his wife. English common law regulated marriage by using this principle. *Coverture* merged a wife's property and identity with those of her husband, and this meant that wives lost the legal rights they had held before marriage.

The Lawes Resolutions of Women's Rights; or The Lawes Provision for Women (London, 1632) gives the following interpretation of the word *coverture:* "When a small brooke or little river incorporateth with Rhodanus, Humber or the Thames, the poor rivulet looseth its name, it is carried and recarried with the new associate, it bereth no sway, it possesseth nothing during coverture." In this way a *feme covert* became legally disabled when she married, becoming with her husband "one person" (that person being the man) in the eyes of the law. This principle of common law was dominant in early America.

By contrast, a single woman or widow *(feme sole)* had more legal rights than her married counterpart. She could control her own property and wages, engage in business, act as an administrator of an estate, and make contracts. Perhaps it was this experience of freedom that led a Pennsylvania widow to make her betrothal to the man she loved conditional on retaining rights to her own property.

The Wealthy Widow

Margaret Erwin was a well-off widow, who owned over fifty-six acres of land. She received an annuity of twenty-five pounds, and expected a large inheritance upon the death of her mother. In 1774, she fell in love with Matthew Henderson and agreed to marry him. Margaret Erwin wanted to ensure that her property, both real and personal, would remain in her family. So the couple made a simple contract giving her the control of her own property *after* the wedding and allowing her to will it to whomever she chose.

However, Pennsylvania law (and American custom) permitted a wife to protect her own property ("separate estate") only if she had a trust—or guardian, usually a male relative—administer it for her. The law assumed wives were incapable of administering property themselves. The Hendersons failed to do this, an oversight that would initiate a legal challenge to Margaret Henderson's will sixteen years later.

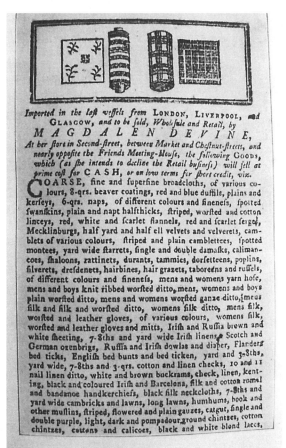

In this 1768 ad from the *Pennsylvania Gazette*, Magdalen Devine offers merchandise for sale at her store. If she married, this property would go to her husband unless the couple made a premarital settlement.

In January 1790, Margaret, who had fallen ill, drafted her final will. Having no children, she bequeathed five shillings to Earles Barnes, her nephew and heir-at-law (the person whom the law says inherits when no will exists). To her other nephews and nieces, she left different amounts. She willed the remainder of the estate to others and appointed Joseph Hart and Nathaniel Erwin as her executors. Two months later, she died.

Hart and Erwin sold their properties. However, Walter White, a tenant (or lessee) of Earles Barnes, brought a legal action (an ejectment) against the other inheritors, hoping to win a share of their real estate.

Can Married Women Make Wills?

To win, White had to challenge Margaret Henderson's will in court. His attorneys—Rawle and Bankson—argued that married women could *not* make wills under common law. They claimed that the pre-marital agreement made by the Hendersons was legal only if *trustees* administered her separate estate. Their evidence was a state law that declared "wills of any manors, lands, tenements or other [inherited property] made by any woman *covert,* shall not be taken to be good or effectual law."

In their argument, Rawle and Bankson made a distinction between common law and "equity law." The cornerstones of the common law are judicial precedents rather than written laws. By contrast, equity law is decided by a judge, and is based on the judge's sense of fairness. Equity law originated in England in reaction to the inability of common law courts to provide a remedy for every injury. For example, equity law introduced the idea of the wife's separate estate. In England, the Court of Chancery handled equity law, and some colonies followed this practice as well.

Under equity law, a prenuptial contract could itemize the property a woman brought into marriage. Wives could also bring lawsuits against husbands who failed to abide by their agreements. However, the courts construed pre-marital contracts narrowly, so most women, unable to finance a lawsuit, continued to lose control of their property after marriage.

In America there were twelve chancery courts, but none in Pennsylvania, Connecticut and Massachusetts. Therefore, in *Barnes v. Hart*, the Supreme Court of Pennsylvania had to decide whether the English use of equity law (decided in the English case *Rippon vs. Dawding)* applied to Henderson's will—specifically as it concerned her real estate.

The Decision

The court debated whether the prenuptial agreement permitted Henderson to will her separate estate to whomever she chose. The court decided agreed that she could.

> It was formerly doubted whether marriage was not such a suspension of the capacity of the wife to execute any effective conveyance [transferring title to real estate to another person] of her property, as deprived her of the power of assenting to any alienation even of real estate. . . . But it is now settled that a wife has a capacity by her consent, of making a valid contract as to her separate estate, and that therefore a mere covenant or agreement between a woman and her intended husband . . . that she shall have a power to dispose of her real estate, without any estate being vested in trustees . . . will bind her heir. . . .

The Pennsylvania jurists had decided to follow the lead of the English chancery court. If a man wanted to agree by contract to permit his wife to dispose of her own real estate, he could. Chief Justice Thomas McKean reasoned:

> There is no Court clothed with chancery powers in Pennsylvania; but equity is part of our law. . . . Why should she not have a right in equity, of disposing of her lands, as incident to her ownership? For she is to be taken, as to the execution of this power, as a *feme sole*.

The court unanimously decided that the Hendersons *could* make a binding pre-marital agreement and that Margaret Henderson could will her lands to whomever she chose. To reach this decision, the court treated her as a single woman *(feme sole)*, who by law held the right to make a will.

As legal scholar Marylynn Salmon has written, "Simple agreements marked an equitable advancement in the law on separate estates." This progress would continue until the passage of the "married woman's property acts" of the mid-nineteenth century. These acts, passed between 1839 and 1848, permanently changed wives' status by giving them the right to control their own separate property, the rents and profits earned from it, their wages, and in some states, equal custody to their children. By the mid-1870s, every Northern state had passed a married woman's property act, and by 1900, Southern states had followed suit. After the introduction of equity law, these acts constituted the most important early advance for women's rights in American legal history.

For Further Reading

Hoffer, Peter Charles. *Law and People in Colonial America*. Baltimore: The Johns Hopkins University Press, 1992.

Salmon, Marylynn. *Women and the Law of Property in Early America*. Chapel Hill: The University of North Carolina Press, 1986.

Wortman, Marlene Stein. *Women in American Law, Vol. 1*. New York: Holmes & Meier Publishers, Inc., 1985.

Scott v. Scott: 1795

Plaintiffs: Creditors of John Scott, deceased **Defendant:** Sarah Scott, widow of the deceased **Plaintiffs' Claim:** That the commissioners appointed by a court of probate and named in a writ of dower should not have awarded Sarah Scott one tractor parcel of land instead of one-third of each separate piece of her husband's real estate, or a sum of money
Chief Lawyers for Defendant: Mr. Pinckney and Mr. Ford
Chief Lawyers for Plaintiffs: Mr. Read and Mr. Pringle **Justices:** Elihu Hall Bay, *Chief Justice John Rutledge* **Place:** South Carolina
Date of Decision: May term, 1795 **Decision:** The widow was entitled to only one-third of each parcel of land or an equivalent sum of money

SIGNIFICANCE

In favoring creditors over widows, this decision was one of the first to put the claims of creditors above those of widows.

U nder English common law, a wife could not own real estate. If her husband died without a will (intestate), she received a one-third "life interest" in his estate. If there were no children to inherit, she could receive one-half. "Life interest" meant that a widow could use the property during her lifetime although she could not sell or will it to others. Husbands, if they wished, could will their wives more generous settlements, but they could not leave them with less than one-third.

To protect a wife's "dower rights," the law forbade husbands to mortgage or sell real estate without their wives' consent. Dower rights also took precedence over the claims of creditors—guaranteeing widows a measure of economic security.

After the American Revolution, however, the value of land increased. Dower rights interfered with men's freedom to buy and sell it. In response, many courts slowly chipped away at widows' rights. Then, in 1795, the Superior Court of South Carolina took the first step in the long road to abolishing them.

Not So Fast

Upon his death, John Scott owned property in town and in the country. A probate court gave John's widow, Sarah, a "life tenancy" in the couple's home instead of her one-third dower right to their lands.

However, John Scott had died in debt. His angry creditors sued to prevent his wife from receiving the town house. Lawyers for the creditors argued that the court ought to have assigned her dower out of each tract of property left by her husband, rather than give her "the most valuable part of the estate." Her right to live in the house "had very much impaired the value of that lot out of which the whole dower was assigned, and rendered it unsaleable and unproductive, being encumbered with her life estate." They said the lands in question "in fact belong to them, and not to the heir," until their bills were paid. They also claimed that under statutes adopted by South Carolina in 1777, court commissioners could only assign dowers by "metes and bounds" (a one-third share of each separate piece of real property owned by the husband). Where this proved impractical, the court should pay a widow a lump-sum of cash equal to one-third of her husband's real estate.

In this mourning embroidery, c. 1805, a widow pays her respects at the grave of her departed husband.

The widow's lawyers argued that the creditors did not have legal standing (a clear personal stake) to sue and that the probate commissioners had acted correctly.

Creditors First

The court upheld the rights of the creditors to be heard in the trial, and eventually ruled in their favor: *only* with the agreement of all those involved could dower rights be assigned in "whole tracts" (the house and lot on which it stood). The court said widows would suffer if they received "an entire tract in some remote and uncultivated part of the state." More importantly, creditors would suffer if they were not paid for their services because an entire property could not be sold.

The Superior Court ordered that the actions of the probate commissioners be set aside. When the commissioners met again they changed Sarah Scott's dower to a lump-sum of cash equivalent to one-third of the estate's value, ending her claim to her husband's property. As a result, the creditors got their money back when the house was sold.

The court's decision reflected the priorities of commerce. Speculators could not trade land at its true market value so long as widows could claim one-third in rents and profits. Of course, some women may have preferred cash payments—which they could spend as they wished—to life-tenancy. Others, however, faced serious economic and emotional distress because they were not free to inherit and dispose of their property because of decisions such as this.

Dower remained the most important way in which the law protected widows until the twentieth century. The custom remained in effect until 1945, when the Administration of Estates Act abolished it.

For Further Reading

Hoffer, Peter Charles. *Law and People in Colonial America*. Baltimore: Johns Hopkins University Press, 1992.

Kerber, Linda K. *Women's America: Refocusing the Past*. New York: Oxford University Press, 1991.

Salmon, Marylynn. *Women and the Law of Property in Early America*. Chapel Hill: University of North Carolina Press, 1986.

Wortman, Marlene Stein. *Women in American Law, Vol. I*. New York: Holmes & Meier Publishers, 1985.

Megrath v. Robertson: 1795

Plaintiff: Catharine Megrath   **Defendant:** Administrators of John Robertson and Ann Robertson   **Plaintiff's Claim:** That Megrath should inherit the estate of her late daughter   **Chief Lawyer for Defendant:** Mr. Ford
Chief Lawyer for Plaintiff: C. C. Pinckney   **Chancellors:** John Mathews and Hugh Rutledge   **Place:** Charleston, South Carolina
Date of Decision: August 1795   **Decision:** Megrath could inherit her daughter's estate because the property had been maintained and run by her with her husband's obvious approval

SIGNIFICANCE

South Carolina, like Maryland and Virginia, was tolerant toward wives who wished to conduct their own business affairs. However, they could do so only with the—at the very least, tacit—agreement of their husbands.

In the colonial period, single females operated their own businesses. Called *feme sole traders*, these women made contracts, brought lawsuits, took on debts, and engaged in other commercial activities. Wives could do none of these things.

However, a few states did allow wives to participate in business, if their husbands approved in writing. *Megrath v. Robertson*, which dates from the Federalist period, shows that South Carolina dealt liberally with wives in trade.

Ahead of Their Time

John and Ann Robertson had lived together for many years in Charleston, South Carolina. Both operated their own businesses, although John had never signed papers permitting Ann to do so. Neither had he signed an agreement that her earnings or profits would belong to her, not him, as was customary under common law.

Yet Ann *did* have her husband's blessing: She had for many years managed her business; collected its profits; bought property in her own name; lent her husband money; and employed a clerk to handle her accounts.

Many instances clearly demonstrate her independence from him. When one of her debtors tried to pay John the money he rightly owned Ann, John told him to settle up with his wife, as she held the note. When John would sometimes caution his wife against overbidding at auctions, she would reply—in front of witnesses—that it was her money to do with as she pleased, and bid as she chose.

When John died without a will (intestate), Ann inherited all of his estate. (Under common law, without a will, widows received one-third to one-half their husband's estates.) She administered the inheritance, inventoried it, and sold it, merging his property with hers. After Ann died—also intestate—her mother, Catharine Megrath, became her "heir-at-law," (the person the common law chose to inherit when there was no will). Megrath assumed she would inherit her daughter's estate, since there were no children or other living close relatives.

However, Ann's administrators, also executors of John's estate, were unsure how to distribute the wealth. They believed Ann's separate estate (from her business) should have been merged with that of her husband, as would normally have been done. So they fought Megrath's claims in the South Carolina Chancery Court.

Hers or His?

Chancery courts exercised "equity" law. In early America, as in Great Britain, chancellors administered equity decisions. In contrast to common law, which turns on precedents, equity jurisprudence rests on the chancellor's sense of equality. He frequently ruled on disputes concerning marital property, for example, whether wives owned property separately from their husbands.

The idea of a "separate estate" evolved in Great Britain as an exception to the common law principle that the husband controlled all of his wife's property. Over the years chancery courts expanded wives' property rights, but the common law courts refused to enforce them. Hence, a dual system developed for establishing the rights of married women: under one, women held equal property rights with men; under the other, none at all.

Opposed by Puritans and Quakers as disruptive of family harmony, chancery courts did not exist in Connecticut, Massachusetts, or Pennsylvania. However, New York, Maryland, Virginia, and South Carolina established them, indicating the region's support for married women's property rights. In the colonies there were about twelve chancery courts.

Tacit Permission Is Enough

A chancery court would decide the question of who would inherit Ann's estate. The lawyer for the administrators, Mr. Ford, claimed that John had left no written authorization for his wife to be in business (or act as a *feme sole* trader). Therefore, she had no separate property—everything belonged to her husband. As for Ann's mother, he claimed that Megrath was a British citizen who could not take possession of the real estate because of her citizenship.

Megrath's attorney, C. C. Pinckney, responded that South Carolina law had no precise prescription for how a wife could become a sole trader. However,

John's tacit consent had allowed Ann to act in this capacity. That Ann incurred debts, which involved lawsuits, indicated that she owned separate property and had been expected to pay what she owed from it.

The judges took time to deliberate these arguments. In the end, they decided that the trial turned on three questions. Did John appoint Ann a sole trader? What benefits resulted to her from it? What portion of Ann's estate should go to her mother?

On the first point, the court concluded that John had tacitly permitted Ann to operate her business. If he had wanted to enforce his common law rights to her profits, he could have done so. The judges felt there was "no law here defining what is a sole dealer, and how a *feme covert* [married woman] can be made a sole trader; . . . if the husband permits his wife to act as such, he relinquishes the control he had at common law."

On the second question, the court ruled that Ann "became sole mistress of the property which she acquired in the character of a sole trader, free from the control of her husband." The judges separated the property in this way: "What was brought home to the house must be considered the husband's, unless shown to be hers by documents, deeds, or [items] employed in her trade; and except her wearing apparel. . . . As to the land, the titles were made to her of her houses; to him of his." Ann was entitled to one-half of John's estate, plus the property she earned as a businesswoman.

Megrath was entitled to "the whole of her [daughter's] personal estate, and to the real [estate] if the British treaty now pending [allowing British subjects to hold American lands], be ratified by our government." (The treaty of November 19, 1794, commonly called Mr. Jay's Treaty, was pending in the U.S. Senate. Under Article 9, it was agreed that "British subjects who now hold lands in the territories of the United States [and American citizens holding in Great Britain] shall continue to hold them, according to the nature and tenure of their respective estates and titles therein; and may grant, sell or devise the same.")

Despite the tolerance of South Carolina's chancery court, few women achieved economic independence. Their business activities remained strictly illegal without the express permission of their spouses. A few other states did allow abandoned wives to act as *feme sole traders;* and some granted this status to certain groups, such as the spouses of seamen. But in general, married women whose husbands supported them could not go out into the world and become breadwinners.

These laws changed by the nineteenth century. In 1821, in *Kenny v. Udall and Kenny* (see page 274) the question was not whether wives were entitled to the wealth they brought with them into marriage, but how much of it could be set aside for their exclusive use. Beginning with the 1830s, the states passed a series of married woman's property acts that gave wives absolute control over their own property. By the turn of the century, the principle had become firmly established throughout the United States.

For Further Reading

Dexter, Elizabeth Anthony. *Colonial Women of Affairs*. Boston: Houghton Mifflin Company, 1924.

Hoffer, Peter Charles. *Law and People in Colonial America*. Baltimore: The Johns Hopkins University Press, 1992.

Kerber, Linda K. *Women's America: Refocusing the Past*. New York: Oxford University Press, 1991.

Salmon, Marylynn. *Women and the Law of Property in Early America*. Chapel Hill: University of North Carolina Press, 1986.

Wortman, Marlene Stein. *Women in American Law, Vol. I*. New York: Holmes & Meier Publishers, 1985.

Beall and King v. Woolford: 1797

Plaintiffs: Hamilton and Leah Beall and John King   **Defendant:** Levin Woolford   **Plaintiff's Claim:** Their mother's will was lawful
Chief Lawyer for Defendant: Luther Martin
Chief Lawyer for Plaintiffs: William Cooke   **Chancellor:** Alexander Contee Hanson   **Place:** Annapolis, Maryland   **Date of Decision:** November 7, 1797
Decision: The court upheld a pre-marital agreement that allowed a wife to will her own property, an advance for married women

SIGNIFICANCE

This was Maryland's first decision upholding a prenuptial agreement executed without trustees (or guardians).

In early America, two conflicting legal principles created different interpretations of the rights of married women. The first was common law, grounded in precedents. The second was equity law, based on the judge's sense of fairness, or equality. A look at disputes tried in equity courts (called courts of chancery) appears to show wives holding nearly equal property rights with men. A glance at rulings made in courts of common law, however, show wives with few property rights at all. Equity law— which gave wives the right to own, manage, transfer the title to (convey), and will (devise) real property—represented a radical breakthrough for women. It was the most significant change in the legal status of women until the "married women's property acts" in the nineteenth century.

From 1750 to 1830, the courts of common law jealously protected a husband's superior rights to his wife's property. He owned her personal property—such as jewelry, clothes, and furniture—and managed her real estate, that is, her lands or houses. However, the courts of chancery allowed wives to keep some rights to their own property. (These courts first appeared in New York, Maryland, Virginia, and South Carolina.) Even in the chancery courts, a wife could not completely control her property unless it was supervised by one or more trustees (or guardians), such as a brother, uncle, or family friend. Short of bringing a lawsuit, a wife could not oppose the decisions of her trustees.

About 1793, a few American courts tested a new British rule of equity law. This rule allowed a married woman to keep control over her own property if she and her fiancé drew up a simple contract before marriage.

The Test Case

In 1797, Maryland for the first time made lawful a pre-marital settlement made *without* the supervision of trustees. The case came before Maryland's Court of Chancery.

Beall and King v. Woolford was the first decision of its kind to support a marriage settlement without trustees. This eighteenth-century coat of arms embroidery depicts the joining through marriage of Judge Samuel Corwin to Abigail Russell in Massachusetts.

Ann Woolford, of Somerset County, had, by an earlier marriage to John King, three children: Whittington, Leah, and John. Later, Ann married a man named Jones. When he died, Levin Woolford proposed to her. On June 19, 1781, the engaged couple agreed in writing that Ann could will (devise) the property she had received from her former husbands to her children. The contract read:

> Know all men by these presents that I Levin Woolford of Somerset County am held and firmly bound unto Ann Jones widow of the County aforesaid on the full and just sum of twenty thousand dollars common money of the State of Maryland . . . which payment well and truly to be made and done. I bind myself, my Heirs, Executors and administrators firmly by these presents sealed with my seal and dated this nineteenth day of June Anno Domini

one thousand seven hundred and eighty one:

The Condition of the above obligation is such that if the above bound Levin Woolford should be the longest liver and should agree that the aforesaid Ann Jones at her death should dispose of her estate hereafter mentioned either by will or deed of gifts as follows, one negro man named Tomey and one named Cesar, one negro woman named Frank[sic], three negro lads Joshua, Jupiter and Jim, two negro girls Rose and Beck [sic], nine young heffers [sic], eighteen head of Sheep, and three beds and furniture if living and not taken from him by the Enemy before her death, provided that the above Levin be cleared from all claims that shall come against the estate by John Kings Heirs or any other person or persons claiming any debts, dues or demands contracted before her marrying the aforesaid Levin Woolford; and farther [sic], the aforesaid Levin Woolford does agree to give the aforesaid Ann Jones, in case she should be the longest liver, four hundred acres of land on the west side of the main road beginning below *where* John Richer now lives and where my line crosses the main road and running up the said road till a north course includes the quantity to the extent of my land, during her widowhood, she committing no waste. Then the above obligation to be void, or else to be and remain in full force virtue and power in Law. Given under my hand and seal the day and year above written. [Signed] L. Woolford

Ten years later, during an illness, Ann told her husband that she wanted to write her will. Levin refused her request. Frightened, Ann, with the help of friends, wrote her will, dated October 19, 1791, in secret:

> I Ann Woolford being of sound mind and memory do make this my last will and Testament in manner and form following . . .: –
>
> . . . I give and bequeath unto my daughter Leah Bell two negros namely Cesar and Tomey and two beds and furniture one to be my small bed: –
>
> Item, I give and bequeath unto my son Whittington King two negros namely Frankey and Beck and one bed and furniture: –
>
> Item, I give and bequeath to my son John King four negroes namely Jupiter, James, Rose, and Jane and two beds and furniture. . . .
>
> Item. It is my will and desire that all the remainder of my estate be Equally divided between my three children Leah Beall, Whittington King and John King.

Ann died a few days later. An angry Levin refused to pay the legacies to Leah and John, and on November 28, 1792, the two brought a lawsuit against him in the Court of Chancery. (Whittington did not join them.)

Levin's Side

Levin's attorney told the court that his client had always looked after Ann's children and treated them with affection. He had paid for their schooling and medical bills and lent them money. Knowing this, he said, Ann had promised Levin she would leave her property to him. He also alleged Levin was away on business on the day Ann made the will and had never seen it, casting doubt on the its authenticity.

Levin said that because he and Ann had made their prenuptial agreement in private, and because it did not mention trustees, the agreement was not lawful. He would, however, dispense the legacies if the children could agree who would divide it.

Women's Rights Under Equity Law

The court considered the question of whether Levin must fulfill the promises he had made to his late wife. Speaking for the court, Chancellor Alexander Hanson said:

> It would appear extraordinary indeed, if this Court should decide that engagement to be void; when the defendant himself admits, that he ought to be bound by it; when it appears too, that he has had the full benefits of that consideration [marriage] for which he entered into the engagement.
>
> As to those parts of his wife's personal estate. . . . The . . . defendant ought to deliver them to the legatees [inheritors], and to make them a compensation for the use of them since her death.
>
> Levin must honor his contact with his late wife.

In 1818, the Court of Chancery again supported marriage settlements without trustees. The chancellors believed that progress was being made in the area of the property rights of wives:

> [The] stern and ungallant general rules of the common law, by which marriage so sinks the wife under the absolute sway of the husband have been made, in many respects, to yield to a better feeling, and have undergone many wholesome modifications chiefly by the direct, or indirect application of the principles of equity.

The next advance came with the passage of the married woman's property acts between 1839 and 1895. Ever since, the rights of wives to their separate property and to jointly-held property have been expanding. In the late twentieth century, only Louisiana left wives so unprotected that they did not own the clothes they wore. (Louisiana followed the Code Napoléon, which discriminated against women more than the English common law.) In 1981, the Supreme Court's decision in *Kirchberg v. Feenstra* (see page 328) strengthened women's property rights in Louisiana, and lent the weight of the U.S. Constitution to the campaign to end male supremacy in property rights throughout America.

For Further Reading

Hoffer, Peter Charles. *Law and People in Colonial America.* Baltimore: Johns Hopkins University Press, 1992.

Kerber, Linda K. *Women's America: Refocusing the Past.* New York: Oxford University Press, 1991.

Salmon, Marylynn. *Women and the Law of Property in Early America.* Chapel Hill: University of North Carolina Press, 1986.

Spruill, Julia Cherry. *Women's Life and Work in the Southern Colonies.* W. W. Norton, 1972.

Wortman, Marlene Stein. *Women in American Law, Vol. I.* New York: Holmes & Meier Publishers, 1985.

Fry v. Derstler: 1798

Plaintiff: John Fry **Defendant:** Adam Derstler **Plaintiff's Claim:** That he was entitled to damages because his wife, from whom he was separated, had "criminal conversation" (adultery) with Adam Derstler
Chief Lawyers for Defendant: William Montgomery and Mr. McKean
Chief Lawyers for Plaintiff: Mr. Smith and Mr. Hopkins **Justices:** Chief Justice Thomas McKean and Justice Edward Shippen, Jr. **Place:** Lancaster, Pennsylvania **Date of Decision:** April 13, 1798 **Decision:** A jury awarded damages to John Fry, apparently believing he did not willingly consent to separating from his wife

SIGNIFICANCE

This trial illustrates the most common form of divorce in early America—a mutual agreement between spouses to separate. It is also a good example of how the common law gave only husbands the right to dissolve a marriage until public opinion demanded change.

Colonial marriage and divorce laws were more flexible than those of England. In the words of historian Peter Charles Hoffer, they were "slightly more open to the needs of a mobile, heterogeneous, opportunistic, fluid society." However, Protestant England kept its earlier Roman Catholic attitude toward divorce: it banned the practice. After 1670, Parliament granted only ninety "legislative" divorces between 1692 and 1785. Most colonists also viewed divorce as a shameful, even immoral practice, and practiced it rarely. Abandoned wives—in desperation—were the most frequent applicants for divorce.

Couples ended their marriage simply by separating. Informally, couples divided their property so that both spouses could have separate households. Where couples could not agree, they went to court.

The courts offered two solutions. One was "absolute" divorce with the right to remarry *(a vinculo matrimonii);* the other was separation "from bed and board" *(a mensa et thoro)* without the right to remarry. Both were more common in colonies under Puritan influence, where residents viewed marriage as a contract, not a sacrament. Massachusetts, for example, permitted absolute divorce on grounds of adultery, cruelty, or desertion. Connecticut was even more liberal. However, these departures from English tradition did not occur else-where. For example, the southern colonies never granted absolute divorces.

After the Revolution many of the new states quickly reformed their divorce laws. In 1785, Pennsylvania passed a law granting jurisdiction over divorce to the state supreme court. Under the statute, men and women could obtain absolute divorces for adultery, desertion, bigamy—and sexual incapacity (if known before the marriage). Couples also won divorces "from bed and board" for these reasons and for cruelty.

Why the unhappy Frys did not go to the supreme court to divorce is unclear, but their actions indicated they—and their neighbors—wanted a simpler solution.

A Do-It-Yourself Divorce

The Frys married in 1785. Within a year or so, Mrs. Fry fell in love with Adam Derstler and had an affair with him. In 1787, she left her husband and went to live in her father's house. Furious, her husband placed ads warning merchants not to allow his wife to buy items on his account and declaring he "was determined never to cohabit with her again."

Mr. Fry sent arbitrators to his father-in-law's house to divide the marital property, receiving:

> 27 [pounds] for doing the work of a farmer, &c. on the father-in-law's plantation, but deducted 12 [pounds] for boarding his wife and keeping his mare, finding a balance due of 15 [pounds] due to the plaintiff, for which his father-in-law gave his note.

The arbitrators—along with neighbors and family alike—agreed that the couple should separate. They declared that "either should be at liberty to marry whom they pleased." However, the law did not allow this. Common law gave husbands the power to decide whether to divorce. As witnesses proved, the separation "was agreed to by Fry with great reluctance, as he wished to take his wife home with him."

Four months after the Frys' separation, the new lovers married. They lived together in Derstler's home and raised two children. Seven years later, unable to forgive or forget, Fry sued Derstler for "criminal conversation" with his wife, demanding payment for damages.

The court instructed the jury that time limits to the adultery charge had long since expired. Besides, both Mr. and Mrs. Fry had agreed to separate. If the jury found that their agreement was mutual, they should find for Derstler. The jury, however, favored Fry, awarding him 227 pounds damages.

The court then ordered a new trial, explaining, "The law is perfectly clear, that where a husband and wife live in a state of separation, an action for criminal conversation cannot be maintained." Derstler should not pay "damages [to Fry] for depriving him of the society of his wife, whom he had before parted with, with his full consent." A new court heard the case in Lancaster on April 13, 1798. The jury still sided with Fry, awarding him 150 pounds in damages.

After the Revolution, Americans wanted more liberal divorce laws. The states—more responsive than the courts—passed statutes granting divorces on certain grounds, such as adultery, desertion, and physical cruelty. For instance, an 1859 Indiana law broadened the grounds for divorce to include drunkenness, cruelty, and abandonment. In 1860, Elizabeth Cady Stanton spoke to the Tenth National Woman's Rights Conference in New York. Her speech urged making getting married harder and divorce easier to obtain. More shocking, she asked that divorce be granted on grounds of mere "incompatibility." Although this suggestion was extremely controversial in the nineteenth century, it would become widely accepted as grounds for divorce in the twentieth century.

For Further Reading

Hoff, Joan. *Law, Gender, and Injustice: A Legal History of U.S. Women.* New York: New York University Press, 1991.

Hoffer, Peter Charles. *Law and People in Colonial America.* Baltimore: Johns Hopkins University Press, 1992.

Kahn, Ada P., and Linda Hughey Holt. *The A-Z of Women's Sexuality.* New York: Facts on File, 1900.

Kerber, Linda K. *Women's America: Refocusing the Past.* New York: Oxford University Press, 1991.

Salmon, Marylynn. *Women and the Law of Property in Early America.* Chapel Hill: University of North Carolina Press, 1986.

Wortman, Marlene Stein. *Women in American Law, Vol. I.* New York: Holmes & Meier Publishers, Inc., 1985.

Griffith v. Griffith's Executors: 1798

Appellant: Martha Griffith   **Appellees:** Heirs of Samuel Griffith
Appellant's Claim: That under Maryland law a widow was entitled to a
dower right of one-third her deceased husband's personal property, as well
as his real property   **Chief Lawyer for Appellees:** Mr. Martin
Chief Lawyer for Appellant: Mr. Winchester   **Justices:** *William Pinkney,*
Mr. Duvall, and Chief Justice Goldsborough   **Place:** Maryland
Dates of Decision: May term, 1798   **Decision:** The court of appeals
awarded Martha Griffith one-third of her husband's personal property clear of
debts—her dower rights to his real property (land, buildings) were not in
question

SIGNIFICANCE

In this landmark decision Maryland allowed a widow a one-third share of her
husband's personal estate as her dower-right. Because of this and other property
decisions, Maryland women held higher status and had more control over their
lives than elsewhere in early America.

From the settlement of Jamestown in 1607 until the married woman's property rights acts of the mid-nineteenth century, the most important laws affecting wives were those that regulated their dower rights.

Because the common law stripped women of their property rights when they married, wives became vulnerable when their husbands died. In colonial America the majority of husbands left no wills, leaving their wives unable to support themselves. In these cases, courts granted widows a minimum of one-third of their husbands' real estate, called "widow's thirds." However, a widow could not own the property in her own name; therefore, she could not sell or will it, but could only live off the rents during her lifetime.

During the eighteenth century this practice changed—first in England, then in the colonies. Widows lost their claims to personal property, although they kept their one-third shares of real estate. Only Maryland and Virginia continued to allow widows a one-third share of personal property, a practice that Martha Griffith challenged in 1798.

Wives' Rights

Martha Griffith went to court because her husband, Samuel, left a will that pointedly excluded her from inheriting his personal property. Other heirs contested her claim.

Samuel's will, dated 12 January 1794, contained only one clause relating to his wife. It read: "I desire my wife *Martha Griffith*, should have the use and benefit of my farm on Swan Creek during her widowhood; provided she claims no thirds of my land in Rumney Neck, and that she commits no waste of timber, which will be left to the discretion of my executors and trustees hereafter named; and after which period the aforesaid farm to be sold, and the money equally divided between my eight children." The rest of the estate went to the children.

At court, Martha's lawyer, Mr. Winchester, cited numerous acts passed by the Maryland assembly allowing widows to claim their dower shares of personal as well as real property. The earliest law, passed in 1638, allowed widows whose husbands died intestate (without a will) "one moiety [half of the] personal estate, after payment of all debts" but if there were no children, the widow inherited everything.

Similarly, by the acts of 1704 and 1715, a widow received one-third of the husband's personal estate after paying his debts, and one-half if there were no children. Under the act of 1729, a widow inherited all the estate if there were no other heirs such as children, grandchildren, brothers, sisters, nieces, or nephews.

In 1798 Maryland's dower law was disputed in *Griffith v. Griffith*. In this mourning picture, c. 1800, a widow visits the grave of her late husband.

Samuel's executors, represented by lawyer Martin, claimed that the acts of the assembly did not apply to such cases. He argued that "The common law of England is the common law of Maryland. The common law of England was adopted in Maryland as it stood at the formation of our government, and it never did deprive the husband of the right to dispose of his personal estate." Maryland women, then, lost their right to personal property when English women did. Martin claimed that the acts of the Maryland assembly were irrelevant aberrations.

The court of appeals agreed with Martha. The court believed that Maryland's 1704 law had specified that widows receive a dower-right to personal property. The bench explained that the colonists who settled Maryland introduced the English common law, which granted widows a one-third interest in personal and real property. Maryland law never reversed this practice.

Justice William Pinkney wrote, "It has for many years . . . been the prevailing idea in this country among lawyers . . . that a husband could not devise [will] away the whole of his personal estate from his wife." He quoted *Blackstone's Commentaries:* "By the common law of England, as it stood in the reign of *Henry II*, a man's personal estate was to be divided in three equal parts; of which one went to his heirs or lineal descendants, another to his wife, and the third was at his own disposal." "The shares of the wife and the children were called their *reasonable parts*," which the husband could not will away from them—this had been the law of England from the time of the *Magna Charta* (1215).

There were many exceptions to Maryland's leniency toward widows. According to historian Joan Hoff, the number of colonial women who died with enough property to be probated "seldom exceeded more than 10 percent of all the probate records in most counties for the entire period before the American Revolution," and probably averaged no more than seven percent. Although inheritance laws improved somewhat for women after the Revolution, dower laws did not. Hoff writes that the percentages of their husband's estates that widows received *declined* from the Revolutionary period until the 1820s. After the Civil War, however, many states gave widows total ownership of their dower-right rather than a life interest. In 1945, the federal Administration of Estates Act (Section 45) abolished dower. Today in most states the traditional one-third percentage unconditionally passes to the widow in the event her husband dies without a will. (A widow's corresponding right of inheritance is called a "curtesy.")

For Further Reading

Hoff, Joan. *Law, Gender, and Injustice: A Legal History of U.S. Women.* New York: New York University Press, 1991.

Hoffer, Peter Charles. *Law and People in Colonial America.* Baltimore: Johns Hopkins University Press, 1992.

Kerber, Linda K. *Women's America: Refocusing the Past.* New York: Oxford University Press, 1991.

Salmon, Marylynn. *Women and the Law of Property in Early America.* Chapel Hill: University of North Carolina Press, 1986.

Wortman, Marlene Stein. *Women in American Law, Vol. I.* New York: Holmes & Meier Publishers, 1985.

Dibble v. Hutton: 1804

Appellant: Nehemiah Dibble   **Appellee:** Mary Hutton
Appellant's Claim: That Executor Dibble should not have to pay Hutton a
share of the proceeds of land she had owned before her marriage
Chief Lawyers for Appellee: Mr. Ingersoll and R. M. Sherman
Chief Lawyer for Appellant: Mr. Smith   **Justices:** John Allen, Aaron Austin,
Jonathan Brace, Joseph P. Cooke, David Dagget, Oliver Ellsworth, Chauncey
Goodrich, William Hillhouse, Roger Newberry, Thomas Seymour, and William
Williams   **Place:** Hartford, Connecticut   **Dates of Decision:** June, 1804
Decision: The court decided not to enforce the Huttons' marital agreement,
which obliged them to share the profits from a land sale

SIGNIFICANCE
The decision set a negative precedent toward the recognition of "separate
property" rights for wives.

Throughout the nineteenth century the question, "What do women want?" echoed from the press and pulpit. A look at the aftermath of the American Revolution suggests an answer. War had brought women new responsibilities: With men away, they had managed households, businesses, and farms. After the war, they lost these responsibilities. Although the war had promised change, historian Marylynn Salmon finds only "a picture of their enforced dependence" after the Revolution. For example, *no* former colony or new state permitted wives "the legal ability to act independently with regard to property." The reason was the common law idea of "coverture."

The old French word *feme* (the modern version is *femme)* occurs in legal parlance as *feme covert,* meaning a married woman. The term meant that a husband, as head of the household, protected or "covered" his wife. English common law regulated marriage by this principle, which in practice meant the merging of a woman's property and identity with that of her husband, called "coverture."

The benefits of this arrangement were one-sided, for only the wife merged with the husband, not the other way around. Coverture meant that a woman's entire personal property passed absolutely to her husband at marriage. Her real estate (land and buildings) went to him to manage and reap the profits thereof, although wives did have to agree to the sale or mortgage of their property.

Each colony differed in regulating how wives "proved" they had consented to these transactions. Would it be by signing a deed? Testifying to a court officer? Privately talking to a judge? New England courts, especially Connecticut's, were unwilling to enforce such protections for wives. Therefore, as historian Marlene Stein Wortman observes, "The effect of the common law on marital property was to distribute the benefits of land speculation to the husband and the risks to the wife." In New England, once a wife consented to the sale or mortgage of her lands, she had no legal way of ensuring she would profit by it.

A nineteenth-century illustration depicts a colonial wedding. (Prints & Photographs Division, Library of Congress)

The Land Agreement

This was the predicament in which Mary Hutton found herself in 1802. Four years earlier, Mary and her husband, Samuel, had held fifty-five acres of land in Norwalk, Connecticut. Mary had owned one-fourth of them before her marriage. Samuel wanted to sell the lands together, claiming he could not sell his alone without losing money. At first Mary refused, but after Samuel promised to pay her one-fourth of the profits, she finally consented.

The couple then made a contract, agreeing to sell the land on condition Mary received one-fourth of the purchase price. On January 6, 1798, the Huttons sold their acres to Caleb Comstock and Benoni St. John in return for notes promising to pay them 192 pounds and 10 shillings plus interest for the lands. Samuel gave some of these notes to Mary who put them into a drawer.

Before the land sale, in 1792, Samuel had drafted a will, appointing Nehemiah Dibble as his executor. In the will he left Mary that part of his estate that the law required (as dower) for her widowhood, about one-third. When Samuel died in 1799, Dibble said this "dower share" was all Mary should receive, ignoring the sale of her lands. Threatening her with a lawsuit, he demanded she return the I.O.U.s. Mary gave them up, but "with an express reserve, that her claims should not be prejudiced thereby."

After Dibble paid Samuel's debts, $20,000 remained, yet still he refused to pay Mary her share of the land sale. This left her dependent on her friends for support. So Mary went to the county court, "praying that the executor might be ordered, within a reasonable time, to pay her one-fourth of the said 192 [pounds] 10 [shillings] with interest." Mary claimed:

> The executor has since received the money upon said notes; the estate of the said Samuel, after payment of his debts, is the value of $20,000; but the petitioner, notwithstanding, is left dependent upon her friends for support, and has received no compensation for her land, and has no remedy at law.

The county court found that the facts of her story were true, and ordered the executor to pay her $211.03 from Samuel's estate. The superior court, on appeal, also supported Mary. However, Dibble won in the Supreme Court of Errors.

Promoting Domestic Tranquillity

Dibble's counsel thought the essential question was "whether a contract, by husband and wife, made during coverture, and to be performed during coverture, is a legal, valid contract." Common law courts would say "no." Equity courts might say "yes." In contrast to common law, which rests on precedents, equity law depends on a judge's sense of fair play. Chancery (or equity) courts, headed by a chancellor, dispensed equity law. Both in England and in some of the southern colonies, they often decided disputes involving a wife's "separate property."

Rhetorically, Smith asked the court, "Are we . . . to take, at once, the last step, which corruption has there introduced, and bury in oblivion the principle, that a *feme covert* has no separate existence [from her husband]? . . . We happily have never heard of . . . relations giving property to married women, to their separate use." He continued: "While husband and wife have but one interest, you may calculate upon the most perfect harmony; but create separate interests, and you destroy domestic tranquillity. While both go to the same purse, it may be expected, that each will promote what is in the interest of both."

Finally, in an often repeated excuse to deny wives property rights, Smith told the court, "If society was here, as in England, and vast estates were depending upon the principle, there might be some reason for adapting it; but, by granting this application, you destroy, at a stroke, one-half of what we have ever deemed a marriage contract. That such a case was never before heard of in Connecticut, shows, that such contracts were never expected to be enforced."

The Husband Is the One

In response, Mary's attorneys argued that even in America some courts had recognized the principle of a separate interest between husband and wife. They cited *Adams v. Kellogg* (1786), a decision in which the Supreme Court of Errors allowed Mary Kellogg to leave real estate she had inherited from her deceased husband to her current one. (Although the court recognized a wife's separate interest in the case, the ruling ran counter to the general trend in Connecticut.) The lawyers asked, "Where, therefore, we find the English rules so clear, and the justice of the case so apparent, and no rule of our own to oppose them; it is important, that their decisions be adopted here . . ."

However, the Supreme Court of Connecticut agreed with Dibble. It rejected developments in England's equity law, assuming that if a wife controlled her own property, she would be more likely to leave her husband: "By the common law, the husband and wife are considered one person in law, the existence of the wife being merged in that of the husband, or suspended during coverture. As a consequence . . . husband and wife cannot contract with each other, nor the husband make a grant or gift to the wife, nor the wife have personal estate, to her sole and separate use. . . ." Property brought by a woman into her marriage had to be controlled by her husband. For "by a kind of fiction, the husband is considered a trustee for the wife."

Historians still debate the effects that the American Revolution had on the legal status of women. Marylynn Salmon found only two changes that occurred as a result of independence: "one involving divorce law and two, the law of inheritance." The major shift in the marital status of women came during 1839–1895. During these years, the states passed the married women's property acts, which permanently changed the property rights of wives. In 1848, the state of New York passed the strongest law. It read in part: "The real and personal property of any female who may hereafter marry, and which she shall own at the time of her marriage, and the rents, issues and profits thereof, shall not be subject to the disposal of her husband nor be liable for his debts and shall continue her sole and separate property as if she were a single female."

In 1848, common law was in force in most of the states. The number of courts of equity law, which treated wives more fairly, had declined. As Susan B. Anthony would note in 1902: "Its treatment of women was a blot on civilization only equalled in blackness by the slavery of the negro." However, at the beginning of the twentieth century, "in not one State does the Common Law now prevail in its entirety." State laws had blended the two forms of jurisprudence, and under them, wives could own and control property, do business and keep their wages, make wills and contracts, sue and be sued, testify in courts, and administer estates.

The idea of community property—that a husband and wife both contribute to the property acquired during their marriage and should therefore share equally in its ownership—was introduced in the nineteenth century, when Idaho and Washington became the first states to adopt such laws. By 1992, twelve states had passed similar statutes. "Equitable distribution" statutes existed in other states to achieve the same ends. Even in these states, however, some discriminatory provisions remained; for instance, four states did not allow wives to devise [in wills] their halves of jointly-held property. Therefore, a husband was entitled to all of his deceased wife's property; a wife to only half of his.

The first major Supreme Court decision to use the Constitution to end male domination over marital property was in 1981 with *Kirchberg v. Feenstra* (see page 328). Congress followed with the Uniform Marital Property Act on January 1, 1986, which very few states adopted. However, today nearly all states have some form of equitable distribution laws.

For Further Reading

Hoffer, Peter Charles. *Law and People in Colonial America*. Baltimore: The Johns Hopkins University Press, 1992.

Salmon, Marylynn. *Women and the Law of Property in Early America*. Chapel Hill: The University of North Carolina Press, 1986.

Wortman, Marlene Stein. *Women in American Law, Vol. 1*. New York: Holmes & Meier Publishers, Inc.

Fitch v. Brainerd: 1805

Appellant: Elizabeth Mary Fitch **Appellee:** Jehu Brainerd
Appellant's Claim: That a probate decision upholding the will of a married
woman was incorrect because a married woman has no right to make a will
Chief Lawyers for Appellee: Jared Ingersoll and Mr. Daggert
Chief Lawyers for Appellant: Mr. Smith and Mr. Edwards **Justices:** John
Allen, Aaron Austin, Jonathan Brace, John Chester, William Edmund, Oliver
Ellsworth, Chauncey Goodrich, Elizur Goodrich, Matthew Griswold, William
Hillhouse, Stephen T. Hosmer, and Roger Newberry **Place:** New Haven,
Connecticut **Date of Decision:** June 1805 **Decision:** A wife cannot make
a will unless a law specifically gives her this power

SIGNIFICANCE

Until the 1820s, most wives could not make wills or own property in their names.
New England was particularly conservative in these matters, as shown by the
refusal of this Connecticut court to allow a woman to make a will leaving property
to her husband.

In England during the feudal system, no person could will his real estate to another. However, in 1541 and 1543, King Henry VIII made two laws granting this right to ". . . all persons . . . except *femes covert* [married women], infants, idiots, and persons of insane memory."

In 1672, with Henry's laws before them, Connecticut wrote its first statute book. In regulating wills, the colonial statute was more liberal:

> . . . all persons of the age of twenty-one years, of right understanding and memory, whether excommunicated or other, shall have full power, authority and liberty to make their wills and testaments, and all other lawful alienations of their lands and other estates. . . .

In 1784, the legislature revised this statute by adding the words "not otherwise legally incapable" after "all persons." Did this mean that wives could now make wills leaving their lands and buildings to whomever they chose? The question came before the Connecticut Supreme Court in 1805.

Can a Married Woman Write a Will?

Elizabeth Mary Fitch appealed a superior court decision approving the will of her aunt, Abigail Mary Brainerd. When Abigail died, Elizabeth expected to inherit her estate, which was due her under common law. However, Abigail had attempted to will her real estate to her husband, Jehu. Both relatives claimed the inheritance. A probate court upheld the will and ruled for Jehu. The Superior Court agreed. Still, Elizabeth would not give up. She appealed to the state supreme court.

Elizabeth's lawyers claimed wives were not "persons" under the law and said the revised law of 1784 never intended by its general language to include them:

> The words "not otherwise legally incapable," were therefore inserted, which were intended, at once, to except *femes covert* [married women]. . . .

The attorneys warned that if wives could make wills, they would be equally able "to give their vote, verdict, or sentence, in any matter or cause; they may vote in freeman's meeting, may be jurors, and may even be judges of the courts. The evident absurdity of such a conclusion is a clear proof, that it was not intended by the legislature.

After reviewing Connecticut's long history of denying property rights to wives, they concluded:

> When our ancestors first settled this country, they looked up to the great Lawgiver of the Universe as their immediate legislator; and from him they learned, that when two persons are married, of twain they become one flesh. But, two persons cannot be formed into one, unless the legal existence of one of them be suspended; and, if a doubt could exist, which of the two should retain the sole legal existence, and be the head of the family; that doubt is solved, by the same high authority. So strongly, indeed, were our ancestors impressed with the necessity of a perfect union between husband and wife, that, without any statute on the subject, they adopted every principle of the ancient common law of England, which went to establish such union. The right of a *feme covert* to hold lands, which, by the English common law, forms an exception to the entire union of husband and wife, was, at the same time, rejected here. Our ancestors admitted of no exception. The whole estate of the wife, both real and personal, vested absolutely in her husband. These principles, being adopted by general consent, became a part of the common law of Connecticut, and so remained for nearly a century.

Fair Is Fair

Jehu's side rejected these arguments:

> It has been strongly insisted that these words ["not otherwise legally incapable"] took away from *femes covert* the power of devising, if they possessed it before. — But is this fair reasoning? It is not to be presumed, that the legislature of 1784 intended to invest an important right by such a clause inserted in the parenthesis, and liable to so much just criticism.

Making a more human point, the attorneys asked: "And why may not a woman, equally with her husband, reward the affectionate treatment of a kind relative, rather than see her property descend to those, who have been perverse, unkind, or cruel?

The counselors cautioned they were not questioning whether women had the right to will *personal* property, but only real property, due to new language of the law of 1784: "We frequently find it said generally, that a woman cannot devise her personal property, because it belongs to her husband. With this principle we have no controversy; for the right of devising never extends to the property of another."

The attorneys cited certain cases in England where wives could devise their own estate, and then took up the question of whether allowing wives to do so in the United States could rend the social fabric:

> It is also said that if our statute does not prohibit *femes covert* from devising, then they are permitted to "give their vote, verdict, or sentence in any matter or cause." To this it is sufficient to answer, that this argument equally destroys the right of a single woman to devise, unless those who urge it will contend, that single women may sit as jurors.

Finally, the lawyers pointed to *Adams v. Kellogg*, a 1788 decision that allowed a wife to will real estate to her husband:

> It is said, also, that precedents are to be regarded only as illustrative of principles. This together with the other objections, really amounts to this; that every court must decide on every question, as though it were new; and, of course, that all former decisions which do not square with the opinion of the judge, must yield to such opinion. Such a doctrine is fraught with mischief. . . . English courts have never hesitated to declare themselves bound by precedents.—They are not ashamed to say, we cannot legislate.

Precedents Lead to Principles

The court's view rested on whether precedents existed for wives to execute wills:

> It being well understood, that a right to devise is not a natural, but a municipal right, it must, so far as it exists, have a statute or custom for its creation. Has it had such creation in favor of a *feme covert*, here, or in the country from which we emigrate?

The court decided no such law existed:

> But does either the statute, or common law of England, recognize the right in question? The only statutes which bear upon the case, those of thirty-second and thirty-fourth of Hen. VIII, which grant generally the right of devising, expressly except *femes covert;* negating, at once, the expediency of extending the right to them, and the fact of their having it before.

As for the common law, "a *feme covert* cannot devise—except by special custom: and even such a custom has been adjudged ill, on the ground, that it could not have had a reasonable commencement."

The court did not find that the newly-revised law of 1784 created a right for wives to make a will: "For, who will say, that all sane persons, twenty-one years old, females as well as males, and *femes covert* as well as *femes sole* [single women], are qualified, in all respects, and have plenary [complete] for all the acts there qualified?"

The court also ruled that the early 1672 law applied to estate holders, and wives at that time could not own estates. To support their opinion, the justices quoted from the preamble of a 1723 law called, "An act for preventing the Sales of the Real Estates of Heiresses, without their Consent," which read:

> The real estate of any person, which either by descent or will, became the estate of his daughters, whether it descended or came to them during their coverture [marriage], became thereby the property and sole estate of their husbands.

Then the court searched Connecticut history for any law or practice that gave wives the right to make a will leaving their real property:

> It remains only to inquire, has there been, from the early settlement of the state, a practice for *femes covert* to devise; . . . Of such as practice there are no memorials or traditions. And we cannot presume from the condition of the early settlers, and still less from their character, that they would have introduced it.

Echoing the position of Elizabeth's attorneys, the court ruled:

> For near a century, *femes covert* had no estate to devise. — The custom for them to devise, if such it may be called, is very recent, as well as very limited—confined, so far as is known, to a few instances, and within the last twenty years.

> There has, indeed, been one ultimate decision, of a divided court, in favor of the right in question, in the case of [*Adams v. Kellogg,* 1786]; but that decision, we are constrained to say, after much deliberation, was not law.

> Whether the refinements of the present age, require a departure from the ancient law upon this subject; or whether the supposed benefits of a change would countervail its obvious mischiefs, are legislative, not judicial questions. — In this case, the court is unanimously of opinion, there must be a reversal.

In 1805, the court overturned the decision made in *Adams v. Kellogg.* Only four years later, lawmakers enacted a statute specifically granting wives the right to make their own wills. Over time, other states followed suit, responding to the needs of an emerging commercial economy.

For Further Reading

Kerber, Linda K. *Women of the Republic: Intellect and Ideology in Revolutionary America.* New York: W. W. Norton, 1980.

Salmon, Marylynn. *Women and the Law of Property in Early America.* Chapel Hill: The University of North Carolina Press, 1986.

Wortman, Marlene Stein. *Women in American Law, Vol. 1.* New York: Holmes & Meier, 1985.

Watson v. Bailey: 1808

Appellants: Mr. Bailey et al. **Appellee:** Mr. and Mrs. Watson and their lessee **Appellants' Claim:** That Margaret Mercer's deed permitting her husband to sell off her lands was valid even though it was improperly executed **Chief Lawyer for Appellee:** Mr. Hopkins
Chief Lawyers for Appellants: Mr. Montgomery and Mr. Tilghman
Justices: Mr. Brackenridge (abstained), Mr. Smith, and *Mr. Yeates*
Place: Philadelphia, Pennsylvania **Date of Decision:** December 31, 1808
Decision: Margaret Mercer's deed was improperly executed and therefore void

SIGNIFICANCE

This decision, which became the ruling principle in Pennsylvania, gave wives greater control over their property.

In early America, northern colonies and states were slow to recognize the right of married women to own separate property. In Pennsylvania, New York, Massachusetts, and Connecticut, a wife's personal property belonged exclusively to her husband; her real estate became his to manage and dispose of as he wished. Therefore, a married woman had little financial security; husbands, tradesmen, and lenders alike could ignore her opinions about business transactions.

Should a husband wish to sell or mortgage his wife's property, he needed only to sign a deed. Only Virginia, Maryland, and South Carolina required judges to privately examine wives to make sure their husbands had not coerced them, physically or otherwise, into going along. Depending on the colony or state, wives swore to the judge, verbally or in writing, that they endorsed the transactions. Sometimes they might have to repeat certain words before a judge or secure the judge's signature on the document itself. Not until 1770 did Pennsylvania begin such reforms.

Even with new laws, changes in everyday practice were slow. Husbands might still intimidate wives into going along with them. As *Watson v. Bailey* illustrates, judges sometimes simply overlooked the fraud.

On February 24, 1770, the Pennsylvania legislature passed "an act for the better confirmation of the estates of persons holding or claiming under feme coverts [wives], and for establishing a mode by which husband and wife may hereafter convey their estates." It stated that, in the future, a wife would have to acknowledge before a judge in private chambers that she had voluntarily signed a deed executed by her husband:

> [The judge] shall examine the wife separate and apart from her husband, and shall read or otherwise make known the full contents of such deed or conveyance to the said wife; and if, upon such separate examination, she shall declare that she did voluntarily, and of her own free will and accord, seal, and as her act and deed deliver, the said deed or conveyance, without any coercion or compulsion of her said husband, every such deed or conveyance shall be, and the same is hereby declared to be, good and valid law. . . .

The act led the way to expanded property rights for Pennsylvania wives. Despite the new law, however, husbands could still ignore their wives' wishes, either by coercing them into signing deeds or selling the property outright without informing them. Fear of their husbands or feelings of shame kept most women silent.

Under the new act, judges had to question spouses to make sure they agreed with their husbands' actions. Wives repeated precisely worded terms and phrases, such as whether they had acted "voluntarily" or consented "without any *coercion* or compassion." In practice, justices often disregarded this requirement. Wives' property rights had been so ignored in the past that judges, who were mostly justices of the peace, were sloppy about recording female words. They might even question wives in front of their husbands, aiding the coercion. It took a state supreme court decision to curtail this behavior in Pennsylvania.

Just Between Us Guys

On May 30, 1785, Margaret and James Mercer sold Nathan Thompson for eight hundred pounds lands Margaret had brought to their marriage years before. The ink was barely dry on the documents that day when Thompson sold the property back to James Mercer for the same amount of money. This sleight of hand deprived Margaret of her rights to the property and bestowed them upon her husband.

On the day the deed was signed, the couple appeared before Henry Slaymaker, a justice of the peace in Lancaster County. He not only reconveyed the property to James but haphazardly endorsed the deed in this way:

> Lancaster county. . . . Personally appeared before me, the subscriber, one of the justices of the court of common pleas for the county aforesaid, the within James Mercer and Margaret, his wife, and acknowledged the above written indenture to be their act and deed, and desired that the same might be recorded. *She the said Margaret being of full age and by me examined apart.* In testimony whereof I have hereunto set my hand and seal, this 30th day of May, anno Domini 1785.

Just One Minute!

Margaret died without a will. Her sister, Sarah Watson, claimed the property, noticing that Margaret had improperly acknowledged the deed. If the deed had conformed to the law of 1770, Sarah would have had no claim. However, as Margaret's "heir-at-law" (the person who inherits when there is no will), Sarah could inherit the lands if her sister had improperly executed the deed.

The chief judge at the 1807 trial declared that Margaret's acknowledgment had been defective and the jury found for Sarah. The court denied a motion for a new trial and the Supreme Court heard the appeal.

The Letter of the Law?

Attorneys Montgomery and Tilghman argued for the appellants that they had obeyed the substance of the law in selling Margaret's lands. (The appellants included a Mr. Bailey, who represented the interests of himself and James Mercer. The trial record does not report Bailey's stake in the case.) The judge of the common pleas had witnessed and signed that Margaret had appeared before him and had acknowledged her agreement to the sale: "She the said Margaret being of full age and by me examined apart." Was not this sufficient to prove that Margaret willingly sold her land?

Attorney Hopkins, advocating Sarah Watson's position, declared it was not, and disputed that Margaret had been examined apart from her husband:

> The joint acknowledgment is nothing; for the wife's is to be separated and apart from the husband. There is therefore no acknowledgment by the wife. The contents are to be made known to her; this does not appear. She is to declare that her acknowledgment is not the effect of coercion or compulsion; this does not appear; and these are the very essence of acknowledgment. It is not even certified that she was examined separate and apart *from her husband.*

With this the court agreed. In the words of Justice Yeates:

> Lord Hardwicke has somewhere said, that the wife may be intimidated by cruelty on the part of the husband, as well as seduced by his flattery and extreme kindness, to do acts, which, on more mature deliberation, she would totally disapprove of. In this acknowledgment, her consent to the deed is not expressed by the justice, which alone could give it validity, without adverting to smaller matters. We may regret the unskillfulness or negligence of the scrivener has led to this error; but we are bound to say . . . the party must abide by the consequences of his own acts.

Yeates declared that Margaret "should have appeared before a proper tribunal, and declared her consent separate and apart from her husband, in the manner pointed out by the laws of the country." He interpreted the act of 1770 to mean that a justice should certify a wife's acknowledgment on the back of the deed, under his hand and seal, together with the date. The justice before whom the Mercers came "had not conformed himself to the directions of the law 'establishing a mode by which husband and wife may convey the estate of the wife, but had materially and substantially failed therein.' " His actions were "not sufficient to pass the wife's estate."

A Nefarious Deed

What angered the court even more was that the sale of the property to Thompson and the resale of the lands from Thompson to Mercer were dated on the same day before the same judge and contained the same purchase price of eight hundred pounds. Said Yeates, "The intention evidently was to devest the wife of her legal right in the lands, and vest it in the husband."

Although traditional practices did not change immediately after *Watson v. Bailey*, Pennsylvania courts were less tolerant of behavior that lessened the protection granted by the legislature to wives retaining control over their separate estates.

For Further Reading

Hoff, Joan. *Law, Gender, and Injustice: A Legal History of U.S. Women*. New York: New York University Press, 1991.

Kerber, Linda K. *Women's America: Refocusing the Past*. New York: Oxford University Press, 1991.

Salmon, Marylynn. *Women and the Law of Property in Early America*. Chapel Hill: University of North Carolina Press, 1986.

Wortman, Marlene Stein. *Women in American Law, Vol. I*. New York: Holmes & Meier Publishers, 1985.

Kempe v. Kennedy: 1809

Appellant: John Den, lessee of Grace Kempe, a subject of Great Britain
Appellees: R. Kennedy and M. Cowell, citizens of New Jersey
Appellant's Claim: That New Jersey illegally confiscated Grace Kempe's land because she had accompanied her husband to his British homeland during the Revolutionary War   **Chief Lawyer for Appellees:** Mr. Lewis
Chief Lawyer for Appellant: Richard Stockton   **Justices:** Samuel Chase, Oliver Ellsworth, William Johnston, Henry B. Livingston, *Chief Justice John Marshall,* Alfred Moore, Thomas Todd, and Bushrod Washington
Place: Washington, D.C.   **Date of Decision:** February 20, 1809
Decision: New Jersey could confiscate Grace Kempe's lands because she followed her husband into exile to Great Britain during the Revolutionary War

SIGNIFICANCE

This 1809 lawsuit was the first post-revolutionary separate-property case to reach the Supreme Court. It sheds light on marital relations at the beginning of the nineteenth century.

Under English common law, broadly adopted by the colonies, brides lost many rights at the altar. Marriage meant a merging of a wife's property and identity with those of her husband. A newlywed's entire personal property—even jewelry, clothing, or books—belonged to her husband. Her real property (lands and buildings) became his to manage and profit from. A wife's inheritance also went to her husband, even if she wanted her child to have it. In the following trial, Grace Kempe could only claim the right to her property by arguing that she was not a citizen.

Before 1772, Grace Coxe of New Jersey married John Tabor Kempe, the king's attorney general for New York City. The rich bride brought choice New Jersey lands into the marriage. This real estate legally came under the authority of her husband. The couple later moved to New York, where they lived before and during the Revolution.

When British troops occupied New York, John returned to Great Britain. The Loyalist Grace accompanied him. Some time later, New Jersey confiscated the couple's lands on grounds of treason and sold them to a resident of New Jersey.

After her husband died in 1792, Grace tried to get the lands back, claiming the state never should have confiscated them. Her case came before the Inferior Court of Common Pleas for Hunterdon County, New Jersey, which decided the current owners of the land, R. Kennedy and M. Cowall, could keep them.

Grace's attorney, Richard Stockton, appealed to the U.S. Supreme Court. He demanded that the land be returned to his client because, under common law, a wife must follow her husband wherever he goes. Therefore, she did not have the legal "capacity" to break the law.

Stockton first maintained that his client did not fall under any of the categories listed as traitorous according to "an act for forfeiting to, and vesting in, the state of New-Jersey, the real estates of certain fugitives and offenders" of December 11, 1778. He reasoned that even if the charges against her husband were valid, Grace had no choice but to follow:

> The inquisition charges, that Kempe and wife are offenders against the act of 11th of December, 1778, in this, "that the said John Tabor Kempe and Grace his wife, *did go* to the enemy, and *took refuge* with them some time in April, 1776, and *still remain with them*," against the form of their allegiance to this state. . . . Take the fact as charged; *she and her husband, i.e., she in company with her husband; and legally by the command and control of her husband*, in April, 1776, went to the British and remained with them.

In this 1829 quit-claim deed, one person transferred property to another. (Litchfield Historical Society, Litchfield, Conn.)

Therefore, Grace was not a traitor but merely an obedient partner, following her husband to his homeland. Stockton then pointed out that no married woman (*feme covert*) fell under the 1778 act because "the only law which existed placed her under the dominion of her husband. He had the right to command, and the power to compel her to go and remain with him, and she had neither right to refuse, nor power to resist."

In short, the seizure of her husband's lands might be legal, but seizing his wife's property was not.

Were Women Citizens?

Stockton's case rested on the fact that women were not citizens on par with men:

A *feme covert* [married woman] cannot properly be called an inhabitant of a state. The *husband* is the inhabitant. By the constitution of New-Jersey, all inhabitants are entitled to vote; but it has never been supposed that a *feme covert* was a legal voter. Single women have been allowed to vote, because the law supposed them to have wills of their own.

Wives, however, did *not* have wills of their own. Legally, Stockton implied, allowing wives to vote would be like giving infants suffrage. Stockton then recalled *Martin v. Massachusetts* (1805) (see page 93), which ruled that a wife did not forfeit her lands by joining the enemy with her husband, because a wife must do as her husband commands.

However, Mr. Lewis, who represented Kennedy and the other defendants, took a different tack, arguing that the confiscation and sale of Grace's lands were "all perfectly regular." However, "even if they were not, the 11th section of the law prevents such error from affecting [the purchaser's title to the lands]."

Therefore, if the original judgment was wrong, it was still in effect until it was reversed. If reversed, Grace's only remedy would be against the state, not the current owners or renters. Lewis also took issue with Stockton's charge that women were not really citizens on the same footing as men.

Chief Justice John Marshall affirmed a lower court's decision, disallowing Grace Kempe to regain her property in America. (Engraving by Alonzo Chappell, Collection of The Supreme Court of the United States)

It is objected that a wife living with her husband cannot be an inhabitant [of a state], but there is nothing inconsistent in the idea. The husband and wife are both inhabitants; and it is evident that the legislature meant to include them, because they speak of "his or *her*" estate." *And the word* "her" comprehends *femes covert* as well as *femes sole* [single women].

Chief Justice John Marshall expressed sympathy with Grace, yet he allowed the judgment to stand, reasoning "it is a judgment, and, until reversed, cannot be disregarded." Thus the Court did not establish a national precedent resolving her property versus her citizenship rights.

This losing lawsuit illustrates the legal subordination of women during the post-revolutionary period. Kempe's attorney built his case on the argument that his client had no will of her own, denying even that she was a legal *inhabitant* of New Jersey. Although his reasoning did not prevail in court, it was an accurate description of the legal liabilities that hobbled married women after the Revolution.

For Further Reading

Hoff, Joan. *Law, Gender, and Injustice: A Legal History of U.S. Women.* New York: New York University Press, 1991.

Hoffer, Peter Charles. *Law and People in Colonial America.* Baltimore: Johns Hopkins University Press, 1993.

Kerber, Linda K. *Women's America: Refocusing the Past.* New York: Oxford University Press, 1991.

Salmon, Marylynn. *Women and the Law of Property in Early America.* Chapel Hill: University of North Carolina Press, 1986.

Wortman, Marlene Stein. *Women in American Law, Vol. I.* New York: Holmes & Meier Publishers, 1985.

Coutts v. Greenhow: 1811

Appellant: Estate of Reuben Coutts   **Appellees:** Dr. James Greenhow et al.
Appellant's Claim: That unpaid creditors may not receive a marriage settlement (a grant of property) made by Coutts for his wife before they wed
Chief Lawyer for Appellees: Mr. Williams
Chief Lawyers for Appellant: Mr. Call and Mr. Wickham   **Judges:** Francis T. Brooke, William H. Cabell, John Coalter, William Fleming, and Spencer Roane (not present)   **Place:** Richmond, Virginia   **Date of Decision:** June 20, 1811   **Decision:** The Supreme Court of Appeals reversed the lower court decision, denying a creditor's claim that a widow must pay the debts of her deceased husband out of her marriage settlement

SIGNIFICANCE
Coutts v. Greenhow illustrates how Virginia courts ensured that some wives were financially secure when their husbands died.

In early America, common law gave wives no rights to their own property (separate estates) or that held jointly with their husbands. However, husbands could provide for their wives' security by transferring property to them in a contract called a marriage settlement. American courts usually supported these agreements, for they brought security to married women and their children when husbands died. However, if the settlement's sole purpose was to avoid the repayment of debts, a popular ruse, courts might invalidate it. In the trial of Reuben Coutts, the court was sorely tested, for it had to consider a marriage settlement made by a "fornicator" as well as a debtor.

Coutts had lived in a "common-law marriage" with Jane New for many years and had five children with her. On September 10, 1799, he drew up a marriage settlement transferring his property to her. It stated that if Reuben died before Jane, all of his rents and profits would go to her up to 1,501 pounds per year. This replaced the widow's dower share (a right to one-third to one-half of her late husband's estate). Upon Jane's death, her children would divide the estate. Reuben then made his will, confirming all the provisions of the marriage settlement. He also left a small part of the estate (most of which Jane had brought to the marriage) to his wife and her heirs. The rest of the estate would go to the children. The couple married seven days later.

Eleven years later Reuben died, leaving bills unpaid. The creditors sued his estate before Virginia's Superior Court of Chancery for the Richmond district. It seems that Coutts had owed 1,541 pounds to Dr. James Greenhow, the collateral for which was land in Kentucky.

The creditors made two key points. First, they said no debtor could create a marriage settlement sheltering his wealth to avoid paying a debt. Second, the inheritance rights of children born out of wedlock were suspect, and could not come before the rights of the creditors to be paid.

The family's attorney responded that Reuben had made the marriage settlement *not* to defraud his creditors but for "a valuable consideration"—the marriage.

However, the court doubted this, and ordered the estate to pay the creditors first:

> Would it not be monstrous to say, that Coutts, who was really an old man, far beyond the prime of his life, after so many years spent with a woman, in a state of fornication, should be allowed to avoid the payment of his debts, by entering into a marriage contract with her? What was the inducement to it but to avoid his creditors? Attend to the circumstances: on the 29th of August, 1799, the debts were contracted; on the 10th September following, a marriage settlement was entered into; and, on or about the 17th of the same month, the marriage was actually celebrated; the consideration of which, was the settlement of all his estate for the purpose of above mentioned, and the children of the marriage, all of whom were born before, and not afterwards. . . . Every aspect of the record shows that Coutts had increased his estate, at least to the amount of these judgments, with a clear intention not to repay them; and although the agreement may be good as between the parties, yet, as to creditors, it is void.

In 1811, the Coutts family appealed this decision to the state's Supreme Court of Appeals. Attorney Call represented them, arguing that neither Reuben's "fornication" nor his indebtedness meant his marriage settlement was unlawful:

> Marriage of itself is a sufficient consideration for a settlement; not marriage and previous chastity. If a man as rich as *Croesus* marries a poor woman worth nothing, and makes a marriage settlement, it is good. Neither is the husband's being in debt of any consequence.

Denying that Reuben had intended to defraud the creditors, Call argued:

> The conveyance [transfer of land] here is good in law. Upon what ground can a court of equity take away the legal right. *Coutt's* motive was one of the most honorable that could be. He had long lived with his intended wife, and had no complaint against her that she had conne[c]tion with any other man; the object of the marriage was to legitimate those children in conformity with the act of the assembly.

In response, Greenhow's counselor, Williams, said children born out of wedlock could not automatically inherit:

> According to the *British* authorities, children born before the marriage are but volunteers, and cannot be preferred to creditors. . . . Does [Virginia law]

change the doctrine? According to [it], the marriage must first take place and *afterwards* the children must be recognized [by their father], to make them legitimate. It does not say they shall be considered as *children of the marriage*, and entitled, as such, to the benefit of a *settlement*. . . .

Jane's second attorney, Wickham, refuted this:

Mrs. Coutts had a good right to *dower:* why not, then, to the benefit of a *settlement?*. . . I believe that, in fact, Mrs. *Coutts* made a bad bargain; the [marriage settlement] being worth less that her dower would have been. But the *plus*, or the *minus*, is a matter of no consequence. Mr. *Williams* admits the decree must be reversed as to *her*. Why not, then, as to her *children?*

He continued defending the children's rights:

Under our act of assembly, (which makes children, *born before* the marriage, and *recognized* by their father, *legitimate,)* the same principle applies in favour of children born *before the marriage, if recognized*. All *such* children must, in this country, be considered *children of the marriage.''* Recognition need not be *after* the marriage: it made *at any time*, it is good: and in this case they are recognized in the settlement itself.

In conclusion, Wickham showed there was no proof that Reuben had been insolvent, and asked that the estate pay his debts before disturbing the children's—or widow's—inheritance. He demanded that the debt owed to Greenhow be paid from remainder of the estate. The court agreed and Judge John Coalter observed:

There can be no doubt whatever but that this deed is good, against creditors, as to the *wife and the issue of the marriage*. The only question is, whether the *children born before the marriage* are mere volunteers, and the deed, as to them, void against creditors.

He concluded that the deed to the children was legitimate:

I shall not be the apologist of the conduct of the parties before their marriage. They have, however, legitimated the innocent offspring of their criminal intercourse, and have made to society all the atonement in their power.

Judge Francis Brooke agreed that the marriage settlement was a valid contract against the creditors, adding:

It does not appear by any thing in the record, that it was the intention of the parties, by executing the marriage settlement, to commit fraud on the creditors of *Reuben Coutts*. On the contrary, it does not appear that there were any debts except the one, the payment of which was provided for by the mortgage of the *Kentucky* lands.

He concluded, "By the civil law, the marriage of the parents legitimated *base born* children."

The appeals court overruled the lower court's decision and supported the marriage settlement against the claims of the creditors. The decision permitted no part of the family's shares to be used to pay Greenhow. The court remanded (sent back) the case to the lower court to decide whether and what part of the remainder of Reuben's estate could be used to pay Greenhow.

Decisions such as this strengthened the property rights of wives. Indeed, more families began using marriage settlements during the 1820s, when a depression—which led to the election of President Andrew Jackson in 1826—made the financial situations of many families desperate. Americans began to feel that it was unfair to use a wife's estate to pay for her husband's debts. Historian Marylynn Salmon writes: "As the economy became increasingly unstable, these sentiments grew until by the middle of the nineteenth century Americans were ready to grant all women, not just those with separate estates, independent property rights." Many states passed new laws, known as the married woman's property acts, which radically elevated the status of women by giving them complete and absolute control of their own property—real and personal—and banning the use of their property to pay husbands' debts. As *Coutts v. Greenhow* shows, these principles existed in American law early in the century.

For Further Reading

Hoffer, Peter Charles. *Law and People in Colonial America*. Baltimore: The Johns Hopkins University Press, 1992.

Salmon, Marylynn. *Women and the Law of Property in Early America*. Chapel Hill: The University of North Carolina Press, 1986.

Spruill, Julia Cherry. *Women's Life and Work in the Southern Colonies*. New York: W. W. Norton, 1966.

Wortman, Marlene Stein. *Women in American Law, Vol. 1*. New York: Holmes & Meier Publishers, Inc.

Webster v. McGinnis: 1812

Appellant: Mr. Webster **Appellee:** Mr. McGinnis **Appellant's Claim:** That Mr. McGinnis, a tavern-keeper, should honor a contract made by his wife to provide hay and oats for stage horses and board for stage drivers
Chief Lawyer for the Appellee: Mr. S. Riddle
Chief Lawyer for Appellant: Mr. Weigley **Justices:** Mr. Brackenridge, *Chief Justice William Tilghman, Jasper Yeates* **Place:** Philadelphia, Pennsylvania **Date of Decision:** September 19, 1812 **Decision:** The Supreme Court of Pennsylvania upheld the decision of a lower court ruling that a wife—although entrusted by her husband to transact the ordinary business of a tavern—has no authority to bind the husband to a special contract

SIGNIFICANCE

In this historic decision, married woman—who normally could not make contracts in their names—could act as agents of their husbands, but *only* for contracts that the men knew of and approved.

Under common law, once a woman married, she underwent a change of legal status akin to civil death: She became a *feme covert*—someone protected or "covered" by another. Husband and wife were, for legal purposes, considered "one person"—and that one person was the husband. Blackstone's *Commentaries* declared in 1765: "By marriage, the husband and wife are one person in law; that is, the very being or legal existence of the woman is suspended during the marriage, or at least is incorporated and consolidated into that of the husband; under whose wing, protection, and cover, she performs everything."

Therefore, once a woman married, she lost the right to sign contracts in her name. The reasoning was that since a married woman owned no property of her own, no court could endorse her agreements. Wives could, however, contract jointly with their husbands. They could also act as their husbands' agents. If a husband should be ill, away on business, or called up for military service, and if his wife ordinarily ran a business in his absence, her ability to enter into legal agreements was essential to the family's economic well-being.

For example, the colonial legislature in Pennsylvania in 1718 awarded the wives of mariners *feme sole* [single woman] legal status during their husbands' absences at sea, with full authority to sign contracts, sue, and be sued. Without such authority, with so many husbands going to sea, a maritime economy would have been in acute distress and the wives would have had an impossible time keeping the home fires burning.

Of course the problem proved a more general and in many ways an intractable one. The difficulty in law was in deciding just how much leeway a wife had in the conduct of her husband's business. The answer given in *Webster v. McGinnis* was "not much."

A Great Deal

Mr. McGinnis ran a tavern in Somerset County, Pennsylvania. It was his custom to have his wife take care of business in his absence. On one such occasion, Mr. Webster, who operated a stage line, contracted with McGinnis' wife to board his stage drivers and to provide hay, oats, and other necessities for his stage horses for several months.

When McGinnis returned, he was angry about his wife's agreement with Webster. She had apparently negotiated a deal with Webster that McGinnis found too generous. He appealed to the Somerset County justice of the peace asking that Webster pay the going price for board already provided his drivers, and for hay and oats fed to his horses. The justice of the peace decided in favor of McGinnis. Webster then appealed the case to the Court of Common Pleas, which again found for McGinnis. Finally Webster took his case to the top: the Supreme Court of Pennsylvania.

In finding again for McGinnis, Chief Justice William Tilghman declared: "It is a well settled principle, that the husband is not bound by the contract of his wife, unless by some act or declaration prior or subsequent to the contract, his consent may be fairly inferred." Even if a husband had entrusted his wife the ordinary business of the tavern, as McGinnis had, this did not confer on her the status or power of acting as his legal agent in transactions outside such common-place actions as the sale of liquor, and the purchase of provisions necessary for operation of the tavern. Since the contract with Webster involved dispensing with the usual prices for board, and for the feeding of horses, and since no evidence existed that McGinnis had assented to the contract, it was not legal.

Justice Jasper Yeates concurred: "The natural idea arising from doing the ordinary business of a country tavern, is that the party furnished the usual provisions, refreshments and provender to travelers, and received payment therefor; but it would be straining the expressions very far, to extend it to any case of contract respecting a public house of entertainment." In a case involving a stage line with board and provender for many months, "we cannot deem the wife the agent or servant of the husband."

In the court's interpretation, a husband who either implicitly or explicitly made his wife his agent, was indeed bound to honor any contracts she made in his name. But because the wife made a contract that was not in the "ordinary" line of business, and because the husband was quick to make his disapproval of her agreement known, he did not have to honor the contract. This decision made the murky legal status of women doing business in their husband's names no clearer. Until wives were legally accountable for the transactions they made, both creditors and debtors were at risk.

For Further Reading

Hoffer, Peter Charles. *Law and People in Colonial America*. Baltimore: Johns Hopkins University Press, 1992.

Kerber, Linda K. *Women's America: Refocusing the Past*. New York: Oxford University Press, 1991.

Salmon, Marylynn. *Women and the Law of Property in Early America*. Chapel Hill: University of North Carolina Press, 1986.

Wortman, Marlene Stein. *Women in American Law, Vol. I*. New York: Holmes & Meier Publishers, 1985.

Pennsylvania v. Addicks: 1813

Plaintiff: Commonwealth of Pennsylvania, upon application of Joseph Lee
Defendant: Barbara Addicks   **Plaintiff's Claim:** That Joseph Lee was entitled to the custody of his two minor daughters
Chief Lawyer for Defendant: Joseph Hopkinson
Chief Lawyer for Plaintiff: J. R. Ingersoll   **Justice:** *Chief Justice William Tilghman*   **Place:** Philadelphia, Pennsylvania   **Date of Decision:** July 10, 1813   **Decision:** The court refused to turn over a child to its father, although he had divorced their mother for adultery

SIGNIFICANCE

This important trial introduced the principle of "the best interests of the child" in determining custody. Before this trial, children always belonged to their fathers. The idea that a child needs the care of its mother during its "tender years" slowly led courts to grant custody to an increasing number of women. In this instance a common-law court began to make law and expand its powers.

In early America, the common law gave fathers custody of their children when marriages dissolved. In practice, colonial courts might allow a very young girl to live with her mother, but they always acknowledged the father's primary custodial right. *Commonwealth v. Addicks* introduced the idea that the "best interests" of children should count as well.

On June 12, 1813, Joseph Lee divorced his wife, Barbara, because she had entered into an adulterous relationship with another man named Addicks. Barbara Lee and Addicks had a child together and later married. They ignored a 1785 law that prohibited a partner who was guilty of adultery from marrying his or her paramour during the lifetime of the spouse.

After Barbara remarried, Joseph went to court to gain custody of his two daughters, now ten and seven. His lawyer said that a father was the "natural guardian" of his children under common law. He also maintained that it would be improper to permit the children to remain with their adulterous mother.

Barbara saw the matter quite differently. As her lawyer explained, she was "at least as unfortunate as she was culpable." For four years before the divorce, Joseph had not supported the family. During this period, Barbara had kept a boarding house, and had educated the children, having had an excellent education herself in Canada. When she remarried, Barbara was ignorant of the 1785 law. She remained devoted to her daughters, whose young ages demanded care.

Joseph admitted that his financial problems had prevented him from supporting his daughters, but he felt he was now able to support them, as he had his son, who had always lived with him.

The court refused to decide who should win guardianship. Chief Justice William Tilghman said:

> We cannot avoid expressing our disapprobation of the mother's conduct, although as far as regards her treatment of her children, she is in no fault. They appear to have been well taken care of in all respects. It is to *them*, that our anxiety is principally directed; and it appears to us, that considering their tender age, they stand in need of that kind of assistance, which can be afforded by none so well as a mother. It is on their account, therefore, that exercising the discretion with which the law has invested us, we think it best, at present, not to take them from her. At the same time, we desire it to be distinctly understood, that the father is not to be prevented from seeing them. If he does not choose to go to the house of their mother, she ought to send them to him, when he desires it, taking it for granted that he will not wish to carry them abroad, so much as to interfere with their education.

Pennsylvania v. Addicks established the "best interests of a child" doctrine: at least temporarily, an infant was best left in the custody of his or her mother. This nineteenth-century drawing shows a weary seamstress taking a moment to rest as she cares for her sleeping child.

The court overlooked Barbara Addicks' adultery and changed the common law. It introduced the idea that children of "tender years" needed the special nurturing of their mother. In 1860, New Jersey turned the "tender years" doctrine into law, requiring prepubescent children to remain in the custody of their mother unless she was "unfit." In the 1879 Rhode Island trial *McKim v. McKim* (see page 300), courts began treating mothers as separate legal entities from their husbands, best able to care for the emotional needs of their children. At the turn of the century, most separated or divorced mothers received custody of their children—though often not the funds to care for them.

For Further Reading

Hoff, Joan. *Law, Gender, and Injustice: A Legal History of U.S. Women.* New York: New York University Press, 1991.

Kerber, Linda K. *Women's America: Refocusing the Past.* New York: Oxford University Press, 1991.

Salmon, Marylynn. *Women and the Law of Property in Early America.* Chapel Hill: University of North Carolina Press, 1986.

Wortman, Marlene Stein. *Women in American Law, Vol. I.* New York: Holmes & Meier Publishers, 1985.

1 8 1 3

Pennsylvania v.

Addicks

Kenny v. Udall and Kenny: 1821

Plaintiff: Eliza S. Kenny   **Defendants:** Richard Udall and Edward M. L. Kenny   **Plaintiff's Claim:** That Eliza Kenny's husband did not have the legal right to sell her bank stock   **Chief Lawyer for Defendants:** Mr. Wells **Chief Lawyer for Plaintiff:** Mr. Slosson   **Justices:** Unknown   **Place:** New York State Court of Chancery   **Date of Decision:** June 2, 1821 **Decision:** A husband cannot waste his wife's fortune without providing for her support

SIGNIFICANCE
As the result of decisions such as this, nineteenth-century courts gradually recognized that wives must have the legal right to support themselves.

Eliza Hewitt was born in 1801. In 1814, her father, Thomas, set up a trust for her, setting aside 310 shares of stock he owned in Bank of America, worth $8,000. Eliza would receive the dividends on the stock until she was twenty-one, then take possession of the principal.

After Thomas died, his widow served as her daughter's guardian until her own death in 1819. Before her death, Mrs. Hewitt arranged that Eliza should become a ward of the court, with a court-appointed trustee to receive the dividends on the $8,000 of stock held in trust for her.

The Child Bride

On January 19, 1818, the sixteen-year-old girl married Edward Kenny—without her mother's consent. Several weeks later, upon petition by Kenny, the dividends from Eliza's stock began coming to him, although the principal remained in trust. Kenny, "embarrassed in his circumstances," wanted it all.

Therefore, he arranged with his friend, Ezra L. Ingraham, to sell the stock to Richard Udall. Udall would pay Kenny $5,000 in cash in exchange for "absolute assignment and transfer of the [$8,000 in] stock" to him. After an initial payment of $450, Udall reneged on the deal. Kenny fell into debt and went to prison. Desperate, Kenny agreed to accept even less from Udall—cash, promissory notes, and a life insurance policy on Eliza. Up to this point, Kenny had spent only about $150 in board and clothing on his wife from the proceeds from the stock. In June 1819, the New York Court of Chancery—in response to another petition from Udall—ordered that he be allowed to receive the dividends on Eliza's stock, which had been accruing since the start of the year.

This was too much for Eliza and her family's friends. In November 1820, E. Elmendorf sued on her behalf to void the court of chancery's order and return the assignment of stock dividends to Eliza. When the dispute came before the court on June 2, 1821, Mr. Slosson, representing Udall, argued that "the husband, at law, has an absolute right to all his wife's personal estate." Eliza could not sue, he said, because her equity in her husband's estate "never interferes with his legal right [of management], but leaves it to the husband undisturbed."

Eliza's second lawyer, Mr. Wells, said that the assignment of stock from her husband to Udall violated the trust agreement drawn up by Eliza's father. He charged Udall with taking advantage of the indebted Kenny in securing the stocks at bargain price.

The Chancellor's Decision

The chancellor agreed that Udall had exploited Kenny's "embarrassed circumstances." Nonetheless, "the wife had an equitable interest in that fund, which could not be defeated by the act of the husband. . . ." Kenny could not simply sell his wife's personal property: "It is now fully settled, that the wife's equity attaches upon her personal property [the stocks]." Either Kenny had to adequately support Eliza or obtain her legal consent before selling the stocks. However, in law Eliza was "still an infant," so her consent could not be legal.

The chancellor did not deny that a husband enjoyed the legal right to control the income of his wife's property: "If the husband lives with his wife, and maintains her, and has not misbehaved himself, the course of the Court has been to leave him the receipt of the interest or dividends of her fortune." However, in this case, where Kenny was guilty of the "prodigal waste of his wife's fortune," leaving her "helpless and destitute," justice demanded that he be denied that right.

The chancellor returned Eliza's entire estate. Kenny's sale of the stock became invalid. Until Eliza became twenty-one, all dividends from the stock went directly to her solicitor. When she reached the legal age of adulthood, she would apply to the court to transfer the shares to her.

The trial foreshadowed a burning legal question of the nineteenth century: How much of a wife's own property can she control? A series of married woman's property acts passed by the states between 1839 and 1895 settled the controversy: wives controlled all of it.

For Further Reading

Hoff, Joan. *Law, Gender, and Injustice: A Legal History of U.S. Women.* New York: New York University Press, 1991.

Hoffer, Peter Charles. *Law and People in Colonial America.* Baltimore: Johns Hopkins University Press, 1992.

Kerber, Linda K. *Women's America: Refocusing the Past.* New York: Oxford University Press, 1991.

Salmon, Marylynn. *Women and the Law of Property in Early America.* Chapel Hill: University of North Carolina Press, 1986.

Wortman, Marlene Stein. *Women in American Law, Vol. I.* New York: Holmes & Meier Publishers, 1985.

Peckford v. Peckford: 1828

Plaintiff: Mrs. Peckford **Defendant:** Mr. Peckford **Plaintiff's Claim:** That having divorced her husband for adultery, she was entitled to alimony payments **Chief Defense Lawyer:** R. Bogardus
Chief Lawyer for Plaintiff: A. L. McDonald **Justices:** Unknown
Place: New York State Court of Chancery **Date of Decision:** December 2, 1828 **Decision:** The court of chancery decided that Mrs. Peckford should receive "alimony"; however, the court also declared that had her conduct (which was perfectly legal) been "discreet, prudent and submissive to her husband," Mrs. Peckford would have been entitled to more

SIGNIFICANCE
Peckford v. Peckford set a precedent for making the "submissiveness" and "proper" conduct of wives determine divorce settlements, weakening the property rights of women.

During the seventeenth and eighteenth centuries, divorce law varied from colony to colony. In parts of the South, divorce did not exist. In New York and Virginia, since divorce was a religious, not a civil, process, it was only granted occasionally. New England and Pennsylvania viewed divorce as a civil matter, but still rarely permitted it.

After the American Revolution, divorce increased dramatically—but not necessarily in a way that made the relations between women and men fair.

Some have argued that the climb in the divorce rate reflected a change in women's expectations of marriage. Increasingly, wives saw marriage as a companionable relationship between equals; when their hopes were dashed, they more readily divorced. Others point to a relaxation of the divorce laws themselves making it easier for either party to end the relationship. Whichever is correct, one question must be answered: Did more divorces signal an improvement in the legal status of women?

Winning and Losing

In 1787, the state of New York adopted its first divorce statute. The new law—a liberalization of earlier laws—granted divorce for adultery.

The penalty for adultery was stiff. Courts allowed the innocent partner to remarry, but not the guilty one, at least until the death of the former spouse. Legal separation was the sole legal remedy for cases involving cruelty or desertion, allowing neither husband nor wife to remarry. Here the law elevated the position of wives, since before 1787, only husbands could decide whether or not to divorce.

Where divorce was now legal, both men and women could sue on relatively equal legal footing. However, when it came to dividing the property, eighteenth- and early nineteenth-century wives faced legal disadvantages. Under common law, they lost their right to own or manage their real property, even if it was theirs before marriage. If a husband died intestate (without a will), his wife could count on inheriting only one-third to one-half of his real estate—and it was hers only during her lifetime. She could neither sell nor will it away. Even when a husband was "at fault" in a divorce, as in *Peckford v. Peckford*, his wife might receive only her dower share of the estate. However, the court of chancery could vary the settlement depending on the situation. For example, it might award cash to the wife and property to the husband.

An Uppity Woman

In 1828, Mrs. Peckford sued for a divorce in New York because of Mr. Peckford's adultery. The court of chancery readily granted it. However, the chancellor disapproved of Mrs. Peckford because she had taken a trip to England without the express permission of her husband, "expos[ing] him to temptation." The chancellor held her responsible for her husband's philandering—that is, if *she* had not gone to England, *he* might not have misbehaved. *Why* she went to England does not seem to have entered into his calculations. Nonetheless, to punish her for her behavior, the chancellor was determined to limit Mrs. Peckford's property settlement to the minimum.

He judged Mr. Peckford's property to be worth $12,000. Had Mrs. Peckford "been perfectly discreet, prudent and submissive to her husband," he declared, "I should have allowed her half of this property." However, Mrs. Peckford had "exposed" her husband "to temptation, which has probably proved the destruction of their connubial happiness." Even after returning to New York, "her indiscretions . . . were such at least as to produce remarks from her more discreet neighbors." One cannot help wondering what those "indiscretions" might have been to so upset the chancellor. In the end, rather than finding herself with $6,000 worth of property, Mrs. Peckford had to settle for much less.

The chancellor granted her only "an annuity equal to the value of one third of the property, at six percent," or about $400 a year for the rest of her life—assuming she lived another twenty-five years—payable in quarterly installments. Thus Mrs. Peckford, who was legally the innocent party, found her own conduct bearing close scrutiny and penalized financially by the court.

Historically, divorce laws have required one partner to be guilty in order for the marriage to end. However, judges applied a double standard to the behavior of wives and husbands, expecting wives to be "pure." This changed in 1969, when all states (except South Dakota) passed reforms in their divorce laws. All made divorce easier to win and gender-neutral. By 1985, fourteen states had "no-fault" divorce laws, which held neither partner "guilty" in order to dissolve a marriage. Nearly all states had passed these by 1995.

For Further Reading

Hoffer, Peter Charles. *Law and People in Colonial America.* Baltimore: Johns Hopkins University Press, 1992.

Kerber, Linda K. *Women's America: Refocusing the Past.* New York: Oxford University Press, 1991.

Salmon, Marylynn. *Women and the Law of Property in Early America.* Chapel Hill: University of North Carolina Press, 1986.

Wortman, Marlene Stein. *Women in American Law, Vol. I.* New York: Holmes & Meier Publishers, 1985.

Prince v. Prince: 1845

Plaintiff: Sarah Prince **Defendant:** George Prince **Plaintiff's Claim:** That she should receive alimony and child support after her husband deserted her, even when he had no property or fixed or permanent income

Chief Lawyers for Defendant: Mr. Magrath and Mr. Yeadon

Chief Lawyer for Plaintiff: Mr. Elliott **Chancellors:** Benjamin F. Dunkin and Mr. Johnson **Place:** South Carolina **Date of Decision:** March 1845

Decision: A husband, when he has the income, is responsible for alimony and child support

SIGNIFICANCE

South Carolina took a fresh look at the idea of support for a deserted wife, deciding that a husband who had the means of supporting his wife, even though he had no visible property or fixed and permanent income, should be responsible for alimony and the support of the couple's children.

Colonial marriages were easy to make but hard to end. A man and woman could marry by simply agreeing to live together. Even couples who preferred a religious ceremony did not need to follow formal procedures. These accepting attitudes lasted until the mid-nineteenth century.

A Step Up

However, different colonies granted divorce either rarely or not at all. New Englanders could divorce for adultery, cruelty, and desertion. However, divorce with the right to remarry was illegal throughout the South. Legal separations took their place—without the right to remarry. South Carolina was particularly rigid, refusing to grant divorces even for a husband's adultery. To allow a woman the right to divorce her husband for his extramarital affairs insulted her husband's honor. This attitude condoned the sexual exploitation of female slaves by their masters.

Prince v. Prince was a step forward for wives in the state. It set a precedent for helping wives financially when husbands abandoned them. Earlier law required husbands to support their estranged wives, but *only* if the men owned property from which to pay them.

An Informal Marriage

Sarah and George Prince married in Portsmouth, England, on March 2, 1835, in the Jewish faith. A simple certificate confirmed the union. Within the year, the couple had a son. Shortly after the baby's birth, George began mistreating Sarah, finally abandoning her for America. There he began living with another woman. As an apothecary, a dealer in botanical medicines, George made from fifteen to twenty dollars each day. He lived in comfort, yet he did not contribute any money to his family, leaving Sarah to support their son alone.

Destitute, Sarah followed him to South Carolina. There she asked the court for alimony, not only for herself, but for her son as well. The case came to trial in Charleston in January 1841. George's attorney claimed that his client was poor, possessing no property from which to pay alimony. George denied that he had ever married Sarah, claiming the child was not his. He produced witnesses who said that under Hebrew law, the certificate signed by the couple was for a betrothal only. Sarah's side called witnesses who swore that the couple had lived together in marriage. Some had carried money from George to Sarah for her bed and board during the early days of their separation.

After listening to testimony about whether the Princes had a real marriage under Jewish law, the court decided that a ceremony *had* taken place. The marriage was valid, though informal. George had *indeed* deserted Sarah.

Benjamin F. Dunkin presided as chancellor during the *Prince v. Prince* trial (1845). (South Caroliniana Library, University of South Carolina)

The only question remaining was whether George had the money to pay her support. Since he was self-employed, he appeared to have no permanent or fixed income and no real property. The court commented, "If the condition in life of the parties is such that neither had property, and they were both to labor for subsistence, it is very questionable whether a case for alimony is presented."

The Court Investigates

Chancellors Dunkin and Johnson then appointed a court assistant ("Master") to investigate George's finances. The Master completed his investigation in 1844 and the case came before the court. The report read:

> The Master does not find any proof that the defendant is in possession of any estate, either real or personal; but from the testimony submitted, he finds that he is in the receipt of money; that he lives comfortably and well; and

that in the Master's own mind there is little doubt that he is in possession of funds sufficient to meet any decree that may be awarded against him.

Then the court reviewed the evidence showing that George had lived the good life:

The evidence reported shows the existence of considerable income. . . . It appears that the defendant has been in the habit of taking boarders; that he vends medicines, and occasionally administers them; that he lives in a hired house, for which he regularly pays considerable rent; and that he supports a woman who lives with him.

The court reasoned George's income might be $1,800 a year. But was he bound to contribute to the support of the wife he had deserted? The court wrote:

By marriage the husband becomes entitled to whatever [property] the wife may possess, and to all her earnings. She is reduced to a state of comparative servitude. She cannot change her situation by another marriage, more agreeable or more beneficial to her. She is deprived of the power of making contracts; and, of course, of the means of accumulating property, or laying by the means of subsistence in sickness or old age. Will it do to say that the husband, entitling himself to all these advantages, and subjecting the wife to all these disabilities, by the marriage, is not bound, by all the means in his power, to sustain her? And if he deserts her, shall his desertion, which is, itself, a wrong, excuse him from the performance of this obligation? Certainly not. It would be a reproach to the law if this were so. God knows, the condition of all women, but especially of married women, is bad enough by the common law of England, and advancing civilization loudly demands its amelioration. But that law, which almost enslaves the wife, makes the husband liable for her support. It is a duty he has undertaken, with her aid, if he chooses to avail himself of it; and for which he is bound, if he rejects that assistance.

George had to pay Sarah alimony and the court told the Master to hear evidence on whether the child was George's or not and, if so, to order that George pay for his education and support as well. George lost his appeal of the decision.

Before this trial, husbands had paid alimony out of the livings they made from their property. *Prince v. Prince* granted alimony out of the husband's earned income. This practice would protect more women. The empathy shown by the court eventually led to more liberal divorce laws in America. Even South Carolina developed rules to provide for a wife's support when the marriage was irretrievable. This reflected a broader change ushered in by Jacksonian democracy, which extended to greater numbers of people the same rights that had formerly been enjoyed by a privileged few.

Suggestions For Further Reading

Hoffer, Peter Charles. *Law and People in Colonial America*. Baltimore: The Johns Hopkins University Press, 1992.

Wortman, Marlene Stein. *Women in American Law, Vol. I*. New York: Holmes & Meier Publishers, 1985.

Shaw v. Shaw: 1845

Plaintiff: Emeline Shaw   **Defendant:** Daniel T. Shaw
Plaintiff's Claim: That she be granted a divorce on the ground of intolerable cruelty   **Chief Lawyers for Defendant:** Mr. Church and Mr. Hubbard
Chief Lawyers for Plaintiff: Mr. Sedgwick and Mr. Seymour
Justices: Joel Hinman, Henry Waite, *Chief Justice Thomas S. Williams* (majority); Samuel Church (dissent); William L. Storrs (absent)
Place: Litchfield, Connecticut   **Date of Decision:** June 1845
Decision: The court denied Shaw her divorce

SIGNIFICANCE

This case illustrates why divorces were so rare during most of American history. Patriarchal rights were a given, spousal rape was not considered bodily harm severe enough to constitute cruelty, and male jealousy justified abuse in the eyes of the courts.

D ivorce, until recently, has been rare in America. During the colonial period, anyone seeking a divorce had to produce written proof of the date of marriage and obtain signed petitions of support. In those days, the most frequent petitioners were abandoned wives. However, after the war for independence, many of the new states reformed their divorce laws, with women successfully suing for divorce as easily as men. In the South, however, courts rarely permitted divorce for any reason. Couples who wanted to separate had three options. The first was divorce *a vinculo matrimonii*, or absolute divorce, which permitted remarriage. Connecticut and Massachusetts granted this type of divorce but only for adultery, cruelty, and desertion. The second option was divorce *a mensa et thoro*, a permanent separation "from bed and board." This arrangement was more common, but did not permit either party to remarry. The third option was a private divorce in which couples simply lived apart.

Connecticut's divorce laws became more liberal than other states' except Massachusetts. In these two states—probably because of the influence of the Puritans who viewed marriage as a civil, not religious, ceremony—marriages were more easily dissolved. Connecticut divorce decrees gave each party the legal status of unmarried persons. Therefore, divorced women could own and control property, sue or be sued, engage in business, and participate in other activities denied to their wives.

Sticks and Stones

In Connecticut, if a wife was in physical danger in her home, her husband had to support her somewhere else. Cruelty was a major cause of legal separation and divorce. However, a woman had to fear injury or death to expect a court to free her from the marriage. *Shaw v. Shaw* illustrates how the courts excused cruelty even up to the mid-nineteenth century.

The Litchfield County Courthouse (c. 1840s) where the divorce trial *Shaw v. Shaw* took place. (The Litchfield Historical Society)

Emeline and Daniel Shaw married on October 24, 1841, and lived together until June 10, 1844. On that day, Emeline left Daniel to live with her mother—and went to court for a divorce charging him with cruelty. At a hearing before Justice Joel Hinman at the February 1845 term of the superior court in Litchfield, she claimed her husband often spoke to her in angry, abusive, and obscene language, even in front of her children (by a former husband). He called her names, such as "old hypocrite," and "ugly devil." He implied she was a slut and accused her of going to New York to have intercourse with other men.

Emeline testified that Daniel was unreasonably jealous of her, and would not allow her to visit her friends or family—particularly with her mother. On one occasion, when her mother-in-law had come to see the ailing Emeline, Daniel turned her away, forbidding her to come again. At another time, when Emeline wanted to sleep overnight at her mother's house—her health being so poor she feared having intercourse with Daniel—he tried to stop her by locking her door. She escaped out a window. On other occasions, Daniel had forced Emeline to have sex with him.

Patriarchal Power

In February 1845, after a preliminary hearing, the dispute went to Connecticut's Supreme Court of Errors.

Daniel's lawyers argued that he was not guilty of "intolerable cruelty" because these words meant "personal violence," resulting in extreme suffering or death—or, at least, endangering one's life or health. Daniel's actions were not "cruel" in either sense—certainly not extreme enough to allow for even a divorce *a mensa et thoro*. Finally, words, however abusive, are not legal cruelty. Daniel's violence did not endanger Emeline's life, injure her, or disturb the peace. For such lesser cruelties, the remedy lay with the legislature, not the courts.

Emeline's lawyers argued that the Supreme Court should permit the Shaws to separate. By endangering his "blameless" wife's health, Daniel had forfeited his right to Emeline's company. Even if Daniel had committed no bodily harm to his wife, his behavior defeated "the great ends of marriage." Especially offensive was his insulting and obscene language in front of the children, the mental "torture" he inflicted upon her by denying her access to her friends and family, and his "barbarous and disgusting abuse of his marital rights" by rape.

For the court, Chief Justice Thomas S. Williams first asked what constituted intolerable cruelty:

> What is that "intolerable cruelty" spoken of in the statue? It doubtless speaks of acts done to the wife herself; and we understand it to impart barbarous, savage, inhuman acts. They must be of that character as to be in fact intolerable, *not to be borne*. The legislature must have had in view acts as cruel at least for those for which, under the head of *extreme cruelty*, the ecclesiastical courts in Great Britain divorce *a mensa et thoro;* and those decisions may furnish some assistance upon the subject. . . .

The chief justice accepted Daniel's lawyers' argument that words, however abusive, did not amount to legal cruelty. He also agreed that Daniel's violence did not endanger his wife's life, injure her, or disturb the peace. Rationalizing Daniel's abusive language, Williams said:

> The first thing to be considered . . . is the language made use of, by this defendant, towards his wife. It is vulgar, obscene, harsh. . . . They were, however, accompanied by no act or menace indicating violence to her person . . . but when we look further, and find, that he was jealous of his wife, it is not so much to be wondered at, as we have been told by authority, that "jealousy is the rage of man." The unfortunate victim of this passion is indeed to be pitied; but the law furnishes no remedy for conduct like this.

Refusing to let Emeline visit her own mother and relatives was "harsh, if not cruel," the court agreed. However, it upheld the rule of patriarchy, concluding:

> As the husband must have the right to say who shall be admitted to his house, and in some measure to regulate the intercourse of his wife, the court cannot draw a line by which his authority can be restrained.

Chief Justice Williams added that even *unreasonable* exercise of a husband's authority was not the kind of cruelty that would warrant a separation. He attributed Daniel's rape of his wife to his ignorance of Emeline's condition. Daniel did not *know* he was hurting her, and besides, she suffered no "real" harm. In conclusion, nothing the husband had done to the wife, rape included, was unlawful:

> Were these acts, such acts of intolerable cruelty as are a cause of separation? No case of this kind is known to have been brought before the court. . . . The cases found in the books, are cases of violence, where the natural consequence would be injurious or dangerous, and where the act, therefore, was unlawful. Here the act in itself was a lawful act—in ordinary circumstances, not injurious nor dangerous. . . . Are we to couple an act of this kind with an act where a violent blow is given, which must greatly injure or endanger, and which was so intended?

Therefore, the court refused to allow Emeline either to divorce or separate from Daniel.

Shaw v. Shaw illustrates how supportive the courts were of the idea that the husband was the head of the house: The "husband must have the right to say who shall be admitted to his house, and in some measure to regulate the intercourse of his wife." His rape of his wife, unlike today, was viewed as neither criminal nor cruel.

In 1978, in all but three states, husbands held immunity from raping their wives. That year, the trial of *Oregon v. Rideout* (see page 73) led many states to abolish marital and cohabitation exemptions to rape.

For Further Reading

Hoff, Joan. *Law, Gender, and Injustice: A Legal History of U.S. Women.* New York: New York University Press, 1991.

Hoffer, Peter Charles. *Law and People in Colonial America.* Baltimore: Johns Hopkins University Press, 1992.

Kerber, Linda K. *Women's America: Refocusing the Past.* New York: Oxford University Press, 1991.

Salmon, Marylynn. *Women and the Law of Property in Early America.* Chapel Hill: University of North Carolina Press, 1986.

Wortman, Marlene Stein. *Women in American Law, Vol. I.* New York: Holmes & Meier Publishers, 1985.

Hair v. Hair: 1858

Appellant: Irvine R. Hair   **Appellee:** Rebecca E. Hair
Appellant's Claim: That Rebecca Hair could not receive alimony because she refused to move with her husband to another state
Chief Lawyer for Appellee: A. P. Aldrich   **Chief Lawyer for Appellant:** J. T. Aldrich   **Chancellors:** *Job Dargan,* Benjamin F. Dunkin, and F. H. Wardlaw   **Place:** Columbia, South Carolina   **Date of Decision:** May 1858
Decision: Irvine Hair did not have to pay alimony to his wife because the appeals court decided that she had deserted *him* by refusing to follow him to another state

SIGNIFICANCE

Until the late twentieth century women lost many legal rights when they married—and one was the freedom to choose where to live. Husbands had an absolute right to select a family's home—by custom and law. *Hair v. Hair* illustrates the consequences for South Carolina wives if they refused to obey.

During the colonial period, legislators turned to their ancestral homeland for rules regulating divorce. England supplied them with two ways to dissolve a marriage. One, like modern divorce, allowed husbands and wives to remarry (divorces *a vinculo matrimonii).* The other permitted couples to separate without remarriage (divorces *a mensa et thoro).* Divorces *a vinculo matrimonii,* also called "absolute divorces," were rare. According to legal historian Marylynn Salmon, no southern colony ever granted it.

After the Revolution most states liberalized their divorce laws. Some granted absolute divorces for adultery, impotence, and imprisonment; others included desertion and bigamy. Only South Carolina remained unchanged. Its assembly passed no statute on divorce and its courts continued to bar absolute divorces and annulments for many years. Judges and lawmakers alike believed that to do so would encourage marital disputes and immorality. Some suggest that as a slave-holding state, South Carolina chose not to recognize divorce because this would have allowed wives to divorce husbands who committed adultery with enslaved women.

Even though divorce was illegal in South Carolina, if a couple separated, the few courts of equity (or chancery) law might grant alimony to the wife. They were more inclined to support wives if there was threat of injury, desertion, or "obscene and revolting indecencies practiced in the family circle." However, to obtain alimony women had to be "blameless," as *Hair v. Hair* illustrates so well.

In 1853, Rebecca Matheney agreed to marry Irvine Hair, on condition that they would never move out of South Carolina without her consent. Irvine—negotiating for Rebecca's lands as much as for her companionship—agreed, and the family blessed the marriage.

The couple married on October 13, and for fourteen months lived with Rebecca's mother. On September 11, 1854, Rebecca delivered a baby girl. The following year, the family bought a small farm one half-mile away. Mrs. Matheney willingly gave the couple two female slaves, Hagar and Ann (who bore a son, Josephus) and one hundred dollars. All of this property became Irvine's, as Rebecca's husband and "guardian."

Before long, Irvine decided he wanted to move to Louisiana. Rebecca refused, reminding him of the promise he had made to her and her mother before they married.

Like a Thief in the Night

Three years later, Irvine secretly rented the land on which his family lived and sold their growing crops, hogs, and other animals. At midnight on Sunday, September 27, 1857, he kidnapped two of their slaves, Ann and Josephus (Hagar escaped), taking them to Louisiana. Eleven days after his desertion, Rebecca filed papers seeking divorce and alimony.

Irvine heard of Rebecca's action and quickly returned to South Carolina. On January 11, 1858, he formally responded, denying he ever promised Rebecca or her mother he would remain in South Carolina (although three witnesses would dispute this claim).

Their battle came before the circuit court in Barnwell, South Carolina. Irvine said that he had wanted to move to Louisiana because that state offered brighter prospects for farming. He claimed that he had made a great effort to have his wife and child accompany him, but that Rebecca had vehemently refused. Finally, he asserted he had left the house at midnight "to avoid a scene." Throughout the trial, Irvine renewed his offer to take his family to Louisiana, but in a manner that Rebecca found insincere. Chancellor F. H. Wardlaw sided firmly with Rebecca:

> I think that, under the circumstances of this case, a wife is not bound to return to the society of a husband who deserted her. His oral offer to take her back was abrupt and rude, and his offer, in the answer, is gingerly.

Wardlaw ruled that Irvine deceptively won his wife and her property by promising not to move from the area. Irvine had the means to support his family comfortably where they were, and therefore had no reason to leave. The chancellor awarded alimony to Rebecca, directing that "allowance should be made out of [Irvine's] estate for the maintenance of [Rebecca] with her child," and that "the allowance to the plaintiff [should] constitute a lien on this estate."

Irvine appealed, urging the South Carolina Court of Equity in Columbia to reverse the lower court's decision. This time he asked how, with divorce illegal in South Carolina, the court could have awarded Rebecca alimony.

Purer Than Caesar's Wife

Job Dargan, the new chancellor, said there were only three grounds for alimony. These were, first, bodily injury inflicted or threatened; second, desertion; and third, "obscene practices" in the home, which would cause the wife to flee "from the polluting presence of that monster, with whom in an evil hour she had united her destinies." Except for these reasons, South Carolina courts had never upheld a suit for alimony. Dargan stated:

> The question is, whether [Rebecca] has made out a case of desertion. That [Irvine] left her and removed to another State, is beyond controversy, and not denied. But did he leave her in an unjustifiable manner? Her own declarations in her bill shew that he most earnestly solicited her for years, to accompany him.

Dargan believed Rebecca was at fault:

> At length, upon her persistent, I may well say, obstinate refusal, he went alone—without his wife and child. Certainly the husband, by our laws, is lord of his own household, and sole arbiter on the question as to where himself and family shall reside.

Regarding Rebecca's point that Irvine had made a prenuptial agreement to jointly decide their place of residence, Dargan responded:

This mid-nineteenth century engraving portrays a family struggling to move west. During this era, husbands dictated where the family lived, despite the circumstances or aftermath of such a move. (Prints & Photographs Division, Library of Congress)

My opinion is that he made the promises in the manner charged in the bill. But they created a moral obligation only. It may be conceded to be very dishonorable in him to commit a breach of the promises he made, in order to obtain the hand of his wife in marriage . . . and by those promises induce [friends and family] to waive a settlement of her property. [However] the contract of matrimony has its well understood and its well defined legal duties, relations and obligations, and it is not competent for the parties to interpolate into the marriage compact any condition in abridgment of the husband's lawful authority over her person, or his claim to her obedience.

Returning to the question of blame, Dargan addressed those assembled in the courtroom:

The simple question is, did the defendant desert his wife, the plaintiff? It must be a legal desertion. It is not every withdrawal of himself by the husband from the society of the wife that constitutes desertion in legal contemplation. The conduct of the wife must be blameless. If she elopes, or commits adultery, or violates or omits to discharge any of the important hymeneal obligations which she has assumed upon herself, the husband may abandon her without providing for her support; and this Court would sustain him in such a course of conduct.

By this reasoning, Dargan concluded that Rebecca had effectively deserted Irvine:

The husband has the right, without the consent of the wife, to establish his domicile in any part of the world, and it is the legal duty of the wife to follow his fortunes, wheresoever he may go. . . . Considering the relative duties and obligations of husband and wife, as defined by law, who, under these circumstances is guilty of desertion? The wife, assuredly.

Dargan reversed the lower court's decision, denying Rebecca alimony. The court, like so many in the nation, had clearly used harsher standards for Rebecca than Irvine, condemning her disobedience more severely than her husband's abandonment. In South Carolina and elsewhere, wives had to toe the line, or suffer stiff consequences.

The husband's right to establish the family's domicile was emphatically upheld as late as 1953 by the Arizona supreme court *(Carlson v. Carlson)*. Today, however, most states permit a wife to establish her own domicile if she is living apart from her husband for cause. A few will allow her to do so for any reason at all.

For Further Reading

Cary, Eve, and Kathleen Willert Peratis. *Woman and the Law*. Skokie, Ill.: National Textbook Company in conjunction with the American Civil Liberties Union, 1981.

Hoffer, Peter Charles. *Law and People in Colonial America*. Baltimore: Johns Hopkins University Press, 1992.

Kerber, Linda K. *Women's America: Refocusing the Past*. New York: Oxford University Press, 1991.

Ross, Susan Deller, et al. *The Rights of Women: The Basic ACLU Guide to Women's Rights*. Carbondale and Edwardsville: Southern Illinois University Press, 1991.

Salmon, Marylynn. *Women and the Law of Property in Early America*. Chapel Hill: University of North Carolina Press, 1986.

Wortman, Marlene Stein. *Women in American Law, Vol. I*. New York: Holmes & Meier Publishers, 1985.

Packard v. Packard: 1864

Plaintiff: Reverend Theophilus Packard, Jr. **Defendant:** Elizabeth Parsons Ware Packard **Plaintiff's Claim:** That his wife was insane and he could confine her at home **Chief Lawyers for Defendant:** Stephen Moore and John W. Orr **Chief Lawyer for Plaintiff:** No record **Judge:** Charles R. Starr **Place:** Kankakee, Illinois **Dates of Trial:** January 13–18, 1864 **Verdict:** Elizabeth Packard was declared sane and restored to liberty

SIGNIFICANCE

In 1864, Illinois law permitted a man to institutionalize his wife "without the evidence of insanity required in other cases." Elizabeth Packard set about to change that law and was instrumental in securing reform in Illinois and Massachusetts (1867), Iowa (1872), and Maine (1874).

In the late autumn of 1863, Elizabeth Packard was discharged from the Illinois State Hospital for the Insane, where her husband, the Reverend Theophilus Packard, had ordered her sent. Soon after she returned home, he locked her away in her children's nursery. Most states in the nineteenth century permitted husbands to use their own judgment in institutionalizing their wives. The law made no mention of a woman's being "put away" *in her own home*, however, and Elizabeth promptly tossed a letter of protest from her window. Elizabeth's friend, Sarah Haslett, brought the letter to Judge Charles R. Starr.

Starr directed Reverend Packard to produce Elizabeth for examination in his chambers. When the Packards appeared, Reverend Packard brought along his written explanation that Elizabeth had been "discharged [from the Illinois State Hospital] . . . and is incurably insane . . . [and] the undersigned has allowed her all the liberty compatible with her welfare and safety." The judge, unconvinced, scheduled a jury trial to decide the question of Elizabeth's sanity.

He Says . . .

Reverend Packard was an austere, uncompromisingly orthodox Calvinist minister. He claimed that his wife's liberal and even mystical interpretations of theological points—as well as her refusal to be guided by the man who was both her minister and her husband—were clear evidence of insanity. In particular, as attorney Stephen Moore wrote (in the only record of the trial known to survive), Elizabeth refused to believe "the Calvinist doctrine of man's total depravity, and that God has preordained some to be saved, others to be damned. She stands fully on the platform of man's free agency and accountability to God for his actions."

She also believed that the Holy Ghost was the female component of the Trinity, and that she herself might be its dwelling place (as might other holy Christian women). Although her husband described these thoughts as both "emanations from the devil" and "the vagaries of a crazed brain," the prosecution's witnesses—this being the nineteenth and not the seventeenth century—addressed only the latter possibility.

Dr. Christopher Knott had interviewed Elizabeth before her husband had committed her to the Hospital for the Insane. He testified that "her mind appeared to be excited on the subject of religion. On all other subjects she was perfectly rational. . . . I take her to be a lady of fine mental abilities. . . . I would say she was insane, the same as I would say Henry Ward Beecher, Spurgeon, Horace Greeley, and like persons are insane."

Dr. J. W. Brown had interviewed Elizabeth in the guise of a traveling sewing machine salesman a few weeks prior to the trial. When he had engaged her in conversation about her husband and religion during his pseudo-sales pitch, she complained that her husband believed "the despotism of man may prevail over the wife." Once religion became their topic of discussion, Dr. Brown testified, he "had not the slightest difficulty in concluding that she was hopelessly insane."

This nineteenth-century drawing depicts the house from which Mrs. Packard was kidnapped on June 18, 1860.

Not only had Elizabeth claimed to be "the personification of the Holy Ghost," but "she found fault that Mr. Packard would not discuss their points of difference in religion in an open manly way instead of going around and denouncing her as crazy to her friends and to the church." Her characterization of Dr. Brown as a copperhead (a northern Democrat sympathetic to the South) and her refusal to shake his hand at the end of their encounter—as well as negative feelings toward her husband—convinced him of her insanity.

When Abijah Dole, Reverend Packard's brother-in-law, took the stand, he testified that Elizabeth had told him that she no longer wished to live with her husband—proof that her mind had become confused. He also said that an essay Elizabeth had written was further evidence of her insanity. Finally, he testified that Elizabeth had taken formal steps to leave her husband's church. One of Elizabeth's attorneys, John W. Orr, immediately demanded: "Was that an indication of insanity?" Dole expressed no doubt: "She would not leave the church unless she was insane."

Sybil Dole also provided "evidence" against her sister-in-law. "She accused Dr. Packard very strangely," she testified, "of depriving her of her rights of conscience— that he would not allow her to think for herself on religious questions because they differed on these topics."

Sarah Rumsey—a mother's helper to Elizabeth—testified, "She wanted the flower beds in the front yard cleaned out and tried to get Mr. Packard to do it. He would not. She put on an old dress and went to work and cleaned out the weeds . . . until she was almost melted down with heat. . . . Then she went to her room and took a bath and dressed herself and lay down exhausted. . . . She was angry and excited and showed ill-will."

Finally, a certificate issued by Dr. Andrew McFarland, superintendent of Illinois State Hospital for the Insane, said that Elizabeth Packard had been discharged from the hospital as incurable.

She Says . . .

Elizabeth Packard's lawyers, Orr and Moore, allowed her to read her Bible class essay to the court. Written in 1860 and entitled "How Godliness is Profitable," it reasoned that "the Christian farmer has no more reason to expect success in his farming operation than the impenitent sinner." It concluded with the observation that while "gain and loss, dollars and cents, are not the coins current in the spiritual world . . . happiness and misery are coins which are current in both worlds," and her belief that a "godly person" may be happier, if not richer, than an "ungodly" one.

Several neighbors testified that they had never found any evidence of insanity in Mrs. Packard. Sarah Haslett described Elizabeth's response to the messy home she returned to upon her release from the Hospital for the Insane: "I called to see her a few days after she returned from Jacksonville. She was in the yard cleaning feather beds. . . . The house needed cleaning. And when I

A lithograph of Elizabeth Parsons Ware Packard during her trial in 1864. (Illinois State Historical Library)

called again it looked as if the mistress of the house was *home.*" Haslett also testified that Reverend Packard had nailed the nursery windows shut in order to confine his wife.

The last witness to testify for the defense was Dr. Duncanson, a physician and theologian. He said, "I did not agree with . . . her on many things, but I do not call people insane because they differ with me. . . . You might with as much propriety call Christ insane . . . or Luther, or Robert Fuller. . . . I pronounce her a sane woman and wish we had a nation of such women."

The jury delivered their verdict after only seven minutes of deliberation on January 18, 1864. "We, the undersigned Jurors in the case of Mrs. Elizabeth P. W. Packard, alleged to be insane, having heard the evidence . . . are satisfied that [she] is sane." Starr ordered that she "be relieved of all restraints incompatible with her condition as a sane woman."

The Packards did not divorce, but remained estranged for the rest of their lives. Elizabeth Packard lectured, wrote, and lobbied on behalf of women's rights and persons committed or alleged to be insane. She was instrumental in securing a married woman's property law in Illinois (1869) and commitment law reform in Illinois and Massachusetts (1867), Iowa (1872), and Maine (1874).

For Further Reading

Burnham, John Chynoweth. "Elizabeth Parsons Ware Packard." In *Notable American Women, 1607– 1950.* Edward T. James, Janet Wilson James, and Paul S. Boyer, eds. Cambridge, Mass.: Belknap Press of Harvard University Press, 1971.

Chicago Tribune, July 28, 1897.

Packard, Elizabeth Parsons Ware. *Great Disclosure of Spiritual Wickedness!! in high places. With an appeal to the government to protect the inalienable rights of married women.* Written under the inspection of Dr. M'Farland, Superintendent of Insane Asylum, Jacksonville, Illinois, 4th ed. Boston: Published by the authoress, 1865.

———. *Marital Power Exemplified in Mrs. Packard's Trial and self-defense from the charge of insanity, or, Three years imprisonment for religious belief, by the arbitrary will of a husband, with an appeal to the government to so change the laws as to afford legal protection to married women.* Hartford, Conn.: Case, Lockwood & Co., 1866.

———. *The Mystic Key; or The Asylum Secret Unlocked.* Hartford, Conn.: Case, Lockwood & Brainard Co., 1866.

———. *The prisoners' hidden life, or Insane asylums unveiled: as demonstrated by the Report of the Investigating Committee of the Legislature of Illinois, together with Mrs. Packard's coadjustors' testimony.* Chicago: The Author; A. B. Case, Printer, 1868.

Sapinsley, Barbara. *The Private War of Mrs. Packard.* New York: Paragon House, 1991.

Birkbeck v. Ackroyd: 1878

Appellant: Edmund Ackroyd   **Appellee:** Thomas Birkbeck
Appellant's Claim: That Birkbeck had no right to sue for the recovery of his
wife's back wages   **Appellee's Lawyer:** W. J. Welsh
Appellant's Lawyer: Herbert Gedney   **Judges:** *Charles Andrews;* Robert
Earl and Judge Miller (absent)   **Place:** New York, New York
Date of Decision: September 17, 1878   **Decision:** Plaintiff could recover
his wife's wages

SIGNIFICANCE

Nineteenth-century courts believed that the combined wealth of husbands and
wives belonged to the male "head of the house." It took state houses in the
Guilded Age (1873–1900) to diminish the rights of husbands.

N ew York State was a center for women's activism in the Victorian Period. At
Seneca Falls, in upstate New York, the first organized convention on behalf
of women's rights took place in 1848. Susan B. Anthony and Elizabeth Cady
Stanton, leaders of the women's rights movement, both lived in New York, and
Stanton testified before the New York legislature on behalf of women's causes.
So it is curious that New York State enforced the married women's property
rights in such a reluctant manner—as is reflected in the 1878 *Birkbeck v. Ackroyd*
decision.

In 1846, thirty-two years before *Birkbeck v. Ackroyd*, New York State abolished its Court of Chancery, which dispensed equity law. Equity procedures had
softened the impact of the common law upon wives. Now this merger of
common law and equity procedures threatened to remove the few rights wives
held under eighteenth-century law.

Two years later, feminists forced New York State to pass the Married
Woman's Property Act of 1848. Later amendments in 1849, 1857, and 1860
strenthened the property rights of wives.

The 1848 law declared with seeming forthrightness that "the real and
personal property, and the rents, issues and profits thereof of any female now
married shall not be subject to the disposal of her husband; but all be her sole
and separate property as if she were a single female. . . ." In practice, the courts

tended to interpret these statutes narrowly, noting in particular that the acts did not change the rule of the common law.

In *Switzer v. Valentine* (1854), the New York Superior Court held that a wife without a separate estate could not make a valid contract. In *Brooks v. Schwerin* (1873), the majority of the New York Superior Court upheld the husband's primary right to his wife's earnings and his right to sue for their recovery. *Birkbeck v. Ackroyd* also would test these new progressive laws.

Does a Husband Own His Wife's Wages?

On June 14, 1878, attorneys for Thomas Birkbeck and Edmund Ackroyd argued an appeal before the New York State Court of Appeals. Birkbeck had worked as a superintendent at a woolen mill owned by Ackroyd. Birkbeck's wife, and several of his adult and minor children, also worked at the mill. In a dispute over back wages, Birkbeck brought suit to recover his own pay, and those of his wife and children.

The New York Supreme Court had found in Birkbeck's favor; on appeal, Ackroyd's attorney, Herbert Gedney, argued that under the Married Women's Property Act, Birkbeck was not entitled to sue. Judge Charles Andrews, writing on behalf of the Court of Appeals, stated that under the 1860 law a wife "may elect to labor on her own account, and thereby entitle herself to her earnings, but in the absence of such an election or of circumstances showing that she intended to avail herself of the privilege and protection conferred by the statute, the husband's common law right to her earnings remains unaffected."

Andrews suggested that if Mrs. Birkbeck had been "living apart" from her husband, or had been "compelled to labor for her own support," or if the "conduct or habits of the husband" endangered her property, Ackroyd could have raised a valid objection to Birkbeck's right to bring suit. However, Andrews concluded that "where the husband and wife are living together, and mutually engaged in providing for the support of themselves and their family . . . and there is nothing to indicate an intention on the part of the wife to separate her earnings from those of her husband, . . . [they] belong . . . to the husband, and he may maintain an action . . . to recover them."

The court thus declined to hold that "irrespective of her intention, [a wife's] earnings, in all cases, belong to her and not to the husband. . . ." While Mrs. Birkbeck was doubtless happy that her husband received her back wages, the decision underlined the continuing uncertainties about the legal status of working wives. In the absence of evidence that a wife wanted to keep her separate estate, courts assumed she was under the disabilities of the common law.

Although jurists interpreted the new property laws narrowly, over time Victorian legislatures did strengthen the ability of married women to protect themselves from their husbands, a role once played by courts of equity.

"Look! the boss has a WOMAN to write his letters"

Birkbeck v. Ackroyd underscored the right of male New Yorkers to sue for their wives' wages. This late nineteenth-century drawing shows a woman working in an office as men in the foreground joke about a woman doing a "man's" job. (National Archives)

For Further Reading

Frost, Elizabeth, and Kathryn Cullen-DuPont. *Women's Suffrage in America: An Eyewitness History.* New York: Facts on File, 1992.

Hoffer, Peter Charles. *Law and People in Colonial America.* Baltimore: The Johns Hopkins University Press, 1992.

Kanowitz, Leo. *Women and the Law: The Unfinished Revolution.* Albuquerque: University of New Mexico Press, 1969.

Salmon, Marylynn. *Women and the Law of Property in Early America.* Chapel Hill: University of North Carolina Press, 1986.

McKim v. McKim: 1879

Plaintiff: Charles F. McKim   **Defendant:** Anne B. McKim
Plaintiff's Claim: That he should have custody of his four-year-old daughter
Chief Lawyer for Defendant: Abraham Payne
Chief Lawyer for Plaintiff: Charles Hart   **Chief Justice:** Charles S. Durfee
Place: Providence County, Rhode Island   **Date of Decision:** November 1,
1879   **Decision:** The court awarded custody of the child to her mother
although custody could change at any time in the future

SIGNIFICANCE

After this trial, American courts slowly began favoring mothers over fathers when
awarding custody of a child of "tender age."

Charles McKim was a successful New York architect with a "cold and imperial style" in both his architecture and personality. Some called him a gentleman of excellent character; others thought he could make a "damn fool" of himself. In October 1874, he married, and seven months later, moved with his wife to Newport, Rhode Island. There Anne McKim bore a daughter on August 13, 1875.

In January 1876, the McKims returned to New York and moved into a house provided and partly furnished by Anne's father. That year Anne's health mysteriously gave way, "as if," in the words of Chief Justice Charles S. Durfee, "it were sapped by secret troubles." In May 1877, Anne packed, dressed her daughter, and left home, returning to her father's house in Newport.

Humiliated and angry, Charles went to court for the return of his daughter. When the hearing began, the girl entered the courtroom looking "delicate and frail." The child's doctor testified that she had suffered from a chronic bronchial disorder and other ailments that would weaken without her mother's care.

During the many months it took the case to move through the Rhode Island courts, Charles claimed his marriage had been "perfectly happy" until after the birth of his daughter. Then he and Anne had hired a baby nurse, Rose Wagner, an old friend of Anne. Rose, Charles thought, had come to "monopolize" his wife.

However, Anne's side argued that it was *not* Rose who broke up her marriage but Charles, who was critical, untruthful, and immoral. Anne implied that he had been unfaithful to her—although she presented no proof.

Charles' attorney, Charles Hart, then raised a new point: He quoted *Commonwealth [of Massachusetts] v. Briggs* (1834) to bolster their case, which had decided that "the unauthorized separation of the wife from the husband without any apparent *justifiable* cause, is a strong reason why the child should not be restored to her." Indeed, the common law had traditionally awarded custody to the father, as the legal head of the household.

The Rhode Island Supreme Court agreed with Anne that the nurse did not break up the marriage. On the second point, the justices thought that Anne had no legal justification for deserting Charles. They believed Charles was "morally fit to have the custody of his child." Still, in a precedent-setting decision, the court concluded:

> The welfare of the child, considering her tender years, her sex, and the delicacy of her constitution, will, in our opinion, be best subserved by leaving her for the present with her mother; and indeed we think that, for the present, to take her from her mother is too hazardous an experiment for us to try, unless the law, in deference to the superior right of the father, requires it of us.

Justice Durfee made his decision based on his review of the history of English and American child custody law. He attempted to show that his decision was not as radical a departure as it really was.

Supreme Court Justice Charles S. Durfee delivered the opinion of the Court in the Rhode Island *McKim* divorce trial of 1879. (Rhode Island Historical Society, All Rights Reserved)

The More Things Change . . .

The landmark *Pennsylvania v. Addicks* (see page 271) decision of 1813 had introduced the "best interests of the child" idea to America. However, in practice, fathers still won custody when they desired it. So Durfee drew from *Rex v. Delaval*, a 1763 English case. He used it to show that although the court recognized the "preferable right of the father," it also had an obligation to consider the good of the child. As the justice explained:

> If the child here, instead of being a girl, were a boy of somewhat riper age, in good health, we might deem it our duty under the law to restore him to his father, even at the risk of tearing the mother's heartstrings asunder. We are

led in this case to leave the child with the mother, not for the mother's sake, but for the good of the child.

However, Durfee gave Charles some hope:

The mother should remember that this decision is not necessarily definitive, and that, while the custody of the child is confided to her, the father's right has not been forfeited.

The court told Anne not to "alienate the child from the father, or to instill into her mind any thought or feeling which a daughter ought not to cherish for her father." If Anne failed to obey this instruction, she could lose her daughter.

Today's Working Mothers

Durfee's ruling was a first step in the direction of granting custody to the mother under the "best interests" of the child doctrine. By the turn of the century, this practice had become the norm. Inevitably many men came to feel that because of their sex, they were at an automatic disadvantage in these disputes. However, by the second half of the twentieth century, most states had ended their assumption that mothers always received custody. This was because more mothers were working than ever before. In 1970, 30.3 percent of mothers with children under the age of six held outside jobs. By 1994, the number had climbed to 61.7 percent.

Beginning in the 1970s, a number of high-profile lawsuits caused working women more concern. In 1975, psychologist Lee Salk and Kersten Salk divorced. Dr. Salk sued for sole custody of their children, which his wife had reared full-time without help. Both were good parents, yet the court awarded custody to the doctor—who would probably need to hire a nanny. Based on a new "affirmative standard," the decision "discounted" Kersten Salk's full-time parenting in favor of Lee Salk's "psychological expertise and 'intellectually exciting' lifestyle." Dr. Salk predicted, "*Salk v. Salk* will touch every child in America [and] give fathers the 'incentive' to seek custody of their children."

In 1994, the deputy chief counsel of the Senate Judiciary Committee, Sharon Prost, lost custody of her two young boys because a judge thought she seemed too "absorbed by her work and her career." In 1995, the estranged husband of Marcia Clark, chief prosecutor in the O.J. Simpson trial, filed a suit demanding temporary custody of the couple's two boys. He claimed Clark "is never home and never has any time to spend with them." He had been unemployed for two years before the couple divorced. A lower court in the famous Michigan trial *Ireland v. Smith* (1995) granted custody of Baby Maranda to the young father, Steven Smith. Macomb Circuit Judge Raymond Cashen felt the child was better off with Smith and his family because the mother, Jennifer Ireland, was a full-time student at the University of Michigan. (The state appeals court later overturned the ruling, which was upheld in 1996 by the Michigan Supreme Court.)

Do such cases signal a new judicial bias against working mothers? Or, as fathers' rights advocates claim, has a "motherhood mystique" held the courts in its grip for too long? A 1989 Massachusetts Supreme Judicial Court study showed that fathers who sought primary custody won in twenty nine percent of the cases compared with seven percent of the mothers. And fathers who sought either primary or joint custody won over seventy percent of the time. The study concluded that where fathers sought custody, the courts held mothers to a higher standard than fathers. Mothers are expected to perform two jobs perfectly, but fathers need only succeed in the workplace. Any job they perform at home is an extra plus.

For Further Reading

Chesler, Phyllis. *Mothers on Trial: The Battle for Children and Custody.* San Diego: Harcourt Brace Jovanovich, 1991.

Fineman, Martha Albertson. *The Neutered Mother, the Sexual Family and Other Twentieth Century Tragedies.* New York: Routledge, 1995.

Hoff, Joan. *Law, Gender, and Injustice: A Legal History of U.S. Women.* New York: New York University Press, 1991.

Kerber, Linda K. *Women's America: Refocusing the Past.* New York: Oxford University Press, 1991.

Salmon, Marylynn. *Women and the Law of Property in Early America.* Chapel Hill: University of North Carolina Press, 1986.

Schabath, Gene. "Judge in Day Care Case Sticks by Decision." *Detroit Journal,* December 10, 1995.

Wortman, Marlene Stein. *Women in American Law, Vol. I.* New York: Holmes & Meier Publishers, 1985.

McGuire v. McGuire: 1953

Appellant: Charles W. McGuire **Appellee:** Lydia McGuire
Appellant's Claim: That the lower court ruling awarding "suitable
maintenance and support" to Lydia McGuire was an "unwarranted usurpation
and invasion of [the husband's] fundamental and constitutional rights"
Chief Lawyer for Appellee: H. D. Addison
Chief Lawyer for Appellant: Mark J. Ryan **Justices:** Paul E. Boslaugh,
Edward F. Carter, Ellwood B. Chappell, *Fred W. Messmore,* Chief Justice
Robert G. Simmons, Adolph E. Wenke (majority); John W. Yeager (dissent)
Place: Lincoln, Nebraska **Date of Decision:** June 26, 1953
Decision: Where a husband and wife live together, maintaining a home, the
law regards the husband as legally supporting his wife regardless of their
actual living standards

SIGNIFICANCE

This trial shows that during the 1950s, a homemaker's right to support from her
husband was only to the bare necessities, a condition not dissimilar to that of
colonial wives.

How much support should a homemaker receive for her services as cook, bottle-washer, and nanny? Legally, "not much," as this trial shows. In 1919, a thirty-three-year-old widow with two daughters married Charles McGuire, a frugal forty-six-year-old bachelor. By the 1950s, Charles had reached eighty or so. He held more than $116,000 in cash assets and $83,000 in real estate. His wife Lydia—sixty-six years old—kept house without indoor plumbing or other conveniences.

Lydia did not want a separation or divorce, but she did want "suitable maintenance and support." So she sued Charles in the district court of Wayne County, Nebraska.

The Simple Life

Neither the McGuires nor their attorneys disagreed about facts of the couple's life together. Charles was not *totally* lacking in concern for Lydia: When she needed three abdominal operations, he "allowed" her to choose her doctor and paid the bills.

He also helped his stepdaughters. By working, and with some financial assistance from Charles and their mother, the daughters graduated from high school and attended a few years of college. However, that seemed to be the limit of his financial generosity.

Lydia was not *completely* bereft of spending money: She and her daughters had inherited an eighty-acre farm from her first husband, and each had a one-third share in the property's rent. In addition, she also kept up to three hundred chickens, buying her clothes and the family's groceries with the proceeds of her egg and poultry sales. Then, several years before the suit, Charles leased his farm land to a tenant, leaving his wife room for only twenty-five chickens and a reduced income.

On balance, Charles seemed to be a miser and Lydia seemed to be in dire straits, although she remained "a dutiful and obedient wife." A court would find she "worked in the fields, did outside chores, cooked and attended to her household duties such as cleaning the house and doing the washing."

Once Lydia's egg money dropped off, Charles began buying the couple's groceries. However, he would give her no wardrobe money. At trial, both agreed that in four years he had bought only one article of clothing for her—a badly needed coat. Her daughters gave her a dress or two a year, but otherwise Lydia made do with little.

Lydia complained her husband was "a poor companion" who had not taken her to one motion picture show during the past twelve years, but she complained even more bitterly about the state of her house and the family car.

As the court record states, Lydia received no money "to purchase furniture or other household necessities . . . the house is not equipped with a bathroom, bathing facilities, or inside toilet. The kitchen is not modern. She does not have a kitchen sink. Hard and soft water is obtained from a well and cistern. . . . There is a pipeless furnace which she testified has not been in good working order for five or six years, and she testified she was tired of scooping coal and ashes . . . a 1929 Ford coupe equipped with a heater which is not efficient . . . and when she goes to see her daughters . . . she uses part of the rent money [from her one-third interest in her first husband's farm] for that purpose, [her husband] providing no funds for such use. . . ."

On the plus side, Charles did drive her to see her mother once a year, and "three years ago he did purchase an electric, wood-and-cob combination stove which was installed in the kitchen, also linoleum floor covering for the kitchen."

The district court ruled that Lydia "was legally entitled to use the credit of the defendant and obligate him to pay for . . . improvements and repairs, furniture, and appliances in the amount of several thousand dollars." The court also ordered Charles to buy a car with a working heater, provide his wife with an allowance of fifty dollars per month, and pay the costs of an annual visit to each of her daughters.

Not the Court's Decision

Charles appealed to the Supreme Court of Nebraska, which reversed the lower court ruling. Justice Fred W. Messmore read the court opinion that Charles' "attitude toward his wife, according to his wealth and circumstances, leaves little to be said in his behalf." Nonetheless, "The living standards of a family are a matter of concern to the household, and not for the courts to determine."

Courts determine spousal support only when the parties "separate or liv[e] apart from each other," Messmore said. In contrast, "As long as the home is maintained and the parties are living as husband and wife it may be said that the husband is legally supporting his wife and the purpose of the marriage relation is being carried out. Public policy," he stated emphatically, "requires such a holding."

A 1950s Decision and the Equal Rights Amendment

The Equal Rights Amendment (ERA), drafted by suffragist Alice Paul, was introduced in Congress in 1923. Section 1 reads as follows: "Equality of rights under the law shall not be denied or abridged by the United States or by any state on account of sex."

In 1970, U.S. congresswoman Martha Griffiths (D-Mich.) brought an end to an almost fifty-year period in which the ERA had been buried in the House Judiciary Committee files. She forced the amendment onto the House floor for a vote. After a long delay, the Senate also passed the ERA by a vote of 84 to 8. By 1973, through the efforts of many groups and individuals, thirty states had ratified the amendment.

During this time, ERA opponents won many homemakers to their side by claiming that the amendment would deprive them of their right to spousal support. ERA supporters responded that homemakers in intact marriages actually *had* no right to support beyond bare necessities. They even distributed pamphlets citing *McGuire v. McGuire* and other cases to illustrate their point. They also pointed out there was sufficient legal precedent to predict that under the ERA the meager spousal support obligations that *did* exist would be expanded to cover the homemaking husbands of wage-earning women.

In the end, however, the inflammatory speeches of Phyllis Schafly and other ERA opponents were more persuasive than the ERA supporters' recitation of case law, and many homemakers did not support the amendment.

As a result, in June 1982 the ERA expired—three states short of ratification.

For Further Reading

Cary, Eve, and Kathleen Willert Peratis. *Woman and the Law*. Skokie, Ill.: National Textbook Company in conjunction with the American Civil Liberties Union, 1977.

Kanowitz, Leo. *Sex Roles in Law and Society*. Albuquerque: University of New Mexico Press, 1973.

Mansbridge, Jane J. *Why We Lost the ERA*. Chicago: University of Chicago Press, 1986.

Steiner, Gilbert Y. *Constitutional Inequality: The Political Fortunes of the Equal Rights Amendment*. Washington, D.C.: The Brookings Institution, 1985.

Frontiero v. Richardson: 1973

Appellants: Sharron A. Frontiero and Joseph Frontiero   **Appellees:** Elliot L. Richardson, secretary of defense, et al.   **Appellants' Claim:** That requiring different criteria for male spouses of female military personnel—as opposed to female spouses—to qualify for benefits is a violation of the Fifth Amendment   **Chief Lawyer for Appellees:** Samuel Huntington
Chief Lawyer for Appellants: Joseph L. Levin, Jr. and Ruth Bader Ginsburg
Justices: Harry A. Blackmun, *William J. Brennan, Jr.,* Chief Justice Warren E. Burger, William O. Douglas, Thurgood Marshall, Lewis F. Powell, Potter Stewart, and Byron R. White (majority); William H. Rehnquist (dissent)
Place: Washington, D.C.   **Date of Decision:** May 14, 1973   **Decision:** The federal statutes violated the Fifth Amendment's due process clause and were overturned

SIGNIFICANCE

The assumption that "the husband in our society is generally the 'breadwinner' in the family [while] the wife [is] typically the 'dependent' partner," was shown to be no longer valid. The justices also came within one vote of finding sex an "inherently suspect" category for equal protection purposes.

In this lawsuit, Sharron Frontiero, a married Air Force lieutenant, and her husband, Joseph, a veteran and full-time college student, challenged a federal statute. The law automatically granted male members of the "uniformed forces" housing and other benefits for their wives. However, it required its female members to demonstrate the "actual dependency" of their husbands before granting the same benefit.

According to the statute, a woman's husband was "actually dependent" if his wife provided more than half of his living expenses. Because Joseph Frontiero received $205 per month in veteran's benefits, Sharron Frontiero paid less than half of his living expenses, which were $354 per month. Denied the increased medical and dental benefits for her husband and the same housing allowance that a married male lieutenant automatically received for his spouse, the Frontieros sued. In 1972, the three-judge United States Court for the Middle District of Alabama denied the Frontieros request for relief. Next the Frontieros appealed to the U.S. Supreme Court.

A Federal Problem

The Frontieros claimed the federal government had abridged their rights. They said that the law violated the Due Process Clause of the Fifth Amendment. (While the Fifth Amendment actually contains only "due process" language and no "equal protection" clause, it had long been interpreted by the Supreme Court to require the federal government to grant the same "equal protection" specifically required of the states by the Fourteenth Amendment.)

Ruth Bader Ginsburg had argued another case on behalf of the Women's Rights Project (WRP) of the American Liberties Union, and the WRP now asked the Frontieros' lawyer, Joseph J. Levin, Jr., if the organization might join his Supreme Court appeal. He agreed. The Court granted special leave for the organization to act as *amicus curiae* (friend of the court), and gave Ginsburg ten of the thirty minutes in which the Frontieros' case would be argued.

A Matter of Convenience

The Court heard arguments on January 17, 1973. Samuel Huntington, representing the federal government, argued that, in the uniformed services, the law treated men and women differently for "administrative convenience." He said that American wives were usually dependent upon their husbands, but that American husbands were not usually dependent upon their wives.

For this reason, Congress had reasonably decided that it was cost effective simply to view all wives as financially dependent without requiring all the male members of the uniformed services to document that fact. In contrast, if most men were not dependent upon their wives, it was cost effective and not administratively burdensome to review each female member's documentation of a husband's actual dependency.

Levin argued that the statute unreasonably discriminated because of sex, which was in violation of the Fifth Amendment. He held that it was discriminatory "as a procedural matter" to require documentation of spousal dependency from women but not from men. In addition, he also pointed out that it was unfair

Joseph and Sharron Frontiero in 1973. (Southern Poverty Law Center, Montgomery, Ala.)

that a male member who provided less than one-half of a wife's living expenses received spousal benefits, while a "similarly situated" female member obtained none.

Ginsburg focused on the *level* of judicial scrutiny applied in sex discrimination cases. The Court viewed all laws discriminating because of race, religion, or national origin as "inherently suspect" and subject to "strict judicial scrutiny." To withstand a constitutional challenge, such laws needed to serve a *necessary* relationship to a *compelling* state interest. Ginsburg asked the Court to find sex discrimination as inherently suspect as discrimination based on race, religion, or national origin, and to apply the strict scrutiny standard in this and future sex discrimination cases.

Strict Scrutiny

On May 14, 1973, the Court—with only Justice William H. Rehnquist dissenting—overturned the federal statute. Four of the justices—William J. Brennan, Jr., William O. Douglas, Thurgood Marshall, and Byron R. White— agreed that laws discriminating because of sex were inherently suspect and subject to strict judicial scrutiny. Brennan detailed the historical similarities in race and sex discrimination in America, and the "accident of birth" common to each person's identity insofar as race and national origin:

> Our statute books gradually became laden with gross, stereotyped distinctions between the sexes and, indeed throughout much of the 19th century the position of women in our society was, in many respects, comparable to that of blacks under the pre-Civil War slave codes. Neither slaves nor women would hold office, serve on juries, or bring suit in their own names, and married women traditionally were denied the legal capacity to hold or convey property or to serve as legal guardians of their own children. . . . And although blacks were guaranteed the right to vote in 1870, women were denied even that right . . . until adoption of the Nineteenth Amendment half a century later. . . . Nevertheless, . . . women still face pervasive, although at times more subtle, discrimination. . . . Moreover, since sex, like race and national origin, is an immutable characteristic determined solely by the accident of birth, the imposition of special disabilities upon the members of a particular sex would seem to violate the basic concept of our system that legal burdens should bear some relationship to individual responsibility . . . statutory distinctions between the sexes often have the effect of relegating the entire class of females to inferior legal status without regard to the actual capabilities of its individual members.

Justice Potter Stewart agreed that the challenged statutes "work an invidious discrimination in violation of the Constitution," but did not address the scrutiny issue. Lewis F. Powell, joined by Warren E. Burger and Harry A. Blackmun, also agreed "that the challenged statutes constitute an unconstitutional discrimination against servicewomen in violation of the Due Process Clause of the Fifth Amendment. However, Powell specifically added that he could not agree that classifications based upon sex were "inherently suspect" like those based on race, religion, and national origin.

Ginsburg failed by one vote to win strict scrutiny in sex discrimination cases. However, in the 1976 trial of *Craig V. Boren* (see page 123), the Court would establish a "mid-level" or "heightened" scrutiny standard. Under this compromise standard, sex discrimination would be tolerated only if such discrimination bore a *substantial* relationship to an *important* governmental interest.

For Further Reading

Cary, Eve, and Kathleen Willert Peratis. *Woman and the Law.* Skokie, Ill.: National Textbook Company in conjunction with the American Civil Liberties Union, 1977.

Goldstein, Leslie Friedman. *The Constitutional Rights of Women: Cases in Law and Social Change*, rev. ed. Madison: The University of Wisconsin Press, 1989.

Hoff, Joan. *Law, Gender, and Injustice: A Legal History of U.S. Women.* New York: New York University Press, 1991.

Von Drehle, David. "A Trailblazer's Step-by-Step Assault on the Status Quo." *The Washington Post National Weekly Edition*, July 26–August 1, 1993.

Weinberger v. Wiesenfeld: 1975

Appellant: Caspar W. Weinberger **Appellee:** Stephen Charles Wiesenfeld

Appellant's Claim: That the District Court erred in its finding that Stephen Wiesenfeld's constitutional rights were violated by Social Security provisions that awarded survivor benefits to widowed mothers, but not to widowed fathers, upon the death of a working spouse

Chief Lawyers for Appellee: Ruth Bader Ginsburg and Melvin Wulf

Chief Lawyer for Appellant: Keith A. Jones **Justices:** Harry A. Blackmun, *William J. Brennan, Jr.,* Chief Justice Warren E. Burger, Thurgood Marshall, Lewis R. Powell, Jr., Potter Stewart, William H. Rehnquist, and Byron R. White; Justice William O. Douglas, due to illness, did not participate

Place: Washington, D.C. **Date of Decision:** March 19, 1975

Decision: That the gender-based distinctions of Section 402(g) of the Social Security Act violated the Due Process Clause of the Fifth Amendment and were therefore unconstitutional

SIGNIFICANCE

This decision discounted two stereotypical views of the marriage partnership: "namely, that male workers' earnings are vital to the support of their families, while the earnings of female wage-earners do not significantly contribute to their families' support," and "women as a group would choose to forego work to care for children while men would not."

ollowing the Supreme Court's 1971 historic decision in *Reed v. Reed* (see page 112) and its subsequent decision in the 1973 *Frontiero v. Richardson* case (see page 308), two cases in which *men* claimed sex discrimination came before the justices. In *Kahn v. Shevin* (1974), the Court ruled that Florida's statute granting widows—but not widowers—an annual five-hundred-dollar exemption from property taxes was constitutional. The Court thought that the exemption bore "a fair and substantial relation to the object of the legislation," that is, to reduce "the disparity between the economic capabilities of a man and a woman" arising from either "overt discrimination or . . . the socialization process of a male-dominated culture."

In *Schlesinger v. Ballard* (1975), the Court upheld a Congressional regulation requiring the honorable discharge of any male navy lieutenant or marine captain who is twice passed over for promotion, while permitting female navy lieutenants and marine captains a minimum of thirteen years of service as unpromoted officers prior to such discharge. In its opinion, the Court ruled that such discrimination was permissible. The regulation reflected "not archaic and overbroad generalizations" but the "demonstrable fact" that female officers—barred as they were in 1975 from combat missions and ships engaged in other than medical and transport activities—"had less opportunity for promotion than did their male counterparts. . . . A longer period of tenure for women officers would, therefore, be consistent with the goal to provide women officers with 'fair and equitable career advancement programs.'" In *Weinberger v. Wiesenfeld*, the court would find no such justifications.

A Breadwinner by Any Other Name

Stephen C. Wiesenfeld and Paula Polatschek married in 1970. Paula had been employed as a schoolteacher for five years prior to her wedding, and she continued to teach following her marriage. She provided most of the couple's economic support during the marriage, earning $10,000 in 1970 and 1971, years in which Stephen earned between $2,000 and $3,000. In 1972, Paula earned $7,000 and Stephen, $2,500. Following Paula's death in childbirth on June 5, 1972, Stephen applied for social security benefits both for their newborn son, Jason Paul, and himself.

The maximum social security contributions had been deducted from Paula's wages in each of her working years, and on Jason's behalf, Stephen was awarded $3,000 per year. A surviving widow in these circumstances would have also been awarded an additional $3,000 per year on her own behalf, a sum that would have been reduced by $1 for every $2 earned over $2400 per year, and eliminated once the widow's earnings reached $8400. However, the widower—because of his sex—received nothing.

In February 1973, Wiesenfeld filed his lawsuit with the three-judge United States District Court for the District of New Jersey. His lawyers, Ruth Bader Ginsburg and Melvin Wulf, filed a summary motion requesting that the court find Section 402(g) of the Social Security Act, under which Wiesenfeld had been denied benefits, unconstitutional insofar as it treated men and women differently.

They also requested an injunction against Secretary of Health, Education, and Welfare Casper Weinberger, prohibiting him from denying benefits on the sole basis of sex, and an award of survivor benefits due to Wiesenfeld from June 1972 forward. The district court issued a summary judgment in Wiesenfeld's favor, on the basis that the provision violated the Due Process Clause of the Fifth Amendment. Weinberger made a direct appeal to the Supreme Court.

A Widower's Right

Ginsburg argued Wiesenfeld's case before the Supreme Court on January 20, 1975. She maintained that Section 402(g) of the Social Security Act discriminated against Wiesenfeld and, just as seriously, against Paula Polatschek Wiesenfeld. Paula, she argued, had contributed to the Social Security program on an equal basis with similarly salaried men, and yet she had not received equal protection for her family.

Attorney Keith A. Jones took another view of the disparate treatment. Arguing for the government, he said the program treated widowed women more benevolently than widowed men in an attempt "to offset the adverse economic situation of women by providing a widow with financial assistance to supplement or substitute for her own efforts in the marketplace."

Justice William J. Brennan, Jr., delivered the opinion of the Court on March 19, 1975. He agreed that the Court, in *Kahn v. Shevin*, had upheld a discriminatory provision on the grounds that it helped to compensate women for the greater financial burdens they generally faced upon the loss of their spouse. He said that provision differed from the social security provision in question, which, "linked as it is directly to responsibility for minor children, was intended to permit women to elect not to work and to devote themselves to the care of children. Since this purpose in no way is premised upon any special disadvantages of women, it cannot serve to justify a gender-based distinction which diminishes the protection afforded to women who do work."

Ruth Bader Ginsburg argued this case on behalf of Charles Stephen Wiesenfeld. (Collection, The Supreme Court Historical Society)

He pointed out that social security provisions denying benefits to widows younger than age 60 and *without* dependent children, was further evidence that "Congress was not concerned in Section 402(g) with the employment problems of women generally but with the principle that children of covered employees are entitled to the personal attention of the surviving parent if that parent chooses not to work."

Quoting from *Reed*, the opinion affirmed the decision of the District Court in favor of Wiesenfeld:

Since the gender-based classification of Section 402(g) cannot be explained as an attempt to provide for the special problems of women, it is indistinguishable from the classification held invalid in *Frontiero*. Like statutes there, "[b]y providing dissimilar treatment for men and women who are . . . similarly situated, the challenged section violates the [Due Process] Clause."

The decision also repudiated two entrenched views of married life, "namely, that male workers' earnings are vital to the support of their families, while the earnings of female wage-earners do not significantly contribute to their families' support," and that "women as a group would choose to forgo work to care for children while men would not." In so doing, it underscored the finding in *Frontiero* that women's financial contributions to their families merited the same consideration as men's. It also set a new precedent: the Court would not view child-care responsibilities or decisions as being bound by gender.

For Further Reading

Cary, Eve, and Kathleen Willert Peratis. *Woman and the Law*. Skokie, Ill.: National Textbook Company in conjunction with the American Civil Liberties Union, 1977.

Goldstein, Leslie Friedman. *The Constitutional Rights of Women*. Madison, Wisconsin: University of Wisconsin Press, rev. ed., 1989.

New York Times, March 20 and 23, 1977.

Lynn, Naomi B., ed. *Women, Politics and the Constitution*. Binghamton, N.Y.: The Harrington Park Press, 1990.

Von Drehle, David. "The Quiet Revolutionary: Ruth Bader Ginsburg's Odyssey from Convention to Crusade." *Washington Post National Weekly Edition*, July 26–August 1, 1993.

——. "A Trailblazer's Step-by-Step Assault on the Status Quo." *Washington Post National Weekly Edition*, July 26–August 1, 1993.

Orr v. Orr: 1979

Appellant: William Herbert Orr **Appellee:** Lillian M. Orr
Appellant's Claim: That Alabama's alimony statutes were unconstitutional
Chief Lawyer for Appellee: W. F. Horsley
Chief Lawyer for the Appellant: John L. Capell, III **Justices:** *William J. Brennan, Jr.,* Thurgood Marshall, Potter Stewart, Byron R. White (majority); Harry A. Blackmun and John P. Stevens, III (concurred, each with a separate opinion); Lewis F. Powell, Jr., William Rehnquist, and Chief Justice Warren E. Burger (dissent) **Place:** Washington, D.C. **Date of Decision:** March 5, 1979 **Decision:** Invalidated Alabama's statutes by which husbands, but not wives, might be required to pay alimony upon divorce

SIGNIFICANCE

Orr v. Orr rejected the premise that married women are necessarily dependent upon their husbands for financial support.

L illian and William Orr divorced in Alabama on February 26, 1974. The judge directed William to pay Lillian $1,240 per month in alimony. Soon William either fell behind or stopped paying altogether, and Lillian brought contempt proceedings against him in the Circuit Court of Lee County, Alabama, demanding back payments.

In defense, William claimed that Alabama's alimony statutes violated the equal protection clause of the Fourteenth Amendment, since they required only husbands—never wives—to pay alimony. Lillian believed the law *was* constitutional. The court agreed with her and ordered William to pay the back alimony plus Lillian's legal fees. William promptly appealed the judgment to the Court of Civil Appeals of Alabama.

On March 16, 1977, the court ruled that Alabama's alimony laws— "designed" to help "the wife of a broken marriage who needs financial assistance"—*were* constitutional. The judgment against William must stand. Aftermore proceedings, William appealed to the U.S. Supreme Court, which agreed to hear the case.

Questions Never Asked

The trial began on November 27, 1978. Lillian's position was curiously single-minded. She *could* have objected to William's standing to sue. She *could* have claimed that his suit came too late; after all, he had not complained at the time of the divorce. And she *could* have argued that since they had both agreed and signed on the dotted line, they were bound by state contract law—so it did not matter whether the alimony laws were constitutional or not. William would still have to pay. However, to the surprise of the justices, she offered none of these arguments. Lillian stood by her original contention that the only issue before the Court was the constitutional one.

Therefore, the Court addressed these unmade arguments for her. First, it granted William standing to sue. Justice William J. Brennan, Jr., said: "There is no question but that Mr. Orr bears a burden he would not bear if he were female. This is highlighted, although not altered, by transposing it to the sphere of race. There is no doubt that a state law imposing alimony obligations on blacks but not on whites could be challenged by a black who was required to pay. The burden alone is sufficient to establish standing."

Second, the Court found that the "unexcused tardiness" of William's challenge "might well have constituted a procedural default under state law, and if Alabama had refused to hear Mr. Orr's constitutional objection on that ground, we might have been without jurisdiction to hear it here."

The third question was whether the Supreme Court should refuse jurisdiction because Alabama's contract laws might have furnished a valid basis for a lower court decision in favor of Lillian. In response, Brennan quoted *Anderson v. Brand* (1938): "We cannot refuse jurisdiction because the state court might have based its decision . . . upon an independent and adequate non-federal ground."

Associate Justice William J. Brennan, Jr., gave the opinion of the Supreme Court in the *Orr v. Orr* alimony trial. (Collection, The Supreme Court Historical Society)

A Woman's Place Is . . .

Turning to the merits of the case, Brennan stressed that recent Supreme Court decisions had established that "classifications by gender must serve important governmental objectives and must be substantially related to achievement of those objectives." He then examined what might have been three objectives of the alimony statutes in question.

William had suggested that Alabama preferred wives to play dependent roles within families and reinforced that model by requiring husbands to pay alimony. As Brennan pointed out—citing the 1975 case *Stanton v. Stanton* (see page 119) as one example—a law intending to further that state objective could not stand.

Brennan then turned to the opinion of the Alabama Court of Civil Appeals that said divorced wives needed financial aid. The legislature might have meant to "provide help for needy spouses" and "use[d] sex as a proxy for need." The legislature might also have had "a goal of compensating women for past discrimination during marriage, which assertedly had left them unprepared to fend for themselves in the working world after divorce. Of course, . . . assisting needy spouses is a legitimate and important governmental objective."

Citing the 1979 case *Califano v. Webster* (see page 324), which upheld a more generous formula for the calculation of women's social security earnings than was used for men's, Brennan remarked that reducing the disparity of incomes between men and women caused by the "long history of discrimination" was an important goal. However, there were other ways to achieve it besides burdening husbands. Alabama required individual hearings before any divorce. These could determine which spouses were "needy" and "which women were in fact discriminated against vis-à-vis their husbands, as well as which family units defied the stereotype and left the husband dependent on the wife."

Brennan concluded his discussion with a few remarks about women's "proper place":

> Legislative classifications which distribute benefits and burdens on the basis of gender carry the inherent risk of reinforcing stereotypes about the "proper place" of women and their need for special protection. . . . Thus, even statutes purportedly designed to compensate for and ameliorate the effects of past discrimination must be carefully tailored. Where, as here, the State's compensatory and ameliorative purposes are as well served by a gender-neutral classification as one that gender classifies and therefore carries with it the baggage of sexual stereotypes, the State cannot be permitted to classify on the basis of sex.

A Divorce Decision Changes the Meaning of Marriage

In settling the Orrs' dispute about their divorce decree, the Supreme Court radically changed the legal basis of marriage in America. As editor Leslie Friedman Goldstein points out, Anglo-American law had held that the "legal core" of marriage was a woman's obligation to provide sexual and domestic services and a man's obligation to provide financial support. The Court's ruling in *Orr v. Orr* was a complete rejection of such assumptions and one that, in Goldstein's words, "seismically altered" the marriage institution.

For Further Reading

Goldstein, Leslie Friedman. *The Constitutional Rights of Women,* rev. ed. Madison: The University of Wisconsin Press, 1989.

New York Times. March 6, 7, and 11, 1979.

Lynn, Naomi B., ed. *Women, Politics and the Constitution.* Binghamton, N.Y.: Harrington Park Press, 1990.

Marvin v. Marvin: 1979

Plaintiff: Michelle Triola Marvin   **Defendant:** Lee Marvin
Plaintiff's Claim: That Michelle Marvin was entitled to support payments for life and to one-half of the moneys Lee Marvin earned during the six years they lived together   **Chief Lawyer for Plaintiff:** Marvin M. Mitchelson
Chief Lawyer for Defendant: Mark A. Goldman   **Judge:** Arthur K. Marshall
Place: Los Angeles, California   **Date of Decision:** April 18, 1979
Verdict: The court rejected Michelle Marvin's claims, but nonetheless, it awarded her $104,000 in "rehabilitative alimony"; this judgment was later rescinded

SIGNIFICANCE

Live-in couples, even if they never marry, can make "palimony" settlements, stated or implied. The California Supreme Court made history by upholding a verbal agreement of support between an unwed couple. While denying Michelle Marvin's claims, the court gave the idea of "rehabilitative alimony" credibility by providing her with a monetary award.

Until recently, when people married, the husband was the family breadwinner and the wife stayed at home to raise children and tend to domesticity. In these unions, a married woman gave up her ability to support herself, in exchange for lifetime support. In the event of a divorce, a full-time homemaker could expect this support to continue as alimony.

Expectations aside, even today divorce can mean poverty for wives and their children, whose income drops approximately seventy percent after divorcing. After many years of marriage, divorced women often find themselves thrust into the job market with no employable—or, at best, atrophied—skills. Once common law marriage was generally abolished (1895 in California), women who lived with men *without* benefit of clergy could find themselves in even a worse situation—with no legal standing to claim alimony. The 1979 decision in *Marvin v. Marvin* provided the modern legal precedent that cohabitating but unwed couples might sue for alimony and a division of property at the end of their relationship.

Come Be With Me . . .

By 1966, open cohabitation had begun to occur with the increasing—albeit reluctant—acceptance of the general public. Even though that "piece of paper,"—the marriage certificate—was missing, many live-in couples still clung to the man-at-work, woman-at-home picture of domestic bliss. When Lee Marvin popped the question to Michelle Triola, it was not marriage he was proposing. Instead, he allegedly promised to support her for the rest of her life if she would just give up her singing and dancing career and come live with him and be his cook, confidante, companion and interior decorator—along with tending to him after bouts of heavy drinking.

For six years, Michelle did just that. At first the two lived together in her apartment. Then after his divorce from his first wife was final, they lived in his beach house—lavishly redecorated by Michelle. They jetted together around the world as he continued his movie acting career. He frequently introduced her to others as his wife and, on occasion, while on a movie-making locale, they shared checking accounts.

After more than five years into the relationship, she legally added his name to hers—even though he joked that she would be better off picking a better known name. Several months later, Lee Marvin married his "childhood sweetheart," leaving Michelle in the lurch. He did, however, pay her the sum of $833 per month for fourteen months. Then, at the same time that he was negotiating lower alimony and child support payments for his former wife, Betty, the money for Michelle came to an abrupt halt.

A Deal Is a Deal

For a while, Michelle supported herself watering plants for friends and with other part-time jobs. Then she met Marvin M. Mitchelson, the lawyer who agreed to take her case on a contingency agreement for one-third of whatever she was awarded. She sued for "palimony"—claiming Lee Marvin's promise to support her for life was a binding contract. The California Superior Court, and then the appeals court, denied her claim because such a contract between two unmarried people was unenforceable.

Michelle and her lawyer pressed on, appealing to the California Supreme Court. Its approach was quite up-to-date. Since "common law" marriage as a legal concept had been abolished in California in 1895, the court decided that the Marvins' actual marital status was irrelevant. The focus must be on whether a contract could exist between the two. It ruled that the courts should enforce express contracts between nonmarital partners except to the extent that the contract is explicitly founded on the consideration of meretricious sexual services.

In short, if having sex were an explicit part of the deal, the court would not enforce that part of the contract since it would mean endorsing prostitution—sex in exchange for money—an illegal act. However, since nonmarital relationships in modern society had become socially acceptable, the court was unwilling to "impose a standard based on alleged moral considerations . . . that have been so widely abandoned by so many." Therefore, "The courts may inquire into the conduct of the parties to determine whether that conduct demonstrates an implied contract or implied agreement of partnership or joint venture, or some other tacit understanding between the parties."

With this reasoning, the California Supreme Court overruled the two lower courts and sent her case back for trial. The lower court would have to decide from the evidence whether the Marvins had a binding contract.

More Than Chief Cook and Bottle Washer

It was now up to Michelle Marvin to convince the court that she did have a binding oral contract with Lee Marvin. She argued that she had done all that could be expected from a wife: She had become pregnant three times by the actor, miscarrying one pregnancy but aborting the other two because he did not want children. She had managed the household accounts and paid all the bills from a weekly allowance he had given her. Her agent testified that that she had heard Lee promise to take care of Michelle and that she should not worry about her career since she had him.

At almost every turn, however, Lee gave an explanation or a rebuttal. She produced love letters; he cheerfully agreed to have written them but claimed they were only "sexual promises rather than promises to spend my life with her." Yes, he *had* given her money for an abortion and *had* registered with her at many hotels as husband and wife and *had* introduced her to many people as his wife. However, he only did that to spare her embarrassment.

Lee insisted that although Michelle was fun to be with and he had enjoyed her company, he had never intended to share his property or the rest of his life with her. Then, adding insult to injury, he called in people from the entertainment business who testified that Michelle had, at best, minimum talent—implying that she had had no career to lose.

Alimony by any Other Name

When all was said and done, the Judge Arthur K. Marshall agreed that there had been no express or implicit contract requiring Lee Marvin to share his assets. However, under the legal principle of "equitable remedy," the judge awarded Michelle Marvin $1,000 a week—the highest salary she had ever earned as an entertainer—for two years so that she might gain the necessary retraining to take up her old career or to learn new skills to make her more employable.

Was this "palimony"—a term for paying alimony to the female half of an unmarried couple? Or was it "rehabilitative alimony"—a short-term payment to support a former wife during the time it takes to prepare her for employment? Or was it just the same old alimony masquerading as something else? As far as the judge was concerned, what the award was called was not the point. He just did not want to resurrect the old concept of "common law" marriage. What he did, instead, was try to compel Lee to put Michelle back on her feet—instead of leaving that onus on the state. Regardless, in 1981, a California State Court of Appeals ruled that there was no basis in law for such a specific figure and overturned the $104,000 award.

Marvin v. Marvin made news coast-to-coast. It so popularized the idea of "palimony" that other unwed couples began to sue for financial support after breaking up. The courts in most other states have followed the reasoning of the California Supreme Court in determining the rights of unwed heterosexual couples. Only a few, however, have applied this thinking to cohabiting homosexual couples.

For Further Reading

Agrest, Susan, Diane Camper, Jerrold K. Footlick, Martin Kasindorf, and Pamela Ellis Simons. "Legal Battle of the Sexes." *Newsweek*, April 30, 1979, p. 68.

Lindsey, Robert. "Lee Marvin Told to Pay $104,000, But Judge Prohibits Property Split." *New York Times*, April 19, 1979, p. A1.

"Man Against Woman." *Time*, April 30, 1979, p. 25.

Mittenthal, Sue. "Aftershocks of Lee Marvin Case." *New York Times*, February 22, 1979, p. C6.

New York Times, January 9, 13, 31; February 21, 25; March 11, 16; April 22; July 20, 1979.

"$6.60 an Hour?" *Time*, May 7, 1979, p. 57.

Van Gelder, Lawrence. "Lawyers Troubled by Rehabilitation Concept in Marvin Decision." *New York Times*, April 20, 1979, p. A18.

Califano v. Westcott: 1979

Appellant: Joseph A. Califano, Jr.   **Appellees:** Cindy and William Westcott
and Susan and John Westwood   **Appellant's Claim:** That the lower court
was incorrect to rule that it was unconstitutional to provide benefits to
families with unemployed fathers, but not to families with unemployed
mothers   **Chief Lawyer for Appellees:** Henry A. Freedman
Chief Lawyer for Appellant: William H. Alsup   **Justices:** *Harry A.
Blackmun,* William J. Brennan, Jr., Thurgood Marshall, John Paul Stevens,
and Byron R. White (majority); Chief Justice Warren E. Burger, Lewis F.
Powell, Jr., William H. Rehnquist, and Potter Stewart (concurring in part;
dissenting in part)   **Place:** Washington, D.C.   **Date of Decision:** June 25,
1979   **Decision:** That it was a violation of both the Fifth and Fourteenth
Amendments to provide benefits to families with unemployed fathers, but not
to families with unemployed mothers

SIGNIFICANCE

The archaic notion that men were the only *real* breadwinners and that women
were working for mere "pin money" was put to rest—at least in the eyes of the
courts. This decision gave full recognition to women as equal contributors to the
family's financial well-being.

W hen Cindy Westcott and Susan Westwood lost their jobs, their families
applied for federally-matching-funded benefits in Massachusetts. Cindy
Westcott and her husband, William, applied through the Department of Public
Welfare for unemployment benefits under the Aid to Families with Dependent
Children, Unemployed Father (AFDC-UF) program. Congress created this
program to provide, among other things, assistance to "a needy child . . . who has
been deprived of parental support or care by reason of the unemployment . . . of
his *father.*"

The Wrong Gender

To qualify for these benefits, an unemployed "father" must work six or
more quarters in any thirteen-quarter period ending within one year prior to the
application for aid. William Westcott was the no-longer-working father of an

infant son, but he had not accrued a sufficient work history to qualify as "unemployed" for the purposes of the program. Cindy Westcott, who had been her family's primary wage earner before the loss of her job, would have met every requirement if she had been her infant son's father instead of his mother. The Westcott family's application was denied.

Susan and John Westwood applied for Medicaid benefits upon Susan's loss of her job. Their experience paralleled that of the Westcott's: John's work history was deemed too scanty to bring him within the program's requirements, while Susan—who qualified in every other respect—was ruled ineligible because she was not her infant son's father, but his mother.

Way Behind the Times

Convinced the program was unconstitutional, the couples filed a class-action suit against Secretary of Health, Education, and Welfare Joseph A. Califano, Jr., whose department administered the federal program, and the commissioner of the Massachusetts Department of Public Welfare (DPW). The district court, without opposition from the defendants, certified the case as a class action brought on behalf of "all those Massachusetts families with two parents in the home and with minor dependent children, born or unborn, who would otherwise be eligible for AFDC under Massachusetts' AFDC program, and hence Medicaid as well, but for sex discrimination."

The Westcotts and Westwoods claimed that AFDC-UF discriminated on the basis of sex in violation of the Fifth and Fourteenth Amendments. In 1978, the district court agreed. Ruling that the gender-based requirements of the program were not substantially related to any important governmental interests, the court described the regulation as the result of an "archaic and overbroad generalization," namely, that "mothers in two parent families are not breadwinners, so that loss of their earnings would not substantially affect the families' well being." The court found the sex classification unconstitutional, and it ordered the DPW commissioner to grant benefits to the families of unemployed mothers "in the same amounts and under the same standards" as such benefits were granted to the families of unemployed fathers.

HEW secretary Joseph Califano was the appellant in the 1979 *Califano v. Westcott* trial.

The DPW commissioner then filed a motion asking the district court to amend its order so that Massachusetts might pay benefits "only to those families where needy children have been deprived of parental support or care by the unemployment of *the family's principal wage-earner* [emphasis added]." The court denied the motion, and the commissioner appealed to the Supreme Court. So did Califano—claiming that the government program was in fact constitutional.

A Rose by Any Other Name

The Supreme Court heard the consolidated cases on April 16, 1979. The Court made short work of the argument that AFDC-UF was "gender-based" but not "gender-biased," since it affected family units rather than women as a class. As Justice Harry A. Blackmun wrote, "This Court has not hesitated to strike down gender classifications that result in benefits being granted or denied to family units on the basis of the sex of the qualifying parent." Referring to 1973's *Frontiero v. Richardson* (see page 308), 1975's *Weinberger v. Wiesenfeld* (see page 312), and 1977's *Califano v. Goldfarb*, from which plurality opinion he quoted, Blackmun said that "here, as in those cases, the statute 'discriminates against one particular category of family—that in which the female spouse is a wage earner.' "

Califano had also argued that any sex discrimination in the present case affected "a noncontributory welfare program" and so, unlike the program requirements invalidated by *Frontiero, Weinberger,* and *Califano v. Goldfarb*, did not "denigrate 'the efforts of women who do work and whose earnings contribute significantly to their families' support.' "

The Court was not persuaded that this was relevant. "Putting labels aside," Blackmun wrote, "the exclusion here is more pernicious than those. . . . AFDC-UF benefits are . . . subsistence payments made available as a last resort to families that would otherwise lack basic necessities." He noted that the gender requirement made certain families absolutely unqualified for help. Therefore, the Court rejected the argument that there was no gender discrimination.

Finally, Califano had argued that restricting benefits to the families of unemployed fathers was designed to discourage unemployed fathers from leaving home so their families would qualify for other aid. The Court rejected that argument as well. Rather, Blackmun wrote, the record "suggests that the gender qualification was part of the general objective . . . to tighten standards for eligibility and reduce program costs." However, this goal was attempted by impermissibly discriminatory means. Blackmun pointed out, "Congress, with an image of the 'traditional family' in mind, simply assumed that the father would be the family breadwinner, and the mother's employment role, if any, would be secondary."

The Court also noted that even if the gender requirement had been introduced to eliminate "the father's incentive to desert," that it would not have been found "substantially related to the stated purpose." Since the gender classification failed to further any "important and statutory goals," but rather reflected the "baggage of sexual stereotypes," the Court found that it violated the due process clause of the Fifth Amendment.

The Court concluded by turning down Massachusetts' request that it be permitted to make benefits available to families in which the primary breadwinner had become unemployed, noting that the district court, in ordering that benefits be paid to unemployed mothers and fathers on equal terms, had "adopted the simplest and most equitable extension possible."

For Further Reading

Goldstein, Leslie Friedman. *The Constitutional Rights of Women: Cases in Law and Social Change*, rev. ed. Madison: The University of Wisconsin Press, 1989.

Hoff, Joan. *Law, Gender & Injustice: A Legal History of U.S. Women*. New York: New York University Press, 1991.

Ross, Susan Deller, Isabelle Katz Pinzler, Deborah A. Ellis, and Kary L. Moss. *The Rights of Women: The Basic ACLU Guide to Women's Rights*. Carbondale: Southern Illinois University Press, 1993.

Sidel, Ruth. *Women and Children Last: The Plight of Poor Women in Affluent America*. New York: Viking, 1986.

Kirchberg v. Feenstra: 1981

Appellant: Karl J. Kirchberg   **Appellee:** Joan Paillot Feenstra
Appellant's Claim: That the lower court erred when it found unconstitutional a Louisiana law that permitted a husband to dispose of marital property without his wife's knowledge or consent
Chief Lawyer for Appellee: Barbara Hausman-Smith
Chief Lawyer for Appellant: Alan F. Schoenberger   **Justices:** Harry A. Blackmun, Warren E. Burger, *Thurgood Marshall,* Lewis F. Powell, William H. Rehnquist, John P. Stevens, III, and Potter Stewart   **Place:** Washington, D.C.
Date of Decision: March 23, 1981   **Decision:** The Louisiana Civil Code of 1870 that gave a husband the right to dispose of jointly owned property, without a wife's knowledge or consent, violated the Fourteenth Amendment

SIGNIFICANCE
This was the first Supreme Court decision to declare unconstitutional a law giving husbands, as "head and master," the unilateral right to control marital property.

In 1974, Joan Feenstra filed a federal complaint charging her husband, Richard, with molesting their minor daughter. Richard, upon his arrest, retained Karl J. Kirchberg as his attorney. To secure Kirchberg's services, Richard signed a promissory note, which he secured by placing a mortgage on the home he jointly owned with his wife.

Joan did not know that Richard had mortgaged her home. Even if she had, she could have done nothing to stop it. The Louisiana Civil Code of 1870 gave husbands the unilateral right to dispose of marital property. As the law would have it:

> The husband is the head and master of the partnership or community of gains; he administers its effects, disposes of the revenues which they produce, and may alienate them . . . without the consent of his wife.

Left Holding the Bag

After Joan dropped the molestation charge against her husband, the two separated and Richard moved out of state. In 1976, Joan discovered Richard had mortgaged her home when Kirchberg demanded that she pay the remaining balance on her estranged husband's promissory note or face foreclosure on her home. Feenstra refused to pay. Kirchberg promptly secured an order for the local sheriff to seize the house for sale.

Kirchberg probably anticipated that Feenstra might raise objections. In March 1976, he filed a suit in the U.S. District Court for the Eastern District of Louisiana, asking for a declaratory judgment that he had not violated the Truth in Lending Act. (This is a federal law requiring disclosures regarding commercial credit transactions and giving borrowers a three-day period to rescind a transaction in which they have pledged real property as security.) He argued that since Louisiana law gave the husband control of a couple's property, his claim was valid.

Feenstra responded by alleging that Kirchberg had indeed violated the Truth in Lending Act. Naming the state and governor as third-party defendants, she also filed a counterclaim that Louisiana had abridged her constitutional rights.

Kirchberg and his governmental co-defendants moved for an immediate judgment against Feenstra on her "head and master" counterclaim. The district court, saying that Feenstra had challenged nothing less than the "bedrock of Louisiana's community property system," obliged by deciding against Feenstra. Kirchberg and Feenstra both dropped their claims under the Truth in Lending Act. However, Feenstra appealed to the Court of Appeals for the Fifth Circuit to declare the "head and master" law unconstitutional. Barbara Hausman-Smith was her attorney.

Barbara Hausman-Smith acted as chief defense counsel for Joan Paillot Feenstra during her 1980–81 trial. The U.S. Supreme Court overturned a Louisiana law that permitted a husband who owned property jointly with his wife the right to dispose of the estate without her consent. (Attorney Barbara Hausman-Smith)

A Change in Law

Before the Appeals Court heard Feenstra's case, the Louisiana legislature changed its laws regarding community property. The new statutes gave equal control over community property to wife and husband, specifically providing that "immovables" could not be "alienated, leased or otherwise encumbered without the concurrence of both spouses."

However, since the law would not go into effect until January 1, 1980, the question remained whether the previous law—under which Feenstra's home had been mortgaged without her knowledge and under which the foreclosure proceedings had begun—violated the equal protection clause of the Fourteenth Amendment.

The Appeals Court, relying on previous Supreme Court decisions, inquired whether Louisiana's gender-based law "was substantially related to an important governmental objective." Louisiana had claimed only that "one of the two spouses had to be designated as the manager of the community."

The court acknowledged that Louisiana had an interest in making standard the manner in which community property transactions were conducted. However, it found that the state could achieve this by means other than discriminating against married women. Therefore, the Appeals Court ruled on December 12, 1979, that the law had breached the equal protection clause of the Fourteenth Amendment.

However, cautioning that "substantial hardship with respect to property rights and obligations within the state of Louisiana" could result from a wholesale application of this decision, the court did not apply it retroactively.

Blaming the Victim

Kirchberg appealed to the Supreme Court. His co-defendants declined to join him. Kirchberg's attorneys defended the constitutionality of the Louisiana law in effect in 1974 by pointing to a provision that would have permitted Feenstra to protect herself.

This provision barred a husband from leasing, mortgaging, or selling an "immovable property" jointly owned with his wife, if she "has made a declaration by authentic act that her authority and consent are required for such lease, sale, or mortgage, and has filed such a declaration in the mortgage and conveyance records of the parish in which the property is situated." Since Feenstra had failed to take these steps, Kirchberg said, she was the "architect of her own predicament" and could not blame Louisiana's law.

Unconstitutional Discrimination

Justice Thurgood Marshall delivered the opinion of the Court. He noted that the "appellant overlooks the critical question: Whether [the law] substantially furthers an important governmental interest." It is up to the person who wants to uphold a law "that expressly discriminates on the basis of sex" to put forth an "exceedingly persuasive justification" for its enforcement.

Finding that Kirchberg had failed to show justification for the discriminatory statute—and noting that the state and governor of Louisiana, by refusing to join the appeal, had presumably "abandoned any claim that an important government objective was served by the statute"—the Court affirmed the Appeals Court's ruling.

Kirchberg had also claimed that his mortgage on the Feenstra home was valid regardless of the constitutionality of the new law. He argued that the Court of Appeals ruling could be construed as not applying to Feenstra, but rather, to only those dispositions of community property made during the days between its December 12, 1979, decision and the implementation of Louisiana's new law on January 1, 1980.

Kirchberg and his attorney, Alan F. Schoenberger, urged the Court to adopt this narrow interpretation, since a broader application would put the validity of many other mortgages into question. The Court found that the status of other mortgages was irrelevant to Feenstra's claim. Marshall wrote:

> We decline to address appellant's concerns about the potential impact of the Court of Appeals' decision on other mortgages executed pursuant to Art. 2404. The only question properly before us is whether the decision of the Court of Appeals applies to the mortgage in this case, and on that we find no ambiguity. . . . Mrs. Feenstra specifically sought as relief "a declaratory judgment that the mortgage executed on [her] home by her husband . . . is void as having been executed and recorded without her consent pursuant to an unconstitutional state statute." Thus, the dispute between the parties at its core involves the validity of a single mortgage, and . . . the Court of Appeals clearly intended to resolve that controversy adversely to appellant. Accordingly, the judgment of the Court of Appeals is affirmed.

The Status of Marital Property Legislation

In many respects, Louisiana law had always been exceptional. This is because Louisiana followed the Code Napoléon instead of English common law. The Code Napoléon's clarity, spirit of equality, and reforms of the rules of property and inheritances had made it a model for many nations. However, its provisions dealing with the relationships between husbands and wives were discriminatory. Indeed, only Louisiana, with its French heritage, left women so unprotected that, as historian Eleanor Flexner writes, a wife "did not even have legal title to the clothes she wore."

Kirchberg v. Feenstra overturned the 1870 Civil Code article that gave husbands as "head and master" of the house the right to dispose of community property. However, it did not invalidate various other discriminatory provisions in state law concerning marital property. Legal historian Joan Hoff writes that other state laws regulating a wife's right to marital property [still] "reflected and perpetuated their dependence and inequality." For example, in 1990, in four of the nation's eight community-property states (California, Idaho, Nevada, and New Mexico), a husband could will his half of the community property to another person, but his wife could not. This meant that when his wife died, her husband inherited all of her community property, but if the husband predeceased his wife, she was entitled only to one-half of his. In 1983, the National Conference of Commissioners on Uniform State Laws recommended that the states replace their own varying marital property codes with the Uniform Marital Property Act, which Congress passed on January 1, 1986. By 1997, only Wisconsin had done so.

For Further Reading

Flexner, Eleanor. *Century of Struggle: The Woman's Rights Movement in the United States*, rev. ed. Cambridge: Harvard University Press, 1975.

Hoff, Joan. *Law, Gender & Injustice: A Legal History of U.S. Women*. New York: New York University Press, 1991.

Lefcourt, Carol H., ed. *Women and the Law*. New York: Clark Boardman, 1987.

Leonard, Frances. *Women & Money*. Reading, Mass.: Addison-Wesley Publishing Company, Inc.

Ross, Susan Deller, Isabelle Katz Pinzler, Deborah A. Ellis, and Kary L. Moss. *The Rights of Women: The Basic ACLU Guide to Women's Rights*. Carbondale: Southern Illinois University Press, 1993.

Ireland v. Smith: 1995

Appellant: Jennifer Ireland   **Appellee:** Steven J. Smith
Appellant's Claim: That a lower court ruling that gave custody of Ireland's daughter to the biological father should be reversed
Chief Lawyer for Appellee: Sharon-Lee Edwards
Chief Lawyer for Appellant: The University of Michigan Law School, Women and the Law Clinic by Julie Kunce Field   **Judges:** *Roman S. Gribbs,* Roy D. Gotham, and Janet T. Neff   **Place:** Detroit, Michigan
Date of Decision: November 7, 1995   **Decision:** An appeals court reversed the trial court's decision to remove Baby Maranda from the custody of her mother because she had put the child in day care; the case went back to the lower court for a retrial and Baby Maranda went back to her mother.

SIGNIFICANCE
A judge's appearance of bias against a mother who put her daughter in child care angered working women across the nation. Many wondered, "Are the courts prejudiced against working mothers?" "Do courts have too much leeway in deciding the 'best interests' of a child?"

In 1990, fifteen-year-old Jennifer Ireland was on the top of the world: a popular cheerleader, straight-A student, and the steady girlfriend of the school football star, Steven Smith. But four days after she told Smith that she was pregnant with his child, he broke up with her. Two months later, she checked into a Michigan clinic for an abortion.

At the clinic, the Catholic teen "started thinking I was going to burn in hell." On April 22, 1991, Ireland gave birth to Maranda Kate Ireland-Smith. Smith did not visit Ireland or his baby until their last day in the hospital. The parents agreed to put their daughter up for adoption.

Three weeks later Ireland changed her mind. With the help of her mother and younger sister, she decided to raise Maranda herself. Smith was so angry he did not attempt to see his daughter for one year.

Moving On

After missing two months of her sophomore year, Ireland returned to Cardinal Mooney Catholic High School in Marine City, Michigan. Both she and Smith resumed their normal activities: cheerleading, sports, dating others, and partying. Ireland finished the 1991 term with a 3.98 average, eventually graduating with the third highest ranking in her class.

In the fall of 1993, Ireland, the recipient of an $11,000 scholarship from the University of Michigan, moved to Ann Arbor. She and Maranda lived in an apartment in the university family housing building. So that she would be free to attend classes, Ireland used her personal savings to put Maranda in the university-approved day care center.

Earlier in the year (January 29), Ireland had filed for child support, winning a modest weekly contribution. Smith countersued for custody of his daughter and, in addition, asked the court to reduce his child support payments to twelve dollars a week. Ireland responded with a domestic violence charge, supposedly back to 1992, against Smith.

The Best Custodial Care

In May and June 1994, the dispute came before sixty-nine-year-old Judge Raymond R. Cashen of Macomb County Circuit Court. Cashen appointed the Psychodiagnostic and Family Services Clinic and the Macomb County Friends of the Court to evaluate Maranda's home life. Both agencies agreed that the three-year-old should remain with her mother.

Nonetheless, Sharon-Lee Edwards, Smith's attorney, implied that Ireland was unfit to raise Maranda. During the custody hearing she alleged Ireland "dated many different boys, had sexual relations with most of them, went to parties, abused drugs, and was never home with her baby." By contrast, Edwards insinuated that Smith was quietly living at home with his father and mother. Maranda's grandmother would care for Maranda while her son attended Macomb County Community College and worked part-time at a local park.

Ireland furiously denied Smith's allegations, claiming that he was the real swinger. She said Smith had no ambition, acted violently, and had taken an interest in Maranda only after she had asked for more child support and brought assault charges against him. Furthermore, Ireland's home was the only one Maranda had ever known, and a change of custody would harm her.

On July 27, 1994, Cashen announced that it would be better for Maranda to be in her paternal grandmother's home, "raised and supervised by blood relations" than put in day care "supervised a great part of the time by strangers."

The judge, a father of seven, concluded, "I went to the heart of the matter, and that is, 'What is the best interest of the child?'" He said that there was no way that a person in a rigorous academic college could do justice to both her studies and her child. In a decision that made headlines across the nation, he stripped Ireland of custody, ordering her to turn Maranda over to the child's father within fifteen days. She could see Maranda every other weekend, holidays, and other occasions. Smith observed, "With more and more women in the workplace, men *have* to raise their children."

Two days after he won custody, Smith was arraigned on the 1992 assault charge. Ireland had claimed that he had grabbed her by the shoulders, shook her, and shoved her against a wall. In Smith's eyes, it had been a mutual shoving match. However, Cashen declared this information "superfluous" and "not pertinent" to the custody decision.

A Public Uproar

People throughout the nation condemned Cashen's ruling. Jacquie Steingod, board member of the National Organization for Women, told the *New York Times* on July 27, "It illustrates an attitude toward women about where they should be—the bedroom, kitchen and those kinds of places, not at college." On July 31, the paper interviewed Carol Bruch, a professor of law at the University of California at Davis. "There is certainly a backlash against women who assert some sort of independence, in favor of fathers who offer, albeit belatedly, some concrete evidence of wanting to be involved with their children," she said.

On August 1, the *New York Times'* lead editorial called it "an affront and threat to the millions of women for whom day care is the difference between ignorance and an education, poverty and a decent income, dependency and self-reliance. In stigmatizing Jennifer Ireland for her ambition and initiative, Judge Cashen stigmatizes all of them."

Some disagreed. Ellen Effron, chair of the American Bar Association's custody committee, told the *Times* on July 31, "Even though the courtroom is supposed to be gender neutral, when I represent the father, it's still an uphill battle." Jeff Atkinson, former chair of the custody committee, agreed, "Some judges are stuck in the 1950s' roles of parents, but I'd say the trend is that most judges are not."

But in the End . . .

Ireland's lawyers immediately filed an appeal and on August 9, 1994, the Michigan Court of Appeals granted Ireland a stay in the transfer of custody of Maranda until they could review the case. Nearly a year later, the court heard arguments. On November 7, 1995, Judge Roman S. Gribbs ruled: "A court may not change the established custodial environment of a child unless clear and convincing evidence is presented that it is in the best interest of the child."

Gribbs continued, "Because there was an established custodial environment in this case, the trial court is prohibited from changing custody." In a clear rebuke to the lower court, he added, "We find no support in the record for the trial court's speculation that there is 'no way that a single parent, attending an academic program at an institution as prestigious as the University of Michigan, can do justice to their studies and to raising of an infant child.' The evidence shows that the child has thrived in the university environment."

Finally, Gribbs pointed out that "the evidence does not support the trial court's judgment that defendant's proposed, but untested, plans for the child's care would be better" than the mother's. "We find the court committed clear legal error in considering the 'acceptability' of the parties' home and child-care arrangements." As for Ireland's charges of violence, the court found the evidence was too conflicting to decide.

Since the state supreme court could not rule on the question of custody itself, the case went back to the circuit court with instructions *not* to consider day care in its decision—and *not* to appoint Cashen to preside over the trial (the case was reassigned to Judge Lido Bucci). The legal fight continued until October 16, 1996, when Ireland and Smith agreed to share custody of Maranda. Ireland announced she would drop out of college and move closer to Smith, thereby allowing Maranda to attend school near the homes of both parents.

Ireland v. Smith galvanized working mothers throughout the country, the majority of whom place their pre-school children in day care some of the time. However, the presumption that the mother is always the better parent may be a legal fiction that will come under more challenges from fathers, which courts can only resolve by examining the stereotypes they share with much of the public.

For Further Reading

Chesler, Phyllis. *Mothers on Trial: The Battle for Children and Custody.* San Diego: Harcourt, Brace, Jovanovich, 1987.

Knappman, Edward W. *Sex, Sin and Mayhem: Notorious Trials of the '90s.* Detroit: Visible Ink Press, 1995.

Hoff, Joan. *Law, Gender, and Injustice: A Legal History of U.S. Women.* New York: New York University Press, 1991.

May, Jeanne. "Parents to Share Maranda Equally," *Detroit Free Press*, October 17, 1996.

Section 6
WOMEN AT WORK

The Civil War quickened the growth of industry in the North, as the Lincoln administration commissioned clothes, weapons, medicines, and supplies for its huge Union army. With men killed and disabled in battle, females flooded the new labor market, mainly working in the sewing trades. Historian Eleanor Flexner reports that in 1850, 225,922 females worked in factories. In 1870, the number rose to 323,370.

Long hours, unsanitary conditions, and low pay stimulated the growth of unions, which had nearly vanished after the 1835 recession. Working women—forced to compete for basement wages—angered men who were trying to better themselves through these national organizations. In 1870, most of the thirty-two unions excluded women. The cigarmakers (1867) and printers (1869) were the first to admit them.

Throughout the nineteenth century, employers hired workers either by the day or by the week. Pay might be two dollars a week for a ten-hour day, or sixty-hour week. In 1865, a group of seamstresses complained to President Abraham Lincoln that their wages of one dollar per dozen army shirts was not enough on which to live. The government paid the contractors $1.75 per dozen.

Although wages were of first importance to workers, after the Civil War unions also stressed the eight-hour day. This battle is clear from a trial involving bakers, *Lochner v. New York* (1905). The bakers claimed their workday of twelve to fourteen hours for six or seven days a week left them no time to be husbands, fathers, or good citizens. They were unable to better themselves through education. Miners, builders, and other low-skilled laborers—most of whom had begun working as children—agreed with the bakers wholeheartedly. By overturning New York's Bakeshop Act, which regulated the number of hours employees could work, the *Lochner* decision also set back protective legislation for women for decades. *Muller v. Oregon* (1908), *Adkins v. Children's Hospital* (1923), and *West Coast Hotel v. Parrish* (1937) demonstrate the Court's changing position on this issue. By 1940, when the Court formally disavowed the *Lochner* decision in *United States v. Darby*, most states had enacted protective legislation for working women and children.

In the mid-twentieth century women began to challenge the same protective legislation that earlier they once had thought progressive. Feminists brought lawsuits challenging laws that "protected" them from lifting heavy weights, laboring at night, owning bars, and working while pregnant, which had led to severe economic discrimination. *Goesaert v. Cleary* (1948) is an early example.

In 1964, the passage of the Civil Rights Act, Title VII, brought the hope of more change. *Weeks v. Southern Bell* (1969), *Bowe v. Colgate-Palmolive* (1969), and *Phillips v. Martin Marietta* (1971) illustrate how women used the new law to fight discrimination in the workplace. The turning point in the equal treatment of women in the workplace came with *United States v. Libbey-Owens-Ford* (1971), when the Supreme Court for the first time sued a company under the act for sex discrimination. *Pittsburgh Press v. Pittsburgh Commission on Human Relations* (1973), *Corning Glass Works v. Brennan* (1974), *Geduldig v. Aiello* (1974), *Dothard v. Rawlinson* (1977), *Los Angeles Department of Water and Power v. Marie Manhart* (1978), *Personnel Administrator v. Feeney* (1979), and *Automobile Workers v. Johnson Controls* (1991) were key decisions in a changing climate.

In the 1980s, the courts began to extend the protections offered to lower-skilled women under the Civil Rights Act to professional women as well. *Hishon v. King & Spaulding* (1984), which applied Title VII to a legal partnership's selection of partners, was the first Supreme Court ruling to find that gender discrimination in partnership decisions was a violation of federal law.

The Supreme Court has also come to view sexual harrassment in the workplace as a form of illegal discrimination. *Meritor Savings Bank v. Vinson* (1986) and *Harris v. Forklift* (1993) demonstrate the Court's new rulings on this issue.

Since the 1970s, the Court has viewed discrimination against pregnant women as illegal. For example, the nation's schools fired teachers when they "showed" *(Cleveland Board of Education v. LaFleur,* 1974). If expectant mothers kept their jobs, they received no time off. In 1987, *California Federal Savings and Loan Association v. Guerra* became the first Supreme Court case to challenge a state statute's validity under the Pregnancy Discrimination Act (PDA). It upheld a women's right to unpaid pregnancy disability leaves.

The Civil Rights struggle of the 1960s led businesses, educational institutions, and government agencies to adopt programs to help remedy past discrimination against minorities and women. Called affirmative-action plans, they posed a number of difficult decisions for the Supreme Court: Can employers consider gender in hiring, firing, and promotion? Should women performing equivalent work to men receive equal pay? How long after an act of discrimination takes place can a woman sue? Are affirmative-action programs acceptable for private but not public jobs? In *Johnson v. Transportation Agency* (1987), the Court held that affirmative action programs do not violate the 1964 Civil Rights Act solely because they favor women or minorities. Today, a newly-constituted Supreme Court seems to disapprove of affirmative action plans as constitutionally unfair.

Overall, except in the armed services, working persons legally receive equal protection under law in employment. However, gender preferences are slow to change. Many women experience "glass ceilings" in corporate life that hold them back even though employers are well aware of the consequences of discrimination. Economists believe that today's promotion and salary differentials relate to two practices. First, many women drop out of the workforce to bear children, and do not return to their jobs years later on the same footing as their colleagues. Second, more women than men choose part-time and service-industry work where pay can be low. Recent men and women college graduates, however, now receive equal pay for equal work, a victory that was a long time in coming.

Lochner v. New York: 1905

Appellant: Joseph Lochner **Appellee:** People of the State of New York

Appellant's Claim: That Lochner had not violated the New York Bakeshop Act because the law was an unreasonable exercise of police power

Chief Lawyer for Appellee: Julius M. Mayer, attorney general of New York

Chief Lawyers for Appellant: Frank Harvey Field and Henry Weismann

Justices: David B. Brewer, Henry Billings Brown, Chief Justice Melville W. Fuller, Joseph McKenna, and *Rufus Peckham* (majority); William R. Day, John Marshall Harlan, Oliver Wendell Holmes, and Edward D. White (dissent)

Place: Washington, D.C. **Date of Decision:** April 17, 1905 **Decision:** In protecting the right to contract for labor, the Court overruled the New York Bakeshop Act, which regulated sanitary conditions and the number of hours that employees could work

SIGNIFICANCE

Lochner v. New York postponed protective legislation for women for decades, becoming one of the most controversial decisions in the history of the Supreme Court.

Lochner v. New York began in the Guilded Age and ended in the Progressive Era when *laissez-faire* capitalism began to clash with a new reforming impulse in America. The conflict embroiled Joseph Lochner, owner of a tiny bakery in Utica, New York, that made biscuits, breads, and cakes for early morning customers. Lochner's employees worked late, sometimes sleeping overnight on the premises. In April 1901, baker Aman Schmitter labored more than sixty hours a week.

Receiving a complaint, police arrested Lochner, charging him with violating New York's Bakeshop Act. The law set minimum standards for sanitation and fixed the number of hours that the mostly male bakers could work—at no more than ten hours a day or sixty hours a week.

Approximately ten months after his arrest, Lochner went to trial in the county court. Lochner refused to plead either guilty or innocent and offered no defense, intending to appeal. This tactic left Judge W. T. Dunmore only two choices: to sentence the defendant to a fifty-dollar fine or fifty days in jail. On the same day of the conviction, Lochner's attorney, William S. Mackie, filed an appeal to the Appellate Division of the Supreme Court of New York.

He argued that the Bakeshop regulations interfered with Lochner's right to earn a living, a liberty protected under the U.S. Constitution. Three of five judges disagreed, believing that the statute was a valid exercise of the state's power. Again Mackie appealed and lost.

Lochner's Home Bakery, in Utica, New York, during the early 1900s. (Oneida County Historical District)

A Baker's Lawyer

Finally, Lochner changed attorneys. His new lawyer, Henry Weismann, was an unlikely advocate. Ten years earlier he had been a lobbyist for the Journeyman Bakers Union and editor of the union's newsletter, the *Bakers' Journal*. He had urged his comrades to agitate for the eight-hour bakeshop law.

Resigning from the *Bakers' Journal* in 1897, Weismann opened two bakeries of his own. He joined forces with the Retail Bakers' Association to dilute the impact of the Bakeshop Act. As he told the *New York Times*, "The truth . . . is that I have never been in sympathy with the radicals in the labor movement."

Weissman, who had not passed the bar, asked attorney Frank Harvey Field to join him. The key argument of the new team was that the Bakeshop law violated a doctrine called "liberty of contract"—meaning the right to operate a business, or contract one's labor, so long as this did not interfere with the equal rights of others. State courts embraced this doctrine during the late nineteenth century. (One example was an 1886 Pennsylvania Supreme Court decision to overrule a law that required coal miners to be paid in cash, not goods.)

However, critics argued that the state already placed restrictions on contracts, such as prohibiting the practice of medicine without a license. They claimed the "liberty of contract" doctrine protected the exploitation of workers, who were the weaker parties in labor contracts.

At the time, the U.S. Supreme Court had only once used "liberty of contract" to overrule a state law (in *Allegyer v. Louisiana*, 1897). Mostly, the Court preferred to leave state laws intact. So Field and Weismann faced an uphill battle when they argued that the Bakeshop Act had violated the liberty of contract of the workers and employers of New York State. Baking was not a dangerous profession, they said, and the Bakeshop Act, as it concerned hours, was never intended to protect the health of employees. Instead it was a prohibitive labor law, an illegitimate use of the police power of the state, because it deprived bakers of their due process rights.

Due Process and Daniel Webster

Back in 1819, Daniel Webster had argued that in nullifying the charter of a private college, New Hampshire had performed a semi-judicial act that had, in effect, deprived Dartmouth of its "substantive due process" rights under the Fifth Amendment of the Constitution.

The Weissman-Field team—elaborating on this theory that a state may not invade the rights of persons or property—posed a series of questions to test whether legislators truly had the health and safety of the public in mind when they passed a law:

Does a danger exist? Is it of sufficient magnitude? Does it concern the public? Does the proposed measure tend to remove it? Is the restraint or requirement in proportion to the danger? Is it possible to secure the object sought without impairing essential rights and principles? Does the choice of a particular measure show that some other interest than safety or health was the actual motive of legislation?

Julius M. Mayer, the newly appointed attorney general, made a surprisingly brief eighteen-page response. He said baking required heavy lifting and carrying; because of the flour dust and germs in the air, lung diseases sickened workers. Tuberculosis killed many of them. Therefore, the state could regulate work hours for the public good.

A Surprise Verdict

By a five-to-four vote the Supreme Court elevated liberty of contract over the rights of employees to a safe workplace and reasonable hours. Speaking for the Court, Justice Rufus Peckham said:

There is no reasonable ground for interfering with the liberty of person or right of free contract, by determining the hours of labor, in the occupation of a baker. . . . A law like the one before us involves neither the safety, the morals, nor the welfare of the public. . . .

Justice John Marshall Harlan, six-feet-two-inches tall—who, according to his wife, "walked as if the whole world belonged to him"—joined Edward D. White and William R. Day in dissenting. Harlan quoted professors and writers who felt baking was a hard occupation, and pointed out that Congress and nearly all the states had passed laws concerning "particular occupations involving the physical strength and safety of workmen. . . . Many, if not most, of those enactments fix eight hours as the proper basis of a day's labor." He was referring to hazardous jobs, such as mining.

Oliver Wendell Holmes, on the Court less than two years, also dissented in a separate opinion that people quoted for years to come. He put his finger on the unspoken assumption of the majority:

The liberty of the citizen to do as he likes so long as he does not interfere with the liberty of others to do the same, which has been a shibboleth for some well-known writers, is interfered with by school laws, by the Post Office, by every state or municipal institution which takes his money for purposes thought desirable, whether he likes it or not.

Effect on Women

For years the economic rights upheld in *Lochner v. New York* were used to invalidate laws regulating the hours, wages, and work conditions of women (for instance, *Adkins v. Children's Hospital* in 1923; see page 352.) During the 1930s, the Court relied on *Lochner* to frustrate the New Deal legislation of President Franklin D. Roosevelt, making it a symbol of unfairness. In 1940, the Court formally disavowed the *Lochner* philosophy in *United States v. Darby*. By this time, most states had already enacted laws protecting women in the workplace. In the climate of reform, few imagined the harmful effects that the laws—despite their immediate relief—would have on women's employment opportunities.

Women working in a bakery during the early 1900s. (National Archives)

Because women were "protected" from performing equally with men in lifting, working night shifts, selling spirits, and working while pregnant—to give a few examples—they suffered economic discrimination. Since they could not compete equally with men, they did not earn equal wages, obtain the same jobs, win promotions, or receive equal benefits. In 1964, the Civil Rights Act, Title

VII, brought the promise of relief from discriminatory workplace laws. Seven years later, the Supreme Court for the first time sued a company under the act for sex-discrimination. The case was *United States v. Libbey-Owens-Ford* (see page 376), and it marked an historic turning point in the equal treatment of women in the workplace.

For Further Reading

Cushman, Robert E. *Leading Constitutional Decisions*. New York: Appleton-Century-Crofts, 1958.

Goldstein. Leslie. *The Constitutional Rights of Women: Cases in Law and Social Change* Madison: University of Wisconsin Press, 1989.

Kens, Paul. *Judicial Power and Reform Politics. The Anatomy of Lochner v. New York*. Lawrence: University Press of Kansas, 1990.

Kanowitz, Leo. *Women and the Law: The Unfinished Revolution*. Albuquerque: University of New Mexico Press, 1969.

Otten, Laura A. *Women's Rights and the Law*. Westport, Conn.: Praeger, 1993.

Tribe, Laurence H. *American Constitutional Law*, 2d ed. Mineola, N.Y.: The Foundation Press, 1988.

Muller v. Oregon: 1908

Appellant: Curt Muller   **Appellee:** State of Oregon
Appellant's Claim: That Oregon's 1903 maximum-hour law for women was unconstitutional   **Chief Lawyers for Appellee:** H. B. Adams and Louis Brandeis   **Chief Lawyers for Appellant:** William D. Fenton and Henry H. Gilfry   **Justices:** *David J. Brewer,* William R. Day, Chief Justice Melville W. Fuller, John H. Harlan, Oliver Wendell Holmes, Joseph McKenna, William H. Moody, Rufus W. Peckham, and Edward D. White   **Place:** Washington, D.C.
Date of Decision: February 24, 1908   **Decision:** That Oregon's maximum-hour law for women was constitutional because females are a ''special class'' in need of protection

SIGNIFICANCE
Pigeonholding women as a special (weaker) class sex in need of minimum wages and maximum hours won the battle but lost the war, perpetuating sex-segregation in the work place. Whether women would be better off with special protections or complete equality with men is a question women are still debating.

On September 18, 1905, an Oregon launderer, Mrs. Elmer Gotcher, brought a complaint against her boss at the Portland Grand Laundry. She claimed Curt Muller had let his overseer, Joe Hazelbock, make her work more than ten hours on September 4. This violated Oregon's ''hour law'' for women, which read ''no female (shall) be employed in any mechanical establishment, or factory, or laundry in this state more than ten hours during any one day.''

The county court agreed, sentencing Muller to pay a ten-dollar fine. He appealed, but the state supreme court affirmed the decision. Believing the state law to be unconstitutional, Muller appealed to the U.S. Supreme Court.

However, he underestimated the forces arrayed against him. When Florence Kelley, executive secretary of the National Consumers' League, and Josephine Goldmark, a Barnard tutor, heard of his appeal, they saw a golden opportunity. They believed that working long hours was harmful to females workers, especially mothers and pregnant women. With hours' laws under legal attack in several states, Kelley and Goldmark decided to test Muller's appeal.

The women faced opposition from two sources. The first was from other feminists. Alice Paul and members of her National Woman Party passionately opposed singling out women as needing special protection, believing that all women needed to compete with men was an equal playing field. If women could end discriminatory laws, especially those denying them the vote, they would achieve equality. Kelley and Goldmark could not count on them for support.

The second was from jurists who honored the idea of "liberty of contract," which included the freedom to contract labor. The courts viewed this doctrine as sacrosanct. They believed that Article I, Section 10, of the Constitution prohibited states from passing any law "impairing the Obligation of Contracts." The due process clauses of the Fifth and Fourteenth Amendments also protected liberty of contract ("nor shall any state deprive any person of life, liberty or property, without due process of law"). Progressives such as Kelley and Goldmark argued that the state had a "special interest" in helping workers who labored in dangerous jobs (mining) or in sweat shops that flourished during America's post-Civil War industrial expansion.

Mrs. Elmer Gotcher brought a complaint against her boss, Curt Miller, proprietor of the Portland Grand Laundry. Muller (center) stands on the front steps of his Lace House Laundry in Portland.

A Clash of Ideas

These two ideas—the state's "special interest" in regulating business and the Constitution's protection of "liberty of contract"—clashed dramatically during the Progressive Era (1900 to World War I). In 1905, the Supreme Court upheld "liberty of contract" in *Lochner v. New York* (see page 341) by overturning a state law setting sixty hours a week as the maximum hours that (mostly male) bakers could work. The *Lochner* decision effectively blocked protective legislation for women. Kelley and Goldmark attempted to circumvent it.

They turned to fifty-one-year-old Louis Brandeis, the husband of Goldmark's sister, Alice. Known as "the people's attorney," Brandeis had made a career of expanding the law to address the social needs of people. He had represented several states whose wages' and hours' laws were under attack.

Brandeis agreed to help on two conditions: Oregon must hire him as its attorney, and the National Consumers' League must within two weeks provide him with a massive amount of statistical information on working women. Goldmark and Kelley, laboring around the clock, gave him a 113-page document. It marshaled facts and figures showing that working long hours affected the health and morality of females. For the first time the Supreme Court would hear an argument based on human welfare instead of legal reasoning. The new argument became known as the "Brandeis brief."

Before the Supreme Court, Muller's side argued that to deny women the right to work more than ten hours a day interfered with their liberty to make contracts and diminished their power to support themselves. Since Oregon law gave married women equal contractual and personal rights to men, the state could not use its police power to infringe these rights.

With modern reasoning, Muller's attorney pointed out that the Oregon law was unconstitutional because "the statute does not apply equally to all persons similarly situated, and is class legislation."

With Friends Like These . . .

Brandeis, however, claimed that women *as a group* needed special protection, using the widespread assumption that women were the "weaker sex." He said it was "common knowledge" that to permit women to work more than ten hours a day in factories, laundries, and the like "is dangerous to public health, safety, morals [and] welfare."

This argument forced the Court to reconsider *Lochner v. New York.* The Court had ruled that New York's law was *not* a legitimate exercise of the police power of the state and interfered with the right of male bakers to contract their labor. Were women any different?

Nineteen state legislatures, under pressure from suffragists and some union leaders, had placed women in a special class, regulating their hours of work. Justice David J. Brewer, speaking for the majority, noted that the laws were "significant of a widespread belief that woman's physical structure, and the functions she performs in consequence thereof, justify special legislation restricting or qualifying the conditions under which she should be permitted to toil."

In a view that seemed progressive for its time but now appears paternalistic, Brewer said:

Attorney Louis D. Brandeis represented the state of Oregon in the 1908 *Muller v. Oregon* trial. The future Supreme Court justice became renowned for writing the Brandeis brief, which supported limited working hours for women. (Harris and Ewing, Collection of the Supreme Court of the United States)

That woman's physical structure . . . place her at a disadvantage in the struggle for subsistence is obvious. This is especially true when the burdens of motherhood are upon her. Even when they are not . . . continuance for a long time on her feet at work, repeating this from day to day, tends to injurious effects upon the body, and, as healthy mothers are essential to vigorous offspring, the physical well-being of woman becomes an object of public interest and care in order to preserve the strength and vigor of the race.

For these reasons, Brewer decided that a woman "is properly placed in a class by herself, and legislation designed for her protection may be sustained." The Court unanimously affirmed the lower court's decision requiring Muller to pay the fine and court costs. The Brandeis brief had been a success.

The Aftermath

After Muller, many states passed wages' and hours' laws and other statutes regulating the conditions of work; but in 1923, the Supreme Court ruled this legislation unconstitutional in *Adkins v. Children's Hospital* (see page 352). Then the Great Depression of the 1930s forced the Court to reverse its decision: In the 1937 case *West Coast Hotel v. Parrish* (see page 357), the Court—drawing on *Muller v. Oregon*—overruled its 1923 decision in *Adkins v. Children's Hospital* to uphold Washington State's minimum wage law for women and minors. The justices had nudged the liberty of contract doctrine off its pedestal.

West Coast Hotel v. Parrish paved the way for the Fair Labor Standards Act of 1938, which extended to men the wages' and hours' laws women had won. In *United States v. Darby* (1941), the Court ruled that minimum wage laws for men were constitutional.

Over time, protective legislation—although it brought relief to millions—kept women in low paying, temporary, unskilled jobs. The laws barred women from working overtime and holding good (male) jobs. For instance, females could not sell spirits, deliver the mail, work in foundries and mines, or run elevators. The American Federation of Labor in 1914 turned its back on its earlier support for protective legislation and used the "weaker sex" argument to keep poorly paid women from working with men. It stopped women from working as printers or streetcar conductors and endorsed unequal pay for the same work.

On February 28, 1908, the *New York Times* wrote of the *Muller* decision, "We leave to the advocates of women suffrage to say whether this decision makes for, or against, the success of their cause." *Muller* gave relief to women and children and opened the door to more humane working conditions for men. However, it further segregated the workplace and provided an excuse for unions and employers alike to keep the wages of women low—trends that have continued into the 1990s.

For Further Reading

Hoff, Joan. *Law, Gender, and Injustice*. New York: New York University Press, 1991.

Goldstein, Leslie Friedman. *The Constitutional Rights of Women*. Madison: The University of Wisconsin Press, 1989.

Kanowitz, Leo. *Women and the Law: The Unfinished Revolution*. Albuquerque: University of New Mexico Press, 1969.

Mezey, Susan Gluck. *In Pursuit of Equality: Women, Public Policy, and the Federal Courts*. New York: St. Martin's Press, 1992.

Adkins v. Children's Hospital: 1923

Appellants: Jesse C. Adkins et al.; Minimum Wage Board of District of Columbia **Appellee:** Children's Hospital of the District of Columbia
Appellants' Claim: That the U.S. Congress has the right to establish minimum wages for women and children
Chief Lawyer for Appellee: Wade H. Ellis
Chief Lawyer for Appellants: Felix Frankfurter **Justices:** Pierce Butler, Joseph McKenna, James C. McReynolds, *George Sutherland,* Willis Van Devanter (majority); Oliver Wendell Holmes, Edward T. Sanford, Chief Justice William Howard Taft (dissent); Louis D. Brandeis (abstained)
Place: Washington, D.C. **Date of Decision:** April 9, 1923
Decision: Minimum wage laws for women *are* unconstitutional because they interfere with the liberty of contract guaranteed by the Fifth and Fourteenth Amendments.

SIGNIFICANCE

The Supreme Court ruled that Congress did not have the power to set minimum wages for women as a special group, slowing down the Consumers' League drive to show that a ceiling on wages without a floor left women vulnerable. It also stopped efforts to equalize pay between men and women, a discrepancy that remained until the Equal Pay Act of 1963.

Willie Lyons, a twenty-one-year-old elevator operator, desperately wanted to keep her job. Lyons worked at the Congress Hall Hotel in Washington D.C., where many members of Congress and their families lived. She felt that the work was easy, the hours short, and the surroundings clean and pleasant. She had been happy at work and with her pay—thirty-five dollars a month, plus two meals a day.

Then the District of Columbia Minimum Wage Board set $16.50 a week as the base pay for all female hotel workers. The Congress Hall Hotel had to fire her, or face legal penalties. Lyons knew she could not find a better job elsewhere for the same salary. So she petitioned the court for an injunction to keep the Board—under Jesse Adkins—from enforcing its orders on the Congress Hall Hotel.

On September 19, 1918, Congress passed a law establishing the District of Columbia Minimum Wage Board. This statute set the minimum wage paid to any woman or child working in the nation's capital. For example, the board had fixed a weekly salary of $16.50 for women employed where food was served, $15.50 for those who worked in printing, and $15 for laundry workers, with beginning laundresses earning $9. Lyons feared her skills could not realistically command these wages in the competitive marketplace, and that her current wages were the best she could earn. If the Congress Hall Hotel fired her, Lyons knew she wouldn't find work elsewhere.

Children's Hospital of the District of Columbia, circa 1900. This medical facility was renamed Children's Hospital National Medical Center in 1969.

At the same time that Lyons was trying to obtain an injunction against the Board's decision, the Children's Hospital of the District of Columbia was having its own problems with the Minimum Wage Board. The hospital employed a large number of women in a variety of different jobs. A few of them earned less than $16.50 a week. Like Lyons, the hospital sued to restrain the Board from enforcing its minimum wage ruling on the ground that it violated the Fifth Amendment's due process clause.

However, in both cases the Supreme Court of the District of Columbia affirmed the constitutionality of the law. On appeal, the Court of Appeals of the District affirmed the lower court's decision. Yet after a rehearing, the court reversed its judgment, and a divided bench declared the law unconstitutional. Further appeals carried the two cases, *Adkins v. Children's Hospital* and *Adkins v. Lyons,* to the Supreme Court of the United States.

The legal questions the court faced were these: has Congress the power to prescribe a minimum wage for women in the District? Or, is such wage-fixing by restricting an individual's "liberty of contract" (protected by due process clauses of the Fifth and Fourteenth amendments) an unconstitutional use of the state's police power? Further, was the law discriminatory because it protected only women?

Legal and political controversy swirled about these questions. In 1905's *Lochner v. New York* (see page 341) the Supreme Court had held that it was unconstitutional for New York to limit the number of hours male bakers could work to ten per day. However, in *Bunting v. Oregon* (1917), the justices had upheld a law setting at ten the maximum hours per day people could work in mills, factories, or manufacturing.

Protective Legislation v. Equality

The First Wave women's movement was also hopelessly divided over the issue of special rights versus equal rights for women, as it had been since 1908, when the Supreme Court upheld Oregon's hours law for women in *Muller v. Oregon* (see page 346). Alice Paul and supporters Anne Henrietta Martin and Burbita Shelton Matthews wanted all inequalities between women and men in the law eradicated from jury service, property, custody, guardianship, marriage, divorce, and work. They recognized immediately the sexism implied in legislation to protect only women workers. Paul's slogan "Equality not Protection" repudiated these statutes.

However, Paul's former colleagues in the suffrage movement—Florence Kelley, Jane Addams, Julia Lathrop, and Margaret Dreir Robbins—championed the new wages and hours laws. Their views were shared by groups such as the League for Women Voters and the National Consumers' League, whose stated goals included social welfare legislation for women and children. They were joined by the National Federation of Business and Professional Women, women in the labor movement, and bureaucrats in the Women's Bureau (part of the Department of Labor) created in 1920. In their minds, support for the Equal Rights Amendment (ERA) would set back the protective legislation for women that had been winning support in the states.

But Are they Constitutional?

After the arguments, Justice George Sutherland, delivered the opinion of a divided Court. With reasoning that is reminiscent of modern jurists such as Ruth Bader Ginsburg, he said:

> We cannot accept the doctrine that women of a mature age . . . may be subjected to restrictions upon their liberty of contract which could not lawfully be imposed in the case of men under similar circumstances.

In arguing that it was unfair to apply minimum wage laws to women but not to men, Sutherland went on:

It is simply and exclusively a price-fixing law, confined to adult women . . . who are legally as capable of contracting for themselves as men.

And,

If women require a minimum wage to preserve their morals men require it to preserve their honesty.

Sutherland also highlighted the inconsistencies of the board's orders, pointing out that if a woman employed to serve food required a minimum wage of $16.50, why should beginning laundresses earn only $9 a week?

Finally, Sutherland concluded:

It may be said, that if in the interest of public welfare the police power may be invoked to justify the fixing of a minimum wage, it may, when the public welfare is thought to require it, be invoked to justify a maximum wage. . . . If in the face of the guarantee of the Fifth Amendment this form of legislation shall be legally justified, the field for the operation of the police power will have been widened to a great and dangerous degree.

Justices William Howard Taft and Edward T. Sanford disagreed, arguing:

Legislatures in limiting freedom of contract between employee and employer . . . proceed on the assumption that employees, in the class receiving less pay, are not upon a full level of equality of choice with their employers and . . . are prone to accept pretty much anything that is offered. They are peculiarly subject to the overreaching of the harsh and greedy employer. The evils of the sweating system and long hours and low wages which are characteristic of it are well known.

While Sutherland had said that the wages paid to an employee was the "heart of the contract," Taft felt that this opinion exaggerated the importance of one part of the contract—wages—over other terms, such as hours.

Justice Oliver Wendell Holmes believed that Congress did have the right to establish minimum rates of pay for women:

The end, to remove conditions leading to ill health, immorality, and the deterioration of the race, no one would deny to be within the scope of constitutional legislation.

Justice Louis D. Brandeis, whose daughter, Elizabeth, was the secretary of the District's minimum wage board, took no part in the decision. This split the court 5-3, with the majority voting to overrule the minimum wage law for women. In 1936, *Morehead v. New York ex. rel. Tipaldo* reaffirmed the *Adkins* decision.

After *Adkins*, union leaders such as Samuel Gompers railed against the court, fuming, "The Court ranges itself on the side of property and against humanity." He insisted that women "not only are . . . less than able to defend themselves on the economic fields, but they are absolutely without means of defense in the political field."

The minimum-wage boards in the states believed their laws should be enforced as if the court had not overruled Congress. Congressmen vowed to curb the court. Senators, such as Simeon Fess (R-Ohio), proposed that two-thirds vote of the Supreme Court be required for decisions from then on. U.S. Senator

William E. Borah (Idaho) wanted agreement among at least seven of the nine judges for future Court decisions. Senator Robert LaFollette wanted to give Congress power to overrule the Supreme Court by reposing a law after an adverse decision. These reformers saw the court as overstepping its boundaries and trying to legislate for Congress.

With the Great Depression of the 1930s, Americans came to agree with them. They swept President Franklin D. Roosevelt into the White House in 1932 on the promise of a New Deal. In 1936, Roosevelt sent Congress his "court-packing" plan, which would have added six judges to the Supreme Court, all appointed by him. The progressives, in the long run, were victorious.

Today, historians are somewhat more sympathetic to the Adkins Court. In 1978, legal scholar Lawrence H. Tribe wrote in *American Constitutional Law:*

> While the Court justified the limitation of women's working hours by reference to the perceived social and biological need to limit the participation of women in the labor force [in *Radice v. New York* (1924), which upheld a law prohibiting the employment of women in restaurants between 10:00 P.M. and 6:00 A.M. because of their "peculiar and natural functions"], the Court initially [in *Adkins v. Children's Hospital]* struck down women's minimum wage laws, which could not so easily be assimilated to sexist assumptions about the nature and role of women.

One thing is certain. *Adkins v. Children's Hospital* and *Adkins v. Lyons* would further the disintegration of the women's movement in the twenties over the issue of equal versus special rights for women. Three years after the passage of the Nineteenth Amendment (1920), and the same year that the Supreme Court ruled in *Adkins v. Children's Hospital* and *Adkins v. Lyons* (1923), Alice Paul and her militant National Woman's Party introduced the Equal Rights Amendment into Congress. Section 1 read: "Equality of rights under the law shall not be abridged by the United States or by any state on account of sex." In 1980, presidential candidate Ronald Reagan forced the Republicans to break from tradition by dropping the ERA plank from its platform, and in 1982, the ERA failed to win the endorsement of the necessary number of the states. This left open many of the issues dividing the women's movement in 1923, issues that have not disappeared and which continue to be debated to this day.

For Further Reading

Goldstein, Leslie Friedman. *The Constitutional Rights of Women*, rev. ed. Madison: University of Wisconsin Press, 1989.

Hoff, Joan. *Law, Gender, and Injustice: A Legal History of U.S. Women.* New York: New York University Press, 1991.

Tribe, Lawrence H. *American Constitutional Law.* Mineola, New York: The Foundation Press, 1988.

West Coast Hotel v. Parrish: 1937

Appellant: West Coast Hotel Company   **Appellee:** Elsie Parrish

Appellant's Claim: That Parrish was not due back pay to bring her up to the level she would have received under Washington's 1913 minimum wage law

Chief Lawyers for Appellant: John W. Roberts and E. L. Skeel

Chief Lawyers for Appellee: C. B. Conner and Sam M. Driver

Justices: Louis Brandeis, Benjamin Cardozo, *Chief Justice Charles Evans Hughes,* Owen Roberts, and Harlan Stone, (majority); Pierce Butler, James C. McReynolds, George Sutherland, and Willis Van DeVanter (dissent)

Place: Washington, D.C.   **Date of Decision:** March 29, 1937

Decision: The public interest in setting a minimum wage for women and children is more important than freedom of contract

SIGNIFICANCE

In one of the rare instances in which the Supreme Court overruled one of its own precedents, *West Coast Hotel v. Parrish* set the stage for the passage of the Fair Labor Standards Act of 1938

In the late nineteenth century, many Americans believed women were a separate class from men—physically, economically, and socially. Wisconsin, presuming females were "handicapped for motherhood" by working long hours, passed the first "hour law" for women in 1867. The statute limited the workday of women to ten hours. By 1907, twenty states had passed similar laws. Five years later, Massachusetts passed the nation's first minimum wage law, and over the next two years fourteen states did the same.

Protective legislation regulating hours and wages clashed with the nineteenth-century understanding of liberty, specifically the right to contract one's labor, called "liberty of contract." Many felt the Constitution guaranteed this right in Article I, Section 10 and in the Fifth and Fourteenth Amendments. The two ideas clashed dramatically in 1905, with *Lochner v. New York* (see page 341), and in 1908, with *Muller v. Oregon* (see page 346).

Most employers and male workers fought change. Lawyers battled in the courtrooms over whether or not "liberty of contract" meant starvation wages for women and children. In both 1923's *Adkins v. Children's Hospital* (see page 552) and 1936's *Morehead v. New York ex rel. Tipaldo,* the Supreme Court had upheld "freedom of contract." In *Morehead*, which invalidated New York's minimum wage law for women and children, the Court had ruled that *any* minimum wage law denied due process.

A Test Case

The Great Depression of the 1930s heated up the debate. Reformers fixed their hopes on Elsie Parrish—a grandmother. In 1933, she had gone to work as a chambermaid at the Cascadian Hotel in Wenatchee, Washington. When her job ended, the hotel offered her seventeen dollars for the balance of her services. Parrish and her husband knew that the state's minimum wage law for women (1913) had set wages at a minimum of $14.50 a week— adequate "for the decent maintenance of women" and "not detrimental to health and morals." Women could work no more than forty-eight-hours a week.

The Cascadian Hotel in Wenatchee, Washington, where Elsie Parrish worked as a chambermaid. (North Central Washington Museum, Wenatchee, Wash.)

The couple sued the hotel for $216.19 back pay due under the new scale. Parrish lost in county court, but the Washington Supreme Court upheld the minimum wage law and ordered payment. The West Coast Hotel Company appealed to the Supreme Court, basing its arguments on *Adkins v. Children's Hospital.* The appeal raised a dilemma for the Court: In the middle of the depression should the justices reverse their decision in *Adkins* to protect working people?

E. L. Skeel, representing West Coast Hotel, went to the heart of the matter: The state could not deprive citizens of their right to contract their labor by passing wage or hour laws. He mocked the idea that lawmakers could get away with this by using the police power of the state. Parrish's side countered this assertion by claiming that the act was a valid and reasonable exercise of the state's police power. Citing *Radice v. New York* (1924), attorneys C. B. Conner and Sam M. Driver claimed the legislature had the right to decide what conditions were of public concern and how best to remedy them.

In delivering the opinion of the majority, Chief Justice Charles Evans Hughes reviewed the minimum wage law of the state of Washington.

> Women and minors [must] be protected from conditions of labor which have a pernicious effect on their health and morals. . . . Inadequate wages and unsanitary conditions of labor exert such pernicious effect.

It shall be unlawful to employ women or minors in any industry or occupation . . . under conditions . . . detrimental to their health or morals; . . . to employ women workers in any industry . . . at wages which are not adequate for their maintenance.

There is hereby created a commission to be known as the "industrial Welfare Commission" . . . to establish such standards of wages and conditions of labor for women and minors . . . .

Hughes then turned his attention to whether or not the Washington law violated a person's freedom of contract. He denied that the Constitution protected freedom of contract. "It speaks of liberty and prohibits the deprivation of liberty without due process of law. But the liberty safeguarded requires the protection of law against the evils which menace the health, safety, morals and welfare of the people." With these few words he rejected an absolute right of freedom of contract where a state had a strong public interest.

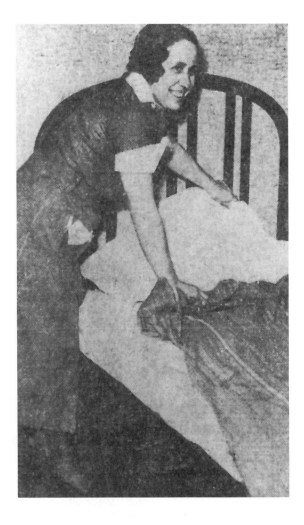

What can be closer to the public interest than the health of women and their protection from unscrupulous and overreaching employers? And if the protection of women is a legitimate end . . . payment of a minimum wage fairly fixed . . . is not admissible to that end? The legislature was clearly entitled to consider the situation of women in employment, the fact that they are in a class receiving the least pay, that their bargaining power is relatively weak, and that they are the ready victims of those who would take advantage of their necessitous circumstances. The legislature was entitled to adopt measures to reduce the evils of the "sweating system," the exploiting of workers at wages so low as to be insufficient to meet the bare cost of living, thus making their very helplessness the occasion of a most injurious competition.

Elsie Parrish makes a bed in 1937. (North Central Washington Museum, Wenatchee, Wash.)

Finally, Hughes said that when women endured exploitation their health suffered, which "casts a direct burden for their support upon the community. What these workers lose in wages the taxpayers are called upon to pay. The bare cost of living must be met."

Justice George Sutherland wrote the dissent. In a curiously modern voice foreshadowing modern feminist arguments, he asked,

> Does the legislation here involved . . . create an arbitrary discrimination? We think it does. Difference of sex affords no reasonable ground for making a restriction applicable to the wage contracts of all working women from which like contracts of all working men are left free. Certainly the suggestion that the bargaining ability of the average woman is not equal to that of the average man would lack substance. The ability to make a fair bargain, as everyone knows, does not depend on sex.

A Close Vote

On March 29, 1937, by a five-to-four vote the Supreme Court upheld the minimum wage law in Washington, ordering the West Coast Hotels Company to pay Parrish the money owed plus court costs. She declared, "I'm not sure I understand all the things but I'm glad its all over."

Two months after *West Coast Hotel v. Parrish*, sixteen states added minimum wage laws to their books. The decision was the beginning of the end of strict judicial adherence to "freedom of contract," which had given employers an advantage probably needed earlier. It also paved the way for the passage of the Fair Labor Standards Act, which one year later extended a minimum wage to workers regardless of gender.

The Fair Labor Standards Act, also called the Wages and Hours Law, established a federal minimum wage of forty cents per hour and a maximum work week of forty hours. It extended to men the benefits women had already won. The act prohibited employing children under the age of sixteen and the hiring of sixteen- to eighteen-year-olds in hazardous occupations. The law applied only to enterprises that engaged in or affected interstate commerce, specifically exempting many other occupations, such as domestic, seasonal, agricultural, and professional jobs.

West Coast Hotel v. Parrish has been called "the switch in time that saved nine" because had the Court *not* overruled itself, President Franklin D. Roosevelt—angry that the Court had voided much of his New Deal legislation—would have "packed" it. Six of his own appointees would then have joined the other nine members in a blatant attempt to manipulate the Court's decisions.

For Further Reading

Cushman, Robert E. *Leading Constitutional Decisions.* New York: Appleton-Century-Crofts, 1958.

Hoff, Joan. *Law, Gender, and Injustice: A Legal History of U.S. Women.* New York: New York University Press, 1991.

Kanowitz, Leo. *Women and the Law: The Unfinished Revolution.* Albuquerque: University of New Mexico Press, 1969.

Otten, Laura A. *Women's Rights and the Law.* Westport, Conn.: Praeger, 1993.

Tribe, Lawrence H. *American Constitutional Law*, 2d ed. Mineola, N.Y.: The Foundation Press, 1992.

Goesaert v. Cleary: 1948

Appellants: Valentine Goesaert, Margaret Goesaert, Gertrude Nadroski, and Caroline McMahon   **Appellees:** Owen J. Cleary, Felix H. H. Flynn, and G. Mennen Williams   **Appellants' Claim:** That the state of Michigan's statute arbitrarily discriminated between male and female owners of liquor establishments and their potential employees
Chief Lawyer for Appellees: Edmund E. Shepherd
Chief Lawyer for the Appellants: Anne R. Davidow   **Justices:** Hugo Black, Harold H. Burton, *Felix Frankfurter,* Robert H. Jackson, Stanley F. Reed, and Chief Justice Fred M. Vinson (majority); William O. Douglas, Frank Murphy, and Wiley B. Rutledge (dissent)   **Place:** Washington, D.C.
Date of Decision: December 20, 1948   **Decision:** Upheld Michigan's law prohibiting women who were not the wife or daughter of a bar's owner from working as a bartender

SIGNIFICANCE

Goesaert v. Cleary is the most interesting trial to go before the Supreme Court to argue that the Fourteenth Amendment protected a woman's right to work wherever she chose.

In 1945, Michigan cities with populations larger than fifty thousand licensed male bartenders, but not females who were not "the wife or daughter of the male owner." (Women *were* permitted to work as waitresses in bars and other establishments that served liquor.) In 1948, four women who wished to be licensed—Valentine Goesaert, Margaret Goesaert, Gertrude Nadroski, and Caroline McMahon—brought suit against three members of the Liquor Control Commission of the State of Michigan.

The women claimed that Michigan's law violated the equal protection clause of the Fourteenth Amendment of the U.S. Constitution. The members of the Liquor Control Commission and their lawyers, along with Michigan's attorney general, Eugene F. Black, defended the state's statute on the basis that men were stronger and better able to contend with heavy drinkers.

Can't Win for Losing

The state supreme court ruled four to three in favor of the state on May 7, 1948. The majority opinion characterized men as the more efficient bartenders and, echoing the state, cited men's strength as an advantage in the event of barroom trouble. The three dissenting judges disagreed, stating, as the *New York Times* summarized it, "that women could do with a word and a smile what men needed fists, biceps and rough talk to accomplish."

Both the majority and dissenting judges also addressed "public welfare" and "morals." The majority said that the licensing of female bartenders would increase the number of female bar patrons. The dissenters, noting that women were permitted to patronize bars and to work as waitresses, asked: "If the claim is that women behind a bar would be a menace to public welfare or morals, how can they be any more of a threat serving liquor from behind the bar than in front of it or anywhere else in the room?"

A three-judge panel of the U.S. District Court for the Eastern District of Michigan, Southern Division, upheld the decision of the state supreme court. The women appealed to the U.S. Supreme Court.

No Equal Protection

The women's case was argued by their attorney, Anne R. Davidow. She described the Michigan law as containing "an unfair and unjust classification as to sex, and an unfair discrimination against women owners of liquor establishments, women bartenders, daughters of female owners of bars, and an unfair discrimination between waitresses and female bartenders."

She challenged its constitutionality on Fourteenth Amendment grounds. "The act complained of is repugnant to the Fourteenth Amendment to the Constitution of the United States in that it creates an unreasonable and arbitrary classification, and denies the plaintiffs the equal protection of the laws."

Appellee lawyer Edmund E. Shepherd argued that "since legislation governing the alcoholic beverage traffic falls into its own peculiar category, a state, in controlling it, may draw finer lines of distinction in classification than might be permitted in regulating a useful occupation." He also claimed that the law neither "set up an arbitrary classification" nor "violate[d] the equal protection clause [of the Fourteenth Amendment]." Finally, he asserted that it was for the legislature, and not the courts, to take up the "fair debate" as to women's fitness for the bartending trade.

Reality Has Nothing to Do With It

Supreme Court Justice Felix Frankfurter, who wrote the majority opinion upholding the Michigan law, appears to have found the issue a humorous one. "Beguiling as the subject is," he wrote, "it need not detain us long. . . . We are, to be sure, dealing with a historic calling. We meet the ale-wife, sprightly and ribald, in Shakespeare. . . ." He added:

> Michigan could . . . forbid all women from working behind the bar. This is so despite the vast changes in the social and legal position of women. The fact that women may now have achieved the virtues that men have long claimed as their prerogatives and now indulge in vices that men have long practiced, does not preclude the States from drawing a sharp line between the sexes, certainly in such matters as the regulation of the liquor traffic. . . . The Constitution does not require legislatures to reflect sociological insight, or shifting social standards, any more than it requires them to keep abreast of the latest scientific standards.

As to whether Michigan could make an exemption for the wives and daughters of bar owners, Frankfurter wrote that "while Michigan may deny to all women opportunities for bartending, Michigan cannot play favorites among women without rhyme or reason." He found that the family relationship between a female bartender and a male bar owner a sufficiently rational basis for differing treatment under the law.

In 1948, *Goesaert v. Cleary* upheld a Michigan law that prohibited women from working as licensed bartenders unless they were wives or daughters of the owners. This decision was overturned in 1976. In 1995 this young woman worked as a bartender in Connecticut. (V. Harlow/ Glockenspiel)

> Michigan evidently believes that the oversight assured through ownership of a bar by a barmaid's husband or father minimizes hazards that confront a barmaid without such protecting oversight. . . . If it is entertainable, as we think it is, Michigan has not violated its duty to afford equal protection. . . . Since the line they [the Michigan legislature] have drawn is not without a basis in reason, we cannot give ear to the suggestion that the real impulse

behind this legislation was an unchivalrous desire of male bartenders to try to monopolize the calling.

Finally, he wrote that it was not "unconstitutional for Michigan to withdraw from women the occupation of bartending [just] because it allows women to serve as waitresses where liquor is dispensed."

Justice Wiley B. Rutledge, in the dissenting opinion joined by William O. Douglas and Frank Murphy, wrote:

> The statute arbitrarily discriminates between male and female owners of liquor establishments. A male owner . . . may employ his wife and daughter as barmaids. A female owner may neither work as a barmaid herself nor employ her daughter in that position, even if a man is always present in the establishment. . . . This . . . belies the assumption that the statute was motivated by a legislative solicitude for the moral and physical well-being of women who . . . would be employed as barmaids. Since there could be no other conceivable justification for such discrimination against women owners of liquor establishments, the statute should be held invalid as a denial of equal protection.

In 1976, the Supreme Court revealed embarrassment about its decision in Footnote 23 to *Goesaert v. Cleary*. *Craig v. Boren* states: "*Goesaert v. Cleary* . . . is disapproved." Today few jobs outside the church or military automatically exclude women.

For Further Reading

Goldstein, Leslie Friedman. *The Constitutional Rights of Women*, rev. ed. Madison: The University of Wisconsin Press, 1989.

Lynn, Naomi B., ed. *Women, Politics and the Constitution*. New York: Harrington Park Press, 1990.

New York Times, May 8 and 25, 1948; December 21, 1948.

Weeks v. Southern Bell: 1969

Appellant: Lorena Weeks   **Appellee:** Southern Bell Telephone and Telegraph Company   **Appellant's Claim:** That Southern Bell discriminated against Weeks because of her sex by refusing her the position of switchman. Limiting weights that women may lift cannot be justified on the basis of a *bona fide occupational qualification (bfoq)* exception to Title VII of the 1964 Civil Rights Act   **Chief Lawyer for Appellee:** David J. Heinsma
Chief Lawyer for Appellant: Sylvia Roberts   **Justices:** Robert A. Ainsworth, Jr., *Frank M. Johnson,* and John Minor Wisdom   **Place:** Atlanta, Georgia
Date of Decision: March 28, 1969   **Decision:** Weight-lifting limits for women stem from gender stereotypes and may not be used as a *bfoq* exception to Title VII of the 1964 Civil Rights Act

SIGNIFICANCE
This decision marked a major triumph in the fight against protective labor laws and company restrictions upon the hours and conditions of women's work and opened many previously male-only jobs to women.

In 1966, Georgian Lorena Weeks, a nineteen-year employee of the Southern Bell Telephone and Telegraph, applied for the job of "switchman." The job entailed maintaining switching equipment. It offered double the salary of her present job. Although she had occasionally replaced the regular switchman, the company denied Weeks the position. In violation of its contract with the union, the company gave the job to a man with less seniority.

The contract plainly stated that all other qualifications being equal, the company must hire the senior bidder. However, Southern Bell told Weeks that they would not assign women to such jobs. They explained that it was contrary to company policy (and state law) to hire women to lift more than thirty pounds—which the switchman's job could require. Weeks complained to the Equal Employment Opportunity Commission (EEOC) and with a court-appointed counsel, went to court.

Weeks was unsuccessful in the district court. Lacking the resources to pursue an appeal, she turned to the National Organization for Women (NOW). NOW's Legal Committee agreed to handle her appeal free of charge if she agreed to continue as an employee of Southern Bell. Weeks accepted—despite hostility and mistreatment that continued during and after the appeals. For NOW, her case was not just potentially historic. If the decision remained unchallenged, it would serve as a precedent for other employers to stop women from working in male-only occupations.

The Trouble with Protection

Protective labor laws for women originated during the Progressive Era from good intentions and in response to appalling workplace conditions of the nineteenth century. But loopholes and poor enforcement prevented the laws from being as effective as they might otherwise have been and many women—principally domestic and agricultural workers—remained excluded from such coverage.

Court decisions also took away women's rights under the guise of protection. 1908's *Muller v. Oregon* decision (see page 346), for example, emphasizing the biological differences between men and women and the latter's role as childbearers, kept women out of juries, state-supported universities, and some professions. Nonetheless, most women's groups supported protective legislation. They did not object to the fact that these laws assumed that women were physically inferior and that child-bearing was their chief responsibility.

The debate over protective legislation had consequences that went far beyond the issue itself. There were the obvious tensions, such as those between two philosophical camps. Supporters of the Equal Rights Amendment (ERA) advocated the achievement of equality through identical treatment. The other believed that protective laws were necessary and compensated for and offset the effects of past discrimination.

The controversy also created class conflict, because supporters of protective legislation were mainly the working classes, and its opponents usually came from the middle and upper classes. Despite occasional efforts at compromise, there was a much-lamented loss of valuable energy because of this fighting among women who otherwise shared many interests.

Some historians have pointed out that protective legislation had profound effects upon the unionization of women as well as the whole American labor movement. Although many American feminists were pro-union, unions themselves were often anti-feminist and generally unenthusiastic or worse on the subject of unionizing women. Women usually held difficult-to-unionize unskilled jobs and were a potential source of competition for male workers. These attitudes understandably robbed women of their interest in unions—ultimately to the detriment of both women, who became trapped in less desirable jobs, and the union movement as a whole.

The best evidence that some people intended to use protective legislation to deliberately limit opportunities for women to enter and advance in certain professions came during the first and second world wars. With men gone to war, many restrictions on women's work ended, indicating confidence in the competence of women workers to perform jobs men's jobs. However, the old "protective" arguments resurrected at the end of the wars when men returned wanting those jobs back.

Tellingly, state protective legislation continued to survive even after the passage of the 1964 Civil Rights Act. Title VII of the act prohibits discrimination by companies, employment agencies, and unions. The law exempts a narrow category, called *bona fide occupational qualifications (bfoq)*, where the need to have a worker of a particular sex can be justified. Even the EEOC's 1969 position against such legislation came only after many years of pressure from feminist groups rather than in an immediate understanding that protective laws were now unlawful.

Stereotypes Discriminate

At the same time the Weeks case was progressing through the courts, Georgia's weight-lifting law preventing women from lifting more than thirty pounds on the job was overturned. Therefore, Weeks's case changed from one challenging the state law to one contesting the *company's* policies, putting the burden of proof upon Southern Bell.

The district court's decision in favor of Southern Bell flowed from its belief that the weight-lifting limit was reasonable. Southern Bell had seemed to demonstrate the "strenuous" nature of the job and pointed to the fact that switchmen were on call twenty-four hours a day and occasionally worked alone at night.

The appeals court, however, objected to the vague nature of the characterization "strenuous." It also frowned on the absence of evidence that the level of strenuousness was so great that all or almost all women would be incapable of successfully holding the job. The EEOC had not found evidence to support this claim, and Weeks testified that she was able to perform the job and offered examples of other women in similar jobs as additional proof.

The court found ample room to dispute the exact degree of the strenuous quality of the job: Only one thirty-one pound piece of equipment was repeatedly used on a regular basis, and there was not much need to lift it. However, the court refused to engage in the technical analysis necessary to fix a definition of "strenuous." It found that simply calling it strenuous was not enough to justify a *bfoq* exception.

To address the question of whether a company can impose a reasonable weight-lifting limitation on its own, the court looked to the EEOC's testimony in *Rosenfeld v. Southern Pacific* (1968), which argued against a broad construction of the *bfoq* exception. The court agreed that allowing wide application of the *bfoq* exception would defeat the purpose of the 1964 Civil Rights Act.

Noting the absence of evidence about the abilities of women to lift weight, the court pointed out that Southern Bell's case stemmed from building on stereotypes about the abilities of men and women. It observed that technique— unrelated to gender—is an important factor in weight-lifting.

To Southern Bell's argument that women might not be able to handle emergencies, the court responded that speculative emergencies should not provide an excuse for employers who wish to discriminate. Rejecting the argument that the unpleasant aspects of the job should be used as reasons for barring women, the court stated,

> Title VII rejects just this type of romantic paternalism as unduly Victorian and instead vests individual women with the power to decide if they should take on unromantic tasks. Men have always had the right to determine whether the incremental increase in pay for strenuous, dangerous, obnoxious, boring or unromantic tasks is worth the candle. The promise of Title VII is that women are now to be on equal footing.

Lorena Weeks and her husband, Billy, in 1990. (Lorena W. Weeks)

After finding in favor of Weeks, the appeals court sent the case back to the district court. It ordered that Weeks be given the position and $31,000 in back pay. In an apparent act of defiance, Southern Bell refused to carry out the court's order. It was only in April 1971, after demonstrations conducted by NOW, that Southern Bell finally followed the court's order.

This case paved the way for women to work in many non-traditional jobs. In 1977, *Dothard v. Rawlinson* (see page 398)—by eliminating height and weight requirements of female job-seekers—would finally force employers to consider women on their individual merits.

For Further Reading

Davis, Flora. *Moving the Mountain: The Women's Movement in America Since 1960.* New York: Simon & Schuster, 1991.

Foner, Philip S., ed. *Women and the American Labor Movement: From the First Trade Unions to the Present.* New York: The Free Press (division of Simon & Schuster), 1979–1980.

Holt, Judith, and Ellen Levine. *Rebirth of Feminism.* New York: Quadrangle, 1971.

Bowe v. Colgate-Palmolive: 1969

Appellants: Thelma Bowe et al. **Appellees:** Colgate-Palmolive Company
and International Chemical Workers Union, Local #15
Appellants' Claim: That companies do not have the right to segregate jobs
on the basis of gender by limiting women to less strenuous jobs
Chief Lawyer for Appellees: Herbert L. Segal
Chief Lawyer for Appellants: Marion W. Garnett **Justices:** Walter J.
Cummings, Otto Kerner, Henry S. Wise **Place:** Chicago, Illinois
Date of Decision: September 26, 1969 **Decision:** Companies may not use
job classification systems that discriminate on the basis of gender. If a
weight-lifting limit is used as a general guideline, it must apply to both men
and women—providing employees the opportunity to demonstrate their
suitability for physically demanding jobs on an individual basis.

SIGNIFICANCE
After this decision, women could work in many jobs that had been for men only—
so long as females could meet the physical requirements. The *bona fide occupational qualification (bfoq)* exception to Title VII—permitting discrimination where it
is reasonably necessary to the job—therefore would no longer be used to exclude
women from most job opportunities.

The passage of Title VII of the 1964 Civil Rights Act raised the hopes of millions of American women who believed they would now receive fair treatment in the workplace. The law makes it "an unlawful employment practice for any employer . . . to discriminate against any individual with respect to his compensation, terms, conditions, or privileges of employment, because of such individual's race, color, religion, sex, or national origin." It took effect in July 1965.

However, the legal battles that accompanied the enforcement of this legislation unearthed sexism unchanged by law. This sexism—sometimes remnants of earlier protective legislation for women—was no longer a legal excuse to exclude women from the work place. Still women had to sue to combat sex discrimination and workplace restrictions.

The experiences of Thelma Bowe, an employee of the Colgate-Palmolive company's plant in Jeffersonville, Indiana, illustrated the challenges that women continued to face in combating sex discrimination that persisted even after the Civil Rights Act.

Protective Legislation

Colgate, like many companies—and states—had placed a weight limit on items female employees might be required to lift. Such restrictions on women could also include maximum hours' rules and prohibitions on nighttime work. These regulations were mostly products of the Progressive Era, which lasted from 1900 to World War I. The women's groups and unions who had promoted these laws had benevolent motives. Unfortunately, like most—if not all—protective laws, this legislation had proven to be a liability to women.

The Colgate company's weight-lifting limit for women dated from World War II and the company's first large-scale influx of women workers as replacements for men in military service. Jobs were specifically fashioned for these women. The work was less physically demanding and did not require the lifting of more than twenty-five pounds.

As the servicemen returned, however, the company and the union continued to set aside less strenuous jobs for women—reserving jobs requiring more physical stamina for men. But by the second wave of feminism in the 1960s, almost all women's groups were unequivocally opposed to these laws and rules, describing them as paternalistic and instrumental in limiting women's job opportunities—not to mention resulting in lower pay.

Gender Segregation

The Colgate company had maintained separate seniority systems for men and women. The seniority ranking affected not only an employee's ability to obtain sought-after assignments, but also, of course, layoffs—women were let go before men with less seniority, and called back the same way. This segregation continued even after the company had made minor changes and relabeled the practices to appear more gender-neutral.

Bowe was one victim of this discrimination. She—and others—filed charges with the Equal Employment Opportunity Commission (EEOC). However, they could not obtain an agreement from Colgate. Therefore, the women brought a class-action lawsuit against the company, heard by the U.S. District Court for the Southern District of Indiana on June 30, 1967. Colgate eventually made conciliation attempts and recalled laid-off plaintiffs after a strike, yet the suit continued over the issue of back pay and the sex-segregation system.

The First Round

The District Court refused to equate racial and sex-based discrimination, and endorsed the idea that the *bfoq* exception does not have to be based on what is absolutely necessary, but rather (quoting the act itself) what is "reasonably necessary." By emphasizing the word "reasonably" and choosing to interpret it to mean that some options are left open for employers, the court found in favor of Colgate's establishment of the weight-lifting limit.

Since the genesis of the weight-lifting restriction was the well-being of female employees, the court declared that Colgate had acted reasonably because it had studied various state weight-lifting regulations before arriving at its own precise limit (rather than determining it in an arbitrary fashion). Furthermore, the court said, it would be impractical to determine weight-lifting ability on an individual basis.

The court's decisions were also fueled by the EEOC's own position at the time: Some protective laws could conceivably be reasonable and therefore should not be overturned. Protective laws—and more discretion for the employer—demanded the adoption of a "common sense" approach, allowing a degree of discretion in hiring even under Title VII.

Appeals Court Overrules

Two years later, the U.S. District Court of Appeals, Seventh Circuit, heard the case in Chicago. On September 26, 1969, the judges reversed most of the lower court's decision. It found that, although a defendant would have to defend himself or herself twice, it was necessary to allow plaintiffs to pursue remedies through both the courts and through arbitration, because each channel might offer different remedies. However, remedies should only be enacted at the end of the entire process so that there was no duplication, which would be unfair to a defendant.

Although the appeals court found the district court's approach to be "carefully reasoned and conscientious," it also concluded that the decision was based on a misunderstanding of the purpose of Title VII. Just because state protective laws could stand as long as they did not conflict with Title VII, the district court could not conclude that those same laws were not affected by Title VII.

The EEOC's position (at the time)—that Congress did not mean to overturn all protective laws—was taken out of context by the lower court. The EEOC's limited interpretation of the *bfoq* exception did not allow the labeling of jobs as "male" or "female," since labeling would exclude men or women from many job opportunities.

The appeals court emphasized that the practice of creating seniority systems that segregate "light" and "heavy" jobs may not be used if they merely disguise gender classifications or make it more difficult for men or women to advance into positions for which they normally would be suitable. The court pointed to three cases coming before *Bowe* in which the EEOC had favored individual testing of weight-lifting ability, rather than weight-lifting limits based on sex.

The court also ruled that since there was a lack of agreement about precisely how much weight women can lift from state to state, and since many of those limits were too old to be relevant to the physical condition of contemporary women, weight-lifting ability should be tested individually. The conditions of work and the manner in which weight-lifting should be performed should also be taken into account.

Colgate could maintain its current thirty-five-pound weight-lifting limit only as it applied to both men and women. Colgate was required to give notice to all employees that they would be regularly granted opportunities to prove their suitability for more physically demanding jobs. Employees who have this capacity must be allowed to pursue any position and be paid appropriately for their level of seniority.

Regarding the other issues, on November 28, 1973, the U.S. Court of Appeals, Seventh Circuit, sent the case back to the district court to create a system in which seniority and other disputes were handled fairly. The court extended the right to receive back pay to additional plaintiffs. It granted the right to sue for back pay even to plaintiffs who had not filed a charge with the EEOC and instructed Colgate to notify employees that this opportunity was available. Title VII suits must, by definition, be class-action suits because they were based on a quality shared by a class of people.

Echoing the views of other courts on Title VII suits and on racial discrimination cases, the court found that Title VII suits were meant to advance public policy endorsed by Congress. The intent of Congress was not just to change a defendant's behavior, but for other types of redress (such as back pay), as well. The goal of Title VII was clearly to end discrimination and to compensate its victims. The most efficient way of achieving this result would be through class-action suits.

For Further Reading

Chafe, William Henry. *The American Woman in the 20th Century*. New York: Oxford University Press, 1991.

De Hart Mathews, Jane, and Linda K. Kerber, eds. *Women's America: Refocusing the Past*. New York: Oxford University Press, 1982.

Lehrer, Susan. *Origins of Protective Labor Legislation for Women. 1905–1925*. Albany: State University of New York Press, 1989.

Phillips v. Martin Marietta: 1971

Plaintiff: Ida Phillips   **Defendant:** Martin Marietta Corporation
Plaintiff's Claim: That hiring based on special requirements for gender is a form of sex discrimination   **Chief Lawyer for Defendant:** Donald T. Senterfitt   **Chief Lawyer for Plaintiff:** William L. Robinson   **Justices:** Hugo L. Black, Harry A. Blackmun, William J. Brennan, Jr., Chief Justice Warren E. Burger, William O. Douglas, John M. Harlan, *Thurgood Marshall,* Potter Stewart, and Byron R. White (per curiam)   **Place:** Washington, D.C.
Date of Decision: January 25, 1971   **Decision:** Companies must set the same hiring standards for both women and men

SIGNIFICANCE

With this case, the Supreme Court began its analysis of Title VII of the 1964 Civil Rights Act. The formerly sanctioned "sex-plus" theory, in which discrimination was permissible when it was based not on gender alone, but on a combination of gender plus another quality, was ruled unlawful.

When Ida Phillips charged the Martin Marietta Corporation with sex discrimination in the late 1960s—she had been denied a job as an assembly trainee because of her sex—the U.S. District Court for the Middle District of Florida summarily dismissed the case. She had no better luck with the Court of Appeals for the Fifth Circuit. It affirmed the lower court's decision and refused to rehear the case.

Martin Marietta had denied any discrimination, pointing out that while the company did refuse to consider job applications from women with pre-school children (although it had hired male employees with children in those ages), at the time of Phillips' application, roughly seventy to seventy-five percent of the applicants and seventy-five to eighty percent of the successful candidates were women.

Sex-Plus Theory Illegal But . . .

The philosophy behind Martin Marietta's rejection of Phillips' job request was named the "sex plus" theory. This idea argued that while discrimination based on gender alone was not legally defensible, gender in conjunction with another characteristic—such as women with pre-school children—provided an acceptable reason not to hire.

The Supreme Court disagreed, finding the relevant portion of the 1964 Civil Rights Act to be perfectly clear: "Persons of like qualifications [must] be given employment opportunities irrespective of their sex." The Court of Appeals was therefore mistaken in its interpretation of the law. Maintaining different hiring policies for men with pre-school-age children and for women in the same situation was contrary to Title VII.

The decision, however, alarmed women's groups with a suggestion that it might be possible to apply the *bona fide occupational qualification (bfoq)* exception in some cases if parenting could be shown to be "demonstrably more relevant to job performance for a woman than for a man." Therefore, since there was insufficient evidence before the Court to indicate whether or not such a *bfoq* exception existed, the matter was returned to the lower court with an instruction that a more extensive review of the issue be undertaken.

A Feminist Perspective

Although Justice Thurgood Marshall agreed that the case was worthy of more consideration, he disagreed with the idea that a *bfoq* exception could be justified by showing that most women with young children have responsibilities at home that are not shared by men—thereby possibly adversely affecting their performance on the job. Marshall pointed out that employers can simply demand certain standards from all their employees and insist that parenting not disrupt an employee's work.

Ida Phillips was the first person to bring a case before the U.S. Supreme Court that dealt with sex discrimination in hiring practices. *(Florida Times-Union)*

Lamenting the Court's failure to endorse this approach, he wrote, "The Court suggests that it would not require such uniform standards. I fear in this case, where the issue is not squarely before us, that the Court has fallen into the trap of assuming that the 1964 Civil Rights Act permits ancient canards about the proper role of women to be a basis for discrimination."

Clearly the law was not intended to allow discrimination based on stereotypes, he stressed. Continuing, he commented, the *bfoq* exception was not intended to completely dilute the effectiveness of the basic law. The Equal Employment Opportunity Commission (EEOC) must be regarded as a principal authority on this issue, and its interpretation was that the *bfoq* exception applied only in cases where physical qualities unique to men or unique to women were involved.

The Motherhood Bias

In the minds of many women's rights activists, the Phillips case underscored the need for an Equal Rights Amendment (ERA). Women were frustrated by the Supreme Court's unwillingness to put men and women on truly equal ground, even after the passage of Title VII. Nonetheless, this decision represented at least a partial triumph, not only in the battle against sex discrimination, but specifically in the struggle against anti-motherhood bias, which some have suggested is a distinct phenomenon.

Discrimination against mothers, historically commonplace, has never been condemned to the same extent as other forms of sex discrimination because it probably originates from the ancient concept that parenting is a uniquely female responsibility.

However, the immediate cultural genesis of discrimination against mothers dates to 1920 with the founding of the Labor Department's Women's Bureau, which played a large part in causing this teaching to become fixed in our culture. The Bureau discouraged wives and mothers from working unless it was financially urgent. However, for most working women, as statistics compiled by the Bureau itself indicated, there were, in fact, financial reasons contributing to their entrance into the workforce.

In any case, the Women's Bureau provided a type of ammunition for anti-feminists who were seeking an excuse for not hiring women—ammunition which was all the more valuable because of its origination from an organization that had been chartered to be concerned about women's issues. This protective philosophy was contagious—exploited by those in the anti-ERA and protective legislation camps as well as by official groups such as the President's Commission on the Status of Women and the Citizens' Advisory Council and ultimately accepted by much of society.

For Further Reading

Cott, Nancy F. *The Grounding of Modern Feminism*. New Haven, Conn.: Yale University Press, 1989.

Nye, Francis Ivan, and Lois Wlapis Hoffman, eds. *The Employed Mother in America*. Chicago, Rand McNally, 1963.

Wertheimer, Barbara Mayer. *We Were There: The Story of Working Women in America*. New York: Pantheon Books, 1977.

United States v. Libbey-Owens-Ford: 1971

Plaintiff: United States   **Defendants:** Libbey-Owens-Ford Company and United Glass and Ceramic Workers of North America AFL-CIO Local #9
Plaintiff's Claim: That the consent order designed to provide relief to women workers was not discriminatory against males even if they were displaced because of the order   **Chief Lawyers for Defendants:** John G. Mattimoe for Libbey-Owens, David Clayman for the Union
Chief Lawyers for Plaintiff: William M. Connelly and Joel Selig
Judge: Don J. Young   **Place:** Toledo, Ohio   **Date:** February 3, 1971
Decision: The court overruled objections to the consent order bringing relief to women workers, leaving the door open to provide relief for male workers who might suffer discriminatory effects as a result of the order

SIGNIFICANCE

For the first time, the U.S. Justice Department sued a company under the sex discrimination clause of Title VII of the 1964 Civil Rights Act, resolving the matter through a consent order. However, the company challenged the order in court. The resulting decision gave working women ammunition in remedying past discrimination. It also marked the birth of an era when activism on women's issues took the form of litigation rather than protests and demonstrations.

In 1970, 157 women working at Libbey-Owens-Ford in Toledo, Ohio, charged that the company hired them for only one of their five plants, putting them in less desirable jobs than men. Libbey-Owens-Ford claimed it could not remedy their situation. The state's protective labor laws for women—including a limit on weight-lifting and workday hours—prohibited the company from hiring women on an equal basis with men.

The Justice Department took the side of the women workers. It demanded Libbey-Owens-Ford adopt a new hiring policy and pay back wages to the female employees. On December 7, 1970, the dispute was resolved by a consent decree. Libbey-Owens-Ford admitted to no wrong-doing but did agree to open up more job opportunities for women, to grant some women immediate promotions, and to provide advice to women about job opportunities.

However, almost no one was happy with these results. Women's organizations objected because the settlement offered no guidance on the legal issues surrounding the conflict between Title VII and state protective legislation, and because workers received no back pay. Also, male employees at Libbey-Owens-Ford objected to some of the agreed upon remedies, and challenged the consent decree in district court.

A Problem of Seniority

Of the 157 women workers (of Libbey-Owens' 5,400 employees) the vast majority, 139, held at least fifteen years of seniority; another twelve had at least ten years of seniority. These women could not take advantage of job opportunities throughout all departments in Libbey-Owens' plants. They constituted a "relief class."

Under the collective bargaining agreement that had been in effect between Libbey-Owens-Ford and the union, workers could only build seniority within one department at a time—in other words, employees transferring from one department to another could not also transfer their level of seniority but must start over. The consent decree would allow women in the relief class to carry their seniority with them as they transferred from one department to another. This seniority issue became the "hot-button" issue (out of twenty-six categories of objections) that soured the consent decree.

The employees who objected pointed out that this was a unique privilege for the relief class; in transferring their seniority from one department to another the females could potentially displace male employees who had more seniority in that department but less in the overall plant. They also complained that the relief class could displace employees with greater *plant* seniority when transferring—and technically it *was* possible a female employee with more departmental seniority *might* displace a man with more plant seniority in those small departments with very few low-seniority employees.

Male employees argued that any displaced male worker under those circumstances would face discrimination because he could not transfer his seniority to another department. The court agreed that the senior employee would suffer some loss, but "only of that privilege or benefit to which the loser was not justly entitled."

The Tables Turned . . . Temporarily

In overriding this objection, the U.S. District Court in Ohio's Northern District looked at the underlying issues surrounding measures intended to provide relief for victims of past discrimination and found a basic justification for these measures so long as they were in effect only for a limited time:

> A system which discriminates against some individuals necessarily discriminates in favor of others. The only way that the discrimination against some can be eliminated is to eliminate that which is in favor of the others. This

does not mean that the former underdog is now top dog, and vice versa, but only that in the future there will be neither.

So, the court apparently viewed the temporary granting of privileges to the relief class as part of a process that would remove the effects of past discrimination that had favored men—simply allowing female employees to achieve positions they would have otherwise filled but for discrimination.

Another complaint about the consent decree concerned the right given solely to female workers to transfer back to their original departments. The court found this privilege, which was intended to allow women to transfer to opportunities in other departments without being very fearful of failure, permissible— as long as it did not continue indefinitely.

An Even-Handed Approach

The court, recognizing the complexity of matters such as seniority systems, did not try to monopolize the right to seek remedies for grievances in this area. It emphasized the suitability of collective bargaining in these cases. While it recognized that its ruling might influence the bargaining process, it believed the warring parties could reach a solution consistent with the law without judicial intervention; no court decision could substitute for collective bargaining.

The court retained the right to intervene in this case for three years. It wanted to ensure that the order, once in effect, did not create unfair results for any of the male employees rather than just eradicating discrimination in their favor. The court outlined a procedure for employees who wished to pursue grievances in the future. After overruling the remaining objections, which were minor, the court allowed the consent decree to stand.

The Libbey-Owens case demonstrated that while anti-discrimination laws themselves were simple, having them enforced was complex. Although the case only obtained mixed results for women, the tendency of female victims of discrimination to head for the courts rather than picket lines became increasingly common. The strategy was fueled even further by legislation that in 1972 gave the Equal Employment Opportunity Commission (EEOC) the right to sue employers, not merely press for voluntary agreements. Because employees often fear going to court, many cases have since been settled by out-of-court settlements favorable to those with grievances.

For Further Reading

Holt, Judith, and Ellen Levine. *Rebirth of Feminism.* New York: Quadrangle, 1971.

Kessler-Harris, Alice. *Out to Work: A History of Wage-Earning Women in the United States.* New York: Oxford University Press, 1982.

Milkman, Ruth, ed. *Women, Work and Protest: A Century of U.S. Women's Labor History.* Boston: Routledge & Kegan Paul, 1985.

Pittsburgh Press v. Pittsburgh Commission on Human Relations: 1973

Appellant: Pittsburgh Press Company   **Appellees:** Pittsburgh Commission on Human Relations et al.   **Appellant's Claim:** That a newspaper may publish gender-segregated help wanted advertising to attract the advertiser's intended audience   **Chief Lawyer for Appellees:** Eugene B. Strassburger, III
Chief Lawyer for Appellant: Charles Richard Volk   **Justices:** William J. Brennan, Jr., Thurgood Marshall, *Lewis F. Powell, Jr.,* William H. Rehnquist, and Byron R. White (majority); Harry A. Blackmun, Warren E. Burger, William O. Douglas, and Potter Stewart (dissent)   **Place:** Washington, D.C.
Date of Decision: June 21, 1973   **Decision:** Newspapers may not use separate male and female columns when publishing help-wanted advertising

SIGNIFICANCE
Eliminating sex-segregated want ads opened the way for women to apply for jobs previously limited to men—often jobs that offered higher pay and more opportunities for advancement.

In 1960, forty percent of women over sixteen worked. Most were secretaries, nurses, or sales clerks, with salaries at the low end. Quotas kept most out of graduate, law, and medical schools. When women looked for jobs in the newspapers, they saw columns titled "Help Wanted, Male" and "Help Wanted, Female." This meant that a female mathematician who looked for a job in the Pittsburgh want ads would find offerings such as "key punch operator" or "kitchen help."

Title VII of the 1964 Civil Rights Act specifically prohibits employment agencies, labor organizations, and employers from indicating a preference for either sex in employment advertising in any form. Yet the Equal Employment Opportunity Commission (EEOC) refused to enforce this aspect of the law when it came to women. This neglect fueled the second wave of feminism.

A Matter of Sex Appeal

In 1965, the EEOC released guidelines clearly prohibiting column headings that classified jobs by race, religion, or national origin. Women's rights groups (as well as the attorney general and several members of the president's cabinet) wanted no less when it came to sex-segregated headings.

The EEOC had expressly allowed sex-segregation of newspaper want ads since 1966. It argued, at first, that the sex-segregation of advertising could take place under Title VII, since some jobs would have more appeal to men and others to women—and the separate headings would make it easier to see which was which. The EEOC had only taken a position on the *content* of the ads. These ads could indicate a gender preference only where the need to have a worker of a different gender could be justified, called a *bona fide occupational qualification (bfoq).*

NOW Steps Up

One particularly passionate advocate on this issue was the National Organization for Women (NOW). In addition to conducting televised demonstrations to sensitize the EEOC to public sentiment against its policy, NOW petitioned the EEOC to hold hearings—a request granted in May of 1967. NOW's view was shared by less militant groups such as Business and Professional Women and in August 1968, feminist efforts paid off. The EEOC changed its guidelines.

At this point, NOW turned its attention to conducting demonstrations against individual newspapers. These demonstrations were a critical factor in the want ads controversy because the EEOC still lacked the authority to enforce its decisions. This fact was underscored by the arguments of the American Newspaper Publishers Association. It brought a lawsuit against the EEOC in September of 1968. Besides the obvious desire to maintain maximum editorial control, fear of financial loss contributed to newspaper resistance: since companies—wishing to attract both male and female job applicants—would occasionally buy ads in both columns, some ad sales would be lost if separate male and female headings were removed.

The earliest success in changing newspapers policies came in December of 1968 when charges filed with the New York Fair Employment Practices Commission yielded the integration of want ad headings in all New York City newspapers. Continuing demonstrations and legal action produced success in other cities too, but the issue was not conclusively resolved until it was examined by the Supreme Court.

Stop the Presses

In 1969, the Pittsburgh Human Relations Commission followed the suggestion of future NOW president Wilma Scott Heide and made sex discrimination illegal through an administrative order. In October of 1969, the Pittsburgh

Help Wanted—Female

MEDICAL SECRETARY
For director of laboratory & research in large hospital; to be in charge of office staff. Excellent working conditions in modern air-cond office. Good salary, knowledge of medical terminology & stenography rqd.
JEWISH CHRONIC DISEASE HOSP
Rutland Rd near Utica Ave, Bklyn

MEDICAL TYPIST
DICTAPHONE, PATHOLOGY, BUSY OFFICE EXP; EXCEL SALARY. ADELPHI HOSPITAL, 50 GREENE AVE, BKLYN.

MEDICAL SECRETARY
Medical terminology, Mon to Fri 9-5, $80. TR 9-9000, ext 7028.

MEDICAL secy, med group Bklyn, steno, medical terminol not nec, 9-5, $80 +
Nassau Med Agency, 33 W 42 CH 4-8101

MERCHANDISING TRAINEE $65
typing BOYLE Agency 4 W 40

MILLINERY, assistant designer fitter, patterns, ARJEF 23 West 56 Street

MODEL SIZE 8 OR 10
5 FT 1-5 FT 2 IN HEELS
LADIES COATS & SUITS
FREISS INC   205 W. 39

MODEL STENO/TYPE $90
Sz 10, 5'5" BOYLE Agency 4 W 40

MODEL /JR DESIGNER $75
size 9, no exp Boyle Agency 4 W 40

MODEL 9 petite dresses. Asst bkkpr, recept, Hit Fashions, 463 7th Ave.

MONITOR board recept decorator $75
H-o-r-n Agency, 505 5th Ave
H-o-r-n Agency, 130 W. 42 St.

MON-Bd recept "Radio-TV-Adv" to $85
Prestige Agencies, 130 W 42 & 160 Bway

MONBO-Rocpts (4) "Furn Shwrm" $75
Immed opngs. Parker Agency, 130 W 42

NCR BOOKKEEPER, $90
"MEDICAL OFFICE"
Hrs to 4:30. No Pressure. Lovely Ofc.
Accurate Agency 15 E 40 (Lobby)

NCR 3200 OP $80
Provident Agency, 7 E. 42nd St., Rm 810

NCR 3200 (8) "AIRLINES" $85
Immed opngs. PARKER agency 130W42

NITE CLKS, FEE PD TO $80
Any 7½ Hrs starting 1-2-3-4-5-6-11 PM,
12-8 AM or 2-10 AM. MANY OPENINGS
PARK AGENCIES (2)
160 BROADWAY   9 EAST 40 ST

NURSES - RN
STAFF & PER DIEM

3 to 11:30 PM & 11:15 PM to 7:15 AM—To work in a new modern hospital in Flushing. Excellent salary, fringe benefits & working conditions. Differential salary for specialty areas in O.R., Delivery Room & for Eves & Nites.

Contact Miss D. Stuart
DIRECTOR OF NURSING
Hillcrest General Hospital—AX 1-1000
NURSES

Help Wanted—Male

MEN-MEN

NO EXP
MANY MEN NEEDED
NITES 6PM-2AM
21 YEARS & UP
Bring draft card 1A-5A. Students OK or service record DD214.
ALPINE AGENCY
115-17 W. 42, Rm 206, LO 4-2600

MEN TRAIN ELEV OPERS $95
Steady work record. Will train.
Smith's Fifth Ave Agency, 489 5th Ave.

Mdse. Trainees $5500
College grads w-wo exp. Investigate these non-selling office career Jobs in Management & Administrative.
FEE PAID OR NEGOTIABLE
Jamaica Agency, 89-31 161 St, JA 6-0258

APRIL 1, 1962.

Help Wanted—Male

CLERKS
CLERKS
CLERKS
CLERKS

WE HAVE TOP NOTCH MANAGEMENT TRAINEES SPOTS FOR BEGINNER CLERKS. NO EXP NEC. MUST HAVE AT LEAST 2 YRS OF HIGH SCHOOL. MANY HAVE FREE LUNCH AND BONUS. $60 TO $90. START YOUR CAREER NOW.

CO PAYS FEE
A & C AGENCIES (2)
198 BWAY   41 E 41 ST

CLERK'S
BROKERAGE
TRAINEES $80-100
COMPANY PAYS FEE
WITH/WITHOUT EXP, BONUS + LCH
Park Agency, 160 Bway

COLLEGE STUDENT
TO ASSIST DEPARTMENT HEAD
FACILITY FOR FIGURES & DETAIL
JANE COLBY, INC
113-4TH AV-COR. 12   2ND FLOOR

Help Wanted—Male-Female

COLL GRAD   ANY MAJOR

CUSTOMER
RELATIONS

FEE PAID $7500-9500
Our client offers a solid future with good growth in a formal customer relations training program. You will be given the opportunity to prove your ability to grow in management. Good grades, draft deferred or vet preferred.

SEE JIM COLT

MICHAELS
2 W 45 St (at 5th Ave)   (agency)

Gal/Man Fri-Mdtwn to $120
FEE PAID
PERSONNEL
Not the usual trainee position which often means doing the tedious work the higher ups hate. This wonderful director of Personnel will involve you in every facet of this fascinating field. You will receive the training here that will enable you to make a career of Personnel. You will have much freedom & oppty to do creative thinking on your own. I worked for this delightful man myself & never had a better boss. Average typing suffices. A spirit of adventure, enthusiasm & intelligence essential.
BY APPOINTMENT ONLY
CALL DI 4-1730
Lorna Saunders
76 BEAVER ST.   (agency)   Suite 1800

GAL/MAN FRIDAY
$100 to $130
Do you like a take charge desk with diversified duties and have good typing skills and light steno? Come join our Park Ave service co. Excel benefits. Call us at 889-6353 Ext. 40.

GAL/MAN-FRIDAY, English trained preferred for world's largest int'l firm in its field. Glamorous-congenial surroundings in prestige Fifth Ave. gallery. Exciting oppty for intelligent & creative person. Possible oppty to travel. Interviews. 9:30 to 10:30 A.M. and 5:30 to 6:30 P.M. only. 2nd floor. Harmer Rooke Bldg. 604 Fifth Ave., NYC

In 1969 Supreme Court justices ruled that segregated want ads led to discriminatory hiring practices. The ads pictured here date from 1962 to 1969.
(New York Times)

chapter of NOW filed a complaint with the commission against the *Pittsburgh Press* over the want ads issue.

The headings used by the *Pittsburgh Press* at that time were "Male Help Wanted" and "Female Help Wanted"; these headings were changed to "Jobs— Male Interest" and "Jobs—Female Interest." The placement of the ads in such columns, however, would result from the preference of the advertiser, sometimes elicited by the paper.

Wilma Scott Heide, former president of NOW, speaks at a press conference in New York one month before the Women's March for Equality in August 1972. (Bettye-Lane Studio)

In 1970, the Human Relations Commission issued a statement declaring that employers had violated the anti-discrimination law by using sex-segregated columns for their help-wanted ads, and that the *Pittsburgh Press* had participated in the process by allowing the columns to appear in the first place. The commission ordered the paper to abandon its practice of publishing separate male and female columns.

The *Press* refused and so the case then began its progress through the courts. Ultimately it reached the Supreme Court, where justices debated whether the law interfered with constitutionally protected liberties.

A Fine Line

The Court emphasized its respect for the freedom of speech and for the freedom of the press. Because of the high status to be accorded these liberties, only the narrowest exceptions may be made in cases that pertain to them.

The defenders of the law carefully adhered to that line. Their argument flowed from the identification of the speech in question as commercial speech and on the doctrine that commercial speech lacks First Amendment protection.

In reviewing the *Pittsburgh Press* case, Justice Lewis F. Powell, Jr., repeatedly made reference to *Valentine v. Chrestensen* (1942), which gave birth to the differentiation between commercial and non-commercial speech for the purposes of constitutional protection. In comparing the *Pittsburgh* case to *Chrestensen*, in which the Court upheld a ban on the hand distribution of submarine tour ads, he emphasized that the key feature of the ad in *Chrestensen* was that it simply suggested a commercial transaction.

Powell observed that simply because newspapers seek to make profit does not make all aspects of newspaper publishing commercial. Advertisements that are political in nature are protected, for example. Of the want ads in question, however, "none expresses a position on whether, as a matter of social policy, certain positions ought to be filled by members of one or the other sex, nor does any of them criticize the ordinance or the commission's enforcement practices. . . . The advertisements are thus classic examples of commercial speech."

Powell noted that while the ordinance does influence the make-up of part of the paper to a degree, it does not damage the press as an institution. There was no reason to believe that the ordinance was passed to prevent the press from presenting ideas. Furthermore, the *Pittsburgh Press* itself did not maintain that its financial well-being or publishing and distribution powers were affected by the ordinance.

The newspaper did argue that editorial judgment—used to decide where the ad was to go—was an exercise of free speech and therefore protected. Powell pointed out that the paper did what the employer wished so far as which heading was being used. If the content of the ad were the issue, it would be protected only if the subject matter was protected.

The Ads and the Headings Are the Same

In fact, since the employers whose ads appeared in sex-segregated columns clearly seemed to be more inclined to discriminate against job-seekers of one sex or the other, it was obvious that the headings themselves were discriminatory. The headings and ads were not sufficiently dissociated from each other to justify separate treatment as far as First Amendment issues were concerned. An ad appearing in a sex-segregated column indicates the same willingness to discriminate as one which openly states its intention to do so.

Powell declared irrelevant the *Press'* alternative argument that, even if an ad and its placement were commercial, commercial speech required greater protection than it was currently given. He found the use of these columns by employers and the publishing of them by newspapers was illegal because sex-segregated columns did in fact assist employers to express unlawful gender preferences. He equated sex discrimination with other illegal activities such as the sale of drugs or the solicitation of prostitutes, and underscored the unquestioned ability of government to forbid advertising of those activities or column headings proposing them.

To the argument that the law was improper because it constituted a prior restraint on expression, which is illegal, Powell responded that the prohibition against prior restraint was intended to prevent systematic censorship, and to prevent material from being rejected for publication before it can be determined whether or not it is constitutionally protected. Clearly in this case the ordinance was narrow in focus and was issued with the understanding of the type of material to be excluded from publication, because the publication of the columns was a regularly repeating practice.

On the Other Hand . . .

Justices Warren E. Burger, William O. Douglas, Potter Stewart, and Harry A. Blackmun wrote dissenting opinions. Burger objected to what he called "a disturbing enlargement of the 'commercial speech' doctrine and a violation of the First Amendment.''

Douglas denounced the exemption of commercial speech from constitutional protection itself. He reminded the Court of the Jeffersonian doctrine that the government may interfere with free speech only when speech was linked to action.

Stewart—and for the most part, Blackmun—saw the issue primarily as freedom of the press. Describing the *Pittsburgh* decision as a perhaps unprecedented sanctioning of governmental intrusion in newspaper composition and layout, Stewart warned that in the future the government may, with noble motives, seek more extensive control of newspapers.

Victory for NOW

NOW had fought a nine-year battle to abolish "male" and "female" want ads in newspapers. They faced entrenched opposition: newspaper chiefs argued they would lose readers if they integrated their want ads; some men claimed that they would be forced to work for female supervisors; others warned of unisex bathrooms and other terrible consequences. However, once the papers integrated their "male" and "female" columns, the only dire result that came to pass was the lessening of overwhelming male dominance in the American workplace.

For Further Reading

Crites, Laura L., and Winifred L. Hepperle, eds. *Women, The Courts and Equality.* New York: Russell Sage, 1987.

Davis, Flora. *Moving the Mountain: The Women's Movement in America Since 1960.* New York: Simon & Schuster, 1991.

Goldstein, Leslie Friedman. *The Constitutional Rights of Women: Cases in Law and Social Change.* Madison: University of Wisconsin Press, 1988.

Cleveland Board of Education v. LaFleur: 1974

Appellants: Cleveland Board of Education and Chesterfield County School Board **Appellees:** Jo Carol LaFleur, Ann Elizabeth Nelson, and Susan Cohen
Appellant's Claim: That it is constitutional for states or boards of education to force pregnant women to take arbitrary maternity leave on the assumption that they are incapable of working in their physical condition
Chief Lawyers for Appellees: Philip J. Hirschkop and Jane M. Picker
Chief Lawyers for Appellants: Charles F. Clarke and Samuel W. Hixon, III
Justices: Harry A. Blackmun, William J. Brennan, William O. Douglas, Thurgood Marshall, Lewis Powell, *Potter Stewart,* Byron R. White (majority); Chief Justice Warren Burger, and William Rehnquist (dissent)
Place: Washington, D.C. **Date of Decision:** January 21, 1974
Decision: Forcing pregnant teachers to take unpaid maternity leave violates the due process clause of the Constitution's Fourteenth Amendment

SIGNIFICANCE
This decision ended a period of public policy-making in which it was common-place for state and local laws to discriminate against pregnant women because of "presumptions" about women's inability to work.

The year 1971 marked a turning point in women's struggle for legal equality. That year, in *Reed v. Reed* (see page 112), the Supreme Court for the first time overruled a statute because it discriminated against women. After *Reed*, the Supreme Court took challenges to state laws that discriminated against women more seriously. They examined most, but not all, such cases in light of the equal protection clause of the Fourteenth Amendment. *Cleveland v. LaFleur* ended a policy that arbitrarily forced women to leave their jobs without pay when they became pregnant.

Jo Carol LaFleur and Ann Elizabeth Nelson taught junior high in the Cleveland, Ohio, public schools. Both became pregnant during the 1970–71 school year, but as they were not due to have their babies until summer (July and August respectively), they wanted to continue teaching until the end of the term. However, the schools refused, forcing them to take unpaid maternity leave in March, during the middle of the term, and to stay out of the classroom until the babies were at least three months old.

Since 1952, the Cleveland Board of Education had required a pregnant teacher to take maternity leave at the end of the fourth month—if she had more than one year seniority. If she had less, she was simply fired. Teachers had to apply for this leave no later than two weeks before the fifth month began. Once on leave, a teacher could not return to work until the beginning of the next regular school semester following her child's three-month birthday. At that point, a doctor had to attest to the teacher's health before she could return to work, and sometimes provide a physical exam. If a teacher did not follow these rules, she could be fired. If she did, she was still not guaranteed her job back.

Denied their jobs and salaries, LaFleur and Nelson filed separate suits in the U.S. District Court for the Northern District of Ohio, challenging the constitutionality of the maternity leave rule. They lost, but won in the U.S. Court of Appeals for the Sixth Circuit. The state appealed to the Supreme Court.

Another County Heard From

Meanwhile, Virginia teacher Susan Cohen was suffering similar treatment under the School Board in Chesterfield County. The rules of that school board were almost the same as Cleveland's so far as taking maternity leave was concerned. However, re-employment was not arbitrary—there was no three-month return rule. A teacher had only to submit a letter from her doctor stating that she was physically fit to teach and assure the board that caring for her child would not interfere with her job.

Cohen told the board in November of 1970, that she was pregnant and expected to give birth about April 1, 1971. She asked that she be able to continue to teach until then. The board rejected her request, forcing her to leave on December 18, 1970, in mid-semester.

An angry Cohen filed suit in the U.S. District Court for the Eastern District of Virginia. The Court ruled that the school board rules violated the equal protection clause of the Fourteenth Amendment. However, in 1973, a divided panel of the Fourth Circuit reversed this decision.

Off to Washington

Therefore, at the same time the Ohio school boards were preparing to appeal their defeat to the Supreme Court, Cohen was also getting ready to challenge the Chesterfield board to the high court in Washington, D.C. In 1973, the Ohio and Virginia cases merged into one case before the Supreme Court.

LaFleur and Nelson's lawyer, Jane M. Picker, told a quiet courtroom that to require a woman to stop teaching because she is pregnant or a new mother was discrimination. Citing *Frontiero v. Richardson* (see page 308), Picker pointed out that the Court should view the maternity leaves as suspect behavior and subjected to strict judicial scrutiny.

Philip J. Hirschkop—Cohen's lawyer—recalled *Reed v. Reed* in arguing that sex-based classifications should be recognized as inherently invidious. The maternity policies clearly curtailed civil rights of one group, he said, and that group was women.

On behalf of the school boards, Charles F. Clarke (Ohio) and Samuel W. Hixon (Virginia) argued that pregnant teachers were physically incapable of performing their jobs properly. Privately Hirschkop admitted that board members had remarked that pregnant women, because of their ungainly size, were fire hazards, blocking the exit of hundreds of children.

Clarke and Hixon claimed that by requiring unpaid maternity leave, the boards were protecting the health of the teacher and her unborn child, as well as assuring students that they had a capable instructor.

In fact, Dr. Mark C. Schinnerer, superintendent of Cleveland's schools, testified in the District court that the schools had adopted the rules in part to save pregnant women from embarrassment in front of giggling students; they had set the cutoff date at the end of the fourth month because this was when the teacher "began to show." One member thought students should not see a pregnant woman "because some of the kids say, my teacher swallowed a watermelon."

Just leaving the U.S. Supreme Court, Jo Carol LaFleur stops to speak with Sidney Picker, the husband of her attorney, Jane M. Picker. (Attorney Jane M. Picker)

Nevertheless, Clarke and Hixon insisted that the schools' motive for forcing teachers to give up their jobs was to maintain "continuity of instruction" for the students. In addition—in an amazing *non sequitur*—Hixon disputed the charge that the maternity rules discriminated against women, insisting that since "only a woman may become pregnant . . . a classification based on pregnancy is not a classification based on sex because it in no way affects males."

Welcome to the Twentieth Century

Justice Potter Stewart—never known for being liberal in his views—wrote the opinion of the Court. He agreed that advanced notice of maternity leave was reasonable for school planning, but pointed out that arbitrary leave dates disrupted education as often as they contributed to its stability. For example, LaFleur and Nelson would have successfully completed the school terms if the Cleveland board had not forced them out in mid-March—deflating the board's claim of preserving continuity in the classroom.

Even granting that the advanced notice of maternity leave was necessary for planning, the solution of forcing teachers out was not. As Stewart wrote, "Neither the necessity for continuity of instruction nor the state interest [in] keeping physically unfit teachers out of the classroom"—the rationales cited by the boards—"can justify the sweeping mandatory leave regulations that the Cleveland and Chesterfield schools boards have adopted."

The Court also questioned the boards' candor in defending maternity leaves, commenting that "whatever may have been the reaction in Queen Victoria's time, pregnancy is no longer a dirty word."

The justices agreed with medical experts who testified that the stage at which a woman becomes physically incapable of doing her job can only be determined on an individual basis. Pin-pointing freedom of personal choice in matters of marriage and family as one of the liberties protected by the due process clause of the Fourteenth Amendment, the justices ruled that the Cleveland requirement that teachers wait three months after giving birth before returning to work was unconstitutional. The rule penalized a pregnant woman for deciding to have a child.

The Supreme Court affirmed the judgment in the LaFleur/Nelson case by seven to two and reversed the decision in the Cohen case. It declined to rest its decision on equal protection grounds, but based its opinion on the Fourteenth Amendment's due process clause.

Just six years after *Cleveland Board of Education v. LaFleur*, nearly one-half of American women holding white-collar jobs worked until their last month of pregnancy. The Court's decision had officially ended a period of discrimination against pregnant women based on stereotypes about their ability to work.

For Further Reading

Hoff, Joan. *Law, Gender, and Injustice: A Legal History of U.S. Women.* New York: New York University Press, 1991.

Mezey, Susan Gluck. *In Pursuit of Equality: Women, Public Policy, and the Federal Courts.* New York: St. Martin's Press, 1992.

Otter, Laura A. *Women's Rights and the Law.* Westport, Conn.: Praeger, 1993.

Tribe, Lawrence H. *American Constitutional Law*, 2d ed. Mineola, N.Y.: The Foundation Press, 1988.

Corning Glass Works v. Brennan: 1974

Petitioner: Corning Glass Works **Respondent:** Peter J. Brennan, U.S. secretary of labor **Petitioner's Claim:** That paying male night inspectors higher base wages than female day inspectors did not abridge the Equal Pay Act **Chief Lawyer for Respondent:** Allan Abbot Tuttle
Chief Lawyer for Petitioner: Scott F. Zimmerman **Justices:** William J. Brennan, William O. Douglas, *Thurgood Marshall,* Lewis F. Powell, Jr., and Byron R. White (majority); Harry A. Blackmun, Chief Justice Warren E. Burger, and William H. Rehnquist (dissent); Potter Stewart did not take part in the case **Place:** Washington, D.C. **Date of Decision:** June 3, 1974
Decision: The wage difference between Corning's female day and male night inspectors violated the Equal Pay Act

SIGNIFICANCE
This was the first Equal Pay Act violation charge that the Supreme Court ever considered.

Before 1925, the Corning Glass Works operated only day shifts. Women workers did all of the quality inspection work, earning between twenty and thirty cents an hour. When the company introduced automatic production techniques in 1925, the volume of Corning products increased, creating the need for a night-time inspection staff. Both New York and Pennsylvania had protective labor laws banning the employment of women between 10:00 P.M. and 6:00 A.M. (New York's law was passed in 1927 and Pennsylvania's in 1913.) Corning therefore turned to its male day workers to fill the night-time inspection shift.

Most of the men worked in the glass blowing room, earning at least forty-eight cents an hour. They objected to the inspection positions as "women's work" and "demeaning." They also refused to work for women's wages. To fill the night-time inspection positions, Corning agreed to pay fifty-three cents an hour to the men. No other group of Corning night-shift employees received this amount.

Corning's workers joined a union in 1944. A collective bargaining agreement resulted in an across-the-board pay increase to all of Corning's night-time production and maintenance workers for the very first time. Although the all-male night inspection staff *already* received a higher wage than their female day-shift counterparts, the new night-shift increase further added to their wages.

Women Join the Night Shift

The New York and Pennsylvania laws forbidding women's night-time employment disappeared between 1947—when Pennsylvania permitted women to work on the night shift *if* the employers provided transportation home—and 1969 when both states removed all special restrictions on women's night-time employment. At the same time, Congress passed another law affecting women's employment: the federal Equal Pay Act of 1963 requiring equal pay for equal work.

Against this complicated background, in June 1966, Corning began to open its night-shift work to women. Seniority lists for men and women, which the company had previously segregated, were now combined. Women could compete for night inspection work on the same basis as men, and when they worked in these positions, they received the same high wages previously earned by men.

Then, three years after the passage of the Equal Pay Act, another bargaining agreement introduced a new policy. Corning would pay all inspectors hired after January 20, 1969, the same base wage, regardless of sex or shift. That is, new night-shift inspectors would still receive the same extra pay as the rest of the company's night-time employees, but they would no longer receive the additional wages originally intended to lure men into "women's positions." However, Corning made an exception for night inspectors hired *before* the contract's effective date. Now called "red circle" employees, they were permitted to keep their traditionally higher wages.

Two States, Two Opinions

U.S. Secretary of Labor Peter J. Brennan sued the two Corning Glass plants, charging violation of the Equal Pay Act and seeking back wages for the female day inspectors. The district court that tried the case involving the Pennsylvania plant found that the Equal Pay Act had not been violated. The Court of Appeals for the Third Circuit agreed.

In New York, the decision went the other way. Both the district court and the appeals court found that the act *had* been violated. The disappointed party in each state appealed to the Supreme Court, which heard the cases together.

Justice Thurgood Marshall read the Court's opinion, saying the tangled case history presented three central questions: "Did Corning ever violate the Equal Pay Act by paying male night shift inspectors more than female day shift inspectors?" "If so, did Corning cure its violation of the Act in 1966 by permitting women to work as night shift inspectors?" And, "Finally, if the violation was not remedied in 1966, did Corning cure its violation in 1969 by equalizing day and night inspector wage rates but establishing higher 'red circle' rates for existing employees working on the night shift?"

Turning to the first question, the Court examined the Equal Pay Act requiring employers to pay men and women equal wages "for equal work on jobs . . . which requires equal skill, effort and responsibility . . . performed under similar working conditions." The act permitted exceptions if companies made payments to male and female employees under "a seniority system," "a merit system," "a system which measures earnings by quantity or quality of production," or "a differential based on any other factor other than sex."

Corning had argued that its higher night-shift wages were necessary because employees did not perform day and night work under similar conditions. The Court rejected this argument. It pointed out that, as Corning had testified at the Congressional hearings during the debate of the Equal Pay Act, the working conditions—"surroundings" and "hazards"—were the same. The night inspection work "at issue in this case," Marshall said, "whether performed during the day or night, is 'equal work' as that term is defined in the Act."

Marshall said that even though night work did not entitle a worker to higher pay under the Equal Pay Act's "working condition" guidelines, night-shift workers *could* be paid higher wages than day workers under the act's catchall exception for pay differentials "based on any other factor other than sex"—provided that no discrimination was involved. In Corning's case, however, the Court ruled that the company had not made the payments "to serve as compensation for night work."

Quoting the district court's opinion in Corning's New York state plant, Marshall stressed that "the higher night rate was in large part the product of the generally higher wage level of male workers and the need to compensate them for performing what were regarded as demeaning tasks."

As Marshall pointed out, the higher rate began when Corning paid no other night-time workers more than the corresponding day workers, and continued long after Corning paid *everyone* more for working at night. The men were paid more because they would not work at the low wages paid women and, in that job market—and in the existing cultural attitude that "women's work" was by definition not worth as much as men's work—Corning could get away with it. Taking advantage of the situation certainly made economic sense, but it was *illegal* "once Congress enacted into law the principle of equal pay for equal work."

Still Taking Advantage

The Court next considered whether Corning had breached the 1963 act after it opened night work to women in 1966—but still paid the day-time female inspectors less. Marshall wrote that the question was not whether men and women were treated equally after 1966 but whether "the company remedied the specific violation of the act which the Secretary [of Labor] proved." The act specifically provided that male and female wages had to be equalized *without* lowering the pay of any employee.

Marshall quoted from the *Congressional Record* and the *House Hearings* to illustrate that virtually all of the legislators involved in the passage of the 1963 act had taken the view that "the only way a violation could be remedied under the bill . . . is for the lower wages to be raised to the higher." Corning clearly had not done so. He quoted the district court's opinion of Corning's violation:

> In light of this apparent congressional understanding, we cannot hold that Corning, by allowing some—or even many—women to move in to the higher paid night jobs, achieved full compliance with the act. Corning's action still left the inspectors on the day shift—virtually all women—earning a lower base wage than the night shift inspectors because of . . . sex. . . . Corning was still taking advantage of the availability of female labor . . . at a deferentially low wage rate not justified by any other factor other than sex.

As for the company's claim that it was in compliance by the effective date of its most recent collective bargaining agreement, Marshall wrote that this "contention . . . need not detain us long." Had the company properly cured its violation prior to that agreement, Marshall noted, Corning's senior day-time inspectors would have qualified for the same "red circle" base wage awarded to the senior night inspectors.

The Next Frontier?

The Equal Pay Act and the Supreme Court's decision in this case addressed the outright discrimination of paying women less than men for the *same* work. A more subtle problem remains unaddressed: Almost half of all wage-earning women work in occupations where eighty percent or more of the employees are women and generally, as the National Committee on Pay Equity reports, "the more women in an occupation, the lower the pay." Should gender-based occupational discrimination be prohibited by a "pay equity act," similar to one passed by Canada's Ontario legislature in 1987? In the 1990s, women and men with similar education and experience received the same pay. However, females who work part-time, or take time off to raise their children, or work in the service industry receive lower pay than women and men who do not. For many, a less rigorous work schedule is worth less pay; for others it is not. The answer will most likely come from individual choices, not group legislation.

For Further Reading

Goldstein, Leslie Friedman. *The Constitutional Rights of Women: Cases in Law and Social Change*, rev. ed. Madison: University of Wisconsin Press, 1989.

Kessler-Haris, Alice. *Out to Work: A History of Wage-Earning Women in the United States*. New York: Oxford University Press, 1982.

Ross, Susan Deller, Isabelle Katz Pinsler, Deborah A. Ellis, and Kary L. Moss. *The Rights of Women: The Basic ACLU Guide to Women's Rights*, 3d ed. Carbondale: Southern Illinois University Press, 1993.

Wertheimer, Barbara Mayer. *We Were There: The Story of Working Women in America*. New York: Pantheon Books, 1977.

Geduldig v. Aiello: 1974

Appellant: Dwight Geduldig, director of the California Department of Human Resources Development   **Appellees:** Carolyn Aiello, Augustina Armendariz, Elizabeth Johnson, and Jacqueline Jaramillo   **Appellant's Claim:** That the district court erred when it ruled that California was required to pay disability benefits to private employees temporarily disabled by their pregnancies
Chief Lawyer for Appellees: Wendy W. Williams
Chief Lawyer for Appellant: Joanne Condas   **Justices:** William J. Brennan, Jr., Chief Justice Warren E. Burger, William H. Rehnquist, *Potter Stewart,* and Byron R. White (majority); Harry A. Blackmun, William O. Douglas, and Thurgood Marshall (dissent)   **Place:** Washington, D.C.
Date of Decision: June 17, 1974

SIGNIFICANCE

This decision, excluding absences due to "normal pregnancy" from medical disability coverage, left women *without* pregnancy problems in an intolerable financial bind. In 1978, Congress finally passed the Pregnancy Discrimination Act, forcing employers to treat a maternity-related absence like any other medical absence.

In the 1940s, California created an Unemployment Compensation Disability Fund to provide benefits to workers temporarily disabled by injuries or illnesses not covered by workers' compensation. California employees contributed one percent of their salaries to the fund, up to an annual maximum of eighty-five dollars. In the 1970s, four women who had contributed the required percentages of their salaries to the fund, sued when they found that the fund excluded pregnancy-related disabilities from coverage.

Four Women, Different Pregnancies

Three of the women had a wide range of pregnancy-related disabilities: Carolyn Aiello suffered an ectopic pregnancy that required surgical termination; Elizabeth Johnson experienced a tubal pregnancy, also necessitating surgical termination; and Augustina Armendariz miscarried. Jacqueline Jaramillo, however, had a normal pregnancy and delivery. All were excluded according to Section 2626 of the Unemployment Insurance Code, which read:

> "Disability" or "disabled" includes both mental or physical illness and mental or physical injury. An individual shall be deemed disabled in any day in which, because of his [or her] physical or mental condition, he [she] is unable to perform his [her] regular or customary work. *In no case shall the term "disability" or "disabled" include any injury or illness caused by or arising in connection with pregnancy up to the termination of such pregnancy and for a period of 28 days thereafter* [emphasis added].

A three-judge panel of the federal district court ruled that the fund's pregnancy exclusion violated the Fourteenth Amendment of the U.S. Constitution. Dwight Geduldig, the director of California's Department of Human Resources Development, appealed to the U.S. Supreme Court, which agreed to hear the case.

Another Court Heard From

Ten days before the district court ruled in *Geduldig*, the California Court of Appeals ruled in a case brought by another woman who had been denied benefits following an ectopic pregnancy. The court of appeals ruled in this case, *Rentzer v. Unemployment Insurance Appeals Board* (1973), that Section 2626 did not prohibit women from receiving benefits if they suffered medical complications of their pregnancies. The regulations were subsequently rewritten to exclude only "maternity benefits" for normal pregnancies and deliveries, and so Aiello, Armendariz, and Johnson—who had suffered ectopic and tubal pregnancies and a miscarriage, respectively—had their claims approved.

Jaramillo, whose disability claim was denied following a normal pregnancy and delivery, did not benefit from the amendment of the fund's requirements. The new regulations, contained in Section 2626.2, provided that:

> Benefits relating to pregnancy shall be paid under this part only in accordance with the following:
>
> (a) Disability benefits shall be paid upon a doctor's certification that the claimant is disabled because of an abnormal and involuntary complication of pregnancy, including but not limited to: puerperal infection, eclampsia, caesarian section delivery, ectopic pregnancy, and toxemia.
>
> (b) Disability benefits shall be paid upon a doctor's certification that a condition possibly arising out of pregnancy would disable the claimant without regard to the pregnancy, including but not limited to: anemia, diabetes, embolism, heart disease, hypertension, phlebitis, phlebothrombosis, pyelonephritis, thrombophlebitis, vaginitis, varicose veins, and venous thrombosis.

On March 26, 1974, the attorneys for Geduldig and Jaramillo presented oral arguments before the Supreme Court. Jaramillo's advocate attorney, Wendy W. Williams, remarked that the continued exclusion of pregnancy-related disability claims arising from normal pregnancy and delivery violated the Fourteenth Amendment. Geduldig's attorney, Joanne Condas, insisted that the exclusion served the important governmental objectives of making the insurance program both self-supporting and affordable to all of the state's employees.

Is Normal Pregnancy a Disability?

In his June 17, 1974, opinion for the majority of the Court, Justice Potter Stewart wrote that the Court had evaluated a number of "variables," including "the benefit level deemed appropriate to compensate employee disability, the risks selected to be insured . . . and the contribution rate chosen to maintain the solvency of the program and at the same time to permit low-income employees to participate. . . ." Stewart said the Court found that the "essential issue in this case is whether the Equal Protection Clause requires such policies to be sacrificed or compromised in order to finance the payment of benefits to those whose disability is attributable to normal pregnancy and delivery."

The Court found that California, in designing its program, had addressed its legitimate governmental interests without engaging in "invidious discrimination under the Equal Protection Clause." Noting that "there is nothing in the Constitution . . . that requires the State to subordinate or compromise its legitimate interests solely to create a more comprehensive social program than it already has," Stewart wrote that the plan included "no risk from which men are protected and women are not. Likewise, there is no risk from which women are protected and men are not." The Court reversed the judgment of the District Court, and permitted California to retain the exclusion for disability claims arising from normal pregnancy and delivery.

Creating a Double Standard

Justice Harry A. Blackmun wrote a spirited dissent, joined by Justices William O. Douglas and Thurgood Marshall:

> The economic effects caused by pregnancy-related disabilities are functionally indistinguishable from the effects caused by any other disability: wages are lost due to a physical inability to work, and medical expenses are incurred for the delivery of the child and for postpartum care. In my view, by singling out for less favorable treatment a gender-linked disability peculiar to women, the State has created a double standard for disability compensation: a limitation is imposed upon the disabilities for which women workers may recover, while men receive full compensation for all disabilities suffered, including those that affect only or primarily their sex, such as prostatectomies, circumcision, hemophilia, and gout.

Congress to the Rescue

In 1976, the female employees of General Electric sued, claiming that the pregnancy exclusions contained in their company's insurance plan violated Title VII of the Civil Rights Act of 1964. Relying on its decision in *Geduldig*, the Supreme Court ruled that private employers did not violate federal law when they chose to deny medical disability payments to workers with maternity-related absences.

In 1978, Congress amended Title VII to include the Pregnancy Discrimination Act. The act specifically provided that "women affected by pregnancy, childbirth, or related medical conditions shall be treated the same for all employment-related purposes, including the receipt of benefits . . . as other persons not so affected but similar in their ability or inability to work. . . ."

For Further Reading

Goldstein, Leslie Friedman. *The Constitutional Rights of Women: Cases in Law and Social Change*, rev. ed. Madison: University of Wisconsin Press, 1989.

Hoff, Joan. *Law, Gender and Injustice: A Legal History of U.S. Women*. New York: New York University Press, 1991.

Ross, Susan Deller, et al. *The Rights of Women: The Basic ACLU Guide to Women's Rights*. Carbondale: Southern Illinois University Press, 1993.

Dothard v. Rawlinson: 1977

Appellant: E. C. Dothard, director of the Department of Public Safety of Alabama   **Appellee:** Dianne Rawlinson   **Appellant's Claim:** That Alabama's height and weight standards for prison guards were job related and necessary *bona fide occupational qualifications (bfoqs)*

Chief Lawyer for Appellant: G. Daniel Evans

Chief Lawyer for Appellee: Pamela S. Horowitz   **Justices:** Harry A. Blackmun, William J. Brennan, Chief Justice Warren E. Burger, Thurgood Marshall, Lewis R. Powell, Jr., William H. Rehnquist, John Paul Stevens, *Potter Stewart,* and Byron R. White   **Place:** Washington, D.C.

Date of Decision: June 27, 1977   **Decision:** Title VII of the Civil Rights Act does not prohibit sex discrimination entirely, because it does permit a narrow category of exemptions where sex is a *bona fide occupational qualification (bfoq)* for a job. This means that employers can discriminate when the need to have a worker of a particular sex can be justified. The Court decided Alabama's height and weight standards were not *bfoq*s for prison guard employment. However, the exclusion of women from prison ''contact'' positions in male penitentiaries was, for security and safety reasons.

SIGNIFICANCE

This decision established that the strength necessary to perform a particular job cannot be assumed on the basis of a particular height or weight and that such requirements are not *bfoq*s permitted under Title VII of the 1964 Civil Rights Act. However, employers could exclude women from certain positions, if their presence might endanger the safety of others.

U pon her graduation from college with a major in correctional psychology, twenty-two-year-old Dianne Rawlinson applied for a position as prison guard trainee (or "correctional counselor" as the guards were called) with the Alabama Board of Corrections. At 115 pounds and five-foot-two inches tall, she lost the job because she did not meet the state's minimum physical weight standards of 120 pounds. (Alabama also had maximum weight standard of 300 pounds.)

Disappointed and angry, Rawlinson filed a Title VII sex-discrimination complaint with the Equal Employment Opportunity Commission (EEOC). Title VII of the 1964 Civil Rights Act, known as the Equal Employment Opportunity section, forbids discrimination by private employers, employment agencies, and unions on the basis of race, color, religion, national origin, or sex. Rawlinson won a right-to-sue letter. She then brought suit against Alabama in the district court on her own behalf and on behalf of all other similarly-situated women.

However, before Rawlinson's case could be tried, the Alabama Board of Corrections passed Administrative Regulation 204, barring women's employment in "contact" positions in all-male maximum security facilities. Rawlinson responded by amending her class-action suit to challenge Regulation 204 as well. The district court ruled in Rawlinson's favor on both counts, and Alabama appealed to the Supreme Court.

Limited Opportunities

There was no dispute about the living conditions of inmates at Alabama's maximum-security prisons. As Justice Potter Stewart would summarize in the Supreme Court's opinion:

> Their intimate living quarters are for the most part large dormitories, with communal showers and toilets that are open to the dormitories and hallways. [Two of the male maximum security] penitentiaries carry on extensive farming operations, making necessary a large number of strip searches for contraband when prisoners re-enter the prison buildings.

As for the working conditions of female prison guards, of the 435 people employed as correctional counselors by Alabama, fifty-six were female. Following the passage of Regulation 204, these female employees continued to work in "contact positions" with male prisoners in *non*-maximum security prisons, inspecting shower and toilet areas.

However, women's job opportunities, said Rawlinson's attorney, Pamela S. Horowitz, were illegally limited in two ways: First, by arbitrary height and weight restrictions, which eliminated 41.13 percent of the female population but only 1 percent of the male population from consideration; and second, by the new regulations, which classified 336 male-maximum security positions (or slightly more than 75 percent of the system's total correction counselor positions) as open only to men.

On the Face of It . . .

The Supreme Court had already heard two cases involving apparently neutral job qualifications which, in fact, "disproportionately excluded Negroes from employment." Stewart stated that "those cases guide our approach here." Quoting from one of the cases, *Griggs v. Duke Power Co.* (1975), Stewart stressed that the Court interpreted Title VII as requiring "the removal of artificial, arbitrary, and unnecessary barriers to employment when the barriers operate invidiously to discriminate on the basis of racial or other impermissible classification." Before the Court would strike down such a barrier, however, it had to address several points.

Rawlinson first had to prove that a *prima facie* case of discrimination, that is, a case of discrimination not requiring any further proof or support, existed. To do this, she needed only to prove that the "facially neutral standards in question select applicants for hire in a significantly discriminatory pattern." Alabama argued that if Rawlinson had presented a statistical study of actual female applicants who had been rejected because of the height and weight standards, no discriminatory pattern would have been found.

The Court rejected this argument. As Stewart wryly noted, "A potential applicant could easily determine her height and weight and conclude that to make an application would be futile." So the Court instead relied on Rawlinson's general population survey, which showed that despite the state's high number of females, few would currently qualify as guards. The Court agreed that the height and weight requirements created a sufficiently discriminatory effect on women applicants to establish a *prima facie* case of sex discrimination.

However, Alabama still could try to show that the job requirements, though discriminatory in impact, were job related. Alabama claimed that height and weight were related to strength and that strength was "essential to effective job performance as a correctional counselor." However, they failed to produce "evidence correlating the height and weight requirements with the requisite amount of strength thought essential. . . ."

Stewart noted that if strength were truly a *bona fide* job requirement, Alabama could both satisfy Title VII and secure a suitably strong workforce by administering a non-discriminatory strength test to all applicants. However, the Court found that Alabama's arbitrary height and weight requirements violated Title VII. They were, therefore, void.

The Court Giveth with One Hand . . .

Alabama defended its barring of women from contact positions in men's maximum security prisons, arguing that the gender requirement fell within Title VII's exception for "instances where . . . sex . . . is a *bona fide* occupational qualification *(bfoq)* reasonably necessary to the normal operation of that particular business or enterprise." On this point, the Supreme Court agreed with Alabama.

Stewart described "the environment in Alabama's penitentiaries [as] a peculiarly inhospitable one for human beings of whatever sex." He also noted that a federal district court had found the conditions for inmates unconstitutional in terms of their "rampant violence" and "jungle atmosphere."

He pointed out that Alabama kept its prisons inadequately staffed and did not separate male maximum security prisoners "according to their offense or level of dangerousness." Also, "the estimated 20 percent of the male prisoners who are sex offenders are scattered throughout the penitentiaries' dormitory facilities." Stewart said the Court could not view Alabama's barring of women from such an environment as "an exercise in 'romantic paternalism,'" or an attempt to "protect" individual female employees:

> More is at stake . . . than an individual woman's decision to weigh and accept the risks of employment in a "contact" position in a maximum-security male prison.
>
> The essence of . . . [the] job is to maintain prison security. A woman's relative ability to maintain order in a male, maximum-security, unclassified penitentiary of the type Alabama now runs could be directly reduced by her womanhood. . . . There are few visible deterrents to inmate assaults on women custodians.
>
> The likelihood that inmates would assault a woman because she was a woman would pose a real threat not only to the victim of the assault but also to the basic control of the penitentiary and protection of its inmates and the other security personnel. The employee's very womanhood would thus directly undermine her capacity to provide the security that is the essence of a correctional counselor's responsibility.

The Supreme Court therefore affirmed the district court's opinion by invalidating Alabama's height and weight requirements for correction counselors, but overturned the decision insofar as it barred women from contact positions in male maximum-security prisons.

The American Civil Liberties Union handbook, *The Rights of Women*, assures its readers that the first half of the decision contains the more important precedent for women hoping to enter previously male fields of employment.

For Further Reading

Goldstein, Leslie Friedman. *The Constitutional Rights of Women: Cases in Law and Social Change*, rev. ed. Madison: The University of Wisconsin Press, 1989.

MacKinnon, Catharine A. *Feminism Unmodified: Discourses on Life and Law*. Cambridge, Mass.: Harvard University Press, 1987.

——. *Sexual Harassment of Working Women*. New Haven, Conn.: Yale University Press, 1979.

Ross, Susan Deller, Isabelle Katz Pinzler, Deborah A. Ellis, Kary L. Moss. *The Rights of Women: The Basic ACLU Guide to Women's Rights*. Carbondale: Southern Illinois University Press, 1993.

Los Angeles Department of Water and Power v. Marie Manhart: 1978

Appellants: City of Los Angeles, Department of Water and Power; members of the Board of Commissioners of the Department; and members of the plan's Board of Administrators **Appellees:** Marie Manhart and all women employed or formerly employed by the Department of Water and Power **Appellants' Claim:** That lower courts were wrong to rule that a pension plan requiring higher contributions from women than from men violated Title VII and that current and past female employees were due a refund
Chief Lawyer for Appellees: Robert M. Dohrmann
Chief Lawyer for Appellants: David J. Oliphant **Justices:** Harry A. Blackmun, Warren E. Burger, Thurgood Marshall, Lewis F. Powell, Jr., William H. Rehnquist, *John Paul Stevens, III,* Potter Stewart, and Byron R. White (William H. Brennan, Jr., did not participate) **Place:** Washington, D.C.
Date of Decision: April 25, 1978 **Decision:** Requiring females to make larger contributions to the pension fund than males was a violation of Title VII, but affected women were not entitled to a refund

SIGNIFICANCE
This decision was the first step in eliminating gender-related cash "penalties" women had been paying by virtue of their sex.

The "feminization of poverty" and, in particular, the poverty experienced by a great many elderly women, has long been a concern of women, and with good reason. As the Women's Research and Education Institute reported in its 1992–93 report, nearly twice as many women as men over the age of sixty-five entered the 1990s in poverty. There are many reasons for this disparity, starting with the lower wages historically paid to many women throughout their working lives.

One cause, however, is rarely examined—pension fund discrimination. Prior to 1978, it was legal—and customary—to withhold a larger share of women's wages for the identical retirement benefits men received. When this practice was outlawed, some companies equalized deductions, but then paid women a smaller monthly benefit than men upon retirement. Although this practice was also eventually outlawed (in *Arizona Governing Committee v. Norris*, 1983), many retired women still receive smaller pension checks than their male counterparts as a result.

Yes, But . . .

In 1973, Marie Manhart, four other women, and the International Brotherhood of Electrical Workers, Local Union No. 18, sued the Los Angeles Department of Water and Power over its discriminatory pension fund practices. The suit, brought in U.S. District Court for the Central District of California, claimed that the department infringed upon Title VII by requiring female workers to make larger pension fund contributions than male workers.

Women's take-home wages and living standards were clearly affected by the policy. One of the women had paid more than $18,000 into her pension fund, compared to the $3,000 that would have been required of an identically employed male worker over the same time period. The women and their labor union therefore wanted not only a stop to the practice, but a refund of any overpayment past and current female workers may have made.

Before the suit went to court, however, the California legislature passed a law forbidding its agencies from employing the challenged contribution scheme. The Department of Water and Power complied and, beginning January 1, 1975, operated its plan without distinctions based on sex.

Later that year, the district court ruled that Title VII had indeed been violated by the plan's original gender-based differential in pension plan contributions. The court also ordered the department to make restitution to all affected women. The U.S. Court of Appeals for the Ninth Circuit affirmed this decision in 1976, and the case was appealed to the Supreme Court.

Arguing the Odds

On January 18, 1978, the Department of Water and Power presented its case, claiming that its pre-1975 policies *were* justified. There were four specific arguments: First, the difference in take-home pay received by employed men and women who worked for the same salary but experienced disparate pension plan withholdings was not discriminatory because women, as a class, lived longer than men. Therefore, although it was true that women effectively received less compensation during their working years, they made up the difference in the end by getting more monthly pension checks than their shorter-lived male counterparts.

Second, the distinction was made for a reason "other than sex" (namely, differing longevity expectations) and was therefore not in violation of the Equal Pay Act.

Third, the department claimed that the Supreme Court's 1976 decision in *General Electric Co. v. Gilbert*—which permitted private employers to exclude pregnancy from their medical disability plans—acted as a precedent to uphold the different treatment of male and female pension plan participants.

Fourth, the department argued that the refunding of a portion of women's pension plan contributions would not be justified, even if the differing requirements were found to violate federal law.

Manhart's attorney, Robert M. Dohrmann, argued that the pre-1975 policies of the water department clearly violated Title VII, which states, "It shall be an unlawful employment practice for an employer . . . to discriminate against any individual with respect to his [her] compensation, terms, conditions, or privileges of employment, because of such individual's race, color, religion, sex, or national origin." Furthermore, he asserted, any woman who had been illegally required to contribute too large a share of her paycheck should be reimbursed for her overpayment.

An End to All That

On April 25, 1978, the Court ruled that the sex-based differential in the department's pension plan violated Title VII. However, no restitution for overpayment was required. Justice John Paul Stevens, writing for the Court, acknowledged that prior to the passage of the Civil Rights Act of 1964, employers could base personnel policies on assumptions about men and women—valid or not. Title VII was designed to put an end to all that, making it illegal to base employment decisions on "mere 'stereotyped' impressions about the characteristics of males or females."

Stevens noted that the department had not based its policy on a "fictional difference," but on "a generalization that the parties accept as unquestionably true: Women, as a class, do live longer than men." However, he said Congress' intent was to prohibit discrimination against *individuals*, not as parts of a class. While actuarial tables proved a generalization about women as a class, there was no proof that any of the females in the department who "received smaller paychecks because of their sex" would fit the generalization.

Stevens pointed out that actuarial tables "could unquestionably identify differences in life expectancy based on race or national origin, as well as sex." However, Title VII intended "to make race irrelevant in the employment market . . . [and] could not reasonably be construed to permit a take-home-pay differential based on a racial classification." The idea that differing longevity was an innate difference between the sexes rather than a result of differing behaviors among individuals was not necessarily true. For example, Stevens pointed to "the social fact that men are heavier smokers than women."

Stevens next turned to the Equal Pay Act, which required employers to pay male and female workers equal wages for equal work—with several exceptions. One of the exceptions was for a "differential based on any other factor other than sex." The department had argued that longevity was such a factor, but the Court disagreed. On this point, he quoted an earlier decision in a lower court: It is impossible to "say that an actuarial distinction based entirely on sex is 'based on any other factor other than sex.' Sex is exactly what it is based on."

The argument that the Supreme Court's 1976 decision in *General Electric v. Gilbert* set a precedent failed as well. Stevens wrote that the exclusion of pregnancy-related claims from a medical disability plan was not "discrimination based upon gender as such."

In the pregnancy cases, Stevens wrote, "the two groups of potential recipients . . . were pregnant women and nonpregnant persons. While the first group is exclusively female, the second includes members of both sexes." Since the employer in the present case divided its employees into two groups defined "entirely and exclusively" by sex, Stevens continued, "This plan discriminates on the basis of sex whereas the General Electric plan discriminated on the basis of a special physical disability."

It's a Matter of Money

Despite its finding that the pension plan had been in violation of federal law, the Court ruled that restitution of overpayment was not required. Stevens wrote that "Title VII does not require a district court to grant any retroactive relief," but that such relief " 'may' be awarded if it is 'appropriate.' " In this case, "pension administrators could reasonably have thought it unfair—or even illegal—to make male employees shoulder more than their 'actuarial share of the pension burden.' "

They also found "no reason to believe the threat of a backpay award is needed to cause other administrators to amend their practices to conform to this decision." The Court reasoned that such an award would have major financial implications not only for an individual pension plan, but for the economy as a whole insofar as a retroactive award would have ramifications for the entire pension and insurance industries.

For Further Reading

Cary, Eve, and Kathleen Willert Peratis. *Woman and the Law*. Skokie, Ill.: National Textbook Company in conjunction with the American Civil Liberties Union, 1977.

Goldstein, Leslie Friedman. *The Constitutional Rights of Women: Cases in Law and Social Change*, rev. ed. Madison: University of Wisconsin Press, 1989.

Hoff, Joan. *Law, Gender & Injustice: A Legal History of U.S. Women*. New York: New York University Press, 1991.

Ross, Susan Deller, Isabelle Katz Pinzler, Deborah A. Ellis, and Kary L. Moss. *The Rights of Women: The Basic ACLU Guide to Women's Rights*. Carbondale and Edwardsville: Southern Illinois University Press, 1993.

Personnel Administrator of Massachusetts v. Feeney: 1979

Appellants: Personnel Administrator of Massachusetts et al.
Appellee: Helen Feeney   **Appellant's Claim:** That state law granting veterans' preference in employment did not discriminate against women
Chief Lawyer for Appellee: Richard P. Ward
Chief Lawyer for Appellants: Thomas R. Kiley   **Justices:** Harry A. Blackmun, Chief Justice Warren E. Burger, Lewis F. Powell, Jr., William H. Rehnquist, John Paul Stevens, *Potter Stewart,* and Byron R. White (majority); Thurgood Marshall and William J. Brennan, Jr. (dissent)   **Place:** Washington, D.C.   **Date of Decision:** June 5, 1979   **Decision:** The U.S. Supreme Court upheld a lifetime preference for veterans—who were mostly male—in state civil service employment

SIGNIFICANCE

The decision shows how even gender-neutral laws can harm women, when the goals of the state conflict with an individual's protection under the Constitution. It also illustrates the new willingness of women during the 1970s to challenge such discriminatory laws.

Since the Civil War the federal government has given special preferences to veterans in appreciation for their valor. In 1944, Congress enacted the first Veterans Preference Act. By the 1970s, forty-one states had added extra points to the civil service scores of veterans—ten points for disabled veterans, five points for able-bodied ones.

During the Vietnam War, Massachusetts was the most pro-veteran state, mandating lifetime preferences in hiring for veterans *and* their families. Massachusetts legislators passed the law in 1889 as an attempt to assist aging Civil War veterans. They rewrote the law six years later to exempt veterans from all merit selection requirements. No other state went this far.

Best Not Good Enough

For twelve years, Dracut resident Helen Feeney worked for the state of Massachusetts. She started out in 1963 as a clerk, four years later moving up to personnel coordinator in the Massachusetts Civil Defense Agency. When legislators abolished the agency in 1975, Feeney was out of a job.

Over the years Feeney had taken civil service tests twice to upgrade her position. Each time her standing dropped as male armed service veterans with lower test scores moved ahead of her. Feeney had very impressive scores, among the highest in the state. In one instance, she received the second highest mark on the exam but was ranked sixth—after five vets; in the second, she won the third highest mark, but ranked only twelfth on the eligibility list when eleven veterans with lower scores jumped the queue.

After the Vietnam War, a large number of veterans were living in Massachusetts—over twenty-five percent of the state's population. Ninety-eight percent of them were male. These men had a head start on jobs that constituted sixty percent of all public sector work available in the state.

Women made up only 1.8 percent of the state's veterans. The Women's Armed Services Integration Act of 1948, which established the women's services, also placed a quota prohibiting women from making up more than two percent of the work force in the armed forces—a policy Congress did not change until 1967.

Once Too Often

Tired of being passed over, Feeney filed a lawsuit in the federal district court, charging that the Massachusetts law discriminated against women. Two of the three judges on the panel agreed, concluding that the unintended consequences of the statute were so devastating for women that the state must find a better way to achieve its goals of compensating veterans.

Although the goal was to help veterans, the legislature must have known that it would freeze women out of a job. As the judges remarked:

> The legislature did not wish to harm women. But the cutting-off of women's opportunities was . . . as inevitable as the proposition that if tails is up, heads must be down. Where a law's consequences are *that* inevitable, can they meaningfully be described as unintended?

Twice the attorney general of Massachusetts appealed the district court ruling to the Supreme Court. The second time, the Court agreed to review it.

Was There Intent?

Feeney argued that the state's absolute lifetime preference for veterans inevitably worked to exclude women from the best civil service jobs, denying them equal protection of the laws under the Fourteenth Amendment. She felt the statute was biased, favoring a status reserved under federal law primarily to men, and that the consequences were too inevitable to have been unintended.

The Massachusetts attorney general conceded that the unintended results of the veterans' preference were disastrous for women. However, he argued that lawmakers had never intended to discriminate against women. Indeed the law defined "veteran" as "any person, male or female, including a nurse." Without the intent to discriminate, the law should stand.

Justice Potter Stewart, speaking for the Court, announced: "The sole question for decision on this appeal is whether Massachusetts, in granting an absolute lifetime preference to veterans, has discriminated against women in violation of the Equal Protection Clause of the Fourteenth Amendment."

His answer, writes historian Laura A. Otten, "reveals, just as did answers from the Court in the late 1800s, much about how the Court saw women's rights and privileges. Women learned that in the eyes of a majority of the Supreme Court, even the Equal Protection Clause is not absolute and that it, too, can be abridged for a compelling state goal."

Stewart conceded that the dispute was unusual since the law was not neutral—by design. There was no question the law preferred veterans—giving them a head start. However, "this legislation choice [is] legitimate." The basic distinction was between veterans and nonveterans, not between women and men—and the goals of such preference were worthy. Therefore, the law "must be analyzed as is any other neutral law that casts a greater burden upon women as a group than upon men as a group." Military enlistment policies may indeed be discriminatory but "the history of discrimination against women in the military is not on trial in this case."

Helen Feeney lost her employment discrimination battle in 1979. *(The Lowell Sun)*

Stewart continued, " 'Discriminatory purpose'... implies that the ... state legislature, selected or reaffirmed a particular course of action at least in part 'because of,' not merely 'in spite of,' its adverse effects upon an identifiable group. Yet nothing in the record demonstrates that this preference for veterans was originally devised or subsequently re-enacted because it would ... [keep] women in a stereotypic and predefined place. ..."

Therefore the Supreme Court held that the test for finding discrimination in a law is clear evidence of *intent* to discriminate. The "substantial edge" Massachusetts gave veterans "may reflect unwise policy," but since its purpose was not to discriminate, it was not unconstitutional.

As the *Feeney* decision makes clear, restricting women's participation in the armed forces has an impact on the civilian jobs open to them. Today women comprise twenty-four percent of the Air Force's recruits, nineteen percent of the Army's recruits, and seventeen percent of the Navy's recruits. In 1993, combat positions began to open for servicewomen. These increasing numbers mean that in the future more women will benefit greatly from the *Feeney* case.

For Further Reading

Goldstein, Leslie Friedman. *The Constitutional Rights of Women: Cases in Law and Social Change.* Madison: The University of Wisconsin Press, 1989.

Otten, Laura A. *Women's Rights and the Law.* Westport, Conn.: Praeger, 1993.

Tribe, Lawrence H. *American Constitutional Law*, 2d ed.: Mineola, N.Y.: The Foundation Press, 1988.

Hishon v. King & Spalding: 1984

Petitioner: Elizabeth Anderson Hishon   **Respondent:** King & Spalding
Petitioner's Claim: That the lower courts erred in dismissing her claim of
sex discrimination without allowing Hishon her day in court
Chief Lawyer for Respondent: Charles Morgan, Jr.
Chief Lawyer for Petitioner: Emmett J. Bondurant, II   **Justices:** Harry A.
Blackmun, William J. Brennan, Jr., *Chief Justice Warren E. Burger,* Thurgood
Marshall, Sandra Day O'Connor, Lewis F. Powell, Jr., William H. Rehnquist,
John P. Stevens, III, and Byron R. White   **Place:** Washington, D.C.
Date of Decision: May 22, 1984   **Decision:** Hishon could go to court to try
to prove her charge of sex discrimination. Title VII *does* apply to a
partnership's selection of partners.

SIGNIFICANCE

This Supreme Court ruling was the first to find that gender discrimination in
partnership decisions was a violation of federal law—providing women with one
small crack in the so-called glass ceiling.

Elizabeth Anderson was a Harlan Fiske Stone scholar at Columbia Law
School, from which she graduated with honors in 1972. She was recruited to
the prestigious and century-old King & Spalding law firm by one of its most
prominent attorneys, Jack H. Watson, Jr., who later became President Jimmy
Carter's chief of staff.

Anderson knew that the only other female attorney who had ever worked
at the firm had done so for twenty-five years without being promoted to
partner—while witnessing the promotions of sixty men younger than she.
Anderson therefore expressed concern about her own future prospects at King &
Spalding. Assured that promotions to partner were "a matter of course" for
associates "who receive[d] satisfactory evaluations" during five or six years of
service and that partnership decisions were always made "on a fair and equal
basis," Anderson agreed to join the firm.

The next five years were rewarding ones, both professionally and personally. Anderson earned more than satisfactory evaluations at King & Spalding
and, in 1977, she married another lawyer (not associated with her firm). Then, in

1978 and 1979, Elizabeth Anderson Hishon was twice rejected for promotion to partnership.

Like many other law firms, King & Spalding had a strict "up or out" policy—associates who were not offered partnership within a certain number of years were told to find employment elsewhere. Since Hishon had not been promoted, she was fired as of December 31, 1979. (The firm's decades-long-employment of its other unpromoted female attorney, who had retired after thirty-three years in 1977, was an exception to the promote-or-fire policy.)

Hishon described herself as "not typically one to march in a[n] [equal rights] parade." However, as she also later said, "There comes a point, and I reached that point, where you have to take a stand." Convinced that she had been a victim of sex discrimination, Hishon filed a complaint with the Equal Employment Opportunity Commission (EEOC) against King & Spalding. The EEOC issued a notice of a right to sue, and in 1980 Hishon filed suit in the U.S. District Court for the Northern District of Georgia. One of her husband's partners, Emmett J. Bondurant, II, acted as her attorney.

No Satisfaction

Hishon quickly found employment with another Atlanta law firm, but she went ahead with her suit against King & Spalding. She claimed that the firm's refusal to promote her was sex discrimination in violation of Title VII. Instead of reinstatement and the promotion, she asked the court to find the law firm's behavior illegal and to order it ended. In addition, she wanted back pay and compensatory damages.

The district court dismissed the action, saying that a partnership's selection of its partners was not governed by Title VII. When this decision was upheld by the U.S. Court of Appeals for the Eleventh Circuit, Hishon petitioned the Supreme Court to review the case and to decide whether Title VII protection extended to a partnership's selection of its partners. If Title VII's anti-discrimination provisions *were* found to apply to partnership decisions, Hishon's case would be sent back to the lower court for reconsideration.

On October 31, 1983, Bondurant argued before the Supreme Court that King & Spalding was an "employer" within the meaning of Title VII, even though it was a partnership. As an employer, he continued, it could not discriminate on the basis of "race, color, religion, sex, or national origin" with regard to "terms, conditions, or privileges of employment." Equal consideration for promotion to partner was certainly one of the "terms, conditions, or privileges of employment." King & Spalding therefore had illegally refused to consider Hishon for promotion on an equal basis with its male employees.

King & Spalding's attorney, Charles Morgan, Jr., argued, in contrast, that promotion to partnership was not one of the "terms, conditions, or privileges of employment," because once such a promotion occurred, the promoted individual was no longer one of the firm's "employees" but one of its "employers." He also asserted that decisions concerning partnership selections were more akin to "a voluntary joinder" like marriage, and therefore Title VII did not apply. He also insisted if Title VII regulated partnership promotions, the First Amendment's guarantee of freedom of expression and association would be violated.

A Promise Is a Contract

The Court ruled unanimously that Title VII protection did extend to the law firm's partnership decisions. Chief Justice Warren E. Burger wrote that the "contractual relationship of employment triggers the provision of Title VII governing 'terms, conditions or privileges of employment'" and that "Title VII in turn forbids discrimination on the basis of "race, color, religion, sex, or national origin." He also said that oral and informal contracts were as valid a trigger of Title VII protection as written or more formal contracts, a point he illustrated by noting that "an informal contract of employment may arise by the simple act of handing a job applicant a shovel and providing a workplace."

If the law firm promised that Hishon would be considered for partnership, Burger continued, "that promise clearly was a term, condition, or privilege of her employment" and "Title VII would then bind respondent to consider petitioner . . . without regard to petitioner's sex." He underscored that the law would still apply even without an express and contractual promise if, as Hishon contended, "the opportunity to become a partner was part and parcel of an associate's status," and "associates could regularly expect to be considered for partnerships at the end of their 'apprenticeships.'"

Rejecting King & Spalding's claim that Title VII did not apply because promotion made the new partner an "employer" and ended the "employee" relationship, Burger stressed that "a benefit need not accrue before a person's employment is completed. . . . Pension benefits, for example, qualify as terms, conditions, or privileges of employment even though they are received only after employment terminates." Burger also refuted King & Spalding's claim that partnership decisions were exempt from Title VII protection, saying simply that where Congress had wanted to grant an employer immunity, "it expressly did so."

Burger flatly rejected the law firm's First Amendment claims as well. Lawyers may make a "distinctive contribution . . . to the ideals and beliefs of our society" but no one had shown how considering Hishon for partnership on her merits would interfere with that function. Moreover, he added, "invidious private discrimination . . . has never been accorded affirmative constitutional protection. . . . There is no constitutional right, for example, to discriminate in the selection of who may attend a private school or join a labor union. . . . Petitioner, therefore, is entitled to her day in court to prove her allegations."

In June 1984, Hishon settled her lawsuit against King & Spalding in return for a financial payment. Hishon, by then a partner in the firm of O'Callaghan, Saunders & Strum, said she hoped the Supreme Court decision would "have a wide impact on women and minorities in the professions."

And Indeed It Did

Another partnership decision made its way to the Supreme Court before the end of the decade. In 1983, the Price Waterhouse accounting firm refused to promote Ann B. Hopkins to partner, even though she consistently brought in more business than any of that year's other—all male—partnership candidates. According to the record, the Price Waterhouse partners who evaluated Hopkins thought she should go to "charm school," dress "more femininely" and wear more makeup and jewelry. Price Waterhouse argued that these comments were "legally irrelevant," but the Court disagreed. In 1989, by a margin of 6-3, the Supreme Court ruled that sexual stereotyping had indeed played a part in her partnership denial.

On May 14, 1990, a federal district judge, after retrying the case, found Price Waterhouse guilty of discrimination. Price Waterhouse appealed but the lower court's ruling that Ann B. Hopkins must be admitted to partnership was upheld.

For Further Reading

Goldstein, Leslie Friedman. *The Constitutional Rights of Women: Cases in Law and Social Change*, rev. ed. Madison: The University of Wisconsin Press, 1989.

Hoff, Joan. *Law, Gender & Injustice: A Legal History of U.S. Women.* New York: New York University Press, 1991.

New York Times, May 23, 27, and 29, 1984; June 15, 1984; and May 2, 1989.

Ross, Susan Deller, Isabelle Katz Pinzler, Deborah A. Ellis, and Kary L. Moss. *The Rights of Women: The Basic ACLU Guide to Women's Rights*, 3rd ed. Carbondale and Edwardsville: Southern Illinois University Press, 1993.

Meritor Savings Bank v. Vinson: 1986

Appellants: Meritor Savings Bank, FSB and Sidney Taylor
Appellees: Mechelle Vinson et al.   **Appellants' Claim:** That the Court of
Appeals erred in ruling that "hostile environment" sex harassment was a
violation of Title VII of the 1964 Civil Rights Act
Chief Lawyers for Appellees: Patricia J. Barry and Catharine A. MacKinnon
Chief Lawyer for Appellants: F. Robert Troll, Jr.   **Justices:** Harry A.
Blackmun, William J. Brennan, Jr., Chief Justice Warren E. Burger, Thurgood
Marshall, Sandra Day O'Connor, Lewis F. Powell, Jr., *William H. Rehnquist,*
John Paul Stevens, Byron R. White   **Place:** Washington, D.C.
Date of Decision: June 19, 1986   **Decision:** A claim of "hostile
environment" sexual harassment *is* a form of sex discrimination actionable
under Title VII of the 1964 Civil Rights Act

SIGNIFICANCE
This decision provided a clearer definition of what constituted sexual harassment
on the job and under what circumstances the employer could be held liable for the
actions of subordinates.

In 1974, Mechelle Vinson joined the Capital City Federal Savings and Loan
Association, located in Washington D.C. Sidney Taylor hired and supervised
her. Between 1974 and 1978, Vinson progressed from teller-trainee, to teller, to
head teller, and then to assistant branch manager, all under Taylor's supervision.
Vinson's promotions had been based exclusively on merit, according to court
records.

In September 1978, Vinson took an indefinite sick leave. The following
month, the bank fired her for her "excessive use of that leave." In 1980, Vinson
sued Taylor and the bank, claiming that she had "constantly been subjected to
sexual harassment" by Taylor in violation of Title VII of the 1964 Civil Rights
Act, which bans discrimination against women and other groups. She sought
injunctive relief and compensatory and punitive damages against both the bank
and Taylor, plus attorney's fees.

He Said, She Said

During the bench trial before the district court, Vinson testified that Taylor behaved in a fatherly manner until her teller-trainee and probationary period ended. When Vinson became a teller, Taylor asked her to dinner. During the meal, he asked her to join him for sex at a motel. After numerous occasions and as many refusals—and because she was afraid of being fired if she didn't comply—she complied with Taylor's request.

Vinson testified that for two-and-a-half-years Taylor continued to press her for sexual favors. Submitting to demands made during and following work hours, she had intercourse with him between forty and fifty times, sometimes under threat of physical force. Vinson also testified that Taylor fondled her—and other female employees—in the presence of coworkers, trailed her into the women's restroom, and exposed himself to her. She did not use the bank's formal complaint procedure, which required her to report the harassment to her supervisor—Taylor himself.

Taylor denied all of Vinson's claims. He said they had never had sexual intercourse. He also claimed never to have requested sexual relations, made suggestive comments, or fondled Vinson. For its part, Capital City Federal Savings and Loan Association denied that any of these things happened and, in any case, said it had not known about, consented to, or approved any such behavior by Taylor.

Round One

In 1980, the district court found that if there were "an intimate or sexual relationship" between Vinson and Taylor during her employment, it was "voluntary" and had no bearing on her promotions or continued employment. She "was not the victim of sexual harassment [or] . . . sexual discrimination."

Despite its finding that Title VII had not been violated, the court examined the issue of employer responsibility. The court pointed out that the bank had a formal anti-discrimination policy and that neither Vinson nor any of her coworkers had ever filed a sexual harassment complaint against Taylor. It concluded that "the bank was without notice and cannot be held liable for the alleged actions of Taylor."

Round Two

In 1985, the Court of Appeals for the District of Columbia Circuit reversed the lower court's decision. Referring to its decision in a 1981 case, *Bundy v. Jackson*, and the Equal Employment Opportunity Commission's (EEOC) Guidelines on Discrimination Because of Sex (1985), the appeals court stressed that *two* forms of sexual harassment were described in Title VII.

The first involved a demand of sexual favors in return for continued employment or other employment-related benefits. The second was sexual harassment sufficient to create a "hostile" or offensive environment, independent of any economic impact. The district court had addressed only the first type of sexual harassment claim, while "Vinson's grievance was clearly of the [hostile environment] type."

The appeals court also questioned the district court's conclusion that any sexual activity between Vinson and her supervisor "was a voluntary one." If "Taylor made Vinson's toleration of sexual harassment a condition of her employment," her compliance "had no materiality whatsoever."

Finally, the appeals court differed with the district court's ruling on employer responsibility. Referring both to the EEOC Guidelines and to Title VII's specific inclusion of "any agent of such a person" within the definition of "employer," the Appeals Court held that regardless of whether an employer knew or should have known about the sexually harassing conduct of one of its supervisors, that employer was still liable for supervisory sexual harassment under Title VII.

Shortly after this decision, the bank merged with Northern Virginia Savings and Loan Association. The newly-merged bank took the name PSFS Savings Bank FSB.

Round Three

The Supreme Court heard the case on March 25, 1986. Attorney F. Robert Troll defended Taylor and PSFS Savings Bank. Patricia J. Barry argued the case for Vinson. Before the Court reached its decision, PSFS changed its name once again, to Meritor Bank.

For more than a dozen years after the 1964 passage of Title VII, federal courts refused to find that sex harassment was a form of sex discrimination. It was not until 1977 that a three-judge panel of the U.S. Court of Appeals for the District of Columbia issued the first federal court ruling that sex harassment was, in fact, sex discrimination, in *Barnes v. Costle*. Catharine A. MacKinnon, who had been one of Paulette Barnes' attorneys in that case, joined Barry's legal team to work on behalf of Vinson.

In her brief for the Supreme Court, MacKinnon addressed the fact that Taylor had not accompanied his harassment with the outright threat or promise of economic consequence. Reiterating arguments presented in her 1979 book *Sexual Harassment of Working Women*, MacKinnon presented "hostile environment" sex discrimination as "on a time line" with *quid pro quo* sex discrimination (sex in direct exchange for continued employment or other benefit). She argued that female employees frequently became *quid pro quo* victims when they could no longer endure being "hostile environment" victims and were fired or forced to quit for sudden non-compliance with sexual demands. If hostile environment harassment was not itself a ground for complaint, MacKinnon reasoned, a woman who is harassed " with enough coerciveness, subtlety, suddenness or one-sidedness, while her job is formally undisturbed, . . . is not considered to have been sexually harassed." For a woman to be required to risk her job in order to ensure that her claim became an actionable one, MacKinnon argued, would amount to her having "to bring intensified injury upon herself in order to demonstrate that she is injured at all."

On June 19, 1986, Justice William H. Rehnquist delivered the unanimous opinion of the Supreme Court's affirmation of the Appeals Court ruling. He first addressed the scope of Title VII's prohibition against sex discrimination in the "terms, conditions, or privileges" of employment. Meritor Savings Bank's contention that the prohibition covered only " 'tangible loss' of 'an economic character,' [and] not 'purely psychological aspects of the workplace environment' " was rejected.

The Court noted that *quid pro quo* harassment was not the issue in this case. The guidelines classified offensive behavior as sexual harassment "whether or not it is directly linked to the grant or denial of an economic *quid pro quo*," if the behavior affects an employee's work performance or makes the environment unworkable. In short, sexual harassment may indeed create a hostile or abusive work environment, and as such is a form of sex discrimination.

Rehnquist quoted a prior case that stated the language of Title VII shows Congress intended "to strike at the entire spectrum of disparate treatment of men and women" in employment. He noted the EEOC's guidelines define sexual harassment as, among other things, "unwelcome sexual advances, requests for sexual favors, and other verbal or physical conduct of a sexual nature."

Holding that "voluntary" behavior was no defense against a sexual harassment suit, Rehnquist sent the case back to the District Court for consideration of Vinson's "hostile environment" claim. The whole point of any such claim, the court ruled, is that the alleged sexual advances were "unwelcome, . . . not whether her actual participation in sexual intercourse was voluntary."

Hoisted on the EEOC's Petard

As for employer liability, the Court "declined the parties' invitation to issue a definitive rule." Instead, it generally agreed that Congress expected the courts to look to the EEOC's principles "for guidance in this area." Rehnquist noted that the courts had thus "consistently held employers liable for the discriminatory discharges of employees by supervisory personnel, whether or not the employer knew, should have known, or approved of the supervisor's actions." He also pointed out that the EEOC, in its brief in *Meritor*, supported "a rule that asks whether a victim of sexual harassment had reasonably available an avenue of complaint regarding such harassment and, . . . whether that procedure was reasonably responsible to the employee's complaint."

The Court rejected the lower court's view "that employers are automatically liable for sexual harassment by their supervisors. One way for employers to avoid liability, for example, would be to prove that a sexually harassed employee had reasonable opportunities to take advantage of a good, clear complaint procedure without reprisal, but had failed to do so.

However, Rehnquist stressed, even those employers with anti-discrimination policies would not automatically be deemed innocent. In Vinson's case, sexual harassment was not specifically included in the Bank's formal procedure for reporting alleged discrimination. Moreover, the first step was to complain to one's supervisor, in this case, the alleged perpetrator—an action the complainant was hardly likely to take under these circumstances, the Court recognized.

Justice Thurgood Marshall, joined by Justices William O. Brennan, Harry A. Blackmun, and John Paul Stevens, concurred. On the issue of employer liability, however, these justices would hold the employer responsible if a supervisor of an employee engaged in sexual harassment "regardless of whether the employee gave 'notice' of the offense." As Marshall pointed out, "discrimination is rarely carried out pursuant to a formal vote of a corporation's board of directors."

For Further Reading

Goldstein, Leslie Friedman. *The Constitutional Rights of Women: Cases in Law and Social Change*, rev. ed. Madison: University of Wisconsin Press, 1989.

Hoff, Joan. *Law, Gender and Injustice: A Legal History of U.S. Women*. New York: New York University Press, 1991.

MacKinnon, Catharine A. *Sexual Harassment of Working Women*. New Haven, Conn.: Yale University Press, 1979.

Strebeigh, Fred. "Defining Law on the Feminist Frontier." *New York Times*, October 6, 1991.

California Federal Savings and Loan Association v. Guerra: 1987

Petitioner: California Federal Savings and Loan Association

Respondent: Guerra, director, Department of Fair Employment and Housing

Petitioner's Claim: That the Pregnancy Discrimination Act (PDA) passed by Congress as an amendment to Title VII of the 1964 Civil Rights Act invalidated California's Fair Employment and Housing Act (FEHA), which required employers to grant unpaid pregnancy disability leaves of up to four months—but did not provide leaves for men with disabilities

Chief Lawyer for Respondent: Marian M. Johnston

Chief Lawyer for Petitioner: Theodore B. Olson   **Justices:** Harry A. Blackmun, William J. Brennan, Jr., *Thurgood Marshall,* Sandra Day O'Connor, Antonin Scalia, and John Paul Stevens, (majority); Lewis F. Powell, Chief Justice William H. Rehnquist, and Byron R. White (dissent)

Place: Washington, D.C.   **Date of Decision:** January 13, 1987

Decision: That Title VII of the Civil Rights Act of 1964, as amended by the PDA, did not preempt a state statute requiring employers to provide leave and reinstatement to employees temporarily disabled by pregnancy

SIGNIFICANCE

The decision, in this first Supreme Court case to challenge a state statute's validity under the PDA, established that the PDA did not conflict with California's law nor did it discriminate against men. Women's rights to unpaid pregnancy disability leaves were upheld.

In January 1982, Lillian Garland took a pregnancy disability leave from her job as a receptionist for the California Federal Savings and Loan Association (Cal Fed). However, when she was ready to return to work the following April, she found that her job had been given to a replacement and that no similar positions were open. Garland filed a complaint with the Department of Fair Employment and Housing, charging Cal Fed with violating California's Fair Employment and Housing Act (FEHA).

One section of FEHA required employers to provide unpaid pregnancy disability leaves of up to four months to their female employees. It was generally understood that employers could replace the pregnant employee if such replacement was a business necessity. However, when the employee returned at the end of her leave, the employer was required to make "sincere attempts" to find a similar position for the employee.

Before a hearing could be held before FEHA, Cal Fed brought its own suit in the U.S. District Court for the Central District of California. Cal Fed claimed that California's law regarding pregnancy disability leave violated Title VII of the Civil Rights Act of 1964, as amended in 1978 by the Pregnancy Disability Act (PDA). The act provided that:

> The terms "because of sex" or "on the basis of sex" include, but are not limited to, because of or on the basis of pregnancy, childbirth, or related medical conditions; and women affected by pregnancy, childbirth, or related medical conditions shall be treated the same for all employment-related purposes, including receipt of benefits under fringe benefit programs, as other persons not so affected but similar in their ability to work, and nothing in section 703(h) of this title shall be interpreted to permit otherwise.

Cal Fed finally found a position for Garland seven months after she had requested reinstatement. Despite the resolution of Garland's situation, Cal Fed argued before the district court that Title VII prohibited the granting of four-month long leaves for pregnancy disability when such leaves were not granted for other medical disabilities.

The district court agreed. Stating that "California employers who comply with state law are subject to reverse discrimination suits under Title VII brought by temporarily disabled males who do not receive the same treatment as female employees disabled by pregnancy," the district court in 1984 declared California's law "null, void, invalid, and inoperative under the supremacy clause of the United States Constitution."

California Fights for Its Law

California appealed to the U.S. Court of Appeals for the Ninth Circuit, which issued a terse opinion in 1985. The appeals court found that the district court's decision that a section of FEHA discriminated against men since they could not be pregnant was a simple violation of "common sense."

Further, such a conclusion misinterpreted case law and "flout[ed] Title VII and the PDA." Pointing out that Congress had passed the PDA to draw a bottom line below which pregnancy disability benefits could not fall—not a limit on how extensive they might be—the appeals court reversed the lower court ruling.

What Congress Meant

Cal Fed appealed to the Supreme Court. The Court heard oral arguments on October 8, 1986 and issued its ruling on January 13, 1987. Justice Thurgood Marshall presented the opinion of the Court, explaining that "in determining whether a state statute is pre-empted by a federal law and therefore invalid under the Supremacy Clause of the Constitution, our sole task is to ascertain the intent of Congress."

After noting that two sections of the 1964 Civil Rights Act, Sections 708 and 1104, specifically provided that "state laws will be pre-empted only if they actually conflict with federal law," Marshall turned to the Congressional hearings and debates surrounding the amendment of the Civil Rights Act by the PDA.

The *Congressional Reports*, Marshall wrote for the Court, "make abundantly clear that Congress intended the PDA to provide relief for working women and to end discrimination against pregnant workers." Moreover, he noted, Congress was fully aware that several states, including California, had laws mandating pregnancy disability leaves, and the "House and Senate *Reports* suggest that these laws would continue to have effect under the PDA."

California's law was not in conflict with the PDA, Marshall continued, but rather "share[s] a common goal," one described by a sponsor of the Act as "guarantee[ing] women the basic right to participate fully and equally in the workforce, without denying them the fundamental right to full participation in family life."

Marshall also noted the differences between California's statute and the type of protective legislation that the Supreme Court had found unconstitutional earlier in the century. California's law, he wrote, is "narrowly drawn to cover only the period of *actual physical disability* on account of pregnancy, childbirth, or related medical condition. Accordingly, unlike . . . protective labor legislation . . . [FEHA] does not reflect archaic or stereotypical notions about pregnancy and the abilities of pregnant workers. A statute based on such stereotypical assumptions would, of course, be inconsistent with Title VII's goal of equal employment opportunity."

The Court concluded that California's FEHA was indeed constitutional and not in conflict with Title VII or the PDA. Marshall reiterated the appeal court's finding that the Civil Rights Act of 1964, as amended by the PDA, established "a floor beneath which pregnancy disability benefits may not fall—not a ceiling above which they may not rise."

The Family and Medical Leave Act of 1993

In 1993, the Family and Medical Leave Act was signed into law by President Bill Clinton. This act, among other things, required that employers of more than fifty employees provide unpaid leaves of up to twelve weeks to

WOMEN'S

RESSES

ON TRIAL

employees with newborn or newly adopted children—and, for most employers, superseded the PDA.

For Further Reading

Chafe, William H. *The American Woman: Her Changing Social, Economic and Political Roles, 1920–1970.* New York: Oxford University Press, 1972.

Cullen-DuPont, Kathryn. *The Encyclopedia of Women's History in America.* New York: Facts on File, 1996.

Davis, Flora. *Moving the Mountain: The Women's Movement in America Since 1960.* New York: Simon & Schuster, 1991.

Frost-Knappman, Elizabeth. *The ABC-CLIO Companion to Women's Progress in America.* Santa Barbara, Calif.: ABC-CLIO, 1995.

Goldstein, Leslie Friedman. *The Constitutional Rights of Women: Cases in Law and Social Change,* rev. ed. Madison: University of Wisconsin Press, 1989.

Hoff, Joan. *Law, Gender and Injustice: A Legal History of U.S. Women.* New York: New York University Press, 1991.

Johnson v. Transportation Agency: 1987

Appellant: Paul Johnson   **Appellee:** Transportation Agency, Santa Clara County, California et al.   **Appellant's Claim:** That the Transportation Agency violated Title VII of the 1964 Civil Rights Act
Chief Lawyer for Appellee: Steven Woodside
Chief Lawyer for Appellant: Constance E. Brooks   **Justices:** Harry Blackmun, *William J. Brennan, Jr.,* Thurgood Marshall, Sandra Day O'Connor, and John Paul Stevens (majority); Chief Justice William Rehnquist, Antonin Scalia, and Byron White (dissent)   **Place:** Washington, D.C.
Date of Decision: March 25, 1987   **Decision:** Affirmative action programs do not violate the Civil Rights Act *solely* because they favor women or minorities

SIGNIFICANCE
The Supreme Court for the first time ruled that voluntary affirmative action programs for women in fields from which they had previously been excluded were constitutional—even when the employer had not been guilty of past discrimination.

Custom and prejudice have kept women out of well-paying jobs throughout American history. In 1980, Diane Joyce decided to do something about it. She had spent four years filling potholes and pouring asphalt at the Transportation Agency of Santa Clara. Tired, she now wanted a desk job. However, no woman held any of the agency's 238 skilled positions.

On December 12, 1979, the agency announced it would hire a new road dispatcher. Although no woman had ever held this job before, Joyce applied, bringing with her nearly ten years of agency experience. Joyce had begun working as an account clerk in 1970. Four years later, she applied for a dispatcher's position. Since she had never been a road maintenance worker, the agency considered her unqualified. In 1975, Joyce joined a road maintenance crew—the first woman to ever hold this position. After four years of road work, with occasional stints as road dispatcher, Joyce reapplied for the dispatcher's position in 1980.

Paul Johnson applied for the same job. He had begun working for the county in 1967 as a road yard clerk. Like Joyce, in 1974 he had unsuccessfully applied for a road dispatcher job. Three years later he also became a road maintenance worker—occasionally working as a dispatcher as well.

Other employees also applied for the job; nine of them were qualified. A two-person panel gave each an interview test. Seven of the employees scored above 70—the eligibility level. Joyce, the only woman in this group, scored 73; Johnson 75. The agency, judging each of these applicants "well qualified," began to schedule a second round of interviews.

Good Reason to Worry

Joyce suspected she might not get a fair hearing. She had disagreed with some members of the second interview panel. For example, her first supervisor in road maintenance had refused to issue her coveralls, but gave them to her male coworkers. As a result, her clothes were ruined on four separate occasions. Her complaints were ignored until she filed a grievance. The next day she received four pairs of coveralls.

As chair of the Roads Operations Safety Committee, Joyce also had debated road safety with a second member of the interview panel. He had described her as "a rebel-rousing, skirt-wearing person."

Joyce was worried that these panel members might prevent her promotion. To add to her concern, about ten days after her application, she still had not received the date for her second interview. After she told the person setting up the interviews that she had a disaster preparedness class the following week, her scheduler set her appointment for that time.

At this point, Joyce contacted Santa Clara County's Affirmative Action Office. Together they reviewed a 1978 Affirmative Action Plan of the Santa Clara County Transit District Board of Supervisors to hire and promote women and minorities. The plan stated that in making promotions to positions in a traditionally segregated job, the agency *could* consider a person's gender.

The office approached the transportation agency's affirmative action coordinator, who recommended to director James Graebner that Joyce be promoted. Graebner, authorized to choose any of the seven people found eligible, also listened to the suggestions of the second interview panel. He chose Joyce for the dispatcher's position, explaining, "I tried to look at the whole picture, the combination of her qualifications and Mr. Johnson's qualifications, their test scores, their expertise, their background, affirmative action matters, things like that. . . ."

Graebner also said that he did not consider it significant that Johnson had scored 75 and Joyce 73 when interviewed by the board. Both she and Johnson were well qualified. Joyce's evaluation read: "Well qualified by virtue of eighteen years of past clerical experience . . . plus almost five years as a [road maintenance worker]."

The evaluation of Johnson stated: "Well qualified applicant; two years of [road maintenance worker] experience plus eleven years of Road Yard Clerk. Has had previous outside Dispatch experience but was thirteen years ago."

Johnson Cries Foul

However, Johnson felt that the county had discriminated against him because he was a man. He believed the affirmative action plan violated the law, specifically Title VII of the 1964 Civil Rights Act. Title VII, known as the Equal Opportunity section, forbids discrimination by private employers, employment agencies, and unions because of race, color, religion, national origin, or sex.

Therefore, in March 1981, Johnson obtained a "right-to-sue" letter from the Equal Employment Opportunity Commission (EEOC) and sued in Federal District Court. The court decided that he was the best qualified, that Joyce's gender was the "determining factor in her selection," and that the agency's affirmative action plan was invalid. However, the Ninth Circuit Court of Appeals reversed this decision.

Johnson then took his case to the Supreme Court. On March 25, 1987, Justice William J. Brennan, Jr., read the majority opinion of the Court—six to three in favor of Santa Clara County. Brennan said that taking into account the gender of job applicants did not violate Title VII of the 1964 Civil Rights Act.

The Court endorsed the agency's affirmative-action plan even where there was no proven history of sex discrimination by the employer. Brennan said that given the "manifest imbalance" in the number of women or minorities holding skilled positions, the agency had taken "a moderate, gradual approach . . . one which establishes realistic guidance for employment decisions, and which visits minimal intrusion on the legitimate expectations of other employees."

Justice Sandra Day O'Connor, the only woman on the Court, agreed with Brennan, but delivered a separate opinion saying the Court's decision should have been less sweeping. Three other justices—William Rehnquist, Byron White, and Antonin Scalia—dissented. Scalia bitterly announced that civil rights cases had "been converted into a powerful engine of racism and sexism." In his scathing dissent, Scalia said "the Court today completes the process of converting [civil-rights law] from a guarantee that race or sex will *not* be the basis for employment determination to a guarantee that it often *will*." The defeated Johnson agreed: "A ruling like this will cause prejudice in people who have never been prejudiced before."

Over the years the Court has been back and forth over the use of quotas. For example, in *Regents of the University of California v. Bakke* (1978), it opposed quotas; but in *United States Steelworkers v. Weber* (1979) and *Local 28 of the Sheet Metal Workers v. EEOC* (1986), it supported them. Then in 1987 the Court made its surprisingly strong ruling for women in the *Johnson* decision. However, during the 1990s, the Court moved toward restricting affirmative action plans to those situations in which employers have been guilty of deliberately discriminating against a group of people.

Road dispatcher Diane Joyce stands next to her truck in Santa Clara County, California. (Diane Joyce)

For Further Reading

Baer, Judith A. *Women in American Law: The Struggle Toward Equality from the New Deal to the Present.* New York: Holmes & Meier, 1991.

"Balancing Act." *Time,* April 6, 1987.

Davis, Flora. *Moving The Mountain: The Women's Movement Since 1960.* New York: Touchstone, 1991.

Hoff, Joan. *Law, Gender, and Injustice: A Legal History of U.S. Women.* New York: New York University Press, 1991.

Mezey, Susan Gluck. *In Pursuit of Equality: Women, Public Policy, and the Federal Courts.* New York: St. Martin's Press, 1992.

Otten, Laura. *Women's Rights and the Law.* Westport, Conn.: Praeger, 1993.

Automobile Workers v. Johnson Controls: 1991

Petitioners: International Union, United Automobile, Aerospace, and Agricultural Implement Workers of America, UAW, et al.
Respondent: Johnson Controls, Inc. **Petitioners' Claim:** That Johnson Controls' "fetal protection policy" is sex discrimination prohibited by the Pregnancy Discrimination Act (PDA)
Chief Lawyer for Respondents: Stanley S. Jaspan
Chief Lawyer for Petitioners: Marsha S. Berzon **Justices:** *Harry A. Blackmun,* Anthony M. Kennedy, Thurgood Marshall, Sandra Day O'Connor, Chief Justice William H. Rehnquist, Antonin Scalia, David Souter, John Paul Stevens, and Byron R. White **Place:** Washington, D.C.
Date of Decision: March 20, 1991 **Decision:** Johnson Controls' fetal protection policy was in violation of Title VII of the Civil Rights Act of 1974, as amended by the PDA

SIGNIFICANCE
This decision gave women the opportunity to make their own reasoned decisions about pregnancy and dangerous work.

A woman who became sterilized in order to keep her job, Mary Craig, sparked a trial that would be the ultimate test of the Pregnancy Discrimination Act (PDA). In 1990, she worked at Johnson Controls, Inc. The company manufactures batteries—a process that utilizes lead as a primary ingredient. Men's and women's exposure to lead may have a negative impact on health, including birth defects in children. Some studies have suggested lead exposure may affect fertility in both men and women.

Before the passage of Title VII of the Civil Rights Act of 1964, Johnson Controls hired men only. Title VII banned this practice. However, once women began working at the company in 1977, it issued an official policy regarding female exposure to lead:

> Since not all women who can become mothers wish to become mothers (or will become mothers), it would appear to be illegal discrimination to treat all who are capable of pregnancy as though they will become pregnant.

Johnson urged women not to apply for lead-exposed positions if they hoped to bear children. However, it made them eligible for this work provided they signed a statement that they understood the risks, including a higher than normal rate of miscarriage.

During the next five years, eight women with blood levels above thirty micrograms per deciliter—the level considered by the Occupational Safety and Health Administration (OSHA) to be the critical threshold for workers hoping to have children—became pregnant. None of the children born of these pregnancies had any apparent birth defects or abnormalities. Still Johnson Controls decided to exclude women of childbearing age from lead-exposed jobs or positions from which one would be eligible for promotion to a lead-exposed job. The policy defined "women . . . capable of bearing children" as "all women except those whose inability to bear children is medically documented."

Women and Children First

Various unions filed a class-action lawsuit claiming that Johnson's fetal-protection policy was sex discrimination. Some employees joined them: Mary Craig, the young woman who became sterilized; Elsie Nason, a fifty-year-old divorcee, who had to transfer to a lower-paying but lead-free position; and Donald Penney, who had been denied leave of absence to lower his lead level before fathering a child.

In its 1985 opinion, the district court stressed there was every likelihood that exposure to lead placed a fetus at risk—as well as affecting the reproductive abilities of would-be parents. However, the court thought the same amount of lead exposure would affect the fetus more.

Therefore, since the union and its employees had not offered an acceptable alternative policy to protect the fetus, the court found that the company's policy had been a "business necessity" and decided in favor of Johnson Controls. The defeated groups appealed.

Defining "Business Necessity"

The Court of Appeals for the Seventh Circuit asked three questions about fetal-protection policies to determine whether they were business necessities. First, was there a substantial health risk to the fetus? Second, was the hazard to the fetus transferred only through women? Third, was there "a less discriminatory alternative equally capable of preventing the health hazard to the fetus?"

In 1989, the court found that there was no dispute about the first question—lead exposure *did* present a hazard to a fetus. Did the father transmit a health risk to the fetus? The court ruled the evidence "at best, speculative and unconvincing." As for a less discriminatory plan, the court found that the union and its employees failed to present an alternative.

Johnson Controls' policy was a business necessity and, therefore, was not illegal under the PDA. The court also decided that such policies could exclude women under the *bona fide occupational qualification (bfoq)* standard exemption of Title VII, which allowed discrimination if gender was critical to the job. None of the other courts of appeals had held this in resolving the fetal protection claims, so the Supreme Court granted *certiorari* to resolve the conflict.

"Outright and Explicit" Discrimination

The opinion of the Supreme Court, delivered by Justice Harry A. Blackmun, found Johnson Controls *had* discriminated against women: "The bias in Johnson Controls' policy is obvious. Fertile men, but not fertile women, are given a choice as to whether they wish to risk their reproductive health for a particular job."

The Court also held that the appeals court's application of the business necessity test was a mistake, because it "is more lenient for the employer" than the test required by Title VII. In an earlier decision, *Wards Cove Packing Co. v. Antonio* (1989), the Supreme Court had ruled that the employee, and not the employer, bore the burden of proving a discriminatory policy was not a "business necessity." However, this "burden" was applicable only in cases where discrimination was a consequence of a neutral policy—never in cases of explicitly gender-based sex discrimination. To make his point clear, Blackmun quoted the Equal Employment Opportunity Commission (EEOC): "For the plaintiff to bear the burden of proof in a case in which there is direct evidence of a facially discriminatory policy is wholly inconsistent with settled Title VII law . . . *bona fide* occupational qualification is the better approach."

The *bfoq* Considered

Title VII permitted an employer to discriminate on the basis of "religion, sex, or national origin" only when a genuine *bfoq* existed that was "reasonably necessary to the normal operation of that particular business or enterprise." Johnson Controls argued that its safety concerns *were* "reasonably related," and that its fetal protection policy discriminated on the basis of a *bfoq* of female sterility.

Blackmun conceded that *bfoq*'s had sometimes been upheld due to safety concerns. Citing a decision in which an airline's mandatory retirement policy had withstood an age discrimination charge, he explained that the safety concerns had "involved the possibility that, because of age-connected debility, a flight engineer might not properly assist the pilot, and might thereby cause a safety emergency." He stressed, however, such policies must prevent dangers to "third parties . . . indispensable to the particular business at issue" to establish a *bfoq*. Johnson Controls' policies did not.

None of Your Business

Recalling 1977's *Dothard v. Rawlinson* (see page 398), Blackmun wrote, "danger to a woman herself does not justify discrimination." Similarly, the risks a pregnant woman assumed on behalf of her fetus were not her employer's concern. On this point, Blackmun cited a number of lower court cases that upheld the layoffs of pregnant flight attendants "at different points during the first five months of pregnancy . . . to ensure the safety of passengers." Two of these opinions, he noted, "pointedly indicated that fetal, as opposed to passenger, safety was best left to the mother."

In 1978, the PDA provided that "women affected by pregnancy, childbirth, or related medical conditions shall be treated the same for all employment-related purposes. . . ." The legislative history of the act confirmed that Congress intended to amend Title VII to prohibit employers from "requir[ing] a pregnant woman to stop working at any time during her pregnancy unless she is unable to do her work. . . . Congress indicated that the employer may take into account only the woman's ability to get her job done."

Any decision regarding work prior to or during pregnancy, Blackmun concluded, "was reserved for each individual woman to make for herself." The Court dismissed Johnson Controls' more general argument that its "moral and ethical concerns about the welfare of the next generation . . . suffice[d] to establish a *bfoq* of female sterility." Such decisions, Blackmun said, "must be left to the parents . . . rather than the employers. . . . Title VII and the PDA simply do not allow a woman's dismissal because of her failure to submit to sterilization."

It's Up to the Women

What about the company's liability if fertile women were not excluded from hazardous work? Blackmun conceded that more than forty states permitted lawsuits to recover for prenatal injuries. However, the right to recover in the cases was uniformly based on negligence or on wrongful death. Johnson Controls had the power, to "comply with the lead standard developed by OSHA and warn its female employees about the damaging effects of lead."

Therefore, Blackmun rejected the tort liability claim, saying: "If . . . Title VII bans sex-specific fetal protection policies, the employer fully informs the women of the risk, and the employer has not acted negligently, the basis for holding an employer liable seems remote at best."

Perhaps anticipating a mixed reaction to this decision, Blackmun concluded that "our holding today that Title VII, as so amended, forbids sex-specific fetal-protection policies is neither remarkable nor unprecedented. Concern for a woman's existing or potential offspring historically has been the excuse for denying women equal employment opportunities. . . . It is no more appropriate for the courts than it is for individual employers to decide whether a woman's reproductive role is more important to herself and her family than her economic role. Congress has left this choice to the woman as hers to make."

For Further Reading

Faludi, Susan. *Backlash: The Undeclared War Against American Women*. New York: Crown Publishers, 1991.

Hoff, Joan. *Law, Gender and Injustice: A Legal History of U.S. Women*. New York: New York University Press, 1991.

Rosen, Ruth. "What Feminist Victory in the Court?" *New York Times*, April 1, 1991.

Harris v. Forklift: 1993

Appellant: Teresa Harris   **Appellee:** Forklift Systems, Inc.
Appellant's Claim: That she was sexually harassed by the owner
Chief Lawyer for Appellee: Stanley M. Chernau
Chief Lawyer for Appellant: Irwin Bennick   **Justices:** Harry A. Blackmun,
Stephen G. Breyer, Ruth Bader Ginsburg, Anthony M. Kennedy, *Sandra Day
O'Connor,* Chief Justice William H. Rehnquist, Antonin Scalia, David H. Souter,
John Paul Stevens, Clarence Thomas, and Byron R. White
Place: Washington, D.C.   **Date of Decision:** November 9, 1993
Decision: The Supreme Court, in a unanimous decision, found that Teresa
Harris *did* work in a sexually abusive environment

SIGNIFICANCE
The Supreme Court defined sexual harassment in the workplace so that workers
today can win lawsuits without having to prove that the offensive behavior left
them psychologically damaged or unable to perform their jobs.

From April 1985 to October 1987, Teresa Harris worked as a manager at Forklift Systems, Inc., of Nashville, Tennessee, an equipment rental company. During this time, her boss, Charles Hardy, subjected her to lewd remarks, sexual put-downs, and suggestive innuendoes.

For example, Hardy told her in the presence of several other workers, "You're a woman, what do you know," "We need a man as the rental manager," and "You're a dumb ass woman." Publicly, he suggested going "to the Holiday Inn to negotiate your raise." He threw items on the floor and demanded the women pick them up. Hardy would even play a variation on "pocket pool" by asking women employees to remove coins from his front pants pockets.

That Did It

Finally, Harris had had enough. She confronted Hardy, who insisted he had only been joking, and promised he would stop. So Harris stayed at her job. Then in early September, Hardy began his cracks anew. While Harris was making a deal with one of Forklift's customers, Hardy asked her, in front of the staff, "What did you do, promise the guy . . . some 'bugger' Saturday night?"

That was enough for Harris, who quit on October 1, 1987—and sued, claiming that Hardy's conduct created an abusive work environment. She felt targeted because of her gender, and filed charges under Title VII of the Civil Rights Act of 1964.

From 1987 to 1992, Harris waged an uphill battle. Declaring this to be a "close case," the U.S. District Court for the Middle District of Tennessee, agreed that Hardy often was "vulgar" and "inane," but not discriminatory. The behavior would offend any "reasonable woman," but Hardy's insults were not:

Teresa Harris, at the time of her U.S. Supreme Court trial in 1987. (Teresa Harris Wilson)

> so severe as to be expected to seriously affect [Harris'] psychological well-being. A reasonable woman manager under like circumstances would have been offended by Hardy, but his conduct would not have risen to the level of interfering with that woman's performance.

The judge also decided, "Although Hardy may at times have genuinely offended [Harris], I do not believe that he created a working environment so poisoned as to be intimidating or abusive to [her]." In other words, Harris had not been so sufficiently traumatized, medically or psychologically, to prove harassment, a standard set by earlier federal courts of appeal. Harris's case was denied.

However, Harris fought to the Supreme Court. The Court, which can often make the simple appear complex, did the opposite in this case. It examined the complicated question and made the answer look easy. In four weeks the justices reached a unanimous decision.

Discrimination by Any Other Name. . .

The Supreme Court's first female justice, Sandra Day O'Connor, wrote the final decision, delivering the six-page ruling on November 9, 1993. She believed that a workplace environment that "would reasonably be perceived, and is perceived, as hostile or abusive" because of sexual harassment *is* a form of sex discrimination. The decision overturned lower federal court rulings that made proof of "severely psychological injury" a critical factor.

Citing the "broad rule of workplace equality" and federal laws against job discrimination, the Court stated that no single factor, such as psychological distress, is an *essential* element. O'Connor wrote that the definition of sexual harassment "by its nature cannot be a mathematically precise test." Rather, courts should look at "all the circumstances" to determine whether a work environment is a hostile one. These circumstances may be "the frequency of the discriminatory conduct; its severity; whether it is physically threatening or humiliating, or a mere offensive utterance; and whether it unreasonably interferes with an employee's work performance." In short, O'Connor emphatically ruled that the Title VII protection "comes into play before the harassing conduct leads to a nervous breakdown."

Ruth Bader Ginsburg's brief was her first since she joined the court in October as its second female member. According to the *New York Times*, Ginsburg "went out of her way to suggest that discrimination on the basis of sex should be taken as seriously by the Court as discrimination on the basis of race."

The *Harris* decision reaffirmed the standard set by *Meritor Savings Bank v. Vinson* (see page 414): an employer violates Title VII of the 1964 Civil Rights Act when the workplace is permeated with discriminatory behavior, creating an unfairly hostile or abusive atmosphere.

The Supreme Court instructed the appeals court to rehear the case for damages, but before the lower court could reach its decision, Harris settled out of court with her former employer. Neither one has ever disclosed the terms. Harris is now an oncology nurse at Vanderbilt University Medical Center in Nashville, Tennessee, working in the Bone Marrow Replacement Unit. Her legal victory is the law of the land.

For Further Reading

"Excerpts From Supreme Court Ruling on Sexual Harassment." *New York Times*, November 10, 1993.

MacKinnon, Catharine A. *Sexual Harassment of Working Women*. New Haven, Conn.: Yale University Press, 1979.

Otten, Laura. *Women's Rights and the Law*. Westport, Conn.: Praeger, 1993.

"A Victory on Workplace Harassment." *New York Times*, November 11, 1993.

The Tailhook Scandal: 1994

Defendants: Las Vegas Hilton and Hilton Hotels Corporation   **Charges:** That Hilton Hotel failed to provide the necessary security that would have prevented the sexual harassment and assault on Lt. Paula Coughlin and many others   **Defense Lawyer:** Eugene Walt   **Lawyer for the Plaintiff:** Dennis Schoville   **Judge:** Philip M. Pro   **Place:** Las Vegas, Nevada **Date of Decision:** October 24, 1994   **Verdict:** Guilty of negligence; Coughlin was initially awarded $6.7 million in compensatory and punitive damages; it was later reduced to $5.2 million

SIGNIFICANCE

Coughlin's action forced the Navy to recognize the continual sexual harassment, rape, and assaults that women in the Navy had been enduring but that the Navy had ignored or hushed up. The other military organizations likewise sat up and took notice—a long overdue first step in rectifying a shameful situation.

In 1993, Lt. Paula Coughlin must have thought she had the world on a string. She was an admiral's aide, and what was more important to her, a helicopter pilot. She thought of the Navy as an extended family and looked forward to attending the annual Tailhook Association convention at the Hilton in Las Vegas, Nevada.

Coughlin might have been aware that "wild partying" went on in some areas during the convention. However, secure in her status as "one of the boys," she was in no way prepared for what happened to her in the third floor hallway of the Hilton. As she stepped off the elevator, she saw a drunken crowd of men. Despite her outraged protests, and amid shouts of "woman on deck" and "admiral's aide," she was forced to run a gauntlet of officers who grabbed at her breasts, her crotch and buttocks, and attempted to tear her clothes from her body.

Officers and Gentlemen

Coughlin was not alone. As a later investigation showed, many others— male and female—had suffered similar indignities at the hands of these "officers and gentlemen." Also devastating to Coughlin was that her boss, Admiral

John W. Snyder, dismissed her complaint with a wave of his hand, remarking, "That's what you get when you go on the third deck full of drunk aviators."

Coughlin, deciding that it was *not* what she deserved, filed formal charges through regular Navy channels but as time wore on and nothing seemed to be happening, she "went public." Seven months later, the Naval Investigative Service (NIS) and the Navy Inspector General delivered their initial reports, describing in excruciating detail what had happened. By February 1994, they had investigated 140 cases of misconduct.

Congress designates officers as "gentlemen," a classification requiring certain behaviors and prohibiting others. However, the descriptions of the orgy and debauchery that had gone on was enough to raise eyebrows above the hairline. While some of the women were there willingly, there were eighty to ninety victims—including six officers' wives—who were not. Secretary of the Navy H. Lawrence Garrett, III, immediately ordered the Navy and Marine Corps to begin disciplinary action against some seventy officers. Over fifty were implicated in forcing women to run the "gauntlet" and six were accused of blocking the investigation.

From the Top

In the military, "chain of command" means that those at the top are responsible for everything that goes on below them in their commands—right down to the lowest-rated sailor or soldier. There were many flag officers—admirals and generals—present at the Tailhook Convention who could and *should* have called a halt to the out-of-hand "partying"—including the chief of Naval Operations, Frank Kelso, as well as Navy Secretary Garrett.

Both men claimed that neither of them had seen anything "untoward" or had been anywhere near the scenes of the indecent "partying." Nevertheless, witnesses later placed both men near the infamous third floor, where the "gauntlet" had taken place. This caused Garrett's immediate resignation (without a thank you from President George Bush) and a humiliating struggle in the Senate over Kelso's early retirement. By a fifty-four to forty-three vote, the Senate allowed Kelso to retire with his four stars in 1994.

The sad irony was that Admiral Kelso was known as a "gentleman of the old school" and both he and Garrett had spent some of their time in office trying to formulate ways of improving the status of women in the military and discouraging sexual harassment. Kelso also tried to open up more opportunities for women in the Navy. For example, in 1992, Kelso had urged the Senate Armed Services Committee to permit women to fly combat aircraft—a big step forward for ambitious women pilots in the military. In 1994, the Navy—perhaps shamed into the decision by the Tailhook debacle—agreed to allow women to serve on combat ships. The *U.S.S Dwight D. Eisenhower*—a carrier—was the first to be outfitted to accommodate the incoming women.

The Fallout

The fallout was blunt and to the point. Coughlin's boss, Snyder, was relieved of duty for ignoring his subordinate's complaints, putting an end to his career. Three admirals were censured (which also meant, most probably, the end of their careers) for failing to prevent or stop the misbehavior of the junior officers at the convention. Thirty other admirals received letters of caution to be placed in their permanent records. Nearly forty lower ranking senior officers (captains and commanders in the Navy; colonels in the Marine Corp) were fined or otherwise disciplined with letters of censure or reprimand—putting a probable end to their careers as well.

Most of the junior officers escaped relatively unscathed. Although 117 officers were "implicated in one or more incidents of indecent assault, indecent exposure, conduct unbecoming an officer, or failure to act in a proper leadership capacity," not one was ultimately court-martialed or otherwise brought to public account. On the other hand, seven lieutenants, two junior-grade lieutenants and one lieutenant commander—all remained unidentified—were issued letters of admonition and each was docked one thousand dollars from their pay.

Unfortunately, some officers were unfairly caught in the cross-fire. One commander, the officer in charge of the Navy's Blue Angels, was denied promotion in 1995. Although he had been initially approved, a Senate committee and Navy Secretary John Dalton changed their minds after discovering that the officer had been in the area when the Tailhook scandal occurred. He had indeed been in Las Vegas during the crucial time, but he went there to receive an award and had been cleared by a Navy court of inquiry of any misconduct. Whether he will be promoted eventually has yet to be decided.

Even though Coughlin was able to identify her main assaulter, there were no corroborating witnesses willing to testify. In addition, in a pre-trial hearing, the accused's lawyer produced a picture of the man—allegedly taken at the time of the Tailhook incident—in different clothing than Coughlin had described, and so the Marine general acting as judge dismissed the case. In addition, apparently all the officers interviewed either lied outright, "couldn't remember" due to overconsumption of alcohol, or they stonewalled, refusing to speak about anything that had happened or to implicate anyone. So in the end, the investigation ground to a halt with not one of the actual perpetrators held accountable for what they had done.

Coughlin v. Las Vegas Hilton

As a consequence, Coughlin (and six of the other victims) sued the Tailhook Association and the Las Vegas Hilton Hotel—and its corporation—for failing to provide the proper security for guests. The Tailhook Association settled with Coughlin before trial for $400,000—and with six other women who likewise had sued charging sexual assault. They settled for an undisclosed amount, though their lawyers did admit to a sum in six figures for each victim.

After seven weeks of testimony, the jury awarded Coughlin $1.7 million in compensatory damages for emotional distress and $5 million in punitive damages. Judge Philip M. Pro later reduced the total amount. He deducted the Tailhook settlement from the $1.7 million compensatory damage and cut back the punitive damages to $3.9 million because Nevada law limited punitive damages to three times the compensatory damages.

The next chief of Naval Operations, the late Michael Boorda, who took over from Kelso when he retired in April 1995, had attempted to help Coughlin by transferring her to his office while he was still head of Naval Personnel. Nevertheless, hounded by hate mail, and emotionally exhausted, Coughlin resigned from the Navy in February 1995. As of May 1995, the Hilton Hotels Corporation appealed the judgment and sought a new trial, so the story is not over.

For Further Reading

Army Times Publications, August 16, 1994.

Glamour, November 1994.

Ladies Home Journal, November 1992.

Navy Times, August 22, 1994.

New York Times, June 14 and 17, 1992; October 22, 1993; March 13, 1995; May 12, 1995; and June 23, 1995.

Time, February 21, 1994; and May 2, 1994.

Glossary

Note: References to other defined terms are set in **bold** type.

Accomplice: one who voluntarily engages with another in the commission or attempted commission of a crime

Alimony: an agreement or court order for periodic support payments to either husband or wife after a marriage has ended

Affirmative action: preferences given one group over another to ease conditions resulting from past discrimination

A mensa et thoro: a form of legal separation in which the spouses remain married but do not live together

Amicus curiae: literally, "friend of the court," an individual or entity not party to the lawsuit whose role is to provide the court with information, typically a legal brief, which might not otherwise be considered by the court

Annulment: a nullification, as of a marriage; when a marriage is annulled, it is as if it never existed, whereas divorce terminates the legal status of the marriage from that point forward

Appellant: the party appealing a decision to a higher, appellate court

Appellate jurisdiction: the power of a superior court or other tribunal to review the judicial actions of lower courts, particularly for legal errors, and to revise their judgments accordingly

Appellee: the party who prevailed in the court below the appellate court and who argues on appeal against setting aside the judgment of the lower court

Bona fide: in good faith

Brief: a written argument used by a lawyer in representing a client

Certiorari: *see* **Writ of *certiorari***

Chancery: law exercised in a court of **equity,** originally by a chancellor (synonymous with equity law)

Chattel: a moveable piece of personal property; a slave was chattel and, until the early 1970s, federal law described female spouses of military personnel as chattel

Circumstantial evidence: indirect, secondary facts from which the existence or non-existence of a fact at issue in a case may be inferred

Civil liberties: rights that are protections from governmental action, reserved for individuals

Civil rights: rights given by positive laws enacted by civilized communities

Claimant: the party, customarily the **plaintiff,** asserting a right, usually to money or property

Class action: a lawsuit brought by a representative individual(s) of a larger group on behalf of all members who share a common interest

Clemency: the act, usually by a chief executive such as a president or governor, of forgiving a criminal liability for his or her actions, as when a **pardon** is granted

Co-conspirator: one who engages in a **conspiracy** with others; the acts and declarations of any one conspirator are admissible as evidence against all his or her co-conspirators

Cohabitation: the act of living together publicly as husband and wife; forbidden in some local and state laws

Common law: principles and rules of action derived from past judicial decisions, as distinct from laws created solely through legislative enactment or **equity** jurisprudence

Community property: in present day terms, everything acquired by either spouse after marriage, except for gifts and inheritances. In earlier times, all "common" property was vested in the husband

Commutation: alteration or substitution, such as when one criminal punishment is substituted for another, more severe one

Conveyance: the transfer of real estate to another person, such as in a sale or mortgage

Conspiracy: the agreement of two or more individuals to commit, through their joint efforts, an unlawful act

Coroner's inquest: an examination by the coroner, often with the aid of a jury, into the causes of a death occurring under suspicious circumstances

Court of chancery: courts that follow rules of **equity,** or general rules of fairness, rather than strictly formulated common law; distinctions between courts of equity and courts of law have essentially disappeared at both the state and federal levels

Cross-examination: questioning a witness, by a party or a lawyer other than the one who called the witness, about testimony the witness gave on **direct examination**

Coverture: the condition of married women who, under common law, gave sexual and housekeeping services to their husbands in return for his protection; in practice, women lost their specific legal identity, property (including their own wages and right to inherit), right to engage in business (make contracts, sue, or be sued), and had a right to the custody of their children

Declarative judgment of relief: a binding adjudication of the rights and status of parties that does not require any further action or relief

Devise: to bequeath property to others in a will

Defamation: speech **(slander)** or writings **(libel)** that damages the reputation of another

Direct evidence: testimony at trial by a witness who actually heard the words or saw the actions that, if believed by the trier of fact, conclusively establish a fact at issue

Direct examination: initial questioning of a witness by the lawyer who called him or her, the purpose of which is to present testimony regarding the facts of the examining party's case

Dower: an inheritance to which a wife is entitled upon the death of her husband, usually amounting to one-third of his estate

Due process: applicable only to actions of state or federal governments and their officials, it guarantees procedural fairness when the state deprives an individual of property or liberty; also, substantive due process requires that all legislation be enacted solely to further legitimize governmental objectives

Ejectment: a legal action brought by one person who claims title to property against another who possesses it, or is a tenant

Equity: a form of justice; developed in England to provide equal treatment where the common law did not

Expert witness: a witness, such as a psychological statistician or ballistics expert, with special knowledge concerning the subject about which he or she will testify

Felony: high crimes, such as burglary, rape, or homicide, which unlike misdemeanors, are often punishable by lengthy jail terms or death

Feme covert: under common law, a married woman

Feme sole: under common law, an unmarried woman

Feme sole trader: a married woman who, by special law, does business on her own, separately from her husband

Habeas corpus: a procedure for a judicial ruling on the legality of an individual's custody, used in a criminal context to challenge a convict's confinement and in a civil context to challenge child custody, deportation, and commitment to a mental institution

Hearsay: a statement, other than one made by a witness at a hearing or trial, offered to prove the truth of a matter asserted at the hearing or trial; such statements are inadmissible as evidence except under certain circumstances

Heir-at-law: when the owner of a property has died without a will or given up the property, it goes to the person to whom the law gives it

Indictment: a formal written accusation drawn up by a public prosecuting attorney and issued by a grand jury against a party charged with a crime

Injunction: a judicial remedy requiring a party to cease or refrain from some specified action

Injunctive relief: an order to stop the enforcement of a law

In re: literally, "in the matter of"; used to signify a legal proceeding where there are no adversaries, but merely a matter, such as an estate, requiring judicial action

Interspousal immunity: a state common law rule, now largely abolished, prohibiting tort actions, or lawsuits concerning certain civil wrongs, between husbands and wives

Judicial notice: recognition by a court during trial of certain facts that are so universally acknowledged or easily verifiable (for instance, historical facts or geographical features) that do not require the production of evidence as proof of their existence

Judicial review: the examination of a trial court decision by an appellate court; power and responsibility of the U.S. Supreme Court and the highest state courts to determine the constitutionality of the acts of the legislatures and executive branches of their respective jurisdictions

Justifiable homicide: the killing of another in self-defense or in the lawful defense of one's property; killing another when the law demands it, such as in execution for a capital crime

Legatee: a person who receives an inheritance

Lessee: a person who holds an estate by lease, such as a tenant

Libel: a method of defamation expressed by false and malicious publication in print for the purpose of damaging the reputation of another

Manslaughter: unlawful killing of another without malice, aforethought, or an intent to cause death, it calls for less severe penalties than murder; most jurisdictions distinguish between voluntary, or intentional, manslaughter, and involuntary manslaughter, such as a death resulting from an automobile accident

Marriage settlement: a contract transferring a husband's property to his wife

Married Women's Property Acts: between 1839 and 1895, a series of married women property laws permanently elevated women's legal status; they guaranteed wives the absolute right to control the property they brought with them into marriage; New York State's Married Woman's Property Act (1848) reads in part: "The real and personal property of any female who may hereafter marry, and which she shall own at the time of her marriage, and the rents, issues and profits thereof, shall not be subject to the disposal of her husband nor be liable for his debts and shall continue her sole and separate property as if she were a single female"

Misdemeanor: any criminal offense less serious than a **felony,** generally punishable by a fine or imprisonment other than in a penitentiary and for a shorter period than would be imposed for a felony

Moot: irrelevant to the discussion even though not settled

Original jurisdiction: the authority to hear a case at its inception and to pass judgment on its law and facts, as opposed to **appellate jurisdiction,** which grants the power to review the decisions of lower tribunals, which can then be affirmed, reversed, or modified

Parole: a conditional release of a prisoner after he or she has served part of a sentence

Pardon: an act, usually of a chief executive such as a president or governor, that relieves a convicted individual from the punishment imposed for his or her crime and restores rights and privileges that have been forfeited because of it

Perjury: the criminal offense of making false statements while under oath

Plaintiff: the party who initiates a lawsuit, seeking a remedy for an injury to his or her rights

Police power of the state: the power of state and local governments to impose upon private rights restrictions that are necessary to the general public welfare

Preliminary injunction: a judicial remedy to keep a party from doing a specific act during trial to maintain the *status quo*

Prima facie: sufficient on its face and not requiring any further proof or support

Prima facie **case:** a case that, because it is supported by the requisite minimum of evidence and is free of obvious defects, can go to the jury; thus the defendant is required to proceed with its case rather than move for dismissal or a directed verdict

Pro bono: when an attorney takes a case without fee "for the public good."

Pro se: representing oneself without counsel

Punitive damages: compensation in excess of actual losses awarded to a successful **plaintiff** who was injured under circumstances involving malicious and willful misconduct on the part of the defendant

Quid pro quo: a required equal exchange

Rational basis test: a constitutional method of discovering whether a challenged law has a rational relationship to a legitimate and reasonable government objective

Reasonable doubt: the degree of certainty required for a juror to find a criminal defendant guilty, meaning that proof of guilt must be so clear that an ordinary person would have no reasonable doubt as to the guilt of the defendant

Reprieve: a temporary relief or postponement of a criminal punishment or sentence

Remand: to send a matter back to the tribunal from which it was appealed; when an appellate court reverses a judgment, the case is usually remanded to the lower court for a new trial

Slander: oral defamation; false and malicious words spoken with the intent to damage another's reputation

Stare decisis: the rule by which courts are slow to interfere with principles announced in former decisions

Statutory rape: the crime of having sexual intercourse with a female under an age set by the state statute

Strict scrutiny: a means of determining the constitutional validity of a law that creates a classification of a group of people

Subordination of perjury: the criminal offense of procuring another to commit **perjury**

Subpoena: a written order issued under court authority compelling the appearance of a witness at a judicial proceeding

Sui juris: one who has come of age and is capable of caring for oneself or is no longer under the care of a guardian

Summary affirmation: a decision that a superior court makes without hearing arguments to uphold a lower court's verdict

Temporary insanity: a criminal defense asserting that, because the accused was legally insane at the time the crime was committed, he or she did not have the necessary mental state to commit it and is therefore not responsible for the alleged criminal conduct

Title VII: part of the Civil Rights Act (1964) which bans discrimination against women and other groups

Voir dire: examination by the court or by lawyers for the parties of prospective jurors; also, a hearing by the court during trial out of the jury's presence to determine initially a question of law

Writ of *certiorari:* a means of gaining appellate review: a written order issued by an appellate court to an inferior tribunal, commanding the latter to forward the record of the proceedings below in a particular case

Writ of *habeas corpus:* a procedure used in criminal contexts to bring a petitioning prisoner before the court to determine the legality of his or her confinement *(see also* **habeas corpus)**

Writ of *mandamus:* an order issued by a court, usually to a lower court, commanding performance of some ministerial act or mandatory duty, or directing the restoration to the petitioner of rights and privileges that have been illegally denied

Appendix of Legal Citations and Sources

Adkins v. Children's Hospital: Adkins v. Children's Hospital of District of Columbia, 43 S Ct 394 (1923).

American Booksellers Association v. Hudnut: American Booksellers Association, Inc. v. Hudnut 771 F.2d 323 (1985); 106 S Ct 1172 (1986).

Automobile Workers v. Johnson Controls: Automobile Workers v. Johnson Controls, Inc., 499 US 187 (1991).

Baby M, Matter of: Matter of Baby M, 537 A.2d 1127 (NJ) 1988.

Barnes v. Hart: Barnes v. Hart, 1 Yeates 221, Pa. (1793).

Beall and King v. Woolford: Beall and King v. Woolford (Md., 1792–97) Chancery Records, 39: 30, MHR.

Birkbeck v. Ackroyd: Birkbeck v. Ackroyd, 29 Sickels 356, NY (1878).

Bowe v. Colgate-Palmolive: Bowe v. Colgate-Palmolive Company, 416 F.2d 711 (1969).

Bradwell v. Illinois: Bradwell v. State of Illinois, 83 US 130 (1873).

Breedlove v. Suttles, Tax Collector: Breedlove v. Suttles, Tax Collector, 302 US 277 (1937).

Buck v. Bell: Buck v. Bell, 47 S Ct 584 (1927).

Burk v. Phips: Burk v. Phips, 1 Root 487, Conn. (1793).

Califano v. Westcott: Califano v. Westcott 442 US 682 (1979).

California Federal Savings and Loan v. Guerra: California Federal Savings & Loan Association v. Guerra, 479 US 272 (1987).

Cammermeyer v. Aspin: Cammermeyer v. Aspin, 850 F.Supp. 910 (W.D. Wash. 1994).

Carroll v. Warren: Carroll v. Warren (Md., 1736), Chancery Records, 7:100, MHR.

Cleveland Board of Education v. LaFleur: Cleveland Board of Education v. LaFleur, 94 S Ct 791 (1974).

Coker v. Georgia: Coker v. Georgia, 433 US 584 (1977).

Corning Glass Works v. Brennan: Corning Glass Works v. Brennan, 417 US 188 (1974).

Coutts v. Greenhow: 2 Munford 363 (VA) 1811.

Craig v. Boren: Craig v. Boren, 97 S Ct 451 (1976).

Crandall v. Connecticut: Crandall v. State of Connecticut, 10 Ct. 339 (1834).

Dibble v. Hutton: Dibble v. Hutton, 1 Day 221 Conn. (1804).

Dothard v. Rawlinson: Dothard v. Rawlinson, 433 US 321 (1977).

Dyer, Mary: Mary Dyer Trials, *Records of the Governor, and Company of the Massachusetts Bay (1853-54)*, IV, pt. 1, pp. 383–90, 419 (ed. Nathaniel B. Shurtleff, Boston: From the Press of William White, Printer to the Commonwealth, 1854).

Eisenstadt v. Baird: Eisenstadt v. Baird, 92 S Ct 1029 (1972).

Fitch v. Brainerd: 2 DAY 163 (Conn.) 1805.

Frontiero v. Richardson: Frontiero v. Richardson, 411 US 677 (1973).

Fry v. Derstler: Fry v. Derstler, 2 Yeats 278 (Pa., 1798).

Geduldig v. Aiello: Geduldig v. Aiello, 417 US 484 (1974).

Goesaert v. Cleary: Goesaert v. Cleary, 69 S Ct 198 (1948).

Griffith v. Griffith's Executors: Griffith v. Griffith's Executors, 4 Harris & McHenry 101, Md. (1798).

Griswold v. Connecticut: Griswold v. Connecticut, 85 S Ct 1678 (1965).

Grove City College v. Bell: Grove City College v. Bell, Secretary of Education, 465 US 555 (1984).

Hair v. Hair: Rebecca E. Hair v. Irvine R. Hair, 10 Rich., S.C. 163 (1858).

Harris v. Forklift: Teresa Harris, Petitioner v. Forklift Systems, Inc., 114 S Ct 367 (1993).

Harris v. McRae: Harris v. McRae, 488 US 297 (1980).

Hishon v. King & Spalding: Hishon v. King & Spalding, 467 US 69 (1984).

Hutchinson, Anne: The Trial of Mrs. Anne Hutchinson at the Court of Newton, Massachusetts *History of New England*, James K. Hosmer, 1908.

Ireland v. Smith: Ireland v. Smith, 542 N.W.2d 344 (Mich. App. 1995).

Johnson v. Transportation Agency: Johnson v. Transportation Agency, Santa Clara County, 480 US 616 (1987).

Kempe v. Kennedy: Kempe's Lessee v. Kennedy, 9 US 173 (1809).

Kenny v. Udall and Kenny: Kenny v. Udall and Kenny, 5 Johnson's Chancery Reports 464, N.Y. (1821).

Kirchberg v. Feenstra: Kirchberg v. Feenstra, 101 S Ct 1195 (1981).

Lochner v. New York: Lochner v. New York, 25 S Ct 539 (1905).

Los Angeles Department of Water and Power v. Marie Manhart: Los Angeles Department of Water and Power v. Marie Manhart, 98 S Ct 1370 (1978).

Los Angeles v. Stately: People v. Stately, 91 Cal. App.2d Supp. 943, 206 P.2d 76 (1949).

Madsen v. Women's Health Center: Madsen v. Women's Health Center, 114 S Ct 2516 (1994).

Martin v. Massachusetts: Martin v. Commonwealth, 1 Williams, Mass. 347 (1805).

Marvin v. Marvin: Marvin v. Marvin, 557 P.2d 106 (1979).

Massachusetts v. Bangs: Massachusetts v. Bangs, 9 Mass. 386 (1812).

Massachusetts v. Fogerty: Commonwealth v. Fogerty, 8 Gray, Mass. 489 (1857).

McGuire v. McGuire: McGuire v. McGuire, 59 N.W.2d 336 (1953).

McKim v. McKim: McKim v. McKim , 12 Green 462, R.I. (1879).

Megrath v. Robertson: Megrath v. Robertson, 1 Desaussure 444 S.C. (1795).

Mendame, Mary: The Case of Mary Mendame, Plymouth Colony Records, Mass. 132 (1639).

Meritor Savings Bank v. Vinson: Meritor Savings Bank, FSB v. Vinson et. al. 477 US 57 (1986).

Michael M. v. Superior Court of Sonoma County: Michael M. v. Superior Court of Sonoma County, 101 S Ct 1200 (1981).

Minor v. Happersett: Minor v. Happersett, 88 US 162 (1875).

Mississippi University for Women v. Hogan: Mississippi University for Women v. Hogan, 458 US 718 (1982).

Missouri v. Celia, a Slave: Missouri v. Celia, a Slave, File 4496, Callaway County Court, October Term, 1855. Calloway County Courthouse, Fulton, Mo.

Muller v. Oregon: Muller v. Oregon, 28 S Ct 324 (1908).

New Bedford Rape Trials: People v. Viera, New Bedford Superior Court Docket No. 12265; People v. Silva, New Bedford Superior Court Docket No. 12266; People v. Cordeiro, New Bedford Superior Court Docket No. 12267; People v. Raposo, New Bedford Superior Court Docket No. 12268 (1984).

New York v. Sanger: New York v. Sanger, 222 N.Y. 192 (1918).

Oregon v. Rideout: 108,866 Circuit Court, County of Marion, Or. (1978).

Orr v. Orr: Orr v. Orr, 99 S Ct 1102 (1979).

Packard v. Packard: Packard v. Packard, 27 FAM LQ 515 (1864).

Pattison v. Pattison: Pattison v. Pattison, Chancery Records 6: 207, Md. (1736-37) MHR.

Paul, Alice and Other National Woman's Party Members: Hunter v. District of Columbia, 47 App. Cas. 406 (D.C.).

Peckford v. Peckford: Peckford v. Peckford, 1 Paige's Chancery Reports 275 (N.Y., 1828).

Pennsylvania v. Addicks: Pennsylvania v. Addicks, 5 Binney Pa. 519 (1813).

Pennsylvania v. Daniel and Douglas: Commonwealth v. Daniel, 232 A.2d 247 (1967).

Personnel Administrator of Massachusetts v. Feeney: Personnel Administrator v. Feeney, 442 US 256 (1979).

Phillips v. Martin Marietta: Phillips v. Martin Marietta, 400 US 542 (1971).

Pittsburgh Press v. Pittsburgh Commission on Human Relations: Pittsburgh Press Co. v. Pittsburgh Commission on Human Relations, 413 US 376 (1973).

Planned Parenthood of Southeastern Pennsylvania v. Casey: Planned Parenthood of Southeastern Pennsylvania v. Casey, 112 S Ct 2791 (1992).

Prince v. Prince: Sarah Prince v. George Prince 1 Rich, S.C. (1845).

Reed v. Reed: Reed v. Reed, 404 US 71 (1971).

Roberts v. United States Jaycees: Roberts v. United States Jaycees, 468 US 609 (1984).

Roe v. Wade: Roe et al. v. Wade, 410 US 113 (1973).

Rostker v. Goldberg: Rostker v. Goldberg, 453 US 57 (1981).

Salem Witchcraft Trials: Salem Witchcraft Trials, Charles W. Upham, *Salem Witchcraft* (Boston: Wiggin and Lunt, 1867).

Scott v. Scott: Scott v. Scott, Widow, 1 Bay's South Carolina Reports 504 (1795).

Shaw v. Shaw: Shaw v. Shaw, 17 Day Conn. 189 (1845).

Sheepey, Charles: The Trial of Charles Sheepey, H. Clay Reed & George J. Miller, Burlington Court Book (1680–1709), 75 N.J. (1687).

Stanton v. Stanton: Stanton v. Stanton, 95 S Ct 1373 (1975).

Tailhook Scandal: Lt. Paula A. Coughlin v. Las Vegas Hilton Hotels Corporation CV-S-93-044-PMP, US District Court of Nevada (1994).

Taylor v. Louisiana: Taylor v. Louisiana, 419 US 522 (1975).

Triangle Shirtwaist Fire: People v. Harris, 74 Misc. 353, NY (1911).

United States v. Virginia: United States v. Commonwealth of Virginia, 976 F.2d 890 (4th Cir. 1992); 1996 Supreme Court citation unavailable.

United States v. Libbey-Owens-Ford: United States v. Libbey-Owens-Ford Co., 3 FEP Cases 372 Oh. (1971).

United States v. One Package: United States v. One Package, 58 US 98 (1936).

United States v. Susan B. Anthony: United States v. Susan B. Anthony, 24 F. Cas 829 N.Y. (1873).

United States v. Vuitch: United States v. Vuitch, 402 US 62 (1971).

Vaughan, Hester: Hester Vaughan, *New York Times*, Dec. 4, 1868; *Philadelphia Inquirer*, Dec. 3 & 4, 1868.

Watson v. Bailey: Watson v. Bailey, 1 Binney 470, Pa. (1808).

Webster v. McGinnis: Webster v. McGinnis, 5 Binney 235, Pa. (1812).

Webster v. Reproductive Health Services: Webster v. Reproductive Health Services, 492 US 490 (1989).

Weeks v. Southern Bell: Weeks v. Southern Bell Telephone and Telegraph Company, 408 F.2d 288 (1969).

Weinberger v. Wiesenfeld: Weinberger v. Wiesenfeld, 95 S Ct 1225 (1975).

West Coast Hotel v. Parrish: West Coast Hotel Company v. Parrish, 300 US 379 (1937).

INDEX

Boldfaced numerals denote an entire section devoted to that subject; *italicized numerals* denote references to illustrations.

A

A mensa et thoro, 241
A vinculo matrimonii, 241, 283
Abandonment, 243, 290
Abbott, George, 220
Abbott, Jane. *See also* Pattison, Jane
Abnormalities, 429
Abolitionists, 16
Abortifacients, 158
Abortion(s), xxix, 30, 41, 149–52, 158, 161, 167–73, 177–78, 181–85, 187–89, 191, 197–200, 202–207, 210–11, 322, 333. *See also* trials in "Reproductive Rights" section
Abortion clinics, 202
Abortion Control Act, 202, 203, 205
Abortionists, 159, 172
Abraham, Lorraine, 192, 193
Absentee act, 93, 94
Accident of birth, 310
Ackroyd, Edmund, 153, 296, 297
ACLU. *See* American Civil Liberties Union (ACLU)
"An act for preventing the Sales of the Real Estates of Heiresses, without Their Consent" (1723), 255
Adams, Andrew, 223
Adams, H. B., 346
Adams, Judge, 17
Adams v. Kellogg (1788), 250, 254, 255
Addams, Jane, 354

Addicks, Barbara, 271–71
Addison, H. D., 304
Adkins, Jesse C., 352
Adkins v. Children's Hospital (1923), 109, 337, 344, 350, **352–56,** 357, 358
Adkins v. Lyons, 353, 356
Administration of Estates Act (Section 45), 232, 246
Administrative Regulation 204, 399
Adoption, 183, 190, 191, 197, 333
Adultery, 39, 43–44, 164, 214, 241–43, 271–72, 277–78, 280, 283, 287, 290
Advertising, gender-segregated help wanted, 379–80
AFDC-UF. *See* Aid to Families with Dependent Children, Unemployed Father (AFDC-UF) program
Affirmative Action Office (Santa Clara County, Cal.), 424
Affirmative action plans, 338, 424, 425
Affirmative action programs, 423
AFL. *See* American Federation of Labor (AFL)
African race. *See* Blacks
After-the-fact appeal, 32
Against Our Will: Men, Women and Rape (Brownmiller), 81
Age, 142, 197, 198
Age discrimination, 430. *See also* Discrimination
Aid to Families with Dependent Children, Unemployed Father (AFDC-UF) program, 324, 325, 326
Aiello, Carolyn, 394, 395
Ainsworth, Robert A., Jr., 365
Alabama Board of Corrections, 399

Alderman, Kate, 58
Aldrich, A. P., 287
Aldrich, J. T., 287
Alienage, 310
Alimony, 119, 214–15, 277, 280–82, 287–
    90, 316–17, 320, 322
Allegyer v. Louisiana (1897), 342
Allen, John, 247, 252
Allgeyer, Gary, 209
Alsup, William H., 324
Alvord, D.W., 53
American Birth Control League, 159, 160
American Booksellers Association v. Hudnut
    (1986), 40, **86–90**
American Civil Liberties Union (ACLU),
    88, 70, 113, 168, 203
American College of Gynecologists and
    Obstetricians, 181
American Constitutional Law (journal), 356
American Federation of Labor (AFL),
    56, 350
American labor movement, 366
American Magazine, xxiv
American Medical Association, 149, 158,
    161
American Medicine (journal), 160
American Newspaper Publishers
    Association, 380
American Revolution, xxi, xxiii, xxiv,
    xxvi, 213, 214, 246, 247, 250, 260,
    268, 277, 283
American Women (1963) (report), 63
amicus curiae, 70, 71, 113, 124, 129, 181,
    197, 198, 309
Amniocentesis, 150
Anderson, Elizabeth. *See* Hishon,
    Elizabeth Anderson
Anderson, Myron E., 112
Anderson v. Brand (1938), 317
Andrews, Charles, 296, 297
Andrews, William S., 29
Annulments, 287
Anthony, Susan B., xxv, xxvi, xxx, 2, 13,
    21–24, *23*, 97–98, *98*, 104–105, 109,
    114, 250, 296. *See also United States v.
    Susan B. Anthony*
Anti-abortion groups, 207; law(s), 149,
    150, 169, 167, 170. *See also* Abortion
Anticontraceptive laws, legislation, 162,
    165. *See also* Contraception

Anti-discrimination laws, 378; policies,
    418. *See also* Discrimination
Anti-feminists, 375. *See also* Feminists
Anti-motherhood bias, 375
Anti-obscenity laws, 158
Anti-pornography law, 86
Arizona Governing Committee v. Norris
    (1983), 403
Arlund, Rick, 119
Armed forces, 127, 338, 407, 409
Armed robbery, 115
Armendariz, Augustina, 394, 395
Army, U.S., 2, 35, 37
Army War College, 34
Artificial insemination, 190, 193
Aspin, Les, 34
Assault and battery, 69, 151, 152, 334,
    335, 486; sexual, 86, 87, 89, 438
"At fault," 278
Atkinson, Jeff, 335
Atlantic Monthly (magazine), 158
Austin, Aaron, 247, 252
Automobile Workers v. Johnson Controls
    (1991), 338, **428–32**
Aware Woman Center for Choice
    (AWCC), 207, 208, 209, 211
AWCC. *See* Aware Woman Center for
    Choice (AWCC)

B

Baby killers, 202, 207
Baby M trial. *See In the Matter of Baby M*
    (1988)
Baby Maranda. *See* Ireland-Smith,
    Maranda Kate
Baby M(elissa). *See In the Matter of Baby
    M* (1988)
Bacon, Judge, 17
Bailey, Mr., 256
Baird, William R., Jr., 172–75, *174*
Baird-Windle, Patricia, 207, 208
Bakers, 337, 347, 348, 354
Bakers' Journal (newsletter), 342
Bakeshop Act, 337
Balliro, Joseph, 172, 173, 175
Bamberger, Michael A., 86
Bangs, Isaiah, 149, 151, 152
Banishment, 5
Bankson, Mr., 226, 228

Barber, Richard, 73, 74
Barker, Sarah Evans, 88
Barnes, Earles, 226, 227
Barnes, Paulette, 416
Barnes v. Costle (1977), 416
Barnes v. Hart (1793), xxiii, 213, **226–29**, *227*
Barrow, Anne Llewellyn, 14
Barry, Patricia J., 414, 416
Bartenders, 361, 362, 363, 364
Basic Educational Opportunity Grants (BEOG), 135, 136, 137
Bathrooms, unisex, 384
Bator, Paul M., 135
Battery. *See* Assault and battery
Bay, Elihu Hall, 230
Beal v. Doe (1977), 186
Beall and King v. Woolford (1797), 214, **237–40**, *238*
Beall, Hamilton, 237–39
Beall, Leah, 237–39
Beecher, Henry Ward, 293
Bell, J. H., 153, 156
Bell, John C., Jr., 63, 67
Bell, Terrel H., 135, 136
Belmont, Alva, 57
Bender, Paul, 143
Benefits, disability, 324, 394, 412
Bennick, Irwin, 433
Benson, George, 17
BEOG. *See* Basic Educational Opportunity Grants (BEOG)
Berzon, Marsha S., 428
Best interests of the child, xxii, 271, 301, 302, 333, 334
Bfoq. See Bona fide occupational qualification (bfoq)
Bible, 187
Bigamy, 242, 287
Bigelow, Judge, 53, 54, 55
Bigotry, 87
Bill of Rights, 127, 165
Birkbeck, Thomas, 296, 297
Birkbeck v. Ackroyd (1878), 213, **296–99**, *298*
Birth control, xxi, 31, 32, 158, 159, 160, 181; clinic, xxix, 2, 29, 30, 159, 163; devices, 172; education, 30; laws, 162, 175; movement, 29, 161
Birth control statutes, 164, 165
Birth defects, 429

Birth mothers, 194
Bishop, Edward T., 61, 62
Bishop, Sarah, 11, 12
Bissell, Clark, 15, 19
Black, Eugene F., 361
Black, Hugo L., 109, 112, 162, 165, 167, 168–69, 361, 373
Black Law, 2, 15, 17, 18, 19
Blackmun, Harry E., 69–70, 77, 86, 112, 115, 119–21, 127, 131, 135, 139, *141*, 197, 203, 207, 308, 310, 312, 324, 326–27, 328, 373, 379, 383–85, 390, 394, 396, 398, 402, 406, 410, 414, 418–19, 423, 428, 430, 433
Blacks, xxv, 17, 21, 50, 82, 102, 107, 250, 310, 317, 399
Blackstone, Sir William, 53, 54
Blackstone's Commentaries, 246
Blackwell's Island, 31, 32
Blake, George, 93
Blanck, Max, 56, 58, 59
Blasphemy, 39
Bogardus, R., 277
Bona fide occupational qualification (bfoq), 365, 367, 369, 370, 371, 374, 375, 380, 398, 400, 430
Bondurant, Emmett J., II, 410, 411
Boorda, Michael, 439
Borah, William E., 356
Boren, David, 123
Boslaugh, Paul E., 304
Bosson, Wiliam, 93
Boston State House, 9
Boston University, 172, 173
Bostwick, Charles S., 56, 58
Boulware, Isaac M., 48, 50
Bowe, Thelma, 369, 370
Bowe v. Colgate-Palmolive (1969), 338, **369–72**
Brace, Jonathan, 247, 252
Brackenridge, Justice, 256, 268
Bradford, William, 226
Bradley, Joseph P., xxvi, 91, 100, 103, 104
Bradwell, Myra, xxvi, xxx, 91, 100, 101, *101*, 102, 103, 114
Bradwell v. Illinois (1873), xxv, xxvi, xxx, 91, **100–103**
Brainerd, Abigail Mary, 253
Brainerd, Jehu, 252, 253
Brandeis brief, xxvii, 348, 349, 350

Brandeis, Louis, D., xxvii, 109, 153, 346, 348–50, *349*, 352, 355, 357

Breadwinners, 215, 235, 308, 320, 324, 325, 327

Breedlove, Nolen R., 109, 110

Breedlove v. Suttles, Tax Collector (1937), 91, **109–11**

Brennan, Peter J., 390

Brennan, William J., Jr., 69, 71, 77, 80, 86, 112, 115, 119, 125, 129, 131, 135, 139, 141, 149, 162, 167, 172, 175, 177, 181–83, 185, 197, 308, 310, 312, 314, 316–18, *317*, 324, 373, 379, 385, 390–94, 398, 402, 406, 410, 414, 418–19, 423, 425

Brewer, David B., xxvii, 341, 346, 348, 350

Breyer, Stephen G., 143, 433

Brodzinsky, David, 192, 194

Bronze Star, 2, 34

Brooke, Francis T., 264, 266

Brooklyn Eagle (newspaper), 31

Brooks, Constance E., 423

Brooks v. Schwerin (1873), 297

Brown, J. W., 293

Brown, John R., 178

Brown v. Board of Education of Topeka (1954), 18

Brownmiller, Susan, 46, 47, 81

Bruch, Carol, 335

Bruner, Fred, 179

Bucci, Lido, 336

Buck, Carrie, 150, 153, 154–55, 156, *156*

Buck, Emma, 153

Buck v. Bell (1927), 150, **153–57**, *154*

Buck v. Priddy. See Buck v. Bell

Buckley, James L., 185

Buffum, Arnold, 16

B.U. News, 172, 173

Bundy v. Jackson (1981), 415

Bunting v. Oregon (1971), 354

Bureau of Fire Prevention (New York, N.Y.), 60

Burger, Warren E., 69, 71, 77, 79, 86, 112, 115, 119, 125–27, 131, 135, 139, *141*, 167, 172, 177, 185, 308, 310, 312, 316, 324, 328, 373, 379, 383–85, 390, 394, 398, 402, 406, 410, 412, 414

Burk, Edward, 223–25

Burk, Mrs., 223–25

Burk v. Phips (1793), xxii, 214, **223–25**, *224*

Burns, Lucy, *26*, 27

Burt, Charles, 73, 75

Burton, Harold H., 361

Bush, George, 144, 198, 203, 437

Business and Professional Women, 380

Business necessity, 429–30

Butler, Pierce, 109, 110–11, 153, 352, 357

Buxton, Charles Lee, 162, 163, *163*, 164

By These Standards, We Are All Unfit Mothers (document), 194

Byrne, Ethel, 30, 31, 159

Byron, Lord, 158

C

Cabell, William H., 264

Cable Act (1922), 109

Cady, George, 17

Cal Fed. *See* California Federal Savings and Loan Association (Cal Fed)

Califano, Joseph A., Jr., 324–27, *325*, *325*

Califano v. Goldfarb (1977), 326

Califano v. Webster (1979), 318

Califano v. Westcott (1979), **324–27**

California Federal Savings and Loan Association (Cal Fed), 419–21

California Federal Savings and Loan Assocation v. Guerra (1987), 338, **419–22**

Call, Mr., 264, 265

Call, The (newspaper), 30

Callaway Hall, *132*

Calvinist, 292

Cammermeyer, Margarethe, 2, 34–37

Cammermeyer v. Aspin (1994), **34–37**

Canterbury Female Boarding School, 15, 19

Capell, John L., III, 316

Capital City Federal Savings and Loan Association, 414, 415

Cardoza, Benjamin N., 29, 109, 357

Carey Population Services, 162

Carey v. Population Services International (1977), 175

Carlson v. Carlson (1953), 290

Carnegie Hall, 31

Carnegie Institute of Washington, 155

Carol L., 86

Carpenter, Matthew H., 100, 102, 103
Carroll, Charles, 217, 218, 219
Carroll v. Warren (1736), xxiii, 213, **217–19**, *218*
Carter, Edward F., 304
Carter, Jimmy, 127, 128, 410
Cascadian Hotel, 358, *358*
Casey, Robert P., 202–203
Cashen, Raymond, R., 302, 334–36
Cassidy, Harold, 190, 192, 194
Cat o'nine tails, 43
Catholic faith. *See* Roman Catholic Church
Celia, 48–52
Century of Struggle (Flexner), xxii
certiorari, 430
Chain of command, 437
Chancery Court(s), xxiii, 234, 235, 249, 265, 275, 277, 287, 296. *See also* Equity courts
Chappell, Ellwood B., 304
Charity, 153
Chase, Amory A., 29
Chase, Salmon P., 100
Chase, Samuel, 260
Chattel, 213
Chernau, Stanley M., 433
Chesebro, Ray L., 61
Chesler, Ellen, 161
Chester, John, 252
Chesterfield (Ohio) County School Board, 385
Chicago Legal News, xxvi, 100, 101, *102*
Children's Hospital of District of Columbia, 352, 353, *353*
Child abuse, 87
Child custody, 63; law(s), 223, 301; support, 119, 280, 334
Childbearers, 366
Childbirth, 182, 186, 187, 189, 191, 200, 397, 420, 431
Children, xxvii, 88, 337, 354, 360, 428–29; unborn, 198
Children's rights, 266
Christ, 5, 295
Church of Boston, 7
Church of the Latter Day Saints, 1
Church, Samuel, 15, 19, 283
Cigarmakers Union, 337
Circumcision, 396
Citadel, 147

Citizens and citizenship, 18, 19, 107; rights and responsibilities of, xxi, 91–92, 100
Civil Death, 268
Civil disobedience, 159
Civil law, 266
Civil rights, 40, 63, 87, 338, 387; law, 425; movement (1960s), 16
Civil Rights Act, 1964, 142, 369, 370, 374, 376, 404
Civil Rights Act: Title VII (1964), xxviii, 338, 344–45, 365, 367–68, 371–73, 375, 377, 379, 396, 399–400, 402–403, 410–12, 414, 416–17, 419–21, 423, 425, 428, 430–31, 433, 435
Civil Rights Restoration Act of 1988, 135, 138
Civil War, xxv, 16, 19, 144, 158, 246, 337, 406
Clark, Joseph B., 162, 164–65
Clark, Tom C., 162
Clarke, Charles F., 385, 388
Class-action lawsuit, 325, 370, 372
Class conflict, 366
Claverack College, 29
Clayman, David, 376
Cleary, Owen J., 361
Cleveland Board of Education, 385
Cleveland Board of Education v. LaFleur (1974), xxix, 338, **385–89**
Cleveland, Deborah, 75
Clifford, Nathan, 100, 104
Clifford, Robert, 190
Clinton, Bill, 143, 145, 421
Coalter, John, 264, 266
Code Napoleon, 240, 331
Coffee, Linda, 150, 177, 178, 179
Cohabitation, 321
Cohen, Herbert B., 63
Cohen, Susan, 385, 386, 388
Coker, Erlich Anthony, 69, 70
Coker v. Georgia (1977), 39, **69–72**
Colao, Flora, 87
Colgate-Palmolive Company, 369, 370
Collective bargaining, 377, 378, 390
Collin, Frederick, 29
Colom, Wilbur O., 131
Colonial America, xxi, xxiii, 13, 287
Color, 369, 398, 411, 412
Colored citizens. *See* Blacks
Columbia Law School, 410

Combat, 129, 133

Combat units, 127, 128

Comley, John, 164

Commentaries (Blackstone), 268

Commentaries on the Laws of England, 53

Commercial speech, 383, 384

"Committee of 100," 31

Common law, xxii, xxiii, 40, 73, 63, 93,
    149, 151, 182, 213–14, 217, 222–23,
    226, 228, 230, 233–35, 237, 240–42,
    244–47, 248–50, 252–54, 260–61, 264,
    268, 271–72, 278, 296–97, 301, 321,
    323, 331, 382

Common sense, 420

Commonwealth [of Massachusetts] v. Biggs
    (1834), 301

Commonwealth of Pennsylvania v. Addicks
    (1813). *See Pennsylvania v. Addicks*
    (1813)

Compensation, 369

Compromise, 366

Comstock Act (1873), 29, 30, 31, 32, 149,
    158, 159

Comstock, Anthony, 158, 159

Comstock, Caleb, 248

Comstockery, 159

Conception, 152, 182, 190, 191, 198, 199,
    201

Condas, Joanne, 394, 395

Conditions, 369

Congregational Church, 17

Congress Hall Hotel, 352, 353

Congressional Record (U.S.), 393

Congressional Reports, 421

Connelly, William M., 376

Conner, C. B., 357, 358

Consent, 45, 203

Consent decree, 377, 378

Consent order, 376

Constitutional rights, 101, 112, 162

Consumers' League, 352

Content, Harold, 30

Contraception, 30, 149, 159, 160, 161,
    173

Contraceptive devices, 158, 159. *See also*
    Anti-contraceptive devices

Contraceptives, xxix, 2, 32, 158, 161, 162,
    164, 165, 172, 173, 175, 200; foam,
    173, 174; information on, 163–64; use
    of, 178. *See also* Anti-contraceptive
    laws

Contracts, xxii, 103, 322, 268, 342, 348,
    412

Contributing to the delinquency of a
    minor, 79

Control, editorial, 380

Conveyance, 228, 265

Cooke, Joseph P., 247

Cooke, William, 237

Copelon, Rhonda, 185, 188

Copperhead, 293

Cordeiro, John, 81, 82, *82*, 83, 84

Corey, Giles, 12

Corning Glass Works, 390

Corning Glass Works v. Brennan (1974),
    xxviii, 338, **390–93**

Correia, Marie, 83

Corwin, Jonathan, 11

Corwin, Samuel, *238*

Cotati, Teresa de la O, 77

Cotton, John, 3, 5

Coughlin, Paula, 436–39

Counseling, pregnancy, 207

County Court (Brooklyn, Conn.), 17

Court of Quarter Sessions of Philadelphia
    County, 67

Court of Special Sessions (Brooklyn,
    N.Y.), 31

Court-packing plan, 356

Coutts, Reuben, 264–67

Coutts v. Greenhow (1811), 213, **264–67**

Covenant of Works (Puritan), 4

Covenant Presbyterian, 208

Covert, 228. *See also* Feme(s) covert

Coverture, xxii, 247, 249, 250, 255

Cowell, M., 260, 261

Coxe, Grace. *See* Kempe, Grace

Craig, Curtis, 123, *124*

Craig, Mary, 428, 429

Craig v. Boren (1976), 77, 79, 92, **123–
    26,** 145, 311, 364

Crain, Thomas C. T., 56, 59

Crandall, Prudence, 2, 15–19, *18*

Crandall v. Connecticut (1834), **15–20**

Crane, Frederick E., 29, 32

Crimes, gender-based, 55; religious, 2;
    violent, 47

Crimes against chastity law (Mass.), 174

Crimes against nature, 39

Crimes of conscience and nonconformity,
    xxi, 1–37

Criminal conversation, 242. *See also* Adultery
Crocker, Gertrude, 25, 27
Croesus, 265
Crowley, Richard, 21, 22–23
Cruel and unusual punishment, 70
Cruelty, 214, 241, 243, 278, 280, 283–85
Cuddeback, William H., 29
Cumming, William, 217
Cummings, Walter J., 369
Curtis, Michael, 218
Curtis, Sarah, 217–219
Custody, xxi, xxii, 190, 192–94, 214–15, 224, 229, 271, 300–302, 333–36, 354
Custody committee, American Bar Association, 335

D

Daggett, David, 15, 18
Daggert, Mr., 247, 252
D'Alemberte, Talbot, 207
Dall, Mark, 86, 88
Dalton, John, 438
Daly, Mary, 181
Damages, compensatory, 439
Dana, Francis, 93, 94, 95
Daniel, Clarence, 67
Daniel, Jane, 63, 64, 65, 67
Dargan, Job, 287, 289–90
Dartmouth, 343
Date rape, 41
Davenport, Rev. John, 3
Davidow, Anne R., 361, 362
Davis, Daniel, 93
Davis, David, 100, 104
Day care, 302, 334, 335
Day, William R., 341, 343, 346
D.C. General Hospital, 168
Dealer, sole, 235
Death, xxii, 53, 191
Death penalty, 46, 69, 72
Debauchery, 437
Declaration of Independence, 22
Declaration of Rights, 100
Declaration of Rights and Sentiments, 223
Declarative relief, 180
Declaratory relief, 178
Deed or Conveyance, 219
Deeds, xxi

Deep Throat (film), 87
Delany, D., 217
Democracy, 26
Demonstrations, 376
Den, John, 260
Department of Education, U.S., 136
Department of Fair Employment and Housing (Cal.), 419
Department of Human Rights (Minn.), 140, 141
Department of Motor Vehicles, 207
Dependency, 335
Derr, Allen R., 112, 113, 114
Derstler, Adam, 241, 242
Desertion, 214, 241, 242, 243, 278, 280, 283, 287, 288, 290
Detamore, Charlie, 156
Deukmejian, George, 77
Devil, 11, 52
Devil's mark, 39
Devine, Magdalen, *227*
Dibble, Nehemiah, 247, 249, 250
Dibble v. Hutton (1804), 213, **247–51, ***248*
Dickinson, Anna, 98
Differences, biological, 366; sex-based, 404
Disability, 395; gender-linked, 396
Disciplinary action, 437
Discrimination, 67, 87, 138, 140, 310, 313, 338, 362, 369–70, 372, 374, 377–78, 388, 392–93, 400, 409, 413–14, 418, 428, 430; age, 430; economic, 344; gender, 326, 338, 393, 410, 430; job, 338, 402, 433; legal, 64; private, 412; racial, 142, 372; reverse, 420; sexual, xxvii, xxxi, 87, 122, 124, 126, 129, 132, 135, 138, 142, 145–46, 310, 315, 325–26, 338, 345, 369–70, 373, 375–76, 380, 383, 398, 400, 410–11, 414; Supreme Court tests to determine, 36
Disobedience, 290
Distress, emotional, 439
Divorces, xxi, 213–15, 219, 241–43, 271, 277–79, 283; *a mensa et thoro*, 187, 283, 285; *a vinculo matrimonii*, 187; absolute, 187; law(s), xxiii, 277, 279; private, 283
Dobbs, Alice, 153
Dobbs, J. T., 153

Doctor-patient relationship, 170

Doctrine of necessities, 220, 222

Doctrine, Puritan, 3

Doe v. Bolton (1973), 183

Doe v. General Hospital of the District of Columbia (1970), 169

Dohrmann, Robert M., 402

Dole, Abijah, 293

Dole, Sybil, 294

Dominion of New England, 13

Donahue, Frank, 190

Dooling, John F., 186–87

Dorrumple, Eleanor, 222

Dorrumple, John, 221

Dorsen, Norman, 167

Dothard, E. C., 398

Dothard v. Rawlinson (1977), xxix, 368, 388, **398–401**, 431

Double standard, 279, 396

Douglas, Daisy, 63, 67

Douglas, William O., 112, 115, 119, 162, 165, 167, 169–70, 172, 177–78, 308, 310, 312, 316, 361, 364, 373, 379, 383–85, 390, 394, 396

Dower, 213, 230, 249, 264, 266, 278

Dower right(s), 230–32, 244–46

Draft registration, 127, 128

Dred Scott decision, 19

Dred Scott v. Sandford, 52, 106–107

Driver, Sam M., 357, 358

Druggists, 159

Drugs, 383

Due process, 164, 169, 186, 343. *See also,* e.g., Fifth Amendment

Dulany, D., 220

Duncanson, Dr., 295

Dunkin, Benjamin F., 280, 281, *281*, 287

Dunmore, W. T., 341

Durfee, Charles S., 300, 301, *301*

Duvall, Justice, 244

Dworkin, Andrea, 40, 86, 87, 194

Dyer, Eliphalet, *223*

Dyer, Mary, 1, 5, **7–10**, *8*

Dyer, William, 9

E

Eagen, Michael J., 63

Eagle, Carrie Buck. *See* Buck, Carrie

Eagle, William Davis, 156, *156*

Earl, Robert, 296

Easterbrook, Frank, 89

Economic discrimination, 344. *See also* Discrimination

Edmund, William, 252

Education Amendments of 1972, Title IX *(also called* Higher Education Act of 1972) 122, 132, 133, 134, 135, 136, 137, 138

Edward I, king of England, 53

Edwards, Mr., 252

Edwards, Sharon-Lee, 333, 334

EEOC. *See* Equal Employment Opportunity Commission (EEOC)

Effron, Ellen, 335

Eighth Amendment, 69, 70, 71

Eisenstadt, Thomas, 172, 173

Eisenstadt v. Baird (1972), xxix, 32, 149, 161, 162, **172–76**, 181

Ejectment, 227

Elders of Boston, 5

Electrocution, 70

Elliott, Mr., 280

Ellis, Wade H., 352

Ellsworth, Oliver, 247, 252, 260

Ellsworth, William Wescott, 15, 17, 18

Elmendorf, E., 275

Embryo, 203

Emergencies, 368

Emerson, Thomas I., 162, 164

Employment, 406

Employment, women's night-time, 391

en banc, 89, 145, 416

Endecott, John, 7, 9

Environment, sexually abusive, 433

Ephron, Nora, 194

Equal Employment Opportunity, xxviii, 398, 421

Equal Employment Opportunity Commission (EEOC), 365, 367, 370–72, 375, 378–80, 399, 411, 425, 430; Guidelines on Discrimination Because of Sex (1985), 415–17

Equal opportunity, 142

Equal Opportunity section of Civil Rights Act (1964). *See* Civil Rights Act: Title VII

Equal Pay Act of 1963, xxviii, 352, 390–93, 404

Equal pay for equal work, 339, 391, 392, 404

Equal protection, xxx, 63, 362, 363

Equal Protection Clause, 65, 112, 113, 124, 125, 144, 145, 186, 215, 408. *See also* Fourteenth Amendment
Equal protection of the laws, 124
Equal rights, 40, 63, 342, 354
Equal Rights Amendment (ERA), xxi, xxx, xxxi, 1, 127, 128, 129, 306, 354, 356, 375
Equal rights for women, 361
Equality, xxx, 336
"Equality not Protection," 354
Equitable distribution statutes, 251
Equitable remedy, 322
Equity courts, xxiii, 249, 265, 287, 289, 297; jurisprudence, xxiii; and the law, xxiii, 228, 234, 237–39, 250, 296. *See also* Chancery Courts
ERA. *See* Equal Rights Amendment (ERA)
Ergot fungus, 13
Ernst, Morris L., 158, 160
Erwin, Margaret. *See* Henderson, Margaret
Erwin, Nathaniel, 227
Espionage Act of 1917, 26
Establishment clause, 189
Estabrook, Arthur, 155
Eugenic sterilization law (Va.), 153
Eugenics, 154
Evans, G. Daniel, 398
Excommunication, 5
Execution, 39
Exile, 5
Expressive association, 141, 142

F

Facism, 425
Fair Employment and Housing Act (FEHA), 419, 420
Fair Labor Standards Act of 1938, 357, 360. *See also* Wages and hours laws
Fairstein, Linda, 72
Family, 171, 388
Family and Medical Leave Act of 1993, 421–22
Family law, 215
Family, traditional, 326
Fathers, contracting, 150; unemployed, 324–27
Fathers' rights advocates, 302

Faulkner, Shannon, 147, *147*
Faux, Marian, 181
Fay, Mr., 151
Federal Jury Selection and Service Act of 1968, 117
Federal obscenity act, 158
Federal tuition aid, 135
Feeblemindedness, 150, 153, 154, 155
Feeney, Helen, 406, 407–409, *408*
Feenstra, Joan Paillot, 328–31
FEHA. *See* Fair Employment and Housing Act (FEHA)
Felonious intimacy, 53
Female sexuality, 30
Feme(s) covert, xxii, 94–95, 101, 103, 213, 226–27, 235, 247, 249, 252–55, 261–62, 268
Feme sole, 101, 224, 229, 268–69; traders, 233, 235
Feminism, 370, 379
Feminist Majority Foundation's 1994 Clinic Violence Survey, 211
Feminists, 69, 190, 296, 337, 346, 366, 378, 393. *See also* Anti-feminists
Feminization of poverty, 402
Fenton, William D., 346
Ferraro, Geraldine, 1
Fertility, 428,
Fess, Simeon, 355
Fetal deformity, 152
Fetal development, 197
Fetal life, 180
Fetal protection policies, 428, 429
Fetal viability, 201
Fetus, 181, 185, 188, 191, 197, 198, 199, 200, 429, 431
Field, Frank Harvey, 341, 342
Field, Julie Kunce, 333
Field, Stephen J., 100, 104
Fifth Amendment, 36, 106, 127, 165, 186, 324–25, 343, 352, 357; due process clause of, 128, 168, 187, 202, 308–10, 312–13, 327, 347, 353–54
Finch, Katherine, 5
First Amendment, 36, 86, 88–89, 127–28, 140, 165, 173, 179–80, 186–88, 207, 209, 382–84, 412
First-degree murder, 97
First Statute of Westminster, The, 53
First trimester, 177
First Wave (women's movement), 354

First women's rights convention (Seneca Falls, N.Y., 1848), 223

Fitch, Elizabeth Mary, 252, 253

Fitch v. Brainerd (1805), 214, **252–55**

Fleming, William, 264

Flexner, Eleanor, xxii, 331, 337

Flogging and whipping, 43, 45

Flowers, Robert, 177

Floyd, Jay, 177, 180, 181

Flynn, Felix H. H., 361

Fogerty, Patrick, 40, 53, 54

Force, 54

Ford, Mr., 230, 233, 234

Forklift Systems, Inc., 433

Fornication, 39, 164

Fortune-telling games, 11

Foster care, 183, 333

Founding Fathers, xxi, 182

Fourteenth Amendment, xxv–xxvi, 23, 63, 65, 79, 91, 92–95, 100–105, 107–10, 112–15, 117, 119–20, 123–24, 129, 131–32, 134, 140, 143–46, 156, 164–65, 179–80, 182, 186, 200, 309, 324–25, 328, 352, 357, 362, 388, 395; equal protection clause of, 316, 329–30, 361, 385, 396; equal protection of the laws under, 407–408

Frankfurter, Felix, xxi, 352, 361, 362–64

Fraud, 256

Frederick, J. Dennis, 119

Free speech, 88, 89, 141, 383, 384

Freedman, Henry A., 324

Freedom of choice, 188

Freedom of contract, 268, 357, 358, 359, 360

Freedom of intimate association, 141

Freedom of personal choice, 388

Freedom of religion, 187

Freedom of speech, 163, 164, 207, 210, 211, 382

Freedom of speech and association, 34

Freedom of the press, 382, 384

Freemen, 18

French, Marilyn, 194

French Revolution, 331

Freschi, Judge, 31

Fried, Charles, 197, 199–200

Friedan, Betty, 194

Fringe benefit program, 420

Frontiero, Joseph, 308–309, *309*

Frontiero, Sharon A., 308–309, *309*

Frontiero v. Richardson (1973), xxx, 125, 126, 145, 215, **308–11**, 312, 315, 386

Fry, John, 241, 242

Fry, Mrs. John, 242

Fry v. Derstler (1798), **241–43**

Fuller, Melville W., 341, 346

Fuller, Robert, 295

Fulton Telegraph (newspaper), 52

G

Gage, Matilda Joslyn, 13

Gardner, Booth, 34

Garibaldi, Marie, 190

Garland, Lillian, 419

Garment-making, 56

Garnett, Marion W., 369

Garrett, H. Lawrence, III, 437

Garrison, William Lloyd, 15, 16, 17

Garrow, David J., 202, 204

Gays, 34

Geary, John W., 97, 98

Gedney, Herbert, 296, 297

Geduldig, Dwight, 394, 395

Geduldig v. Aiello (1974), 338, **394–97**

Geis, Dr. Gilbert, 74

Gender, 315, 317, 326, 365, 369, 373, 424, 430; classification, 371; neutral, 335; segregation, 92

Gender-based law(s), 312, 325, 329

Gender-biased laws, 364

Gender discrimination, 326, 338, 393, 410, 430. *See also* Discrimination

General Electric Co., 396, 403, 405

General Electric Co. v. Gilbert, 403, 405

George (a slave), 48, 49

Gerard, Justinian, 218

Gerard, Sarah. *See* Curtis, Sarah

Gesell, Gerhard A., 168, 169

Gestation, 186

Gholson, Hunter M., 131

Gilbert, Frederick P., 124, 125

Gilfry, Henry H., 346

Ginsburg, Ruth Bader, xxxi, 70–72, 92, 112–13, 123–25, 143, 145–47, 207, 215, 308–11, 312–14, *314*, 354, 433, 435

Glass ceiling, 410

Glass, David M., 34

God, 3, 4, 12, 100, 293

Goddard, Calvin, 17, 18

Godfrey, Jackie, 74–75

Goesaert, Margaret, 361

Goesaert v. Cleary (1948), 338, **361–64,** *363*

Goesaert, Valentine, 361

Goldberg, Arthur, 162, 164–65

Goldberg, Irving S., 178, 179, 180

Goldberg, Robert L., 127, 129

Goldman, Mark A., 320

Goldmark, Josephine, xxvii, 346, 347, 348

Goldsborough, Justice, 244

Goldsmith, Judy, 128

Goldstein, Jonah J., 29, 31, 32

Goldstein, Leslie Friedman, 318

Gompers, Samuel, 56

Good-faith decisions, 169

Goodrich, Chauncey, 247, 252

Goodrich, Elizur, 252

Good, Sarah, 11, 12

Gordon, Bennett, 155, 156

Gormley, Kenneth, 83

Gortmaker, Gary D., 73

Gotcher, Mrs. Elmer, 346, 347

Gotham, Roy D., 333

Gout, 396

Grace, Sandra, 83

Grassley, Charles E., 72

Gray, James, H., 124

Great Depression (1930s), 350, 356, 358

Greeley, Horace, 293

Greenhow, James, 264, 265

Greif, Judith Brown, 192, 194

Greiner, Gladys, 25, 27

Gribbs, Roman S., 333, 335–36

Grievances, 378

Griffith, Martha, 244, 245

Griffith, Samuel, 244

Griffith v. Griffith's Executors (1798), 213, **244–46,** *245*

Griffiths, Martha, 128, 306

Griggs v. Duke Power Co. (1975), 399

Grindle, B. Dean, Jr., 69, 70

Griswold, Estelle T., 162, 163, *163*, 164

Griswold, Matthew, 252

Griswold v. Connecticut (1964), xxix, 32, 149, 161, **162–66,** 170, 171, 172, 175, 178, 199–200

Grove City College, 135

Grove City College v. Bell (1984), **135–38**

Guardian ad litem, 192

Guardianship, 354

Guerra (FEHA director), 419

Guforth, John, 96

Guidelines on Discrimination Because of Sex. *See* Equal Employment Opportunity Commission (EEOC)

Guilded Age (1873–1900), 296, 341

Gunn, David, 209

H

Habeas corpus, 22, 28, 173, 175, 271, 292

Hair, Irvine R., 287, 288–90

Hair, Rebecca E., 287, 288–90

Hair v. Hair (1858), 214, **287–91,** *289*

Hale, Matthew, 74

Half-way citizenship, 106

Hall, Carl D., Jr., 139, 141

Hall, David, 14

Hall, William, 48, 51

Hallford, Dr. James, 179

Hallucinogenic, 13

Hammond, Ann Eliza, 16

Hammond, Phillip[a], 5

Hand, Augustus H., 158

Hand, Learned, 158

Handler, Alan B., 190

Hanson, Alexander Contee, 237, 239–40

Happersett, Reese, 104, 106

Harassment, sexual. *See* Sexual harassment

Hardy, Charles, 433

Hardy, Lamar, 158

Harlan, John Marshall, 112, 162, 167, 341, 343, 346, 373

Harrington, Edward F., 81, 83

Harris, Isaac, 56, 58, 59

Harris, Patricia R., 185, 186, 187

Harris, Sarah, 15

Harris, Teresa, 433–35, *434*

Harris v. Forklift (1993), 338, **433–35**

Harris v. McRae (1980), 150, 183, **185–89**

Hart, Charles, 300–301

Hart, Joseph, 227

Hart, Mr., 25, 27

Hart, Solomon, 226

Haslett, Sarah, 292, 294

Hausman-Smith, Barbara, 328, 329, *329*

Hawthorne, John, 11

Hazards, fire, 387

Hazelbock, Joe, 346

Heart of Atlanta Motel, Inc., v. United States (1964), 142
Hebrew law, 281
Heide, Wilma Scott, 380, *382*
Height, 368
Heightened scrutiny, 311
Heinsma, David J., 365
Heir-at-law, 234, 258
Heir at Law, The (Davisson), xxiv
Helms, Jesse A., 185
Hemophilia, 396
Hendersen, John B., 104
Henderson, Margaret, 227–29
Henderson, Matthew, 227
Henry II, king of England, 246
Henry VIII, king of England, 252, 254
Hereditary Health Law (Germany), 157
Heresy, 4
Hewitt, Eliza. *See* Kenny, Eliza S.
Hewitt, Thomas, 274
Higgins, Margaret Louise. *See* Sanger, Margaret
Higher Education Act of 1972, Title IX. *See* Education Amendments of 1972
Hilles, Florence Bayard, 26
Hillhouse, William, 247, 252
Hilton Hotels Corporation, 436, 439
Himes, Michael H., 34
Hinkle, Jack, 75
Hinnan, Joel, 283, 284
Hiring standards, 373
Hirschkop, Philip J., 385, 387
Hiscock, Frank H., 29
Hishon, Elizabeth, 410–12
Hishon v. King & Spalding (1984), 388, **410–13**
Historia Placitorum Coronae, A History of the Pleas to the Crown (1736), 74
History of Women Suffrage (book), 13
Hixon, Samuel W., III, 385, 387, 388
Hoff, Joan, 246, 331
Hoffer, Peter Charles, 39, 241
Hoffman, J. Sydney, 64
Hogan, Joe, 131, 134
Hogan, John W., 29
Holman, Lucy, 149, 151
Holmes, Oliver Wendell, 153, 156, 341, 343–44, 346, 352, 355
Holy Ghost, 3, 293
Homicide, justifiable, 51
Homosexuality, 2, 35, 36

Hopkins, Allison Turnbull, 26
Hopkins, Ann B., 413
Hopkins, Mr., 241, 256, 258
Hopkinson, Joseph, 271
Horowitz, Pamela S., 398, 399
Horsley, W. F., 316
Hosmer, Stephen T., 252
Hours, workday, 346, 357, 365, 376
House Hearings, U.S., 393
Howe, Isaac P., 50
Hoyt v. Florida (1961), 117, 118
Hubbard, Mr., 283
Hudnut, William H., III, 86, 88
Hudson River Institute, 29
Hughes, Charles Evans, 109, 357, 358–59
Hughes, Sarah Tigham, 178, 180
Human Rights Act, 140
Human Rights Act (Minn.), 139
Human Rights Amendment, 142
Human welfare, 348
Hunger strike, 28, 32, 31
Hunt, Ward, xxvi, 21, 22, 23, 24, 104
Huntington, Samuel, 167, 308, 309
Hutcheson, Elizabeth, 45
Hutcheson, Martha, 45
Hutchinson, Anne, 1, **3–6,** 7
Hutton, Mary, 247, 248–50
Hutton, Samuel, 248–49
Hyde Amendment, 185, 186, 188, 189
Hyde, Henry J., 185

I

IGLWU. *See* International Ladies Garment Workers' Union (IGLWU)
Illinois' Act of 1869, 101, 102
Illinois Revised Statutes, 100
IMPACT. *See* Institute of Mobilized Prophetic Activated Christian Training (IMPACT)
Incest, 152, 186, 189, 335
Indians, xxiii
Indigency, 189
Industrial homes, 66
Industrial Welfare Commission, 359
Infants, xxiv, 252
Ingersoll, Jared, 247, 252, 271
Ingraham, Ezra L., 274
Inheritance, xxii, 234
"Inherently suspect," 124
Injunctive relief, 178, 180

Insanity, xxiv, 252, 292, 293, 294
Insemination, artificial, 190, 193
Institute of Mobilized Prophetic
     Activated Christian Training
     (IMPACT), 208, 209
Intercourse, sexual, 46, 51, 73, 75, 78, 79,
     80, 165, 415
International Brotherhood of Electrical
     Workers, Local Union No. 18, 403
International Chemical Workers Union,
     Local #15, 369
International Ladies Garment Workers'
     Union (IGLWU), 56, 58, 59
International Union, United Automobile,
     Aerospace, and Agricultural
     Implement Workers of America
     (UAW), 428
Interstate commerce, 360
Intervenor-defendants, 185
Intestate, 234, 245
In the Matter of Baby M (1988), 150, **190–
     96**
In the Matter of Karen Ann Quinlan (1975),
     162
Ireland, Jennifer, 302, 333–37
Ireland v. Smith (1995), 214, 302, **333–37**
Ireland-Smith, Maranda Kate, 302, 333–37

J

Jacksonian democracy, 282
Jackson, Robert H., 361
Jackson v. Transportation Agency (1987),
     338
James II, king of England, 13
Jameson, John, 48, 50, 51, 52
Jaramillo, Jacqueline, 394
Jaspan, Stanley S., 428
Jaycees, 92, 139–42
Jaycees, Minneapolis and St. Paul, 140
Jealousy, 214, 283
Jeninger, Edward, 220
Jewish faith, 81, 182, 187, 281
Jilka, Gregory F., 77
Job discrimination, 338, 402, 433. *See also*
     Discrimination
Jobs, civil service, 407
John Scopes Trial (1925) (The Monkey
     Trial), 117
Johns, Isaac, 221
Johnson Controls, Inc., 428

Johnson, Elizabeth, 394, 395
Johnson, Frank M., 365
Johnson, Mr., 280, 281
Johnson, Paul, 423–25
Johnson, Richard, 67
Johnson, Sonia, 1
Johnson v. Transportation Agency (1987),
     423–27
Johnston, Marion M., 419
Johnston, William, 260
Joint Commission on the Accreditation of
     Hospitals, 183
Joint venture, 322
Jones, Ann. *See* Woolford, Ann
Jones, Benjamin R., 63
Jones, Beverly W., 23
Jones, Jefferson, 50
Jones, Keith A., 312, 314
Jordan, Joseph, 173
Journeyman Bakers Union, 342
Joyce, Diane, 423–26, *427*
Judicial scrutiny, 215
Judson, Andrew T., 15, 16, 17, 18
Jukes in 1915, The (research study), 155
Julian, Anthony J., 173, 175
Junior Chamber of Commerce. *See*
     United States Jaycees
Jury service, xxi, xxix, 63, 115, 116, 354

K

Kahn v. Shevin (1974), 312, 314
Karlsen, Carol, 14
Keane, Noel, 191
Kelley, Florence, xxvii, 346, 347, 348,
     354
Kellogg, Mary, 250
Kelso, Frank, 437, 439
Kempe, Grace, 260–63
Kempe, John Tabor, 260
Kempe v. Kennedy (1809), 95, 213, **260–
     63**, *261*, *262*
Kendall, David E., 69
Kennedy, Anthony M., 143, 197, 199–
     200, 202–204, 207, 428, 433
Kennedy, John F., 40, 63
Kennedy, R., 260, 261, 262
Kenny, Edward M. L., 274–75
Kenny, Eliza S., 274–76
Kenny v. Udall and Kenny (1821), 214,
     235, **274–76**

Kerner, Otto, 369
Kidnapping, 69, 87, 115, 116
Kiley, Thomas R., 406
King & Spalding, 410–12
King, John, 237, 238–39
King, William M., 115, 116
Kirchberg, Karl J., 328–31
Kirchberg v. Feenstra (1981), xxx, 213, 240, 251, **328–32**
Knott, Christopher, 293
Knout, 43
Kolbert, Kathryn, 203
Koshin-Kintigh, Nancy, 208
Kouns, Nathan Chapman, 48, 50
Krieger, Sandy R., 77, *78*
Ku Klux Klan, 89

L

Labor, 228, 390
Labor laws, 365, 366, 376
Labor market, 337
Lacey, J. Robert, 163, 164
Ladies' Home Journal (magazine), 160
LaFleur, Jo Carol, 385, 386, 387, *387*, 388
LaFollette, Robert, 356
Laissez-faire, 341
Land agreement, 248
Las Vegas Hilton Hotel, 436, 438
Lascell, David M., 135
Lathrop, Julia, 354
Laughlin, Harry H., 154
Law, Anglo-American, 318
Law of inheritance, 250
Law, weight-lifting, 367
Lawley, Frank P., Jr., 63
Lawes Resolutions of Women's Rights; or The Lawes Provision for Women, The, xxii, 348
Laws, alimony, 316, 317; divorce, 283, 287; gender-neutral, 406; protective, 371
Layoffs, 370
Lead exposure, 428
Leaders, union, 348
League for Women Voters, 354
Leaves, maternity, xxix, 385–39; pregnancy disability, 338, 419, 420, 421
Leaves of absence, 429
Ledbetter, Les, 74
Lee, Joseph, 271–72
Lee, Sergeant, 27

Legal discrimination, 64. *See also* Discrimination
Legal separation(s), 278, 280
Legislation, protective, xxi, 337, 350, 367; labor, 421; social welfare, 354; state protective, 377
Lemlich, Clara, 56
Leonard, Abiel, 52
Lesbianism, 2, 34
Letter, right-to-sue, 425
Levin, Joseph L., Jr., 308, 309–10
Lewis, Harry E., 29
Lewis, Mr., 260, 262
Liability, employer, 418
Libbey-Owens-Ford Company, xxviii, 376–78
Liberator, The (newspaper), 15, 16
Liberty, 347, 359
Liberty of contract, xxvii, 342, 347, 352, 354, 357
Liberty, religious, 3
Life, 198, 347
Life expectancy, 404
Life imprisonment, 69
Life interest, 230
Life tenancy, 231, 232
Life-threatening situations, 152
Lincoln, Abraham, 337
Lindahl, Judith, 81
Liquor Control Commission of the State of Michigan, 361
Liquor trade, 124
Litchfield County Courthouse, *284*
Literature, pornographic, 158
Lobetkin, Esther, 57
Local 28 of the Sheet Metal Workers v. EEOC (1986), 425
Lochner, Joseph, 341
Lochner v. New York (1905), 337, **341– 45**, *342, 344*, 347, 348, 354, 357
Los Angeles, City of, Board of Commissioners of, 402
Los Angeles, City of, Department of Water and Power, 402, 403
Los Angeles Department of Water and Power v. Marie Manhart (1978), xxix, 338, **402–405**
Los Angeles v. Stately (1949), 40, **61–62**
Louisiana Civil Code of 1870, 328, 331
Lowe, David, 74
Lozier, Dr. Clemence, 97

Ludow, James Riley, 96
Lynn, Sherri, 119
Lyons, Willie, 352–53

M

Macaulay, Donald B., 173
McCorvey, Norma. *See* Roe, Jane (Norma
    McCorvey)
McCree, Wade H., Jr., 129, 185, 187
McDonald, A. L., 277
McFarland, Andrew, 294
McGinnis, Mr., 268, 269
McGregor, Robert, 209
McGuire, Charles W., 304–306
McGuire, Lydia, 304–306
McGuire v. McGuire (1953), 214, **304–307**
Machado, Carlos, 83
McIntosh, Millicent, 181
Mackall, Barbara, 222
McKean, Mr., 241
McKean, Thomas, 226, 229, 241
McKenna, Joseph, 341, 346, 352
Mackie, William S., 342
McKim, Anne B., 300
McKim, Charles F., 300
McKim v. McKim (1879), xxii, 214, 272,
    300–303
MacKinnon, Catharine, A., 40, 86, 87,
    414, 416–16
Macomb County Community College, 334
Macomb County Friend of the Court, 334
McLaurin, Melton, 51
McMahon, Caroline, 361
McRae, Cora, 185, 186
McRee, Wade H., Jr., 127
McReynolds, James C., 109, 153, 352,
    357
Madsen, Judy, 207, 208
Madsen v. Women's Health Center (1994),
    207–11
Magistrates of Massachusetts, 3
Magna Charta (1215), 246
Magrath, Mr., 280
Maher v. Roe (1977), 186, 188
Mahon, George, *180*
Majority, age of, xxx, 119, 120, 121. *See
    also Stanton v. Stanton* (1975)
Malone, Dudley Field, 25, 27, 28
Manhart, Marie, 402, 403
Mansfield, Arabella, 101

Manslaughter, 56, 59
Marine Corps, U.S., 437, 438
Marital agreement, 247
Marital privilege, 73
Marital property, 251
Marital status,197
Marot, Helen, 57
Marriage, xxxi–xxiii, 63, 165, 171, 213–
    15, 217, 226, 228, 243, 247, 250–51,
    265, 277, 280–81, 283, 318, 354, 388
Marriage certificate, 321
Marriage contract, 250
Marriage Disability, 100–101
Marriage settlement, 264, 265
Married Woman's Property Act of 1848
    (amended in 1849, 1857, and 1860),
    229, 237, 244, 250, 267, 275, 296, 297,
    331
Married woman's property rights, 235, 292
Marshall, Arthur K., 320, 322–23
Marshall, John, 95, 213, 260, 262, *262*
Marshall, Thurgood, 18, 69, 71, 77, 80,
    86, 112, 115, 119, 127, 131, 135, 139,
    167, 172, 177, 185, 197, 308, 310, 312,
    324, 328, 330–31, 373–75, 379, 385,
    390, 394, 396, 398, 402, 406, 410, 414,
    418, 419, 421, 423, 428
Martez, Julius, 163
Martin, Anna, xxiv, 93, 94
Martin, Anne Henrietta, 354
Martin, James, 51, 93, 95
Martin, Luther, 237
Martin Marietta Corporation, 373
Martin, Mr., 244, 245
Martin v. Massachusetts (1805), xxiv, 91,
    93–95, 213, 262
Martin, William, 93, 94
Marvin, Lee, 320, 322, 323
Marvin, Michelle Triola, 320, 321, 322, 323
Marvin v. Marvin (1979), 215, **320–23**
Mary Baldwin College, 145, 146
Mary, queen of England, 13
Massachusetts Bay Colony, 1, 3, 7, 9, 11
Masschusetts Civil Defense Agency, 407
Massachusetts Department of Public
    Welfare (DPW), 325–26
Massachusetts, Personnel Administrator
    of, 406
Massachusetts v. Bangs (1812), **151–52**
Massachusetts v. Fogerty (1857), xxii, 40,
    53–55, *54*

Matheney, Rebecca. *See* Hair, Rebecca
Matthews, Burbita Shelton, 354
Matthews, John, 233
Mattimoe, John G., 376
Maturity, lung, 198
Maximum hours, 354; law for women (1903), xxvii, xxviii, 346–51; rules, 370
Maximum wage, 354
Maximum work week, 360
May, Samuel J., 16, 17, 19
Mayer, Julius M., 341, 343
Mead, Margaret, 181
Medeiros, José, 81, 82, 83, 84
Medeiros, Virgilio, 81, 82, 83, 84
Medicaid, 185, 186, 188, 189, 325
Megrath, Catharine, 233, 234, 235
Megrath v. Robertson (1795), xxii, 213, **233–36**
Men, xxviii, xxxi, 88, 354, 361–62, 366–74, 376, 378, 384, 391, 396, 402–404, 407–408, 419–20, 428, 430, 435
Mendame, Mary, xxi, 39, **43–44**
Mendame, Robert, 44
Mental defectives, 154
Mercer, James, 256, 257, 258, 259
Mercer, Margaret, 256, 257, 258, 259
Meritor Savings Bank, 414–16, 417
Meritor Savings Bank v. Vinson (1986), 338, **414–18**, 435
Merrill, Roy, 179
Messmore, Fred W., 304, 306
"Metes and Bounds," 231
Michael M., 77, 79, 80
Michael M. v. Superior Court of Sonoma County (1981), 40, **77–80**
Military Selective Service Act, 129
Miller, Samuel F., 100, 104
Mindell, Fania, 30, 31
Miners, 337
Minimum-maximum sentence, 67
Minimum wage, 352, 353, 354, 357, 360
Minimum Wage Board of District of Columbia, 352, 353
Minimum wage laws, 109, 350, 350, 354, 357, 360; women's, 356, 358
Minor, Francis, xxv–xxvi, 21, 104, 105
Minor v. Happersett (1875), 21, 91, **104–108**, *106*, *107*
Minor, Virginia, xxx, 21, 92, 114, 104, 105

Minorities, 338, 412, 424, 425
Minors, 79, 358, 359
Miscarriage, 191, 395, 429
Misdemeanor, 44
Mississippi Industrial Institute and College for the Education of White Girls of the State of Mississippi. *See* Mississippi University for Women
Mississippi University for Women (MUW), 131, 132, *132*, 133, 134
Mississippi University for Women v. Hogan (1982), xxx, 92, **131–34**, 146
Missouri v. Celia, a Slave (1855), 40, **48–52**, *49*
Mitchelson, Marvin M., 320, 321
Mondale, Walter, 1
Montgomery, Mr., 256, 258
Montgomery, William, 241
Moody, William H., 346
Moore, Alfred, 260
Moore, S. Clark, 77
Moore, Stephen, 292, 293, 294
Morals, 348, 359, 362
Morehead v. New York ex. rel. Tipaldo (1936), 355, 357–58
Morgan, Anne, 57
Morgan, Charles, Jr., 410, 411
Morgenthau, Mrs. Henry, 57
Mormon Church. *See* Church of the Latter Day Saints
Mortgage, 331
Moscowitz, Grover, 160
Mother, surrogate, 150; and Jay's Treaty, 235; unemployed, 324, 325, 327
Motherhood mystique, 302
Mrs. Warren's Profession (play), 159
Muller, Curt, 346, 347, *347*
Muller v. Oregon (1808), xxvii, 337, **346–51**, 354, 357, 366
Mullowney, Alexander, 25, 26
Multiple sclerosis, 192
Muncy Act (1913), 63, 64, 65, 67
Mungo, Raymond, 173
Murder, 69, 96
Murphy, Frank, 361, 364
Musmanno, Michael, 63
MUW. *See* Mississippi University for Women (MUW)

N

NAACP. *See* National Association for the Advancement of Colored Persons (NAACP)

Nadroski, Gertrude, 361

Narcissistic personality disorder, 194

NARAL. *See* National Abortion Rights Action League (NARAL)

Nason, Elsie, 429

National Abortion Rights Action League (NARAL), 168

National Association for the Advancement of Colored Persons (NAACP), 18

National Birth Control League, 31

National Committee on Maternal Health, 160

National Committee on Pay Equity, 393

National Conference of Commissioners on Uniform State Law, 331

National Consumers' League, xxvii, 346, 348, 354

National Federation of Business and Professional Women, 354

National Guard Bureau (U.S.), 34, 35

National Guard (Washington), 35, 36

National origin, 124, 142, 215, 310, 369, 380, 398, 411, 412, 430

National Organization for Women (NOW), 128, 129, 181, 335, 365–66, 368, 379, 380, 382

National Woman Suffrage Association, 98

National Women's Party, 2, 25, 346, 356

Native Americans, 5

Naval Investigative Service (NIS), 437

Navy, U.S., 436, 437, 438, 439

Nazis, 89

Necessaries, 220

Neff, Janet T., 333

Negroes. *See* Blacks

Nellis, Joseph L., 167

Nelson, Ann Elizabeth, 385, 386, 388

Neuberger, Maurine B., 181

New Bedford Rape Trials (1984), 40, **81– 85**, *82, 84*

New Bedford Women's Center, 84

New Deal Legislation, 360

New England Anti-Slavery Society, 16

New, Jane, 264

New York Academy of Medicine, 181

New York Bakeshop Act, 341

New York City Health and Hospitals Corporation, 185

New York Fair Employment Practices Commission, 380

New York State Club Association, Inc. v. New York City (1988), 142

New York Times, 31, 74, 81, 164, 194, 204, 335, 342, 350

New York v. Sanger (1918), **29–33**

New York's Married Woman's Property Act (1848), 214

Newberry, Roger, 247, 252

Newcombe, Mary, 34

Newgate Prison, 43

Newman, Pauline, 57

Newsom, David, 49, 50

Newsom, Harry, 49

Newsom, Mary, 48, 49

Newsom, Robert, 48, 50

Newsom, Virginia, 48, 49

Niemeyer, Paul V., 144, 145

Nighttime work, prohibitions on, 370

Nineteenth Amendment (1920), xxvi, 24, 28, 95, 106, 109–11, 149, 164–65, 175, 178–82, 186, 310, 356

Ninth Amendment, xxix

NIS. *See* Naval Investigative Service (NIS)

No fault divorce laws, 215, 279, 290

Noel Keane's Infertility Center of New York, 190

Nolan, Joseph R., 172, 173, 175

Nonveterans, 408

Northcutt, W. S., 109

Northern Virginia Savings and Loan Association. *See* Meritor Savings Bank

NOW. *See* National Organization for Women (NOW)

Noyes, Nicholas, 1, 12

Nuns, Roman Catholic, 1

Nurse, Rebecca, 1, 11, 12

Nurses, 379

O

Obligation of Contracts, 347

Obscenity Law, 32. *See also* Anti-obscenity laws

O'Brien, Henry X., 63

O'Callaghan, Saunders & Strum, 412

Occoquan Workhouse, 27, 28
Occupational Safety and Health
    Administration (OSHA), 60, 429, 431
O'Connor, Agnes, 40, 53, 54
O'Connor, Sandra Day, 86, 104, 131,
    133–35, 139, *141*, 143, 146–47, 197,
    200, 202–204, *204*, 207, 410, 414, 419,
    423, 425, 428, 433–35
Ogle, Saymuel, 217, 220
O'Horn, Daniel, 190
Okrand, Fred, 170
Old Testament, 54
Oliphant, David J., 402
Olsen, Theodore B., 143, 419
Operation Goliath, 208
Operation Rescue, 202, 207, 208, 209
Ordinary felony murder, 181
Oregon v. Rideout (1978), 40, 55, **73–76**,
    286
O'Reilly, Leonora, 60
Orr, John W., 292, 294
Orr, Lillian M., 316–18
Orr v. Orr (1979), xxix, 214, **316–19**
Orr, William Herbert, 316–18
Osborn, Sarah, 11, 12
OSHA. *See* Occupational Safety and
    Health Administration (OSHA)
Otten, Laura A., 408
Out of wedlock, xxiv, 265

P

Packard, Elizabeth Parsons Ware, 292–
    95, *294*
Packard, Theophilus, Jr., 93–95, *94*
Packard v. Packard (1864), **292–95**, *293*
Packers and Stockyards' bill (1921), 109
Paine House, 15, 17
Palimony, 320, 321, 322–23
Parenting, xxi, 213–15
Parker, Isaac, 151
Parole, 45
Parrish, Elsie, 357, 358, *359*, 360
Parsons, Theophilus, xxiv, 93, 94, 151,
    213
Partnerships, 322, 410, 413
Pattison, Jane, 220–22
Pattison, Jeremiah, 220–22
Pattison v. Pattison (1737), 213, **220–22**,
    221, 222
Patty Cake test, 194

Paul, Alice, 2, 25–28, *26, 27*, 306, 346,
    354, 356
Paul, Jason, 313
Pay equity act, 393
Pay, take-home, 403
Payne, Abraham, 300
PDA. *See* Pregnancy Discrimination Act
    (PDA)
Pearl, Philip, 19
Peckford, Mr. and Mrs., 277–79
Peckford v. Peckford (1828), 214, **277–79**
Peckham, Rufus, 341, 343, 346
Pelvic disease, 154
Penal Code, 62, 78, 79
Penney, Donald, 429
Pennsylvania Board of Probation and
    Parole, 67
Pennsylvania v. Addicks (1813), 214, 224,
    271–73, *272*, 301
Pennsylvania v. Daniel and Douglas (1967),
    40, **63–68**
People v. Leon P. Belous (1969), 170
People's attorney, 348
*Personnel Administrator of Massachusetts v.
    Feeney* (1979), 338, **406–409**
Pessaries, 149, 159, 160
Peter, Raymond A., 170
Philadelphia Inquirer, 96
Philleo, Rev. Calvin, 19
Phillips, Ida, 373, *374*
Phillips v. Martin Marietta (1971), 338,
    373–75
Phips, Mr., 223–25
Phips, William, 13
Physical cruelty, 243
Picker, Jane M., 385, 386–87
Picker, Sidney, *387*
Picketing, 2, 25, 26, 27, 378
Pilpel, Harriet, 164
Pina, Ronald A., 81
Pinckney, C. C., 233, 234
Pinkney, William, 244, 246
Pittsburgh Commission on Human
    Relations, 379, 380, 382
Pittsburgh Glass Company, 379
Pittsburgh Human Relations
    Commission, 380, 382
Pittsburgh Press (newspaper), 382–84
*Pittsburgh Press v. Pittsburgh Commission on
    Human Relations* (1973), xxix, 338,
    379–84, *381*

Planned Parenthood, 162, 163, 181, 198

Planned Parenthood of Southeastern Pennsylvania v. Casey (1992), xxix, 150, 183, 201, 202–206

Plymouth Colony Records, The, 44

Polatschek, Paula. *See* Wiesenfeld, Paula

Police, 57

Poll tax, 91, 109, 110, 111

Pollack, Herman I., 63, 64

Pollock, Stewart G., 190

Popish inquisitors, 9

Pornography, 40, 86–89, 158. *See also* Anti-pornography laws

Portland Grand Laundry, 346, 347

Post, Melville Davisson, xxiv

Pound, Cuthbert W., 29

Pounders, William R., 77

Poverty, 31, 335, 402

Powell, Lewis F., Jr., 69, 71, 77, 79, 115, 119, 127, 131, 135, 139, 172, 177, 181, 185, 308, 310, 312, 316, 324, 328, 379, 382–83, 385, 390, 398, 402, 406, 410, 414

Powell, William, 49, 51

Preate, Ernest D., Jr., 202, 203

Pregnancy(ies), 150, 167, 170, 175, 179–83, 188, 191, 197–98, 203–204, 322, 338, 388, 397, 404–405, 420–21, 428, 431; ectopic, 394–95; normal, 394; teenage, 79; term, 186; tubal, 394–95; unwanted, 31

Pregnancy Discrimination Act (PDA), 338, 394, 397, 420, 428, 429, 431

Premarital agreements, 214, 226, 228, 229, 237, 238. *See also* Prenuptial agreements

Prenuptial agreements, 237, 239, 289–90; contract, 228. *See also* Premarital agreements

President's Commission on the Status of Women (1961), 40, 63

President's Commission on the Status of Women and the Citizens' Advisory Council, 375

Presumed coercion, 40, 61, 62

Prewitt, Robert, 48, 50

Price-fixing law, 355

Price Waterhouse, 413

Priddy, Albert, 154, 155

Prima facie, 400

Primogeniture, xxiii

Prince, George, 280, 281

Pringle, Mr., 230

Prince, Sarah, 280, 281

Prince v. Prince (1845), 214, **280–82**

Printers Union, 337

Prisoners, political, 2

Privacy, 164, 180, 182; rights, xxi, 149, 199

Private discrimination, 412. *See also* Discrimination

Pro-choice, 1, 203

Procreational rights, 200

Progressive Era, 341, 347, 360, 370

Pro-life movement, 202

Promiscuity, 173

Promissory note, 328

Pro, Philip M., 436, 439

Pro se, 197

Property, xxii, xxiv, xxx, 14, 40, 51, 63, 119, 217, 226, 247, 252, 264, 290, 322, 347, 354; acts, xxiv; community, 215, 250–51, 329, 331; laws, 297; marital, 248, 328, 331; personal, xxiii, 237, 244–45, 254, 256, 260, 275; private, 213; rights, 218, 234, 237, 240, 244, 250, 253, 256, 267, 331; separate, 219. *See also* Real estate; Real property

Prost, Sharon, 302

Prostatectomies, 396

Prostitution, 87, 153, 155, 311, 383

Protestants, 182, 187

Protests, 376

PSFS Savings Bank. *See* Meritor Savings Bank

Psychodiagnostic and Family Services Clinic, 334

Psychological distress, 434

Public accommodation laws, 142

Public alms, 213

Public bathrooms, 128

Public health, 348

Public welfare, 354, 362

Puritan Founders, 7

Puritan theology, 1

Puritans, xxiii, 3, 9, 217, 234, 283

Q

Quack doctors, 158

Quakers, 1, 7, 9, 234

Quickening, 151, 152

Quid pro quo, 416, 417
Quit-claim, 261
Quota(s), 379, 407

R

Race, 124–25, 143, 197, 215, 310, 317, 369, 380, 398, 404, 411–12, 425
Racial discrimination, 142, 372. *See also* Discrimination
Radice v. New York (1924), 356, 358
Rape, 39, 45–47, 51, 53–54, 69, 87, 89, 115, 152, 186, 189, 214, 285; aggravated, 81–82, 84, 436; first-degree, 73; gang, 81; spousal, 283
Raposo, Victor, 81, 82, *82*, 83, 84
Rational relationship tests, 36, 125
Rawle, Mr., 226, 228
Rawlinson, Dianne, 398–400
Read, Mr., 230
Reagan, Ronald, 356
Real estate, xxiii, 218, 230, 234–35, 237, 244, 247–48, 252, 254–55, 260. *See also* Property; Real property
Real property, 93, 217, 230, 244, 250, 254–55, 260, 278, 281. *See also* Property; Real estate
Reason, 260
Reasonable doubt, 76
Red circle employees, 391
Records of the Governor, 7
Reed, Cecil, 112, 113
Reed, Sally, xxix–xxx, 112, 113, *113*
Reed, Stanley F., 361
Reed v. Reed (1971), xxiv, xxvii–xxviii, 24, 91, 103, **112–14**, 124, 125, 145, 312, 314–15, 385, 387
Reformatories for women, 66
Regents of the University of California v. Bakke (1978), 425
Registration, men-only, 129
Rehnquist, William H., 69, 71, 77, 79–80, 86, 115, 119, 122, 125–27, 131, 135, *141*, 197–98, 316, 324, 328, 379, 385, 390, 394, 398, 402, 406, 410, 414, 417, 419, 423, 425
Reisch, Jenny, 75
Relief class, 377, 378
Religion, 124, 143, 180, 215, 310, 369, 380, 398, 404, 411–12, 430
Religious freedom, 7, 9

Rentzer v. Unemployment Insurance Appeals Board (1973), 395
Reproductive Health Services, 197, 198
Reproductive rights, xxi, 149–50
Reproductive technology, 190
Restrictions, workplace, 369
Retail Bakers' Association, 342
Retirement, 402
Reverse discrimination, 420. *See also* Discrimination
Revolution (newspaper), 21, 98, 105
Revolution. *See* American Revolution
Revolutionary War. *See* American Revolution
Rex v. Deleval (1763), 301
Richardson, Elliot L., 308
Riddle, Mr., 268
Rideout, Greta, 73, 74, 75, *75*, 76
Rideout, John J., 73, *74*, 76
Rigby, J., 222
Right of association, 141
Right to liberty, 164
Right-to-life, 150, 207
Right to privacy, 162, 165, 170, 172, 175, 178, 179, 182
Right to remarry, 241
Right to vote, 310
Rights of husbands, 296
Rights, patriarchal, 214, 283
Rippon v. Dawding (1769), 228
Rita M., 86
Road Operations Safety Committee, 424
Roane, Spencer, 264
Robbery, 67
Robbins, Margaret Dreir, 354
Roberts, John W., 357
Roberts, Kathryn R., 139, 141
Roberts, Owen J., 109, 357
Roberts, Samuel J., 63
Robertson, Ann, 233
Robertson, John, 233
Roberts, Sylvia, 365
Roberts v. United States Jaycees (1984), 92, **139–42**
Robida, Lizetta, 83
Robins, Margaret Dreier, 56
Robinson, William, 7, 9
Robinson, William L., 373
Roe, Bryce E., 119
Roe, Jane (Norma McCorvey), 150, 177, 183

Roe v. Wade (1973), xxix, 150, 152, 162, 167, 169, 175, **177–84,** 185, 186, 188, 197, 198, 199, 202, 203, 204
Roman Catholic Church, 180, 182, 186, 189
Roosevelt, Franklin D., 60, 344, 356, 360
Root, Jesse, 223
Roraback, Catherine G., 163, 164
Rosenfeld v. Southern Pacific (1968), 367
Rostker, Bernard, 127, 129
Rostker v. Goldberg (1981), 92, **127–30**
Rotary International v. Rotary Club of Duarte (1987), 142
Rubin, J. Robert, 56, 58
Rufus, Judge, 17
Rum, John M., 104
Rumsey, Sarah, 294
Russell, Abigail, *238*
Rutledge, Hugh, 233
Rutledge, John, 230
Rutledge, Wiley B., 361, 364
Ryan, Mark J., 304

S

Safety, 348, 359
St. John, Benoni, 248
Salem, Mass., 11
Salem widows, 14
Salem Witchcraft Trials (1692 and 1693), xxi, 1, **11–14,** *13*
Sales clerks, 379
Salk, Kersten, 302
Salk, Lee, 103, 302
Salk v. Salk (1975), 302
Salmon, Marylynn, xxii, xxiii, 229, 247, 250, 267
Sanford, Edward T., 153, 352, 355
Sanger, Margaret H., xxix, 2, 29–32, 159, 160, 161
Sanger, William, 29, 159
Sayers, Lewis, 75
Scalia, Antonin, 143, 147, 197, 200–201, 202, 207, 210–11, 419, 423, 425, 428, 433
Scarborough, T. Ed, 61
Schafly, Phyllis, 306
Schechter, Marshall, 193–94
Schinnerer, Mark C., 387
Schlesinger v. Ballard (1975), 133, 313
Schmitter, Aman, 341
Schoenberger, Alan F., 328, 331

Schoville, Dennis, 436
Schwartz, Margaret, 58, 59
Scott, John, 230, 231
Scott, Sarah, 230, 231
Scott v. Scott (1795), 213, **230–32,** *231*
Scrutiny, 36, 125, 215, 310–11
Sears Roebuck catalog, 160
Second-class citizens, 95
Second Statute of Westminster, The, 53
Second trimester, 177
Sedgwick, Mr., 283
Sedgwick, Thomas, 93, 94, 95
Sedition, 4, 23
Segal, Herbert L., 369
Segregation, 370, 393
Selden, Henry R., 21, 22
Selective Service System, 127, 129
Self-defense arguments, 51
Self-reliance, 335
Selig, Joel, 376
Senate Armed Services Committee, 437
Seneca Falls Convention (1848), 25, 61
Seniority, 370, 377, 378, 385
Senterfitt, Donald T., 373
Separate estates, 217, 223, 227
Separate property case, 260
Separation of church and state, 2
Separations, 214, 217, 219, 241, 242, 286, 340; legal, 284
Sergeant, Mr., 226
Settlements, out-of-court, 378
Sewall, Samuel, 93, 151
Sex, 87, 125, 142–43, 171, 309–10, 318, 321, 346, 356, 360, 362, 365, 369, 371, 373–74, 383, 388, 391, 398, 402–405, 411. *See also* Sexual discrimination
Sex Crimes Unit (Manhattan, N.Y.), 72
Sex offenses, xxi, 39
Sex-plus theory, 373
Sex-segregated (newspaper) columns, 382, 383
Sex-segregated want ads, xxix, 379, 380. *See also Pittsburgh Press v. Pittsburgh Commission on Human Relations* (1973)
Sex-segregation, 346, 370
Sexism, 369, 425
Sexual abuse, 79
Sexual assaults. *See* Assault and battery
Sexual discrimination, xxvii, xxix–xxx, 87, 122, 124, 126, 129, 132, 135, 138, 142, 145–46, 310, 315, 325–26, 338,

345, 369–70, 373, 375–76, 380, 383, 398, 400, 410–11, 414. *See also* Discrimination

Sexual harassment, xxi, 338, 414–18, 433, 434, 436, 437

Sexual Harassment of Working Women (MacKinnon), 416

Sexual license, 173

Sexual orientation, 34

Seymour, Moses, *222*

Seymour, Mr., 283

Seymour, Thomas, 247

Shapleigh, Dr., 96

Sharon, 77–78

Shaw, Daniel T., 283, 284

Shaw, Emeline, 283, 284

Shaw, George Bernard, 159

Shaw, Hartley, 61

Shaw v. Shaw (1845), 214, **283–86**, *284*

Sheats, E. Harold, 109

Sheepey, Charles, 39, **45–47**

Shepherd, Edmund E., 361, 362

Sheppard Towner Act (1921), 109

Sherman, R. M., 247

Shippen, Edward, *226*, 241

Shoatman, Thomas, 50, 51

Sick leave, 414

Silva, Daniel, 81, 82, *82*, 83, 84

Silverman, Phyllis, 194

Simmons, Robert G., 304

Simon, Carly, 194

Simpson, O.J., 302

Single-gender enrollment, 144

Sixth Amendment, 115, 117, 118

Skeel, E. L., 357, 358

Skoloff, Gary, 190, 191

Slaughter-House decision, 107

Slave-holders, 19

Slavery, 107, 144, 250, 310

Slaymaker, Henry, 257

Slosson, Mr., 274, 275

Smith, Judith, 5

Smith, Mr., 241, 247, 249, 252, 256

Smith, Stephen J., 302, 333–37

Smith, Susan, 97

Snell, William T., 50

Snyder, John W., 436–37

Socialist Party, 30

Social needs, 348

Social Security, xxx, 63

Social Security Act, 312, 313, 314; Title XIX, 186

Society of Friends. *See* Quakers

Solitary confinement, 28

Somerveill, James, 221

Sontag, Susan, 194

Sorkow, Harvey, 192, 194

Souter, David H., 143, 202, 203, 204, 205, *205*, 207, 428, 433

Southern Bell Telephone and Telegraph Company, 365, 367, 368

Special interest, 347

Specter, Arlen, 66, *66*

Speerstra, Pauline, 76

Spencer, Caroline, 25, 27

Spousal support, 306

Stanton, Elizabeth Cady, xxvi, 13, 21, 97, *97*, 98, 104, 105, 119, 121, 243, 296

Stanton, James Lawrence, Jr., 119

Stanton, Thelma B., 119, *121*

Stanton v. Stanton (1975), xxx, 79, 92, **119–22**, 318

Stare decisis, 205

Starr, Charles R., 292, 295

Starr, Kenneth W., 203, 204

State Industrial Home for Women Act. *See* Muncy Act (1913)

Stately, Cora Elizabeth, 61

Statutes of Westminster, 46, 53

Statutory rape, 53; laws, 77, 78, 80

Staver, Matthew D., 207

Stay of execution, 52

Stearns, G. M., 53, 54

Steinem, Gloria, 194

Stein, Gary S., 190

Steingod, Jacquie, 335

Stephens, Jess E., 61

Stephenson, Marmaduke, 7, 9

Stereotyping, sexual, 413

Sterility, female, 431

Sterilization, 153, 154, 431; compulsory, 156; forcible, 150, 156; involuntary, 157

Sterilization act, 154

Stern, Elizabeth, 190–94

Stern, James L., 64

Stern, Melissa Elizabeth, 190, 191

Stern, William, 150, 190–93, 196

Steuer, Max D., 56, 58

Stevens, John Paul, III, 69–70, 77, 80, 86, 131, 135, 139, 143, 185, 197, 202–

203, 207, 324, 328, 398, 402, 404–406,
410, 414, 418–19, 423, 428, 433
Stewart, Potter, 69–70, 77, 79, 112, 115,
119, 162, 164–65, 167, 172, 177, 185,
188–89, 308, 310, 312, 316, 324, 328,
373, 379, 383–85, 388, 390, 394–95,
398–402, 408
Stillbirth, 52
Stockton, Richard, 95, 213, 260, 261
Stone, Hannah M., 140, 158, 159, 160,
160, 161
Stone, Harlan Fiske, 109, 153, 357
Stone, Lucy, 104
STOP-ERA, 128
Storrs, William L., 283
Stout, Charles S., 112
Stowe, Harriet Beecher, 158
Strassburger, Eugene B., III, 379
Streep, Meryl, 194
Strict scrutiny, 36, 125, 215, 310–11
Strode, Aubrey, 153, 154, 155, 156
Strong, Henry, 17
Strong, Simon, 93
Strong, William, 100, 104
Stuyvesant, Elizabeth, 30
Substantive due process rights, 343
Suffrage, xxv–xxvi, 2, 21–28, 91, 98;
black male, 104; parade, 60; women,
105–108
Suffragists, 25, 27, 28, 104, 306, 348
Suicide, 169
Sullivan, James, 93
Sullivan, Kenneth, 81
Summary affirmation, 89
Summary judgment, 36, 176
Support, 320; spousal, 214, 215
Supremacy, male, 240
Surnames, 215
Surrogacy, 190–96
Surrogate Parenting Agreement, 190
Susman, Frank, 197, *198*, 200
Sutherland, George, 109, 153, 352, 354–
55, 357, 360
Suttles, T. Earl, 109, 110
Swan, Thomas, 158
Swayne, Noah H., 100, 104
Sweat shops, 56, 60, 346
Sweating system, 359
"Switch in time that saved nine," 360
Switchman, 365, 367
Switzer v. Valentine (1854), 297

Syphillis, 30

T

Taft, Helen, 57
Taft, William Howard, 153, 352, 355
Tailhook Association, 436, 438
Tailhook Convention 437
Tailhook Scandal (1994), **436–39**
Taney, Roger, 107
Tappen, Arthur, 16, 17
Tariff Act (1930), 158, 159, 160
Taxation without representation, 22
Taxes, property, 312
Taylor, Billy Jean, 115, 117
Taylor, Sidney, 414–16
Taylor v. Louisiana (1975), xxx, 91, 196,
98, **115–18**, *116, 117*
Taylor, William McLaughlin, 178
Temin, Carolyn E., 64, *65*
Temple, Thomas, 9
Tender age, 300
Tenth National Woman's Rights
Conference, 243
Terms, 369
Tests, civil service, 407
Thacher, George, 93
Third Amendment, 165
Third-party gestator, 193
Thomas, Clarence, 143, 202, 207, 433
Thompson, Nathan, 257, 259
Thompson, Patsy, 35
Tilden, Jeffrey I., 34
Tilghman, Mr., 256, 258
Tilghman, William, 268, 269, 271, 272
Tinsin, 44
Title VII. *See* Civil Rights Act: Title VII
Title IX. *See* Education Amendments of
1972: Title IX
Tituba, 11
Titus, 4
Todd, Thomas, 260
Tolle, John, 177, 178, 179, 180
Trader, sole, 234, 235
Transportation Agency, Santa Clara
County (Cal.), 423
Transsexuals, 88
Treason, 93
Treatment, fair, 369
Trespass, 51

Trials of Allice Paul and Other National Woman's Party Members (1917), **25–28**

Triangle Shirtwaist Factory, 56, 57, *58, 59*

Triangle Shirtwaist Fire (1911), **56–60**

Tribe, Lawrence H., 356

Trimesters, 177

Triola, Michelle. *See* Marvin, Michelle Triola

Troll, F. Robert, Jr., 414, 416

Trust, 226, 227

Truth in Lending Act, 329

Tuberculosis, 343

Tuition, 136, 137

Tuttle, Allan Abbot, 390

Twenty-first Amendment, 124

Twenty-fourth Amendment, 111

Tydings, Joseph D., 172, 175

U

UAW, 428

Udall, Richard, 274–75

Unemployment Compensation Disability Fund (Cal.), 394

Unemployment Insurance Code, 394–95

Uniform Marital Property Act (1986), 251, 331

Unionist, The (newspaper), 17

Unions, 337, 350, 365, 367, 370

Unitarian Churches, 209

United Glass and Ceramic Workers of North America AFL-CIO Local #9, xxviii, 376

United States Jaycees, 139, 141

United States Steelworkers v. Weber (1979), 425

United States v. Darby, 337, 344

United States v. Libbey-Owens-Ford (1971), xxviii, 338, 345, **376–78**

United States v. One Package (1936), 32, 149, **158–61**

United States v. Susan B. Anthony (1873), xxv, **21–24**

United States v. Virginia (1996), xxi, xxx, 92, 131, 134, **143–47**

United States v. Vuitch (1971), **167–71**

University of Arkansas, 197

Unmarried people, 172

Uprising of the 20,000, 56–57

U.S. Constitution, 18, 19, 21, 30, 40, 86, 88, 89, 92, 104, 105, 406; supremacy clause of, 421

U.S. Post Office, 149

U.S.S. Dwight D. Eisenhower (carrier), 437

Utah Code Annotated 1953, Section 15-20-1, 119

V

Vaccination, compulsory, 156

Valentine v. Chrestensen (1942), 382

Van Devanter, Willis, 153, 352, 357

Van Voorhis, John, 21

Varco, Richard L., Jr., 139, 141, *141*

Vaughan, Hester, 91, **96–99**

Veary, Raymond P., 81, 82

Venereal disease, 31, 32, 164

Veterans, 406, 407, 408, 409

Veterans Preference Act (1944), 406

Viability, 205

Vick, Kendall L., 115

Victoria, queen of England, 388

Victorian Era, xxiv, 296

Vieira, Joseph, 81, 82, 83, 84

Vietnam War, 128, 406, 407

Vinson, Fred M., 361

Vinson, Mechelle, 414–16

Violence, 86, 88, 211, 285, 286, 335

Violence Against Women Act, 55

Virginia Colony for Epileptics and Feebleminded, 153

Virginia Military Institute (V.M.I.), 92, 143, 145, 146, 147

Visitation, 292

Volk, Charles Richard, 379

Vuitch, Milan, 167–68, *170*

W

Waddy, Joseph, 169

Wade, Henry B., 177, 178

Wage contracts, 360

Wages, 335, 355, 357, 392; minimum, 346

Wages and hours laws, 354, 348, 350. *See also* Fair Labor Standards Act of 1938

Waite, Henry, 283

Waite, Morrison R., 104, 108

Walker, Mark, 123

Walt, Eugene, 436

War Message Speech, 26

War powers clause, 92, 127, 129
Ward, Richard, P., 406
Wardlaw, F. H., 287, 288
Wards Cove Packing Co. v. Antonio (1989), 430
Ware Correctional Institution, 69
Warner Brothers, 74
Warren, Earl, 162
Warren, John, 217, 218
Washington, Bushrod, 260
Watson, Jack H., Jr., 410
Watson, Kathryn A., 86, 87, 88
Watson, Mr., 256
Watson, Sarah, 258
Watson v. Bailey (1808), 213, **256–59**
Waxler, David, 81
Waynescot, Coffee, 49
Waynescot, Virginia, 50
Weaker sex, 348, 350
Webster, Daniel, 343
Webster, Mr., 268, 269
Webster v. McGinnis (1812), 214, **268–70**
Webster v. Reproductive Health Services (1989), 150, 183, **197–201,** 204
Webster, William L., 197, 198, 199
Weddington, Sarah, 150, 177, 178, 179, *180,* 181
Weeks, Billy, *368*
Weeks, Lorena, 365, *368*
Weeks v. Southern Bell (1969), 338, **365–68**
Weight, lifting, xxix, 198, 368, 369, 370, 372, 376
Weigley, Mr., 268
Weinberg, Donald L., 127, 129
Weinberger, Casper W., 312, 313
Weinberger v. Wiesenfeld (1975), xxx, 215, **312–15,** 326
Weismann, Henry, 341, 342
Welfare, 325, 348, 359
Wells, Mr., 274–75
Welsh, W. J., 296
Wenke, Adolph E., 304
West Coast Hotel v. Parrish (1937), 337, 350, **357–60**
West Coast Hotels Company, 357, 358, 360
Westcott, Cindy, 324–27
Westcott, William, 324–27
Westwood, John, 324–27
Westwood, Susan, 324–27

What Every Girl Should Know (article), 31
Wheelwright, John, 4
Whipping and flogging, 43, 45
White, Edward D., 341, 343, 346
White, Byron R., 69–70, 77, 80, 112, 115, 117, 119, 127, 131, 135, 139, *141,* 162, 167, 172, 177, 185, 197, 201–202, 308, 310, 312, 316, 324, 373, 379, 385, 390, 394, 398, 402, 406, 410, 414, 419, 423, 425, 428
White Plains Hospital, 29, 159
White, Walter, 228
White, William, 226
Whitehead, Irving, 153, 154, 156
Whitehead, Mary Beth, 150, 190–96, *195*
Whitehead, Richard, 190–91
Whitehead, Sara Elizabeth, 191–92
Whitehurst, "Mrs.", 30
Whitener, Carolyn, 123, 124
Whites, 17, 81, 102, 317
Whitman, Charles, 31
Whole tracts, 232
Whyte, D. M., 50
Wickham, Mr., 264, 266
Widow's rights, 230
Widow's thirds, 244
Wiesenfeld, Stephen Charles, 312–15
Wilcocks, Mr., 226
Wilder, Lawrence Douglas, 143
Wilentz, Robert N., 190, 196
Wilhelm, Caroline, 155
Wills, xxi, xxiv, 214, 226, 227, 228, 229, 234, 244, 246, 249, 252, 252–55, 264
William, King, 13
Williams, G. Mennen, 361
Williams, Mr., 264, 265, 266
Williams, Thomas Scott, 15, 19, 283, 285–86
Williams, Vera B., 194
Williams v. United States (1943), 168
Williams, Wendy W., 394, 395
Williams, William, 247
Williamson, Samuel, 218, 219
Wilson, Woodrow, 25, 26, 27
Winchester, Mr., 244, 245
Winkler, Jack R., 77
Winslow, Rose, 28
Winthrop, John, 3, 4, 9
Wirin, A. L., 170
Wisdom, John Minor, 365
Wise, Henry S., 369

Witches. *See Salem Witchcraft Trials* (1692 and 1693)

Wives, abandoned, 283; battered, 41; working, 297

Wives' Rights, 245

Wizard, 12

Wolcott, Erastus, 223

Wolf, Randy, 190, 193

Woman Rebel, The (magazine), 30

Woman Suffrage Association of Missouri, 21, 105

Woman's brief, 181

Women and the Law Clinic, University of Michigan, 333

Women and the Law of Property in Early America, xxiii

Women's Armed Services Integration Act of 1948, 407

Women's Bureau, 354, 375

Women's movement, 61, 356

Women's Research and Education Institute, 402

Women's rights movement, 296

Women's Rights Project, 113, 309

Women's Trade Union League (WTUL), 56, 57, 58

"Women's work," xxviii, 392

Woodhull, Victoria, xxv

Woodside, Steven, 423

Woolford, Ann, 238–39

Woolford, Levin, 237, 238–40

Working mothers, 302, 337, 354

Working Women's National Association, 97

World War I, 25

World War II, 127, 350

Wortman, Marlene Stein, 247

Writ of certiorari, 316

Writ of dower. See Dower

Writ of habeas corpus. See Habeas corpus

WTUL. *See* Women's Trade Union League (WTUL)

Wulf, Melvin, 312, 313

Y

Yeadon, Mr., 280

Yeager, John W., 304

Yeates, Jasper, 226, 256, 258–59, 268, 269

Young, Don J., 376

Young, William G., 81, 84

Younger, Evelle J., 77

Z

Zilly, Thomas, 2, 34, 36, 37

Zimmerman, Scott F., 390